Recent Developments in Law and Economics
Volume II

The International Library of Critical Writings in Economics

Series Editor: Mark Blaug

Professor Emeritus, University of London, UK
Professor Emeritus, University of Buckingham, UK

This series is an essential reference source for students, researchers and lecturers in economics. It presents by theme a selection of the most important articles across the entire spectrum of economics. Each volume has been prepared by a leading specialist who has written an authoritative introduction to the literature included.

Wherever possible, the articles in these volumes have been reproduced as originally published using facsimile reproduction, inclusive of footnotes and pagination to facilitate ease of reference.

For a full list of published and future titles in this series
and a list of all Edward Elgar published titles visit our site on the World Wide Web at
www.e-elgar.com

Recent Developments in Law and Economics
Volume II

Edited by

Robert D. Cooter

Herman F. Selvin Professor of Law
University of California, Berkeley, USA

and

Francesco Parisi

Oppenheimer Wolff and Donnelly Professor of Law
University of Minnesota, USA
and Professor of Economics
University of Bologna, Italy

THE INTERNATIONAL LIBRARY OF CRITICAL WRITINGS IN ECONOMICS

An Elgar Reference Collection
Cheltenham, UK • Northampton, MA, USA

Published by
Edward Elgar Publishing Limited
The Lypiatts
15 Lansdown Road
Cheltenham
Glos GL50 2JA
UK

Edward Elgar Publishing, Inc.
William Pratt House
9 Dewey Court
Northampton
Massachusetts 01060
USA

A catalogue record for this book is available from the British Library

Library of Congress Control Number: 2009936737

Mixed Sources
Product group from well-managed
forests and other controlled sources
www.fsc.org Cert no. SA-COC-1565
© 1996 Forest Stewardship Council
FSC

ISBN 978 1 84542 326 1 (3 Volume Set)

Printed and bound by MPG Books Group, UK

Contents

PART III   CRIMINAL LAW

Acknowledgements

The editors and publishers wish to thank the authors and the following publishers who have kindly given permission for the use of copyright material.

Berkeley Electronic Press for articles: Robert D. Cooter and Ariel Porat (2006), 'Liability Externalities and Mandatory Choices: Should Doctors Pay Less?', *Journal of Tort Law*, **1** (1), Abstract, 1–25; Guido Calabresi (2007), 'Toward a Unified Theory of Torts', *Journal of Tort Law*, **1** (3), Abstract, 1–9.

Gary S. Becker for article: Gary S. Becker, Kevin K. Murphy and Michael Grossman (2004), 'The Economic Theory of Illegal Goods: The Case of Drugs', *NBER Working Paper No. 10976*, Abstract, December, 1–35.

Harvard Law Review via the Copyright Clearance Center for articles: Louis Kaplow and Steven Shavell (1996), 'Property Rules versus Liability Rules: An Economic Analysis', *Harvard Law Review*, **109** (4), February, 713–90; A. Mitchell Polinsky and Steven Shavell (1998), 'Punitive Damages: An Economic Analysis', *Harvard Law Review*, **111** (4), February, 869–962.

Michigan Law Review for articles: Richard Craswell (1999), 'Deterrence and Damages: The Multiplier Principle and its Alternatives', *Michigan Law Review*, **97** (7), June, 2185–238; Abraham Bell and Gideon Parchomovsky (2002), 'Pliability Rules', *Michigan Law Review*, **101** (1), October, 1–79.

MIT Press for article: John J. Donohue III and Steven D. Levitt (2001), 'The Impact of Legalized Abortion on Crime', *Quarterly Journal of Economics*, **CXVI** (2), May, 379–420.

Oxford University Press for article: Francesco Parisi and Vincy Fon (2004), 'Comparative Causation', *American Law and Economics Review*, **6**, 345–68.

The RAND Corporation for articles: A. Mitchell Polinsky and Yeon-Koo Che (1991), 'Decoupling Liability: Optimal Incentives for Care and Litigation', *RAND Journal of Economics*, **22** (4), June, 562–70; Yeon-Koo Che and Tai-Yeong Chung (1999), 'Contract Damages and Cooperative Investments', *RAND Journal of Economics*, **30** (1), Spring, 84–105.

University of Chicago Press via the Copyright Clearance Center for article: Daniel Kessler and Steven D. Levitt (1999), 'Using Sentence Enhancements to Distinguish Between Deterrence and Incapacitation', *Journal of Law and Economics*, **42** (1), April, 343–63.

Calabresi: Toward A Unified Theory of Torts

For at least the last 50 years two ways of looking at tort law have struggled for dominance. One characterized by system-builders, as Izhak England so felicitously termed us; the other by those who have seen in tort law the highest manifestation of the common law tradition of responding to breaches in non-criminal, often non-contractual interpersonal relationships.

In this paper, I would like to explore the relationship between these two approaches, which I will suggest, find their common law antecedents – where else but -- in the forms of actions, from which so much of modern Anglo-American private law derives. I will suggest that both approaches have always been there and that they have affected and shaped each other over the centuries and continue to do so today.

In a recent conference, marking the 35th anniversary of my book *The Costs of Accidents*, Jules Coleman asserted that while one cannot conceive of a legal world without criminal law or contract, one can conceive of a legal world without torts.

He went on to suggest that the system builders had come close to reconfiguring the legal world to bring about just that. He then added that if that were to happen, if the assertion of duty relationships, which demand and promote personal responsibility in the furtherance of individualized corrective justice were to disappear, something significant would be lost. The gap created would have to be filled, because, unless it was, something would be lost in terms of interpersonal relationships at law. Another area of law would have to concern itself with: (a) duty, (b) breach of that duty, (c) causing, (d) damages, *i.e.*, the hornbook definition of liability. Somehow, somewhere, that highly personalized, interlocking, doctrinal structure would need to be re-established.

My reaction at the time was: Yes, all that can go out of torts, but tort law won't cease being. Because for me the essence of tort law is not that set of interlocking doctrines or the values these doctrines supposedly represent. No, for me what characterizes tort law is the liability rule. For me, tort law and the liability rule are the middle way between contract law and criminal law/regulation.

Contract law reflects the most libertarian set of relationships, in which – once an entitlement has been given or recognized by the polity – that entitlement can only be transferred if the parties themselves agree to do so at an individually determined price. Regulation/criminal law represents the most collective set of relationships in which the State not only decides who owns what, but determines, under pain of criminal sanction, when that entitlement can be removed, transferred or abrogated.

Torts and other related rules permit the involuntary transfer or destruction of entitlements so long as a collectively determined price is assessed as a result of that transfer or destruction. In torts, entitlements are allowed to be shifted or destroyed so long as someone is made to pay damages determined by the State,

Journal of Tort Law, Vol. 1 [2007], Iss. 3, Art. 1

that is, if someone pays a *collectively determined* price. That collectively fixed price can be individually compensatory or super-compensatory, but it is neither a criminal sanction nor an amount the affected parties have agreed to *ex ante*. It is a way of changing, destroying, or shifting entitlements, which is halfway between criminal law and contracts.

If that is torts, I mused, it is in no more danger of extinction than is contract law, which is not characterized by any individual set of (mutable) doctrinal rules, but is characterized rather by the fact that individuals have to negotiate with each other to shift entitlements. It is no more in danger of extinction than is criminal law, which is not characterized by any particular set of penal rules, but is instead characterized by the fact that the State determines not only who owns what, but also which changes in entitlements, if any, will take place.

Rather, tort law viewed in this way is characterized by a set of rules which determine when entitlements, when ownerships, can be shifted not as a result of direct agreement of the parties, nor as a result of direct decisions by the State, but as a result of the willingness of parties to take part in activities which will be charged a price determined by the State, a price which will, as a result, both limit the number and type of transfers that occur, and yet permit such transfers.

As I have written in an article called "Torts – The Law of the Mixed Society":[1] "...all societies use all three of these methods all the time." Thus, the most libertarian 19th century societies had criminal law. And the most socialistic, collectivistic societies have had some contract law. And, all of them, in a variety of ways, have also used the middle ground. Whether it is eminent domain, that permits transfers as a result of paying a collectively set price, or tort law, they have all employed the liability rule. Moreover, to the extent that our societies have become more social-democratic, more mixed, then this way, the tort law way, far from disappearing, has become one of the dominant elements in the legal structure of our societies. It has come to be more important than either of the other ways.

From this point of view let me recall an observation made by the great legal scholar, Leon Lipson. He said that most of the legal philosophers in the 19th Century West came out of contract law. Contract law was the paradigm, the most popular of these three approaches. He added that most of the great legal philosophers from the, so-called, socialist countries (Soviet Law was his field), came out of criminal law. The predominantly collective approach was dominant in those countries, and hence in the minds of their leading thinkers. And he

---

[1] *In* AMERICAN LAW: THE THIRD CENTURY 103 (B. Schwartz ed., 1976); 56 TEX. L. REV. 519 (1978).

Calabresi: Toward A Unified Theory of Torts

wondered whether in the modern Social-Democratic State the legal philosophers would come out of torts.[2]

But is it really this liability rule relationship that characterizes torts? That's what I say it is. Is it really that, or is it rather the furtherance of individualized corrective justice, characterized by a relationship of duty, of breach of that duty, which causes a harm that must be corrected? Perhaps historically it is an odd admixture of both of these!

Let me go back to one of the great cases in the common law of torts and hence of the forms of action, *Scott v. Shepherd,* 3 Wils. 403, Common Pleas 1773. It was decided in 1773, three years before *The Wealth of Nations* and the Declaration of Independence.

What happened in that case? It is well known to all torts scholars. Someone, it may have been a child, it may have a mentally handicapped person (not clear, but he had a guardian), tossed a lighted squib, a firecracker. (I always say to my class, a lighted octopus because squib sounds like an octopus and I have this vision of somebody throwing a lighted octopus into a crowd.) Somebody sees it coming at him, and immediately tosses it away, towards someone else. This person does likewise. And the squib explodes, injuring the plaintiff, who sues the original thrower.

An action in Trespass was brought against the original thrower. But the problem was that an action in Trespass should not have lain. Why? Because Trespass lay for direct injuries and this injury did not fit past definitions of direct. At that time, as far as an action in Trespass was concerned, intent didn't matter, fault didn't matter, non-fault didn't matter. If I hit you, you had a right to recover from me. (It sounds an awful lot like corrective justice, doesn't it? And it was.) But the injury had to be direct.

An action for *Trespass on the Case* also didn't lie, however. Actions on the Case lay for certain categories of injuries, whether direct or indirect, faulty or non-faulty. Thus, one could sue in Case for nuisance, or innkeeper liability. Case lay for husband-wife and for master-servant liability. Fault was not a necessary element of an action on the case. Moreover, an injury could be direct or indirect, and recovery in Case might still be available. Case has been called a catch-all because it covered many things. But as I hope to show in a bit, Case was not a catch-all at all. The one thing, however, that an action on the Case did not cover was *intentional* wrong doing.

In *Scott v. Shepherd* there was an *intentional, indirect* wrong, which didn't seem to lie either in Trespass or in Case. And to the 18th century judges this seemed absurd. Why should it be that plaintiffs could recover if they were *negligently* injured indirectly, but could not recover if they were *intentionally*

---

[2] Conversation between the author and Professor Leon Lipson.

injured indirectly? It made no sense. And, when things don't make sense to judges, judges usually do something about it, although they often don't quite know what they are doing or why they are doing it. But they do try to make sense out of the situation they face.

The law at the time of *Scott v. Shepherd* made no sense to them, and so some judges tried to create new categories of law that would allow recovery. Others, instead, tried to fit the facts into old categories so that recovery would be possible. These said, well, it's like a bouncing ball so it is direct (which it wasn't). But Blackstone, who was on the panel, said: No, no, no, it doesn't fit. I will not change the law.

Had the suit been brought on the Case there would probably have been the same reaction. Some judges would have said, since the person needed a guardian it wasn't really intentional so we'll let an action on the Case lie, etc. Judges would have stretched, because they believed there was something absurd about not giving recovery.

But one must always ask when something is absurd, why was it there? How did it happen that the law had come to require a result that seemed so silly to the 18th century? It is through thinking about that silliness that I believe that we can come to understand the relationship between corrective justice and system building.

Let me suggest to you that an action in Trespass was simply an action in corrective justice. It said: you injure me directly – I have a right to be compensated by you. It doesn't matter whether you are at fault, whether you are not at fault, whether it was intentional, negligent, or anything else, I have a right to be compensated by you because you have injured me directly.

Why the requirement of *direct* injury? Well, there has to be some limit on corrective justice, otherwise – absent limits such as fault, which did not apply, or something akin to directness or proximity, which did -- all of us would be responsible for everything that happens anywhere in the world. So it is perfectly understandable that an early society would say: corrective justice gives me an almost absolute right to recover from you when you injure me, but only if the injury is closely linked to your act, if it is, in other words, direct. It is equally understandable that such a society would not be particularly interested in fault or non-fault, and that deterrence and punishment had little or nothing to do with this right to recover. It wasn't a matter of whether the society wanted to punish somebody. A direct injurer might well not be at fault. Nor was it that the society wanted to deter such injurers. It was entirely a matter of personalized, individual relationships.[3]

---

[3] While the existence of corrective justice imperatives has been recognized at least since Aristotle, just what those imperatives were for any given society has been extraordinarily mutable.

Calabresi: Toward A Unified Theory of Torts

But corrective justice through Trespass was not the only thing that our ancestral tort law dealt with. There were also any number of activities that early societies wanted to deter or to limit, activities as to which incentives for safety were needed. The common law wanted to make innkeepers be more careful. It wanted to limit the amount of stink that stink-works emitted. It wanted to make employers more careful, and make them responsible for costs imposed by their employees. All of these things were also desired at common law.

And the deterrence the common law sought was the category deterrence that the system-builders have discussed as the key to what is achieved through liability rules. Induce deterrence by charging people or categories collectively determined prices. That will lead them to behave more carefully in situations that cannot, and should not, be reached by criminal law.

The early common law societies didn't want to hang an innkeeper because somebody stole goods from a guest. They didn't want to whip a husband because his wife behaved negligently, or an employer for the carelessness of his employees. Heaven forbid! They wanted to deter, but not punish criminally. And that was the basis of the action on the case. That's why it was *anything* but a catch-all; it had a very clear rhyme and reason!

Compensation to the victim was not a *necessary* part of it. And indeed, tort-like remedies that existed around the same time may not have contemplated compensation at all. The Hundred (the neighborhood) was assessed if a thief was not caught. The Hundred was charged the amount of the thievery. But this amount didn't necessarily go to the person whose property had been stolen. Compensation was not the essence of what was going on. It was not a matter of somebody's right to recover. It was system-building, not corrective justice. Why then, in an action on the Case did one give the victim the right to recover from the innkeeper, husband, nuisanceor, and so on? I would guess that one gave that right because giving recovery to the victim was a highly efficient way of structuring system-building. [4]

If one allowed individuals to recover, the victims would sue and the costs of the harm would be put on the activities that the rudimentary system builders wanted to charge. It was like having a whole lot of private Attorneys General. Compensation was not in the beginning what Case was about; compensation was simply an effective way of charging activities with their costs. [5]

---

[4] The requirement of *but for* cause, shown more probably than not, in the action on the Case played a similar, highly effective, role in bringing about correct category deterrence in a simple common law system. *See generally*, Guido Calabresi, *Concerning Cause and The Law of Torts*, 43 U. CHI. L. REV. 69 (1975).

[5] In this respect the common law and the action on the Case were every bit as sophisticated as I sought to be in discussing category deterrence in *The Costs of Accidents*. The common law's choice of level of category on which to put the incentive, *i.e.*, the innkeeper, the employer, the

Journal of Tort Law, Vol. 1 [2007], Iss. 3, Art. 1

But what happened? When one permits people to recover for an injury, even if one does it in order to accomplish something other than compensation, the injured people very quickly get used to getting the recovery. They come to think of it as their right. I have been injured on account of your negligence. I can sue. It's my right to recover. I have been injured on account of husband-wife, master-servant relationships. Whatever: I have a right to recover.

My expectations are that I will recover, and soon enough recovery becomes my right. When it becomes my right it readily becomes part of that society's notion of corrective justice. And people start to believe that not only do they have a corrective justice right to recover when they are injured directly (and regardless of fault), but that they also have a corrective justice right to be made whole when injured – whether directly or indirectly -- through someone's negligence, or through that person's activity as an innkeeper or as a creator of a nuisance, or as a result of that person's husband-wife relationship.

When that happens it is not long before people say: Good heavens, if I have a right in corrective justice to recover when you injure me indirectly on account of your negligence, surely I should have a right in corrective justice to recover when you injure me through an intentional wrong, even if indirectly. [6]

And that is how we come to the problem of *Scott v. Shepherd*, to the paradox that at common law, there would have been no recovery on the facts of that case, and yet "everyone" believed there should be. Why did it take so long for the paradox to become troublesome? Why did not the law say much earlier: if you injure me intentionally but indirectly, *you should be deterred through an action* on the Case? If one thinks about it the answer is easy. When someone injured somebody else *intentionally*, even if indirectly, the injurer was hanged or whipped. It was an intentional wrong. It was a crime. The state hanged the wrongdoer; it whipped the malefactor. Later it deported the criminal.

Individual deterrence through the criminal law was draconic, and there was no need for category deterrence at all! And since there was no need for category deterrence, there was no need for an action on the Case. Nor was there any reason for compensation. The injury was indirect, and the original common law, directness-limited, notion of when corrective justice compensation was justified,

---

polluter, stands up very well to modern economic analysis. *See, generally*, GUIDO CALABRESI, THE COSTS OF ACCIDENTS: A LEGAL AND ECONOMIC ANALYSIS (1970).

[6] Not surprisingly, the requirement of *but for cause, see* note 4, *supra*, so beloved of the corrective justice scholars, came to accrue to itself an analogous justice gloss. And this gloss remains there, even in the face (a) of various classic system-building-justified exceptions to an absolute requirement of *sine qua non* causation, *see, e.g.,* Corey v. Havener, 182 Mass 250 (1902); Summers v. Tice, 33 Cal.2d 80 (1948), and (b) of the more recent, occasional use of statistical cause, *see, e.g.,* Sindell v. Abbott Labs., 26 Cal. 3d 588 (1980), Hymonowitz v. Eli Lilly & Co., 73 N.Y.2d 487 (1989).

Calabresi: Toward A Unified Theory of Torts

remained. Corrective justice required compensation, whenever a victim was injured – regardless of fault – but only if he was injured *directly*!

It made perfectly good sense until the need for deterrence in areas where the society did not want to hang, draw and quarter, and so on, led to the action on the Case, led, that is, to negligence based (and occasionally status-based) liability with compensation to indirect as well as direct victims. Society wanted to charge injury costs – whether they were direct or indirect – to some activities, and, for efficiency reasons, it did so by giving people a right to sue. People came to expect compensation. And expectations, of course, are always at the root of corrective justice. Little wonder that the paradox developed.

I cannot tell you whether this description is fantasy or is actually true. Who can tell what people in ancient time really were thinking? It has been said that lawyers always imagine the past in order to remember the future. So it may be that my description is completely fanciful. But it's the only one I have found that makes any sense of what was going on. And it is a description that has, I think, great consequences for the present, and for the relationship between system-building and corrective justice.

At another conference, in Rome, a speaker said that one of the problems legal systems have with the kind of system building that Calabresi is associated with – he spoke of me in the third person, even though I was there – is that system building creates *expectations* that are too costly, or even impossible, for the society to meet. I don't know if it creates expectations that are impossible. But it certainly has the effect of creating expectations, *i.e.*, of altering our corrective justice notions.

In other words, if – in order to deter by charging certain activities "their costs" – a society gives people the right to recover, such recoveries will surely affect what people think their *rights* are. And that in turn will surely affect that society's notions of corrective justice, just as happened between Case and Trespass in the 18th century.

At that point, the corrective justice scholars in that society will say, it is absurd not to give recovery in similar or related situations. And soon enough that society will begin giving recovery in circumstances in which recovery is not justified from a "deterrence" point of view and hadn't been from an original or earlier corrective justice standpoint either.

I believe this kind of interplay has affected our view of punitive damages, as well as of emotional damages and other non-economic damages. Let me just say a few words about these, to indicate my line of thinking.

System-builders may want to charge more to activities that cause emotional damages. If there is a terrible accident on the street, when I drive by I feel sick. Why isn't this a cost properly charged to those who caused that accident? It is. But if society gives me a cause of action in that situation, I don't just feel sick for

Journal of Tort Law, Vol. 1 [2007], Iss. 3, Art. 1

a few minutes. I feel sick for days. And it's not that I am malingering. I feel sick for days because society has given me a right to feel sick! Once the legal system has given me a *right*, I insist upon that right and cherish that right. That's what corrective justice is all about. We are back to the 18th century paradox.

It is similar with punitive damages. In order properly to deter an activity, we must often award a multiple of the damages suffered by the particular plaintiff. This is because a defendant may not get caught or held liable each time that defendant imposes such social costs.[7] But if these "socially compensatory" costs are awarded to the plaintiff because it is an efficient way of assessing costs on defendants, in due course plaintiffs will come to view such damages as their right. And soon enough they will feel cheated if they do not get them.

What is the solution? Well, one solution would be if we could split off completely the right to recover (limiting that according to our then extant notions of corrective justice), from the charging of those activities that we want to have pay so that they will have incentives to be safer. If we could make people pay according to the incentives that we want them to face, and give recovery only if, and when, pre-existing notions of corrective justice justify recovery, and if we could do both completely separately from each other, the *Scott v. Shepherd* paradox would be avoided.[8]

I sometimes call that New Zealand with steroids – the New Zealand system but worked out in a far more articulated way. If we did that we might not have the constant tension between corrective justice and the system-building that has characterized tort law over the centuries. We would avoid situations in which each is pushing and pulling the other.[9] But it is not easy to do, and I am not sure

---

[7] The multiplier, its *raison d'etre* and its limits, have been analyzed with great ability and thoroughness by Sharkey, Shavell and Polinsky, and Hylton. *See* Catherine M. Sharkey, *Punitive Damages as Societal Damages*, 113 YALE L.J. 347 (2003); A. Mitchell Polinsky & Steven Shavell, *Punitive Damages -- An Economic Analysis*, 111 HARV. L. REV. 870 (1998); Keith N. Hylton, *Punitive Damages and the Economic Theory of Penalties*, 87 GEO. L.J. 421, 456 (1998). It is also discussed in opinions of Judge Richard Posner, and of the author. See, Keemezy v. Peters, 79 F.3d 33 (7th Cir. 1996); Ciraolo v. New York, 216 F.3d 236, 242 (2d Cir. 2000) (Calabresi J., concurring).

For a general discussion of the various reasons why punitive damages may be deemed worth awarding, only some of which start out involving a plaintiff's right to recover such damages, *see* Guido Calabresi, *The Complexity of Torts – The Case of Punitive Damages*, *in* EXPLORING TORT LAW (M. Stuart Madden ed., 2005).

[8] Of course, the placing of correct economic incentives may also require compensation of victims, and that makes such a separation much harder.

[9] While in this paper I have been primarily concerned with how system-building affects corrective justice, it is equally important to examine how shifting notions of corrective justice affect system-building. As our values, tastes, and sense of justice change so will the allocations of incentives that most efficiently serve them. Thus, if individuals value something – their sense of ownership in their homes say – so that they would be grievously hurt if that ownership could be

Calabresi: Toward A Unified Theory of Torts

that would be what a society would want anyway. Maybe legal-political systems like that kind of pushing and pulling. Indeed, they may depend on just such pushes and pulls to further what they view as desirable change.

I was on the verge of working on these things when I became Dean and stopped thinking. Perhaps some day I may go back and try to outline a system that separates the two. And then I would analyze and criticize that system. I would do so because I believe that somewhere in that line of thought lies the link between corrective justice with its personal responsibility requirements, and the requirements of system-building deterrence.

The corrective justice scholars are quite right to say that we would lose something of value if we were to lose that which corrective justice represents. For at any given moment the justice imperatives that the corrective justice notions of a given society represent must be served. And that is the reason for the continuing survival and appeal of such scholarship.

But we would lose something just as essential if we were to abandon general deterrence and liability-rule system-building. For if corrective justice is crucial to certain notions of personal responsibility in human relationships, so is the liability rule essential to deterring activities done by people whom we do not want to hang – people who, if they were subject to criminal punishment, would not simply fail to do things that are too dangerous, but would, instead, fail to get into the activity which entails danger. We don't want people to drive negligently. But if we jailed people who have negligent accidents, people would not simply drive more carefully or drive safer cars, they would not drive at all!

Somewhere in that line of thought, and in the 18th century lighted squib case, lies a unified field theory of torts, the kind of theory to which I believe our scholarship should increasingly turn.

---

taken away even by a fully adequate eminent domain payment, it is incorrect to say that such liability rule protection is more efficient than property rule protection simply because, absent that special taste or value, the pie would be bigger if the property were taken, and compensation paid. It is, in fact, identical to saying to people who like caviar that they could be fed more cheaply if they ate potatoes. That would undoubtedly be true, but it tells us nothing about efficiency. *See generally*, Guido Calabresi & A. Douglas Melamed, *Property Rules, Liability Rules, and Inalienability: One View of the Cathedral*, 85 HARV. L. REV. 1089 (1972). And so it is with some "expensive" tastes that reflect a given society's sense of justice.

[2]

VOLUME 111   FEBRUARY 1998   NUMBER 4

HARVARD LAW REVIEW

ARTICLE

PUNITIVE DAMAGES: AN ECONOMIC ANALYSIS

A. Mitchell Polinsky and Steven Shavell

TABLE OF CONTENTS

PUNITIVE DAMAGES: AN ECONOMIC ANALYSIS

A. Mitchell Polinsky and Steven Shavell[*]

The imposition of punitive damages is one of the more controversial features of the American legal system. Trial and appellate courts have struggled for many years to develop coherent principles for addressing the questions of when punitive damages should be awarded, and at what level. In this Article, Professors Polinsky and Shavell use economic reasoning to provide a relatively simple set of principles for answering these questions, given the goals of deterrence and punishment. With respect to the deterrence objective, on which their Article focuses, they argue that punitive damages ordinarily should be awarded if, and only if, an injurer has a significant chance of escaping liability for the harm he caused. When this condition holds, punitive damages are needed to offset the deterrence-diluting effect of the chance of escaping liability. (They mention as well a deterrence rationale for punitive damages that does not rest on the possibility of escape from liability — that punitive damages may be needed to deprive individuals of the socially illicit gains that they obtain from malicious acts.) Professors Polinsky and Shavell also discuss the tension between the implications of the deterrence objective and present punitive damages law, including the law's emphasis on the reprehensibility of a defendant's conduct and on a defendant's wealth. With respect to the punishment objective, Professors Polinsky and Shavell stress that the imposition of punitive damages on corporations may fail to serve its intended purpose (although the imposition of punitive damages on individual defendants accomplishes punishment in a straightforward manner). Punitive damages against corporations may be ineffective primarily because the payment of punitive damages awards by corporations often does not lead to greater punishment of culpable employees, but instead punishes the corporation's shareholders and customers.

I. INTRODUCTION

One of the more controversial features of the American legal system is the imposition of punitive damages. Courts have struggled for years to develop a rational set of principles for the imposition of punitive damages,[1] legislative bodies have passed or considered a variety of

---

[*] A. Mitchell Polinsky is the Josephine Scott Crocker Professor of Law and Economics, Stanford Law School. Steven Shavell is Professor of Law and Economics, Harvard Law School. Research for this Article was supported by Exxon Corporation. (Exxon is appealing a punitive damages judgment against it in the Exxon Valdez oil spill litigation; we have served as consultants to Exxon in connection with this litigation.) The views expressed below are our own and do not necessarily represent those of Exxon. We received helpful comments on an earlier draft of this Article from Janet Alexander, Daniel Capra, Richard Craswell, Peter Diamond, Aaron Edlin, Jill Fisch, Jesse Fried, Victor Fuchs, Robert Hall, Louis Kaplow, Daniel Klerman, Thomas Krattenmaker, Richard McAdams, Ivan Png, Kenneth Simons, and participants at seminars given at a number of law schools. We also benefited from research assistance from Jennifer Brosnahan, Patrick O'Reilly, Janine Scancarelli, Debra Volland, and Sherri Lynn Wolson.

[1] The United States Supreme Court's struggle to develop coherent principles in this area is exemplified by the skeptical views expressed by various Justices on the rationality of punitive damages. Most recently, in *BMW of North America, Inc. v. Gore*, 116 S. Ct. 1589 (1996), Justice Scalia, in a pointed dissent, described the Court's guideposts for assessing punitive damages as "provid[ing] no real guidance at all." *Id.* at 1613 (Scalia, J., dissenting); *see also* TXO Prod. Corp.

statutes to remedy perceived problems with punitive damages,[2] academic commentators have debated the theory behind, and significance of, punitive damages,[3] and the press has expressed strongly divergent

---

v. Alliance Resources Corp., 509 U.S. 443, 475 (1993) (O'Connor, J., dissenting) ("[T]he lack of clear guidance heightens the risk that arbitrariness, passion, or bias will replace dispassionate deliberation as the basis for the jury's verdict."); *id.* at 466–67 (Kennedy, J., concurring in part and concurring in the judgment) (arguing that the Court's vague formulation of a "reasonableness" standard for punitive damages awards is unsatisfactory and that "[t]his type of review, far from imposing meaningful, law-like restraints on jury excess, could become as fickle as the process it is designed to superintend. Furthermore, it might give the illusion of judicial certainty where none in fact exists.") (internal quotation marks omitted); Browning-Ferris Indus., Inc. v. Kelco Disposal, Inc., 492 U.S. 257, 281 (1989) (Brennan, J., concurring) ("Without statutory (or at least common-law) standards for the determination of how large an award of punitive damages is appropriate in a given case, juries are left largely to themselves in making this important, and potentially devastating, decision."). Justice Brennan also noted that the instructions typically given to jurors, which advise them to consider the character and wealth of the defendant and the nature of the defendant's conduct, provide guidance that is "scarcely better than no guidance at all." *Id.*

2 The statutes to which we are referring are generally aimed at reducing the number of punitive damages claims and the level of punitive damages awards. Notably, many states have enacted legislation imposing limits on the magnitude of punitive damages awards. Another type of statutory reform implemented by several states is the payment of a fraction of punitive damages to a state agency rather than to the plaintiff. Such legislation obviously reduces the incentive to bring suit for punitive damages (but does not impose a ceiling on defendants' payments). For a list of current and proposed statutes on punitive damages caps and payment of punitive damages to state agencies, see *Gore*, 116 S. Ct. at 1618–20 (Ginsburg, J., dissenting); RICHARD L. BLATT, ROBERT W. HAMMESFAHR & LORI S. NUGENT, PUNITIVE DAMAGES: A STATE-BY-STATE GUIDE TO LAW AND PRACTICE (1991). Also, one state has passed legislation requiring post-trial review of punitive damages awards. *See* MONT. CODE ANN. § 27-1-221(7)(c) (1996).

Additionally, as part of its tort reform efforts, Congress has considered legislation curbing punitive damages. Several bills have been proposed limiting punitive damages recovery to cases in which the plaintiff can demonstrate by "clear and convincing" evidence that the defendant displayed a conscious indifference to safety. *See* H.R. 956, 104th Cong. § 201(a) (1995); H.R. 955, 104th Cong. § 8(a), (c) (1995); H.R. 917, 104th Cong. § 6(c)(1) (1995). Most of the bills have proposed some sort of cap on punitive damages in civil cases, usually $250,000 or three times the plaintiff's economic injury, whichever is greater. *See* H.R. 956, 104th Cong. § 201(b) (1995); H.R. 955, 104th Cong. § 8(b) (1995); H.R. 917, 104th Cong. § 6(c)(2) (1995); H.R. 10, 104th Cong. § 103(c)(2) (1995). The proposed tort reform legislation is reviewed in Note, *"Common Sense" Legislation: The Birth of Neoclassical Tort Reform*, 109 HARV. L. REV. 1765, 1769–82 (1996); *see also* Neil A. Lewis, *Senate, 61-37, Approves Narrow Punitive-Damages Curb*, N.Y. TIMES, May 11, 1995, at B10 (reporting that the House of Representatives voted to limit punitive damages to the greater of $250,000 or three times the economic damages, and that the Senate voted for a narrower proposal that would limit punitive damages only in products liability cases to $250,000 or twice the amount of economic damages and pain and suffering damages).

3 With respect to the theory of punitive damages, commentators have disagreed, for instance, about the relevance of the wealth of the defendant. *Compare, e.g.,* Michael Rustad & Thomas Koenig, *The Historical Continuity of Punitive Damages Awards: Reforming the Tort Reformers*, 42 AM. U. L. REV. 1269, 1317–18 (1993) (endorsing the scaling of punitive damages to defendants' wealth because larger sanctions are required to influence the rich than the poor), *with* Kenneth S. Abraham & John C. Jeffries, Jr., *Punitive Damages and the Rule of Law: The Role of Defendant's Wealth*, 18 J. LEGAL STUD. 415, 415 (1989) (concluding that a "defendant's wealth is irrelevant to the goal of deterring socially undesirable conduct and is an improper consideration in assessing the basis for retribution"), *and* Clarence Morris, *Punitive Damages in Tort Cases*, 44 HARV. L. REV. 1173, 1191 (1931) (noting that evidence of a defendant's wealth, "instead of aiding the jury to assess a proper verdict, may prejudice them against the defendant and prevent an impartial judgment"). Additionally, commentators emphasize different goals in their consideration of puni-

opinions about the merits of punitive damages.[4]

---

tive damages. *Compare, e.g.*, Thomas C. Galligan, Jr., *Augmented Awards: The Efficient Evolution of Punitive Damages*, 51 LA. L. REV. 3, 6–14 (1990) (proposing a system of extracompensatory damages based solely on deterrence), *and* Dan B. Dobbs, *Ending Punishment in "Punitive" Damages: Deterrence-Measured Remedies*, 40 ALA. L. REV. 831, 853–63 (1989) (same), *with* Marc Galanter & David Luban, *Poetic Justice: Punitive Damages and Legal Pluralism*, 42 AM. U. L. REV. 1393, 1432–40, 1447–51 (1993) (discussing both punishment and deterrence goals), *and* David G. Owen, *The Moral Foundations of Punitive Damages*, 40 ALA. L. REV. 705, 713 (1989) (same), *and* Jacqueline Perczek, Note, *On Efficiency, Punishment, Deterrence, and Fairness: A Survey of Punitive Damages Law and a Proposed Jury Instruction*, 27 SUFFOLK U. L. REV. 825, 856–64 (1993) (same).

The empirical importance of punitive damages is also the subject of dispute among academic commentators. A number of commentators suggest that punitive damages are widespread and problematic. *See, e.g.*, Dorsey D. Ellis, Jr., *Punitive Damages, Due Process, and the Jury*, 40 ALA. L. REV. 975, 975–77, 987–88 (1989) (arguing that "courts . . . have continued to uphold ever larger awards in cases in which defendants' conduct falls far short of the intentionally injurious behavior that traditionally characterized punitive damages cases") (footnote omitted); Peter Huber, *No-Fault Punishment*, 40 ALA. L. REV. 1037, 1037–47 (1989) ("As the new tort revolution has taken hold, courts and juries have developed an even sharper, and for plaintiffs more lucrative, sense of outrage."); John Calvin Jeffries, Jr., *A Comment on the Constitutionality of Punitive Damages*, 72 VA. L. REV. 139, 139 (1986) (arguing that "punitive damages are out of control"); *see also* ERIK MOLLER, NICHOLAS M. PACE & STEPHEN J. CARROLL, PUNITIVE DAMAGES IN FINANCIAL INJURY JURY VERDICTS 25–27 (Institute for Civil Justice, RAND Corp., No. MR-888-ICJ, 1997) (finding that, in lawsuits concerning financial injury, the percentage of verdicts in which punitive damages were awarded fell between the period 1985–1989 and the period 1990–1994, but that the average award and the portion of all damages represented by punitive damages rose); MARK PETERSON, SYAM SARMA & MICHAEL SHANLEY, PUNITIVE DAMAGES: EMPIRICAL FINDINGS 65 (Institute for Civil Justice, RAND Corp., No. R-3311-ICJ, 1987) (concluding that punitive damages awards for business/contract cases are increasing, while punitive damages awards for personal injury cases are stable). Others suggest that the fraction of cases in which punitive damages are awarded is not significant. *See* Stephen Daniels & Joanne Martin, *Myth and Reality in Punitive Damages*, 75 MINN. L. REV. 1, 61–62 (1990) (concluding that the magnitude of the punitive damages problem is overstated by reformers); William M. Landes & Richard A. Posner, *New Light on Punitive Damages*, REGULATION, Sept.-Oct. 1986, at 33, 33 (suggesting that "the incidence of punitive-damage awards may be exaggerated"); Michael Rustad, *In Defense of Punitive Damages in Products Liability: Testing Tort Anecdotes with Empirical Data*, 78 IOWA L. REV. 1, 24 (1992) (concluding that there are very few punitive damages awards in product liability cases). These and other studies are reviewed by Marc Galanter, *Real World Torts: An Antidote to Anecdote*, 55 MD. L. REV. 1093, 1126–40 (1996). The most thorough, recent empirical study of punitive damages also emphasizes this point. *See* Theodore Eisenberg, John Goerdt, Brian Ostrom, David Rottman & Martin T. Wells, *The Predictability of Punitive Damages*, 26 J. LEGAL STUD. 623, 623–25, 633 (1997). *But see* A. Mitchell Polinsky, *Are Punitive Damages Really Insignificant, Predictable, and Rational? A Comment on Eisenberg et al.*, 26 J. LEGAL STUD. 663, 664–71 (1997) (explaining in part that the study by Eisenberg et al. may understate the significance of punitive damages by ignoring the effects of such damages on settlements).

[4] *Compare Curtailing Civil Justice*, N.Y. TIMES, Apr. 8, 1995, at 22 (noting that "[p]unitive damages are often the best deterrent to destructive corporate behavior" and arguing against arbitrarily low limits on awards), *and* Editorial, ST. PETERSBURG TIMES, May 23, 1996, at 14A ("Punitive damages clearly have a place in society. They are designed to punish and awaken."), *and* Long Shadow of the Exxon Valdez, N.Y. TIMES, Sept. 21, 1994, at A22 ("[T]he jury . . . clearly understood that only a sizable civil penalty would accomplish the purpose for which punitive damages are designed: to penalize flagrant wrongdoing and deter others from similar gross negligence."), *with Trial Lawyers' Triumph*, WASH. POST, Mar. 19, 1996, at A16 (stating that "[l]egislation is needed because punitive damages are wildly unpredictable, so arbitrary as to be

Our goal in this Article is to develop a coherent and relatively simple set of principles for determining when punitive damages should be awarded and, in circumstances in which they are appropriate, what their level should be. We separately consider two social objectives: deterrence and punishment.[5] Our methodology is economic in the sense that we organize our inquiry around an examination of how rational parties will respond to the threat of punitive damages, and whether their response will promote, or fail to promote, social welfare.[6]

The analysis of the deterrence objective comprises the first and major part of the Article. Our conclusions in this part flow from the basic principle that, to achieve appropriate deterrence, injurers should be made to pay for the harm their conduct generates, not less, not more. If injurers pay less than for the harm they cause, underdeterrence may result — that is, precautions may be inadequate, product prices may be too low, and risk-producing activities may be excessive. Conversely, if injurers are made to pay more than for the harm they cause, wasteful precautions may be taken, product prices may be inappropriately high, and risky but socially beneficial activities may be undesirably curtailed.

It follows from these observations that a crucial question for consideration is whether injurers sometimes escape liability for harms for

---

unfair"), *and Sue? Just Say No*, WALL ST. J., Sept. 28, 1994, at A18 (noting that punitive damages suits "have widespread, silent costs in frivolous filings being 'settled out' and legitimate business activities curtailed for fear of exposure to jury risk"), *and No Paint, No Gain*, ECONOMIST, May 25, 1996, at 67 (arguing that the current punitive damages system yields "bizarre" and excessive awards that keep useful products off the United States market and chill research and development of new products).

[5] Deterrence and punishment are traditionally said to be the goals of punitive damages. *See* City of Newport v. Fact Concerts, Inc., 453 U.S. 247, 266–67 (1981) ("Punitive damages . . . are . . . intended to . . . punish the tortfeasor whose wrongful action was intentional or malicious, and to deter him and others from similar extreme conduct."); Gertz v. Robert Welch, Inc., 418 U.S. 323, 350 (1974) ("[Punitive damages] are . . . private fines levied by civil juries to punish reprehensible conduct and to deter its future occurrence.").

[6] The concept of rationality in individual decisionmaking is discussed, for example, in Amartya Sen, *Rational Behaviour*, *in* 4 THE NEW PALGRAVE: A DICTIONARY OF ECONOMICS 68–76 (John Eatwell, Murray Milgate & Peter Newman eds., 1987). The notion of social welfare is reviewed, for instance, in DAVID M. KREPS, A COURSE IN MICROECONOMIC THEORY 149–82 (1990), and Amartya Sen, *Social Choice*, *in* 4 THE NEW PALGRAVE: A DICTIONARY OF ECONOMICS, *supra*, at 382–93. Social welfare is determined by the well-being of individuals. Thus, social welfare generally rises if individuals' well-being rises, and falls if individuals' well-being falls. In particular, social welfare reflects the deterrence objective of punitive damages, for the avoidance of harm preserves the well-being of persons; and social welfare reflects the punishment objective of punitive damages, for the punishment of wrongdoers may be desired by individuals. We should add that, from the viewpoint of economics, no objective basis exists for saying that a specific formulation of social welfare (such as utilitarianism, which defines social welfare as the sum of individuals' utilities) is correct. Any measure of social welfare can be studied to determine what social policies or legal rules are best with respect to that measure. However, certain relatively simple measures of social welfare are often investigated for analytical convenience.

which they are responsible. If they do,[7] the level of liability imposed on them when they *are* found liable needs to exceed compensatory damages so that, on average, they will pay for the harm that they cause. This excess liability can be labeled "punitive damages," and failure to impose it would result in inadequate deterrence. In summary, *punitive damages ordinarily should be awarded if, and only if, an injurer has a chance of escaping liability for the harm he causes.*[8]

This principle often will have transparent implications for the circumstances in which punitive damages should be awarded in practice. Consider a company that is responsible for trucking toxic waste to a dump site where it will be charged disposal fees. To reduce its fees, suppose the company allows some of the waste to leak onto the highway, because it knows that the leak is unlikely to be noticed and traced to its source. Under our analysis, punitive damages obviously would be called for because of the significant chance that the company will escape liability for the harm it caused. Alternatively, suppose the gross negligence of the firm that is responsible for treating the waste at the dump site leads to a substantial and highly visible spill from the firm's waste storage tanks. Punitive damages would not be appropriate because the firm is unlikely to escape detection and liability for this harm.

When an injurer has a chance of escaping liability, the proper level of *total damages* to impose on him, if he is found liable, is the harm caused multiplied by the reciprocal of the probability of being found liable. Thus, for example, if the harm is $100,000 and there is a twenty-five percent chance that the injurer will be found liable for the harm for which he is legally responsible, the harm should be multiplied by $1/.25$, or 4, so total damages should be $400,000. Because the injurer will pay this amount every fourth time he generates harm, his average payment will be $100,000 (= $400,000/4).[9] Thus, on average, the injurer will pay for the harm he causes, and appropriate deterrence will result. Once the proper level of total damages is calculated in this way, punitive damages can be determined by subtracting compensa-

---

[7] We discuss below several reasons that injurers might be able to escape liability: the difficulty of detecting harm, the inability to identify the injurer, problems in proving that the injurer is liable even if he can be identified, and the plaintiff's failure to sue because of the costs of litigation. *See infra* p. 888.

[8] We say "ordinarily" because we discuss circumstances in which it might not be desirable or necessary to impose punitive damages even if a chance exists of escaping liability (punitive damages might not be desirable when the probability of escaping liability is low, *see infra* pp. 895–96, and they might not be necessary when harm occurs to purchasers of products, *see infra* section III.J). We also discuss reasons that punitive damages might be desirable even if there is no chance of escaping liability (specifically, when the injurer's act is malicious, *see infra* p. 875 and section III.A).

[9] We are presuming here that the injurer engages in repetitive conduct. Our point, however, applies even if the injurer commits the harmful act only once. It is still true then that the probability-discounted or "expected" value of what he pays is $100,000. *See infra* note 46.

tory damages from the total. In the example, because compensatory damages would equal the harm of $100,000, punitive damages would equal $300,000 (= $400,000 - $100,000).

If punitive damages are needed according to this theory, we believe that courts and juries often will be able to obtain enough information about the likelihood of escaping liability to apply the theory reasonably well. We will discuss how our analysis relates to several leading punitive damages cases,[10] and we will provide model jury instructions that can be used to aid jurors in applying the principles that we develop.

We also will relate our analysis of the deterrence rationale for punitive damages to the criteria commonly applied by courts in imposing such damages. Importantly, we will explain that the reprehensibility of a corporate defendant's conduct generally should not be a factor in deciding whether, and to what extent, to impose punitive damages for purposes of promoting deterrence (although the reprehensibility of the conduct of a person who is a defendant may be relevant to punitive damages and deterrence). In addition, we will argue that the wealth of a corporate defendant presumptively should not be taken into account in determining the level of punitive damages (although again the conclusion may be different in the case of a person who is a defendant). We also will consider other aspects of punitive damages policy from the perspective of deterrence, including the appropriateness of caps on punitive damages, the relevance of potential harm for punitive damages, the insurability of punitive damages, and the importance for punitive damages of the distinction between victims who are customers of an injurer and victims who are strangers to the injurer.

One further observation about our analysis of deterrence is worth noting. We ordinarily assume that the benefits that injurers derive from engaging in the conduct that gives rise to harm is included in the calculation of social welfare. We also will discuss, however, the possibility that such benefits should not be included — notably, when a wrongdoer derives pleasure from his victim's suffering. We will explain that, if the injurer's benefits are excluded from social welfare, punitive damages may be needed for proper deterrence even when there is no chance of escaping liability.[11]

In our discussion of the second objective of punitive damages — punishment — we focus on the assumption that the underlying goal of society is to penalize especially blameworthy *individuals*. Achieving this goal is reasonably straightforward if the defendant is a person who has been found to have acted culpably — after all, imposing punitive damages on that person punishes him. But if the defendant is a corporation, imposing punitive damages on it may or may not lead to

---

[10] *See infra* section II.D.
[11] *See infra* section III.A.

the punishment of blameworthy individuals within the corporation, for a variety of reasons that we will discuss. To the extent that such individuals are not punished, imposing punitive damages on the corporation does not advance the punishment goal. Moreover, we will explain that much of the sting from imposing punitive damages on corporations may be borne by individuals who are usually not thought to be culpable, namely, shareholders and customers. In the light of these points, we conclude that the extent to which imposing punitive damages promotes the punishment goal may be significantly different when defendants are corporations from when they are individuals, and that the importance of punitive damages as a form of punishment may be considerably attenuated for corporate defendants.

The plan of our Article is as follows. In Part II, we review the economic theory of deterrence and develop the basic principles determining when punitive damages should be awarded, and at what level. We also apply these principles to certain aspects of punitive damages law and legislation, as well as to several prominent punitive damages cases. Part III relates the basic principles to a number of criteria that are employed by the courts to determine the appropriateness and magnitude of punitive damages awards, and also examines a variety of other factors and policies that bear on punitive damages. Part IV discusses the punishment goal of punitive damages. Part V briefly summarizes our main points.[12] An Appendix contains the model jury instructions for use in awarding punitive damages.

---

[12] Our article builds on many other contributions. The general point that, to achieve proper deterrence, sanctions must be inflated if injurers can escape liability dates at least from Bentham, see JEREMY BENTHAM, *Principles of Penal Law*, *in* 1 THE WORKS OF JEREMY BENTHAM 365, 401–02 (John Bowring ed., 1962) (1838–43), and has been applied to the subject of punitive damages by many commentators. The first explicit references to the factor of escaping liability as a justification for punitive damages apparently are RICHARD A. POSNER, ECONOMIC ANALYSIS OF LAW 77–78 (1st ed. 1972), and Dorsey D. Ellis, Jr., *Fairness and Efficiency in the Law of Punitive Damages*, 56 S. CAL. L. REV. 1, 25–26 (1982). This justification for punitive damages has been developed most thoroughly by Robert D. Cooter, *Punitive Damages for Deterrence: When and How Much?*, 40 ALA. L. REV. 1143, 1149–66 (1989) [hereinafter Cooter, *Deterrence*].

In addition to the works cited in the previous paragraph, there are many others in which punitive damages are considered using economic analysis. Those in print include Darryl Biggar, *A Model of Punitive Damages in Tort*, 15 INT'L REV. LAW & ECON. 1 (1995); James Boyd & Daniel E. Ingberman, *Noncompensatory Damages and Potential Insolvency*, 23 J. LEGAL STUD. 895 (1994); Bruce Chapman & Michael Trebilcock, *Punitive Damages: Divergence in Search of a Rationale*, 40 ALA. L. REV. 741 (1989); Robert D. Cooter, *Economic Analysis of Punitive Damages*, 56 S. CAL. L. REV. 79 (1982) [hereinafter Cooter, *Economic Analysis*]; Richard Craswell, *Damage Multipliers in Market Relationships*, 25 J. LEGAL STUD. 463 (1996); Andrew F. Daughety & Jennifer F. Reinganum, *Everybody Out of the Pool: Products Liability, Punitive Damages and Competition*, 12 J.L. ECON. & ORG. 410 (1997) [hereinafter Daughety & Reinganum, *Products Liability*]; David Friedman, *An Economic Explanation of Punitive Damages*, 40 ALA. L. REV. 1125 (1989); Galligan, *supra* note 3; David D. Haddock, Fred S. McChesney & Menahem Spiegel, *An Ordinary Economic Rationale for Extraordinary Legal Sanctions*, 78 CAL. L. REV. 1 (1990); Jason S. Johnston, *Punitive Liability: A New Paradigm of Efficiency in Tort Law*, 87 COLUM. L. REV. 1385 (1987); Marcel Kahan & Bruce Tuckman, *Special Levies on Punitive Damages: Decoupling,*

II. DETERRENCE: THE BASIC THEORY

In this Part, we summarize the basic principles of the economic theory of deterrence and explain what these principles imply for the use of punitive damages. By deterrence, we mean what is often called *general deterrence*, namely, the effect that the prospect of having to pay damages will have on the behavior of similarly situated parties in the future (not just on the behavior of the defendant at hand).[13]

We should add that the basic theory that we are about to review is the standard theory of deterrence, on which economically oriented scholars widely agree.[14] As noted, we will usually make the conven-

---

Agency Problems, and Litigation Expenditures, 15 INT'L. REV. LAW & ECON. 175 (1995); William M. Landes & Richard A. Posner, *An Economic Theory of Intentional Torts*, 1 INT'L REV. LAW & ECON. 127 (1981); George L. Priest, *Insurability and Punitive Damages*, 40 ALA. L. REV. 1009 (1989) [hereinafter Priest, *Insurability*]; George L. Priest, *Punitive Damages and Enterprise Liability*, 56 S. CAL. L. REV. 123 (1982); Paul H. Rubin, John E. Calfee & Mark F. Grady, BMW v Gore: *Mitigating The Punitive Economics of Punitive Damages*, 5 SUP. CT. ECON. REV. 179 (1997).

Recent unpublished articles include James Boyd & Daniel E. Ingberman, Do Punitive Damages Promote Deterrence? (Mar. 20, 1996) (unpublished manuscript, on file with the Harvard Law School Library); Andrew F. Daughety & Jennifer F. Reinganum, Settlement, Deterrence and the Economics of Punitive Damages Reform (Mar. 1997) (Department of Economics & Business Administration, Vanderbilt University Working Paper No. 97-W04) [hereinafter Daughety & Reinganum, Settlement]; Peter Diamond, Efficiency Effects of Punitive Damages (Sept. 1997) (Department of Economics, Massachusetts Institute of Technology, Working Paper No. 97-17) [hereinafter Diamond, Efficiency Effects]; Peter Diamond, Integrating Punishment and Efficiency Concerns in Punitive Damages for Reckless Disregard of Risks to Others (Oct. 1997) (Department of Economics, Massachusetts Institute of Technology, Working Paper No. 97-19) [hereinafter Diamond, Punishment and Efficiency]; Keith N. Hylton, Punitive Damages and the Economic Theory of Penalties (Dec. 1997) (unpublished manuscript, on file with the Harvard Law School Library); Alan O. Sykes, Constitutionalizing Punitive Damages (Dec. 1997) (unpublished manuscript, on file with the Harvard Law School Library).

Our treatment of deterrence and punitive damages is more comprehensive than that of these earlier economically oriented articles, and our analysis of certain issues that have been considered previously differs from what has been written. Moreover, our examination of punishment and punitive damages is substantially different from what is found in the literature on punitive damages. We discuss the relationship between our Article and some of the preceding literature in notes 14, 48, 95, 118, 131, 165, 183, 194, 205, 207, 220, 244, and 272.

[13] General deterrence may be contrasted with *specific deterrence*, which is the effect that the imposition of a sanction on a party will have on *that* party's future behavior. *See generally* BENTHAM, *supra* note 12, at 396 (contrasting particular and general deterrence); HERBERT L. PACKER, THE LIMITS OF THE CRIMINAL SANCTION 39–48 (1968) (discussing special and general deterrence as justifications for criminal punishment).

[14] The theory of deterrence — the elaboration of the effect on rational actors of the possible imposition of sanctions for violations of law — was first articulated in detail by Jeremy Bentham, *see* BENTHAM, *supra* note 12, at 365–580, and has been developed intensively in the last several decades, stimulated largely by an important article by Gary S. Becker, *Crime and Punishment: An Economic Approach*, 76 J. POL. ECON. 169 (1968). This literature is synthesized and surveyed in, for example, R.A. CARR-HILL & N.H. STERN, CRIME, THE POLICE AND CRIMINAL STATISTICS (1979); WILLIAM A. LUKSETICH & MICHAEL D. WHITE, CRIME AND PUBLIC POLICY (1982); DAVID J. PYLE, THE ECONOMICS OF CRIME AND LAW ENFORCEMENT (1983). For a collection of more recent contributions, up to 1992, see BIBLIOGRAPHY OF LAW AND ECONOMICS 504–26 (Boudewijn Bouckaert & Gerrit De Geest eds., 1992).

Beginning with GUIDO CALABRESI, THE COSTS OF ACCIDENTS (1970), many writers have

tional assumption that the benefits that injurers obtain from engaging in the conduct that gives rise to harm are credited in social welfare.[15] Thus, for example, we will assume that the time saved by a speeding driver, or the cost saved by a company that chooses not to purchase certain pollution control equipment, constitutes a social benefit that is to be weighed against the harm from speeding or polluting. We will consider the implications for punitive damages of the alternative assumption — that the benefits from harmful conduct do not count in social welfare — when we examine the reprehensibility criterion in section III.A.

We first discuss deterrence in a very simple setting in which a party will be sanctioned whenever he causes harm. We then discuss the situation in which parties sometimes escape sanctions for harms for which they are responsible. It is in this latter case, as we indicated above, that damages exceeding harm should be imposed, and punitive damages thus used.

A. Optimal Damages When the Defendant Is Found Liable with Certainty

The central point that we want to explain here is that, if a defendant will definitely be found liable for the harm for which he is responsible, the proper magnitude of damages is equal to the harm the defendant has caused.[16] If damages are either lower or higher than the harm, various socially undesirable consequences will result, as described below. We first illustrate these points when liability is strict —

---

applied the general theory of deterrence to the subject of tort liability. For an integrated presentation of this literature, see WILLIAM M. LANDES & RICHARD A. POSNER, THE ECONOMIC STRUCTURE OF TORT LAW (1987), and STEVEN SHAVELL, ECONOMIC ANALYSIS OF ACCIDENT LAW (1987).

[15] This assumption is consistent with a standard definition of social welfare employed in deterrence theory, in which social welfare equals the benefits that parties obtain from their activities, less various costs (including the expense of precautions taken to avoid harm, the harm that does occur, and any costs associated with the use of the legal system).

Note that this definition of social welfare does not incorporate the compensation of victims as a social benefit, even though most individuals consider compensation to be a social goal. Accounting for the compensation goal in measuring social welfare would be relatively straightforward, but doing so is unnecessary for our purposes for several reasons. First, and most importantly, punitive damages are generally extracompensatory; thus, whether or not they are paid typically does not affect fulfillment of the compensation objective. Second, victims often have insurance — so-called "first-party" insurance — that compensates them for their losses, at least partially, so that the extent to which it is necessary to rely on the liability system to achieve the compensation goal may be limited. Third, the insurance system is generally a much less expensive way to achieve compensation than the liability system. *See, e.g.*, DON DEWEES, DAVID DUFF & MICHAEL TREBILCOCK, EXPLORING THE DOMAIN OF ACCIDENT LAW: TAKING THE FACTS SERIOUSLY 421–24 (1996) (summarizing empirical findings concerning the relative cost of the insurance system and the liability system in providing compensation to accident victims).

[16] Readers familiar with the economic logic supporting this claim may want to proceed directly to section II.B.

an injurer is supposed to be liable for any harm caused[17] — and then when liability is fault-based (in which case our conclusions are somewhat qualified). We assume for the purpose of this discussion that harm is properly measured.[18]

There are a number of reasons why it is best for damages to equal harm under strict liability. One concerns the *level of precautions* taken by parties when engaging in their activities. We interpret the term "precautions" very generally. For example, it can refer to safety devices — such as valves to release excess pressure on tanks used to store dangerous chemicals — or to the actions of individuals that reduce harm — such as inspecting the brakes of trucks. Additionally, and importantly, precautions include the variety of ways in which firms monitor and screen their employees — such as an airline testing its pilots for their use of controlled substances. Any action that reduces the risk or the level of harm constitutes a precaution under our interpretation.

If damages equal harm, potential injurers will in theory have socially correct incentives to take precautions. Specifically, they will be induced to spend money on precautions if the expenditure is socially worthwhile in the sense that the expenditure reduces the harm by a greater amount. Suppose, for example, that by spending $50,000 on a precaution, a firm can prevent a harm of $100,000. It is socially desirable that such a precaution be taken. If the level of liability is equal to the harm of $100,000, a firm will be led to spend $50,000 to prevent harm. But if the level of liability is less than $100,000, a firm might not take precautions when it should. For instance, if the level of liability is only $30,000, then a firm would not take the precaution costing $50,000, even though this precaution is socially desirable.[19]

Conversely, if damages exceed harm, firms might be led to take socially excessive precautions. A socially excessive precaution is one that costs more than the reduction of harm produced by it. In the previous example, suppose that the precaution costs $250,000 instead of $50,000. Such a precaution would be socially excessive because it would be wasteful to spend $250,000 to avoid a harm of $100,000. Yet if damages exceed harm, a firm might be led to take the precaution. Assume, for instance, that punitive damages of $200,000 are added to the compensatory damages of $100,000, so that the firm's total damages will be $300,000 if it does not take the precaution. Because the

---

[17] For ease of analysis, we will presume that issues of contributory negligence do not arise.

[18] We discuss below the possibility that compensatory damages do not correctly reflect the harm that actually occurred. *See infra* section III.L. We also observe that the total social harm caused by an adverse event includes litigation costs. *See infra* note 168. For simplicity, we will not take this refinement into account in Part II.

[19] In this example, and in those in the remainder of the Article, we consider relatively simple fact situations. The principles that these examples illustrate apply to more complicated and realistic circumstances.

cost of the precaution is $250,000, the firm will be led to take it, even though the precaution is socially wasteful.

Although the notion of excessive spending on precautions might seem counterintuitive to the reader, it is quite real, and often recognized as such. For example, commentators frequently make reference to "defensive medicine," by which is meant physicians' wasteful use of tests and diagnostic procedures in response to the threat of liability.[20] On reflection, it is not difficult to imagine that excessive expenditures could be made on safety precautions in almost any context. Consider, for instance, how much could be spent on cement traffic dividers for city streets (suppose that all streets had dividers), on additional personnel to monitor employees' safety practices at oil refineries (each employee at a refinery could be accompanied by another watching over his activities), or on sensors to detect switching problems on railroad tracks (a costly sensor might be installed on every switch on every track).[21]

In our numerical examples, we have discussed precautions as if they would completely eliminate the risk of harm. However, everything we have said applies to situations in which precautions reduce, but do not eliminate, the risk of harm. In particular, the proper magnitude of damages continues to be the harm the defendant has caused.[22] This level of damages again induces potential injurers to take appropriate precautions, but the determination of appropriate precautions now involves a comparison of the cost of the precaution with the reduction in the *expected harm* that results if the precaution is

---

[20] Some studies show this to be an important phenomenon. *See, e.g.,* Daniel Kessler & Mark McClellan, *Do Doctors Practice Defensive Medicine?,* 111 Q.J. ECON. 353, 386 (1996) (finding that malpractice "reforms that directly limit liability ... reduce hospital expenditures by 5 to 9 percent" with no "consequential differences in mortality or the occurrence of serious complications"); Roger A. Reynolds, John A. Rizzo & Martin L. Gonzalez, *The Cost of Medical Professional Liability,* 257 JAMA 2776–81 (1987) (finding that defensive medicine has generated substantial costs). Other studies, however, have not found support for the notion of defensive medicine. *See, e.g.,* Laura-Mae Baldwin, L. Gary Hart, Michael Lloyd, Meredith Fordyce & Roger A. Rosenblatt, *Defensive Medicine and Obstetrics,* 274 JAMA 1606, 1609 (1995) (finding no evidence of "an association between the malpractice claims experience or exposure of individual physicians and an increase in the use of prenatal resources or cesarean deliveries for the care of low-risk obstetric patients").

[21] For example, the Federal Railroad Administration has studied proposals for sensor systems to prevent derailments on railroad bridges, but it concluded that they would cost as much as $40,000 per bridge to install. Overall, the cost could be billions of dollars for installation and $60 million more per year for operation and maintenance. *See* Richard Pérez-Peña, *Rail Accident Stirs Debate About Sensors,* N.Y. TIMES, Nov. 29, 1996, at B1. The Federal Railroad Administration determined that the cost was too high because of the low frequency of railroad accidents that occur on bridges. *See id.*

[22] This proposition assumes that individuals are *risk neutral.* We discuss the meaning of this assumption, and the justification for making it below. *See infra* pp. 886–87.

taken, where expected harm refers to the harm multiplied by the probability of its occurrence.[23]

Note that, even when proper precautions are exercised, some accidents will occur because of residual, hard-to-eliminate risks. For example, even the safest automobile tire may blow out and cause an accident. That a blowout occurs does not necessarily mean that the manufacturer took inadequate precautions in the design and manufacture of the tire. Likewise, even if employers screen and monitor employees with appropriate vigilance, occasional employee misbehavior will still occur, possibly egregious in character.[24] It is important to stress that such misbehavior does not necessarily signal a lack of proper oversight by the employer.[25]

Let us now turn to a second reason that it is best for damages to equal harm. This reason concerns the extent to which individuals and firms participate in risky activities — what we will refer to as their *level of activity*.[26] A party's level of activity affects the magnitude of expected harm, whatever precautions the party takes when engaging in the activity. For example, the more miles a person drives — his level of activity — the greater the number of accidents that he is likely to cause, whatever his level of care when he drives. (Of course, the more care he takes when driving, the lower will be the expected number of accidents per mile driven.) Similarly, the more units of a risky product a firm produces and sells — its level of activity — the greater the number of accidents that will be caused by the product, whatever are its safety features.

---

[23] For example, if a harm of $10,000 occurs with a probability of 20%, the expected harm is $2000 (= 20% x $10,000). This expected harm also can be interpreted as the average harm per instance of some conduct that, each time it occurs, has a 20% chance of causing a $10,000 harm. More generally, the expected harm is the sum of products of each possible magnitude of harm and its probability. Thus, if there is a 20% chance of a $10,000 harm, as well as a 5% chance of a $30,000 harm, the expected harm is $3500 (= (20% x $10,000) + (5% x $30,000)).

[24] An example may clarify this point. Suppose that 3% of the applicants for employment at a firm are "rotten apples" who will misbehave on the job and cause a $100,000 accident; that by spending $500 per applicant on investigating the applicant's background it is possible to detect one-third of the rotten apples; that by instead spending $4000 per applicant on more intensive screening, it is possible to detect two-thirds of the rotten apples; but that it is impossible to detect the remaining one-third of the rotten apples. In this example, it is socially desirable for the firm to spend $500 per applicant on screening. A firm spending this much would have a 1% chance of detecting a rotten apple (because one-third of the 3% of rotten apples in the applicant pool are identified) and of thereby avoiding a $100,000 harm. In other words, it would reduce the expected harm by $1000 (= 1% x $100,000) per applicant screened in this way. It is not socially worthwhile, however, to spend $4000 per applicant, because spending this higher amount would reduce the expected harm by only $2000 (= 2% x $100,000) per applicant. Significantly, whichever amount is spent, there will still be at least a 1% chance of employee misconduct.

[25] In the example in the previous footnote, the occurrence of employee misconduct does not necessarily imply that the employer's screening activity was improper because, under the best available screening process, at least 1% of the rotten apples will remain undetected.

[26] The distinction between level of activity and level of care to be explained here was first emphasized by Steven Shavell, *Strict Liability Versus Negligence*, 9 J. LEGAL STUD. 1 (1980).

If damages equal harm, potential injurers will have the socially correct incentives to engage in risky activities. In particular, they will engage in an activity if and only if the benefit they derive exceeds the additional harm caused by their decision to engage in it. If damages equal harm, an individual will tend to participate in an activity such as hunting if and only if the benefit he obtains from this activity exceeds the expected accident costs that hunting imposes on others. Likewise, a firm will produce a product if and only if the product's value, as reflected in the willingness of customers to pay for it, exceeds the full costs of its production, including accident losses. Specifically, if damages equal harm, the cost of production will include the harm. To cover its costs, a firm will have to sell its product at a higher price — a price that reflects the average harm caused per unit of output. Therefore, consumers will only buy the product if they value it more highly than its full cost of production, including the harm. Their consumption of the product will therefore be socially correct. In other words, the fact that the product price will rise in response to the firm's liability costs is desirable because, if damages equal harm, this price increase appropriately discourages consumers of the product from, in effect, causing an excessive number of accidents by consuming too much of the product.

It follows that, if damages are less than harm, parties will engage in activities to an excessive extent — that is, they will engage in activities even when the benefits are outweighed by the harms caused. Conversely, if damages exceed harm, parties may be led to curtail their activities to an inappropriate extent — to refrain from engaging in them even when the benefits exceed the harms caused. In particular, a firm might be induced to withdraw its product from the marketplace even though consumers place a higher value on the product than its full cost of production, which includes the average harm caused by the product.

The preceding possibilities — engaging excessively or inadequately in activities that cause harm — are realistic. For instance, some studies indicate that much of the harm from automobile pollution is not reflected in the price of gasoline or automobiles.[27] Hence, individuals will tend to drive too much.[28] Conversely, some evidence suggests that manufacturers of certain socially desirable products — for example,

---

[27] *See, e.g.*, Kenneth A. Small & Camilla Kazimi, *On the Costs of Air Pollution from Motor Vehicles*, 29 J. TRANSP. ECON. & POL'Y 7, 27 (1995) (demonstrating that an additional tax of about 50% on the price of gasoline would be required to account for air pollution costs).

[28] *See* JAMES J. MACKENZIE, ROGER C. DOWER, & DONALD D.T. CHEN, THE GOING RATE: WHAT IT REALLY COSTS TO DRIVE 5 (1992) ("The net effect of [federal and state] policies is to make driving seem cheaper than it really is and to encourage the excessive use of automobiles and trucks.").

childhood vaccines — may have stopped selling their products because of the prospect of damages exceeding harm.[29]

We have now explained the fundamental reasons that damages should equal harm under strict liability. We next discuss why we assume that damages should equal harm under the negligence rule.

By definition of the negligence rule, if a potential injurer fails to take proper precautions — does not meet the negligence standard — he is said to be negligent and must pay damages.[30] The economic interpretation of the proper negligence standard involves comparing the cost of taking the precaution with the expected reduction in harm that results from taking it: if the former amount is less than the latter, the precaution should be taken and the failure to do so is negligent.[31] It would be negligent not to take a precaution costing $50,000 that would prevent a harm of $100,000.

---

[29] A number of articles have discussed the withdrawal of products from the marketplace in response to actual or prospective liability costs (including liability insurance premiums). *See* DEWEES, DUFF & TREBILCOCK, *supra* note 15, at 241–42 (1996) (discussing the reduction of vaccine manufacturing because of the expansion of liability); W. KIP VISCUSI, REFORMING PRODUCTS LIABILITY 8 (1991) (noting product liability litigation has forced some companies to stop producing private airplanes); Louis Lasagna, *The Chilling Effect of Product Liability on New Drug Development, in* THE LIABILITY MAZE: THE IMPACT OF LIABILITY LAW ON SAFETY AND INNOVATION 334, 337–41 (Peter W. Huber & Robert E. Litan eds., 1991) (describing the litigation that led to the voluntary withdrawal of the anti-morning sickness drug, Bendectin); Robert Martin, *General Aviation Manufacturing: An Industry Under Siege, in* THE LIABILITY MAZE: THE IMPACT OF LIABILITY LAW ON SAFETY AND INNOVATION, *supra,* at 478, 478 (concluding that product liability litigation "threatens the very existence" of the corporate and private airplane industry). These discussions do not address the question whether the reduction in productive activity was due to the imposition of damages exceeding harm. However, if, as some commentators believe, product liability is socially excessive, *see, e.g.,* PETER W. HUBER, LIABILITY: THE LEGAL REVOLUTION AND ITS CONSEQUENCES 9–11 (1988) (arguing that the sharp increases in tort awards in the 1980s have led to the curtailment of socially beneficial activities such as vaccinations, ambulance services, and waste cleanup), such reductions in the availability of products may be partially attributable to excessive damages.

[30] *See* RESTATEMENT (SECOND) OF TORTS § 282 (1965) ("[N]egligence is . . . conduct which falls below the standard established by law for the protection of others against unreasonable risk of harm." (citation and internal quotation marks omitted)); PROSSER AND KEETON ON THE LAW OF TORTS, § 31, at 169 (Dan B. Dobbs, Robert E. Keeton, W. Page Keeton & David G. Owen eds., 5th ed. 1984) ("[N]egligence is not necessarily the absence of solicitude for those who may be adversely affected by one's actions but is instead behavior which should be recognized as involving unreasonable danger to others.").

[31] Judge Learned Hand's algebraic formula for determining the due care standard encapsulates the economic interpretation of the negligence rule. In his opinion in *United States v. Carroll Towing Co.,* 159 F.2d 169 (2d Cir. 1947), Judge Hand said that a party is negligent if he fails to take a precaution when the burden of the precaution is less than the reduction of the expected loss occasioned by taking the precaution — in other words, if $B < PL$, where B is the burden of taking the precaution, P is the probability of the loss if the precaution is not taken, and L is the magnitude of the loss. *See id.* at 173. For further development of this idea, see, for example, John Prather Brown, *Toward an Economic Theory of Liability,* 2 J. LEGAL STUD. 323 (1973). *See also* William M. Landes and Richard A. Posner, *The Positive Economic Theory of Tort Law,* 15 GA. L. REV. 851, 892–903 (1981) (arguing that judicial practice is consistent with the economic interpretation of the negligence rule).

Under the negligence rule, if damages equal harm, potential injurers will be led to comply with the negligence standard (assuming that it is chosen properly) and thus to take appropriate precautions. If a precaution costing $50,000 would prevent a harm of $100,000, the threat of having to pay damages of $100,000 for not taking the precaution would induce a party to spend $50,000 on the precaution. However, if damages are less than harm, the negligence standard might not be met and underdeterrence would result. In the example, if damages are only $40,000 (even though harm is $100,000), the party would not be led to take the precaution costing $50,000.[32] Conversely, if damages exceed harm, a potential injurer will have a stronger motive to meet the negligence standard than if damages equal harm. If damages are $200,000 (even though harm is $100,000), a party will have a greater incentive to spend $50,000 on the precaution than if damages are $100,000. But he will not take more precautions than are required to meet the negligence standard, assuming that the negligence determination is not erroneous. In the absence of errors, a party has no incentive to do more than satisfy the negligence standard, even if the damages that would be imposed if negligence is found far exceed the harm, because there is no chance that such damages will be imposed against him.

Realistically, however, errors will occur in the negligence determination, which suggests that damages exceeding harm could lead to excessive precautions. For several reasons, parties attempting to act non-negligently may be found liable under the negligence rule. Notably, they may inaccurately assess what the negligence standard is, or courts may inaccurately observe the parties' behavior and find them negligent when they were not. Because of the risk of mistakes, parties may well have an incentive to take greater precautions than they otherwise would have, in order to reduce the chance that they will incorrectly be found negligent.[33] If, as a result, they take socially excessive precau-

---

[32] Note that damages must be sufficiently less than the harm before the party would find it worthwhile to act negligently. If damages exceeded the $50,000 cost of the precaution, the party would be induced to take the precaution even if damages were less than the harm of $100,000.

[33] Although parties will generally reduce the chance of being found negligent by mistake by taking greater care, they will not necessarily take more care than they would if there were no mistakes in the determination of negligence. The reason is that, to the extent that there is a random component in the assessment of care, the exercise of greater care will be only partially rewarded. For instance, if half the time a party's care is not observed and courts make a guess about its level, increasing the level of care would benefit the party only half the time. The condition under which parties will take greater care is, roughly, that the assessment of care is not too imprecise. For details, see John E. Calfee & Richard Craswell, *Some Effects of Uncertainty on Compliance with Legal Standards*, 70 VA. L. REV. 965 (1984), and Richard Craswell and John E. Calfee, *Deterrence and Uncertain Legal Standards*, 2 J.L. ECON. & ORG. 279 (1986). *See also* SHAVELL, *supra* note 14, at 93–99 (arguing that injurers will exercise more than due care in the presence of errors in the assessment of their level of care). *But see* Mark F. Grady, *A New Positive Economic Theory of Negligence*, 92 YALE L.J. 799, 817–21 (1983) (showing that, under a different but plausible interpretation of the negligence rule, mistakes will not cause parties to take excessive care);

tions, raising the level of damages imposed on them will only exacerbate this problem.

Next, consider the relationship between damages and the level of activity under the negligence rule. In this regard, observe that, in the absence of mistakes, the negligence rule may result in parties participating in risky activities to a socially excessive extent.[34] This excessive participation results because, once a party takes the precautions required by the negligence standard, he will not be found liable for any harms that he causes. For example, a person who drives with reasonable care will not be found negligent, and therefore will not have to pay for any harm caused by his driving; consequently, he will drive more than is socially desirable. Or a manufacturer that takes appropriate care in the design of its product will not be liable under a negligence rule for harms that result if its product nonetheless turns out to be flawed; as a result, too much of the product will tend to be produced.[35]

However, because non-negligent parties sometimes will be found liable by mistake, they will sometimes bear damages. In principle, this erroneous imposition of liability could mitigate the problem that the negligence rule may induce parties to participate in risky activities to an excessive degree. However, finding parties negligent by mistake may result in their bearing damages in excess of the harm they have caused,[36] and thereby discourage their participation in the activity to an inappropriate extent. This effect, if it occurs, will be exacerbated by raising the level of damages.

This discussion of the negligence rule shows that the optimal level of damages is not as easily determined as under the strict liability rule.

Marcel Kahan, *Causation and Incentives To Take Care Under the Negligence Rule*, 18 J. LEGAL STUD. 427, 437–39 (1989) (same).

[34] The result that the negligence rule leads to socially excessive participation in risky activities was originally developed in Shavell, cited above in note 26. *See also* A. Mitchell Polinsky, *Strict Liability vs. Negligence in a Market Setting*, 70 AM. ECON. REV. 363 (1980) (demonstrating the result in market settings).

[35] The point of this paragraph may be clarified by a numerical illustration. Suppose that taking proper precautions would cost an individual $100 each time he engages in an activity and would reduce to 1/2% the risk of an accident that would cause harm of $100,000. Assuming that the individual would take the precautions in order to avoid liability for negligence, he will engage in the activity whenever the benefit to him exceeds the $100 cost of precautions. However, each time he engages in the activity, he causes total social costs of $600: the $100 cost of precautions, *plus* the expected harm of $500 (= 1/2% × $100,000). Consequently, from society's perspective, he should engage in the activity only if his benefit exceeds $600. If his benefit lies between $100 and $600, however, he will engage in the activity even though doing so is socially undesirable.

[36] More precisely, expected damages could exceed harm for two reasons. First, a party who caused harm but who was not negligent might be found negligent by mistake and made to pay such a high level of damages that, on average, he will pay for more than the harm he caused. Second, a party who did not cause harm might mistakenly be found both to be the cause of harm and to be negligent. Obviously, any damages imposed on such a party are excessive and will chill participation in activities in which such mistakes occur.

Under strict liability, we concluded that damages should equal harm. Under the negligence rule, we have observed that, in the absence of mistakes, damages equal to harm will appropriately encourage parties to take precautions, but so will higher levels of damages.[37] In the presence of mistakes, the optimal level of damages under the negligence rule is difficult to ascertain, although it is clear from what we have said that if damages are set too high, parties will tend to be induced to take excessive precautions; moreover, they will not participate in their activities to an appropriate degree. In the light of the preceding points, and recognizing that there is not a simple, theoretically correct answer to the question of what level of damages is optimal under the negligence rule, we will assume for the purpose of our analysis that optimal damages under the negligence rule equal harm.[38]

This concludes our review of the implications of deterrence theory for the optimal level of damages under the rules of strict liability and negligence when injurers will be found liable with certainty. Because damages should equal harm under the strict liability rule, and because we assume that damages should equal harm under the negligence rule for the reasons given, we generally will not distinguish between the rules in our subsequent discussion.

In passing, we want to note that the principal conclusion reached in this section — that damages should equal harm — depends on how potential injurers respond to risk. We have implicitly assumed that they are *risk neutral*. This means that, in considering situations of risk, parties care only about the expected value of a risky situation — that is, the magnitude of a potential loss or gain multiplied by the probability of the loss or gain occurring.[39] If injurers are *risk averse* (they dislike uncertainty itself)[40] and cannot purchase liability insurance, the optimal level of damages tends to be lower than the harm: setting damages below the harm reduces the imposition of risk on in-

---

[37] Some lower levels of damages also will properly induce parties to take precautions provided that these levels still exceed the cost of precautions. *See supra* note 32.

[38] This assumption is made mostly for convenience and does not affect our main point that the benchmark level of damages — the level that would be appropriate for deterrence if injurers were definitely found liable — should be inflated using a specific multiplier formula if injurers can sometimes escape liability. If the benchmark level of damages is different from harm, this benchmark quantum, whatever its magnitude, should be inflated by the multiplier we give below in order for deterrence to be appropriate when injurers can escape liability. *See infra* section II.B.

[39] A risk-neutral injurer would be indifferent between paying certain damages of, say, $10,000, and facing a risky situation in which he will pay either nothing or $20,000 with equal probability, because the risky situation involves an expected payment of $10,000 (= 50% × $20,000). *See generally* ROBERT S. PINDYCK & DANIEL L. RUBINFELD, MICROECONOMICS 146 (3d ed. 1995) (discussing the concept of risk neutrality).

[40] A risk-averse injurer would prefer to pay certain damages of $10,000 than to face a risky situation in which he will have to pay either nothing or $20,000 with equal probability, even though the risky situation involves an expected payment of $10,000. *See generally id.* (discussing risk aversion).

jurers, and damages do not need to be as great as the harm to induce injurers to behave appropriately.[41]

Notwithstanding this last point, we will usually assume in our subsequent analysis that, when injurers are found liable for sure, the level of damages that is optimal with respect to deterrence is equal to harm,[42] for two reasons. First, even if parties are risk averse, if they can purchase liability insurance, it can be shown that the optimal level of damages still equals harm.[43] Second, it can be demonstrated that publicly held firms should be treated as approximately risk neutral — implying that damages should equal harm — if their shareholders have well-diversified portfolios, which often, if not usually, will be the case.[44]

B. *Optimal Damages When the Defendant Can Sometimes Escape Liability*

The main point that we will develop in this section is that *if a defendant can sometimes escape liability for the harm for which he is responsible, the proper magnitude of damages is the harm the defendant has caused, multiplied by a factor reflecting the probability of his escaping liability.* As we will explain, use of such a multiplier will make defendants pay on average for harm actually done and thus will lead

---

[41] This result is demonstrated in SHAVELL, cited above in note 14, at 218–21, and Steven Shavell, *On Liability and Insurance*, 13 BELL J. ECON. 120, 124–26 (1982). The optimal level of damages depends on the degree of risk aversion of injurers and on whether victims are insured or, if not, how risk averse they are.

[42] In Part III, we will discuss two situations in which this assumption is not appropriate. One is, as we have noted, when behavior is malicious; then optimal damages may exceed harm. *See infra* section III.A. The second situation is when victims of harm are customers of the defendant and are relatively well informed about risk, in which case it may not be necessary to impose damages equal to harm to achieve optimal deterrence. *See infra* section III.J.

[43] This conclusion is formally demonstrated in SHAVELL, cited above in note 14, at 222–27, and Shavell, cited above in note 41, at 126–30. It should seem intuitively plausible if injurers purchase full coverage against liability, for then their risk aversion is irrelevant. If injurers do not purchase full coverage (suppose there is coinsurance or a deductible), the conclusion is not obvious because injurers do bear residual risk, but it is true nonetheless for reasons explained in the sources cited in this note.

[44] The point that diversified shareholders will want a firm to be operated in an approximately risk-neutral manner is well-accepted in the economic literature concerning corporate finance. *See, e.g.*, RICHARD A. BREALEY & STEWART C. MYERS, PRINCIPLES OF CORPORATE FINANCE 148–49 (4th ed. 1991). The reason shareholders desire that firms operate in a risk-neutral manner is, roughly speaking, that each shareholder, holding a diversified portfolio, will not worry about the riskiness of any particular firm in which he has ownership rights; thus, he will vote to have the firm maximize its expected return. The result that the optimal level of damages equals harm when shareholders want the firm to act in a risk-neutral way follows directly from reasoning in Harry A. Newman & David W. Wright, *Strict Liability in a Principal-Agent Model*, 10 INT'L REV. L. & ECON. 219 (1990). This result holds even though employees of firms will generally be risk averse and cannot be controlled perfectly by shareholders. (The point of this footnote may not apply if the wealth of the owners of a particular firm depends in a significant way on the profitability of that firm, as would often be the case for privately held firms owned by relatively few individuals.)

to socially desirable behavior in terms of precautions and participation in risky activities.

There are several reasons that injurers sometimes escape liability for harms for which they should be liable. First, the victim may have difficulty determining that the harm was the result of some party's act — as opposed to simply being the result of nature, of bad luck. For instance, an individual may develop a form of cancer that could have been caused by exposure to a naturally occurring carcinogen, such as radon gas, but which was in fact caused by exposure to a manmade carcinogen that was released by the injurer.

Second, even if the victim knows that he was injured by some party's conduct, he may have difficulty proving who caused the harm. The owner of a parked car that was damaged might know that it had been struck by another vehicle, but not be able to identify the injurer. Those living near a polluted lake might know both that pollution is responsible for an unusually high rate of disease in their neighborhood and who the polluters are, but not be able to establish causation in court.

Third, even if the victim knows both that he was wrongfully injured and who injured him, he might not sue the injurer. A person will tend not to bring a suit if the legal cost and the value of the time and effort he would have to devote to the suit exceed the expected gain. The decision to forgo suit will often occur when the harm the victim has suffered is relatively small or the likelihood of establishing causation is low. (Additionally, a victim might not sue if he has a distaste for the legal process.)

For one or more of the above reasons, injurers will sometimes be able to escape liability for harms for which they should be held responsible.[45] The consequences of this possibility are clear: *if damages merely equal harm, injurers' incentives to take precautions will be inadequate and their incentive to participate in risky activities will be excessive.* Suppose that there is only a one-in-four chance that an injurer will be found liable for a $100,000 harm, for which he would have to pay damages of $100,000. On average, then, the injurer will

---

[45] Consider, for example, the following evidence. The likelihood of obtaining compensation for medical negligence has been found to be about 6%. *See* HARVARD MEDICAL PRACTICE STUDY, PATIENTS, DOCTORS, AND LAWYERS: MEDICAL INJURY, MALPRACTICE LITIGATION, AND PATIENT COMPENSATION IN NEW YORK 7-1 (1990). The average probability that an oil spill in excess of 10,000 gallons will be detected and traced to its source is approximately 60%. *See* Mark A. Cohen, *Optimal Enforcement Strategy To Prevent Oil Spills: An Application of a Principal-Agent Model with Moral Hazard*, 30 J.L. & ECON. 23, 44–45 (1987). The average probability of the detection of fraud is estimated to be 30%. *See* Jonathan M. Karpoff & John R. Lott, Jr., *The Reputational Penalty Firms Bear from Committing Criminal Fraud*, 36 J.L. & ECON. 757, 789–90 (1993).

We should also note that parties may sometimes be found liable for harms for which they are *not* responsible. Although we do not consider this possibility in our analysis, were we to do so, it would often lower the level of damages that otherwise would be optimal.

pay $25,000 when he causes the harm — only a fraction of the harm caused. If the harm could have been prevented each time by taking a $50,000 precaution, the injurer will not have an adequate incentive to take the precaution, because the precaution cost will exceed his average liability cost by a substantial margin. Moreover, because the injurer will pay only $25,000 on average for a $100,000 harm, he will engage in the risky activity to an excessive degree. If the injurer is a firm, the price of its product will rise by an amount reflecting only one-quarter of the harm caused, leading consumers of the product to buy more of it, and thereby cause more harm, than is socially desirable.

To remedy these problems of underdeterrence, damages that are imposed in those instances in which injurers are found liable should be raised sufficiently so that injurers' average damages will equal the harm they cause. In the example in the preceding paragraph, in which the chance of being found liable for having caused a $100,000 harm is only one in four, damages should be raised to $400,000. Then, on average, the injurer will pay $100,000 when he causes the harm — on average, every four times he causes harm, he will be found liable once for $400,000. Equivalently, his total damages will tend to equal the total amount of harm that he has caused.[46] As we emphasized above,[47] making injurers liable for the harm they cause will induce them to take proper precautions and participate appropriately in risky activities.

This discussion suggests a simple formula for assuring that injurers will pay for the harms they cause: *the total damages imposed on an injurer should equal the harm multiplied by the reciprocal of the probability that the injurer will be found liable when he ought to be.*[48] We will refer to this multiplier as the *total damages multiplier.* In the example in the preceding paragraph, the probability that the injurer would be found liable was one in four, or .25; thus, the multiplier is 1/.25, or 4. Because the harm was $100,000, this formula will result in total damages imposed on the injurer of $400,000. Similarly, if the in-

---

[46] If the injurer does not engage in an activity repeatedly, but, say, only once, the injurer obviously will not pay for the harm done, even approximately: he either will pay $400,000 in this one instance (more than the $100,000 harm he caused) or will escape liability altogether. However, the injurer's *expected* damages — the damages he will have to pay if he is found liable, multiplied by the probability of being found liable — equal the harm of $100,000 (because he has a one-in-four chance of being found liable and made to pay $400,000).

[47] *See supra* section II.A.

[48] It may be helpful to state this formula algebraically. If H is the harm and P is the probability of being found liable, then the injurer should pay $H \times 1/P$ — that is, H/P — when he is found liable. Thus, the injurer's expected damages will be $P \times (H/P) = H$. The earliest reference to this formula (although in words) apparently is in Jeremy Bentham, *An Introduction to the Principles of Morals and Legislation,* in THE UTILITARIANS 173 (1961) (1789). For other references to this formula, see ROBERT COOTER & THOMAS ULEN, LAW AND ECONOMICS 391–92 (1st ed. 1988); POSNER, cited above in note 12, at 77; and SHAVELL, cited above in note 14, at 148, 161–62.

jurer would be found liable with a one-in-two chance, damages should be $200,000 — the $100,000 harm multiplied by 2 (= 1/.5). And if the chance of liability is only one in ten, damages should be $1,000,000 — the $100,000 harm multiplied by 10 (=1/.1). The application of this formula will guarantee that, on average, injurers will pay for the harm they cause, and therefore take proper precautions and appropriately participate in risky activities.[49]

It is important to stress that the level of damages given by the formula is optimal not only because this level remedies problems of underdeterrence, but also because it avoids problems of overdeterrence. The latter problems, described above,[50] would arise if damages were to exceed the optimal amount.

We will refer to the excess of total damages over compensatory damages as *punitive damages*. Thus, the *optimal* level of punitive damages from the perspective of deterrence is the level of total damages determined by the formula, less compensatory damages. If an injurer has a one-in-four chance of being found liable for causing a $100,000 harm, the formula implies that total damages should be $400,000. Because $100,000 of this total represents compensatory damages, the $300,000 remainder is the optimal amount of punitive damages.

The optimal level of punitive damages also can be described as a multiple of harm or, equivalently, a multiple of compensatory damages. Specifically, punitive damages should equal the harm multiplied by a factor that we will refer to as the *punitive damages multiplier*: the ratio of the injurer's chance of escaping liability to his chance of being found liable.[51] In the example in the previous paragraph, the injurer has a three-in-four chance of escaping liability and a one-in-four chance of being found liable. The punitive damages multiplier is therefore .75/.25, or 3. Because the harm was $100,000, punitive damages should be three times this amount, or $300,000.

Although we refer to the excess of total damages over compensatory damages as punitive damages, the adjective "punitive" may sometimes be misleading. This is because extracompensatory damages may

---

[49] Two qualifications should be mentioned. First, total damages should be less than the amount given by the formula in this paragraph if injurers are risk averse and cannot obtain liability insurance. This conclusion follows from our discussion above. *See supra* pp. 886–87. Second, if an injurer's subjective belief about the probability of being found liable differs from the true probability, the former should in principle be used in the formula. For simplicity, we assume in this Article that parties are aware of the actual probability of being found liable.

[50] *See supra* section II.A.

[51] To see that this level of damages is the correct one, recall from note 48, above, that the proper level of *total* damages is H/P, where H is the magnitude of harm and P is the probability that the injurer will be found liable. This amount would comprise a payment of H in compensatory damages and $(H/P) - H$ in punitive damages. The punitive payment can be rewritten as $[(1 - P)/P]H$. The term in brackets is the punitive damages multiplier to which we refer in the text.

be needed for deterrence purposes in circumstances in which the behavior of the defendant would not call for *punishment*. As we have
explained, the deterrence goal leads us to impose such damages when
injurers may escape liability. But injurers might escape liability even
when their conduct is not strongly blameworthy. Suppose an injurer
accidentally (perhaps even non-negligently) causes harm, but the victim does not sue, either because he is unable to trace the harm to its
source or because of the cost of litigation. In other words, non-
blameworthy conduct might still call for punitive damages to achieve
proper deterrence.[52] Despite a certain inappropriateness, therefore, in
using the label "punitive damages" to refer to extracompensatory damages needed for deterrence reasons, we will continue to employ it because it is the common term for extracompensatory damages in private
civil litigation.[53]

We have several comments to make about the punitive damages
formula presented in this section. First, judges and juries[54] often will
be able to apply the formula without difficulty because the formula
transparently (if trivially) implies that no punitive damages are needed.
In other words, in many situations, it will be obvious that the injurer
has virtually no chance of escaping liability — say because the harm
occurred openly and the magnitude of the harm is such that the victims almost surely will bring suit. Examples of such situations are
when a building collapses as a result of a plainly defective design[55]
and when a supertanker runs aground and spills a large quantity of oil
on the shoreline, where the oil is observed by many people.[56] In such
cases, the proper total damages multiplier is one — that is, total damages should equal harm. Punitive damages are not needed for proper
deterrence, and imposing them would result in the problems of overdeterrence discussed above.[57]

Second, in other circumstances, when the chance of escaping liability is clearly positive, the probability of liability still might be relatively easily calculated. For example, suppose a firm dumps toxic
waste at night along an infrequently used road, but is caught as a result of the report of a driver who happened to notice the firm's activities. In such a case, pressure-sensitive recording devices laid across the

---

[52] We will elaborate on this point when we discuss the reprehensibility criterion in the context
of deterrence. *See infra* section III.A.

[53] For essentially the reasons we have given, Galligan prefers the term "augmented awards" to
"punitive damages." *See* Galligan, *supra* note 3, at 12–13.

[54] For simplicity, we sometimes will refer hereafter to courts, when we mean both courts and
juries.

[55] Consider, for example, the collapse of two pedestrian skywalks at the Hyatt Regency Hotel
in Kansas City in 1981. *See In re* Federal Skywalk Cases, 97 F.R.D. 380 (W.D. Mo. 1983). The
defendants in that case agreed not to contest liability. *See id.* at 389.

[56] *See infra* pp. 903–04 (discussing the Exxon Valdez oil spill litigation).

[57] *See supra* section II.A.

road could be used to determine the volume of traffic on the road at night, and the resulting data could be employed to calculate the odds that someone would drive by during a particular interval of time. The reciprocal of this probability could then be used as the total damages multiplier.[58] In general, a careful consideration of the facts in a case often will allow a jury to make a reasonable estimate of the probability of escaping liability.[59] The testimony of expert witnesses also may be helpful in calculating this probability.[60]

Third, circumstances in which the chance of escaping liability is difficult to estimate will inevitably arise. To reduce the decisionmaking burden on jurors, a judge could present them with a table with a limited number of values for the probability, such as 0.1 through 0.9 by increments of one-tenth, from which to choose.[61] Although such a simplification would not directly resolve the problem of determining the probability of detection, it may aid jurors in settling on a single number.[62] Even if jurors make significant errors in estimating the probability, such errors will not necessarily create a serious problem for achieving optimal deterrence: provided that the errors are not systematically biased upwards or downwards, a potential injurer will know that the assessment of juries will be approximately correct on average, which will induce the injurer to behave properly. Another

---

[58] Some estimate also would have to be made of the probability that a driver who observed suspicious behavior would report it. Obviously, the lower this probability, the higher the proper damages multiplier. (If this consideration is ignored because of the difficulty of estimating the probability, the multiplier discussed in the text would be a lower bound for the ideal multiplier.)

[59] We discuss a number of punitive damages cases below and explain how the facts in those cases bear on determining the appropriate damages multiplier. *See infra* section II.D.

[60] It should be noted that juries are often required to consider and determine probabilities in contexts other than those discussed here, for example in assessing negligence. In deciding whether a person is negligent, a jury must ascertain how much an additional precaution would lower the probability of harm. If the reduction in the probability, multiplied by the harm, exceeds the cost of the precaution, it is negligent not to have taken it. *See* RESTATEMENT (SECOND) OF TORTS § 291 (1965) ("Where an act is one which a reasonable man would recognize as involving a risk of harm to another, the risk is unreasonable and the act is negligent if the risk is of such magnitude as to outweigh what the law regards as the utility of the act or of the particular manner in which it is done."). Thus, when a jury considers whether the failure to install a safety device was negligent, it must determine how much the device would have lowered the accident probability. No reason exists to believe that juries would have more difficulty in appraising probabilities in the context of calculating punitive damages than in the context of determining negligence, which is not thought to be especially problematic. However, some evidence suggests that individuals do have problems with estimating probabilities in many circumstances. *See, e.g.,* JUDGMENT UNDER UNCERTAINTY: HEURISTICS AND BIASES 3–20 (Daniel Kahneman, Paul Slovic & Amos Tversky eds., 1982) (documenting the manner in which people rely on heuristics to facilitate the assessment of probability).

[61] Such a table is provided below. *See infra* Appendix.

[62] A byproduct of restricting attention to a limited number of probabilities is that this prevents the jury from picking a damages multiplier above a certain value — for example, the damages multiplier cannot exceed 10 if the lowest probability offered is 0.1. We discuss caps on punitive damages below and point out that they cannot be justified as a matter of principle. *See infra* p. 900.

option is for the legislature to set damages multipliers for separate categories of wrongful conduct, based on rough assessments of the different chances of escaping liability in the various settings. This approach might be desirable if one believes that jury determination of the probabilities, and therefore of the damages multipliers, would be systematically biased. (Such an approach, however, would prevent juries from making use of any information they have about particular cases.[63])

Fourth, it might seem problematic for the application of the multiplier formula that the probability of escaping liability, and thus the multiplier, may depend on the way in which an accident is categorized. For example, consider a spill of dangerous chemicals from a tanker truck on a highway. Such a spill can be categorized either relatively narrowly — one category might be a spill resulting from the rupture of the tank and another category might be a spill resulting from a slow leak of the tank — or relatively broadly — one category encompassing both types of accident. A spill obviously will be much more easily detected if it is the consequence of a rupture than of a slow leak. Thus, if a rupture-caused spill is treated as a separate category, a lower multiplier would be used than if it is treated as an instance of a broader category of spills that includes leaks. How, then, should the categorization of an accident be determined for the purpose of deterrence? Should categorization be narrow, with separate multipliers employed for different types of chemical spills, or be broad, with a single multiplier employed? The answer is, essentially, that narrow definitions of accidents and separate multipliers should be used, other things being equal. Otherwise, incentives to prevent specific types of chemical spills would tend to be distorted. This is because the multiplier used for a specific type of accident would not be tailored to it, but instead would reflect the likelihood of escaping liability for a broader category of accidents. If a single multiplier is employed for all chemical spills, then, because it would exceed one, firms would have excessive incentives to avoid chemical spills for which they would definitely be found liable; thus, they might spend excessively on reinforcing the tanks or on testing the tanks' pressure (say, every fifteen minutes rather than every trip). Further, because the multiplier would be lower than is appropriate for slow leaks that are very likely to escape notice, firms would have inadequate incentives to prevent these spills; for instance, they might not check frequently enough for cracks in difficult-to-inspect parts of the tanks. The general point, then, is that when actors

---

[63] Juries could be given limited discretion to use such information if legislatures select a range for the punitive damages multiplier rather than a specific multiplier.

can take precautions that are particular to a type of accident, the categorization of the accident should be narrow.[64]

Fifth, an important question about the multiplier formula arises in cases in which the defendant is a firm: should the damages multiplier be based on the probability that the firm will be found liable, or on the generally lower likelihood that the responsible employee will be found liable? The answer is that the firm's probability is the relevant one. Consider a situation in which a firm definitely would be found liable for a harm resulting, say, from an explosion of a chemical storage tank, but the employee whose actions led to the explosion might be difficult to identify. Because the firm will have to pay for the harm for sure, punitive damages are not needed: the firm's product price and its incentives to take precautions will be correct because it will be paying for all of the harm it causes if it pays just compensatory damages. That the particular employee who caused the explosion might not be caught does not alter this point — the employee's escaping responsibility does not free the firm from liability. Were the firm to face puni-

---

[64] If, however, all precautions are general rather than specific to a kind of accident, it does not matter whether accidents are categorized narrowly. Failing to categorize narrowly will not distort which type of precaution is taken if there are no specific types of precaution to take.

To illustrate, suppose that there is one type of precaution and two kinds of accident, A and B; that the two kinds of accident are equally likely to occur; that each would cause harm of $10,000; that if A occurs, no likelihood of escaping liability exists; and that if B occurs, the likelihood of escaping liability is 50%. Under these assumptions, we will show that an injurer's expected damages if an accident occurs will equal the harm of $10,000 regardless of whether accidents are categorized narrowly or broadly. If the categorization is narrow, the multiplier for an accident of type A will be 1, and the multiplier for an accident of type B will be 2. Thus, if an accident of type A occurs, the injurer's expected damages will be $10,000 because he will definitely pay $10,000; and if an accident of type B occurs, his expected damages will also be $10,000 because he will pay $20,000 with a probability of 50%. If the categorization is broad, including both kinds of accident, the multiplier will be 1.3333 because the probability of being found liable for an accident of some type is 75% (the average of 100% and 50%). Hence, damages when the injurer is found liable will be $13,333 (= 1.3333 × $10,000). The injurer's expected damages for an accident will again be $10,000, comprising a 50% chance that a type A accident will occur, in which case the injurer will definitely be found liable for $13,333, plus a 50% chance that a type B accident will occur, in which case the injurer will be found liable for $13,333 with a 50% probability (in other words, [50% × (100% × $13,333)] + [50% × (50% × $13,333)] = $10,000). Accordingly, whichever categorization is used to determine the multiplier, the injurer's incentives will be correct, and no issue of distortion of the types of precaution taken will arise because, by hypothesis, only one type exists.

If there were two separate types of precaution, one reducing the frequency of type A accidents and the other reducing the frequency of type B accidents, then under the broad categorization, with a multiplier of 1.3333, a potential injurer would take an excessive degree of care to reduce type A accidents and too little care to reduce type B accidents. (We note, however, that the following point can be demonstrated: if the single multiplier used under the broad categorization is always adjusted to reflect the relative likelihoods of type A and type B accidents — they would not necessarily be equally likely when there are different types of precaution — use of a single multiplier would not distort incentives to take different types of precaution. Nevertheless, making such an adjustment would be administratively difficult, to say the least.)

tive damages because of the employee's chance of escaping liability, overdeterrence would result.[65]

Sixth, it should be observed that the award of punitive damages may itself raise the probability of suit, which would reduce the probability that the defendant will escape liability. This effect, when applicable, must be taken into account and will tend to lower the appropriate level of punitive damages. Suppose, for example, that the probability of suit for a $100,000 harm for which a party should be liable would be one-third if damages are compensatory, but would rise to one-half if damages are twice compensatory damages, $200,000. Suppose also that, if a suit is brought, the plaintiff will definitely prevail. If the damages multiplier is based on the one-third probability of suit, it would call for total damages of $300,000. But this level of damages would be too high because the probability of suit increases to one-half (or greater) when damages are $300,000: expected damages would be $150,000 (or greater), far exceeding the harm. In fact, damages of $200,000 would be appropriate because the probability of suit would then be one-half and expected damages would be $100,000. In general, a level of damages will exist that, given the resulting probability of suit, will lead to optimal deterrence.[66] Basing punitive damages on the relatively low probability of suit that would occur if only compensatory damages were awarded, however, will tend to lead to excessive damages.

Seventh, it might seem that the analysis in this section would virtually always call for *some* punitive damages award, because some chance of escaping liability will almost always exist.[67] But such a conclusion ignores a factor that we have not yet mentioned, namely, the costs associated with the use of the legal system.[68] Were every case to involve the calculation of the proper multiplier of harm, a new and potentially costly-to-decide issue would be introduced into litigation. This additional cost suggests that the domain of cases in which the multiplier inquiry is made should be limited. Specifically, our formula should be applied only if the likelihood of escaping liability surpasses some threshold, for that is when the problem of dilution of deterrence

---

[65] Although punitive damages should not be imposed on the firm, the firm may want, in effect, to impose punitive internal sanctions on its employees in order to deter them from acting in ways that cause harm. Additionally, the greater the likelihood that employees would escape such sanctions, the more the firm may want to spend on its monitoring and screening efforts.

[66] To state matters formally, let D be damages and let $P(D)$ be the probability of suit, which rises as D rises and which is less than one. The claim in the text is that there exists a D such that $P(D)D = H$, where H is the harm. Because the function $P(D)D$ is continuous in D, there must exist such a D between H and $H/P(H)$ because $P(H)H < H$ and $P(H/P(H))[H/P(H)] > P(H)[H/P(H)] = H$ (the asserted D is unique because $P(D)D$ is strictly rising in D). We comment further on the connection between damages and the probability of suit below. *See infra* section III.E.

[67] *See* David G. Owen, *Civil Punishment and the Public Good*, 56 S. CAL. L. REV. 103, 113 (1982).

[68] We discuss this consideration in more detail below. *See infra* section III.E.

will be significant, making it socially worthwhile to incur the additional litigation costs associated with calculating a corrective multiplier.[69]

Finally, it should be noted that we have assumed that when parties are found liable, they pay for all of the harm that they have caused. In practice, though, parties may escape having to pay for some of the harm. To the extent that this occurs, an argument can be made that the level of damages should be higher than that called for by our multiplier formula, to make up both for the chance of escaping liability altogether and for the chance of not having to pay for the full harm. The most likely circumstance in which the full harm would not be assessed against the defendant arises when a particular component of harm (say, some type of non-pecuniary loss) is excluded from compensatory damages. For reasons explained below, however, we believe that punitive damages should not be raised to make up for an excluded component of harm.[70]

C. *Consistency of Punitive Damages Law with the Basic Theory of Deterrence*

We now will relate our analysis to certain important aspects of legal doctrine concerning punitive damages, and also to legislation imposing caps on punitive damages.

As noted above,[71] one of the two main purposes of punitive damages is deterrence. The courts state, for example, that punitive damages are intended "to deter the wrongdoer and others from committing similar wrongs in the future."[72] Given that achieving proper deterrence is an avowed goal of courts, *it follows from the logic of deter-*

---

[69] Actually, this statement oversimplifies matters. To decide when it is worthwhile to calculate a damages multiplier, one would in principle need to take into account not just the probability of escaping liability, but also the magnitude of the harm and the costs of precautions. For even if the probability of escaping liability is high, if the harm is very low or if the costs of additional precautions are very high, it may not be worthwhile to incur the additional litigation costs in order to determine the proper damages multiplier.

Additionally, if the determination of punitive damages is not done on a case-by-case basis, it might be desirable to award punitive damages even when the probability of escaping liability is low. Suppose a fixed multiplier is applied in all cases in which the probability is small but positive. Then no additional litigation costs would be associated with calculating the multiplier in each case; and if the fixed multiplier is set appropriately, incentives will be improved overall relative to what they would be if no multiplier were employed.

[70] *See infra* section III.L.

[71] *See supra* p. 873.

[72] Green Oil Co. v. Hornsby, 539 So. 2d 218, 222 (Ala. 1989). The United States Supreme Court has endorsed the criteria for evaluating punitive damages discussed in this case. *See* Pacific Mut. Life Ins. Co. v. Haslip, 499 U.S. 1, 20–24 (1991). For further support for the proposition that deterrence is one of the central purposes of punitive damages, see also the cases cited above in note 5. Indeed, in Maine, deterrence is the only justification for punitive damages. *See* Foss v. Maine Turnpike Auth., 309 A.2d 339, 345 (Me. 1973) (citing Allen v. Rossi, 146 A. 692, 694 (Me. 1929)).

rence theory that courts should take the punitive damages formula pre-sented above into explicit account. Otherwise, courts cannot responsibly weigh the proper punitive damages amount for achieving deterrence against the proper amount for achieving the other main purpose of punitive damages, punishment.[73]

However, courts' determinations of punitive damages do not reflect in any clear manner the formula that achieves optimal deterrence. Although courts do consider the magnitude of harm in assessing the proper level of punitive damages, they do not use harm as the base to be multiplied by an appropriate damages multiplier. Rather, courts take harm into account in a vague way, through application of the general principle that punitive damages should bear a "reasonable relationship" to compensatory damages.[74] They do not explain what this relationship should be and, even when they identify a ratio of punitive damages to compensatory damages that they find excessive, they do not supply a basis for selecting the particular ratio identified.[75]

---

[73] How the deterrence goal and the punishment goal should be reconciled when they are in conflict is discussed below. *See infra* Part V and Appendix.

[74] 1 LINDA L. SCHLUETER & KENNETH R. REDDEN, PUNITIVE DAMAGES § 6.1(C), at 334 (3d ed. 1995). "As a general rule, the punitive damages award must bear a reasonable relation to the amount of actual damages awarded." *Id.* The United States Supreme Court has endorsed the reasonable-relationship notion in its decisions. *See, e.g.,* BMW of N. Am., Inc. v. Gore, 116 S. Ct. 1589, 1601 (1996) (stating that "[t]he principle that exemplary damages must bear a 'reasonable relationship' to compensatory damages has a long pedigree," and citing cases dating from 1852); *Haslip,* 499 U.S. at 21–22 (endorsing Alabama's criteria for the post-verdict review of punitive damages, which include "whether there is a reasonable relationship between the punitive damages award and the harm likely to result from the defendant's conduct as well as the harm that actually has occurred," and stating that the "review ensures that punitive damages awards . . . have some understandable relationship to compensatory damages").

[75] The United States Supreme Court has recently presented three "guideposts" for determining whether a punitive damages award is excessive. *See Gore,* 116 S. Ct. at 1598. "The second [of these guideposts,] and perhaps [the] most commonly cited indicium of an unreasonable or excessive punitive damages award is its ratio to the actual harm inflicted on the plaintiff." *Id.* at 1601. The Court, however, rejects the possibility that excessiveness can be determined by "a simple mathematical formula, even one that compares actual and potential damages to the punitive award." *Id.* at 1602 (citing TXO Prod. Corp. v. Alliance Resources Corp., 509 U.S. 443, 458 (1993)). In his concurrence in *Gore,* Justice Breyer points to problems with the reasonable-relationship standard, arguing that, at least as it is interpreted by the Alabama courts, it "does little to guide a determination of what counts as a 'reasonable' relationship . . . . To find a 'reasonable relationship' between purely economic harm totaling $56,000, without significant evidence of future repetition, and a punitive award of $2 million is to empty the 'reasonable relationship' test of meaningful content." *Id.* at 1606 (Breyer, J., concurring).

Courts often make statements of the following sort: "[A]lthough there is no fixed ratio by which to determine the propriety of a punitive damage award, punitive damages should bear a reasonable relationship to the compensatory damages awarded." Little v. Stuyvesant Life Ins. Co., 136 Cal. Rptr. 653, 663 (Cal. Ct. App. 1977). The *Little* court followed that sentence with the observation that "[h]ere, the ratio of punitive damages to compensatory damages is in excess of 14 to 1 and in dollar amount the punitive damage award exceeds the compensatory award by almost two and a third million dollars," and the court relied on these facts, among others, in concluding that the punitive damages award in the case was excessive. *Id.* at 664.

In an important early article on punitive damages, Clarence Morris criticized approaches like that of the *Little* court:

As the reader knows, our analysis implies a simple and precise relationship between punitive damages and harm: punitive damages should equal the harm multiplied by what we refer to as the punitive damages multiplier. If punitive damages are to achieve appropriate deterrence, the "reasonable relationship" criterion must be interpreted in this specific way. Any other relationship between punitive damages and compensatory damages will lead to either inadequate or excessive deterrence.

Courts also do not pay systematic attention to the probability of escaping liability, even though this probability is the central element in determining the appropriate damages multiplier for the purpose of achieving proper deterrence. Courts sometimes allude to the possibility of escaping liability, but they rarely recognize its importance with respect to deterrence. For example, in determining the level of punitive damages, courts occasionally consider whether the defendant has attempted to conceal his conduct.[76] Courts usually do so, however, in assessing the reprehensibility of the defendant's conduct;[77] they generally do not appreciate that evidence of attempted concealment should influence the calculation of the defendant's chance of escaping liability. Additionally, courts sometimes mention that the cost of litigation should be taken into account "so as to encourage plaintiffs to bring wrongdoers to trial."[78] This factor is obviously related to the injurer's chance of escaping liability because one reason an injurer might not be

---

Courts often insist that "punitive damages must bear some relation to actual damages," and attempt to test verdicts in terms of mathematical ratios. The opinions contain statements to the effect that a verdict for punitive damages *x* times as great as the actual damages is clearly excessive....

This test is probably more often a rationalization of results than a means of obtaining them. The proper ratio between actual damages and punitive damages is placed at a figure which supports the judge's view of the verdict ....

Clarence Morris, *Punitive Damages in Tort Cases*, 44 HARV. L. REV. 1173, 1180 (1931).

[76] *See, e.g., Green Oil*, 539 So. 2d at 223 (considering concealment and cover-up in determining degree of reprehensibility, which influences the level of punitive damages); Gamble v. Stevenson, 406 S.E.2d 350, 354 (S.C. 1991) (establishing "defendant's awareness or concealment" as one factor to consider in the post-trial review of jury awards of punitive damages).

[77] *See, e.g., Green Oil*, 539 So. 2d at 223; *see also* Garnes v. Fleming Landfill, Inc., 413 S.E.2d 897, 909 (W. Va. 1991) (stating that, in determining the reprehensibility of defendant's conduct, the jury should consider "whether he attempted to conceal or cover up his actions or the harm caused by them").

[78] *Green Oil*, 539 So. 2d at 223; *see also Garnes*, 413 S.E.2d at 909 (instructing trial courts to consider the costs of litigation in reviewing punitive damages awards, because "[w]e want to encourage plaintiffs to bring wrongdoers to trial"). In the same vein, a Texas Court of Appeals affirmed an award of $4500 in exemplary damages, in an action for invasion of privacy from telephone harassment, when actual damages were $2 and attorney fees were $4462.52. *See* Donnel v. Lara, 703 S.W.2d 257, 258, 262 (Tex. App. 1985), *superseded by* TEX. CIV. PRAC. & REM. CODE ANN. § 41.004 (West 1997). The court noted that the plaintiffs "had obligated themselves to pay reasonable attorney fees as a necessary prerequisite for obtaining relief through the courts," and held that "the amount exemplified an accurate application of the purposes for exemplary damages — to punish and deter similar wrongs in the future." *Id.* at 262.

found liable is that he is not sued.[79] Thus, courts occasionally refer to considerations that bear on the probability that a defendant would have escaped liability. But they rarely explain in a direct and systematic way how this probability should be used to determine the proper level of damages for deterrence purposes.[80]

Further, courts generally pay insufficient attention to the potential problem of overdeterrence. Judicial opinions mention this issue only infrequently,[81] and none of the lists of factors used by courts in determining punitive damages includes overdeterrence as a consideration.[82] As we have emphasized,[83] however, damages that exceed the level in-

---

[79] *See supra* p. 888.

[80] A few courts have explicitly recognized the importance of the defendant's chance of escaping liability. *See, e.g.,* Kemezy v. Peters, 79 F.3d 33, 35 (7th Cir. 1996) (Posner, C.J.). In that case, the court noted:

> When a tortious act is concealable, a judgment equal to the harm done by the act will underdeter. Suppose a person who goes around assaulting other people is caught only half the time. Then in comparing the costs, in the form of anticipated damages, of the assaults with the benefits to him, he will discount the costs (but not the benefits, because they are realized in every assault) by 50 percent, and so in deciding whether to commit the next assault he will not be confronted by the full social cost of his activity.

Id.; see also Zazú Designs v. L'Oréal, S.A., 979 F.2d 499, 508 (7th Cir. 1992) (Easterbrook, J.) ("Punitive damages are appropriate when some wrongful conduct evades detection; a multiplier then both compensates and deters.")

In *FDIC v. W.R. Grace & Co.*, 877 F.2d 614 (7th Cir. 1989) (Posner, J.), the court stated:

> The most straightforward rationale for punitive damages . . . is that they are necessary to deter torts or crimes that are concealable. Suppose the average defrauder is brought to book only half the time. To confront him with a sanction that will make fraud worthless to him and thus deter him, it is necessary that when he is caught he be made to pay twice as much as his profits.

Id. at 623; *see also* BMW of N. Am., Inc. v. Gore, 116 S. Ct. 1589, 1602 (1996) (Stevens, J.) ("A higher ratio [of punitive damages to compensatory damages] may also be justified in cases in which the injury is hard to detect . . . ."). Justice Breyer's concurrence in *Gore* mentions economic theories of punitive damages that focus on ensuring that a wrongdoer pays for the total cost of the harm caused. *See id.* at 1607 (Breyer, J., concurring). He correctly interprets these theories as permitting juries "to calculate punitive damages by making a rough estimate of global harm [and] dividing that estimate by a similarly rough estimate of the number of successful lawsuits that would likely be brought." *Id.*

[81] One exception is Justice Breyer's concurrence in *Gore*, in which he observes that damages greater than the total harm caused will "'over-deter' by leading potential defendants to spend more to prevent the activity that causes the economic harm, say, through employee training, than the cost of the harm itself." *Gore*, 116 S. Ct. at 1607–08 (Breyer, J., concurring); *see also* Jones v. Reagan, 696 F.2d 551, 554 (7th Cir. 1983) (Posner, J.) ("[I]f considerations of deterrence are to be brought to center stage, the potential for overdeterrence must also be considered . . . ."); Roginsky v. Richardson-Merrell, Inc., 378 F.2d 832, 839–41 (2d Cir. 1967) (Friendly, J.) (noting that allowing multiple punitive damages awards for negligence in the manufacture of goods gives rise to the danger of "overkill" and "needless" deterrence).

[82] For example, the *Green Oil* factors, which were endorsed by the United States Supreme Court in *Pacific Mutual Life Insurance Co. v. Haslip*, 491 U.S. 1, 21–22 (1991), fail to mention overdeterrence. *See Green Oil*, 539 So. 2d at 223–24. Nor do state statutes outlining the factors to be considered in awarding punitive damages include the danger of overdeterrence. *See* KAN. STAT. ANN. § 60-3701(b) (1994); MINN. STAT. ANN. § 549.20 subd. 3 (West 1988); MONT. CODE ANN. § 27-1-221(7)(b) (1995); OR. REV. STAT. § 30.925(2) (1995).

[83] *See supra* section II.A.

dicated by the formula may result in wasteful precautions and the withdrawal of socially valuable products and services from the marketplace.

Not only do courts usually fail to consider correctly the factors that *are* relevant to proper deterrence, but they also err in considering a variety of factors that generally *are not* relevant to deterrence, including the reprehensibility of defendants' conduct and defendants' wealth. We will discuss at some length why these factors ordinarily should not be taken into account if the goal is to promote proper deterrence,[84] but the point we want to make here is that consideration of these factors in awarding punitive damages causes such damages to deviate further from the level given by our formula.

Some aspects of legislation governing punitive damages are also inconsistent with deterrence theory. Notably, many states have imposed caps of various kinds on punitive damages awards: an absolute ceiling (for example, $350,000 in Virginia), a maximum ratio of punitive damages to compensatory damages (for example, three times compensatory damages in Florida), or both.[85] Such caps cannot be justified on deterrence grounds because they might preclude the proper award of punitive damages. For example, suppose that the harm caused by an injurer is $100,000 and that he has only a one-in-ten chance of being found liable. The optimal level of punitive damages is then $900,000, or nine times compensatory damages (because the optimal level of total damages, including compensatory damages, is ten times the harm). This absolute amount and this ratio would exceed punitive damages caps in the majority of states that have them,[86] yet under the circumstances posited, a punitive damages award of this magnitude, and that has this relationship to compensatory damages, is needed for proper deterrence.

Our criticism of caps is not meant to deny that, if jury awards of punitive damages are thought to be systematically excessive, caps might beneficially constrain such awards.[87] But in the absence of systematic bias, caps are inappropriate.

---

[84] *See infra* Part III.

[85] *See Gore*, 116 S. Ct. at 1618–19 (Ginsburg, J., dissenting) (surveying state caps on punitive damage awards).

[86] Justice Ginsburg lists 16 states in which caps on punitive damages have been enacted or proposed. In 13 of those states (Colorado, Connecticut, Delaware, Florida, Georgia, Illinois, Indiana, Maryland, Nevada, New Jersey, North Dakota, Texas, and Virginia), the award described in the text would exceed the cap. *See id.*

[87] *See, e.g.,* Dan Quayle, *Civil Justice Reform*, 41 AM. U. L. REV. 559, 564–65 (1992) (arguing that "the current approach to punitive damages will continue to generate disproportionately high awards in a random and capricious manner" and that one aspect of reform should be to limit the amount of punitive damages to "the full amount of compensatory damages").

D. Punitive Damages Cases

We briefly consider here three prominent punitive damages cases in the light of the deterrence principles discussed above. Our primary objective is to state what deterrence theory suggests about the appropriate level of punitive damages in these cases, given their facts and circumstances, not to analyze the legal doctrines that were applied or developed in them.[88]

  1. BMW of North America, Inc. v. Gore.[89] — In this case, the plaintiff, Ira Gore, Jr., purchased a new BMW sedan from an Alabama dealer. He subsequently learned that the defendant, BMW of North America, had repainted part of the car because of damage to the car before its arrival in the United States, although BMW had not disclosed this fact. The jury awarded Gore compensatory damages of $4000 for diminution in the value of the car, and punitive damages of $4 million. The Alabama Supreme Court reduced the punitive award to $2 million, but the United States Supreme Court held even this award to be grossly excessive. On reconsideration, the Alabama Supreme Court reduced the punitive award to $50,000.[90]

Consider the probability that BMW would escape liability for having sold a repainted car as new. The determination of this probability involves two factors. One is the possibility that BMW would escape notice for having repainted a car, and the other is the likelihood that a purchaser who did discover that his car had been repainted would sue. Gore drove the car for nine months without detecting any abnormalities in the paint on his car. It was only after he took his car to a detail shop that he learned that it had been repainted. It seems reasonable to suppose, therefore, that many purchasers of repainted cars sold as new would never discover that their cars had been repainted.

Whether an owner who did discover that his car had been repainted would sue depends on the costs to him of suit (time and out-of-pocket expense) and the amount that he could collect. If the harm is as low as the jury found in *Gore*, $4000, it would seem that many owners — or the lawyers they might hire on a contingency fee — would not have a sufficient financial incentive to sue. There may have been a significant chance, therefore, that BMW would have escaped liability if damages were merely compensatory, because of victims' inadequate motive to sue.

In *Gore*, information that would be useful in estimating the probability of BMW's being found liable was provided. Among the facts

---

[88] We have commented on the legal doctrine governing punitive damages to some degree above in section II.C and will discuss it more extensively below in Part III.

[89] 116 S. Ct. 1589 (1996).

[90] *See Alabama Court Slashes Punitive Award in Case Involving Repainted BMW Car*, WALL ST. J., May 12, 1997, at B10.

established at trial were that fourteen new BMW cars in Alabama had been repainted, including Gore's, and one prior suit had been brought against BMW by an owner of one of these cars.[91] If none of the other Alabama victims of repainting were to sue,[92] the probability of detection and liability might be thought to be two in fourteen,[93] in which case the total damages should be seven times the $4000 harm, or $28,000.[94] Of that total, $4000 would represent compensatory damages, and $24,000 would represent punitive damages. By this reasoning, the $2 million punitive award initially approved by the Alabama Supreme Court was grossly excessive, and the reduced award of $50,000 was much more reasonable.[95]

2. *Pacific Mutual Life Insurance Co. v. Haslip.*[96] — This case involved an insurance agent who misappropriated premium payments. The insurance policy in question was a group health plan sold to the municipality of Roosevelt City, Alabama. When Cleopatra Haslip, a city employee, was hospitalized, she apparently did not know that the policy had lapsed because of the agent's misappropriation. When the hospital and her physician sought payment from her, she and other Roosevelt City employees sued the agent and the Pacific Mutual Life Insurance Company for fraud.[97] The jury awarded her total damages

---

[91] *See Gore*, 116 S. Ct. at 1593. The other plaintiff, Thomas Yates, was awarded $4600 in compensatory damages but nothing in punitive damages. *See Yates v. BMW of N. Am., Inc.*, 642 So. 2d 937, 938 (Ala. Civ. App.), *cert. quashed*, 642 So. 2d 937 (Ala. 1993). It should be noted that in the entire United States, BMW had sold 983 cars as new after repainting. *See Gore*, 116 S. Ct. at 1593. In this example, we are restricting our attention to the subset of cars sold in Alabama because the Alabama Supreme Court, in reviewing *Gore*, limited consideration in this way. It essentially makes no difference whether the multiplier is calculated separately for each state or instead is calculated for the entire country (based on appropriate national statistics, such as the figure of 983 cars in *Gore*). Under either method, a firm's expected damage payments would equal the harm caused nationally.

[92] In fact, other suits were brought. *See BMW of N. Am., Inc. v. Gore*, 646 So. 2d 619, 626 n.4 (Ala. 1994) (listing the 25 cases brought by Gore's attorney against BMW for similar conduct). The assumption in the text that only two suits were brought is made for illustrative purposes.

[93] In general, the proper approach to calculating the probability of liability would be to use all available information about the likelihood of detection and suit. Such information might include, for example, information about the frequency of suit against BMW under similar circumstances in other states, the frequency with which car owners take their cars to detail shops, and the likelihood of lawyers taking cases with higher or lower stakes.

[94] In fact, the calculation of the multiplier may be more complicated because the award of punitive damages will itself affect the probability of suit. As we observed above, total damages should be such that the probability of suit induced by that award of damages results in expected damages equal to harm. *See supra* p. 895. Therefore, if an award of $28,000 would induce more than two plaintiffs to sue, the proper multiplier might be less than seven.

[95] For another economically oriented discussion of *Gore*, see Rubin, Calfee & Grady, cited above in note 12. Their discussion, however, does not emphasize the point that we make here.

[96] 499 U.S. 1 (1991).

[97] *See id.* at 4–5. In fact, the insurance policy that lapsed was not Pacific Mutual Life's policy, but rather the policy of another company, Union Fidelity Life Insurance Company, which the agent was also representing. *See id.* However, premiums for the Union policy were collected through Pacific Mutual Life's Birmingham office. *See id.* at 5. Pacific Mutual Life was sued for fraud under a theory of respondeat superior. *See id.* at 6.

of $1,040,000, of which $200,000 appears to have been assessed as compensatory damages and $840,000 as punitive damages.[98]   The award was affirmed by the trial court, the Alabama Supreme Court, and the United States Supreme Court.[99]

The key issue relating to deterrence in this case is whether a significant chance exists that an insurance company whose agent misappropriates premiums will escape liability for coverage that individuals expected to have. (The focus should be on the company's chance of escaping liability, rather than the agent's, for the reason we explained above.[100]) Obviously, if a policy has been invalidated because of an agent's misappropriation of premium payments, the invalidation will come to the attention of a person who applies for coverage under that policy. If the insurance company does not pay the individual voluntarily, the individual probably would sue the company, provided the amount at stake is large enough.

In the present case, the compensatory damages were, as noted, $200,000. However, less than $4000 of this amount represented out-of-pocket expenditures, the rest apparently consisting of non-economic losses such as emotional distress.[101]   It seems reasonable to suppose that recovery of the $4000 out-of-pocket loss is more probable than recovery of the $196,000 non-economic loss. If the likelihood of the latter recovery is sufficiently low, an individual probably would not bring a lawsuit. Conversely, if this likelihood is high, a lawsuit would be much more certain. A related consideration is that three other Roosevelt City employees joined Haslip in suing the defendants. Their awards totaled approximately $38,000.[102] Clearly, the prospect of obtaining this additional amount would increase the incentive to sue. On balance, therefore, although a suit seems reasonably likely in the circumstances of *Haslip*, some countervailing considerations might justify a modest punitive damages award, to offset the chance that a lawsuit would not be brought.

3. In re The Exxon Valdez.[103] — In this case, the defendant's supertanker, the Exxon Valdez, ran aground on a reef in Prince William Sound in Alaska, spilling 11 million gallons of oil[104] and polluting over

---

[98] Although it was not entirely clear how the jury apportioned the total award between compensatory and punitive damages, the United States Supreme Court presumed that not more than $200,000 of the total represented compensatory damages and not less than $840,000 represented punitive damages. *Id.* at 7 n.2.

[99] *See* Pacific Mutual Life Ins. Co. v. Haslip, No. CV-82-2453 (Ala. Cir. Ct. Jefferson County 1987); Pacific Mutual Life Ins. Co. v. Haslip, 553 So. 2d 537, 543 (Ala. 1989); *Haslip*, 499 U.S. at 24.

[100] *See supra* pp. 894–95.

[101] Haslip's out-of-pocket expenses were "less than $4,000." *Id.*

[102] The jury awarded compensatory damages for the other respondents in the following amounts: Hargrove $10,288; Craig $12,400; and Calhoun $15,290. *See id.* at 7.

[103] No. A89-0095-CV (D. Alaska Sept. 24, 1996).

[104] *See, e.g.,* Charles McCoy, *Exxon Corp.'s Settlement Gets Court Approval,* WALL ST. J., Oct. 9, 1991, at A3.

1,000 miles of Alaskan coastline.[105] The supertanker's captain, Joseph Hazelwood, had previously been treated for alcohol abuse and, in connection with the accident at issue, was found to have violated regulations governing alcohol consumption.[106] In the private civil litigation against Exxon stemming from the accident, the plaintiffs — various classes of fishermen and Alaskan natives — were awarded several hundred million dollars in compensatory damages[107] and $5 billion in punitive damages.[108] The punitive damages award was affirmed by the trial judge and is being appealed.[109]

It seems clear that in the circumstances of the Exxon Valdez accident, there was essentially no chance that the defendant company, Exxon Corporation, could escape liability. An accident of this magnitude obviously would have been noticed. Moreover, because the tanker was stuck on a reef, the identity of the injurer was plain. And given the substantial compensatory damages involved, in the hundreds of millions of dollars, a lawsuit certainly could be expected. Thus, according to our analysis, no punitive damages are needed, or appropriate, in the circumstances of this case because the injurer could not have escaped liability for compensatory damages. (In other contexts involving oil spills — such as the intentional dumping of small amounts of waste oil that is unlikely to be detected or traced to the spiller — some punitive damages would be appropriate.[110])

III. DETERRENCE: EXTENSIONS OF THE BASIC THEORY

In this Part, we will discuss several important doctrinal and policy issues in punitive damages law from the perspective of the deterrence principles developed above.[111] Most of these topics (such as the repre-

---

[105] *See Fishermen Block Tankers*, WASH. POST, Aug. 22, 1993, at A9 (noting that the Exxon Valdez "polluted thousands of miles of coastline").

[106] *See* Seth Mydans, *Captain in Alaska Oil Spill Loses License for Nine Months*, N.Y. TIMES, July 26, 1990, at A12 (noting that an administrative law judge for the Coast Guard found Hazelwood guilty of consuming alcohol within four hours of sailing and that Hazelwood had pleaded no contest to the charge); *A Question Recurs: Was Hazelwood Drunk?*, N.Y. TIMES, Feb. 25, 1990, at 29.

[107] The jury awarded $287 million as compensation for fishing losses. *See In re* The Exxon Valdez, No. A89-0095-CV, 1995 WL 527988, at *5 (D. Alaska Jan. 27, 1995). The court noted that, including other verdicts and settlements, the dollar amount of harm caused by the spill was between $288.7 million and $418.7 million (including the $287 million verdict). *See id.*

[108] *See* Caleb Solomon, *Exxon Is Told To Pay $5 Billion for Valdez Spill*, WALL ST. J., Sept. 19, 1994, at A3.

[109] In June 1997, Exxon appealed the $5 billion punitive damages award entered against it in the Exxon Valdez case. *See Exxon Corp. Submits Brief Outlining Valdez Appeal*, WALL ST. J., June 20, 1997, at A4.

[110] Punitive damages would be appropriate, for example, in the circumstances described in Matthew L. Wald, *Royal Caribbean Cruise Line Indicted on Charges of Dumping Oil*, N.Y. TIMES, Dec. 20, 1996, at A26 (cruise line indicted for "routinely dump[ing] waste oil from five of its ships for years and falsif[ying] its log books to hide its activities").

[111] *See supra* Part II.

hensibility of the defendant's conduct) have received substantial attention in judicial opinions, others (whether the state should receive a portion of a punitive damages award) have been considered primarily in a legislative context, and still others (the status of the plaintiff as a customer or a third party) apparently have not been addressed in either setting.

A. *Reprehensibility of Conduct*

The law requires that a defendant be found to have acted in a reprehensible manner — in a way that is egregious, malicious, or undertaken with reckless disregard for the rights of others — before punitive damages can be imposed on him.[112] If a defendant is found to have so acted, the degree of his reprehensibility is often treated as a key factor in determining the level of punitive damages.[113] Indeed, the United States Supreme Court in *Gore* observed that this factor is "[p]erhaps [the] most important" indicium of the reasonableness of a punitive damages award.[114] The reprehensibility of the defendant's conduct was also one of the factors listed by the Court in *Haslip*.[115]

Should reprehensibility per se affect the imposition of punitive damages, given the goal of deterrence?[116] In this section, we explain

---

[112] *See* 1 SCHLUETER & REDDEN, *supra* note 74, at 264 ("In order to receive punitive damages, a plaintiff must show that the defendant acted with malice, either actual or legal."); *see also* Masaki v. General Motors Corp., 780 P.2d 566, 570 (Haw. 1989) (noting that punitive damages "are awarded only when the egregious nature of the defendant's conduct makes such a remedy appropriate"); Barnhouse v. Hawkeye State Bank, 406 N.W.2d 181, 184 (Iowa 1987) ("An award of punitive damages is appropriate when a party acts with actual or legal malice.") (citations omitted); Nappe v. Anschelewitz, Barr, Ansell & Bonello, 477 A.2d 1224, 1230 (N.J. 1984) ("To warrant a punitive award, the defendant's conduct must have been wantonly reckless or malicious.") (citations omitted); Hood v. Fulkerson, 699 P.2d 608, 611 (N.M. 1985) ("[Punitive damages] may be awarded only when the conduct of the wrongdoer may be said to be maliciously intentional, fraudulent, oppressive, or committed recklessly or with a wanton disregard to the plaintiffs' rights." (quoting Loucks v. Albuquerque Nat'l Bank, 418 P.2d 191, 199 (N.M. 1966) (internal quotation marks omitted))).

[113] *See, e.g.*, Green Oil Co. v. Hornsby, 539 So. 2d 218, 223 (Ala. 1989) ("The degree of reprehensibility of the defendant's conduct should be considered" when "determining whether the jury award of punitive damages is excessive or inadequate"), *endorsed in* Pacific Mut. Life Ins. Co. v. Haslip, 499 U.S. 1, 21 (1991); Neal v. Farmers Ins. Exch., 582 P.2d 980, 990 (Cal. 1978) (stating that, among factors to consider in assessing punitive damages is "the particular nature of the defendant's acts in light of the whole record; clearly, different acts may be of varying degrees of reprehensibility, and the more reprehensible the act, the greater the appropriate punishment, assuming all other factors are equal."); McNeill v. Allen, 534 P.2d 813, 820 (Colo. Ct. App. 1975) ("[T]he purpose of punishment and deterrence may best be served by relatively higher or relatively lower exemplary damages according to the nature of the wrongful conduct.") (citation omitted); Ultimate Chem. Co. v. Surface Transp. Int'l, Inc., 658 P.2d 1008, 1012 (Kan. 1983) (listing among the factors to consider in assessing punitive damages "the nature, extent, and enormity of the wrong").

[114] BMW of N. Am., Inc. v. Gore, 116 S. Ct. 1589, 1599 (1996).

[115] *See supra* note 113.

[116] As previously noted, we discuss below the significance of the reprehensibility criterion to the punishment goal of punitive damages. *See infra* pp. 952–953.

that it generally should not.[117] However, an important exception to this conclusion occurs when injurers' gains do not count in social welfare, which we believe is often the case when injurers act maliciously.[118] This exception, we will suggest, only possibly applies to individual defendants, and not to corporate defendants.

As discussed above,[119] under standard assumptions, the imposition of damages equal to harm, appropriately multiplied to reflect the probability of escaping liability, achieves proper deterrence. That a defendant's conduct can be described as reprehensible is in itself irrelevant. Rather, the focus in determining punitive damages should be on the injurer's chance of escaping liability.

Making punitive damages depend on reprehensibility will distort deterrence in two ways. First, excessive damages may be imposed when reprehensible conduct occurs in situations in which an injurer is virtually certain to be found liable. Suppose that a surgeon, through extreme negligence, fails to remove a surgical tool from the body of a patient and that this omission leads to great pain and suffering. If a high probability exists that the surgeon will be sued and found liable because of the magnitude of the patient's harm and the unmistakable error of the surgeon, extracompensatory damages are neither necessary nor appropriate. Similarly, consider a newspaper reporter who, out of reckless disregard for the truth, confuses one firm's safe product with another firm's dangerous product, substantially damaging the former firm's business reputation and profitability. Here, too, we might expect that suit and a finding of liability would be very likely, in which case extracompensatory damages would be excessive. Thus, *even for conduct that is reprehensible*, if little chance of escaping liability exists, compensatory damages alone will achieve appropriate deterrence, and punitive damages will result in overdeterrence.

One might wonder, though, how overdeterrence of reprehensible acts can occur, because society evidently has an interest in deterring such acts completely. To illustrate that overdeterrence still can occur, consider the example of the surgeon. If the magnitude of damages is very high, we can imagine that, to reduce the chance of leaving a surgical tool in a patient, he might hire another medical professional to monitor his actions or he might dramatically increase the time he

---

[117] For the most part, other commentators who have considered punitive damages in terms of the deterrence goal have agreed that the reprehensibility of the defendant's conduct is not a relevant factor. *See, e.g.*, Dobbs, *supra* note 3, at 860–63; Galligan, *supra* note 3, at 62–64.

[118] In their respective discussions of punitive damages, Dorsey Ellis and Robert Cooter also find that the reprehensibility of a defendant's conduct is relevant to deterrence when injurers' gains do not count in social welfare — that is, when their gains are socially illicit. *See* Cooter, *Economic Analysis, supra* note 12, at 86–89; Ellis, *supra* note 12, at 31–33. For more formal treatments of illicit utility, also in the context of punitive damages, see SHAVELL, *supra* note 14, at 146, 159–61; Diamond, *Efficiency Effects, supra* note 12, at 8–12.

[119] *See supra* Part II.

spends on each operation. Even if such responses would succeed in preventing the recurrence of this event, they may be at too great a cost, especially if the likelihood of leaving a surgical tool in a patient is very low anyway. In other words, it might not be socially worthwhile for the surgeon to take the measures needed to eliminate the possibility of his being extremely negligent. Yet a level of liability in excess of that given by the damages formula would improperly encourage him to take these measures.[120]

The problem of overdeterrence also can arise in connection with the reprehensible acts of employees of corporations. Employees obviously cannot be controlled perfectly by a corporation, even though a corporation can improve its ability to prevent employees from committing reprehensible acts by screening them before hiring them and monitoring their conduct afterwards. If damages exceed the level determined by the damages formula, however, the corporations may be led to spend excessively on screening and monitoring efforts in order to forestall reprehensible behavior.[121] This might be true of a newspaper, for instance, if it faced punitive damages for false reporting because of extreme negligence, as in our example of the reporter who confused two firms' products. In response, the newspaper might assign two reporters to every story even if doing so is not socially worthwhile given the cost of this practice and the reduction in risk of reprehensible behavior that would be accomplished.

Not only can attention to reprehensibility result in the imposition of punitive damages that are excessive, but such attention may also lead to the converse problem: the failure to employ punitive damages when they are needed for proper deterrence. This problem will occur if an individual engages in conduct that is harmful, though *not* reprehensible, and he is likely to escape liability. Suppose that a toxic waste disposal truck develops a leak (say, from rust) that results in waste spilling onto a highway at night, when no one is likely to notice it. The driver of the truck may have performed a proper inspection before de-

---

[120] If, unlike in the example we have been discussing, a reprehensible act is purely intentional, overdeterrence cannot occur. Suppose a surgeon intentionally left a surgical tool in the patient. (Although this example may seem unbelievable, we use it to contrast the conclusion in this footnote with that in the text.) Threatening the surgeon with punitive damages in addition to compensatory damages would further discourage the surgeon from intentionally leaving the surgical tool in a patient. Overdeterrence could not occur. But if the surgeon's act was the result of his failure to take adequate precautions — that is, if his act was accidental — the imposition of punitive damages can affect the level of care he exercises. As we explained in the text, this level of care can be excessive.

[121] For example, in the illustration of a firm's screening decision in note 24, above, if damages exceed the amount determined by the damages formula, the firm might be led to spend $4000 per applicant on screening, which would be socially excessive given the assumed benefit from this level of screening. On the point that the imposition of punitive damages may lead corporations to spend excessively in order to forestall reprehensible behavior by their employees, see Daniel R. Fischel & Alan O. Sykes, *Corporate Crime*, 25 J. LEGAL STUD. 319, 348 (1996).

parting, and the company may have reasonable maintenance policies. Although the leak is not caused by anyone's reprehensible behavior, substantial extracompensatory damages may be appropriate if the leak is discovered, to offset the significant likelihood that the injurer would not be identified and held responsible for the harm.

It is clear from the foregoing discussion that the stress courts place on reprehensibility of conduct in considering punitive damages cannot be justified on grounds of deterrence. A minor qualification of this point is that, as we observed earlier,[122] courts treat attempts by the defendant to conceal wrongdoing as a factor that enhances reprehensibility, and thus the level of punitive damages. This response makes rough sense because such behavior clearly reduces the probability of liability. But, as suggested above, the link that courts make between this behavior and punitive damages is vague in nature.[123] We believe that it would be preferable to use evidence of concealment directly to aid in the determination of the chance that the defendant might have escaped liability, rather than as a factor in determining reprehensibility.

Finally, although the reprehensibility of a defendant's conduct should not be used per se as a basis for imposing punitive damages to achieve proper deterrence, such conduct may sometimes provide useful information about the defendant's chance of escaping liability. Everything else being equal, the lower the chance of being found liable, the lower will be an individual's level of care. Therefore, a low care level may suggest a low probability of liability[124] and thus a higher level of punitive damages according to our formula.

Let us now turn to the important exception to our general conclusion about reprehensibility, which, as noted above, arises if injurers'

---

[122] *See supra* section II.C.

[123] *See supra* pp. 898–99. For example, in *Green Oil Co. v. Hornsby*, 539 So. 2d 218 (Ala. 1989), because reference to concealment occurs in the context of the reprehensibility criterion, *see id.* at 223, it is difficult to infer how such behavior should affect punitive damages. This difficulty is partially due to the *Green Oil* court's failure to discuss how the degree of reprehensibility should affect the level of punitive damages. *See id.* at 223–24. Additionally, *Green Oil* offers no guidance concerning how evidence of concealment should affect the degree of reprehensibility, including how much weight concealment should be given in relation to the other factors mentioned that bear on the degree of reprehensibility (such as the duration of the conduct). *See id.* Thus, although *Green Oil* suggests that concealment should be a basis for raising the level of punitive damages, the extent to which punitive damages should be raised is unclear.

[124] For example, consider a firm that believes that any pollution that it generates will be very difficult to detect. Such a firm might not invest in any pollution control equipment — and thus its conduct would be considered reprehensible. In contrast, an otherwise identical firm that believes that its pollution will be detected with a high probability would make reasonable investments in pollution control equipment — its conduct would not be reprehensible. Consequently, if a court does not have direct information about a firm's chance of escaping liability, the court might be able to infer from a firm's level of investment in pollution control equipment — that is, from whether its conduct was reprehensible or not — whether the firm faced a low or high chance of escaping liability.

gains are not counted in social welfare. Suppose that a person, out of spite, punches another individual; his purpose is to cause harm to the victim. Society might well treat the pleasure the injurer obtains from this act as *socially illicit*, not to be counted in social welfare.[125] If so, the act should be deterred completely because it produces no social gain, only harm. To achieve this goal, damages must exceed the injurer's utility from committing the act. Because the injurer's illicit utility could be greater than the harm suffered by the victim, the level of damages needed for proper deterrence might be in excess of harm.[126] In other words, punitive damages might be socially desirable even if there is no chance that the injurer could have escaped liability.

When are the benefits from harmful conduct likely to be considered socially illicit? We suggest that benefits tend to be treated as illicit when the injurer's utility derives from causing harm itself, as when a person punches another out of spite or defames another to see him suffer. The injurer benefits *because* the victim suffers harm. Situations with this characteristic fit under the general rubric of maliciousness and would be considered reprehensible. Thus, *some reprehensible conduct — malicious conduct — could give rise to gains that are not counted in social welfare, in which case punitive damages may be justified even in the absence of a chance of escaping liability,* for the reasons discussed in the previous paragraph.

But many acts that are reprehensible do not seem to be associated with socially illicit utility; they are not undertaken with malice. Consider a person who drives at 60 miles per hour through a residential area in order to arrive at work on time and causes a fatal accident. We would call this act reprehensible because of the driver's wanton disregard for the safety of others. Yet because the purpose of the act is not to cause harm, but rather to arrive at work on time, a perfectly legitimate objective, it does not appear that the utility from the act would be classified as socially illicit. In general, we surmise that reprehensible acts that are not undertaken with the objective of causing

---

[125] We believe that the notion of socially illicit utility reflects how people often would characterize the utility that individuals derive from certain reprehensible acts (such as rape). But because no theoretical basis exists for determining which categories of utility are socially illicit, we are not suggesting below that particular categories of utility are necessarily socially illicit. Which categories of utility from wrongful conduct are socially illicit is an empirical question, determined by what society wants to count in social welfare. The notion of socially illicit utility has been considered by some commentators in the context of punitive damages. *See* sources cited *supra* note 118. It also has been mentioned in the economic literature on law enforcement. *See, e.g.,* George J. Stigler, *The Optimum Enforcement of Laws,* 78 J. POL. ECON. 526, 527 (1970).

[126] For example, suppose an individual obtains a utility gain worth $2000 to him from maliciously hitting someone in the nose, and that the harm to the victim is equivalent to $500 (because $500 would fully compensate the victim for his pain and medical costs). Then, even if the injurer would definitely be found liable, punitive damages of at least $1500 would be required to deter him. (Clearly, if there is a chance that he can escape liability, the punitive damages amount would have to be higher.)

harm, but rather that happen to cause it as a highly likely byproduct, usually are not associated with socially illicit utility. Thus, for these kinds of acts, punitive damages should not be imposed unless the injurer has a significant chance of escaping liability — our usual conclusion.[127]

Note that because the goal of corporations is to make a profit, rather than to cause harm to others, their gains presumably do count in social welfare. Hence, by the foregoing reasoning, if a corporation engages in conduct labeled as reprehensible, this fact per se should not affect the level of its damages. Rather, its damages should be based on the harm it caused and the chance that it might have escaped liability, with punitive damages awarded only if the latter chance is significant.

In summary, we believe that the reprehensibility of a defendant's conduct generally should not be taken into account for the purpose of determining optimal damages for deterrence. The notable exception to this conclusion occurs when the defendant is an individual whose conduct is motivated by malice and whose gains consequently are not included in social welfare.

B. *Wealth of Defendants*

The courts often state that a defendant's financial condition is a relevant factor in setting a punitive damages award, with the understanding that higher punitive damages may be appropriate for defendants with higher wealth.[128] Jury instructions also frequently include the defendant's wealth as a factor that jurors may take into account in determining the level of punitive damages.[129] Not surprisingly, plain-

---

[127] We do not mean to suggest that an injurer's gain necessarily counts in social welfare if his conduct is undertaken without malice. It may well be that the utility from certain types of *non-malicious* reprehensible conduct also would be treated as socially illicit. Consider, for example, a person who gets pleasure from "joyriding" on city streets (driving on them at high speed for fun). Our conclusions regarding the appropriateness of punitive damages for malicious conduct would apply to any category of conduct in which an injurer's gain does not count in social welfare.

[128] *See, e.g., Green Oil,* 539 So. 2d at 222 ("The defendant's financial position is . . . a consideration essential to a post-judgment critique of a punitive damages award." (citation omitted)). The United States Supreme Court endorsed the *Green Oil* approach of including the defendant's financial position as one factor to consider in determining whether an award of punitive damages is excessive or inadequate. *See* Pacific Mut. Life Ins. Co. v. Haslip, 499 U.S. 1, 22 (1991). Other state court decisions have endorsed the consideration of wealth in punitive damages assessments. *See, e.g.,* Neal v. Farmers Ins. Exch., 582 P.2d 980, 990 (Cal. 1978) ("Also to be considered is the wealth of the particular defendant; obviously, the function of deterrence . . . will not be served if the wealth of the defendant allows him to absorb the award with little or no discomfort."); Ultimate Chem. Co. v. Surface Transp. Int'l, Inc., 658 P.2d 1008, 1012 (Kan. 1983) (stating that among the factors to consider in assessing punitive damages is the "defendant's financial condition").

[129] *See, e.g.,* ARK. MODEL JURY INSTRUCTIONS § 2217 (West Supp. 1995); CAL. JURY INSTRUCTIONS: CIVIL § 14.71 (8th ed. 1994); WIS. JURY INSTRUCTIONS: CIVIL § 1707.1 (1995).

tiffs tend to emphasize this factor when defendants are wealthy, especially when the defendants are large corporations.[130]

Should defendants with greater wealth pay higher punitive damages? Our main conclusion in this section is that, from the perspective of achieving proper deterrence, a defendant's wealth generally should not be considered when the defendant is a corporation. We also conclude that the wealth criterion frequently should not be considered when the defendant is an individual, although we discuss certain circumstances in which an individual's wealth should be taken into account in imposing punitive damages.[131]

We explained above that, if damages equal harm multiplied by a factor reflecting the chance of escaping liability, defendants, including corporations, would be induced to take optimal precautions and to participate in risky activities to the proper extent.[132] It follows from this basic conclusion that, if damages are raised above the magnitude given by our formula when corporations are relatively wealthy, those corporations will be led to take excessive precautions, will undesirably curtail their activities, and will set prices above the proper level, chilling consumption of their products. In an extreme case, such corporations might even withdraw their products from the marketplace despite the value of the products to society.

An additional point reinforces the conclusion that corporate wealth should not influence punitive damages: imposing punitive damages on the basis of corporate wealth effectively imposes a tax on corporate size and success, thereby discouraging growth and development. This effect can be important in industries in which liability costs are a significant component of total cost (such as in the pharmaceutical and

---

[130] For example, in the Exxon Valdez case, Exxon's wealth was "virtually the exclusive focus of plaintiffs' Phase III [punitive damages] case." *In re* The Exxon Valdez, No. A89-0095-CV, 1995 WL 527988, at *7 (D. Alaska Jan. 27, 1995). The evidence of Exxon's wealth introduced by the plaintiffs included Exxon's 1990 Annual Report, which claimed that "Exxon's consistently strong earnings performance has enabled the company to achieve and maintain a position of extraordinary financial strength and flexibility. For example, over the past ten years, Exxon's internal cash generation from operations amounted to more than $100 billion." *Id.* at *8 n.16.

[131] Our conclusions about punitive damages and wealth are similar to those of other economically oriented writers on punitive damages. *See* Abraham & Jeffries, *supra* note 3, at 415 ("In our view, the defendant's wealth is irrelevant to the goal of deterring socially undesirable conduct ...."); Chapman & Trebilcock, *supra* note 12, at 824 ("In the case of economic wrongs, the conventional economic theory of deterrence ... suggests no role for corporate wealth in structuring an optimal deterrence regime ...." (footnote omitted)); Cooter, *Deterrence, supra* note 12, at 1177 (stating that the total assets or wealth of the defendant "is typically inappropriate to deterrence of economically self-interested decisionmakers"); Galligan, *supra* note 3, at 65 ("Considering the defendant's wealth has simply no articulable efficiency justification."); Gary T. Schwartz, *Deterrence and Punishment in the Common Law of Punitive Damages: A Comment*, 56 S. CAL. L. REV. 133, 140 (1982) ("The wealth of the defendant bears no obvious relationship to deterrence goals ...." (internal quotation marks omitted)).

[132] *See supra* Part II.

general aviation aircraft industries).[133] Of course, retarding the natural growth of corporations can have adverse consequences, notably, that society forgoes economies of scale in production and in research and development. It also may mean that the risk of harm increases, because small firms may not have enough at stake to make it worthwhile to them to spend a socially proper amount on precautions.

Our discussion of the inappropriateness of taking corporate wealth into account presumes that all corporations — large and small — will, if required to pay for the harms they cause, tend to balance correctly the costs of precautions against the resulting reduction in harm. An argument sometimes is made, however, that because bigger corporations are more bureaucratic, they will not adequately respond to liability risks unless the damages imposed on them are especially high. According to this argument, higher damages are needed against large corporations to attract the attention of senior management.[134] This view is mistaken, as we now discuss.

Although large corporations typically have complicated organizational structures, with senior management at some remove from the level of operations, it does not follow that large corporations will tend to be insufficiently attentive to the reduction of risk. If the cost of a precaution is less than the damages incurred by not taking it, a large firm will want someone employed by it to recognize that fact and take the precaution — because the firm's goal is to maximize profits. A large grocery chain, for example, will want some employee at each of its stores to inspect that store's floor after it is mopped in order to ensure that it is safe. The company will delegate this responsibility to an employee low in the corporate hierarchy, such as an assistant store manager. That this task does not receive the attention of top management, as it might in the case of a firm consisting of only one or two grocery stores, does not mean that the task will be neglected or attended to inadequately. As long as a corporation — large or small — expects to have to pay for the harms it causes, it will have a socially appropriate incentive to reduce the harms.[135]

---

[133] *See supra* note 29 (describing industries in which productive activity may have declined as a result of liability costs).

[134] Sometimes this view is expressed as a need to send a message to headquarters. *See, e.g.,* Browning-Ferris Indus., Inc. v. Kelco Disposal, Inc., 492 U.S. 257, 261 (1989) ("Kelco's attorney urged the jury to return an award of punitive damages, asking the jurors to 'deliver a message to Houston [BFI's headquarters].'" (quoting trial transcript)).

[135] Although we have just emphasized the point that large corporations will take appropriate steps to reduce risk through the delegation of risk-reduction responsibilities, we are not claiming that large corporations will necessarily take the *same* precautions that small corporations do. They may take different precautions — perhaps greater, perhaps not — as a result of their different organizational and decisionmaking structures. But the precautions taken by large corporations will still be socially appropriate because of the basic principle that parties will behave properly if they are made to pay for the harms their actions cause.

Now consider the question of the relevance of wealth for the imposition of punitive damages on individuals. Again, the general arguments we made above imply that punitive damages should not depend on an individual's wealth; rather, punitive damages should depend only on the level of harm and the chance of escaping liability, so that, applying the damages multiplier formula, expected damages equal harm.[136] However, two qualifications to this conclusion suggest that wealth might be relevant in certain circumstances.

The first concerns risk aversion and the unavailability of insurance against punitive damages. We noted above that if potential injurers are risk averse and do not have access to liability insurance, appropriate deterrence will be accomplished with a lower level of damages than if they are risk neutral.[137] Further, the more risk averse an individual is, the lower the optimal level of damages. Assuming that poor individuals are more risk averse than rich ones,[138] the optimal level of punitive damages will be lower for poorer individuals. Equivalently, punitive damages should be higher for wealthier individuals. However, even for the wealthiest individuals, punitive damages should not exceed the level determined by our formula.[139] The relevance of these observations, we reiterate, is limited to situations in which insurance against punitive damages is not available.

The second circumstance in which the level of an individual's wealth may be relevant to the calculation of punitive damages is when the individual's gain from committing the harmful act is socially illicit. We explained above that punitive damages may be needed to offset illicit benefits.[140] To accomplish this, punitive damages generally will have to rise with the wealth of an individual, because the value of money tends to decline with wealth.[141] For example, to offset the utility a rich person would obtain from slandering someone he disliked, we might need to impose $10,000 in punitive damages, whereas to deter a person with only modest assets, $1000 in punitive damages might suffice.

---

[136] *See supra* section II.B.

[137] *See supra* pp. 886–87.

[138] This proposition means, for example, that a poor person would be more averse to a 50% chance of losing $100 than a rich person.

[139] The explanation for this claim is that the bearing of risk by uninsured risk-averse individuals makes it socially desirable to *reduce* damages from the level implied by our formula. *See* pp. 886–87. Thus, although damages should rise with wealth for the reasons just discussed, the highest level of damages — imposed on the wealthiest individuals, who are presumed to be the least risk averse — should still not exceed the level called for by our formula.

[140] *See supra* section III.A.

[141] That the value of a dollar declines with the level of wealth is a standard assumption of economists, reflecting the view that individuals first fulfill their most important needs and desires, then spend on successively less important things. *See, e.g.*, PINDYCK & RUBINFELD, *supra* note 39, at 144–45.

We believe that the foregoing point underlies the common intuition that punitive damages should be linked to wealth. However, this point has a very limited scope, applying only to individuals whose benefit from causing harm is socially illicit, which we generally associate with conduct whose goal is to cause harm. Otherwise, the point of the previous paragraph does not apply to individuals. Moreover, the point does not apply to firms because firms are motivated by profits, rather than by a desire to cause harm.

C. *Potential Harm*

In reviewing the appropriateness of a punitive damages award, some courts have considered not only the harm that has actually occurred, but also the harm that might have occurred — the potential harm.[142] According to these courts, the higher the potential harm, the higher the level of punitive damages that can be justified.[143] The United States Supreme Court endorsed this idea in *Haslip*, as well as in *TXO Production Corp. v. Alliance Resources Corp.*[144] Potential harm also served as a basis for the trial court's upholding the $5 billion punitive damages verdict in the Exxon Valdez oil spill litigation; the court noted that, although 11 million gallons of oil spilled, another 45 million gallons in the Exxon Valdez could have spilled, making the potential harm much higher.[145]

We conclude, however, that a policy of taking potential harm into account in the determination of punitive damages is undesirable given the goal of deterrence. To explain the reasoning behind this conclusion, it will be convenient first to discuss why damages should be

---

[142] *See, e.g.,* Bemer Aviation, Inc. v. Hughes Helicopter, Inc., 621 F. Supp. 290, 300 (E.D. Pa. 1985), *aff'd*, 802 F.2d 445 (3d Cir. 1986) (stating that, in assessing an award of punitive damages, juries may consider "the potential harm that a defendant's conduct poses"); Green Oil Co. v. Hornsby, 539 So. 2d 218, 223 (Ala. 1989); Levine v. Knowles, 197 So. 2d 329, 331 (Fla. Dist. Ct. App. 1967) ("The seriousness of the probable result of the defendant's conduct ... is the yardstick for determining the advisability of discouraging such behavior in the future, rather than the seriousness of the damage actually caused.").

[143] The first of the seven *Green Oil* factors for evaluating punitive damages awards states:

Punitive damages should bear a reasonable relationship to the harm that is likely to occur from the defendant's conduct as well as to the harm that actually has occurred. If the actual or likely harm is slight, the damages should be relatively small. If grievous, the damages should be much greater.

Green Oil, 539 So. 2d at 223 (quoting Aetna Life Ins. Co. v. Lavoie, 505 So. 2d 1050, 1062 (Ala. 1987) (Houston, J., concurring specially)).

[144] *See* Pacific Mut. Life Ins. Co. v. Haslip, 499 U.S. 1, 21–22 (1991) (endorsing the *Green Oil* factors); *see also* TXO Prod. Corp. v. Alliance Resources Corp., 509 U.S. 443, 460 (1993) ("It is appropriate to consider the magnitude of the *potential harm* that the defendant's conduct would have caused . . . .").

[145] "The evidence established that the *Exxon Valdez* spilled 11,000,000 gallons of crude oil, approximately one-fifth of its cargo. Had the remaining 45,000,000 gallons of oil spilled, the disaster and harm would have been many times greater." *In re* The Exxon Valdez, No. A89-0095-CV, 1995 WL 527988, at *6 (D. Alaska Jan. 27, 1995).

based on actual rather than potential harm when there is no chance of escaping liability and the issue of punitive damages does not arise.

Consider an example in which an injurer's act will result in either a low or high level of harm, and the injurer does not know in advance which level will occur. Let the two levels of harm be $1 million and $5 million, which occur with equal probability. This example raises the issue of potential harm because, when a $1 million harm occurs, the harm could have been $5 million. Note that the injurer's act entails an expected harm of $3 million (= (.5 × $1 million) + (.5 × $5 million)). To achieve proper deterrence, therefore, the injurer's expected damages should equal $3 million.

Given our assumption that injurers will be found liable when they cause harm, observe that *deterrence will be optimal if damages are always set equal to actual harm.* For when an injurer engages in the harmful activity, he will expect to have to pay $1 million in damages half of the time and $5 million in damages half of the time. Hence, his average damage payment will be $3 million or, stated differently, the expected value of his damage payment is $3 million (= (.5 × $1 million) + (.5 × $5 million)). As noted in the previous paragraph, this amount is what is needed for proper deterrence.

Nevertheless, if actual harm turns out to be low, one might wonder why basing damages on actual harm does not result in inadequate deterrence. In our example, if the harm is $1 million and the injurer is made to pay this amount, he will be paying relatively little compared to the $5 million harm that his act might have caused. (The difference between actual harm and potential harm could be much greater — indeed, a person may act very dangerously but cause *no* harm, and thus pay *no* damages, if damages are based on actual harm.) The reason that inadequate deterrence is not a problem, however, should be apparent: when a potential injurer chooses whether to engage in a harmful act, he *does not know* what the harm — and therefore what his damages — will be. The injurer in our example cannot predict whether his damages will be $1 million or $5 million. Consequently, he will decide whether to commit the harmful act on the basis of having to pay the average or expected damage amount, which is $3 million. It would be a mistake, therefore, to think that he will be inadequately deterred if the actual harm in a particular case turns out to be $1 million, and he has to pay only this amount. The possibility that the harm and his damages might have been $5 million also will influence his behavior, in an appropriate way.

Now suppose that, instead of basing damages solely on actual harm, courts take potential harm into account by raising damages when the actual harm is unusually low — because it could have been much higher — but do not lower damages when the actual harm is high. (Such an interpretation of how courts use the potential harm factor in practice is plausible, at least in the context of punitive damages.[146]) The point we want to emphasize is that such a policy imparts a systematic upward bias to the level of damages and results in injurers bearing damages in excess of actual harm. Suppose that damages in the example are raised to $3 million when the actual harm is $1 million — on the ground that the former amount is the average harm — but that damages are not lowered when the actual harm is $5 million. Then the injurer will pay on average $4 million ($3 million half of the time and $5 million half of the time), even though the average harm is $3 million. Making injurers pay damages in excess of harm will have the undesirable consequences associated with overdeterrence that we have discussed previously.

Potential harm could be taken into account in another way, however, that would not cause damages to exceed harm systematically. Specifically, suppose that damages are set equal to the average, or expected, harm *regardless* of whether the actual harm is below or above this amount. Thus, in the example, damages would be set equal to $3 million regardless of whether the actual harm is $1 million or $5 million. In effect, this policy recognizes both that, when actual harm is low, it could have been higher, and that, when actual harm is high, it could have been lower. Such a policy would result in proper deterrence because the injurer will be paying on average for the harm he causes: each time he commits the harmful act he pays $3 million and causes, on average, harm of $3 million. Whether this policy would be employed in practice is questionable, however. One might be skeptical that, when the actual harm is high, juries and courts would reduce damages because the harm might have been lower.[147]

Even if a policy of basing damages on average or expected harm were applied consistently, a strong argument exists, based on administrative considerations, for relying solely on actual harm. For the courts to be able to calculate *expected* harm, they would have to determine each level of harm that could have occurred and its probability of occurrence. Such amounts ordinarily would be far more difficult to establish than the harm that actually did occur.[148] Additionally, the more open-ended scope of inquiry into expected harm seems likely to lead to more disputes between the parties, for it is easier to disagree

---

[146] For example, Judge Holland observed that more oil might have spilled from the Exxon Valdez, *see supra* note 145, but he did not mention the possibility that less might have spilled.

[147] To illustrate, imagine the response to the Union Carbide Company if, in the Bhopal disaster in which 4,000 people were killed and thousands of others were injured, *see* Kenneth J. Cooper, *Slums Sprawl in Shadow of Bhopal Gas Leak*, WASH. POST, June 27, 1996, at A19, Union Carbide had argued that damages should be reduced because a gas leak of the kind that occurred ordinarily would be expected to kill and injure a much smaller number of people. *See also supra* note 146 (discussing related issues in the Exxon Valdez case).

[148] In some cases, however, it might be easier to calculate expected or average harm than the particular harm in the case at hand. For example, it might be easier to determine the average value of the contents of a house that burned down than to ascertain the actual value of the contents (because much of the contents may have been consumed in the fire).

about what might have happened, and the odds of it happening, than about what actually did happen. These observations suggest that the courts will bear greater administrative expense, and the parties will bear greater litigation costs, if the goal is to calculate expected harm rather than to ascertain only the actual harm in the instant case.[149]

To summarize, there are two reasons that potential harm generally should not be taken into account in determining damages. First, we envision that the potential harm factor would be used in practice to raise damages when harm is low but not to lower damages when harm is high, thus causing overdeterrence. Second, even if potential harm were considered in the theoretically correct way — by always setting damages equal to average or expected harm — such a policy would require an inquiry into what might have occurred, and is therefore likely to increase the public and private costs of resolving legal disputes.[150]

As noted at the beginning of this section, we assumed for simplicity that the injurer is definitely found liable. The arguments for basing damages on actual harm rather than on potential harm or expected harm are essentially the same if the injurer might escape liability. The discussion then would be framed in terms of a comparison between actual harm, appropriately increased to make up for the chance of escaping liability, and potential harm or expected harm, also so increased. Our point about courts' tendencies to apply the potential harm factor in a way that leads to overdeterrence still holds, as does the point about the greater administrative complexity of determining expected harm. Thus, when the injurer has a significant chance of escaping liability, and punitive damages therefore are needed to achieve proper deterrence, such damages generally should be an appropriate multiple of actual harm, not of expected harm or potential harm. In punitive damages law, potential harm usually should be ignored.

---

[149] This conclusion also would apply if courts attempt to take potential harm into account in some other, less sophisticated, way than by calculating the expected harm.

[150] We have discussed what we believe to be the main arguments bearing on the desirability of taking potential harm into account in calculating damages, but there are other considerations, some of which reinforce our conclusions and some of which do not. Among these additional points, we note two. The first point, which supports our conclusion, is that if damages are based on potential harm rather than on actual harm, the incentive to limit actual harm will be dulled. For example, an oil company would have less incentive to curtail the leakage of oil from a grounded tanker if damages are based on the total amount of oil in the vessel rather than on the amount that actually leaks. The second point, which favors basing punitive damages on potential harm, is that such a policy can reduce the dilution of incentives because of the judgment-proof problem. Specifically, because consideration of potential harm in determining damages means that parties will pay larger amounts than otherwise when actual harm is low, their not being able to pay higher damages when actual harm is high (because of the judgment-proof problem) will tend to be counteracted.

D. Gain of Defendants

When punitive damages are imposed, their level is sometimes influenced by application of the principle that the defendant should not gain from his wrongful conduct.[151] If setting damages equal to harm would not remove the defendant's gain, the argument is that damages should include a sufficient punitive component to offset his gain. The notion that the defendant's gain should be a factor in calculating punitive damages was endorsed by the United States Supreme Court in *Haslip*.[152]

Does it make sense in terms of deterrence to ensure that the defendant's gain is disgorged, or should damages be based solely on harm (abstracting from the issue of the chance of escaping liability[153])? We conclude in this section that setting damages equal to harm generally results in proper deterrence even when the harm is less than the defendant's gain; a policy of removing the defendant's gain may result in overdeterrence. An exception arises, however, when the defendant's gain is socially illicit, in which case extracting the defendant's gain is desirable.[154]

The question whether punitive damages should be imposed to remove the defendant's gain arises only when his gain exceeds the victim's harm (otherwise, compensatory damages would eliminate the gain). One situation in which gain could exceed harm is when the

---

[151] The third *Green Oil* factor states: "If the wrongful conduct was profitable to the defendant, the punitive damages should remove the profit and should be in excess of the profit, so that the defendant recognizes a loss." Green Oil Co. v. Hornsby, 539 So. 2d 218, 223 (Ala. 1989) (quoting Aetna Life Ins. Co. v. Lavoie, 505 So. 2d 1050, 1062 (Ala. 1987) (Houston, J., concurring)) (internal quotation marks omitted); *see also* Estate of Hartz v. Nelson, 437 N.W.2d 749, 755–56 (Minn. Ct. App. 1989) (noting that, under MINN. STAT. § 549.20 (1994), punitive damages should be measured, in part, by "the profitability of the misconduct to the defendant"); Tindall v. Konitz Contracting, Inc., 783 P.2d 1376, 1382–83 (Mont. 1989) (noting that, under MONT. CODE ANN. § 27-1-221(7)(b)(iv) (1997), the awarder of punitive damages must consider "the profitability of the defendant's wrongdoing, if applicable").

[152] *See* Pacific Mut. Life Ins. Co. v. Haslip, 499 U.S. 1, 21–22 (1991) (citing favorably the third *Green Oil* factor).

[153] The arguments that we make in this section do not depend on whether a defendant might escape liability. *See infra* note 161. Thus, for convenience, we assume here that defendants never escape liability.

[154] Although there has been some scholarly discussion regarding whether to base liability on harm or gain, the points developed in this literature differ from the points that we present here. Our focus, as the reader will see, is on a measure of damages equal to the greater of gain or harm. Previous literature studies the measure of damages equal to the gain and compares it to the measure of damages equal to the harm. *See* Richard S. Gruner, *Just Punishment and Adequate Deterrence for Organizational Misconduct: Scaling Economic Penalties Under the New Corporate Sentencing Guidelines*, 66 S. CAL. L. REV. 225, 234–66 (1992); Jeffrey S. Parker, *Criminal Sentencing Policy for Organizations: The Unifying Approach of Optimal Penalties*, 26 AM. CRIM. L. REV. 513, 552–81 (1989); A. Mitchell Polinsky & Steven Shavell, *Should Liability Be Based on the Harm to the Victim or the Gain to the Injurer?*, 10 J. L. ECON. & ORG. 427 (1994); Donald Wittman, *Liability for Harm or Restitution for Benefit?*, 13 J. LEGAL STUD. 57 (1984); Donald Wittman, *Should Compensation Be Based on Costs or Benefits?*, 5 INT'L REV. LAW & ECON. 173 (1985).

level of harm is uncertain and, by chance, turns out to be low — and less than the injurer's gain.[155]   Such a situation could occur even though the *expected harm* exceeds the gain. For example, suppose that a firm would save $100,000, and thus would gain that amount, by not purchasing a safety device; that the expected harm from failing to purchase the device is $1 million; but that only $10,000 in harm occurs. Here the firm's $100,000 gain exceeds the unusually low harm of $10,000.

Using this example, we first want to show that basing damages on harm *will* accomplish proper deterrence even though the defendant's gain exceeds the harm: at the time the firm decides whether to buy the $100,000 safety device, it does not know what the harm will be. If damages always are set equal to harm and the expected harm is $1 million, then the firm's *expected* damages will be $1 million, which of course will induce it to spend $100,000 on the safety device. It is not necessary to impose punitive damages just because the harm turns out to be unusually low and below the injurer's gain. (Note that the point of this paragraph is analogous to the point we made above about potential harm.[156])

If the standard policy of imposing damages equal to harm appropriately deters, is there a disadvantage of imposing higher damages — namely, to remove the defendant's gain — when gain turns out to exceed harm? The answer is in the affirmative because overdeterrence may result. Specifically, if damages are set equal to harm when the harm exceeds the injurer's gain, but damages are set equal to gain when gain exceeds harm, then expected damages will exceed the expected harm, resulting in the usual problems of excessive liability.

If damages are set so as to remove gains, an additional reason that overdeterrence may result is that the basis for measuring the injurer's gains might be interpreted too expansively. In the example above, the firm's gains might be construed to be its profits from the entire line of activity that gave rise to the accident (say, the profits from manufacturing automobiles at a particular plant), rather than just the saving from not taking the particular precaution (say, not purchasing a $100,000 instrument to test the integrity of the automobiles' brakes). If gains are erroneously measured in this way, a policy of setting damages equal to gain will be even more likely to result in excessive liability.

---

[155] If both harm and gain were certain, it would be unlikely that the gain would exceed the harm in a punitive damages case: if the gain is known to exceed the harm, the act would likely be regarded as socially desirable, or at least not one calling for imposition of punitive damages. Hence, we here consider the possibility that harm is uncertain, and below that gain is uncertain. *See infra* p. 920.

[156] *See supra* section III.C.

Another circumstance in which a defendant's gain might exceed the victim's harm is when the level of gain is uncertain[157] and, by happenstance, turns out to be high even though the expected gain is low and less than harm.[158] For example, suppose that the cost of re-engineering an assembly line to make production safer ordinarily is $200,000, but unforeseen complications could raise the cost to $800,000. If the assembly line is modified, harm of $500,000 will be avoided. Thus, although the expected gain from forgoing the safety improvements is less than the $500,000 harm,[159] the actual gain could be $800,000 and greater than the harm. The analysis of this situation is similar to that when the uncertainty concerned harm; again, it can be shown that setting damages equal to harm will create appropriate deterrence and that imposing punitive damages to remove injurers' gains will tend to result in overdeterrence.

Finally, consider the possibility that the injurer's gain is socially illicit, as when a person acts out of malice. We noted above that it is desirable to deter an injurer whose gain is illicit even if his gain exceeds the victim's harm, and that such a goal implies that punitive damages may be needed to offset the injurer's gain.[160] Thus, in the case of socially illicit utility, the notion of using punitive damages to ensure that the defendant's gain is removed is justifiable with respect to the goal of deterrence. As we also observed previously, this justification for removing the defendant's gain does not apply to individuals acting non-maliciously or to corporations.

In sum, then, removing the defendant's gain is potentially appropriate and necessary only when the defendant is an individual who acted maliciously and obtained a socially illicit gain. Otherwise, the usual policy of setting damages equal to harm is desirable for achieving deterrence, and imposing damages so as to remove gains will tend to cause overdeterrence.[161]

---

[157] For simplicity, we assume now that harm is certain.

[158] If the expected gain exceeded the harm, imposition of punitive damages would be unlikely.

[159] This statement will be true if the $200,000 cost of re-engineering the assembly line is more likely than the $800,000 cost, which is what we mean by saying that the cost ordinarily is the lower amount. For then the expected cost will be less than $500,000, which is equivalent to saying that the expected gain from not re-engineering the assembly line is less than $500,000.

[160] *See supra* section III.A.

[161] We suggested above in note 153 that the arguments in this section apply without substantial modification to situations in which defendants might escape liability. To illustrate, consider the initial point that imposing damages equal to harm, whatever its magnitude, will cause expected damages to equal expected harm. The analogue of this point when defendants can escape liability is that imposing damages according to our multiplier formula will result in expected damages equal to expected harm, essentially for the reasons given in the text.

E. Litigation Costs

Several courts have suggested that the plaintiff's litigation costs should be a factor in the determination of punitive damages,[162] and, as noted previously, some have stated that such costs should be included as a component of punitive damages in order to encourage victims to sue injurers.[163]

Should litigation costs bear on the calculation of punitive damages to achieve proper deterrence? Our answer in this section emphasizes two points. The first is that litigation costs may cause the probability of suit to be low and thus justify a punitive damages award according to the damage formula presented earlier.[164] The second point is that punitive damages generally should not be augmented for the purpose of inducing suits that otherwise might not be brought because of the cost of litigation. Raising the probability of suit is usually unnecessary to achieve proper deterrence, and encouraging suits has the disadvantage of increasing the litigation costs borne by society. Indeed, we argue that a policy adopted in many states of *decoupling* punitive damages — giving the plaintiff only a fraction of the punitive damages paid by the defendant, with the remainder going to the state — may be desirable because it can reduce the volume of litigation without compromising deterrence.[165]

The first point, that litigation costs may be relevant to the calculation of punitive damages because they influence the probability of suit, and therefore the chance of escaping liability, is one that we have made previously.[166] We observed that, if litigation costs are significant relative to the expected gain from suit, the probability of suit may be low, and this fact may justify imposing punitive damages on the injurer. For example, we suggested that in the circumstances of *Gore*, litigation costs may have led to a low likelihood of suit because the

---

[162] *See, e.g.*, Ultimate Chem. Co. v. Surface Transp. Int'l, Inc., 658 P.2d 1008, 1012 (Kan. 1983) ("A jury may also consider ... the probable litigation expenses."); Fischer v. Johns-Manville Corp., 512 A.2d 466, 482 (N.J. 1986) (explaining that "the plaintiff's litigation expenses" is a factor to be considered in determining the size of a punitive damages award).

[163] *See supra* note 78.

[164] *See supra* section II.B.

[165] A number of articles on the economics of litigation are relevant to the conclusions that we reach in this section. On the general topic of how to structure the legal system given that litigation is costly, see A. Mitchell Polinsky & Yeon-Koo Che, *Decoupling Liability: Optimal Incentives for Care and Litigation*, 22 RAND J. ECON. 562 (1991); A. Mitchell Polinsky & Daniel L. Rubinfeld, *The Welfare Implications of Costly Litigation for the Level of Liability*, 17 J. LEGAL STUD. 151 (1988); Steven Shavell, *The Fundamental Divergence Between the Private and the Social Motive To Use the Legal System*, 26 J. LEGAL STUD. 575 (1997) [hereinafter Shavell, *Divergence*]; Steven Shavell, *The Social Versus the Private Incentive To Bring Suit in a Costly Legal System*, 11 J. LEGAL STUD. 333 (1982). *See also* Friedman, *supra* note 12 (suggesting that punitive damages may beneficially lower litigation costs by discouraging harmful behavior); Kahan & Tuckman, *supra* note 12 (addressing specifically the decoupling of punitive damages).

[166] *See supra* section II.B.

harm to the plaintiff was found to be only $4000. However, in other circumstances, like those in the Exxon Valdez case, litigation costs are likely to be insignificant in relation to the expected gain from suit, so that the probability of suit may be presumed to be very high. Then, consideration of litigation costs does not provide a basis for imposing punitive damages.

Note that when punitive damages are justified because of litigation costs, they should not necessarily be set equal to litigation costs. Proper punitive damages are determined by the multiplier formula, which calls for a level of punitive damages that generally differs from litigation costs. For instance, suppose harm is $10,000 and the plaintiff's litigation costs are $5000 and lead to a twenty-five percent likelihood of suit. Then total damages should be four times the harm, or $40,000, and punitive damages should be $30,000, not the $5000 amount of litigation costs.

Let us now turn to our second point. Because the punitive damages formula is *designed* to achieve appropriate deterrence when suit does not always occur, it is not necessary to raise punitive damages awards for the specific purpose of raising the probability of suit (provided that at least some suits are brought).[167] If suit occurs only half of the time because of the discouraging effect of litigation costs, total damages according to our formula would be twice the harm, and deterrence will be appropriate; there is no need to increase punitive damages to make suit occur more frequently. Moreover, encouraging lawsuits would increase social costs. Obviously, the greater the number of suits, the higher the legal costs borne by the parties and the administrative costs borne by the court system.[168] Raising damages to induce suits also will cause parties to spend more litigating each suit.[169] Thus, awarding punitive damages to spur suit is socially undesirable, other things being equal.

---

[167] If no suits are brought, deterrence obviously cannot be achieved. But if a positive probability of suit exists, deterrence will be optimal if damages are set according to our formula. There are two reasons, however, that the probability of suit should not be too low, or equivalently, that the level of punitive damages implied by our formula should not be too high. One reason is that high damages impose risk, which lowers social welfare to the extent that parties are risk averse. *See generally* A. Mitchell Polinsky & Steven Shavell, *The Optimal Tradeoff Between the Probability and Magnitude of Fines*, 69 AM. ECON. REV. 880, 884–85 (1979) (demonstrating that risk aversion may make moderate sanctions optimal). The other reason is that high damages might exceed the assets of injurers, rendering the damages ineffective as a deterrent. Assuming that the likelihood of suit is great enough so that neither of these reasons is important, our point is that there is no need for it to be higher in order to accomplish proper deterrence.

[168] Indeed, because litigation is costly, the full social harm due to an accident is the direct harm *plus* the costs associated with use of the legal system. Hence, for the injurer to have correct incentives, he should, in principle, pay damages equal to the direct harm plus these additional costs. *See* Shavell, *Divergence*, *supra* note 165, at 588. As noted previously, we have ignored this refinement in the text for simplicity. *See supra* note 18.

[169] This intuitively plausible proposition has been confirmed in research undertaken by scholars at the Institute for Civil Justice at the RAND Corporation. *See* JAMES S. KAKALIK, PATRICIA

The tendency of higher damage awards to increase litigation costs lends appeal to the policy of decoupling punitive damages. As noted above, under this policy, the plaintiff is awarded only a part of the punitive damages judgment paid by the defendant, with the remainder going to the state.[170] Decoupling mitigates the propensity of punitive damages awards to encourage unnecessary litigation, but does not dilute deterrence because defendants' damage payments are unaffected.[171]

Several states have adopted statutes that decouple punitive damages.[172] For example, in Iowa, twenty-five percent of the punitive damages amount paid by the defendant in certain circumstances is given to the plaintiff, and in Kansas, fifty percent is given to the plaintiff.[173] For the reasons stated in the previous paragraph, decoupling schemes of this sort are beneficial.

In summary, the main justification for considering litigation costs is in connection with estimating the chance that a defendant might have escaped liability because he would not be sued. Punitive damages should be awarded to make up for the chance of escaping liability for this reason, but not as a general matter to encourage the bringing of lawsuits. Decoupling punitive damages may allow proper deterrence to be achieved without inducing needless litigation.

F. Related Private Litigation

A defendant sometimes may be the subject of multiple suits because he engages in the same type of harmful conduct repeatedly, or because he commits a single act that injures many individuals. The circumstances of *Gore* exemplify the former possibility: a car manufacturer that engages in the practice of repainting damaged cars and selling them as new may be sued by different purchasers of these cars. A case involving the dumping of toxic waste that infiltrates an aquifer illustrates the latter possibility: the dumping, a single act, may give rise

---

A. EBENER, WILLIAM L.F. FELSTINER, GUS W. HAGGSTROM & MICHAEL G. SHANLEY, VARIATION IN ASBESTOS LITIGATION COMPENSATION AND EXPENSES 86–91 (Institute for Civil Justice, RAND Corp., No. R-3132-ICJ, 1984).

[170] When we use the term "decoupling," we presume that the defendant pays more than the plaintiff receives, even though, as a logical matter, the plaintiff could be awarded more than the defendant pays.

[171] Because some of the damages paid by defendants go to the state, plaintiffs' incentives to sue will lessen. However, the punitive damages amount determined by our formula will automatically rise to reflect any decrease in the probability of suit. Thus, the expected damages borne by defendants will not decline if our formula for punitive damages is applied.

[172] *See generally* BMW of N. Am., Inc. v. Gore, 116 S. Ct. 1589, 1619 app. (1996) (Ginsburg, J., dissenting) (listing state provisions that allocate a portion of punitive damages awards to state agencies). Although the statutes that describe these allocation arrangements do not use the term "decoupling," this term is employed in some of the economic literature analyzing litigation. *See, e.g.*, Polinsky & Che, *supra* note 165, at 562.

[173] *See* IOWA CODE ANN. § 668A.1(2)(b) (West 1987); KAN. STAT. ANN. § 60-3402(e) (1994).

to suits by many different parties who have been harmed. When there have been prior judgments against a defendant for the same conduct, the United States Supreme Court has endorsed the notion that these judgments should be taken into account in mitigation of a punitive damages award against the defendant.[174]

In this section, we discuss the application of our punitive damages formula when multiple plaintiffs bring suits against the same defendant, and we observe that the formula's implications generally comport with the view that punitive damages should be lowered in the light of other private judgments against a defendant. We also note that multiple punitive damages claims against a defendant for the same or related conduct may result in his paying for more than the harm he caused, and we discuss a mechanism — punitive damages escrow accounts — that can be used to address this problem.

Let us first consider the proper level of punitive damages when multiple suits may be brought because of repeated harmful conduct, as in *Gore*. Whether prior suits have been brought may be relevant in assessing the probability of suit, and thus in determining the punitive damages multiplier. If few (or no) suits have been brought even though harm had occurred in the past, that fact suggests that the likelihood of suit is low, implying that the multiplier should be high. Conversely, if a large number of prior suits have occurred, the usual inference would be that the likelihood of suit is significant, and therefore the multiplier should be low. Note that these points mean that punitive damages in a particular case should be mitigated on the basis of the number of prior suits.[175]

That few (or no) suits have been brought prior to the instant case does not necessarily mean, however, that there will be a paucity of liti-

---

[174] The seventh *Green Oil* factor states: "If there have been other civil actions against the same defendant, based on the same conduct, this should be taken into account in mitigation of the punitive damages award." Green Oil Co. v. Hornsby, 539 So. 2d 218, 224 (Ala. 1989) (quoting Aetna Life Ins. Co. v. Lavoie, 505 So. 2d 1050, 1062 (Ala. 1987) (Houston, J., concurring specially). The United States Supreme Court endorsed the *Green Oil* test in *Haslip*. *See* Pacific Mut. Life Ins. Co. v. Haslip, 499 U.S. 1, 22 (1991). This factor is echoed in the Restatement:

> Another factor that may affect the amount of punitive damages is the existence of multiple claims by numerous persons affected by the wrongdoer's conduct. It seems appropriate to take into consideration both the punitive damages that have been awarded in prior suits and those that may be granted in the future, with greater weight being given to the prior awards.

RESTATEMENT (SECOND) OF TORTS § 908 cmt. e (1979). However, when the harm that originates from the defendant's conduct is repetitive, as in *Gore*, it is not clear whether prior judgments against the defendant would be taken into account. *See* BMW of N. Am., Inc. v. Gore, 116 S. Ct. 1589, 1607 (1996) (Breyer, J., concurring) (noting that the existence of prior actions was not a factor in *Gore*).

[175] It is not just the number of prior suits that matters to the punitive damages multiplier in a case. The magnitude of the awards in prior suits matters as well. The higher the prior awards, everything else being equal, the lower punitive damages should be in the case in question, because the goal of deterrence is to make the injurer's payments equal to the total harm.

gation in the future. For example, publicity about the current suit may engender future suits, or an award of punitive damages in the current suit may stimulate litigation.

Because of the difficulty of predicting the amount of future litigation, courts might mistakenly believe that relatively few suits will be brought, and therefore perceive a greater need for punitive damages than is appropriate. (Although courts also could incorrectly expect that many suits will occur in the future, this error does not give rise to the problem we are about to discuss.[176]) If such a mistake occurs, a defendant may be made to pay more than the harm that he caused. For example, in circumstances like those in *Gore*, suppose that the court in which the first case is filed believes that only ten percent of similarly harmed car purchasers will sue in the future. The punitive damages formula then would imply that the court should impose total damages on the manufacturer equal to ten times the current plaintiff's harm. If, however, the truth is that much more than ten percent of the other victims will eventually bring suit, the car manufacturer may ultimately pay for more than the harm that it has caused, because of the excessive initial award of punitive damages.

A way to avoid the problem of excessive damages when there are multiple suits is to use *escrow accounts* for punitive damages. Under this approach, the defendant would pay punitive damages into an escrow account rather than immediately to the plaintiff.[177] If, over time, more plaintiffs bring suits than the court had anticipated, the damage awards to the plaintiffs can be financed from the escrow account rather than charged to the defendant. In this way, the defendant will not be made to pay more in total damages than the harm done. If, at some natural termination date,[178] funds remain in the escrow account, they can be distributed to plaintiffs whose punitive damages awards had been placed in escrow.[179]

Finally, let us turn briefly to the situation in which multiple suits arise because the defendant has committed a single harmful act that injured many individuals (as in the example involving the dumping of

---

[176] If courts overestimate the likelihood of suit in the future, punitive damages will be lower than they should be in the case at hand. This problem can be corrected, however, by raising punitive damages in future cases. *See infra* note 179.

[177] *See* Margaret I. Lyle, Note, *Mass Tort Claims and the Corporate Tortfeasor: Bankruptcy Reorganization and Legislative Compensation Versus the Common-Law Tort System*, 61 TEX. L. REV. 1297, 1349 n.250 (1983) (suggesting that a court might order "an equitable stay on collection of a punitive damage award for a number of years if it seems likely that the collection of too many of these awards early in the litigation of a mass tort might deprive later plaintiffs of compensatory damages").

[178] For example, a termination date might be the expiration of the statute of limitations period for the bringing of suits.

[179] Conversely, if the funds in the escrow account are exhausted before the termination date, a defendant could be made to pay additional punitive damages so that his total payments over time to the escrow account equal the total harm caused.

toxic waste). Here, our points are analogous to those discussed above. Again, whether prior suits have been brought may be relevant to evaluating the probability of suit: a greater number of prior suits should raise the estimated likelihood of suit, reduce the punitive damages multiplier, and thereby lead a court to impose lower punitive damages. Similarly, an escrow account for punitive damages can be used to avoid imposing excessive damages on the defendant.

G. Related Public Penalties

Another question of interest is whether public penalties that may be imposed for the type of wrongful conduct at issue in a private suit should affect the determination of punitive damages in that suit. Courts have answered this question in two ways. First, some have stated that punitive damages should be reduced to reflect any public penalties that the defendant has paid for the same conduct.[180] Second, the United States Supreme Court has argued in *Gore* that the level of punitive damages should reflect the level of public penalties that *could be* imposed for comparable misconduct — the higher the possible public sanctions, the higher punitive damages should be.[181]

How do these positions relate to our conclusions about punitive damages and deterrence? In this section we observe that the view that courts should reduce punitive damages if the defendant has already paid public sanctions has a straightforward justification. However, we

---

[180] The sixth *Green Oil* factor states: "If criminal sanctions have been imposed on the defendant for his conduct, this should be taken into account in mitigation of the punitive damages award." Green Oil Co. v. Hornsby, 539 So. 2d 218, 223–24 (Ala. 1989) (quoting Aetna Life Ins. Co. v. Lavoie, 505 So. 2d 1050, 1062 (Ala. 1987) (Houston, J., concurring specially)). The United States Supreme Court has endorsed the use of this factor. *See* Pacific Mut. Life Ins. Co. v. Haslip, 499 U.S. 1, 22 (1991).

[181] In *Gore*, the Court expressed this as follows: "Comparing the punitive damages award and the civil or criminal penalties that could be imposed for comparable misconduct provides a third indicium of excessiveness." BMW of N. Am., Inc. v. Gore, 116 S. Ct. 1589, 1603 (1996).

Lower courts have applied this standard. For example, in *Lee v. Edwards*, 101 F.3d 805 (2d Cir. 1996), the court found that punitive damages of $200,000 awarded by the jury in a § 1983 claim were excessive. *See id.* at 813. In reducing the award to $75,000 (if plaintiff agreed to remittitur), the court noted the plaintiff's assertion that the defendant's conduct "could have exposed him to a charge of making a false statement"; if convicted, the defendant "would have faced imprisonment of up to one year and/or a fine of up to $2,000." *Id.* at 811. The court noted that although imprisonment is "a serious sanction, . . . the maximum fine of $2,000 gives little warning that the offense could entail a $200,000 civil award." *Id.* The award of $75,000 was justified in part because the defendant was a police officer and therefore on "notice as to the gravity of misconduct under color of his official authority." *Id.* Also, in *Management Computer Services, Inc. v. Hawkins, Ash, Baptie & Co.*, 557 N.W.2d 67 (Wis. 1996), involving the unauthorized copying and use of computer software, the court reduced a punitive damages award from $1.75 million to $650,000. *See id.* at 83. As part of its *Gore* analysis, the court noted that the defendant's wrongdoing resulted in damages of $65,000 to the plaintiff, and that "the potential criminal penalty for copying computer programs if the damage is greater than $2,500 is a fine not exceeding $10,000." *Id.* at 82–83.

suggest that the view taken in *Gore*, that potential public penalties should serve as a benchmark for punitive damages, is problematic.

To begin, there is an obvious basis for subtracting any public penalties already incurred by the defendant from the level of punitive damages that otherwise would be appropriate: such a policy is necessary to ensure that the defendant's total payment is the proper amount for the purpose of deterrence. As the reader knows, the defendant's total payment should be such that his expected payment equals the harm done. If punitive damages are not reduced from the amount implied by our formula to reflect public penalties borne by the defendant, the defendant's combined private and public payments would result in his expected payments exceeding the harm done.[182]

Now consider the use of public penalties as a benchmark for setting punitive damages, as suggested in *Gore*. This role for public penalties makes sense only if their level conveys information relevant to determining the proper amount of punitive damages. The question naturally arises, therefore, whether the level of public penalties implies something about, among other things, the chance of escaping liability. Ostensibly, the answer is yes. For example, suppose that significant public penalties are imposed on restaurants for food poisoning because food poisoning often will not lead to suit. A court reviewing a punitive damages judgment in a case against a restaurant for food poisoning might use this information about the likelihood of suit, inferred from the magnitude of the public penalties, to justify the award.[183]

Nevertheless, we are skeptical whether the information that generally can be inferred from public penalties will be very useful, given the information that courts already will have about a case. In the course of a trial, a court will typically obtain information particular to that case about the defendant's likelihood of escaping liability. For example, a court might learn whether it would be easy to link harm from food poisoning to the defendant's restaurant (the type of poisoning

---

[182] This statement presumes for simplicity that the outcomes of the private and the public suits are identical — they either both succeed or they both fail. Otherwise, the proper adjustment of the amount implied by our formula does not necessarily involve simply subtracting the amount paid as a public penalty. To illustrate, consider the following example. Suppose that the harm suffered by the victim is $5000 and that the injurer has a 10% chance of being found liable as a result of a private suit. Suppose also that the government will impose a $1000 fine on the injurer with certainty. (It is not essential to this example that the fine is certain, only that it is imposed with a higher probability than the private plaintiff's probability of prevailing against the defendant.) Let A be the amount awarded to the private plaintiff if he prevails, with A set such that the defendant's combined expected public and private payments equal the harm caused. In other words, A is set such that $1000 + .1A = 5000$. Solving for A yields $40,000 as the proper private award. If instead our formula were applied and the public penalty were simply subtracted from the amount implied by our formula, the private award would be $49,000: the $50,000 award implied by our formula (= $5000/.1), less the $1000 public penalty.

[183] The point of this paragraph — that public penalties can serve as useful guidelines for the setting of punitive damages — is discussed by Cooter, *Deterrence*, cited above in note 12, at 1179–80.

may or may not make identification straightforward), or whether the magnitude of the harm from the poisoning would be sufficient to induce suit (the poisoning may or may not result in expensive hospitalization and substantial lost wages). In contrast, the information implicit in public sanctions for food poisoning reflects, one presumes, only the average likelihood of liability over the range of cases of food poisoning.

Further difficulties are involved in inferring useful information from the level of public penalties. Such penalties are influenced in part by political factors — interest group pressures, logrolling, and the like. Consequently, courts would find it hard to determine in any precise way what legislators thought about the likelihood of escaping liability when they set the level of public sanctions. Another complication is that public penalties may themselves be influenced by the possibility of punitive damages awards in private suits: public penalties might be low precisely because legislators believed that punitive damages awards would create effective deterrence. If the courts then constrain such awards on the ground that public penalties for comparable conduct are low, deterrence will tend to be inadequate, because of a kind of circularity — the legislature relying on the courts and the courts relying on the legislature.[184] Because of the possibility of such circularity, the information that courts infer from the level of public penalties may be misleading.

For the foregoing reasons, we believe that courts generally should not use public sanctions as a benchmark in setting punitive damages. Such sanctions should be used, however, as an offset: any public penalties paid for the same conduct at issue in a private suit should reduce the magnitude of punitive damages calculated according to our formula.

H. Tax Treatment of Punitive Damages

If a defendant bears punitive damages as a result of his engaging in some business or other income-earning activity, he generally can deduct such damages from taxable income, just as he can deduct compensatory damages in those circumstances.[185] But neither punitive nor compensatory damages are deductible if they are incurred as a result of the defendant's engaging in a non-business or personal activity.[186]

---

[184] A different type of circularity could result in excessive deterrence. Suppose the legislature sets public penalties at high levels because it expects inadequate use of punitive damages. If the courts then impose substantial punitive damages because public penalties are high, deterrence could be excessive.

[185] *See* 2 STUART M. SPEISER, CHARLES F. KRAUSE & ALFRED W. GANS, THE AMERICAN LAW OF TORTS § 8:64, at 297 (Supp. 1997); ROBERT W. WOOD, TAXATION OF DAMAGE AWARDS AND SETTLEMENT PAYMENTS ¶ 6.292, at 6-14 to 6-15 (1991 & Supp. 1996).

[186] *See* WOOD, *supra* note 185, ¶ 6.6, at 6-31.

We explain here that these policies are desirable, given the goal of creating appropriate deterrence.[187] In the business context, the essence of the argument for the deductibility of punitive damages is that, were they not deductible, overdeterrence would result because the punitive damages component of liability would be more significant than it should be. Conversely, in the non-business or personal context, if punitive damages were deductible, underdeterrence would result.[188]

To see why damages should be deductible in a business context, consider a simple example in which a harm of $10,000 can be prevented by taking a precaution. It is socially desirable that the precaution is taken only if it costs less than $10,000. We first will show that if the injurer always will be sued and have to pay $10,000 in compensatory damages, precautions will be taken precisely when they should be if the damage payment is deductible. Suppose that the precaution costs $8000 and it is not taken. Then the defendant will pay damages of $10,000, and if these are deductible at, say, a forty percent tax rate, the defendant will bear after-tax damages of $6000. If the defendant does take the precaution, he pays $8000 for it, but because this is a deductible expense, the after-tax cost of the precaution is $4800. Hence, he will take the precaution. Alternatively, if the precaution costs more than $10,000, the defendant is better off paying damages of $10,000 and deducting this amount than spending more on the precaution. Thus, the defendant will act optimally.

To put the point differently, because the defendant is able to deduct all of his expenses, whether damages or precautions, he will want to act so as to minimize his after-tax costs and thus will choose the precaution if and only if its cost after taxes is less than the damages the defendant would bear after taxes. Because the tax rate is the same whether applied to deducting precaution costs or damages, the defendant's behavior is equivalent to his choosing the precaution if and only if its cost is less than the damages (putting tax considerations aside), which is the behavior that is desired.

If damages were not deductible, a business actor might take precautions even when they cost more than the harm. Consider a firm in a forty percent tax bracket that is deciding whether to take a precaution that costs $15,000 and would prevent a harm of $10,000. The

---

[187] Because our focus is on properly deterring potential injurers, we do not consider the tax treatment of *plaintiffs' receipts* of punitive damages awards. However, whether punitive damages are taxable income to the recipient may affect a plaintiff's incentive to sue. In this indirect way, the tax treatment of the receipt of punitive damages might affect deterrence.

[188] *See* I.P.L. Png & Eric M. Zolt, *Efficient Deterrence and the Tax Treatment of Monetary Sanctions*, 9 INT'L REV. L. & ECON. 209, 209 (1989) (noting the different possible tax treatments of monetary sanctions and arguing that, to avoid overdeterrence, monetary sanctions should be deductible or the amount of the sanction should be adjusted to account for the offender's tax rate); Eric M. Zolt, *Deterrence Via Taxation: A Critical Analysis of Tax Penalty Provisions*, 37 UCLA L. REV. 343, 364–68 (1989) (expanding on the analysis presented in the Png & Zolt article).

firm will take the precaution if damages are not deductible: the after-tax cost of the precaution is $9000, which is less than the after-tax cost of non-deductible compensatory damages, $10,000. This decision is socially undesirable because the cost to society of the precaution is $15,000, while the benefit to society is $10,000.

The reason that the firm is led to take a socially wasteful precaution is that damages are not deductible, but the precaution cost is, so that the effective cost of the damages to the firm is heightened. Indeed, with a tax rate of forty percent, damages appear to be one-and-two-thirds as important to eliminate as they would be if they were deductible, meaning that the firm would be willing to spend up to $16,667 to eliminate a $10,000 harm.[189]

The explanation that we have provided for the desirability of allowing compensatory damages to be deducted in a business context applies equally to punitive damages. Punitive damages are just another form of damages that are intended to make the expected damages of injurers equal to the harm they cause. If punitive damages were not deductible, but precaution costs were, overdeterrence would result for essentially the same reason as that discussed above: the non-deductibility of punitive damages would make causing harm more costly to business actors than expenditures to prevent harm, so that such actors would be induced to spend too much to reduce harm.[190]

---

[189] To demonstrate this point, let C be the cost of the precaution, H the harm, and T the tax rate. Ideally, the precaution should be taken if $C < H$. If both the precaution cost and damages are deductible, the firm will take the precaution if $(1 - T)C < (1 - T)H$, which is equivalent to $C < H$. But if damages are not deductible, the firm will take the precaution if $(1 - T)C < H$, which is equivalent to $C < H/(1 - T)$. Thus, if $H = \$10,000$ and $T = .4$, the firm would be willing to spend up to $\$10,000/(1 - .4) = \$16,667$ to eliminate the harm. In other words, for every dollar of harm, the firm would be induced to spend up to $\$1/(1 - .4) = \$1.67$ to eliminate it. Hence, damages appear to be one-and-two-thirds more important to eliminate than they would be if they were deductible.

   Note that the logic of our discussion in the text implies that, if damages were not deductible but were reduced appropriately, the firm could be induced to take optimal precautions. If the tax rate is 40% and the harm is $10,000, reducing damages to $6000 and not allowing damages to be deductible would be equivalent to keeping damages at $10,000 but allowing their deductibility. Reducing damages by the precise amount that would be necessary to avoid distortions is functionally equivalent to allowing deductibility. But a policy of allowing deductibility may be preferable on administrative grounds because it obviates the need to determine the defendant's marginal tax bracket in order to calculate damages properly.

[190] For instance, in the example that we considered in which the harm is $10,000, suppose that the defendant is caught one time out of three, so that a third of the time he pays $30,000, consisting of $10,000 in compensatory damages and $20,000 in punitive damages. If the punitive damages component is not deductible and the defendant is in a 40% tax bracket, his after-tax liability cost if a judgment is rendered against him is $26,000 (the sum of an after-tax cost of $6000 associated with the compensatory damages component and an after-tax cost of $20,000 associated with the punitive damages component). Because there is a one-third chance that he will bear this amount, his expected after-tax liability cost is $8667 (that is, $26,000 divided by 3). Because his precaution expenditures are deductible and he is in a 40% tax bracket, he would be willing to spend up to one-and-two-thirds of this amount in order to avoid this liability cost. In other words, he would be willing to spend up to $14,445 (= (5/3) × $8667). But the harm is only

The importance of allowing punitive damages to be deductible in a business context may be substantial because the tax rate for corporations and other business actors is relatively high. As we noted, at a tax rate of forty percent,[191] if damages were not deductible, a potential injurer might be induced to spend up to one-and-two-thirds the harm to prevent it.[192] Thus, if the deductibility of punitive damages in a business setting were disallowed, significant overdeterrence could result.

The explanation for why punitive damages should not be deductible in a non-business or personal context is the converse of that for why they should be deductible in a business context. In a non-business or personal setting, the cost of precautions is not deductible. Hence, if punitive damages also are not deductible, a potential injurer will properly balance the cost of precautions against the reduction in harm from taking the precaution. If punitive damages were deductible, a potential injurer would not give sufficient weight to the reduction in harm from taking precautions, resulting in underdeterrence.

I. *Insurability of Punitive Damages*

Policies regarding the insurability of punitive damages vary among states. Most states allow punitive damages to be covered by liability insurance, but some do not.[193]

$10,000, so many instances could arise in which he will be induced to spend substantially more than $10,000 in order to avoid imposing a harm of $10,000 — a socially wasteful outcome caused by the non-deductibility of punitive damages.

[191] Under the federal tax code, taxable corporate income in excess of $75,000, but not in excess of $10 million, is taxed at a 34% rate. *See* 26 U.S.C. § 11(b)(1)(C) (1994). Taxable corporate income in excess of $10 million is taxed at a 35% rate. *See id.* § 11(b)(1)(D). The use of a 40% tax rate as an illustration in the text is reasonable in light of the additional state income taxes that corporations often have to pay. *See, e.g.*, CAL. REV. & TAX. CODE § 23151(e) (West Supp. 1997) (8.84% of net income for 1997 and beyond); 35 ILL. COMP. STAT. 5/201(b)(7), (d) (West 1996) (7.3% of net income); N.Y. TAX LAW § 210.1(a) (McKinney 1986 & Supp. 1997) (9% of net income).

[192] The explanation for why the injurer would be induced to spend up to one-and-two-thirds of the harm now is complicated by the fact that the fraction of total damages that is accounted for by punitive damages — and therefore the portion of total damages that is not deductible — depends on the chance of escaping liability. In note 190, above, we showed that, if the chance of catching the injurer is one in three, he would be induced to spend $14,445 in order to prevent a harm of $10,000 — that is, 1.44 times the harm. By similar logic, it can be demonstrated that if the chance of detection is sufficiently small — so that nearly all of the damages paid by the injurer are punitive damages and not deductible — the injurer will be induced to spend up to 1.67 times the harm to prevent it.

[193] A majority of jurisdictions follow the approach exemplified in *Lazenby v. Universal Underwriters Insurance Co.*, 383 S.W.2d 1 (Tenn. 1964), under which punitive damages are insurable. *See id.* at 5; *see also* Ellis, *supra* note 12, at 71 (noting that most, though not all, courts have held that punitive damages are insurable). In general, however, insureds cannot indemnify themselves against punitive damages assessed for intentional misconduct. *See, e.g.*, Harrell v. Travelers Indem. Co., 567 P.2d 1013, 1017–19 (Or. 1977) (en banc). A minority of jurisdictions follow the approach taken in *Northwestern Nat'l Cas. Co. v. McNulty*, 307 F.2d 432 (5th Cir. 1962), under which insurance coverage of punitive damages is disallowed because it would violate public policy (on the ground that such coverage would permit wrongdoers to escape punishment and also would compromise deterrence). *See id.* at 442. Even these jurisdictions, however, generally allow

Should punitive damages be insurable? The basic answer to this question is yes, although we qualify this conclusion below. The reason that it is generally desirable to allow insurance for punitive damages is best understood by recognizing that punitive damages are, according to our theory, a way to make defendants pay for the harm they do when they have a chance of escaping liability. Thus, the question whether punitive damages should be insurable is essentially the same as the question whether compensatory damages should be insurable.[194]

Of course, compensatory damages *are* insurable, but what reason can be given for allowing them to be? Consider this question when liability is strict and harm is entirely monetary. In this case, allowing the purchase of liability insurance is socially desirable. Liability insurance raises the well-being of potential injurers, which is why they choose to buy it, and the availability of such insurance does not affect the welfare of victims, who will be fully compensated anyway. Even if the purchase of liability insurance causes injurers to take less care and thereby increases the frequency of accidents, victims will not be affected because they are fully compensated.[195]

However, if losses are nonmonetary, victims might not be fully compensated, or if the negligence rule applies, might not be compensated at all.[196] Consequently, their welfare would be adversely affected if liability insurance leads to an increase in the frequency of accidents. Nevertheless, it can be shown that such insurance often is socially desirable even then, because the value of the insurance to insureds may exceed the loss of welfare to victims.[197] Further, the victims' losses are mitigated because liability insurers have a financial incentive to structure coverage and premiums to control risks. For example, insurers may make insurance premiums depend on an in-

---

insurance coverage of punitive damages in cases of vicarious liability. *See, e.g.,* Ohio Cas. Ins. Co. v. Welfare Fin. Co., 75 F.2d 58, 59–60 (8th Cir. 1934). For further discussion of the insurability of punitive damages, and summaries of the relevant law among the states, see generally ROBERT G. SCHLOERB, RICHARD L. BLATT, ROBERT W. HAMMESFAHR & LORI S. NUGENT, PUNITIVE DAMAGES: A GUIDE TO THE INSURABILITY OF PUNITIVE DAMAGES IN THE UNITED STATES AND ITS TERRITORIES 32–46, 61–308 (1988); 2 SCHLUETER & REDDEN, cited above in note 74, § 17.2, at 233–47; 2 SPEISER, KRAUSE & GANS, cited above in note 185, § 8:54, at 907.

[194] For economically oriented discussion of the question of the social desirability of liability insurance for punitive damages, see Chapman & Trebilcock, cited above in note 12, at 821–22; Cooter, *Deterrence,* cited above in note 12, at 1182–85; Ellis, cited above in note 12, at 71–76; and Priest, *Insurability,* cited above in note 12, at 1011–14.

[195] The argument in this paragraph is based on Shavell, cited above in note 41, which first formally analyzed the social desirability of liability insurance. *See also* SHAVELL, *supra* note 14, at 206–27 (extending the argument). These references show that, in the standard model of accidents, both injurers and victims will be made better off if the sale of liability insurance is permitted.

[196] Victims might not be fully compensated if their losses are nonmonetary because, among other reasons, full compensation may be impossible (for instance, if the loss is of a person's life). Victims may not be compensated at all under the negligence rule because the injurer may not have been negligent.

[197] *See* SHAVELL, *supra* note 14, at 251–52.

sured's history of claims, may only offer partial coverage, or may require that the insured take certain steps to reduce risks. As a result, the purchase of liability insurance may not significantly reduce the insured's incentives to exercise precautions.

Moreover, if liability insurance were disallowed, not only would the well-being of potential injurers decrease, but such injurers also might forgo engaging in some socially beneficial activities that pose liability risks. For example, surgeons might refuse to perform certain operations, or general-aviation aircraft companies might cease making planes. Even when services and products continue to be offered, prices would rise to cover the liability risks that such providers would now have to bear directly, and the resulting price increase generally would exceed that which would have resulted from the purchase of liability insurance.[198] Both of these consequences of disallowing liability insurance — the possible withdrawal from certain activities and the increased price of other activities — hurt consumers of the affected products and services. This consideration lends support to the case for allowing the sale of liability insurance.

A major complication in the preceding discussion concerning the desirability of liability insurance arises from the judgment-proof problem.[199] If injurers can avoid having to pay for some of the harm they cause because their assets are limited, they will have a reduced incentive both to take precautions and to moderate their participation in risky activities. (In the extreme case, an injurer with no assets would have no liability-related incentive to reduce risks.) Depending on insurers' ability to control insureds, the sale of liability insurance could either worsen or ameliorate this problem. If insurers are substantially unable to control the risky behavior of insureds because insurers cannot easily observe insureds' risk-taking behavior and link policy features, such as premium rates, to insureds' behavior, liability insurance would tend to exacerbate the judgment-proof problem. It might then be beneficial to forbid the sale of such insurance. Conversely, if insurers can relatively easily observe and control the behavior of insureds, liability insurance could lessen the judgment-proof problem. For in-

---

[198] To illustrate, suppose that a risk-averse firm with direct production costs of $20 per unit purchases liability insurance whose premium equals the expected damages of $10 per unit of the product sold. In a competitive environment, the price of the product will equal $30, including the $10 liability insurance cost. If the firm cannot purchase liability insurance, the price it charges must not only compensate it for the $10 in expected damages it bears directly, but also for being subject to risk — something it does not like, being risk averse. Thus, the price of the product would have to exceed $30 for the firm to be willing to sell it.

[199] Before discussing this complication, we want to observe that a common view is that, if there is a chance that injurers will be unable to pay for harm, liability insurance is socially desirable because it enhances the ability of victims to collect damages from injurers. We do not consider this reason for liability insurance to be a strong one; as we have noted previously, we believe that first-party insurance is a superior way to provide compensation to victims because it is administratively cheaper than the tort system. *See supra* note 15.

934   *HARVARD LAW REVIEW*   [Vol. 111:869

stance, insurers might require that a restaurant install fire extinguish-
ers and a sprinkler system to reduce fire risks. In this case, not only
might it be desirable to allow the sale of liability insurance, but it
might even be beneficial to require its purchase.[200]

We have now explained that, with some qualifications, it is generally desirable to allow potential injurers to purchase liability insurance
for compensatory damages. Because punitive damages, by our formula, substitute for compensatory damages when injurers can escape
liability, essentially the same arguments support the conclusion that it
is generally desirable also to allow the sale of insurance for punitive
damages, as the majority of states already do.

J. Third Party Versus Consumer Victims

Our analysis of punitive damages has assumed implicitly that the
parties harmed by the injurer are "third parties" — that is, parties who
have no market or contractual relationship with the defendant. Such
was the case, for example, with respect to the fishermen and Alaskan
natives whose livelihood was affected by the Exxon Valdez oil spill. In
many situations, however, the victims are customers of the defendant,
as in *Gore*, in which the plaintiff was a purchaser of a car made by the
defendant.[201]

When determining punitive damages, courts devote little attention
to whether the plaintiff was a third party or a consumer.[202] The list of
factors in *Haslip*, for example, does not include this distinction, nor
does any other similar list or authoritative source of which we are
aware.[203]

---

[200] The conclusions of this paragraph are based on an economic analysis of the judgment-proof
problem and insurance in Steven Shavell, *The Judgment Proof Problem*, 6 INT'L REV. LAW &
ECON. 45 (1986), which is distilled in SHAVELL, cited above in note 14, at 240–43.

[201] *See* BMW of N. Am., Inc. v. Gore, 116 S. Ct. 1589, 1593 (1996); *see also* Sears, Roebuck &
Co. v. Harris, 630 So. 2d 1018, 1022 (Ala. 1994) (customer harmed from self-installed gas water
heater); Moore v. Jewel Tea Co., 253 N.E.2d 636, 639 (Ill. App. Ct. 1969) (customer harmed when
unopened can of drain cleaner exploded), *aff'd*, 263 N.E.2d 103 (Ill. 1970); Leibeck v. McDonald's
Corp., No. CV-93-2419 (N.M. Dist. Ct. 1994) (customer burned by hot coffee).

[202] This difference is not emphasized, for example, in any of the major United States Supreme
Court cases on punitive damages. *See Gore*, 116 S. Ct. at 1589; Honda Motor Co. v. Oberg, 512
U.S. 415 (1994); TXO Prod. Corp. v. Alliance Resources Corp., 509 U.S. 443 (1993); Pacific Mut.
Life Ins. Co. v. Haslip, 499 U.S. 1 (1991); Browning-Ferris Indus. of Vt., Inc. v. Kelco Disposal,
Inc., 492 U.S. 257 (1989). The *Gore* Court, however, mentioned the market relationship between
the plaintiff and the defendant as a factor that would lessen the need for affirmative disclosure
requirements "because the self-interest of those involved in the automobile trade in developing
and maintaining the goodwill of their customers will motivate them to make voluntary disclosures
or to refrain from selling cars that do not comply with self-imposed standards." *Gore*, 116 S. Ct.
at 1596.

[203] The Restatement (Second) of Torts does not mention this distinction explicitly, nor do commentators. *See* RESTATEMENT (SECOND) OF TORTS §§ 908–909 (1977); JAMES D. GHIARDI &
JOHN J. KIRCHER, PUNITIVE DAMAGES LAW AND PRACTICE (1985), SCHLUETER & REDDEN,
supra note 74. This distinction is also absent from cases that provide factors for the jury to consider in determining the amount of punitive damages. *See, e.g.*, Estate of Hartz v. Nelson, 437

However, the status of victims as third parties or consumers is important to consider, for when victims are consumers, the need for punitive damages is lessened. The reason is that, when individuals might be harmed by the products (or services) they buy, producers will tend to be concerned that customers may not be willing to pay as much for the products or that they may stop purchasing the products altogether. Given that producers have this market-based incentive to be attentive to the risk of harm to their customers, the need for liability in general, and for punitive damages in particular, to control their behavior is diminished.[204] Obviously, this market mechanism cannot operate if the victims are not customers of the defendant — that is, if they are third parties.[205]

The extent to which market forces reduce the need for liability as a deterrent depends on how much customers know about product or service hazards. In some circumstances, customers will not be able to discipline firms effectively because of their lack of knowledge of such risks.[206] Because travelers probably would not know much about the chance of suffering food poisoning from eating at a family-owned restaurant at a turnpike stop, the restaurant would not be likely to fear loss of clientele if food poisoning were to occur. Thus, the threat of liability, including punitive damages, might be desirable to induce the restaurant to reduce this risk.[207]

In many settings, however, consumer information about the dangers of products and services is relatively good.[208] This may be be-

---

N.W.2d 749, 755–56 (Minn. Ct. App. 1989); Fischer v. Johns-Manville Corp., 512 A.2d 466, 481–82 (N.J. 1986).

[204] To the extent that liability is unnecessary to promote product safety, imposing liability would be redundant and the costs associated with litigation would be socially wasteful.

[205] Craswell discusses the role of damages multipliers in market relationships, although he does not emphasize the point that we do — that producers have a market-based incentive to be attentive to the risk of harm to their customers. *See* Craswell, *supra* note 12.

[206] For the view that consumers are not well informed about product risks, see Howard Latin, *"Good" Warnings, Bad Products, and Cognitive Limitations,* 41 UCLA L. REV. 1193, 1234 (1994). Latin argues that knowledge of "the great majority of product risks cannot be available to product users." *Id.*

[207] Daughety and Reinganum study the role of punitive damages in reducing product risks when consumers do not have direct information about the risks. *See* Daughety & Reinganum, *Products Liability, supra* note 12; Daughety & Reinganum, Settlement, *supra* note 12.

[208] *See* Patricia M. Danzon, *Comments on Landes and Posner: A Positive Economic Analysis of Products Liability,* 14 J. LEGAL STUD. 569, 572 (1985) (arguing that the cost of obtaining information about product hazards could be low in many circumstances and that the value of such information is high for consumer goods that are purchased repeatedly, durable consumer goods, and producer goods); Alan Schwartz, *Proposals for Products Liability Reform: A Theoretical Synthesis,* 97 YALE L.J. 353, 380 (1988) (arguing that "evidence drawn from surveys and actual market behavior more strongly supports the view that consumers are informed than the view that they are ignorant"). Even if consumer information about the risks of products and services is not widespread, markets may work reasonably well if a sufficiently large fraction of the population of potential consumers is well-informed. *See* Alan Schwartz & Louis L. Wilde, *Intervening in Mar-*

cause the risks have a fairly obvious character, because they have been publicized by the media,[209] or because the customers are repeat purchasers and have learned about them from experience. In such circumstances, the threat of liability would be relatively unimportant in controlling risk. Indeed, if consumer information about risk were perfect, liability to improve product safety would be unnecessary: consumers would reduce their willingness to pay for a firm's product or service by precisely the amount of the expected harm to which the product or service exposed them, which in turn would cause firms to invest in any cost-justified precautions.

Our conclusion, therefore, is that in deciding on punitive damages, courts should take into account whether the victims are third parties or customers and, if the latter, whether market forces are likely to lead sellers to reduce risk properly. A skeptical approach to imposing punitive damages should be adopted when consumers are relatively well-informed about the risk of the seller's product or service.[210]

K. Breach of Contract

Although we have been discussing the imposition of punitive damages in situations governed by tort law, punitive damages sometimes can be levied in contractual disputes as well.[211] Indeed, there seems to be an increasing tendency to employ such damages in this context[212] — for example, in employment termination and insurance litigation.[213]

We will explain that the award of punitive damages sometimes can promote the interests of contracting parties — when a non-performing

---

kets on the Basis of Imperfect Information: A Legal and Economic Analysis, 127 U. PA. L. REV. 630, 637–39 (1979).

[209] For example, we would expect problems with automobiles, as in *Gore, see supra* p. 901, to come to the attention of consumers through stories in newspapers, evaluations in *Consumer Reports*, and the like.

[210] A similar conclusion applies when the victims of accidents are employees, rather than customers. To the degree that employees are aware of workplace risks, they will insist on higher wages (or seek employment elsewhere). Thus, market forces will tend to induce employers to increase workplace safety even in the absence of liability.

[211] Although punitive damages traditionally are not awarded in contract cases, exceptions often are made when the wrongful conduct is also considered to be a tort. *See* 1 SCHLUETER & REDDEN, *supra* note 74, § 7.2, at 371, § 7.3(A), at 377.

[212] *See id.* § 7.0, at 369 ("[O]ver the last twenty years, the courts have broken down the traditional doctrinal barriers between contracts and torts. The result is a growing list of exceptions to the general rule and a growing recognition of punitive damages within the law of contracts."); *see also* Mark Pennington, *Punitive Damages for Breach of Contract: A Core Sample from the Decisions of the Last Ten Years*, 42 ARK. L. REV. 31, 46–60 (1989) (noting departures from the traditional rule against awarding punitive damages for breach of contract); John A. Sebert, Jr., *Punitive and Nonpecuniary Damages in Actions Based upon Contract: Toward Achieving the Objective of Full Compensation*, 33 UCLA L. REV. 1565, 1600–47 (1986) (noting a trend toward allowing punitive damages in contract cases).

[213] *See* 2 SCHLUETER & REDDEN, *supra* note 74, § 13.3(B), at 118 (discussing punitive damages in the employment context); *id.* § 17.3(A), at 247–49, § 17.4(A), at 266 (discussing punitive damages in insurance cases with respect to contract theories).

party has a chance of escaping detection and liability. However, such circumstances do not give rise to the imposition of punitive damages in contract cases in practice, with the result that the interests of contracting parties may be harmed by actual punitive damages policy.[214]

Parties would benefit from the imposition of punitive damages when such damages are necessary to induce the promisor to perform adequately.[215] For example, consider a company that contracts with a city to replace its burned-out streetlights. Suppose that the company would have to pay punitive damages of $200, in addition to compensatory damages of $50, if the city discovers that a light was not replaced in a timely manner (say, one week after burning out). The reason we can imagine that the parties would want punitive damages in this situation is that they both recognize that the city will not discover most of the lights that burn out and that are not repaired on a timely basis. They realize that setting total damages for breach in excess of the loss from breach will give the repair company a stronger and more appropriate motive to search for and replace burned-out streetlights than would compensatory damages alone. Because the city will be willing to pay more to the company for its better service, both parties to the contract can benefit from imposition of punitive damages.[216]

---

[214] Several commentators have discussed the general economic role of punitive damages in breach of contract disputes. *See, e.g.,* Daniel A. Farber, *Reassessing the Economic Efficiency of Compensatory Damages for Breach of Contract,* 66 VA. L. REV. 1443 (1980); Barry Perlstein, *Crossing the Contract-Tort Boundary: An Economic Argument for the Imposition of Extracompensatory Damages for Opportunistic Breach of Contract,* 58 BROOK. L. REV. 877 (1992); Alan Schwartz, *The Myth That Promisees Prefer Supracompensatory Remedies: An Analysis of Contracting for Damage Measures,* 100 YALE L.J. 369, 370–72, 395–405 (1990).

[215] The argument that we are about to make, that parties might benefit from imposition of punitive damages, also means that they might benefit from including a penalty clause in their contract — that is, an extracompensatory level of damages for breach. In practice, however, provisions detailing the damages paid in the event of breach — liquidated damage clauses — are not enforced by courts if they are determined to exceed compensatory damages. *See* RESTATEMENT (SECOND) OF CONTRACTS § 356 (1979) (stating that a liquidated damages clause will be enforced if the contract specifies "an amount that is reasonable in the light of the anticipated or actual loss caused by the breach and the difficulties of proof of loss," but "[a] term fixing unreasonably large liquidated damages is unenforceable on grounds of public policy as a penalty"); *see also* U.C.C. § 2-718(1) (1996) (allowing for liquidated damages provisions but rendering them void if unreasonably large).

[216] To illustrate, suppose that: (a) each light will definitely fail at some time during the year; (b) the value to the city of timely repair of a light is $50; (c) the cost to the contractor of assuring timely repair is $25; (d) the cost to the contractor of less-than-timely repairs is $5 (the contractor does not have to check lights as frequently); (e) the likelihood that the city detects a breach (the contractor's failure to repair a light on a timely basis) is 20%; (f) the city's payment to the contractor is $35 per light per year; and (g) the damages for breach are compensatory, equal to $50 (the value of timely repair).

Note that the contractor will not be induced to spend an extra $20 — $25 instead of $5 — to assure timely repair, because the extra cost to assure timely repair, $20, exceeds the expected damages per light of $10 (= 20% × $50). Thus, the contractor's profit per light will be $20 — the city's payment of $35, less the $5 cost of repairs and the $10 expected damage payment. The city's total cost per light is $75 — its $35 payment to the contractor, plus its $50 loss of value as a result of the contractor's failure to repair the light on a timely basis, less the $10 it receives in expected

Note that the circumstances in this example are analogous to those in the tort settings in which we have said that punitive damages are desirable — namely, when there is a probability that a party will not be found liable if he does harm (in the present context, by committing a breach). Thus, the role of the penalty for breach in the example resembles the role of punitive damages in tort situations — to make up for the chance of escaping liability.[217]

Parties may want punitive damages to be paid for breach in two contexts in which a breaching party may escape liability. The first situation is when the breached-against party does not automatically observe whether performance has occurred, as in the streetlight example.[218] The second situation is when the breached-against party knows that performance has been deficient, but may not be able to prove this in court or lacks a financial incentive to sue. For instance, if an insurance company fabricates a reason for not paying a small claim, the insured may not sue because of the uncertainty of success and the cost of a lawsuit. But because insureds would in principle be willing to pay higher premiums if an insurance company can be deterred from acting in this way, the insurer may benefit from an agreement to pay punitive damages when it is found liable for falsely denying a small claim.

In many circumstances, however, parties will not want damages for breach of contract to exceed the compensatory level because the breach is obvious, the nature of the breach is such that it easily can be proven in court, and the amount at stake is large enough to justify suit. To the degree that courts impose punitive damages in these situa-

---

damage payments.

We want to show that *both* parties can benefit if punitive damages of $200 are also imposed for breach, so that total damages now are $250. Given this level of total damages, the contractor will assure timely repair because the expected damages of $50 (= 20% × $250) exceed the extra cost of assuring timely repair, $20. Consequently, no breach will occur, and no damages will actually be paid. Because timely repair is assured, the city will be willing to pay the contractor more. Suppose the payment is raised to $55 per light. Then the contractor's profits per light will be $30 ($55 less the $25 cost of repair), so he will be better off (because his profits had been $20 per light). The city's cost per light now will be $55 (just the fee), so it will be better off too (because its cost had been $75).

The source of the mutual benefit for the parties is the threat of $200 in punitive damages, which induces the contractor to create a $50 benefit for the city at only an extra $20 cost to itself. This enables the city to make a payment sufficiently higher to make the contractor better off and still leave itself better off.

[217] We should distinguish the present discussion from that in the previous section, which concerned injured parties who were customers. There we assumed that buyers' knowledge of product risks might induce sellers to take appropriate precautions. Here we are *not* making the analogous assumption. In our present example, we did not consider the possibility that the contractor would repair street lights on a timely basis out of a concern that his business reputation might otherwise suffer. Rather, we implicitly assumed that the prospect of damages for breach of contract is needed to motivate the contractor to repair lights on a timely basis.

[218] More generally, whenever a party buys a large quantity of a product and does not inspect every unit to determine whether the product complies with the specifications in the contract, a problem of detecting a breach can arise.

tions, such damages will result in excessive and expensive performance (the analogue of overdeterrence), thereby lowering the welfare of the contracting parties.

In conclusion, courts should be cautious about awarding punitive damages for breach of contract. This point is worth noting because the law governing the imposition of punitive damages for breach of contract does not restrict their award to cases in which the likelihood of escaping liability for breach is substantial.[219]

L. *Components of Harm Not Included in Compensatory Damages*

It is often suggested that punitive damages should be awarded to compensate plaintiffs for non-economic and other losses that would not otherwise be incorporated into compensatory damages.[220] Many courts have endorsed this justification for punitive damages.[221]

Although we recognize that awarding punitive damages as a substitute for a missing component of harm has a potential rationale in terms of assuring proper deterrence, we suggest in this section that remedies for missing components of harm would be best pursued through revision of the rules used to calculate compensatory damages.

As the reader knows, our basic analysis of deterrence implies that injurers should have to pay for the entire harm they cause, in order that injurers take appropriate precautions and that prices and participation in risky activities are proper. Thus, if there is a component of

---

[219] For example, courts have awarded punitive damages in contract cases in which there exists a "special relationship between the parties." 1 SCHLUETER & REDDEN, *supra* note 74, § 7.3(A), at 388 (internal quotation marks omitted). These relationships include: "bank and depositor, employer and employee, franchiser and franchisee, lawyer and client, public utility and customer, and security broker and customer." *Id.* § 7.3(A), at 386 (footnotes omitted). The courts argue that punitive damages are appropriate because one party has greater bargaining power. *See id.* § 7.3(A), at 385. But this superior position, in and of itself, does not suggest that the party with the upper hand will escape liability for a breach of contract.

[220] *See* Chapman & Trebilcock, *supra* note 12, at 768–69 (suggesting that punitive damages serve as a means of compensating for dignitary loss); Ellis, *supra* note 12, at 3 (noting that compensating victims for otherwise uncompensable losses and paying the plaintiff's legal fees are reasons often cited by legal commentators and courts for imposing punitive damages); Dorsey D. Ellis, Jr., *Punitive Damages in Iowa Law: A Critical Assessment*, 66 IOWA L. REV. 1003, 1007, 1010 (1981) (noting the use of punitive damages as compensation for nonpecuniary harms); Galligan, *supra* note 3, at 40–83 (emphasizing that compensatory damages generally should be augmented to reflect otherwise missing elements of harm); David G. Owen, *Punitive Damages in Products Liability Litigation*, 74 MICH. L. REV. 1257, 1295–96 (1976) ("[P]unitive damages do indeed play an important — even if usually residual — compensatory role.").

[221] *See* 1 SCHLUETER & REDDEN, *supra* note 74, § 2.2, at 27. For example, in Connecticut, "exemplary damages cannot exceed plaintiff's expenses, and therefore, in fact and effect are considered compensatory." *Id.* § 2.2, at 27 n.1 (citing Doroszka v. Lavine, 150 A. 692, 692–93 (Conn. 1930), and Craney v. Donovan, 102 A. 640, 641 (Conn. 1917)). In Michigan, "exemplary damages are granted to compensate the plaintiff and not to punish the defendant." *Id.* (citing Oppenhuizen v. Wennersten, 139 N.W.2d 765, 770 (Mich. Ct. App. 1966)).

harm that otherwise would be omitted, a policy of including it in the form of punitive damages would seem to be beneficial.[222]

Notwithstanding this point, employing punitive damages as a substitute for missing components of compensatory damages is problematic. Namely, a component of harm might be excluded from compensatory damages because of the difficulties and expense that would be encountered in estimating it. Consider, for example, the pain and suffering experienced by the friends of a person who dies. If this category of harm were included in compensatory awards, the number of claimants in cases of wrongful death could become quite large, and the cost of litigation would also increase as a result of parties contesting the magnitude of their psychological losses. It may be best, then, for the law to exclude from compensatory damages many such speculative, difficult-to-determine elements of harm, even though these elements are real and their omission does undesirably dilute deterrence.[223]

If a component of loss is excluded from compensatory damages for these reasons, it arguably should be excluded from punitive damages as well. The disadvantages of attempting to ascertain the missing component of harm would not be lessened just because it is calculated under a different head of damages. It will be no easier to determine the pain and suffering due to the death of a friend just because this loss is imported into punitive damages. Indeed, the accuracy of measurement of this loss would be expected to be worse because the calculation of punitive damages is not disciplined by the procedures and evidentiary requirements common to the determination of compensatory damages.[224]

Of course, if a component of loss should have been included in compensatory damages despite the costs of doing so, the natural response is to rectify the mistake by incorporating it in compensatory damages. If the component of loss is instead included as part of punitive damages, not only will it be less accurately measured for the reason noted in the previous paragraph, but there will also be another problem: the component will be omitted in the large majority of cases, those in which only compensatory damages are awarded. Specifically,

---

[222] More precisely, the principle would be to include a multiple of the missing component, with the multiplier determined by the defendant's chance of escaping liability.

[223] The costs of estimating such elements of harm on a case-by-case basis could be largely avoided, however, if courts were to use a table listing standard values of the missing components. This method would be an inexpensive (essentially costless) way to include missing components of damages, and it would be preferable to excluding them.

[224] Juries are given broad discretion over the award of punitive damages. *See* 1 GHIARDI & KIRCHER, *supra* note 203, § 5.38, at 132 ("It is a generally accepted rule that once a court determines that the evidence merits submission of the punitive damages issue to the jury, it is entirely within the discretion of the jury to determine whether those damages should be awarded and to determine the amount which should be awarded."); 1 SCHLUETER & REDDEN, *supra* note 74, § 6.1(A), at 331 (referring to the jury as "less restricted in awarding punitive damages than in awarding compensatory damages").

the component will be omitted in the approximately ninety-four percent of cases in which punitive damages are not awarded.[225]

M. Economic Loss Versus Personal Injury

Several courts have expressed the view that the level of punitive damages should depend on whether the plaintiff's harm involved personal injury or was entirely economic.[226] For example, much was made of this distinction in *Gore*, in which the United States Supreme Court contrasted the "purely economic" harm inflicted by the defendant with instances of "reckless disregard for the health and safety of others," implying that the latter acts should be subject to higher punitive damages.[227]

Does it make sense for punitive damages to be influenced by whether the harm consists of a personal injury, as opposed to an economic loss? The answer is basically no. If the amount that courts award as compensatory damages in personal injury cases is proper,[228] the formula that we have advanced for the determination of punitive damages should apply without modification: the level of compensatory damages for the personal injury should be multiplied by the inverse of the probability of being found liable.

We recognize, however, that the level of compensatory damages awards in personal injury cases may be too low in practice to accomplish proper deterrence.[229] For example, it has been calculated that in

---

[225] *See* Eisenberg, Goerdt, Ostrom, Rottman & Wells, *supra* note 3, at 633 (finding that punitive damages are awarded in approximately 6% of the cases in which plaintiffs prevail).

[226] *See, e.g.*, Lightning v. Roadway Express, Inc., 60 F.3d 1551, 1559 (11th Cir. 1995) ("In determining the reasonableness of an award of punitive damages, courts should consider whether . . . the misconduct caused personal injury or merely damage to property . . . ."); Eisert v. Greenberg Roofing & Sheet Metal Co., 314 N.W.2d 226, 229 (Minn. 1982) (stating that the nature of the plaintiff's injury "may reasonably be taken into account in deciding where punitive damages will be allowed . . . . Where that injury is limited to property damage, the public interest in punishment and deterrence is largely satisfied by the plaintiff's recovery of compensatory damages."); 1 SCHLUETER & REDDEN, *supra* note 74, § 9.5(A), at 536 ("[C]ourts distinguish between whether property damage or personal injury was the result of the defendant's wrongdoing.").

[227] BMW of N. Am., Inc. v. Gore, 116 S. Ct. 1589, 1599 (1996).

[228] In this context, by the proper amount of compensatory damages, we mean the amount of damages that induces a potential injurer to take optimal precautions to prevent personal injury. This amount might not compensate the victim for an injury — indeed, such compensation might be impossible, as in the case of loss of life. Thus, the term "compensatory damages" may be a misnomer when applied to personal injuries, but we employ it because it is used to describe the usual level of damages.

[229] Notably, compensatory damages in wrongful death cases are generally calculated as a survivor's financial loss. *See* CHARLES T. MCCORMICK, HANDBOOK ON THE LAW OF DAMAGES §§ 93–106, at 335–74 (1935). This amount usually will not lead to proper deterrence. For example, if a child or a non-working spouse is killed, the financial loss will be low, but the event is one for which expensive preventive measures are justified to reduce risk. Such measures may not be taken if damages are based solely on the financial loss. For discussion of this and related points about the distinction between optimal compensation for non-monetary losses and optimal deterrence, see SHAVELL, *supra* note 14, at 228–35; Philip J. Cook & Daniel A. Graham, *The Demand for Insurance and Protection: The Case of Irreplaceable Commodities*, 91 Q.J. ECON. 143,

wrongful death cases, the amount that an injurer should pay is between $3 million and $6 million,[230] whereas actual awards are usually substantially lower.[231] If compensatory damages are too low in personal injury cases, they should be raised appropriately.[232] Punitive damages should not be awarded to correct for inadequate compensatory damages, for reasons analogous to those discussed in the previous section.[233]

N. Externalization of Risk Through Independent Contractors

An effect of imposing liability that we have not yet discussed is what we will call *externalization of risk*. By externalization of risk, we mean the ability of potential injurers to avoid liability by hiring independent contractors to undertake risky tasks that they would otherwise perform themselves. The motive to externalize risks results to some extent from the threat of compensatory damages alone, but it is accentuated if punitive damages are awarded. To our knowledge, courts do not consider this factor in the determination of punitive damages.[234]

In this section, we discuss two socially undesirable consequences of externalization of risk. First, the number of accidents that occur tends to be higher because the independent contractors who are engaged generally do not operate as safely as the firms hiring them. Second,

---

144–55 (1977); and A. Michael Spence, *Consumer Misperceptions, Product Failure, and Producer Liability*, 64 REV. ECON. STUD. 561, 563–71 (1977).

[230] *See* VISCUSI, *supra* note 29, at 108 (using the observed risk-dollar tradeoff of blue-collar workers to calculate that the implicit value of life is between $3 million and $6 million); Michael J. Moore & W. Kip Viscusi, *The Quality-Adjusted Value of Life*, 26 ECON. INQUIRY 369, 386 (1988) (finding an implicit value of life of $6 million).

[231] *See, e.g.*, JAMES S. KAKALIK, ELIZABETH M. KING, MICHAEL TRAYNER, PATRICIA A. EBNER & LARRY PICUS, COSTS AND COMPENSATION PAID IN AVIATION ACCIDENT LITIGATION (Institute for Civil Justice, RAND Corp., No. R-3421-ICJ, 1988). In this study of 25 major airline accidents occurring between 1970 and 1984, *see id.* at 4, the authors calculated that the average compensation for airline accident deaths was $321,300 from 1970 to 1976, and $408,500 from 1977 to 1982 (measured in constant 1986 dollars), *see id.* at 20. *See also* Randall R. Bovbjerg, Frank A. Sloan & James F. Blumstein, *Valuing Life and Limb in Tort: Scheduling "Pain and Suffering"*, 83 NW. U. L. REV. 908, 920–23 (1989) (surveying Florida and Kansas City jury verdicts and finding the median loss of life award to be $620,000, and the mean loss of life award to be $1,224,000).

[232] We here presume that problems of implementation, or considerations of cost, do not subvert this recommendation. If they do, a table of standard values for different types of personal injuries could be used instead. *See supra* note 223.

[233] Although the conclusion of this section is that, given the goal of deterrence, the award of punitive damages should not depend on whether the plaintiff's harm involved personal injury, the conclusion might be different with respect to the punishment objective. Notably, when personal injury occurs, members of society may well experience a stronger desire to see the defendant punished than when the harm caused by the defendant is purely economic.

[234] For example, the issue of externalizing risk is not mentioned in any of the recent major Supreme Court cases discussing punitive damages. *See* BMW of N. Am., Inc. v. Gore, 116 S. Ct. 1589 (1996); Honda Motor Co. v. Oberg, 512 U.S. 415 (1994); TXO Prod. Corp. v. Alliance Resources Corp., 509 U.S. 443 (1993); Pacific Mut. Life Ins. Co. v. Haslip, 499 U.S. 1 (1991); Browning-Ferris Indus., Inc. v. Kelco Disposal, Inc., 492 U.S. 257 (1989).

society sacrifices the economic benefits that would have accrued if the firms had carried out certain tasks themselves instead of having them performed by independent contractors. We conclude that when externalization of risk is a relevant factor, it argues for lower punitive damages than would otherwise be appropriate.

Let us amplify on these points. It is well recognized that firms often can avoid liability by hiring independent contractors to undertake risky tasks.[235] For example, a firm that is transporting its toxic waste in its own trucks may be able to hire another company to transport the waste and thereby avoid liability for spills.[236]

However, the incentive of a firm to transfer liability to an independent contractor is more complicated than may at first appear because, if an independent contractor assumes liability by undertaking risky tasks for a firm, the contractor will charge the firm more for performing these tasks. An independent contractor that is hired to haul a firm's toxic waste clearly will charge the firm an amount reflecting its expected damages for spillage of the waste. Thus, the firm might in the end pay for the accident risks it creates even though it hires an independent contractor. It is apparent, therefore, that the firm will want to hire an independent contractor only if the contractor would charge the firm less for assuming liability than the firm would have borne itself.

In fact, an independent contractor might be willing to charge a firm less. The reason is that an independent contractor might not have assets sufficient to cover the full liability it may incur, so that its effective expected damages would be lower than the firm's — assuming that the firm has sufficient assets to pay the full judgment it would have faced, or at least more assets than the contractor. For example, suppose that potential damages are $10 million and that the risk of an accident and liability is five percent. If a firm with assets of $10 million undertakes the risky task itself, its expected damages would be $500,000 (= 5% × $10 million). However, if the firm hires an independent contractor with assets of only $1 million, the contractor's expected damages would be $50,000 (= 5% × $1 million). Hence, the in-

---

[235] *See* RESTATEMENT (SECOND) OF TORTS § 409 (1965) ("[E]mployer of an independent contractor is not liable for physical harm caused to another by an act or omission of the contractor or his servants."); PROSSER AND KEETON ON THE LAW OF TORTS, *supra* note 30, § 71, at 509 ("For the torts of an independent contractor, . . . it has long been said to be the general rule that there is no vicarious liability upon the employer.").

[236] However, this strategy may not always work. For example, in *Kenney v. Scientific, Inc.*, 497 A.2d 1310 (N.J. Super. Ct. Law Div. 1985), the court held the defendant liable for an independent contractor's transportation of toxic waste. *See id.* at 1323–24. The court stated that "[a] company which creates the Frankenstein monster of abnormally dangerous waste should not expect to be relieved of accountability for the depredations of its creature merely because the company entrusts the monster's care to another, even an independent contractor." *Id.* at 1320–21. Notwithstanding such exceptions, we will address situations in which it is possible to shift liability by hiring an independent contractor.

dependent contractor only needs to add $50,000 to the price it charges the firm to be compensated for its expected damages. Accordingly, the firm could in effect reduce its expected damages from $500,000 to $50,000 by hiring the independent contractor.[237]

We have explained that firms might benefit by externalizing their liability risks to independent contractors with assets less than the harm resulting from accidents. It should be emphasized that because firms secure an advantage by dealing with such contractors, they will seek them out and favor them over contractors with greater assets, other things being equal.[238]

The externalization of risk to potentially judgment-proof contractors has an important implication. These contractors will tend to conduct their activities with less care than will actors with more at stake. In the example above, the independent contractor with assets of only $1 million clearly will not have as great an incentive to invest in precautions as the firm that could pay $10 million.[239] Therefore, the frequency of accidents will increase as a result of the externalization of risk.[240]

---

[237] The point of this example holds even if the firm does not have assets sufficient to pay for the full $10 million in damages; as long as its assets exceed those of the independent contractor, a potential gain to the firm still exists from externalizing the risk to the contractor. For instance, suppose that the firm has assets of only $5 million. Its expected liability would then be $250,000 (= 5% × $5 million), which still exceeds the independent contractor's expected liability of $50,000. Thus, the firm will continue to have an incentive to externalize its risk. (The general condition for when it will be advantageous to the firm to use an independent contractor to externalize its risk is twofold: the contractor's assets must be less than the firm's, and there must exist a positive probability that the judgment will exceed the contractor's assets.)

[238] Evidence from the oil industry is consistent with the view that firms have an incentive to externalize some of their liability risks to less well-capitalized independent contractors. For example, after the Exxon Valdez oil spill, Shell shifted some responsibility for the transport of oil from its own tanker fleet to vessels owned by independent contractors. *See* William J. Cook, *An Easy Way Out of This Mess*, U.S. NEWS & WORLD REP., June 25, 1990, at 15; Caleb Solomon & Joann S. Lublin, *Tanker Fire Raises Serious Questions About Liabilities in Oil Spills Off U.S.*, WALL ST. J., June 12, 1990, at A3. Such contractors, who might own just a few supertankers (or even only one), generally are vastly smaller than the major oil companies. *See* Eric Nalder, *Oil Firms Trying to Shield Assets from Liability for Costly Spills*, SEATTLE TIMES, Sept. 26, 1991, at A6 (stating that the assets of independent transporters "are about 25 times smaller than the holdings of the oil giants"). One can think of many other industries, including those involved in the transport or disposal of hazardous materials, in which risks can be externalized to independent contractors that are much smaller than the firms that hire them.

[239] For instance, consider a safety device that would reduce the magnitude of harm from an accident from $10 million to $5 million. This device would be of value to the firm if the firm is exposed to liability, because it would reduce the firm's expected damages by half; however, the device would be of no value to the independent contractor, for the contractor is only capable of paying $1 million. Similarly, consider a safety device that reduces the likelihood of a $10 million accident by 1%. This device will be worth $100,000 to the firm (= 1% × $10 million), so the firm will pay up to $100,000 for the device, but it will be worth only $10,000 to the independent contractor (= 1% × $1 million), so that the contractor might not buy the device when the firm would have.

[240] In the oil industry, for example, it is plausible that tankers owned by independent contractors are more prone to accidents than tankers owned by large oil companies. *Compare* Cook, *su-*

An increase in the number of accidents is not the only socially undesirable consequence of the externalization of risk. The economic advantages firms gain by undertaking certain tasks themselves, rather than contracting with others to perform the tasks, will be lost if firms hire independent contractors to avoid liability. In our example, the advantages that the firm would lose if it hires an independent contractor might include its ability (given its superior knowledge of its own situation) to purchase the most suitable truck for transporting its waste and the opportunity to schedule waste disposal more efficiently.[241]

The two problems caused by the externalization of risk — the increased number of accidents and the loss of economic efficiencies — are exacerbated by the imposition of punitive damages, for such damages increase the desire of firms to externalize their risks. Moreover, the judicial tendency to impose higher punitive damages on wealthier firms[242] has the perverse consequence of increasing the incentive of such firms to externalize risks despite their being more likely to take appropriate precautions (because they are less likely to be judgment-proof). Our conclusion, therefore, is that the increased externalization of risk induced by punitive damages argues for a lower level of punitive damages than would otherwise be appropriate.

O. *Encouraging Market Transactions*

In some circumstances a potential injurer can communicate with a potential victim before causing harm, for example, when a firm deliberately infringes on another's copyright, or when an individual regularly trespasses on someone's property. If prior communication is possible, a potential injurer could negotiate in advance with the potential victim to purchase the right to engage in the harm-creating conduct, rather than first causing the harm and then paying damages. The firm contemplating a copyright violation could secure a license to use the copyrighted material, or the trespasser could obtain an easement. Obviously, the greater the level of damages that would be imposed on an injurer who causes harm without having purchased the right to engage in the harm-creating conduct, the greater the incentive to purchase the right. In this sense, punitive damages can be said to encourage market

---

pra note 238, at 15 (describing independent tankers as "clunkers" operating under "lax standards" with "badly trained crews"), *with* Daniel Southerland, *Mobilizing the Fleet: Oil Giant Hopes Emphasis on Tanker Safety Also Will Produce Profits*, WASH. POST, June 23, 1996, at H1 (emphasizing the high safety standards maintained by Mobil's shipping subsidiary).

[241] For a discussion of the advantages of performing tasks within a firm, rather than delegating them to independent contractors, see, for example, R.H. Coase, *The Nature of the Firm*, 4 ECONOMICA 386, 390–92 (1937); OLIVER HART, FIRMS, CONTRACTS, AND FINANCIAL STRUCTURE 1–92 (1995); and JEAN TIROLE, THE THEORY OF INDUSTRIAL ORGANIZATION 15–60 (1988).

[242] *See supra* pp. 910–11.

transactions. To our knowledge, courts rarely mention this effect of imposing punitive damages.[243]

In this section, we explain that it may be desirable to impose punitive damages in order to encourage market transactions. The reason in essence is that inducing potential injurers to bargain may better lead them to take harm into account and may reduce parties' wasteful efforts to try to take and protect property. Additionally, market exchange may be cheaper than litigation. A qualification to this discussion, however, is that imposing punitive damages when the parties are *not* easily able to bargain may overdeter injurers. Note that the rationale for punitive damages discussed in this section does not presume that a party who causes harm is able to escape liability with positive probability. In other words, the present rationale is independent of the escaping-liability rationale for punitive damages that has been the focus of our Article.[244]

To elaborate, suppose that compensatory damages alone are employed and that they are underestimated. A potential injurer then might cause harm when doing so is socially undesirable — because the benefit to the injurer might be less than the harm done but greater than the low estimate of compensatory damages.[245] In general, as we observed above,[246] an excessive amount of harm will be caused if damages are too low.

Additional undesirable repercussions, similar to those associated with the theft of property, may arise when compensatory damages are underestimated. If injurers can take property from victims without having to pay for its full value, potential injurers will devote effort to identifying and taking such property, and potential victims will expend effort to prevent their property from being taken. Copyright violators, for example, will devote resources to copying others' protected material, and copyright owners will take steps to stop such illicit copying. Such efforts are socially wasteful.

---

[243] The only reference to this effect of which we are aware is in *Kemezy v. Peters*, 79 F.3d 33 (7th Cir. 1996), in which Chief Judge Posner noted in dictum that "[p]unitive damages are necessary in some cases to make sure that people channel transactions through the market when the costs of voluntary transactions are low." *Id.* at 34.

[244] The point that inducing market transactions may better lead potential injurers to take harm into account was made by Guido Calabresi and A. Douglas Melamed. *See* Guido Calabresi & A. Douglas Melamed, *Property Rules, Liability Rules, and Inalienability: One View of the Cathedral,* 85 HARV. L. REV. 1089, 1115–24 (1972). This point has been developed by others. *See* Biggar, *supra* note 12; Haddock, McChesney & Spiegel, *supra* note 12; Louis Kaplow & Steven Shavell, *Property Rules Versus Liability Rules: An Economic Analysis,* 109 HARV. L. REV. 713 (1996); Landes & Posner, *supra* note 12.

[245] In these circumstances, a potential victim would have an incentive to pay a potential injurer not to cause harm. Such a payment might not occur, however. For example, if there are many potential injurers, paying one not to cause harm would not forestall others from causing harm. *See* Kaplow & Shavell, *supra* note 244, at 722.

[246] *See supra* p. 879.

The foregoing problems — an excessive amount of harm and wasteful efforts to take and protect property — can be avoided if punitive damages are imposed. If punitive damages are set so that total damages substantially exceed the value of the attractive property, a person who might otherwise simply take the property will instead bargain with its owner, because it would be cheaper to pay an agreed-on price than to pay damages. Consequently, property will be exchanged only if the buyer values it more than the property owner, and the incentive to take and protect property whose value might be underestimated by compensatory damages will be eliminated.

Another possible reason to employ punitive damages in order to encourage market transactions concerns administrative costs. If compensatory damages are used alone, exchange often will be mediated through the legal system by the bringing of a lawsuit; the cost of exchange then will be the cost of litigation (though this cost is frequently reduced because of settlement). But if punitive damages are used in addition, exchange will be much more likely to occur through voluntary transactions, which may be much less costly than litigation.

The arguments that we have discussed in favor of using punitive damages to promote market exchange obviously do not apply if bargaining between parties is not possible or there are substantial impediments to bargaining. Suppose, for instance, that a hiker lost in the mountains discovers an unoccupied cabin. The benefit he would obtain from using the cabin and consuming the food in it presumably would exceed the loss borne by the cabin's owner. But because there is no opportunity for the hiker to bargain with the owner, the effect of punitive damages might be to discourage the hiker from using the cabin. Hence, when parties cannot bargain, it may be better to employ compensatory damages alone (despite the possibility of errors in estimation); punitive damages would tend to overdeter injurers' conduct. Moreover, even if bargaining is feasible, there may be other impediments to efficient exchange — such as bargaining failures due to strategic behavior — that also could justify relying solely on compensatory damages.[247]

We conclude that punitive damages may sometimes have appeal when it is possible for a potential injurer to communicate with a potential victim before causing harm, in order to encourage market transactions. As we noted above, this rationale for punitive damages, when applicable, is independent of the escaping-liability rationale.[248]

---

[247] For example, suppose a seller holds out for a high price and ultimately refuses to sell to a potential buyer who places a much greater value on the item at issue. In such circumstances, it may be better to set damages equal to harm and allow the "buyer" to take the item and pay damages than to encourage bargaining. See Calabresi & Melamed, *supra* note 244, at 1106–07.

[248] If there is a probability of escaping liability, the punitive damages amount that is appropriate for the purpose of encouraging market transactions should itself be inflated according to the multiplier formula that we developed above. See *supra* section II.B.

IV. PUNISHMENT

By the punishment objective we refer to society's goal of imposing appropriate sanctions on blameworthy parties.[249] We equate blameworthiness with the reprehensibility of a party's conduct, that is, with its maliciousness or the extent to which it reflects disregard for the well-being of others.[250] We assume that the punishment objective derives ultimately from the pleasure or satisfaction people obtain from seeing blameworthy parties punished[251] (although our essential conclusions do not depend on this assumption[252]).

When the defendant is an individual, the connection between the imposition of punitive damages and the accomplishment of the punishment objective is conceptually straightforward: if, after assessing the blameworthiness of an individual's act, appropriate punitive damages are levied, the punishment objective is achieved.[253]

However, when the defendant is a firm, the relationship between punitive damages and the punishment objective is more complex. In this regard, we will develop three points. The first is that there are different ways of viewing the objective of punishment: the goal may be to punish firms as *entities*, that is, independently of whether blameworthy individuals within the firms are penalized; or the goal may be

---

[249] *See* GEORGE P. FLETCHER, RETHINKING CRIMINAL LAW § 6.3.2, at 417 (1978) ("[T]he offender is duty-bound to suffer punishment, for his offense creates an imbalance of benefits and burdens in the society as a whole." (citing HERBERT MORRIS, ON GUILT AND INNOCENCE 34–36 (1976))); WALTER MOBERLY, THE ETHICS OF PUNISHMENT 95 (1968) (stating that, under a retributive theory, "punishment should serve both to express and to deepen the horror with which certain types of action ought to be regarded"); HERBERT L. PACKER, THE LIMITS OF THE CRIMINAL SANCTION 37 (1968) ("The retributive view [of punishment] rests on the idea that it is right for the wicked to be punished: because man is responsible for his actions, he ought to receive his just deserts."); C.L. TEN, CRIME, GUILT, AND PUNISHMENT: A PHILOSOPHICAL INTRODUCTION 2 (1987) ("Punishment involves the infliction of some unpleasantness on the offender . . . made to express disapproval or condemnation of the offender's conduct which is a breach of what is regarded as a desirable and obligatory standard of conduct.").

[250] It is not necessary for our purposes to settle on a more refined definition of blameworthiness or culpability.

[251] A formal interpretation of this assumption is that an individual's utility depends on, and increases with, the magnitude of a variable that measures the extent to which a party who committed a reprehensible act is appropriately punished. (To describe this variable — call it V — more precisely, let S denote the level of the actual sanction, let R be the reprehensibility of the act, and let $S(R)$ represent the ideal punishment given R. Then V is higher the closer S is to $S(R)$.) Because social welfare depends on individual welfare, social welfare is advanced by punishing reprehensible parties appropriately.

The relationship between the punishment objective and the deterrence objective is discussed below. *See infra* notes 272–273 and accompanying text.

[252] It will be evident that, for the most part, our arguments will also hold if the punishment objective derives its force not from individual pleasure and satisfaction at seeing blameworthy parties punished, but from an abstract philosophical principle calling for retribution.

[253] A qualification to this statement concerns liability insurance. If the punished party is insured, the degree to which he is punished depends on the extent to which his coverage is incomplete (because of, for example, deductibles or coinsurance) and the possibility that his premiums will rise in the future.

to punish firms only as a means of punishing culpable *individuals* in the firms. Our second point is that the imposition of punitive damages on firms may not lead to the punishment of blameworthy individuals within them; thus, the goal of punishing blameworthy employees may not be well promoted by imposing punitive damages on firms. The final point is that the imposition of punitive damages on firms often penalizes individuals who are unlikely to be considered culpable, namely, shareholders and customers. We conclude that, to the extent that the goal is to punish culpable individuals within firms, and not firms as entities, the utility of punitive damages in achieving the punishment objective is significantly attenuated.

Consider the possibility that the punishment objective might be furthered because people obtain satisfaction directly from the punishment of a blameworthy firm as an organization, without regard to whether anyone within the firm behaved inappropriately or is punished.[254] We find this conception of the punishment goal unappealing both because it requires a definition of blameworthiness of a firm that is divorced from the behavior of any individuals who are affiliated with it, and because it necessitates believing that people would, after reflecting on the matter, want to impose a penalty on what ultimately is an artificial legal construct. The notion that individuals would want to punish firms per se strikes us as not entirely different from the idea that individuals would want to punish inanimate objects for causing harm (such as trees that fall on people).[255]

Notwithstanding these reservations, it is possible that individuals do want to personify firms and punish them as entities, and the reader can make up his or her mind about the importance of this way of defining the punishment objective. To the extent that it is important, the

---

[254] A number of authors have discussed the punishment rationale in relation to corporations as entities. *See, e.g.,* Albert W. Alschuler, *Ancient Law and the Punishment of Corporations: Of Frankpledge and Deodand,* 71 B.U. L. REV. 307, 312 (1991) (arguing that corporate criminal responsibility is the unwise result of a "superstitious" hatred of the inanimate corporation); V.S. Khanna, *Corporate Criminal Liability: What Purpose Does It Serve?,* 109 HARV. L. REV. 1477, 1494 n.91 (1996) (describing "[t]he notion that society has a retributive need so great that it must punish nonhuman entities and label them criminal" as "implausible"); *Developments in the Law — Corporate Crime: Regulating Corporate Behavior Through Criminal Sanctions,* 92 HARV. L. REV. 1227, 1237 (1979) ("Even though deterrence clearly plays a critical role in the justification of corporate criminal sanctions, the argument that retribution cannot be involved is unconvincing."). As Christopher Stone notes:

> Corporate penalties often impose losses in circumstances when no one appears blameworthy . . . . True, we allow some of these same innocents to suffer . . . when corporate agents wrongfully break a contract or commit a tort . . . . But it seems one thing to make a blameless investor help absorb ordinary damages . . . and quite another thing to reduce his investment further by imposing a penalty.

Christopher D. Stone, *The Place of Enterprise Liability in the Control of Corporate Conduct,* 90 YALE L.J. 1, 27 (1980).

[255] For a similar reaction to the idea of corporate punishment, see Alschuler, cited above in note 254, at 312–13.

imposition of punitive damages on a blameworthy firm directly promotes the punishment objective, much as it does when the defendant
is a culpable individual.[256]

Now consider the alternative reason for punishing firms — to punish blameworthy individuals within them. Supposing that this is the
purpose of punishment, we turn to our second point, about the extent
to which the imposition of punitive damages on firms will actually result in the punishment of blameworthy employees. Because firms
clearly have an interest in discouraging culpable conduct by their employees that could give rise to punitive damages, they can be expected
to seek to control such conduct through the use of internal sanctions,
such as demotion or dismissal. However, two considerations suggest
that the imposition of punitive damages on firms will lead to less punishment of blameworthy employees than might at first be supposed.

First, culpable employees may not be punished by firms because
the firms may have difficulty identifying them. Such individuals may
be able to obfuscate their role in decisionmaking or conceal their behavior in a variety of ways. For example, an employee responsible for
checking a safety valve on a tank storing dangerous chemicals that
subsequently explodes because of a defective valve may claim that he
performed the inspection even if he did not, and may place a false entry in his record book attesting to the inspection. A manager whose
judgment is impaired by alcohol and who gives oral instructions to a
subordinate that lead to an accident may deny ever having told the
subordinate to do what the subordinate did.[257]

Second, even if culpable individuals within a firm can be identified
and punished by the firm, imposing punitive damages on firms often
will have little or no *marginal effect* on their punishment. That is, the
internal sanction imposed on such employees may not be much (if at
all) greater as a result of the firm's bearing both punitive and compensatory damages than if the firm had borne compensatory damages
alone. When a firm incurs high compensatory damages because of the
blameworthy conduct of an identifiable employee, it may want to levy
whatever sanctions on him that it can; imposing punitive damages on

---

[256] Because the punishment objective is, according to our approach, derived from the desire of
individuals to punish culpable parties, the importance of the view that corporations per se should
be punished is an empirical matter, dependent on how many individuals hold this position and
how strongly. We would not be surprised to find that many individuals firmly believe that it is
proper to punish corporations as entities, but we also suspect that, were these individuals to consider seriously the distinction between that goal and the goal of punishing only culpable employees, they would soften, if not reverse, their position.

[257] Although firms may have difficulty identifying culpable employees for the reasons discussed
in this paragraph, imposition of punitive damages might induce firms to take additional steps to
discover such individuals. If punitive damages have this effect, their imposition could help to
satisfy the punishment objective.

the firm then would not result in additional punishment of the employee.[258]

The preceding discussion presupposed that there exist culpable employees in the firm. But in some situations there may not be any. If a significant delay occurs between misconduct and the manifestation of harm and litigation (as was the case, for instance, in connection with the use of asbestos in products), blameworthy individuals may have changed jobs, retired, or died.[259] Also, because decisions in firms often are made by many individuals, it may be that no one individual has the requisite knowledge of risk and of the consequences of his behavior to be considered culpable. One person may decide to put a toxic liquid in a storage tank, believing that the tank can never leak, and another person may leave the tank in a state in which a leak can occur, thinking that the liquid in the tank is not toxic, so that a leak would not cause harm. Here, each decision considered by itself may not be blameworthy because each person believes that what he is doing does not create a risk of a harmful accident.[260]

Let us now consider the third point, concerning how imposing punitive damages on firms often penalizes the firms' shareholders and customers. Shareholders, as residual claimants of a firm's profits, obviously will be made worse off when punitive damages are levied on a firm.[261] Indeed, they usually can be expected to bear a major fraction of the burden of punitive damages.[262] Given that shareholders are punished by punitive damages, the question whether they are blameworthy must be considered. If a shareholder owns a significant fraction of a firm's stock, participated actively in the firm's decisions and acted egregiously, his position would be much like that of a blamewor-

---

[258] It may be worth elaborating on this point. If employees are risk neutral (which we assume here for simplicity), a firm would seek to make an employee pay for any damages he caused the firm to bear; such a practice would make the employee's incentives to prevent harm correct from the firm's perspective. Thus, if damages are $1000, the employee would pay this amount to the firm. But because an employee's assets are limited, the firm's ability to punish an employee will be exhausted as soon as the judgment against the firm exceeds the employee's assets. Thus, if the employee's assets are $10,000, no marginal effect of higher damages will occur once the total damages exceed $10,000. (The situation just described ignores other possible responses of the firm to higher damages. For example, firms might increase their efforts to detect employee misconduct and thereby increase the expected punishment of employees. But our basic point would still apply.)

[259] However, individuals who have changed jobs or retired might be subject to punishment by their former employer because the employer might be able to sue them for acts done when employed.

[260] Of course, some other person within the firm may have been responsible for directing the flow of information, but that person also may not have acted culpably.

[261] Other stakeholders of the firm also will suffer, such as unsecured creditors who are less likely to be repaid if the firm's assets are diminished because of the payment of punitive damages.

[262] Because blameworthy employees generally will bear only a small part of a punitive damages judgment (on account of their limited assets), shareholders and customers will suffer the major part. Under certain circumstances, moreover, customers will not bear much of the burden of punitive damages. *See infra* note 264.

thy employee with decisionmaking power; each would be culpable. But if a shareholder owns a minuscule fraction of the stock of the firm and was a passive investor with no direct involvement in the firm's decisionmaking processes, his degree of blameworthiness would be small, if not nonexistent.[263]

A firm's customers also will be made worse off as a result of the imposition of punitive damages on the firm if such damages cause the prices of the firm's products or services to rise. Firms may regard punitive damages as an additional cost of doing business — a cost that, with a positive probability, will be borne by them in addition to their ordinary costs. To cover the added cost of punitive damages, firms will tend to raise their prices, which will cause the welfare of their customers to decline.[264] Customers, however, would not ordinarily be considered blameworthy, because they do not exert direct control over the actions of firms that pose risks to other persons.[265] Consequently, to the extent that customers pay higher prices as a result of the imposition of punitive damages on firms, innocent parties are penalized.[266]

We can summarize our discussion of the punishment of firms as follows. The view that a firm should be punished per se — without reference to the punishment of individuals within it — is a possible view, but one that we find problematic. Another view is that the punishment goal is promoted *only* by punishing blameworthy individuals within firms. We have explained, however, that imposing punitive damages on firms often will not result in the punishment (or at least any additional punishment) of blameworthy employees, so the use of such damages might not advance the punishment goal very much. Moreover, imposing punitive damages frequently will penalize shareholders and customers, parties who are not likely to be considered blameworthy. This adverse consequence of punitive damages must be weighed against the beneficial effects of such damages in furthering the punishment goal.

Having addressed punitive damages and punishment in general terms, we now briefly consider how the reprehensibility of the defen-

---

[263] If one does believe that each shareholder is slightly blameworthy, the fact that each bears a small portion of punitive damages might be thought to be desirable.

[264] If, however, a particular firm bears punitive damages for a reason not generally applicable to other firms in its industry, these other firms would not have a reason to raise their prices. Consequently, the firm paying the punitive damages would not be able to raise the price of its products (because consumers would purchase from the other firms).

[265] However, it might be thought that customers are partially blameworthy for harms caused by firms because, in the absence of customer interest in firms' products, production and harms would not occur.

[266] For a complementary discussion of the effects of corporate sanctions on a firm's shareholders, bondholders, employees, and customers, see John C. Coffee, Jr., *"No Soul to Damn: No Body to Kick": An Unscandalized Inquiry into the Problem of Corporate Punishment*, 79 MICH. L. REV. 386, 401–02 (1981). Coffee observes that "the costs of [corporate] deterrence tend to spill over onto parties who cannot be characterized as culpable." *Id.*

dant's conduct and the wealth of the defendant should influence punitive damages with respect to the punishment objective.[267] Regarding reprehensibility, we merely observe that the punishment objective will, by definition, be met if sanctions are imposed on those who have acted reprehensibly. Hence, determining the reprehensibility of the defendant's conduct is intrinsic to satisfaction of the punishment objective, and the law's focus on reprehensibility obviously makes sense given this objective. In the case of firms, however, the connection between reprehensibility and punishment may be attenuated for reasons discussed above — the imposition of punitive damages on a firm may not result in the punishment of individuals within the firm who acted reprehensibly.

Concerning defendants' wealth and the appropriate level of damages from the perspective of punishment, consider first the situation when defendants are individuals. In this case, the common belief that punitive damages should be higher for wealthier defendants can be justified. The punishment goal is furthered if a proper punishment is imposed on a culpable individual, which we interpret to mean reducing the individual's utility by a particular amount. To accomplish this, it is generally necessary to assess a higher penalty if the individual is wealthy than if he is poor, because money is worth less to him if he is wealthy.[268]

When the defendant is a firm, the relevance of the defendant's wealth depends on whether the punishment goal is viewed in terms of punishing the firm as an entity or punishing culpable individuals within the firm. Under the first view, the firm's wealth might be thought to be relevant to the proper level of damages for punishment purposes.[269] Under the second view, however, the firm's wealth generally would not be relevant: the level of damages needed to induce a firm to punish its culpable employees ordinarily would not depend on its wealth. A $100 million firm and a $10 million firm would both be expected to impose the same sanction on an employee for misconduct that resulted in a punitive damages award of a given amount. The reason is that, as we have said, rational firms will develop a policy of

---

[267] We will not, however, re-examine the other topics in Part III in relation to punishment. For the most part, what can be said about these topics is clear. Consider, for example, the issue of the tax deductibility of punitive damages. Allowing punitive damages to be deductible would reduce their sting, and so might be undesirable in terms of accomplishing the punishment objective. Likewise, allowing liability insurance coverage against punitive damages also might be undesirable from the perspective of punishment.

[268] We mentioned this point above. *See supra* note 138 and accompanying text. How much the penalty must rise will be determined by the rate at which the marginal utility of money declines with wealth for the individual. In particular, there is no reason to believe that the proper penalty for purposes of punishment would be proportional to wealth.

[269] We say "might" because the first view is not well articulated, and therefore it is unclear what this view would imply about the proper relationship between the level of punitive damages and a corporation's wealth.

punishing employee misbehavior to lower their liability expenses. This policy should depend on variables other than the firm's wealth — notably, the damages that the firm will bear as a result of employee misbehavior.[270] To the extent that the internal sanctions that firms impose on culpable employees do not depend on the firm's wealth, the punishment objective will not be advanced by making punitive damages depend on its wealth.[271]

V. CONCLUSION

In this Article, we have discussed the two fundamental purposes of punitive damages — deterrence and punishment — and have come to conclusions regarding each objective that we now briefly review.

Our central conclusion about punitive damages and deterrence is conceptually simple. Punitive damages should be imposed when deterrence otherwise would be inadequate because of the possibility that injurers would escape liability. In particular, punitive damages should be set at a level such that the expected damages of defendants equal the harm they have caused, for then their damage payments will, in an average sense, equal the harm. This implies a simple formula for calculating punitive damages, according to which harm is multiplied by a factor reflecting the likelihood of escaping liability. If punitive damages are calculated according to this multiplier formula, precautions will tend to be optimal — neither inadequate nor excessive — as will product prices and the incentive to participate in risky activities. These conclusions about punitive damages, and the importance of the role of the defendant's chance of escaping liability, flow from the standard and well-accepted theory of deterrence. We also discussed a deterrence rationale for punitive damages that is not based on the possibility of escaping liability: that punitive damages may be needed to offset the socially illicit utility that individuals obtain from committing malicious acts. This rationale, as we noted, does not apply to firms.

The theory of deterrence not only yields a multiplier formula for computing punitive damages, but also provides guidance regarding a range of important doctrinal and policy issues concerning punitive damages. Notably, we discussed the point that the reprehensibility of a party's conduct generally should not be a factor in the assessment of punitive damages (except in the case of an individual's malicious act),

---

[270] The reasoning behind this statement is essentially that used above when we explained that a firm's wealth will not affect its incentive to invest in safety precautions. *See supra* section III.B.

[271] We have not addressed in this Part the institutional question of who should determine the proper level of damages for purposes of promoting the punishment goal of punitive damages. For an interesting empirical examination and discussion of this question, see Cass R. Sunstein, Daniel Kahneman & David Schkade, *Assessing Punitive Damages (With Notes on Cognition and Valuation in Law)*, 107 YALE L.J. (forthcoming May 1998).

as well as the point that the wealth of a defendant usually should not influence punitive damages (subject to the same exception).

A corollary of our analysis is that the imposition of punitive damages when they are not justified on deterrence grounds generally has socially detrimental consequences. These consequences can take the form of excessive precautionary measures and inappropriate discouragement of participation in socially beneficial activities. In the case of firms, the latter effect may manifest itself in the form of undesirably high prices and the withdrawal of products from markets.

With respect to the punishment objective, we observed that the connection between punitive damages and punishment is relatively straightforward if the defendant is an individual, or if the defendant is a firm and the goal is to punish firms as entities (although we found this latter goal problematic). We came to a different conclusion, however, when the defendant is a firm and the objective is to punish culpable employees. Because the imposition of punitive damages on firms may not result in the punishment of blameworthy employees, but often will penalize shareholders and customers — parties who are not likely to be blameworthy — the ability of punitive damages to advance the punishment goal in the case of firms is limited.

We have not yet commented on how the level of punitive damages should be determined when the objectives of deterrence and punishment have different implications for the proper measure of punitive damages. It is evident that the best level of punitive damages should be a compromise between the levels that are optimal when each objective is considered independently.[272] (The quantities of punitive damages that are separately optimal with respect to the two objectives should not be added to each other.[273]) The weights to be used in the

---

[272] For example, suppose that the level of damages that is best with respect to deterrence is $1 million and that the amount that is best with respect to punishment is $2 million. The optimal amount, taking account of both objectives, must be between $1 and $2 million. As damages are increased from $1 million to $2 million, overdeterrence occurs, but punishment is better promoted. It is optimal to stop raising damages when the marginal social loss from overdeterrence begins to outweigh the marginal social gain from better punishment. (To complete the explanation, observe that optimal damages cannot be less than $1 million or more than $2 million: were damages less than $1 million, the outcome would be worse with respect to both the deterrence and the punishment goals than if damages were $1 million; and were damages in excess of $2 million, the outcome would be worse with respect to both goals than if damages were $2 million.) For further discussion regarding the choice of the level of punitive damages that best balances the deterrence and punishment goals, see Diamond, Punishment and Efficiency, *supra* note 12, at 11–14.

[273] In essence, the amounts should not be added because the punitive damages amount that is proper for the purpose of deterrence also punishes, and the punitive damages amount that is proper for the purpose of punishment also deters.

It is easy to see in the example in the preceding note that it would not be correct to add the $1 million amount that is best for deterrence to the $2 million amount that is best for punishment and impose damages of $3 million. To amplify on what we stated parenthetically in that note, if damages of $2 million are best with respect to punishment, then damages of $3 million would

determination of the compromise will reflect the relative importance accorded to the goals of deterrence and punishment.

Whatever are the weights that policymakers, judges, or juries place on these two goals, we hope that the conceptual framework developed in this Article will aid them in determining the appropriate amount of punitive damages.

---

punish excessively and thus would be worse than damages of $2 million; that is, damages of $2 million are superior to $3 million in terms of punishment. Also, damages of $2 million are superior to damages of $3 million in terms of deterrence, for $3 million overdeters more than $2 million overdeters. Hence, damages of $3 million cannot be optimal: damages of $2 million are superior from the perspectives of both punishment and deterrence (and, as we argued in the preceding note, the *optimal* level of damages must be between $1 million and $2 million).

APPENDIX: MODEL JURY INSTRUCTIONS

The following model jury instructions encapsulate many of the conclusions of our Article. Three sets of instructions are presented: for individuals who have not committed malicious acts; for individuals who have committed malicious acts; and for firms. With regard to the instructions for firms, we have assumed that the goal of punishment is to penalize blameworthy employees, not to punish firms as entities. (The instructions can be modified to reflect a different assumption.)

* * *

FOR INDIVIDUALS WHO HAVE NOT COMMITTED MALICIOUS ACTS

These instructions apply to defendants who have not committed malicious acts. An act is malicious only if it was done for the *purpose* of causing harm.

In considering the imposition of punitive damages on the defendant, you should determine three dollar amounts: (A) an amount to accomplish deterrence; (B) an amount to accomplish punishment; (C) a final amount — your punitive damages award — between the first two amounts.

A. *Deterrence*

1. Punitive damages fulfill the deterrence objective to the extent that they serve as a message and warning to the defendant and to other similarly situated individuals to take appropriate steps in order to prevent harm in the future. But punitive damages will not fulfill the deterrence objective if they cause individuals to take wasteful steps to prevent harm or if they cause individuals to refrain from engaging in socially desirable activities.

2. Your principal task is to estimate the likelihood that the defendant might have escaped having to pay for the harm for which he or she should be responsible. Thus, for example, if the harm was noticeable and likely to lead to a lawsuit, your estimate of the likelihood of escaping liability would be relatively low. But if the harm might not have been attributed to the defendant, or if the defendant tried to conceal his or her harmful conduct, your estimate of the likelihood of escaping liability would be relatively high.

3. You should use the Table below to determine the punitive damages multiplier that corresponds to your estimated probability of escaping liability. Then multiply the compensatory damages amount by your punitive damages multiplier. The resulting number is the *base punitive damages amount.*

4. The base punitive damages amount *should be lowered* if the defendant has paid other private judgments or settlements, or public penalties, for the harm at issue in the present case. If the defendant

has made such payments, the base punitive damages amount should be lowered by the amount of these payments.

5.   The base punitive damages amount *should not be adjusted* because of any of the following considerations:

(a) reprehensibility of the defendant's conduct;

(b) net worth or income of the defendant;

(c) potential harm, that is, the harm that might have been caused by the defendant's conduct;

(d) gain or profit that the defendant might have obtained from his or her harmful conduct;

(e) litigation costs borne by the plaintiff;

(f) components of harm that you did not include in compensatory damages;

(g) whether the harm included personal injury.

B. Punishment

1.   Punitive damages fulfill the punishment objective to the extent that they penalize blameworthy defendants for reprehensible behavior. You should determine the amount of punitive damages that you believe will accomplish proper punishment.

2.   In considering punishment, keep in mind that the defendant's payment of compensatory damages already punishes the defendant to some extent. The amount of punitive damages that you believe will accomplish proper punishment should be what you think must be added to compensatory damages to accomplish the punishment objective, if any additional damages are necessary.

C. Determination of Punitive Damages

Punitive damages should be an amount *between* the amount that you found appropriate for the purpose of deterrence and the amount that you found appropriate for the purpose of punishment. If you attach greater importance to the deterrence objective, punitive damages should be closer to the amount that you found best to promote deterrence. If you attach greater importance to the punishment objective, punitive damages should be closer to the amount that you found best to promote punishment.

* * *

FOR INDIVIDUALS WHO HAVE COMMITTED MALICIOUS ACTS

These instructions apply to defendants who have committed malicious acts. An act is malicious if it was done for the *purpose* of causing harm.

In considering the imposition of punitive damages on the defendant, you should determine three dollar amounts: (A) an amount to accomplish deterrence; (B) an amount to accomplish punishment; (C) a final amount — your punitive damages award — between the first two amounts.

A. Deterrence

1. Punitive damages fulfill the deterrence objective to the extent that they serve as a message and warning to the defendant and to other similarly situated individuals not to commit malicious acts in the future. But punitive damages will not fulfill the deterrence objective if they cause individuals to take wasteful steps to avoid possible liability or if they cause individuals to refrain from engaging in socially desirable activities.

2. Your principal task is to estimate the likelihood that the defendant might have escaped having to pay for the harm for which he or she should be responsible. Thus, for example, if the harm was noticeable and likely to lead to a lawsuit, your estimate of the likelihood of escaping liability would be relatively low. But if the harm might not have been attributed to the defendant, or if the defendant tried to conceal his or her harmful conduct, your estimate of the likelihood of escaping liability would be relatively high.

3. You should use the Table below to determine the punitive damages multiplier that corresponds to your estimated probability of escaping liability.   Then determine the amount that you believe is equivalent to the gain that the defendant obtained from his or her conduct. Multiply this amount by your punitive damages multiplier. The resulting number is the *base punitive damages amount*.

4. The base punitive damages amount *should be lowered* if the defendant has paid other private judgments or settlements, or public penalties, for the harm at issue in the present case. If the defendant has made such payments, the base punitive damages amount should be lowered by the amount of these payments.

5. The base punitive damages amount *should not be adjusted* because of any of the following considerations:

(a) potential harm, that is, the harm that might have been caused by the defendant's conduct;

(b) litigation costs borne by the plaintiff;

(c) components of harm that you did not include in compensatory damages.

B. Punishment

1. Punitive damages fulfill the punishment objective to the extent that they penalize blameworthy defendants for reprehensible behavior. You should determine the amount of punitive damages that you believe will accomplish proper punishment.

2. In considering punishment, keep in mind that the defendant's payment of compensatory damages already punishes the defendant to some extent. The amount of punitive damages that you believe will accomplish proper punishment should be what you think must be added to compensatory damages to accomplish the punishment objective, if any additional damages are necessary.

C. Determination of Punitive Damages

Punitive damages should be an amount *between* the amount that you found appropriate for the purpose of deterrence and the amount that you found appropriate for the purpose of punishment. If you attach greater importance to the deterrence objective, punitive damages should be closer to the amount that you found best to promote deterrence. If you attach greater importance to the punishment objective, punitive damages should be closer to the amount that you found best to promote punishment.

* * *

FOR FIRMS

In considering the imposition of punitive damages on the defendant, you should determine three dollar amounts: (A) an amount to accomplish deterrence; (B) an amount to accomplish punishment; (C) a final amount — your punitive damages award — between the first two amounts.

A. Deterrence

1. Punitive damages fulfill the deterrence objective to the extent that they serve as a message and warning to the defendant and to other similarly situated firms to take appropriate steps to prevent harm in the future. But punitive damages will not fulfill the deterrence objective if they cause firms to take wasteful steps to prevent harm, if they cause the prices of products and services to rise excessively, or if they cause firms to withdraw socially valuable products or services from the market.

2. To achieve the deterrence objective, your principal task is to estimate the likelihood that the defendant might have escaped having to pay for the harm for which it should be responsible. Thus, for example, if the harm was noticeable and likely to lead to a lawsuit, your estimate of the likelihood of escaping liability would be relatively low. But if the harm might not have been attributed to the defendant, or if the defendant tried to conceal its harmful conduct, your estimate of the likelihood of escaping liability would be relatively high.

3. You should use the Table below to determine the punitive damages multiplier that corresponds to your estimated probability of

escaping liability. Then multiply the compensatory damages amount by your punitive damages multiplier. The resulting number is the *base punitive damages amount.*

4. The base punitive damages amount *should be lowered* if the defendant has paid other private judgments or settlements, or public penalties, for the harm at issue in the present case. If the defendant has made such payments, the base punitive damages amount should be lowered by the amount of these payments.

5. The base punitive damages amount also *may be lowered* if the plaintiff was a customer of the defendant. If the plaintiff was a customer and you believe that customers are, or will become, aware of accidents of the type at issue in this case, the base punitive damages amount should be lowered. The more knowledgeable customers are, the more the base punitive damages amount should be lowered.

6. The base punitive damages amount *should not be adjusted* because of any of the following considerations:

(a) reprehensibility of the defendant's conduct;

(b) net worth, revenues, or profits of the defendant;

(c) potential harm, that is, the harm that might have been caused by the defendant's conduct;

(d) gain or profit that the defendant might have obtained from its harmful conduct;

(e) litigation costs borne by the plaintiff;

(f) components of harm that you did not include in compensatory damages;

(g) whether the harm included personal injury.

B. Punishment

1. Punitive damages fulfill the punishment objective to the extent that they cause defendants to penalize their *blameworthy employees* for reprehensible behavior.

2. In considering punishment, you should keep in mind that the defendant's payment of compensatory damages already may lead to the punishment of blameworthy employees to some extent.

3. In considering how well the imposition of punitive damages will fulfill the punishment objective, you should also bear the following in mind:

(a) the extent to which you believe blameworthy employees can be identified and penalized by the defendant. The easier this identification is, the higher should be the level of punitive damages.

(b) the extent to which you believe that innocent parties will suffer as a result of the imposition of punitive damages on the defendant; such parties might include shareholders as well as customers, who may have to pay higher prices for the defendant's products or services. The more likely it is that innocent parties will be punished, the lower should be the level of punitive damages.

4.   In the light of these considerations, you should determine the amount of punitive damages that you believe will accomplish proper punishment.

C.   Determination of Punitive Damages

Punitive damages should be an amount *between* the amount that you found appropriate for the purpose of deterrence and the amount that you found appropriate for the purpose of punishment. If you attach greater importance to the deterrence objective, punitive damages should be closer to the amount that you found best to promote deterrence. If you attach greater importance to the punishment objective, punitive damages should be closer to the amount that you found best to promote punishment.

* * *

TABLE[274]

Probability of Escaping Liability	Punitive Damages Multiplier
0%	0
10%	.11
20%	.25
30%	.43
40%	.67
50%	1.00
60%	1.50
70%	2.33
80%	4.00
90%	9.00

[274] The multipliers in the Table are derived as follows. Let P be the probability of being found liable; thus, the probability of escaping liability is $1 - P$. The multiplier then equals $(1 - P)/P$.

[3]

DETERRENCE AND DAMAGES: THE MULTIPLIER PRINCIPLE AND ITS ALTERNATIVES

*Richard Craswell**

TABLE OF CONTENTS

* Professor of Law, Stanford University. B.A. 1974, Michigan State; J.D. 1977, University of Chicago. —Ed. I am grateful for comments from Howard F. Chang, Marc A. Franklin, Keith N. Hylton, Louis Kaplow, Daniel Klerman, Tracey L. Meares, A. Mitchell Polinsky, Richard A. Posner, James F. Strnad, Steven Shavell, Alan O. Sykes, and participants in workshops at the Harvard, Stanford, and University of Chicago law schools.

V. CONCLUSIONS 2237

One purpose of fines and damage awards is to deter harmful behavior. When enforcement is imperfect, however, so the probability that any given violation will be punished is less than 100%, the law's deterrent effect is usually thought to be reduced. Thus, it is often said that the ideal penalty (insofar as deterrence is concerned) equals the harm caused by the violation multiplied by one over the probability of punishment. For example, if a violation faces only a 25% (or one-in-four) chance of being punished, on this view the optimal penalty would be four times the harm caused by the violation.

This prescription, which I will call the "multiplier principle," has a long pedigree.[1] It figures prominently in texts on law and economics,[2] and has been discussed in many scholarly works.[3] Indeed, in the law review literature the multiplier principle is now routinely cited as part of standard deterrence theory.[4] The

---

1. In modern economics, the multiplier principle owes much of its prominence to Gary S. Becker, *Crime and Punishment: An Economic Approach*, 76 J. POL. ECON. 169 (1968). An early version of the multiplier principle can be found in CESARE BECCARIA, ON CRIMES AND PUNISHMENTS 46 (David Young ed., 1986) (1766), and more explicitly in JEREMY BENTHAM, A THEORY OF LEGISLATION 325-26 (R. Hildreth trans., London, Trübner & Co. 1864) (1802). For a further discussion of these historical roots, see Keith N. Hylton, *Punitive Damages and the Economic Theory of Penalties*, 87 GEO. L.J. 421, 425-27 (1998).

2. *See, e.g.,* ROBERT COOTER & THOMAS ULEN, LAW AND ECONOMICS 390-95 (1988); A. MITCHELL POLINSKY, AN INTRODUCTION TO LAW AND ECONOMICS 77-78 (2d ed. 1989); RICHARD A. POSNER, ECONOMIC ANALYSIS OF LAW § 7.1, at 241 (5th ed. 1998).

3. The most recent and most comprehensive of these is A. Mitchell Polinsky & Steven Shavell, *Punitive Damages: An Economic Analysis*, 111 HARV. L. REV. 869 (1998). Earlier analyses, in addition to the textbooks cited *supra* note 2, include WILLIAM M. LANDES & RICHARD A. POSNER, THE ECONOMIC STRUCTURE OF TORT LAW 160 (1987); Bruce Chapman & Michael Trebilcock, *Punitive Damages: Divergence in Search of a Rationale*, 40 ALA. L. REV. 741, 808-19 (1989); Robert D. Cooter, *Punitive Damages for Deterrence: When and How Much?*, 40 ALA. L. REV. 1143, 1149-61 (1989); and Dorsey D. Ellis, Jr., *Fairness and Efficiency in the Law of Punitive Damages*, 56 S. CAL. L. REV. 1, 25-26 (1982).

4. Examples published in just the last two years include Tom Baker, *Reconsidering Insurance for Punitive Damages*, 1998 WIS. L. REV. 101, 106-07; Roger D. Blair & Thomas F. Cotter, *An Economic Analysis of Damage Rules in Intellectual Property Law*, 39 WM. & MARY L. REV. 1585, 1619-20 (1998); David Crump, *Evidence, Economics, and Ethics: What Information Should Jurors Be Given to Determine the Amount of a Punitive-Damage Award?*, 57 MD. L. REV. 174, 187 nn.82-83 (1998); Antony W. Dnes & Jonathan S. Seaton, *An Exploration of the Tort-Criminal Boundary Using Manslaughter and Negligence Cases*, 17 INTL. REV. L. & ECON. 537, 539 (1997); C. Douglas Floyd, *Antitrust Victims Without Antitrust Remedies: The Narrowing of Standing in Private Antitrust Actions*, 82 MINN. L. REV. 1, 5 (1997); Thomas Koenig & Michael Rustad, *"Crimtorts" as Corporate Just Deserts*, 31 U. MICH. J.L. REFORM 289, 315 & nn.115-16 (1998); Dale A. Nance, *Guidance Rules and Enforcement Rules: A Better View of the Cathedral*, 83 VA. L. REV. 837 app. at 934 (1997); Paul H. Rubin et al., *BMW v. Gore: Mitigating the Punitive Economics of Punitive Damages*, 5 SUP. CT. ECON. REV. 179, 186 (1997); John K. Setear, *Responses to Breach of a Treaty and Rationalist International Relations Theory: The Rules of Release and Remediation in the Law of Treaties and the Law of State Responsibility*, 83 VA. L. REV. 1, 81-86 (1997); Cass R. Sunstein et al., *Assessing Punitive Damages (with Notes on Cognition and Valuation in Law)*,

multiplier principle has also begun to be recognized by courts — especially by economically sophisticated judges — as a possible rationale for punitive damages.[5]

What is less widely appreciated, however, is that the multiplier principle is almost never *necessary* to achieving optimal deterrence. Even when the probability of punishment is less than 100%, more recent work in law and economics has identified several other remedies that could also achieve optimal deterrence.[6] These alternative remedies are often significantly less than those called for by the multiplier principle. In some cases, the alternative remedies could even be less than the harm caused by the violation, implying that optimal deterrence could be achieved if damages were reduced.

My principal aims in this article are to explain why the multiplier principle is not necessary for optimal deterrence and to begin a discussion of the alternatives. While the mathematical analysis behind the recent work is often quite technical, the basic principles are not hard to grasp, and they can be illustrated with simple numerical examples. Thus, a secondary aim is to familiarize a larger audience with the conclusions of this technical body of work. Since this work identifies alternatives to the multiplier principle, its significance is potentially as broad as that of the multiplier principle itself.

Part I begins by reviewing how optimal deterrence is achieved by what I will call the "traditional multiplier principle," in which the harm caused by a defendant's offense is multiplied by one over the probability of punishment. When the probability of punishment is the same no matter how badly a defendant has behaved, such a multiplier is relatively easy to administer. In most contexts in which enforcement is imperfect, however, the probability of punishment any particular defendant faces depends in part on the nature of his or her violation. That is, in most legal regimes, defendants who commit only marginal offenses are less likely to be punished than those who commit more serious or egregious ones. Whenever this is the case, Part I shows that the traditional multiplier principle can

---

107 YALE L.J. 2071, 2082-84 (1998); and W. Kip Viscusi, *The Social Costs of Punitive Damages Against Corporations in Environmental and Safety Torts*, 87 GEO. L.J. 285, 312-13 (1998).

5. *See, e.g.,* BMW of N. Am., Inc. v. Gore, 517 U.S. 559, 592-94 (1996) (Breyer, J., concurring); Kemezy v. Peters, 79 F.3d 33, 35 (7th Cir. 1996) (Posner, C.J.); Zazú Designs v. L'Oréal, S.A., 979 F.2d 499, 508 (7th Cir. 1992) (Easterbrook, J.); FDIC v. W.R. Grace & Co., 877 F.2d 614, 623 (7th Cir. 1989) (Posner, J.).

6. I discuss this work *infra* in Part II.

achieve optimal levels of deterrence *only if the multiplier is calculated on a case-by-case basis,* so that the multiplier varies with each defendant's probability of punishment.

Significantly, few legal regimes follow the traditional multiplier in this respect, for few (if any) use multipliers that are calculated case-by-case. Often no multiplier is used and only compensatory damages are awarded, as in most civil suits under the common law. When the law does use a multiplier, it is often set at a single value that is the same for all defendants, as in the treble damage rule of antitrust law.[7] And when criminal or administrative penalties are used, it is common to set a single fine for all violations of a certain type (e.g., $100 for failing to stop at a stop sign), regardless of either the harm caused or the probability of punishment. Obviously, none of these systems of punishment satisfies the traditional, case-by-case multiplier principle.

The fact that real legal systems usually use some alternative to a case-by-case multiplier raises two questions for those interested in deterrence. First, when (if ever) might these alternatives be superior to the case-by-case multiplier? Second, whether or not they are superior, at what level should the fines or penalties be set (under each of these alternatives) to get the best deterrence possible? A naïve view might hold that when the law uses one of the alternatives, the best policy would still set the fine or other penalty *as close as possible* to the level of the case-by-case multiplier. But this naïve view is incorrect, for — as recent work in law and economics has also shown — each of these alternatives requires a different level of penalties to achieve optimal deterrence. Unfortunately, these differences are not widely understood in mainstream legal analysis, which continues to be fixed on the more traditional theory in which the multiplier is adjusted case by case.

Part II explores these differences by identifying the optimal fines or damage awards[8] under each of the possible alternatives. If the law uses the same multiplier for all defendants, optimal deterrence will usually require a penalty below the traditional multiplier principle. If the law instead uses a single *fine* for all defendants, as opposed to a single *multiplier,* the optimal fine could be either above or below the level of the multiplier principle,

---

7. 15 U.S.C. § 15(a) (1994).

8. In most of the article, I will speak of fines and damage awards interchangeably, without regard to whether they are paid to the victims (the usual rule for damages) or to the state (the usual rule for fines). While there are of course important differences between each of these penalties, most of those differences do not alter the resulting deterrent effect.

depending on (among other things) how rapidly the probability of punishment changes if a defendant commits a more or a less egregious offense. Indeed, this last factor — the responsiveness of the probability of punishment to *changes* in the egregiousness of an offense — is an important determinant of the optimal penalty under each of the alternatives discussed here. For this reason, Part III of the article discusses the factors that could make the probability of punishment more or less responsive to the degree of a defendant's offense.

Finally, Part IV addresses the first question identified above, by assessing the advantages and disadvantages of these alternatives relative to a case-by-case multiplier. The alternatives clearly differ in their computational complexity, and in the informational and other demands they place on judges and juries (or on legislatures). They may also differ in other key respects, such as their effect on litigation costs or on defendants' overall levels of activity, or on the law's symbolic or expressive effects. In the end, I conclude that remedies based on the traditional multiplier principle may well be useful, and may even dominate the alternatives, in a fairly small set of cases. In other cases, however, the balance of advantages and disadvantages is harder to assess.

I. THE TRADITIONAL MULTIPLIER PRINCIPLE

At the outset, it will help to distinguish between two ways of achieving optimal deterrence: by adjusting the penalty, and by adjusting the substantive legal standard. Suppose, for example, that we wish to reduce the risk of leaks of toxic waste, and that the optimal level of precautions would reduce that risk to exactly 1%. One way to achieve this goal is to set a substantive legal standard under which defendants are liable if but only if their risk exceeds that level. If the substantive standard is set correctly, and if it can be applied with no risk of error — two qualifications that will become important below — it may not matter if the penalty for violating the standard is set according to the multiplier principle. In such a regime, all that matters is that the penalty be large enough to deter defendants from violating the substantive legal standard, so any penalty set at this level *or higher* will achieve optimal deterrence. Indeed, as long as defendants who comply with the substantive standard can be assured of not paying any penalties at all, the penalty could (in theory) be increased to infinity without inducing overdeterrence, because defendants could always avoid any penalty by complying with the substantive standard. In such a regime, therefore, any increases in the penalty above the minimum level needed to induce compliance with the standard would not affect the behavior chosen by defendants.[9]

In most legal regimes, however, the size of the penalty will have a continuous effect on defendants' behavior. For example, if the law holds defendants strictly liable for *every* leak, it will then be impossible for defendants to insulate themselves from liability simply by complying with any substantive legal standard. The same is true if there is no official rule of strict liability but if the substantive standard is applied with some risk of error, so that even a defendant whose leaks are within the officially permitted level still faces some chance of being held liable. As long as defendants face some chance of being held liable, every increase in the penalty will strengthen the incentive to reduce their number of leaks. At some point, then, if the penalty is set too high, the incentive will grow too strong and there will be too much deterrence. In short, optimal deterrence in such a regime requires that the penalty be set at exactly the right level, not merely that it be at or above some minimum.

My focus in this article is on regimes of the second type, for that is where the multiplier principle is most relevant.[10] Whenever defendants cannot avoid any chance of liability, the *average* or *expected* liability is what governs the deterrence incentives. For example, if there is only one chance in four that they will actually be found liable, defendants will discount the penalty by 25% in calculating how much they could save by reducing their leaks. This discounting supplies the rationale for the multiplier principle, for it seems to imply that deterrence will be reduced unless the penalty is multiplied by four, to offset the 25% probability of punishment.

However, this conclusion (that the law's deterrent effect will be reduced without a multiplier) requires one additional assumption: that the probability of punishment is unaltered by any changes in a defendant's behavior. Subsection I.A below shows the role this assumption plays in the traditional analysis of multipliers. Subsection I.B then relaxes this assumption, to show why the multiplier principle is not necessary for optimal deterrence if the assumption is invalid.

---

9. This point is developed at more length in Robert Cooter, *Prices and Sanctions*, 84 COLUM. L. REV. 1523, 1524-27 (1984). I will return to it *infra* in section II.C.

10. The application of the multiplier principle (and of punitive damages generally) to regimes of the first sort is discussed in Hylton, *supra* note 1.

A. *Assuming the Probability of Punishment Stays Constant*

Suppose that a firm's activities pose a 1% risk of leaking toxic waste in a way that would cause $6 million worth of damages.[11] The average or expected costs of this activity would thus be $60,000 (.01 × $6,000,000). Suppose, though, that the firm could alter its operations to eliminate that risk and replace it with a 1% risk of a less serious leak that would cause only $5 million in damages, thus reducing the expected costs to $50,000 (.01 × $5,000,000). This means that the alteration would reduce the expected social costs of this activity by $10,000 ($60,000 − $50,000). The alteration is therefore socially efficient if, but only if, its cost is less than $10,000.

If enforcement is perfect — that is, if the firm knows that it will have to pay for all damages its leaks cause — then the firm's average liability will be $60,000 if it does not alter its operations and $50,000 if it does. By altering its operations, the firm can thus save $10,000 in expected liability ($60,000 − $50,000). Since $10,000 is also the social benefit from the alteration, the firm's incentives will be socially optimal. That is, the firm will have an incentive to make the alteration if, but only if, the cost of doing so is less than $10,000.

Now suppose that enforcement is instead imperfect, and that even if there is a leak the firm faces only a 25% chance of being held liable. The firm might then reason as follows: "If we do not alter our operations, then whenever there is a leak (i.e., in 1% of the cases) we will face a 25% probability of having to pay $6 million in damages. This is equivalent to an expected liability of $15,000 (.01 × .25 × $6,000,000). If we instead alter our operations, we will face a 25% chance of having to pay only $5 million, so our expected liability will decline to $12,500 (.01 × .25 × $5,000,000). But this shows that altering our operations would reduce our expected liability by only $2,500 ($15,000 − $12,5000)." This provides too little incentive for the firm to alter its operations, since the social gain from the alteration would still be $10,000 (not $2,500). This is the reasoning behind the multiplier principle: if the chance of having to pay damages is only 25%, the firm will discount the expected penalties undesirably, and the incentive to improve its behavior will be weakened.[12]

---

11. This example is similar to one used by Polinsky & Shavell, *supra* note 3, at 879-80. Like them, I assume that all the relevant costs and benefits can be measured (or at least approximated) numerically.

12. More precisely, the deterrent effect will be reduced if the firm *believes* that the probability of punishment is only 25%: it is the firm's beliefs about the probability that matter. In the discussion that follows, this qualification will be assumed. For a further dis-

This example also shows that if the measure of damages were multiplied by four, the firm's incentives would be optimal again. If damages were multiplied by four, the firm would then have to pay $24 million (4 × $6,000,000) if it caused a leak and had not altered its operations, and would have to pay $20 million (4 × $5,000,000) if it had altered its operations. This gives the firm an average or expected liability of $60,000 without the alteration (.01 × .25 × $24,000,000), compared to $50,000 with the alteration (.01 × .25 × $20,000,000), so the alteration would reduce the firm's expected liability by $10,000 ($60,000 − $50,000). A multiplier of four thus restores the equality between the private gain to the firm and the gain to society at large. This is because a multiplier of four exactly compensates for the 25% chance of being held liable.

Examples such as this are what give the multiplier principle its air of inevitability. Notice, though, that this example assumed that the probability of punishment stayed fixed at 25% *whether or not* the firm altered its operations. The firm's expected liability was calculated on the assumption that if it failed to make any alterations, it faced a 25% probability of paying $24 million in damages; while if it did make the alterations, it faced the same 25% probability of paying $20 million in damages. In other words, the example assumed that the probability of having to pay damages stayed the same regardless of the firm's actual behavior.

As noted earlier, more recent work in law and economics has relaxed this assumption by considering legal regimes in which the probability of punishment depends in part on how well the defendant has behaved.[13] The following subsection explains the implica-

---

cussion of this aspect of deterrence theory, see Steven Garber, *Product Liability, Punitive Damages, Business Decisions and Economic Outcomes*, 1998 WIS. L. REV. 237, 247-51.

13. The earliest analyses include CHARLES J. GOETZ, CASES AND MATERIALS ON LAW AND ECONOMICS 299-303 (1984); STEVEN SHAVELL, ECONOMIC ANALYSIS OF ACCIDENT LAW 93-99 (1987); John E. Calfee & Richard Craswell, *Some Effects of Uncertainty on Compliance with Legal Standards*, 70 VA. L. REV. 965 (1984); and Richard Craswell & John E. Calfee, *Deterrence and Uncertain Legal Standards*, 2 J.L. ECON. & ORG. 279 (1986). Other work will be cited below where it is relevant.

Another (and much larger) line of literature addresses the fact that the probability of punishment can also be altered by increased expenditures on detection and enforcement, or by other improvements to the enforcement system as a whole. For examples of this literature — a literature that also traces its origins to Becker, *supra* note 1 — see A. Mitchell Polinsky & Steven Shavell, *The Optimal Tradeoff between the Probability and Magnitude of Fines*, 69 AM. ECON. REV. 880 (1979); or Steven Shavell, *Specific Versus General Enforcement of Law*, 99 J. POL. ECON. 1088 (1991). My concern in this article, however, is with the extent to which the probability of punishment varies with changes *in an individual defendant's behavior*. I therefore will not address any policies that might alter the probability of punishment across the board, while still leaving that probability unaffected by changes in an individual defendant's behavior.

tions of this work, and shows why the multiplier principle may no longer be necessary for optimal deterrence.

B. *Relaxing the Constant Probability Assumption*

In many contexts, the probability of punishment declines if defendants reduce the riskiness of their behavior or if they behave better along any other dimension. Some reasons for the lower probability of punishment will be discussed in Part III — for example, the public authorities may be less likely to prosecute a firm that appears to be making a good-faith effort to reduce the severity of its leaks, or such a firm might be better able to convince a court that it has not violated the applicable legal standard. For now, the exact reason for the reduced probability of punishment does not matter, as long as the probability does in fact decline.

If the probability of punishment does decline when a defendant improves its behavior, this produces two offsetting effects. The fact that the probability of punishment is still less than 100% will weaken the law's deterrent effect, just as in the earlier example. But if the probability of punishment falls even lower when the defendant improves its behavior, this will *strengthen* the law's deterrent effect, because improved behavior will then bring an extra "reward" in the form of a lower probability of punishment. And since there is no logical connection between the size of these two effects, it is possible for either one to outweigh the other, leading either to a net weakening effect (and net underdeterrence) or a net strengthening effect (net overdeterrence). Indeed, it is even possible for both effects to exactly offset, leaving deterrence at just the optimal level.[14]

These possibilities can all be illustrated using the toxic waste example. Let us now suppose that the probability of punishment is still 25% if the firm does not alter its operations, but only 10% if it does. If no multiplier is used, the firm will still face an expected liability of $15,000 if it does not alter its operations (.01 × .25 × $6,000,000), but if it does alter its operations its expected liability will fall to $5,000 (.01 × .10 × $5,000,000). This means that altering its operations will reduce the firm's expected liability by $10,000 ($15,000 – $5,000). But $10,000 is also the social gain from the alteration, so the firm's private savings will once again equal the social savings. In other words, even with imperfect enforcement

---

14. For a mathematical demonstration of all three possibilities, see Craswell & Calfee, *supra* note 13, at 284 tbl.1.

and no damage multiplier at all, it is still possible for the firm's incentives to be optimal.

Of course, it is only by coincidence (or by careful selection of the hypothetical numbers) that the firm's incentives would be exactly optimal. If extra precautions did not reduce the probability of punishment quite as much, so that probability fell from 25% to some figure above 10%, the firm's savings in expected liability would then be less than $10,000, which would give the firm too weak an incentive (net underdeterrence). Conversely, if the extra precautions reduced the probability of punishment even more, to some figure even less than 10%, the firm's savings would then be more than $10,000, and the firm would have too strong an incentive (net overdeterrence). The net effect on the firm's incentives thus depends critically on the *rate* at which the probability of punishment falls as the firm improves its behavior. In economic terms, it is the marginal *change* in the expected penalty, and not its absolute level, that governs the firm's incentives.

C. *Adjusting the Multiplier Case-by-Case*

Even when the multiplier principle is not strictly *necessary* for optimal deterrence, it could still provide one way of achieving that goal. To be sure, we just saw that if extra precautions reduced the probability of punishment from 25% to 10%, then defendants would have optimal incentives without any multiplier at all. In such a case, it might seem that any multiplier would be a bad idea, because it could only strengthen the deterrent effect and lead to overdeterrence. However, this intuition must be discarded when the probability of punishment is not a constant. In this section, I show that optimal deterrence can still be achieved using the traditional multiplier principle, but only *if the multiplier is calculated separately for each defendant,* based on each defendant's actual probability of punishment.

Consider again the example from the preceding subsection. In that example, defendants who did not take extra precautions faced a 25% probability of punishment. If the multiplier is recalculated case by case, these defendants will still be given a multiplier of four, so they will still have to pay $24 million (4 × $6,000,000) if they are found liable. Their average or expected liability will thus be $60,000 (.01 × .25 × $24,000,000). However, if defendants who do take the extra precautions face only a 10% probability of punishment, they would be assigned a multiplier of ten (if the multiplier is recalculated case by case). These defendants will therefore have to pay $50 million (10 × $5,000,000) whenever they are found liable, so their expected liability will be $50,000 (.01 × .10 × $50,000,000).[15] This means that defendants' incentives will be optimal again, because taking the extra precautions will reduce their expected liability by $10,000 ($60,000 − $50,000), which just equals the social gain from those precautions.

In short, even when the multiplier principle is not absolutely *necessary* for optimal deterrence, it may still be *sufficient* to achieve that goal. As long as the probability of punishment (whether 25% or 10%) is offset by just the right multiplier, the effect will be the same as if enforcement were perfect, and defendants will be made to feel the full costs of their behavior.

1.   *Case-by-Case Multipliers as "Taxes" on Improvements*

It is instructive to compare this conclusion with the one reached in the preceding subsection, when optimal deterrence was achieved even without any damage multiplier. In the preceding subsection, we saw that the decline in the probability of punishment (from 25% to 10%) could itself be enough to create optimal incentives, thus achieving optimal deterrence even though defendants paid only the actual costs of their behavior ($6 million and $5 million, respectively).[16] Yet the example just discussed showed that optimal deterrence could also be achieved if the penalties were increased through a multiplier — and increased quite dramatically, to $24 million and $50 million respectively. But this might seem paradoxical: How can a dramatic increase in penalties leave the law with the same deterrent effect?

The explanation lies in the fact that, while a case-by-case multiplier does increase penalties overall, it also introduces a new factor that checks any tendency to overdeterrence. If the multiplier is recalculated in every case, defendants who improve their behavior will (in effect) be "taxed" on that improvement, by being subjected to a larger multiplier if and when they are found liable. In the example just discussed, defendants who took extra precautions reduced their probability of punishment (from 25% to 10%) and thereby *increased* their multiplier (from four to ten). This tax, in the form of a higher multiplier, counteracted what would otherwise

---

15. Notice that the penalty assessed against these defendants ($50 million) will be larger than the penalty assessed against defendants who did *not* take the extra precautions ($24 million). The possibility that this relationship might offend notions of corrective justice will be discussed *infra* in section IV.G.

16. *See supra* text following note 14.

be an incentive for overdeterrence. As long as the multiplier is re-calculated whenever the probability of punishment declines, the net effects should exactly offset and defendants should have just the optimal incentives.[17]

Indeed, the same analysis would apply even if the original incentives (in the absence of any multiplier) had favored *over*deterrence. For example, if taking extra precautions reduced the probability of punishment from 25% to less than 10%, the reward for taking those precautions would then be even greater (in the absence of a multiplier), leading to too much deterrence. But if a multiplier is used, and if the multiplier is calculated separately for each defendant, defendants who take extra precautions would then face an even higher tax, for their new multiplier would be even greater than ten (because their probability of punishment would be less than 10%). Paradoxical as it may seem, *increasing* penalties can sometimes *reduce* the law's deterrent effect, as long as the extent of the increase itself responds (through changes in the multiplier) to each change in a defendant's behavior.

2.   *The Effect of a Constant Multiplier*

The preceding analysis also shows why the multiplier, to have this effect, *must* be recalculated in every case, so that it changes with each defendant's actual behavior. If the multiplier is instead fixed at some constant level, it no longer leads to optimal deterrence.

The toxic waste example can illustrate this point as well. In that example, the average probability of punishment was somewhere between 10% and 25%. Suppose, for the sake of concreteness, that this average was exactly 20% (as would be the case if one-third of all defendants took the extra precautions but two-thirds did not). If the damage multiplier were set at a constant based on this average probability of punishment, all defendants would be given a multiplier of five. This means that defendants who did not take extra precautions would have to pay $30 million in damages (5 × $6,000,000) each time they were caught, while defendants who did take extra precautions would have to pay only $25 million in damages (5 × $5,000,000).

Unfortunately, these penalties will create too much deterrence. Defendants who do not take extra precautions will now face expected liabilities of $75,000 (.01 × .25 × $30,000,000), while defend-

---

17. For a mathematical proof, see Craswell & Calfee, *supra* note 13, at 292 n.18.

ants who do take extra precautions will face expected liabilities of $25,000 (.01 × .10 × $25,000,000). Thus, defendants who take the extra precautions will be rewarded with a $50,000 reduction in their expected liability ($75,000 − $25,000). But the true social savings from these precautions are still only $10,000 ($60,000 − $50,000), so this $50,000 reward is too large and will lead to overdeterrence.

Notice, too, that the problem is not just that a constant multiplier will not be sufficiently fine-tuned, in the sense that any constant will be too high for some defendants and too low for others.[18] To the contrary, overdeterrence can still be a problem even if the constant multiplier is set at a level that is not "too high" (according to the traditional principle) for any individual defendant. In the example just considered, the highest probability of punishment was 25%, for defendants who did not take the extra precautions. If we follow the traditional multiplier analysis, a multiplier of four would be just right for those defendants and too low for all others (those for whom the probability of punishment was only 10%). And if a multiplier of four is just right for some and too low for others, it might seem as though that multiplier would have to yield too little deterrence on balance.

In fact, though, a multiplier of four will still produce too much deterrence *if it is applied as a constant.* With a constant multiplier of four, defendants who do not take the precautions will have to pay $24 million in damages (4 × $6,000,000) each time they are caught, while defendants who do take the precautions will have to pay $20 million (4 × $5,000,000). This means that defendants who do not take the precautions now face an expected liability of $60,000 (.01 × .25 × $24,000,000), while defendants who do take the precautions face an expected liability of $20,000 (.01 × .10 × $20,000,000). As a result, defendants can now save $40,000 in expected liability ($60,000 − $20,000) by taking the precautions, and this is still far more than the $10,000 social value of the precautions. Thus, a constant multiplier can still lead to overdeterrence even when it seems "just right" for some defendants (according to the traditional multiplier principle) and "too low" for all others.

While this conclusion, too, may seem paradoxical, it follows directly from the earlier analysis. The reason is that constant multipliers — even ones set at relatively low levels — eliminate the "tax" referred to earlier. As we have seen, a case-by-case multiplier taxes

---

18. Polinsky and Shavell emphasize this objection to constant multipliers. *See* Polinsky & Shavell, *supra* note 3, at 893.

defendants whose behavior improves by giving them a higher multi-plier (to correspond to their lower probability of punishment). A constant multiplier eliminates this "tax," but it still increases the overall deterrent effect by increasing all penalties across the board. By thus increasing the size of all penalties without any offsetting "tax," constant multipliers can easily produce too much deterrence, just as in the example above. In fact, to achieve the optimal level of deterrence a constant multiplier will usually have to be set *below* the traditional multiplier principle (as the following Part will discuss).

II. ALTERNATIVE ROUTES TO OPTIMAL DETERRENCE

As noted in the introduction,[19] most legal systems do not use multipliers that are calculated case by case. Instead, they use multi-pliers set at the same level for all defendants, or fines set at the same level for all defendants, or compensatory damages with no multipliers at all. Accordingly, it is important to understand how penalties should be set to achieve optimal deterrence under each of these alternative approaches — and how those penalties would dif-fer from the more familiar, case-by-case multiplier principle.

In this Part, I show that constant multipliers can achieve optimal deterrence if they are set at some suitably lower level (lower, that is, than the traditional multiplier principle). Constant fines can also achieve optimal deterrence, usually by being set below the tradi-tional multiplier principle, but sometimes by being set above that level. Optimal deterrence might also be achieved by reforms that do not involve any multiplier at all — for example, by caps on the highest possible damage awards, or by changing the substantive legal standard. Thus, while the traditional multiplier principle may perhaps be *sufficient* for optimal deterrence, it is not at all *necessary*.

A. *The Optimal Constant Multiplier*

The toxic waste example has already shown how a constant mul-tiplier set at 1.0 could still achieve optimal deterrence. In that ex-ample, extra precautions reduced the probability of punishment from 25% to 10%, and that effect by itself was enough to reduce defendants' expected liability by $10,000.[20] Since $10,000 was also the social benefit produced by the extra precautions, this meant

---

19. *See supra* text accompanying note 7.
20. *See supra* text following note 14.

that defendants had the optimal incentives even with no multiplier at all. But using no multiplier at all, and merely awarding compensatory damages, is equivalent to multiplying the damages by one in every case. And if enforcement is imperfect, a multiplier of one will be below the level recommended by the traditional multiplier principle, which in this example would have been between four and ten (because the probability of punishment ranged from 25% to 10%). In short, we have already seen one example where optimal deterrence was achieved using a constant multiplier below the optimal case-by-case multiplier.

Of course, there is no reason to think that the optimal constant multiplier will always equal one. Indeed, if we change the example slightly, so extra precautions reduce the probability of punishment from 25% to only 20%, the constant multiplier will then have to be larger. In this revised example, defendants who take no extra precautions will face expected liability of $15,000 (.01 × .25 × $6,000,000) if no multiplier is used, but defendants who do take the precautions will face expected liability of $10,000 (.01 × .20 × $5,000,000). Defendants who take the precautions will thus be rewarded with only a $5,000 reduction in expected liability ($15,000 − $10,000), and this reward is less than the social value of the precautions, which is still $10,000 ($60,000 − $50,000). In this case, then, defendants will have too little incentive to take the extra precautions. To correct this problem, the multiplier must be greater than one in order to magnify the reward for taking extra precautions. In this example, the optimal constant multiplier happens to be exactly two.[21]

To be sure, a constant multiplier of two is still less than the optimal *case-by-case* multiplier under the traditional multiplier principle, for that multiplier would now be somewhere between four and five (based on a probability of punishment ranging from 25% to 20%). In this new example, though, the optimal constant multiplier is not as far below the lower end of this range as it was in the original example, where the optimal constant multiplier was only one. This is because the new example features a probability of punishment that is less responsive to improvements in defendants' behav-

---

21. The full calculations are as follows. With a constant multiplier of two, defendants who do not take extra precautions will have to pay $12 million when they are caught (2 × $6,000,000), while defendants who do take extra precautions will have to pay $10 million (2 × $5,000,000). This gives defendants an expected liability of $30,000 if they do not take precautions (.01 × .25 × $12,000,000), as compared to an expected liability of $20,000 (.01 × .20 × $10,000,000) if they do take precautions. The savings in expected liability is therefore $10,000 ($30,000 − $20,000), which again equals the social benefit from the precautions.

2200   *Michigan Law Review*   [Vol. 97:2185

ior: taking extra precautions in the new example brings just a slight reduction in the probability of punishment, from 25% to 20%. The lesson here is that the rate at which the probability of punishment declines is a key factor in determining how low a constant multiplier should be.

Indeed, if the probability of punishment were to decline even faster with each improvement in a defendant's behavior, the optimal constant multiplier would be even smaller — and could even be less than one, implying that even compensatory damages would be too high. To see this, let us alter the example so that extra precautions reduce the probability of punishment from 25% all the way down to 5%. If no multiplier is used, defendants who do not take the precautions would still face expected liabilities of $15,000 (just as before), but defendants who do take the precautions would face expected liabilities of $2,500 (.01 × .05 × $5,000,000). This gives each defendant who takes the precautions a $12,500 reduction in its expected liability ($15,000 − $2,500). But this $12,500 reward is greater than the social value of those precautions (which is still $10,000), so these penalties will lead to overdeterrence. To dampen defendants' incentives and achieve optimal deterrence, any constant multiplier would have to be set at some value less than one. In this example, the optimal constant multiplier happens to be 0.80, which is equivalent to holding defendants liable for only 80% of the harm caused by their behavior. Even though defendants are clearly paying less than the full social costs of their behavior, their incentives are still socially optimal.[22]

Of course, a multiplier of 0.80 is *much* less than the traditional case-by-case multiplier, which in this example would be somewhere between four and twenty (based on probabilities of punishment between 25% and 5%). In general, the more the probability of punishment declines with any improvement in a defendant's behavior, the greater will be the divergence between the optimal constant multiplier and the optimal case-by-case multiplier. As long as the probability of punishment declines at all, though, the optimal constant multiplier will almost always be less than the optimal case-by-case multiplier. More precisely, the optimal constant multiplier will

---

22. With a constant multiplier of 0.80, defendants who do not take extra precautions will have to pay only $4.8 million each time they are caught (.80 × $6,000,000), while defendants who do take extra precautions will have to pay $4 million (.80 × $5,000,000). This gives defendants an expected liability of $12,000 if they do not take the extra precautions (.01 × .25 × $4,800,000), compared to an expected liability of only $2,000 (.01 × .05 × $4,000,000) if they do take extra precautions. This makes the savings in expected liability again equal to $10,000 ($12,000 − $2,000), which is still the social value of the extra precautions.

never be greater than the optimal case-by-case multiplier, and will usually be less.[23]

The reason for this follows from the analysis given earlier. We have already seen that the traditional multiplier will create optimal incentives *if* that multiplier is adjusted on a case-by-case basis to reflect each improvement in a defendant's behavior. We have also seen that this case-by-case adjustment operates as a kind of a tax, which penalizes defendants whose behavior improves by making them face a larger multiplier (to correspond to their reduced probability of punishment). Making the multiplier a constant takes away this tax on improvements and thus strengthens the incentives to make such improvements. But if the case-by-case multiplier (including the tax on improvements) had been creating exactly the optimal incentives, any change that strengthens those incentives will make them too strong, leading to net overdeterrence. The only way to correct this problem (while still employing a constant multiplier) is to reduce the size of the multiplier, reducing the deterrent effect. This is why the optimal constant multiplier will usually be less than, and can never be greater than, the optimal case-by-case multiplier.

The size of the optimal constant multiplier will also depend on the expected damage award facing a defendant whose behavior is at or very near the socially optimal level. In the original toxic waste example, defendants who took the socially efficient level of precautions expected that a leak would occur in 1% of all cases, and that they would then face a 10% chance of having to pay damages of $5 million (before any multiplier was applied). This prospect left these defendants facing an expected liability of $50,000 (.01 × .10 × $5,000,000). But if that figure were either higher or lower, the law's deterrent effect would be altered, requiring a corresponding adjustment in the size of the constant multiplier.

To see this, let us change the original example to make the toxic waste slightly more hazardous, so that a leak now causes $8 million in damages (rather than $6 million) if no extra precautions are taken, and $7 million in damages (rather than $5 million) if the defendant does take extra precautions. Since both figures have increased by the same amount, the social efficiency of the precautions will be just what it was before: the precautions will still reduce

---

23. For a mathematical proof, see Craswell & Calfee, *supra* note 13, at 297 & n.25.

expected social costs by $10,000.[24] However, this change in the absolute levels of harm reduces the optimal constant multiplier. In the earlier example where the damage caused by a leak was either $6 million or $5 million, and extra precautions reduced the probability of punishment from 25% to only 20%, we saw that the optimal constant multiplier was exactly two.[25] If we use these same probabilities in this new example, though, the optimal constant multiplier falls to 1.67.[26]

The reason why the absolute size of the damages matter is that this affects the *significance* (to the defendant) of the rate at which the probability of punishment declines. In both of these examples, the extra precautions reduced the probability of punishment by the same amount, from 25% to 20%. In the first example, though, this represented a reduction of five percentage points in the probability of paying $6 or $7 million (before any multiplier was applied), while in the second case it represented a reduction of five percentage points in the probability of having to pay $7 or $8 million. Obviously, the second reduction is more valuable to defendants than the first, so the second offers stronger incentives for defendants to improve their behavior. As a result, any constant multiplier that was optimal in the first case will be too strong in the second case, and therefore will have to be reduced. This is just what happened in the example itself: the optimal constant multiplier fell from 2.0 to 1.67. This shows that the optimal level for a constant multiplier depends both on the rate at which the probability of punishment declines *and* on the absolute level of damages that are expected when defendants behave optimally.

Of course, the absolute level of these damages depends partly on the technology of the defendant's activity — for example, what kind of waste is involved, and just how toxic is it? But the level of damages may also be affected by other legal rules, especially the rules governing causation. For example, if a defendant who failed

---

24. In this new example, the expected social costs of the defendants' behavior are $80,000 (.01 × $8,000,000) if they do not take the extra precautions, and $70,000 (.01 × $7,000,000) if they do. The social value of the extra precautions is therefore $10,000 ($80,000 – $70,000).

25. *See supra* text accompanying note 21.

26. With a constant multiplier of 1.67, defendants who do not take the extra precautions will have to pay $13.33 million each time they are caught (1.67 × $8,000,000), while defendants who do take the precautions will have to pay $11.67 million (1.6 × $7,000,000). This gives defendants an expected liability of $33,333 if they do not take the precautions (.01 × .25 × $13,333,333), compared to an expected liability of $23,333 (.01 × .20 × $11,666,667) if they do, so defendants can save $10,000 in expected liability by taking the precautions ($33,333 – $23,333). This $10,000 savings exactly equals the precautions' social value, so defendants' incentives will be socially optimal.

to take the appropriate precautions can prove that the same leak would have occurred even if all appropriate precautions had been taken, and that the same victims would still have suffered $7 million in damages (rather than the $8 million in damages they actually suffered), the rules of causation will sometimes reduce such a defendant's liability to only $1 million, reflecting the *incremental* harm attributable to its failure to take proper care.[27] If damages are consistently reduced in this way, the optimal constant multiplier will be larger, because a larger multiplier will be needed to achieve the same deterrent effect. In this example, the optimal constant multiplier would equal four.[28] Of course, a multiplier of four would also satisfy the traditional multiplier principle, based on a probability of punishment of 25%.

This conclusion holds more generally: whenever a causation rule of this sort is applied without error, the optimal constant multiplier will always be just as great as (though no greater than) the optimal case-by-case multiplier.[29] If such a causation rule is perfectly applied, a defendant who takes the socially optimal level of care should never have to pay any damages at all. Such a defendant will therefore be unconcerned with the probability that it might be held liable, and will thus be unaffected by the rate at which that probability might change if the defendant were to deviate slightly from the socially efficient level of care. But if the deterrent effect will be the same regardless of the rate at which that probability changes, this means that the deterrent effect will be the same as it would have been in a world where the probability of punishment did not change at all. And in a world where the probability of punishment did not change at all, there would be no difference between the optimal constant multiplier and the optimal case-by-case multiplier, because in such a world no case-by-case adjustments would ever be required. This is why a perfectly applied causation rule sup-

---

27. *See* sources cited *infra* note 30.

28. The full calculations are as follows. Defendants who do not take extra precautions will be charged with incremental damages of $1 million, for the reasons discussed in the text. A multiplier of four means that these defendants will have to pay $4 million each time they are caught (4 × $1,000,000), leaving them with an expected liability of $10,000 (.01 × .25 × $4,000,000). However, defendants who do take extra precautions will not be charged with any losses at all (under this incremental damage rule), so their expected liability will be zero. This means that defendants can save $10,000 in expected liability ($10,000 minus 0) by taking the precautions — which is just what the socially optimal incentives require.

29. For mathematical analyses of this relationship, see Craswell & Calfee, *supra* note 13, at 295-97; Marcel Kahan, *Causation and Incentives to Take Care Under the Negligence Rule*, 18 J. LEGAL STUD. 427, 437-39 (1989). For a more qualitative discussion, see Mark F. Grady, *Punitive Damages and State of Mind: A Positive Economic Theory*, 40 ALA. L. REV. 1197, 1201-09 (1989).

plies the limiting case in which there is no effective difference between the optimal constant multiplier and the optimal case-by-case multiplier.

It should be stressed, however, that this is indeed a limiting case. If the causation rule is not applied perfectly, but instead involves any risk of error, then even defendants who take socially efficient precautions will always face at least some expected liability, so they will care about the rate at which the probability of punishment changes. More important, the rules of causation often are not applied in precisely the way that the earlier example assumed.[30] For instance, if the efficient level of care would have led to a different *kind* of accident, or to an accident whose losses would have fallen on different victims, defendants' liability generally is not limited to the incremental losses above and beyond those that would have been imposed if they had taken the efficient level of care. The same is true when the expected losses (at any level of care) are entirely probabilistic, so the most that defendants can show is that a similar accident *might* have happened even if they had taken the efficient level of care. In such a case, defendants' liability usually is not reduced by the statistical or expected value of the losses that might have occurred even if they had behaved efficiently. Obviously, there will also be no reduction of their liability in any regime of strict liability, where defendants are held liable for the full costs regardless of whether they behaved efficiently. And if (for any of these reasons) defendants' liability is not limited to the purely incremental losses, the optimal constant multiplier will then be *less* than the multiplier principle. Often it will be less by a considerable margin, as in most of the examples considered above.

To summarize, the optimal constant multiplier can never exceed the optimal case-by-case multiplier, and only rarely will it equal that level. Instead, in most cases the optimal constant multiplier will be less than the optimal case-by-case multiplier, meaning that a constant multiplier can achieve optimal levels of deterrence without satisfying the multiplier principle. Moreover, the extent to which the optimal constant multiplier falls below the multiplier principle depends on two factors: (a) the rate at which the probability of punishment falls with improvements in a defendant's behavior, and (b) the absolute level of expected damages facing a defendant who

---

30. For discussions of the actual legal rules, see Cooter, *supra* note 3; Grady, *supra* note 29; David Rosenberg, *The Causal Connection in Mass Exposure Cases: A "Public Law" Vision of the Tort System,* 97 HARV. L. REV. 849, 862-66 (1984). I discuss the deterrent effect of other causation rules at more length *infra* in section III.D.

behaves in the socially optimal way. Only when one of these factors is eliminated — that is, when the probability of punishment never changes at all, or when defendants who behave optimally can be assured of paying no damages — only then will the optimal constant multiplier be the same as the optimal case-by-case multiplier.

B. *The Optimal Constant Fine*

Another route to optimal deterrence involves the use of a constant fine, in which every defendant who is found liable pays the same total amount. For example, traffic laws often impose the same fine for every violation of a certain type, regardless of the actual damage caused by the violation. A constant fine is slightly different from the constant multiplier discussed in the preceding section, for a constant multiplier allows the total penalty (the multiplier times the harm caused) to vary from defendant to defendant. By contrast, a constant fine keeps the total penalty the same for all defendants.

The significance of this distinction is that a constant multiplier gives defendants two reasons to improve their behavior, while a constant fine gives them only one. Under a constant multiplier, defendants who improve their behavior will be rewarded with a lower probability of being punished, as emphasized in the preceding sections of this article. But defendants who improve their behavior will also be rewarded with a reduction in the damages to which any multiplier will be applied, because improved behavior should (if it is truly an "improvement") inflict lower social costs. Indeed, both of these effects can be seen in the toxic waste example discussed earlier, because in every example there were two reasons why defendants who took the extra precautions faced a lower expected liability. Defendants who took extra precautions benefited from a reduction in the probability of punishment, from 25% to some lower value; but they also benefited from a reduction in the social losses to which any multiplier would be applied, from $6 million down to $5 million (or from $8 million down to $7 million, depending on the example).

The key point for present purposes is that a constant fine eliminates the second of these effects. If the law uses a constant fine, defendants who improve their behavior may still be rewarded with a reduction in the probability of being penalized at all, but this will be their *only* reward: the amount they will have to pay if they are penalized will stay constant. It follows that the deterrent effects of a constant fine will always be less than the deterrent effects of an equivalent constant multiplier. To offset this reduction in deterrent effect, the optimal constant fine will have to be larger than the optimal constant multiplier.[31]

This conclusion, too, is easy to see using a concrete example. In the toxic waste scenario, we calculated earlier that if extra precautions reduced the probability of punishment from 25% to only 20%, the optimal constant multiplier would be exactly two.[32] Using such a multiplier, defendants who do not take the extra precautions will have to pay $12 million each time they are caught (2 × $6,000,000), while defendants who do take the precautions will have to pay $10 million (2 × $5,000,000). If the legal system instead uses a constant fine, however, optimal deterrence will be achieved only if the fine is set at $20 million.[33] Obviously, this $20 million fine is larger than the $12 million and $10 million penalties that would have been optimal under a constant multiplier regime.

At the same time, a $20 million fine is below the penalty called for by the traditional multiplier principle. In this example, defendants who do not take extra precautions still face a 25% probability of punishment, so the traditional multiplier principle would require a multiplier of four, resulting in a total penalty of $24 million (4 × $6,000,000). Similarly, defendants who do take the extra precautions face only a 20% probability of punishment in this example, so for these defendants the multiplier principle requires a multiplier of five and a total penalty of $25 million (5 × $5,000,000). As we have seen, the optimal constant fine is only $20 million, which is less than either $24 million or $25 million.

However, the optimal constant fine may not always be less than the optimal case-by-case multiplier. The optimal constant fine will always be greater than the optimal *constant* multiplier, and the optimal *case-by-case* multiplier will also be greater than (or equal to) the optimal constant multiplier. However, the relationship between the optimal constant fine and the optimal case-by-case multiplier is more difficult to characterize. The most that can be said is that the optimal constant fine will be less than the optimal case-by-case mul-

---

31. For a mathematical proof, compare Craswell & Calfee, *supra* note 13, at 294 (deriving the value of the optimal constant multiplier) with *id.* at 297 (deriving the value of the optimal constant fine).

32. *See supra* text accompanying note 21.

33. With a constant fine set at $20 million, defendants will face an expected liability of $50,000 (.01 × .25 × $20,000,000) if they do not take the extra precautions, but an expected liability of only $40,000 (.01 × .20 × $20,000,000) if they do take the extra precautions. The savings in expected liability therefore equals $10,000 ($50,000 − $40,000), which is also the social value of the extra precautions.

tiplier whenever the probability of punishment is relatively responsive to improvements in a defendant's behavior. In particular, if the
probability of punishment declines quite rapidly with each improvement in a defendant's behavior — so much that the defendant's
incentives would be optimal, or not too suboptimal, with no multiplier at all — then the optimal constant fine will always be less than
the optimal case-by-case multiplier.[34] But if the probability of punishment is somewhat less responsive to improvements in a defendant's behavior, the deterrent effect of a constant fine will then be
reduced, which means that the absolute level of the fine will have to
be raised in order to keep deterrence optimal. At some point, if the
probability of punishment is extremely *un*responsive to improvements in a defendant's behavior, the optimal constant fine could
even surpass the optimal case-by-case multiplier. In short, the *rate*
at which the probability of punishment responds is again a key variable — in this case, the variable that determines the size of the
optimal fine.

C. *Adjustments to the Substantive Standard*

Another method of achieving optimal deterrence, at least under
some legal regimes, is to raise or lower the substantive threshold for
liability.[35] For example, suppose that the optimal risk of toxic leaks
is exactly 1% — but suppose that the net incentives with no multiplier at all favor underdeterrence, so firms choose instead to permit
a 1.5% risk. One way of correcting this underdeterrence is to make
the substantive standard more strict, to permit no more than (say) a
0.75% risk of toxic leaks. At this lower substantive standard, any
firm that continued to permit a 1.5% risk would now face a higher
probability of detection and/or conviction, as its behavior would
more obviously violate the new substantive standard. This increase
in the probability of detection or conviction would give firms a
stronger reason to reduce their levels of risk, thus increasing the
law's deterrent effect and moving firms back toward the socially
optimal risk of 1%. If firms still permitted a risk of more than 1%,

---

34. A mathematical proof is available from the author upon request.

35. The possibility of changing the substantive standard to adjust for imperfect enforcement is discussed in Calfee & Craswell, *supra* note 13, at 997-99; and in Jason S. Johnston,
Punitive Liability: A New Paradigm of Efficiency in Tort Law, 87 COLUM. L. REV. 1385
(1987) [hereinafter Johnston, *Punitive Liability*]. Note, too, that the substantive standard
could also be raised or lowered indirectly by (for example) changing the evidentiary rules or
the burdens of proof. For discussions of this approach, see Craswell & Calfee, *supra* note 13,
at 290-92; Jason S. Johnston, *Bayesian Fact-Finding and Efficiency: Toward an Economic
Theory of Liability Under Uncertainty*, 61 S. CAL. L. REV. 137 (1987).

then the substantive standard could be lowered even further, until the resulting probability of punishment gave defendants an incentive to choose exactly the 1% level.

Of course, if the net incentives without any multiplier instead favored overdeterrence, the appropriate response would require relaxing rather than tightening the substantive standard. Either way, though, we could still achieve optimal deterrence without satisfying the traditional multiplier principle. That is, there should be some adjustment to the substantive legal standard that can achieve optimal deterrence even if the probability of punishment remains less than one, and even if the fines or damage awards remain at purely compensatory levels (and thus fail to satisfy the traditional multiplier principle). This shows, again, that satisfaction of the multiplier principle is not always necessary for optimal deterrence.

In addition, if the substantive standard were relaxed sufficiently, optimal deterrence might also be achieved with penalties *above* the multiplier principle. This can be achieved if the substantive standard is defined in such a way that it could never be applied, even through judicial error, to a defendant who had behaved efficiently. Penalties of this sort — referred to by Robert Cooter as "sanctions"[36] — thus require a triggering test such as "egregious behavior," "gross negligence" or "reckless disregard for human safety," to ensure that they are never applied to efficient behavior.[37] If the probability of the higher penalty is literally zero for any defendant who behaves efficiently, there will be no danger of inducing too many precautions, because a defendant who is already behaving efficiently will (by hypothesis) face no risk of having to pay the higher penalty. As further increases in the penalty should have no effect on these defendants, the penalty could (in theory) be increased indefinitely without deterring beyond the optimal level.[38]

Since this approach permits the imposition of penalties that are *larger* than the multiplier principle (rather than penalties that are smaller, as under most of the other alternatives discussed here), it

---

36. *See* Cooter, *supra* note 9, *passim.* By contrast, penalties calculated according to the multiplier principle are referred to by Cooter as "prices," because they achieve deterrence by making defendants pay the full social costs of their behavior (no more, and no less) as the "price" of that behavior. *See id.* at 1528.

37. *Compare* Polinsky & Shavell, *supra* note 3, at 905-08 (arguing that the reprehensibility of the defendant's conduct should be irrelevant when damages are calculated by the multiplier principle, because under the multiplier principle the only relevant factors are the amount of the harm and the probability of punishment).

38. *See* Cooter, *supra* note 9, at 1524-27.

raises distinct issues that I will not address further.[39] Still, the possibility of optimal deterrence with even larger penalties does reinforce the general lesson of this article — i.e., that the multiplier principle is sufficient but not necessary for optimal deterrence.

D. Caps on Damages, and Other Possible Adjustments

Finally, optimal deterrence can also be achieved by leaving the substantive standard unchanged, but starting with compensatory damages and adding or subtracting (rather than multiplying) a constant amount to each award. The size of the optimal addition or subtraction is harder to express mathematically,[40] but its general character depends on the same factors that characterize the optimal constant multiplier. That is, whenever the optimal constant multiplier would be greater than one (implying that compensatory damages need to be increased), optimal deterrence can be achieved by *adding* some amount to each compensatory award. Similarly, whenever the optimal constant multiplier would be less than one, optimal deterrence can be achieved by *subtracting* some amount from each compensatory award. Either way, the size of the amount to be added or subtracted will be greater or less depending on just how much the optimal constant multiplier would have been greater or lesser than one.

For a similar reason, optimal deterrence could also be achieved by placing a cap on the maximum size of the award — a move that several states have enacted or considered in recent years.[41] Placing a cap on the largest possible award is similar in many respects to subtracting something from the *expected value* of the damage award. That is, if defendants face uncertainty about how damages will be measured (in addition to uncertainty about whether they will be liable at all), an upper limit on the maximum possible award will cut off the upper end of that distribution. This will reduce the average award, thereby reducing the deterrent effect.

To be sure, these reductions would make little sense if optimal deterrence were being pursued by means of the traditional multiplier principle. Under the traditional multiplier principle, we must be prepared to increase damage awards to almost any level, espe-

---

39. For further discussions of this approach as it might apply to punitive damages, see Hylton, *supra* note 1; and Johnston, *Punitive Liability, supra* note 35.

40. For a mathematical model, see A. Mitchell Polinsky & Daniel Rubinfeld, *The Welfare Implications of Costly Litigation for the Level of Liability*, 17 J. LEGAL STUD. 151, 159-60, 163 app. (1988).

41. For citations to the various legislative proposals, see *BMW of North America, Inc. v. Gore*, 517 U.S. 559 app. (1996) (Ginsburg, J., dissenting).

cially when the probability of punishment is relatively small (so that the optimal case-by-case multiplier is large). As Polinsky and Shavell have recently argued, caps on the largest possible award could interfere with this goal, leading to less than optimal deterrence.[42]

If optimal deterrence is instead being pursued by some other route, however, it is harder to condemn such caps a priori. For example, if the law instead aims to achieve optimal deterrence by approximating the optimal constant multiplier, we have already seen that this typically requires awards that are lower than those called for by the traditional multiplier principle.[43] Viewed with this goal in mind, a cap on the highest possible awards could be seen as moving the average or expected award in just the right direction. In other words, a reform that seems obviously unsound from the standpoint of one route to optimal deterrence could be perfectly sound from the standpoint of another.

Of course, to say that caps on damage awards *could* be justified is not to say that any particular proposal is a good idea. Calculating the exact size of the optimal adjustment will often be difficult, in which case it may be hard to say whether any particular cap goes too far or not far enough. Indeed, calculation problems arise under each of the alternatives — as, of course, they arise to some extent under the multiplier principle itself. These calculation problems, and other issues surrounding the administration of each set of remedies, will be discussed below in Part IV.

For now, my point is simply that the existence of alternative routes must first be recognized before we can even begin to consider which is easiest to calculate, or which is best on any other grounds. If we instead assume that the traditional multiplier represents the *only* means of achieving optimal deterrence — as much of the legal literature implicitly assumes today — we will never reach the question of which route is on balance superior, because only one route will even be considered. This accounts for my goal in the first two parts of this article: to show that the multiplier principle is sufficient, but not necessary, for optimal deterrence.

III. THE RESPONSIVENESS OF THE EXPECTED PUNISHMENT

Part IV will discuss the actual advantages and disadvantages of the alternative routes to optimal deterrence. Before beginning that

---

42. *See* Polinsky & Shavell, *supra* note 3, at 900.
43. *See supra* section II.A.

discussion, though, this Part will say more about just when (and why) the expected punishment might respond to changes in a defendant's behavior. As we have already seen, the rate at which the probability of punishment declines is a key factor in determining just how much lower a constant multiplier or a constant fine should be to achieve optimal deterrence. Thus, the responsiveness of the probability of punishment will play a key role in the comparisons in Part IV of this article.

To see how the expected punishment responds to changes in a defendant's behavior, it will be helpful to isolate several components. Before a defendant can be punished, several events must occur: (a) the defendant's offense must be detected by someone; (b) a plaintiff, or a government prosecutor, must decide to file suit; (c) the court, or some other adjudicative body, must find the defendant liable; and (d) the appropriate fine or measure of damages must be assessed. Since all four events must occur before the defendant will be punished, the expected penalty depends on the combined probability of all four — that is, on the probability of detection *times* the probability of prosecution *times* the probability of a finding of liability *times* the expected fine or damage award. Each of these component probabilities will be discussed below.

A. *The Probability of Detection*

In some contexts, the probability of detecting any given offense will be completely *un*responsive to the defendant's behavior. For example, whether a speeding violation is detected typically depends entirely on whether a police officer is present. Moreover, the probability of a police officer being present is normally unaffected by how fast the driver drives, and thus is unresponsive to any improvement in the driver's behavior. In such a case, where the probability of punishment depends *only* on the probability the offense is detected, that probability will not respond to any improvements in a defendant's behavior.[44]

In some cases, though, even the probability of detection may respond to the seriousness of the defendant's behavior. For example, if it is easy to detect that toxic waste has been leaked but hard to detect who was responsible for the leak, the investigating authorities may spend more time tracking down large leaks than tracking

---

44. Interestingly, many analyses of the traditional multiplier principle assumed the only reason for imperfect enforcement was a low probability of *detection*. This is clearly true of the earliest writers such as Beccaria and Bentham, cited *supra* in note 1. It is also true of most of the examples in the recent article by Polinsky & Shavell, *supra* note 3.

down small ones. If so, then manufacturers who permit the risk of large leaks will effectively face a higher probability of detection than will manufacturers who take more precautions and whose leaks are likely to be small.[45] In that event, even the probability of detection will respond to changes in a defendant's behavior.

More important, even when the probability of *detection* is unresponsive to the defendant's behavior, the final probability of punishment will also depend on the probability of prosecution and conviction. As the following subsections demonstrate, these probabilities are almost always responsive to changes in a defendant's behavior.

B.   *The Probability of Litigation*

1.   *The Probability of Prosecution in Systems of Public Enforcement*

Public prosecutors have limited resources, so the probability that a detected offense will be prosecuted is typically less than 100%. While this will reduce the law's deterrent effect, the important point (for present purposes) is that the lower probability will not normally be the same for all defendants, and thus will not be a *constant.* Prosecutors usually have discretion to decide which cases they pursue, and they often try to concentrate their limited prosecutorial resources on the most serious offenses. If so, defendants who improve their behavior will be rewarded with a lower probability of prosecution.

Indeed, it is hard to imagine systems of public prosecution in which this is not true. Police officers, for example, are more likely to stop a speeder who is thirty miles per hour over the speed limit than one who is only five miles per hour over; and pollution authorities are more likely to seek penalties for a huge leak of toxic waste than they are for a small one. Some of this responsiveness may be because it will be easier to win a case against the larger offender than against the marginal one, thus implicating the probability of success at trial (to be discussed in the following subsection). But even if conviction were certain, one would still expect prosecutors to devote the most resources to prosecuting those defendants

---

45. On the other hand, manufacturers who permit large leaks (or commit other serious offenses) may also take greater pains to try to conceal their offense, thereby reducing the probability of punishment. For a formal model of this effect — but one assuming that the probability of punishment does not also vary with the egregiousness of the defendant's behavior, and considering deterrence only by means of a constant fine — see Arun S. Malik, *Avoidance, Screening and Optimum Enforcement,* 21 RAND J. ECON. 341 (1990).

whose violations were the most serious. In any system of public enforcement, then, we should expect the probability of prosecution to decline with improvements in a defendant's behavior. The exact rate of the decline will depend on the extent of the prosecutorial discretion, and on the political and other factors that influence how that discretion is exercised.[46]

2. *The Probability of Litigation Under Private Enforcement*

If enforcement instead depends on private lawsuits, there may be no public-spirited reasons for plaintiffs to concentrate their efforts on the most serious offenses. There may, however, be private motives for them to do so. In particular, if the most serious offenses are also the ones that cause the most damage to their victims, then the victims of the most serious offenses will expect the largest damage awards. All else equal, then, victims of the most serious offenses will also be the ones most likely to find it worthwhile to hire a lawyer and sue. If so, then the most serious offenders will again face the highest probability of suit.[47]

Of course, some kinds of improvements may not have this effect, if they reduce the probability of an accident but do not alter the injury that results if an accident occurs.[48] In that event, since the improvements will not affect the amount that is likely to be recoverable at trial, they also will not affect the probability of litigation. In many cases, though, extra precautions *will* reduce the injury likely to be caused by an accident, and thus will also reduce the amount likely to be recoverable at trial. For example, driving at a lower speed typically reduces the magnitude of any injuries likely to be suffered, as well as reducing the likelihood of any accident at all. Similarly, improvements in a manufacturer's system of quality control often will reduce the average severity of any defects that happen to slip through the system, as well as reducing the likelihood of any defect at all. Whenever improvements in a defendant's

---

46. This suggests that a fruitful line of research might investigate the extent to which, under different systems of punishments, it would be optimal for prosecutors to *try* to make the probability of litigation more or less responsive to changes in a defendant's behavior. I am grateful to Howard Chang for this suggestion.

47. For a mathematical model of just such a system, see Polinsky & Rubinfeld, *supra* note 40. The same argument is also made in A. Mitchell Polinsky, *Are Punitive Damages Really Insignificant, Predictable, and Rational? A Comment on Eisenberg et al.,* 26 J. LEGAL STUD. 663, 675-76 (1997).

48. For a mathematical model employing this alternative assumption, see Keith N. Hylton, *The Influence of Litigation Costs on Deterrence Under Strict Liability and Under Negligence,* 10 INTL. REV. L. & ECON. 161 (1991).

care do reduce the damages victims will suffer, they should also reduce the probability that any victim will bother to sue.

I should note that, when extra precautions do reduce the probability that a victim will sue, there is an additional reason why optimal penalties *could* depart from the traditional multiplier principle. My analysis so far has interpreted the socially efficient level of precautions as the level that minimizes the total accident costs plus the total cost of precautions. However, if litigation is costly then it may be more plausible to define the efficient level of precautions as the level that minimizes the sum of accident costs, precaution costs, *and* litigation costs.[49] If so, reducing the size of the penalty may produce additional benefits by reducing the number of suits that are filed, thus reducing total litigation costs. On the other hand, if the reduced penalty led to fewer precautions and hence a larger number of accidents, then the total number of suits might actually rise (even if the probability that *any given accident* would lead to a suit had declined). As a result, it is hard to say which way penalties should be adjusted to optimize the effect on the total amount of litigation.[50]

Nevertheless, even if the effect on the absolute level of litigation is indeterminate, it remains true that the probability of litigation facing any individual defendant will usually be somewhat responsive to that defendant's behavior. This is enough to give rise to all of the effects analyzed in earlier sections of this article. That is, if the probability of litigation is itself responsive to defendants' behavior, then the overall probability of punishment will also be responsive, because the probability of litigation is simply one component of the overall probability of punishment. And if the overall probability of punishment is responsive to defendants' behavior, then the optimal constant multiplier will again diverge from the optimal case-by-case multiplier, and each of these will diverge from the optimal fine (or the optimal adjustment in any substantive legal standard). In other words, if the probability of litigation responds to improvements in a defendant's behavior, satisfaction of the mul-

---

49. This is the goal assumed in *id.* at 164; and by Polinsky & Rubinfeld, *supra* note 40. For a discussion of these (and other) goals more generally, see Guido Calabresi, The Cost of Accidents: A Legal and Economic Analysis 26-33 (1970).

50. As Polinsky and Rubinfeld conclude, "[t]he optimal adjustment to compensatory damages takes both of these considerations into account, and may be positive or negative." Polinsky & Rubinfeld, *supra* note 40, at 153. For a qualitatively similar analysis, see David D. Friedman, *An Economic Analysis of Punitive Damages*, 40 Ala. L. Rev. 1125, 1133-34 (1989).

Litigation costs could also rise if the amount spent on each suit increased, even if the total number of suits did not. This possibility will be discussed *infra* in section IV.F.

tiplier principle will again be sufficient but not necessary for optimal deterrence.

C. The Probability of Conviction

The effects just discussed will be even more pronounced if improvements in a defendant's behavior also affect the probability of an adverse decision in any case in which a lawsuit has been filed. For simplicity, I will refer to this as "the probability of conviction," though I intend it to include unfavorable decisions in both public prosecutions and private damage actions (where "probability of a finding of liability" would be a more appropriate but more cumbersome label). As the probability of conviction depends largely on the underlying legal standard, I discuss legal regimes based on strict liability separately from those based on negligence.

1. The Probability of Conviction Under Strict Liability

If the legal regime is truly one of strict liability, the probability of conviction may be unresponsive to a defendant's behavior. The probability of conviction may not be 100%, for even regimes of "strict liability" usually require proof of certain elements (was the defendant engaged in the activity? did that activity cause this plaintiff's harm?), and the chance of judicial error on one of these elements may leave defendants facing a probability of punishment below 100%. Still, as long as the chance of error is not correlated with the defendant's level of care, or with the social desirability of any other dimension of the defendant's behavior, the probability of conviction will still be unresponsive to any *improvements* in the defendant's behavior.[51] If so, then any responsiveness in the overall probability of punishment will have to come from other components of that probability, such as the probability of detection or the probability of litigation.

2. The Probability of Conviction Under Negligence

If the legal regime is based on negligence, though, a different picture emerges. A "negligence" regime, as I use that term, is one that conditions liability on whether the defendant conformed to some legally determined standard of behavior. Under such a regime, the probability of conviction should be extremely responsive to improvements in a defendant's behavior.

---

51. Some reasons why this probability might indeed be correlated with the social desirability of the defendant's behavior will be discussed *infra* in subsection III.D.

Indeed, the standard economic analysis of negligence rules has already recognized many of the points made in this article.[52] The earliest analyses focused on perfectly applied negligence rules, in which defendants' liability depended solely on whether they had complied with the legal standard of care. This meant that the probability of punishment declined instantly and dramatically, from 100% all the way to 0%, as soon as defendants came into compliance with the legal standard. A perfectly functioning negligence regime is thus the most extreme case of the phenomenon of interest here, for it yields a probability of punishment that is *extremely* responsive to improvements in a defendant's behavior.

Significantly, analyses of perfect negligence standards have long recognized that the expected measure of damages (if and when liability is found) need not satisfy the traditional multiplier principle.[53] To the contrary, if the probability of punishment falls instantaneously to zero, there will usually be a broad range of fines or damage awards that will suffice to induce compliance with the legal standard. Because defendants who comply with such a standard are rewarded by having their liability eliminated entirely, they will have an incentive to do so as long as the penalty (if they do not comply) equals or exceeds the cost of complying, so any penalty at *or above* that level should lead to optimal deterrence.[54] In other words, under a perfect negligence standard, satisfaction of the multiplier principle clearly is sufficient but not necessary for optimal deterrence.

Of course, most real-world negligence standards are not perfect, and compliance with the standard will not change the probability of conviction from 100% to zero. More realistically, even defendants who comply with the standard might still be held liable through legal error, though that risk will normally decline as they take more care (i.e., as they take precautions well in excess of the legal standard).[55] On the other side of the line, even defendants who do not comply will sometimes be exonerated through judicial error, though

---

52. For a nontechnical discussion, see Cooter, *supra* note 9, at 1526-27, 1538-39.

53. *See, e.g., id.*

54. *See id.* Of course, compliance with the legal standard will produce socially optimal deterrence only if the legal standard is set at the socially efficient level of care.

55. Note that if there were no error or uncertainty of this sort, then defendants would always comply with the negligence standard and would never be found liable, so it would never be worthwhile for plaintiffs to bring suit. In other words, a negligence system with perfect compliance and no uncertainty or error is not a sustainable equilibrium. For mathematical analyses of this aspect of a negligence system, see Keith N. Hylton, *Costly Litigation and Legal Error Under Negligence*, 6 J.L. ECON. & ORG. 433 (1990); Janusz A. Ordover, *Costly Litigation in the Model of Single Activity Accidents*, 7 J. LEGAL STUD. 243 (1978).

this possibility will typically decline as they take less care (i.e., as they fall obviously short of the legal standard). In other words, under most real-world negligence standards, defendants face a continuously declining probability of conviction that varies with the amount of care they actually take.

This continuously declining probability of punishment is precisely what I have assumed throughout the body of this article. That is, in this sort of regime defendants who improve their level of precautions will see their probability of conviction fall from 25% to 20%, or 10%, or some other lower figure (depending on the rate of legal error). Under such a regime, there will no longer be an entire range of punishments that induce compliance with the optimal standard of care, as there would have been under a perfect negligence system. Instead, as we have already seen, there will only be *one* constant multiplier that will create the optimal incentives, just as there will only be one constant fine that is optimal (and only one optimal case-by-case multiplier). And since the optimal case-by-case multiplier will then diverge from the optimal constant multiplier (as well as from the optimal constant fine), there will again be more than one route to optimal deterrence.

It is important to remember, too, that "negligence" as it is used here is a term of art that covers more than its usual legal meaning. That is, in economic analyses of law, "negligence" is used to refer to any regime in which defendants are legally liable for the harm they cause if, but only if, some aspect of their behavior is judged by a court to fall short of some socially desirable level.[56] This term is usually used to mark a contrast with regimes of "strict liability" (another term of art) in which defendants are legally liable without regard to the social desirability of any dimension of their behavior, so the probability of conviction is truly unresponsive to improvements in a defendant's behavior.

Under these definitions, many bodies of law — probably most — are "negligence" regimes. For example, many pollution laws hold defendants liable if (but only if) their pollution exceeds a legally permitted level.[57] Similarly, the law of predatory pricing prohibits monopolists from cutting prices under certain circumstances, if (but only if) the new prices fall below a legally permitted level.[58]

---

56. For a rigorous mathematical definition, see SHAVELL, *supra* note 13, at 8.

57. *See, e.g.,* 40 C.F.R. pts. 425-71 (1998) (EPA effluent guidelines and standards under the Federal Water Pollution Control Act); 33 U.S.C. § 1319 (1994) (penalties for violation of same).

58. For an overview of the relevant legal standards, see Michael L. Denger & John A. Herfort, *Predatory Pricing Claims After* Brooke Group, 62 ANTITRUST L.J. 541 (1994).

And the law of fraud holds defendants liable if (but only if) the allegedly fraudulent statements would have been interpreted by a "reasonable" listener as asserting a false claim, where the judge or jury must decide whether any given statement violates that standard (or whether the statement should instead have been discounted as mere "puffing").[59] This makes each of these doctrines a "negligence" regime, according to the economic definition of that term.

Indeed, even legal doctrines described by courts as "strict liability" are sometimes negligence regimes for purposes of this definition. For example, it is often said that manufacturers are "strictly" liable for all defects that leave their products in an unreasonably dangerous state. When the alleged defect consists of a dangerous design, however, the court must decide whether the design was so bad as to produce an *unreasonably* dangerous product, and the manufacturer will be legally liable if (but only if) the product's design falls short of the standard adopted by the court.[60] This makes the regime one of "negligence" rather than "strict liability" (according to the economic definition), for the defendant's liability depends on the social desirability of its product design choices. By contrast, in strict liability regimes the defendant's liability may depend on how it behaved, but not on the social desirability of its behavior.[61]

My purpose here is not to quibble with the economic definitions, which do serve a useful analytic purpose. Instead, my point is simply that under the vast majority of legal standards — whatever

---

59. When a fraud claim rests on the defendant's failure to disclose information adequately, the court must also decide whether the undisclosed information would have been "material" to a reasonable listener — in other words, whether the defendant's behavior went far enough in disclosing all the information that might have been disclosed. Fleming James, Jr. & Oscar S. Gray, *Misrepresentation* (pt. 2), 37 MD. L. REV. 488, 497-502 (1978). The analogous issues raised in public prosecutions for false advertising are discussed in Richard Craswell, *Interpreting Deceptive Advertising*, 65 B.U. L. REV. 657, 679-81, 696-714 (1985).

60. The same is true if the manufacturer's liability rests on an alleged failure to provide users with an *adequate* warning of the product's risks (thus raising disclosure issues similar to those raised by some claims of "fraud," discussed *supra* in note 59). For more complete discussions of the relationship between "strict liability" and "negligence" in the products liability context see, e.g., Sheila L. Birnbaum, *Unmasking the Test for Design Defect: From Negligence [to Warranty] to Strict Liability to Negligence*, 33 VAND. L. REV. 593 (1980); David G. Owen, *Defectiveness Restated: Exploding the "Strict" Products Liability Myth*, 1996 U. ILL. L. REV. 743.

61. For example, strict liability for ultrahazardous activities (such as dynamiting) attaches only to defendants who engage in that activity, so even this liability is conditional on how the defendant behaved. However, it is not conditional on any judgment about the *social desirability* of the relevant behavior — for example, there is no scrutiny of the desirability of a defendant's decision to engage in dynamiting. This is what makes liability for ultrahazardous activities a regime of "strict liability" even under the economic definition.

label we use to characterize them — the probability of conviction will be highly responsive to changes in a defendant's behavior. Companies whose products impose only slight dangers, or dangers only slightly in excess of their acknowledged benefits, are surely more likely to escape liability than are manufacturers whose products impose greater dangers. Similarly, sellers who disclose all of the most important facts, and omit only a few arguably relevant ones, are more likely to escape liability than are those who disclose nothing whatsoever, omitting even those facts whose importance is obvious. In short, these are all regimes in which the probability of a conviction changes with improvements in a defendant's behavior, and this is enough to generate the effects discussed earlier in this article. (Of course, if the probability of detection and/or the probability of filing suit are *also* responsive to changes in a defendants' behavior, these same effects will be present even in regimes of true strict liability.)

D. *The Probability of Different Damage Awards*

Finally, the legal doctrines governing the measurement of damages can produce similar effects. Moreover, these effects may be present whether the regime is based on negligence or on strict liability. True, the measurement of damages will be irrelevant in any system employing a constant fine, where (by definition) the penalty does not depend on the damages in any particular case. Whenever the penalty does depend on the damages in each case, however, the rules for measuring damages can alter the deterrent effect.

The most relevant doctrines here are those that exclude certain elements from the legally recoverable damages. Sometimes losses are excluded if they were not reasonably foreseeable to the defendant,[62] or if their amount could not be proven with an acceptable degree of precision.[63] Sometimes whole categories of losses may be excluded, as with economic losses in some tort cases,[64] or damages for mental suffering and emotional distress in most breaches of contract.[65] In still other cases, if the defendant's behavior contributed to the victim's harm in only a probabilistic way (by increasing the

---

62. *See, e.g.,* Palsgraf v. Long Island R.R., 162 N.E. 99 (N.Y. 1928); Hadley v. Baxendale, 9 Exch. 341, 156 Eng. Rep. 145 (1854).

63. *See* 4 FOWLER V. HARPER ET AL., THE LAW OF TORTS § 25.3 (2d ed. 1986).

64. *See* 4 *id.* § 25.18a.

65. *See* RESTATEMENT (SECOND) OF CONTRACTS § 353 (1979).

risk of an injury), recovery may be disallowed under the rules governing causation.[66]

Insofar as these exclusions reduce defendants' expected liability, they will reduce the deterrent effect. Indeed, the need to make up for such exclusions from "compensatory" damages has itself been cited as one possible rationale for punitive awards.[67] What is less often noted, however, is that these exclusionary doctrines are often applied in a way that makes them highly responsive to changes in a defendant's underlying behavior. And this responsiveness creates an offsetting effect that *increases* the law's deterrent effect, for all of the reasons discussed earlier in this article.

For example, in cases where the defendant's conduct merely increased the risk of a probabilistic injury, it is often said that a defendant will be liable only if it is "more likely than not" that the defendant's negligence actually caused the plaintiff's injury. In economic analyses, it is sometimes assumed that this rule makes defendants liable if their negligence increased the probability of an injury by more than 50%.[68] If such a 50% cutoff could be applied perfectly, then defendants' expected liability would drop instantaneously to zero once their behavior improved to the point where their contribution to the risk fell below that threshold. In other words, a perfectly applied 50% rule would produce effects very similar to those of the perfectly applied negligence standard discussed earlier.[69] But if there is instead any uncertainty in the application of the 50% cutoff — for example, if defendants cannot know in advance precisely how much of the probability a judge or jury will ascribe to their particular behavior — then the expected punishment will fall more gradually, as defendants who improve their behavior face an increasing likelihood that their behavior will be

---

66. *See* 4 HARPER ET AL., *supra* note 63, § 20.2, at 93-101, 107-10. For economic analyses of this rule, see William M. Landes & Richard A. Posner, *Causation in Tort Law: An Economic Approach*, 12 J. LEGAL STUD. 109 (1983); Rosenberg, *supra* note 30; Steven Shavell, *Uncertainty over Causation and the Determination of Civil Liability*, 28 J.L. & ECON. 587 (1985).

67. *See, e.g.*, Chapman & Trebilcock, *supra* note 3, at 768-69; Thomas C. Galligan, Jr., *Augmented Awards: The Efficient Evolution of Punitive Damages*, 51 LA. L. REV. 3, 39 (1990); *see also* Polinsky & Shavell, *supra* note 3, at 896 ("To the extent that [certain losses are excluded from compensatory damages], an argument can be made that the level of damages should be *higher* than that called for by our multiplier formula . . . ." (emphasis added)). Polinsky and Shavell ultimately recommend that these excluded losses not be used to justify punitive awards, but only because the cost of measuring them will often be too high, and because (when the cost is not too high) a superior solution would be to revise the rules so that those losses were no longer excluded. *See id.* at 939-41.

68. *See, e.g.*, Shavell, *supra* note 66, at 588.

69. *See supra* text accompanying note 52.

found to fall below the relevant cutoff.[70] In other words, defendants who improve their behavior are more likely to be exonerated on causal grounds from full responsibility for all of the losses they may have caused.

More generally, defendants who improve their behavior may also be more likely to receive the benefit of the doubt under most of the other doctrines governing the measurement of damages. In some cases, the categorical exclusion of certain kinds of damages may be relaxed against defendants who behaved in a particularly egregious way.[71] In other cases, the responsiveness may come less from an explicit legal rule and more from biases in the application of a vague legal standard, such as the requirement that losses be proven with *reasonable* certainty,[72] or that the losses have been *reasonably* foreseeable to the defendant.[73] Defendants who behaved well may be more likely to get the benefit of the doubt from the judge (or jury) in these matters, while defendants who behaved badly may be treated more harshly.[74]

The reason this is important, of course, is that if a limit on the recoverability of damages is applied in a way that itself responds to changes in a defendant's behavior, this will increase the law's deterrent effect. That is, even if the absolute level of damages is still less than the harm caused by the violation (because some losses are still being excluded from the measure of damages), there can still be an

---

70. For cases suggesting that the actual rule is applied quite flexibly, see 4 HARPER ET AL., *supra* note 63, § 20.2, at 93-101.

71. *See, e.g.,* Dold v. Outrigger Hotel, 501 P.2d 368, 372 (Haw. 1972) (damages for emotional distress not normally recoverable for breach of contract, but held recoverable in tort if the defendant breached "in a wanton or reckless manner"), *overruled by* Francis v. Lee Enters., Inc., 971 P.2d 707 (Haw. 1999). For discussions of other similar doctrines, see George M. Cohen, *The Fault Lines in Contract Damages,* 80 VA. L. REV. 1225 (1994); and Patricia H. Marschall, *Willfulness: A Crucial Factor in Choosing Remedies for Breach of Contract,* 24 ARIZ. L. REV. 733 (1982).

72. Harper, James, and Gray note an increasing liberality in allowing plaintiffs to recover without proving their loss with literal certainty. They also report that "the tendency is greatest where the nature and impact of defendant's act is such as to make likely the kind of harm that plaintiff is claiming, or to be *especially offensive in light of public policy considerations.*" 4 HARPER ET AL., *supra* note 63, § 25.3, at 510 (emphasis added) (footnote omitted).

73. *See* L.L. Fuller & William R. Perdue, Jr., *The Reliance Interest in Contract Damages* (pt. 1), 46 YALE L.J. 52, 85 (1936) ("As in the case of all 'reasonable man' standards, there is an element of circularity about the test of foreseeability. 'For what items of damages should the court hold the defaulting promisor? Those which he should as a reasonable man have foreseen. But what should he have foreseen as a reasonable man? Those items of damages for which the court feels he ought to pay.'").

74. This aspect of legal bias was often noted by the legal realists. *See, e.g.,* Ralph S. Bauer, *The Degree of Moral Fault as Affecting Defendant's Liability,* 81 U. PA. L. REV. 586 (1933); Fuller & Perdue, *supra* note 73, at 77. For more recent evidence consistent with this view, see Stephan Landsman et al., *Be Careful What You Wish For: The Paradoxical Effects of Bifurcating Claims for Punitive Damages,* 1998 WIS. L. REV. 297, 334-35.

increased marginal incentive if the damages respond sufficiently to *changes* in a defendant's behavior. Here, too, it is the rate of change in the expected liability, rather than the absolute level of liability, that matters for deterrence.

An example will serve to illustrate. In the toxic waste scenario, we originally assumed that each leak would cause $6 million in damages if no extra precautions were taken, and $5 million if the precautions were taken. Suppose now that many of these damages are difficult to measure, or are difficult to attribute to any particular defendant. But suppose, too, that more of these losses will be attributed to defendants who did not take any extra precautions than to defendants who did take precautions, simply because the former are less likely to get the benefit of any doubt. For concreteness, suppose that defendants who did not take the precautions will be assessed $5 million in damages each time they are caught (as compared to the $6 million in damages their activity actually caused), while defendants who did take precautions will be charged with only $1 million in damages (as compared to the $5 million they actually caused). In other words, suppose that both types of defendants get away with paying less than the full social costs of their behavior, but that this shortfall is greatest for defendants who took the extra precautions.

In such a case, even if the probability of punishment is 25% for both defendants (and thus is completely *un*responsive to changes in their behavior), defendants will still have an incentive to take the optimal level of care. It might seem as though their incentives in this case would have to favor underdeterrence, since neither defendant is being charged with the full social costs of its behavior, and since both defendants are discounting these already-low penalties by the same 25% probability of punishment. However, in this example defendants who do not take the extra precautions will face an expected liability of $12,500 ($.01 \times .25 \times \$5,000,000$), while defendants who do take the precautions will see their expected liability fall to $2,500 ($.01 \times .25 \times \$1,000,000$). This means that the precautions can save defendants $10,000 in expected liability ($12,500 − $2,500), which just equals the social value of the precautions and thus achieves optimal deterrence.

The lesson here is the same as it was in preceding subsections of this article. That is, it is not simply the absolute level of expected liability that matters, but rather the *rate* at which that expected liability declines with improvements in a defendant's behavior. It will be relatively rare for that decline to come from changes in the mere probability of detection, but it should be quite common — the rule, rather than the exception — for improvements in a defendant's behavior to reduce the probability of prosecution, the probability of conviction, and/or the likely damage award. Declines in any of these factors will cause a divergence between the optimal case-by-case multiplier and the optimal constant multiplier (or the optimal constant fine). As a result, satisfaction of the traditional multiplier principle will be sufficient but not necessary for optimal deterrence — and this conclusion, too, should be considered the rule rather than the exception.

IV. CHOOSING AMONG THE ALTERNATIVES

We are now in a position to compare the strengths and weak-nesses of case-by-case multipliers, constant multipliers, and the other alternative penalty systems discussed above. While any of these systems could, in theory, lead to optimal levels of deterrence, they differ in many other respects that could make them more or less desirable. In this final Part of the article, I consider differences based on their relative ease of administration; their effect on other economically relevant variables, such as the level of overall activity or the optimal allocation of risk; and their possible symbolic or ex-pressive effects.

A. *Ease of Calculation*

One virtue of the traditional multiplier principle is that it is con-ceptually simple and, therefore, easy to explain to a judge or jury. The case-by-case multiplier requires only two pieces of information: the actual harm caused by the defendant's behavior, and the actual probability of punishment that the defendant faced. And while it will rarely be possible to measure either of these elements precisely, in many cases it should be possible to come to a rough estimate.[75] Moreover, all that really matters under this approach is that the average or *expected* penalty equal the actual harm divided by the probability of punishment, so it may not even matter if juries err as long as their errors are not systematically biased in either direction.[76]

By contrast, many of the alternative remedies are more difficult to calculate. For example, to determine the optimal constant multi-

---

75. *See* Polinsky & Shavell, *supra* note 3, at 891-93. For somewhat more skeptical views, based on the psychology of jury decision-making, see Sunstein et al., *supra* note 4, at 2111-12; Viscusi, *supra* note 4, at 327-32.

76. *See* Polinsky & Shavell, *supra* note 3, at 892.

plier, the decisionmaker must know several factors in addition to the actual harm caused by the defendant's behavior and the actual probability of punishment. In addition, the decisionmaker must be able to estimate the actual harm that would have been present, and the probability of punishment the defendant would have faced, if the defendant had instead committed a slightly more or slightly less serious violation. In particular, the decisionmaker must be able to measure each set of factors with sufficient precision to estimate the *difference* between the two violations, in order to calculate the rate of *change* in the relevant variables. Finally, once these estimates have been made, they must then be combined through a formula that is more complicated than simply multiplying by one over the probability of punishment.[77] Thus, the optimal constant multiplier will always be harder to calculate than the optimal case-by-case multiplier.

The same objection can be raised against many of the other alternatives discussed above. For example, calculating the optimal constant to add or subtract from a compensatory award, or the optimal amount by which to adjust the substantive legal standard, is just as complex as calculating the optimal constant multiplier.[78] Calculating the optimal constant fine is slightly simpler conceptually, for this requires knowledge of only (a) the rate at which the probability of punishment changes in response to changes in defendants' behavior, and (b) the rate at which the expected social costs change in response to changes in defendants' behavior.[79] But information about these hypothetical rates of change will often be hard to come by, compared to information about the actual social harm and the actual probability of punishment. As a result, the case-by-case multiplier will surely rank highest in ease of calculation.

---

77. If x represents the defendant's level of precautions, $H(x)$ represents the expected social harm at any particular level of precautions, and $P(x)$ represents the probability of punishment at any particular level of precautions, then the optimal case-by-case multiplier is given by a simple fraction: $1/P(x)$. To calculate the optimal constant multiplier, we need to let x^* represent the socially optimal level of precautions, and $H'(x^*)$ and $P'(x^*)$ represent the *rate* at which the social harm and the probability of punishment change with slight deviations from the optimal level of precautions. The optimal constant multiplier can then be written as the following complex formula:

$$\frac{H'(x^*)}{H'(x^*)\ P(x^*) + H(x^*)\ P'(x^*)}$$

See Craswell & Calfee, *supra* note 13, at 294. Obviously, this complex formula would be more difficult to present to a judge or jury.

78. *See* Polinsky & Rubinfeld, *supra* note 40, at 159-60, app.

79. Using the notation introduced *supra* in note 77, the optimal constant fine can be represented by the simple fraction $H'(x^*)/P'(x^*)$. *See* Craswell & Calfee, *supra* note 13, at 297.

B. *Institutional Responsibility*

Another difference is that a case-by-case multiplier, by its very nature, must be calculated separately for each defendant, so all the calculations must be made by a judge or jury. By contrast, a constant multiplier could be set once by a legislature or administrative agency, leaving judges and juries with only the task (in each individual case) of measuring the losses to which the constant multiplier would be applied. If a constant fine were used, the judge or jury would not even need to calculate the actual losses in each case, thus shifting even more of the work to a centralized body.

The ability to make such calculations centrally *could* be an advantage. Obviously, it is sometimes cheaper to have calculations made once by a centralized body, rather than making them anew in every case. A centralized body may also be able to assemble more expertise than a judge or a jury — for example, it could commission statistical studies of the probability of punishment and the rate at which it changes. A centralized body can also benefit from the ability to "fine tune" a constant multiplier or a constant fine (or an adjustment to the substantive legal standard), raising or lowering it until the desired level of deterrence is achieved. Finally, in some contexts (or from some perspectives) a centralized body might be seen as more "democratic" or politically accountable.

On the other hand, there are also drawbacks to a centralized decision process, which may make these advantages moot. A centralized body may be more prone to political "capture" by groups favorable to plaintiffs or defendants.[80] Also, even a well-motivated central body must face the practical problem of defining, in advance, the exact class of cases to which any particular fine or multiplier would be applied. After all, the constant multiplier that is optimal for malpractice cases is unlikely to be the same as the one that is optimal for products liability cases; it may also be different for some malpractice cases than for others. Thus, any centralized solution must either (a) define a separate penalty for many different categories of cases, with the attendant difficulty of defining the boundaries of each; or (b) rely on a smaller number of relatively crude categories, recognizing that the penalty selected for each category will not be ideal for every case within that category.

By contrast, one advantage of a decentralized system is that it is unnecessary to define such categories in advance. As Polinsky and

---

80. The legislatively enacted caps on punitive damage awards, discussed *supra* in the text following note 41, may be an example of this.

Shavell pointed out in their analysis of the case-by-case multiplier, courts can estimate the probability of punishment facing any particular defendant without having to assign that defendant to some a priori category: they can define that probability based on whatever is known about this individual defendant's characteristics.[81] To be sure, this does not mean that judges or juries will necessarily get the probability right, for (as the preceding subsection discussed) even case-by-case calculations cannot be based on anything more than a rough estimate of the relevant variables. But since judges and juries decide cases after the fact, they will at least be spared the cost of trying to define relevant categories *in advance,* which is an unavoidable cost of any centralized calculation.

In short, there may be cases where the appropriate penalty can best be calculated centrally, and in those cases the traditional case-by-case multiplier will be inferior (insofar as ease of calculation is concerned). In many cases, though, the costs of centralization will be too high, so both the case-by-case multiplier and the possible alternatives will have to be estimated in every case by individual judges or juries. In that event, the advantage in terms of ease of calculation will usually rest with the traditional case-by-case multiplier, for the reasons discussed in the preceding subsection.

C. *Optimal Levels of Activity*

In addition, whenever it is important to optimize defendants' levels of activity, the case-by-case multiplier may well be superior. As Steven Shavell first emphasized, many social costs can be reduced by carrying on an activity more carefully *or* by reducing the frequency of the activity itself.[82] For example, drivers can reduce the number of auto accidents by driving more carefully, but they can also reduce the number of accidents by using their cars less fre-

---

81. *See* Polinsky & Shavell, *supra* note 3, at 893. More precisely, the probability can be estimated based on (1) all facts that were known to the defendant at the time it chose its level of care, together with (2) any other facts that did not become known until later, but only if those facts were just as likely to raise the probability as to lower it. The qualification is important because it would not be correct, under the traditional multiplier principle, to calculate the probability of punishment for a narrow category defined as "all defendants who behaved in the following way *and* who happened to leave evidence that allowed their victim to bring suit and prevail at trial." The probability of punishment for defendants who are defined in this way is, of course, exactly one, so calculating the multiplier on this basis would be the same as employing no multiplier at all.

For a more general discussion of the choice between categorical and individualized judgments, see Louis Kaplow, *Rules Versus Standards: An Economic Analysis,* 42 DUKE L.J. 557 (1992).

82. *See* Steven Shavell, *Strict Liability Versus Negligence,* 9 J. LEGAL STUD. 1, 2-3 (1980).

quently. Thus, optimizing the level of activity can also be a legitimate goal of deterrence policy.

Significantly, negligence regimes often do not give defendants any direct incentive to constrain their levels of activity. Negligence regimes can easily condition liability on whether a driver was exercising appropriate care, and this gives drivers an incentive to choose their care appropriately. But such regimes rarely condition liability on whether a defendant drove with unnecessary frequency (probably because of the difficulty of determining a "reasonable" frequency), so they give drivers no incentive to limit their total amount of driving. In terms of the analysis used in this article, the probability of being held liable (for any given accident) usually is not responsive at all to any change in the number of miles the defendant drove.

If enforcement is perfect, strict liability regimes can improve defendants' incentives to adjust their levels of activity. In theory, strict liability forces defendants to internalize all of the social costs caused by their activity, and thus gives them an incentive to think about *every* way of reducing those costs, including engaging in the activity less frequently.[83] Even under a regime of strict liability, however, imperfect enforcement will dilute a defendant's incentives. That is, if a driver (or a firm employing a fleet of drivers) should be liable for every accident that results, but if there is only a 25% chance that any given accident will lead to a successful suit, the firm's liability will reflect only 25% of the costs its activity imposes, thus giving it too weak an incentive to reduce its amount of driving. In such a case, the traditional multiplier can restore the optimal incentives by multiplying the firm's expected liability by four, thus making the firm again bear the full social costs of its driving activity.

It might seem, then, that whenever the level of the defendant's activity can affect social costs, the traditional multiplier would always be the better way of achieving optimal deterrence. However, this conclusion is subject to three important limitations. First, the traditional multiplier only produces this effect in regimes of "strict liability," as that term was defined earlier.[84] In "negligence" regimes, defendants will still escape responsibility for the social costs of their activities whenever they are found to have complied with the legal standard, so even a traditional multiplier will not optimize

---

83. *See id.*
84. *See supra* text accompanying note 56.

levels of activity. And since most legal regimes really are "negligence" regimes (under the definition used here), this argument for the traditional multiplier is of limited applicability.

Second, even under regimes of "strict liability," there are a few cases in which increases in the level of activity could increase the probability of punishment per violation. For example, if one of a company's trucks is detected leaking toxic chemicals, the authorities may then decide to inspect all the other trucks owned by that firm. If so, the per-violation probability of punishment will indeed respond to changes in the overall quantity of driving, because increased driving brings a greater probability that at least one of the firm's trucks will be detected leaking chemicals, thus triggering an inspection of all the trucks. While this form of interdependence is probably not very common, it sometimes occurs in the investigation of criminal activities (tax fraud, racketeering, drug rings, etc.), where detection of one offense triggers close investigation of all of a defendant's activities.

Third, even when the traditional multiplier is superior in its effect on levels of activity, it may give rise to other problems that outweigh this benefit. After all, the level of activity is only one of the dimensions of social cost with which the law should be concerned. As the remaining subsections will discuss, there are other dimensions along which a case-by-case multiplier might sometimes be inferior to the alternative routes to optimal deterrence.

D.   *Optimal Levels of Risk*

As noted earlier, the optimal case-by-case multiplier will typically be greater than (and will never be any less than) the optimal constant multiplier. This could make the case-by-case multiplier inferior from the standpoint of optimal levels of risk, quite independently of any effect the multiplier might have on levels of deterrence. If either defendants or their victims are risk averse, there will be benefits from keeping the total amount of risk in the system at a minimum. In a world of imperfect enforcement, however, a case-by-case multiplier increases the risk in the system because it presents defendants with the risk of paying even larger penalties. This could be a drawback in either of two situations.

First, as Polinsky and Shavell have noted, the effect on risk is a drawback if defendants are risk averse and full insurance is unavailable.[85] If defendants are risk averse, a 25% chance of having to pay $20 million in damages (as the traditional multiplier would recommend) will press on them more than four times as heavily as a 25% chance of having to pay only $5 million. The larger award thus could produce too much of a deterrent effect; and the larger award could also reduce total welfare directly, by forcing defendants to bear the disutility of this increased risk. However, the significance of these drawbacks are limited by the fact that they apply only to defendants who are risk averse, and even then only if they cannot get liability insurance (which would transfer the risk to a risk neutral insurance company). Most damage awards are legally insurable.[86] Even when they are not, many defendants are publicly held corporations who can usually be presumed to be risk neutral, or capable of self insurance through diversification of their shareholders' portfolios.[87]

Even when insurance is readily available, however, the effect on risk may still be a drawback if *victims* are risk averse, at least when the defendant and its victims stand in a market relationship (such as seller-customer or employer-employee). To be sure, there is sometimes no need for any liability at all when the defendant and its victims stand in a market relationship, if the victims are well informed about the risks and so the defendant will have adequate market incentives to improve its behavior.[88] In some markets, though, potential victims may not be quite so well-informed, in which case market incentives alone may be inadequate for optimal deterrence. This, at least, is the standard argument for any form of liability for deterrence purposes when defendants and their victims stand in a market relationship.[89] And if the enforcement of such liability is imperfect, the same arguments that would call for a dam-

---

85. *See* Polinsky & Shavell, *supra* note 3, at 886-87. For more technical economic analyses, see Louis A. Kaplow, *The Optimal Probability and Magnitude of Fines for Acts That Definitely Are Undesirable,* 12 INTL. REV. L. & ECON. 3, 6-8 (1992); A. Mitchell Polinsky & Steven Shavell, *The Optimal Tradeoff Between the Probability and Magnitude of Fines,* 69 AM. ECON. REV. 880, 884-85 (1979); Steven Shavell, *On Liability and Insurance,* 13 BELL J. ECON. 120, 124-26 (1982).

86. Even punitive damage awards are insurable in some states. *See* Polinsky & Shavell, *supra* note 3, at 931 n.193.

87. *See id.* at 887 n.44. Obviously, this conclusion would not apply to the extent that the risk in question was systematic (e.g., the risk of a change in legal rules that would increase the expected liability of *all* corporations).

88. *See id.* at 935-36.

89. For formal economic models, see, e.g., Shavell, *supra* note 82, at 14-17; Michael Spence, *Consumer Misperceptions, Product Failure and Producer Liability,* 44 REV. ECON. STUD. 561 (1977).

age multiplier in other contexts would appear to call for a multiplier in market relationships as well.[90]

The important point about market relationships, though, is that defendants' expected liability will ultimately have to be borne by consumers in the form of higher prices.[91] For example, if product defects cause $5 million in damages but defendants are held liable only 25% of the time, a premium will have to be added to the product's price to cover the defendant's expected liability of $1.25 million (.25 × $5,000,000). If the legal system then adopts the traditional case-by-case multiplier, thus making defendants pay $20 million every time they are caught (4 × $5,000,000), their expected liability will rise to $5 million (.25 × 4 × $5,000,000), so the price premium will have to be four times as large. In other words, the good news is that those consumers who are lucky enough to bring a successful lawsuit will have their recovery increased by a factor of four, but the bad news is that all consumers will have to pay an up-front price that includes a premium that is four times as large. In effect, the introduction of a multiplier turns the liability component of the price into a lottery ticket, with a bigger price up front supporting the chance of a bigger payoff at the end.

If customers are risk neutral, they will be indifferent toward this lottery; and if they are risk-preferring then they might actually like this sort of a gamble. It is more plausible, though, to assume that customers are risk averse, at least with respect to this sort of contingency. Those who would like some additional gamble can always go to the race track or play the state lottery, and it would be odd to posit a taste for gambling that could only be satisfied by wagering on a particular product defect. For most customers, then, the introduction of this extra lottery element will make the product less attractive, causing an additional welfare loss.[92]

Moreover, this effect (unlike the effect on risk averse *defendants*) will not disappear with the purchase of insurance. While full insurance can protect parties from many forms of risk, in this context consumers could be protected only by purchasing "reverse" insurance of a sort that is rarely available. That is, consumers

---

90. Polinsky & Shavell, *supra* note 3, at 935; *see also id.* at 938 (making the same argument for punitive damages in breach of contract cases). Breach of contract cases, by definition, always involve defendants and victims who were in a market relationship.

91. For a review of the literature on this point, see Richard Craswell, *Passing On the Costs of Legal Rules: Efficiency and Distribution in Buyer-Seller Relationships*, 43 STAN. L. REV. 361 (1991).

92. I develop this point at more length in Richard Craswell, *Damage Multipliers in Market Relationships*, 25 J. LEGAL STUD. 463 (1994).

would need a policy in which the insurance company paid the consumer up front (rather than the consumer paying an insurance premium), in return for which the consumer would assign to the insurance company his or her right to the punitive portion of any damage award. In theory, the up-front payment by the insurance company would exactly compensate the consumer for that part of the higher product price that reflected the punitive portion of the defendant's expected liability. Such a policy would thus have the same effect as restoring consumers to the premultiplier regime, in which they paid a lower price and were limited to compensatory damages if they sued. But since this sort of reverse insurance is rarely available, most consumers will have no way to insulate themselves from the risk-increasing effect of the larger, case-by-case multiplier.[93]

Of course, even when this risk-increasing effect is a drawback, that may not be sufficient reason to reject the traditional multiplier. If damage multipliers are used only rarely, the effect on total risk-bearing costs is not likely to be very large.[94] Moreover, the effect on risk averse parties is only one of the relevant consequences the law must consider, and a slight negative effect on risk averse consumers might be outweighed by greater improvements in (say) the ease of administration, or the effects on defendants' levels of activity. My point here is simply that *all* of these effects must be considered before any overall decision is reached — and that in evaluating this totality of effects, the effect on risk averse consumers will usually count as a negative.

E. *Practical Constraints on the Maximum Penalty*

The traditional, case-by-case multiplier may also be less desirable if defendants have limited assets, and would be unable to pay a fine as high as that required by the multiplier principle. This constraint is particularly likely to be a problem when the probability of punishment is small, so the penalty required under a case-by-case multiplier would be large. For example, if a violation causes $5 mil-

---

93. One possible way of providing such insurance might be a market in which consumers could sell their right to recovery in advance, at the same time they purchased the product. For a discussion of how this market might work, see Robert Cooter, *Towards a Market in Unmatured Tort Claims*, 75 VA. L. REV. 383 (1989). As Cooter points out, though, these transactions are illegal under current law. *See id.* at 383 & n.1.

94. For empirical evidence consistent with this view, at least where punitive damages are concerned, see Jonathan M. Karpoff & John R. Lott, Jr., *Punitive Damages: Their Determinants, Effects on Firm Value, and the Impact of Supreme Court and Congressional Attempts to Limit Awards*, 52 J.L. & ECON. (forthcoming 1999).

lion worth of damages but brings only a 25% probability of punishment, the optimal case-by-case multiplier would require a fine of $20 million (4 × $5,000,000). But if many defendants are thinly capitalized firms, the threat of an $20 million penalty may have no more effect than the threat of a $9 or $10 million penalty, if $9 or $10 million is the most they could possibly pay. Indeed, in some cases the adoption of larger penalties could even *reduce* deterrence, by giving potential defendants an incentive to operate with even less capital than they otherwise might. This would make it even more likely that these defendants would not have to pay the full legal penalty (because they would not have enough money to pay it), and so would further reduce the law's deterrent effect.[95]

One possible solution to this problem is to (1) raise the penalty as high as possible, then (2) make up for any remaining underdeterrence by improving the enforcement system to raise the probability of punishment.[96] In the above example, if the maximum fine that could possibly be collected is only $10 million, optimal incentives could still be achieved if the enforcement system were improved to raise the probability of punishment from 25% to 50%, since that would make the expected penalty equal the expected social harm (.50 × $10,000,000 = $5,000,000). However, improving the enforcement system has costs of its own that must also be taken into account. As a result, this solution usually leads to a compromise in which the probability of punishment is raised to some extent (at some cost), but it is not raised high enough to satisfy the multiplier principle.[97]

What is less often noted, though, is that the alternative routes to optimal deterrence may provide another solution to this problem. As we have seen, alternatives such as a constant multiplier or a constant fine typically require smaller penalties than those required by the case-by-case multiplier. As a result, the fines or damage awards required under these alternatives are less likely to run up against

---

95. For an economic model of this effect, see James Boyd & Daniel E. Ingberman, *Do Punitive Damages Promote Deterrence?*, 19 INTL. REV. L. & ECON. 47 (1999). For an analysis of the effect of limited capital on deterrence generally, see S. Shavell, *The Judgment-Proof Problem*, 6 INTL. REV. L. & ECON. 45 (1986).

96. Polinsky & Shavell, *supra* note 3, allude to this possibility at 922 n.167.

97. For mathematical analyses of these trade-offs, see A. Mitchell Polinsky & Steven Shavell, *A Note on Optimal Fines When Wealth Varies Among Individuals*, 81 AM. ECON. REV. 618 (1991); A. Mitchell Polinsky & Steven Shavell, *supra* note 85, 69 AM. ECON. REV. 883 (1979); A. Mitchell Polinsky & Steven Shavell, *The Optimal Use of Fines and Imprisonment*, 24 J. PUB. ECON. 89 (1984) [hereinafter Polinsky & Shavell, *Fines and Imprisonment*]. As the second of these articles indicates, another possible solution to the problem of defendants with limited assets — albeit a solution with costs of its own — is to resort to nonmonetary sanctions such as imprisonment. *See* Polinsky & Shavell, *Fines and Imprisonment, supra*.

the constraints imposed by defendants' limited assets. Where limited assets are a problem, then, these alternatives may actually be superior to the traditional multiplier.

Moreover, there are other factors besides limited assets that may constrain the maximum penalty. Jurors (even judges or prosecutors) are sometimes reluctant to impose penalties that seem "too large," thus constraining the maximum penalty through jury nullification (or through the exercise of prosecutorial discretion).[98] Whenever this is likely, the effect will be the same as if the maximum penalty were constrained for any other reason. In particular, if this constraint is below the size of the penalty required by the multiplier principle, the case-by-case multiplier will lead to underdeterrence. Here, too, there may be an advantage to one of the alternatives that can achieve optimal deterrence with smaller penalties.

F. *Litigation Costs*

Because of their smaller size, the alternatives to the traditional multiplier may also reduce the amount spent on litigation in any particular case.[99] This is so for two reasons: the total stakes will be lower, and not as much will turn on establishing any particular probability of punishment.

First, a traditional multiplier raises the stakes involved in litigating other issues, such as the amount of damages to which the multiplier will be applied (or the underlying issue of liability itself). Under a system with no multiplier at all, defendants obviously will have some incentive to try to convince the court that their behavior did not do very much harm, or that they should not be found liable at all. But if case-by-case multipliers are used, every reduction in the measure of damages will be three times as valuable to the defendant if the multiplier is three, or five times or ten times as valuable (if the multiplier is five or ten). To be sure, the measure of damages and the question of underlying liability will also take on greater importance under any regime using a constant multiplier, as long as that multiplier is greater than one. But since the optimal constant multiplier will almost always be less than the optimal

---

98. An economic model with some of these features — specifically, a model in which finders of fact implicitly raise the burden of proof when higher sanctions are sought — is presented in James Andreoni, *Reasonable Doubt and the Optimal Magnitude of Fines: Should the Punishment Fit the Crime?*, 22 RAND J. ECON. 385 (1991).

99. The effect on *total* litigation costs, by increasing or decreasing the number of suits that are filed, was discussed in *supra* text accompanying notes 49-50.

case-by-case multiplier, the incentive to spend on litigation should at least be lower if a constant multiplier is used (and similarly for a constant fine, or for an adjustment to the substantive standard with no adjustment in liability).

Second, a case-by-case multiplier also gives parties an incentive to spend money litigating the size of the multiplier itself. Consider, for example, a defendant who caused $5 million worth of damages, and for whom the probability of punishment was somewhere around 20%. If the court finds that the probability of punishment was exactly 20%, the case-by-case multiplier will be set at five and the defendant will have to pay $25 million in damages (5 × $5,000,000). But if the defendant persuades the court that the probability of punishment was really 25%, the case-by-case multiplier will then be set at four, and the damage award will be reduced to $20 million (4 × $5,000,000). In other words, the defendant can save $5 million in liability ($25,000,000 – $20,000,000) just by altering the court's perception of the probability by five percentage points. This is the same as the amount the defendant could gain by establishing that it was not liable at all, thus reducing its liability from $5,000,000 to 0, in a regime that did not use any multipliers. For many litigants, then, it will pay to spend just as much litigating the probability of punishment (in a system with case-by-case multipliers) as they would spend contesting liability itself (in a system with purely compensatory damages).

Of course, if there is a chance they could alter the court's finding on probability even more — say, by raising it from 20% to 33%, thus reducing the multiplier from five to three — they will have an incentive to spend even more. By contrast, this incentive will be eliminated in any system employing a constant multiplier or a constant fine. For all of these reasons, then, the amount spent litigating each case should be significantly higher under the traditional case-by-case multiplier.

G. *Symbolic or Expressive Effects*

Finally, the alternatives to the case-by-case multiplier may also have symbolic or expressive advantages. Recall that, when the probability of punishment declines with improvements in a defendant's behavior (as it usually will), the case-by-case multiplier has to be largest for those defendants who behaved relatively well (to make up for their low probability of punishment), and smallest for defendants who behaved relatively badly. For instance, in one of the examples discussed earlier, defendants who took extra precautions saw their probability of punishment fall from 25% to 10%, thus increasing the case-by-case multiplier from four to ten.[100] The actual damages in that example were $6 million without the extra precautions and $5 million with the precautions. With a case-by-case multiplier, however, defendants who took the extra precautions had to pay $50 million every time they were caught (10 × $5,000,000), while defendants who did not take the precautions had to pay only $24 million (4 × $6,000,000).

A possible objection is that this inverts the "fair" or "just" relation between wrongfulness of behavior and severity of punishment, by punishing those who behave well more harshly than those who behave badly. The objection is not that this will distort such parties' incentives, because incentives depend on the *expected* levels of punishment, and the expected punishment is more severe for defendants who do not take precautions (.25 × 4 × $6,000,000 = $6,000,000) than for defendants who do (.10 × 10 × $5,000,000 = $5,000,000). But it is sometimes argued that justice places independent constraints on the penalties that can be meted out by the state — independent, that is, of any utilitarian or deterrence-related goals — and that the regime described here would run afoul of those constraints.[101] Indeed, the Supreme Court has suggested (though without addressing this precise issue) that some proportionality between the size of the penalty and the wrongfulness of the defendant's conduct may even be constitutionally required.[102]

Moreover, even those who object to deontological constraints on the size of the permissible penalties might still worry that bad consequences would follow from a regime that punished mild offenses more severely than egregious ones. It is sometimes said that one function of law is to educate its citizens and to instill appropriate attitudes concerning right and wrong.[103] Presumably, this expressive or educative function includes expressing appropriate at-

---

100. *See supra* text following note 14.

101. *Cf.* IMMANUEL KANT, THE METAPHYSICAL ELEMENTS OF JUSTICE 100 (John Ladd trans., Bobbs-Merril Co. 1965) (1916) ("The law concerning punishment is a categorical imperative, and woe to him who rummages around in the winding paths of a theory of happiness [i.e:, utility] looking for some advantage to be gained. . . ."). For modern discussions of this position, describing in more detail its conflict with the multiplier principle, see Chapman & Trebilcock, *supra* note 3, at 779-98; Alan H. Goldman, *The Paradox of Punishment,* 9 PHIL. & PUB. AFF. 42 (1979).

102. *See* BMW of N. Am., Inc. v. Gore, 517 U.S. 559, 575-76, 580-81 (1996).

103. Paul H. Robinson & John M. Darley, *The Utility of Desert,* 91 NW. U. L. REV. 453, 472-73 (1997). For further development of this idea in connection with punitive damages, see Marc Galanter & David Luban, *Poetic Justice: Punitive Damages and Legal Pluralism,* 42 AM. U. L. REV. 1393, 1430-40 (1993).

titudes about relative *degrees* of wrongfulness. But the regime described above could send the wrong signal in this regard, as it could suggest that defendants who took the extra precautions (and therefore had to pay $50 million) had behaved worse than the defendants who did not take the extra precautions (and who only had to pay $24 million).[104] If citizens' attitudes are shaped by this incorrect signal, that could affect the citizens' willingness to reduce their own pollution (or even their willingness to comply with laws in general), thus raising the cost of achieving any given level of deterrence.

To be sure, each of these arguments has difficulties of its own. It is controversial (to say the least) whether we ought to accept purely deontological constraints on the size of permissible punishments. Moreover, the argument that inverted penalties will send the wrong moral message depends on a kind of misperception on the part of the audience of the signal. That is, if citizens realized that the regime described above was adopted solely for its deterrent virtues, and that the difference in penalties therefore expressed only the fact that the probability of punishment was different for the two defendants, there would then be no reason for citizens to draw an incorrect moral lesson. Indeed, if citizens realized that the *expected* penalty was actually harsher for defendants who did not take extra precautions, they might continue to draw the correct moral lesson, in which case the law's expressive or educative effect would be reinforced. The concern that citizens will draw the wrong moral lesson thus rests on an implicit assumption of "noise" or miscommunication between the message intended by the drafters of the policy and the message understood by the citizenry. And while such errors or misperceptions are no doubt common, it is notoriously difficult to predict the exact form they will take.

Still, the fact that such misperceptions are possible means that this concern cannot be dismissed out of hand. My only point here is that, to the extent this danger is real, it too can be avoided by using one of the alternatives to the traditional multiplier principle. Since these alternatives all allow the actual penalties (not just the expected penalties) to increase in severity with the egregiousness of the defendant's behavior, they would not pose any risk of the moral misperception at issue here.

---

104. This very objection is made by Galanter & Luban, *supra* note 103, at 1449-50.

V. CONCLUSIONS

As we have seen, the traditional multiplier of one over the probability of punishment can achieve optimal deterrence if it is recalculated on a case-by-case basis, to reflect the probability of punishment facing each individual defendant. Moreover, if it is applied in this way, the traditional multiplier will be optimal in a wide variety of circumstances, regardless of whether the premultiplier incentives favored under- or overdeterrence. Because a case-by-case multiplier can achieve optimal deterrence using a relatively simple formula under so broad a range of conditions, it is perhaps not surprising that the law review literature has focused almost exclusively on this method of correcting for imperfect enforcement.

In fact, though, the law uses a variety of other methods that do not fit the traditional multiplier principle. Sometimes the law uses a constant multiplier; sometimes it uses constant fines; and sometimes it uses adjustments to the substantive legal standard. Indeed, while all of these methods are relatively common, it is very difficult to find examples of a true case-by-case multiplier, in which defendants whose conduct faces a high probability of punishment are "rewarded" with a multiplier lower than that given to defendants whose conduct is less likely to be punished. Unfortunately, the legal literature has focused so much on the case-by-case multiplier principle that it has not even begun to address the pros and cons of these alternative (and much more common) systems of deterrence. This article is an attempt to begin to fill that gap. While its conclusions are necessarily tentative, several points can be made.

First, the traditional analysis is still perfectly valid whenever the probability of punishment is essentially unresponsive to changes in a defendant's behavior. This is most likely to be the case when the probability of punishment depends entirely on whether the defendant's offense is detected. In other words, the traditional analysis is strongest if, once the offense is detected, prosecution and conviction (or litigation and civil liability) are virtually sure to follow. If, in addition, the probability of detection depends purely on chance, rather than on a prosecutorial decision to allocate more resources to detecting serious offenses; and if any rules excluding certain losses from the fine or damage award are applied no more harshly against defendants who behaved badly than against defendants who behaved well, the expected punishment will then be completely independent of any improvements in a defendant's behavior. In such a case, there will be no difference between the optimal case-by-case multiplier and the optimal constant multiplier (or the optimal constant fine), and all of them will have to satisfy the traditional multiplier principle.

In all other cases, however, the probability of punishment will respond to improvements in defendants' behavior. In these cases, as we have seen, satisfaction of the multiplier principle will no longer be necessary for optimal deterrence (though it may still be sufficient). For example, the optimal constant multiplier will generally be less than the level called for by the multiplier principle, perhaps even at or below compensatory levels. The optimal fine, too, could also be less than the traditional multiplier principle, though in some cases it could be greater. Moreover, if adjustments to the substantive legal standard are also employed, the optimal fine or damage award could be even less. On the other hand, if the substantive standard is relaxed considerably, to the point where a defendant who behaves optimally faces no risk whatsoever of being found in violation of the standard, the penalties for those found in violation could then be substantially *raised* without interfering with optimal deterrence.

In any of these cases, the law faces a choice about which strategy to use to achieve optimal deterrence. This is the choice whose investigation I have tried to begin. Preliminarily, I can suggest that the case-by-case multiplier will work best whenever it is extremely important to optimize defendants' levels of activity as well as their levels of care, and/or if it is more efficient to have all the calculations needed for deterrence made anew by a judge or jury in each individual case. On the other hand, one of the other strategies will probably be best if it is more efficient to have these calculations made by a central legislative or administrative body, and/or if there are practical constraints on the maximum penalty the law can assess, thus requiring penalties below the traditional multiplier. One of the alternative strategies may also be best if it is important to preserve a direct relationship between the harmfulness of a defendant's conduct and the size of the actual penalty that is imposed, either because such proportionality is constitutionally required, or because it is desirable in order to send the proper symbolic message.

I have stressed that these conclusions are tentative, and doubtless they could be improved or refined through further analysis. Until we recognize that there is a choice to be made, however, no progress on these issues will even be possible. It is time to recognize that the multiplier principle is sufficient but not necessary for optimal deterrence.

[4]

Comparative Causation

Francesco Parisi, *George Mason University*, and
Vincy Fon, *George Washington University*

This article examines the criterion of comparative causation according to which an
accident loss is apportioned between a faultless tortfeasor and an innocent victim on the
basis of their relative causal contributions to the loss. To explain the rule's structural
features, we consider a scenario where liability is allocated on the basis of causation,
regardless of fault. While this model brings to light several interesting features, it also
unveils the limits of such a criterion with respect to induced activity and care levels.
Next we extend the model to consider the comparative causation rule in conjunction
with negligence rules. Applying the comparative causation rule under a negligence
regime induces a combination of incentives that is not provided by any known
liability rule.

Under most liability rules, if neither party is at fault, the loss is either
entirely borne by the victim (e.g., in a negligence-based system) or is shifted
entirely onto the tortfeasor (e.g., in a strict liability system). Existing legal
rules lack explicit ways to apportion the loss between a faultless victim and a
faultless tortfeasor.[1]

Law and economics scholars have provided convincing rationales as to
when it may be efficient to let some losses rest where they fall (i.e., leaving

---

We would like to thank Erin Ruane Karsman for her valuable research assistance and
Guido Calabresi, Izhak Englard, and Dan Milkove for valuable comments. We also thank
David A. Bragdon and Robert D. Cooter for insightful conversations during the early
development of this project.

Send correspondence to: Francesco Parisi, George Mason University, School of Law,
Arlington, VA 22201; Fax: (703) 993-8088; E-mail: parisi@gmu.edu.

1. Loss-sharing generally takes place under comparative negligence whenever both
parties have failed to meet their minimum standards of care in their conduct: see Schwartz
(1978); Cooter and Ulen (1986); and Rubinfeld (1987).

American Law and Economics Review Vol. 6 No. 2,
ι American Law and Economics Association 2004; all rights reserved.   doi:10.1093/aler/ahh011

346   American Law and Economics Review V6 N2 2004 (345–368)

the victim's loss uncompensated), and when, instead, efficiency dictates shifting the loss onto the tortfeasor. Yet, as Calabresi (1996) and Calabresi and Cooper (1996) lamented, little consideration has been given to the idea of distributing the loss between a faultless tortfeasor and an innocent victim according to their relative causal contribution to the loss.[2] In recent years, some jurisdictions revived a forgotten paradigm of causal apportionment of liability in cases where the traditional subjective elements of a tort were either inapplicable or failed to provide a satisfactory answer. In the mid-1980s the issue of causal apportionment of the loss was also debated in the legal and economic literature (Kaye and Aickin, 1984; Kruskal, 1986; Landes and Posner, 1983; Rizzo and Arnold, 1980, 1986; Wright, 1985). Most of these studies looked at appropriate ways to assess causation when joint causes are at work. But as Kaye and Aickin (1984, p. 205) critically noted, no systematic framework had been developed for assessing the effect of a causal apportionment of the loss on the parties' incentives for care and activity levels. Analyzing the efficiency effects of this paradigm of liability, which we call "comparative causation," is the object of this article.

Section 1 presents a brief intellectual history of the comparative causation criterion and provides some illustrations of the modern revival of such paradigm of liability. Section 2 develops a positive economic model of pure comparative causation, in which liability is borne by the parties on the basis of their respective causal contributions to the loss, regardless of fault. We look at the incentive effects of the rule. The model brings to light some interesting features of the rule and unveils its limits in achieving efficient care and activity levels, for both tortfeasors and victims. In section 3, we apply comparative causation in conjunction with negligence-based liability. The economic model of this rule allows us to

---

2. In his address as a dinner speaker at the Sixth Annual Meeting of the American Law and Economics Association, held in Chicago, May 10–11, 1996, Guido Calabresi suggested comparative causation as a fertile field for research. Instead of determining who is at fault, the courts would assign liability to each party to the degree that each party was the cause of the accident. Calabresi and Cooper (1996, p. 877) write as follows: "There may be situations in which neither side was negligent, but each side could have done something to avoid the loss and did not. In these situations, too, we might want to split the loss. But we are, in fact, nowhere near ready to do that yet, across the board. And so where neither side is at fault, we still remain subject to all-or-nothing rules. In the absence of defendant fault, innocent plaintiffs bear the whole loss in most areas, while in so-called non-fault liability areas, defendants bear the entire loss where neither party is at fault."

evaluate advantages and limitations of the comparative causation principle, providing an explanation for the emergence and actual scope of application of this rule in historical and contemporary legal systems. Section 4 concludes with some considerations on the dilemma of casual apportionment of damages.

1. The Rise and Fall of Comparative Causation in Tort Law

In this section, we present a brief intellectual history of the comparative causation criterion, offering some historical and modern illustrations of the principle of compensation, and its practical corollary, the principle of causal apportionment of liability. In the following, we refer to the application of these principles as the *criterion of comparative causation*.

1.1. Origins of Causal Apportionment of the Loss in European Tort Law

The problem of apportioning losses between faultless parties has long been debated in legal theory. Fourteenth-century legal scholars and fifteenth-century legal humanists first explicitly considered the problem of apportioning losses among faultless parties.[3] In later times, seventeenth-century natural law scholars such as Hugo Grotius (1583–1645) and Samuel Pufendorf (1632–1694) critically revisited the Romanistic principle of fault, according to which a tortfeasor is responsible for losses that he occasioned only if he is at fault. These scholars challenged the underlying assumptions of the fault principle by asking why a victim should bear losses occasioned by another, even when the victim was not at fault, and formulated an alternative paradigm of liability known as the principle of compensation. The tension between the fault principle and the compensation principle became apparent in the jurisprudential writings of Hugo Grotius, who considered the practical implications of these alternative criteria of liability. Grotius' work is suffused with awareness that the faultiness of an act must be considered independently from the consequences of the act. Grotius proposed moving away from the *fault principle* by adopting the *compensation principle*, suggesting that, absent fault, there is no reason to let the loss fall on the

---

3. For a broader historical analysis of the evolution of these criteria of liability in medieval Europe, see Parisi (1992).

348   American Law and Economics Review V6 N2 2004 (345–368)

innocent victim, just as there is no obvious reason to shift it onto the tortfeasor.[4]

In many ways, Grotius' work exemplifies seventeenth-century scholars' uneasiness with existing paradigms of liability, with an all-or-nothing approach to the apportionment of liability. Even when damages cannot be apportioned on the basis of the relative fault of the parties (e.g., when neither party is at fault and the loss cannot be spread on the basis of comparative negligence), equitable principles may require spreading the loss between parties. In this context, Grotius observed that, according to laws in force in many nations at the time of his writings (i.e., before 1625), damages were usually divided between both parties when neither party was negligent or there were difficulties in deciding who was at fault in the case (Grotius, 1625, sec. 2.17.21). In these situations, notions of causal contribution provided a viable basis for spreading a loss between the parties.

In the following, we consider the mixed fortune of such a criterion of causal apportionment of the loss.

1.2. The Troubled Evolution of Comparative Causation in Modern Tort Law

The historical doctrines of comparative causation that surfaced in Grotius's times left little mark on subsequent restatements of Western tort law. The idea of an equitable apportionment of a loss among nonnegligent parties was not shared by later jurists, such as Domat (1625–1696) and Pothier (1699–1772), and was consequently ignored in the subsequent European codifications of tort law, which remained based solely on the classical principle of fault (e.g., Art. 1382 of the French *Code Civil* of 1804; para. 823 of the German BGB of 1900). Whoever by his fault caused damage to another was bound to compensate the other. Lacking any fault—or evidence thereof—the loss was to lie where it fell, without any room for causal apportionment of the loss or other forms of equitable adjustment of liability.

---

4. The criterion of causal apportionment of the loss was an important, and possibly unavoidable, corollary of Grotius's equitable approach to liability. In a passage of his *De Iure Belli ac Pacis*, Grotius (1625, sec. 2.17.13) examined cases in which the link between liability and faultiness was not clearly assessed.

In spite of the abandonment of the historical doctrines of comparative causation by modern European codes, in recent decades the doctrine of comparative causation has been revived in several jurisdictions. Some developments are quite remarkable, in light of the greater constraints that civil law (as opposed to common law) courts face when introducing new legal principles in established areas of law, such as torts.

France and Germany have adopted causal apportionment standards since the 1800s (Prentice, 1995, n. 44). Current French jurisprudence continues to reflect a causal basis of apportioning liability (Palmer, 1988, p. 1327). The French *Cour de Cassation*, the French Supreme Court, applies all liability defenses on a causal basis and does not recognize "fault" of the victim in isolation in most circumstances. Thus, for example, the "causal impact" of the parties' negligent conduct becomes a relevant factor for apportioning damages under a comparative negligence regime.

Due to the influence of civil law jurisprudence, the principle of comparative causation has reached further than Europe. Traditionally, Japanese courts are committed to finding equitable solution to hard cases. Criteria of causal contribution provide a valid basis for an equitable allocation of damages in tort cases. With causal apportionment, equitable loss-spreading can be achieved, whenever traditional criteria of liability would otherwise lead to all-or-nothing outcomes (Yoshihsa, 1999; Yu, 2000). Legal developments in Europe have also focused on this criterion of liability in the field of environmental law. The *Hoge Raad*, the Supreme Court of the Netherlands, applied negligence and comparative causation principles to a series of environmental liability cases in the 1980s.[5]

In recent years, the rule of comparative causation has emerged in the United States in the midst of liability systems based on fault or strict liability. The revival of the concept of comparative causation in American courts is, however, driven by more pragmatic necessities. Comparative causation has at times been applied when it was difficult to evaluate fault (e.g., liability of incapable individuals) or when it was otherwise desirable to apportion the loss between tortfeasor and victim on the basis of causal imputability (e.g., loss jointly occasioned by faultless individuals).[6]

---

5. For further references on Dutch and Japanese trends, see Yu (2000) and Hondius (1999).

6. For some discussion of recent judicial applications of the comparative causation paradigm, see Gershonowitz (1986) and Clark (1989).

350   American Law and Economics Review V6 N2 2004 (345–368)

These historical and doctrinal illustrations share a common methodo-logical foundation, given the use of causation for the spreading of the loss among faultless parties. In section 2, we consider an economic model of comparative causation in which parties respond on the basis of causation, regardless of fault. We refer to this regime as *pure comparative causation*.[7] We study the effects of this rule of comparative causation on the parties' incentives for care and activity levels. In section 3, we consider a second, more complex version of the comparative causation model used in conjunc-tion with a negligence rule. Under this regime, liability is primarily appor-tioned on the basis of negligence, and only residually on the basis of causation. When only one party is at fault, liability is borne entirely by the negligent individual. When both parties are at fault or when neither party is at fault, the loss is instead split between the parties on the basis of their respective causal contribution to the loss. We refer to this second regime of comparative causation as *comparative causation under negligence*.

2. A Model of Pure Comparative Causation

In this section, we consider a model to highlight the essence of comparat-ive causation. Parties are made to bear a loss proportional to their causal contribution to the loss, regardless of their fault. Three elements contribute to the overall social cost of accidents: the cost of harm occasioned by an accident, the cost of taking precaution, and the cost of reducing the parties' activity levels. All such costs are relevant for the design of liability rules. Social benefits that accrue when parties engage in risk-creating activities are assumed to be fully internalized by the agents.

---

7. Some scholars have analogized the notion of comparative causation to a system of comparative strict liability. Palmer (1988) suggests that we must recognize the possibility that strict liability can be used as a sliding scale, rather than an exact point of reference. Viewed from this perspective, causation can also be thought of as a continuum, and, when multiple causes contribute to a given loss (e.g., tortfeasor's activity and victim's activity, multiple tortfeasors, etc.), comparative causation becomes a potential instrument for apportioning losses among the contributing parties. See also Parisi and Frezza (1998, 1999).

Following conventional notation, define the benefit function $w(z,x)$ as the injurer's expected income from undertaking activity level z with care x. Increasing care is costly to the injurer and leads to decreasing benefits; hence, assume $w_x < 0$ and $w_{xx} < 0$ for all z. Activity level increases benefits up to a point; thus w_z is initially positive but ultimately negative, with w reaching a maximum at $z_p(x)$, and $w_{zz} < 0$.[8] Since increasing care x decreases w, $|w_x|$ is the marginal cost of engaging in additional care. Clearly, w_z is the marginal benefit of engaging in activity level z.

Likewise, let $b(u,y)$ be the benefit function of the victim, where u is the activity level and y is the level of care undertaken by the victim. Assume that b has similar properties to the injurer's benefit function: $b_y < 0$ and $b_{yy} < 0$ for all u; b_u is initially positive but eventually negative, with b reaching a maximum at $u_p(y)$; and $b_{uu} < 0$. Hence, increasing care is always costly to the victim, and in the relevant range an increase in activity level increases the victim's benefit.

Let $D(x,y)$ be the expected damages per unit of activity where levels of care reduce expected accident costs at a diminishing rate, and the levels of care taken by the two parties are substitutes: $D_x < 0, D_y < 0, D_{xx} > 0, D_{yy} > 0$, and $D_{xy} > 0$.[9] Total damages are assumed to be $zuD(x,y)$.[10] Since increasing care x decreases D, $|zuD_x|$ can be interpreted as the (social) marginal benefit of an increased level of care x.

Turning our attention to causation, we note that several variables, including the parties' activity level and the parties' care, affect the causation of an accident. For example, decreasing a party's activity level or increasing a party's precaution makes an accident less likely to occur.[11] Our model

---

8. The signs of the second-order derivatives in our model follow the literature (see, e.g., Shavell, 1987; Landes and Posner, 1987; and Miceli 1997). In general, it is assumed that the second-order sufficient conditions hold for our problems.

9. Our results do not depend on the assumption that the two parties' levels of care are substitutes. This assumption was adopted and conditions the result in several bilateral precautions models. For example, see Miceli (1997, p. 18).

10. The product of activity levels zu follows the formulation of Shavell (1980b).

11. Generally, causation is something that each party affects but no one fully controls. For example, additional precaution or reduced activity levels make it less likely for a party to "cause" an accident, but we assume that no positive and finite value of care or activity can bring causation to zero.

352   American Law and Economics Review V6 N2 2004 (345–368)

considers the general case in which each party's behavior potentially
contributes to causing a loss. We refer to the parties' individual causal
contributions to the accident as *causal inputs*. The causal inputs positively
depend on activity and care levels: $c^I(z,x)$ and $c^V(u,y)$, where the superscripts
I and *V* refer to the injurer and the victim, respectively.[12] Further, we assume
that $c^I_z > 0$, $c^V_u > 0$, $c^I_x < 0$, and $c^V_y < 0$. This means that the lower the activity
level undertaken by one party, the smaller the corresponding causal contribution to a resulting accident. Likewise, the greater the care of one party,
the less the party's causal contribution to a resulting loss.

As has been extensively debated in the literature, each party's causal input
should not be evaluated in isolation, since in some cases both inputs affect
causation of an accident additively, while in other cases they do so multi-
plicatively, or a mix thereof (Kaye and Aickin, 1984; Kruskal, 1986; Landes
and Posner, 1983; Rizzo and Arnold, 1980 and 1986; Wright, 1985).[13] We
illustrate our results with respect to cases in which causal inputs are complements and in which they are substitutes. The case of causal complements is
illustrated by a multiplicative causal relationship: the overall causation factor
is given by the product of the parties' causal inputs, $c^I(z,x)c^V(u,y)$.[14] The case
of causal substitutes is illustrated by an additive causal relationship: the
overall causation factor is given by the sum of the parties' causal inputs,

---

12. This formulation encompasses the case of other particular liability regimes
according to which a loss is apportioned on the basis of factors (e.g., market
share) that are related to the parties' activity levels. In the following discussion,
we thus think of the criterion of comparative causation as representative of this broader
class of liability regimes. Although different labels (e.g., comparative causation, comparative strict liability, market share liability) would best describe the resulting liability
regime in these other cases, qualitatively similar results would obtain from an economic point of view.

13. A comparative causation rule would generally consider the causal potency of
different actions or potential sources of harm with knowledge of how events unfolded.
Scholars have considered the problem and formulated practical frameworks for the comparative ascertainment of causation. See, for example, Martin (1989) and Pearl (2000).
Absent information about actual causation, application of comparative causation rests on
probabilistic information alone (e.g., the likely incidence of a given conduct on the probability of an accident).

14. Strassfeld (1992) notes, however, that this approach needs evidence such as
scientific laws, or statistical, historical, and psychological generalizations. In other
words, comparative causation analysis requires evidence regarding either divisibility
of the harm suffered, or availability of substitutes for one or more causes.

$c^I(z, x) + c^V(u, y)$.[15] In both cases, the causation factor operates as a scale that is multiplied by total damage.

In our model of pure comparative causation, the injurer and the victim share a loss on the basis of their respective causal contributions to the loss, regardless of fault. We now consider the effect of this apportionment rule on the parties' incentives, looking at the cases of causal complements and causal substitutes in turn.

2.1. Causal Complements

We begin by considering the case in which the parties' behaviors act as complements for the causation of a loss and assume a multiplicative causal relationship given by the product of the parties' inputs: $c^I(z, x)c^V(u, y)$. The social optimization problem is then given by

$$\max_{z,x,u,y} w(z, x) + b(u, y) - c^I(z, x)c^V(u, y)zuD(x, y). \tag{1}$$

Suppressing the arguments inside all functions, we give the socially optimal levels z^*, x^*, u^*, y^* by the following first-order conditions:

$$w_z = c_z^I c^V zuD + c^I c^V uD, \tag{2}$$

$$|w_x| = |c_x^I c^V zuD| + |c^I c^V zuD_x|, \tag{3}$$

$$b_u = c^I c_u^V zuD + c^I c^V zD, \tag{4}$$

$$|b_y| = |c^I c_y^V zuD| + |c^I c^V zuD_y|. \tag{5}$$

Each equation expresses the standard optimality condition according to which social marginal benefit equals social marginal cost.[16] In particular, equation (2) indicates that the social marginal benefit of the injurer's activity equals the social marginal cost, SMC_Z, of his activity level.[17] The first term of SMC_Z originates from the fact that an increase in the injurer's activity level increases the likely causation of an accident, while the second term denotes

---

15. Where the causes are apparent and the causal effects are additive, it is easy to apportion liability on the amount of causation. Strassfeld (1992, pp. 937, 941–44) finds that causal apportionment in additive cases allows the court to consider causes of each impact independently, facilitating a more workable comparison. Whenever possible, the importance of one cause in the actual case should be determined on the basis of its actual contribution or impact, rather than on mere statistical information.

16. We assume that second-order conditions hold for this social optimization problem.

17. This equation implies $w_z(z^*, x^*) > 0$, which in turn implies $z^* < z_p(x^*)$.

354   American Law and Economics Review V6 N2 2004 (345–368)

that an increase in activity level z increases the expected accident loss. Both effects of an increase in z are socially relevant, since they increase the overall cost of accidents. Since all partials in equation (3) are negative, we expressed all such terms in absolute values. Equation (3) says that, at the social optimum, the private marginal cost of the injurer's care should equal the social marginal benefit of increased care chosen by the injurer. The social marginal benefit of increased care, SMB_X, has two parts. The first part is the impact of care on the causation of an accident, while the second part represents the impact of injurer's care on total damages.

In a regime of pure comparative causation, we assume that the shares of damage borne by the injurer and the victim are $c^I(z,x)/[c^I(z,x) + c^V(u,y)]$ and $c^V(u,y)/[c^I(z,x) + c^V(u,y)]$, respectively. Note that each damage share is affected by the parties' choice of care and activity level. Hence, the greater the care of one party, the less the party's share of the resulting loss. Likewise, the less the activity level undertaken by one party, the smaller the share of damages borne by the party.[18]

Under this regime of liability, the optimization problem confronting a potential injurer is given by

$$\max_{z,x} w(z,x) - \frac{c^I(z,x)}{c^I(z,x) + c^V(u,y)} c^I(z,x)c^V(u,y)zuD(x,y). \quad (6)$$

Suppressing the arguments inside the functions, we give the first-order conditions characterizing the levels of z and x, given u and y, chosen by the injurer in the following.[19]

$$w_z = (c^{I^2} + 2c^I c^V)/(c^I + c^V)^2 \cdot c^I_z c^V zuD + c^I/(c^I + c^V) \cdot c^I c^V uD, \quad (7)$$

$$|w_x| = (c^{I^2} + 2c^I c^V)/(c^I + c^V)^2 \cdot |c^I_x c^V zuD| + c^I/(c^I + c^V) \cdot |c^I c^V zuD_x|, \quad (8)$$

---

18. This model can easily be adapted to study the workings of market share liability and related criteria of liability, such as liability based on industrial output, annual mileage, and the like. In recent case law, the imposition of liability according to such a "market share" basis is not uncommon. This often happens when a victim cannot identify the specific tortfeasor, but can nevertheless identify the class of product that occasioned the injury, (see, e.g., *Sindell v. Abbott Laboratories; Hymowitz v. Lilly*). In assessing liability in these cases, courts held defendants liable in proportion to their shares of market sales. This bears a close analogy to our hypothetical rule, by which harm is allocated between two parties on the basis of their respective shares of activity level.

19. We assume that second-order conditions hold for this private optimization problem.

If one compares (7) to (2), the left-hand side of each represents marginal benefit from the activity. Note that each term on the right-hand side of (7) is a fraction of the two terms on the right-hand side of (2). Thus, the injurer's private marginal cost of activity falls short of the corresponding social marginal cost. Hence, potential injurers undertake too much activity compared to the social optimum. That is, the injurer's private choice of activity level, z_{CS}, exceeds the social optimum, z^*, because potential tortfeasors expect to share the loss with their victims upon occurrence of an accident.

Next compare equations (8) and (3). The left-hand side of (3) and (8) represent the marginal cost of the injurer's care. The right-hand side of (8), the private marginal benefit of increased care, is again a fraction of the corresponding social marginal benefit, the right-hand side of (3), since each component of private marginal benefit is a fraction of the corresponding component of social marginal benefit. Since private marginal benefit falls short of social marginal benefit, the potential injurer undertakes less care than is socially desirable. That is, the injurer's care level, x_{CS}, is less than the socially optimal level x^*, because a potential tortfeasor does not fully internalize the social marginal benefit of his care level.

For similar reasons, in a regime of pure comparative causation, the victim also rationally undertakes less than optimal care and engages in too much activity, regardless of the care and activity choices of the tortfeasor.[20] The comparative causation equilibrium results from such dominant strategies of the victim and the tortfeasor in adopting care and activity levels.[21] Private incentives induce each party to choose inadequate levels of care and excessive activity levels because both parties expect to share a portion of the loss with the other party.

2.2. Causal Substitutes

We now study the alternative case, in which the parties' actions can be considered substitute inputs in the causation of a loss. We illustrate this case with an additive causal relationship. The causation of an accident is determined by the sum of the parties' causal inputs, $c^J(z, x) + c^V(u, y)$.

---

20. Miceli (1997, pp. 28–29) observes that if both parties cannot simultaneously bear the full liability in equilibrium, they cannot be induced to choose optimal activity levels at the same time.

21. This similarity renders any labeling of the parties as "victim" or "tortfeasor" unnecessary, given that both bear the loss in case of an accident.

356   American Law and Economics Review V6 N2 2004 (345–368)

Under this scenario, the social optimization problem is given by

$$\max_{z,x,u,y} w(z,x) + b(u,y) - [c^I(z,x) + c^V(u,y)]zuD(x,y). \qquad (9)$$

Suppressing arguments inside the functions, we give the socially optimal levels z^*, x^*, u^*, y^* by the following first-order conditions:

$$w_z = c_z^I zuD + (c^I + c^V)uD, \qquad (10)$$

$$|w_x| = |c_x^I zuD| + |(c^I + c^V)zuD_x|, \qquad (11)$$

$$b_u = c_u^V zuD + (c^I + c^V)zD, \qquad (12)$$

$$|b_y| = |c_y^V zuD| + |(c^I + c^V)zuD_y|. \qquad (13)$$

As in the causal complements case, the social marginal cost of the parties' activity level has two components. The first originates from the fact that an increase in activity levels increases the likely causation of an accident. The second follows because an increase in activity level may also increase the expected accident loss. Similarly, the social marginal benefit of care for the two parties has two components, one arising from the impact of the parties' care on causation, and the other from a resulting decrease in accident loss.

The injurer's private problem is then

$$\max_{z,x} w(z,x) - \frac{c^I(z,x)}{c^I(z,x) + c^V(u,y)} [c^I(z,x) + c^V(u,y)]zuD(x,y). \qquad (14)$$

This is equivalent to

$$\max_{z,x} w(z,x) - c^I(z,x)zuD(x,y). \qquad (15)$$

The private choice of the injurer is characterized by the following conditions:

$$w_z = c_z^I zuD + c^I uD, \qquad (16)$$

$$|w_x| = |c_x^I zuD| + |c^I zuD_x|. \qquad (17)$$

Comparing equation (16) to the socially optimal condition (10), we see that only the second terms on the right-hand side are different. In particular, the second term on the right-hand side of (16) is part of the second term on the right-hand side of (10). Hence, as before, the injurer internalizes only part of the social marginal cost of his activity level and thus carries out too much activity. Likewise, the second term on the right-hand side of (17) is smaller than the second term on the right-hand side of (11). This suggests that the injurer internalizes only part of the social marginal benefit of his care level and thus undertakes too little care.

In this regime, the victim rationally undertakes less than optimal care and engages in too much activity. These strategies are dominant and occur regardless of the care and activity choices of the tortfeasor. Thus, the comparative causation equilibrium with causal substitutes is qualitatively similar to the equilibrium identified in the case of causal complements: both parties choose inadequate levels of care and excessive activity levels, because each party expects to share the loss with the other party in equilibrium.

2.3. Pure Comparative Causation versus Traditional Liability Regimes

Turning our attention to differences between models of pure comparative causation and other regimes of liability, we first compare the comparative causation rule to negligence rules. The various negligence-based liability regimes, such as negligence, comparative negligence, and negligence with contributory negligence have similar effects on the parties' care and activity level incentives. We therefore consider these systems conjunctively and refer to them as "negligence-based regimes," denoting the relevant values with the subscript N. In all negligence-based regimes, the victim bears the full loss in equilibrium, given the Nash strategy of the tortfeasors. This induces the victim to take efficient care: $y_N = y^*$. In turn, this induces the potential tortfeasor to take efficient precautions in order to avoid his primary liability: $x_N = x^*$ (see, e.g., Landes and Posner, 1987; Miceli, 1997; Shavell, 1987). In a comparative causation regime, this is not so. Parties face full liability only in the limiting case in which the other party's causation is reduced to zero—an implausible scenario, given positive marginal values of the activity for both parties. This expectation of partial liability by the parties dilutes incentives to undertake optimal care: $x_{CS} < x_N = x^*$ and $y_{CS} < y_N = y^*$.

A similar dilution of incentives occurs with respect to the parties' activity levels. In this dimension, however, the results of comparative causation are not necessarily dominated by negligence-based regimes. Under comparative causation both parties face positive expected liability, although their

358   American Law and Economics Review V6 N2 2004 (345–368)

expectation of liability is less than the total accident loss. As a consequence, the tortfeasor's activity level under comparative causation represents an improvement over the equilibrium level induced by negligence-based regimes: $z_{CS} < z_N$. This is because the tortfeasor internalizes some of the benefit from reducing his activity level. Such improvement, however, comes at the expense of the victim's activity level, since under comparative causation the victim no longer faces the full loss in equilibrium: $u^* = u_N < u_{CS}$.

Symmetrical conclusions are obtained by contrasting the pure comparative causation rule to strict liability with a defense of contributory negligence. We denote the values obtained under this latter regime with the subscript S. In a strict liability regime with a defense of contributory negligence, both parties face optimal care incentives. Under pure comparative causation, given the expectation of partial liability for both parties, the incentives to undertake optimal care are diluted: $x_{CS} < x_S = x^*$ and $y_{CS} < y_S = y^*$. A similar dilution of incentives occurs with respect to the parties' activity levels. This creates a tradeoff between improved victim's incentives, $u^* < u_{CS} < u_S$, and reduced tortfeasor's incentives to mitigate activity levels, $z^* = z_S < z_{CS}$.

In conclusion, our comparison of pure comparative causation with traditional liability regimes reveals weaknesses of the comparative causation regime. Unlike traditional liability regimes that induce both parties to adopt optimal levels of care, pure comparative causation generates suboptimal care incentives for both parties, as neither party faces full expected liability. In comparison to traditional liability regimes, pure comparative causation spreads activity level incentives between parties, rather than concentrating such incentives on one or the other party, yielding mixed results with respect to activity levels.

3. Comparative Causation under Negligence

As noted before, comparative causation historically emerges in the midst of legal systems based on negligence, in response to the conviction that, absent fault, there is no obvious reason to let the loss fall on the innocent victim, just as there is no reason to shift it onto the tortfeasor. Loss spreading among faultless parties, in application of the so-called compensation principle, was thus carried out by invoking criteria of causal loss apportionment. In those early applications, the comparative causation rule was invoked in bilateral precaution situations, under negligence-based regimes.[22] The original formulations of the principle of compensation advocated the criterion of comparative causation only when neither the tortfeasor nor the victim was found negligent. Thus the principle of comparative causation operated only as a residual basis of liability in the presence of faultless parties, avoiding the all-or-nothing allocation of liability generated by traditional rules.[23]

This section extends the economic model of pure comparative causation to consider comparative causation in conjunction with fault-based liability. We refer to this regime as *comparative causation under negligence*, since comparative causation is applied with conventional negligence rules. Before presenting the model, we consider difficulties associated with combining negligence rules with sharing rules that utilize causation variables.

3.1. Missing Thresholds and the Troublesome Design of Loss-Sharing Rules

A point of discontinuity in the liability curves faced by the parties must be created to entice both parties to choose optimal care and activity levels. With respect to care, this is generally done by identifying a socially optimal care level and utilizing such level to mark the boundaries between diligence and negligence. Landes and Posner (1987, pp. 70–71) and Gilles (1992) suggest that courts take into account activity levels in their assessment of negligence whenever it is feasible to do so. However, no threshold of "optimal activity level" is generally invoked by legal rules as a liability allocation mechanism.[24] The reason for this omission is due to the difficulty of pinpointing a critical value to separate efficient from inefficient activity levels. Absent such critical threshold, no discontinuity in the parties' expected liability can be created.

---

22. Comparative causation first emerged in legal systems of the civil law tradition that based liability on fault and generally followed the criterion of comparative negligence for apportioning liability among negligent parties. The civil law tradition adopted a comparative negligence rule in much earlier times than the common law. See Parisi (1992).

23. When neither party is at fault, the comparative negligence criterion does not allow loss-spreading between parties. In such a scenario, the entire loss is borne by the victim.

24. If the due standard of efficient behavior for injurers and victims could also be formulated with respect to optimal activity levels, then liability rules could induce optimal care and activity levels for both parties (Miceli, 1997). The historical emergence of rules of comparative causation partially reflects the difficulties of implementing such an ideal rule.

360   American Law and Economics Review V6 N2 2004 (345–368)

The difficulty of specifying optimal activity levels is because the value of such activities can be ascertained only from private information of the parties.[25] Unlike optimal levels of care, which largely depend on the objective cost of precaution and the expected gravity of harm, optimal activity levels rely on values that are harder to ascertain by a third-party decision maker, since they include the subjective value of the individual that carries out the risk-creating (or risk-bearing) activity.[26] In the absence of such a threshold, it is difficult to induce both parties to internalize the full social cost of their activity levels in equilibrium.

3.2. A Model of Comparative Causation under Negligence

We now present a model of comparative causation under negligence. In this regime, parties share damages only when no unilateral negligence is established. When either the tortfeasor or the victim is found unilaterally negligent, the entire loss is borne by the party at fault. In cases where parties are either both negligent or both diligent, loss-sharing instead follows on the basis of comparative causation. This preserves some essential features of traditional negligence regimes yet allows loss-spreading via comparative causation as a residual basis for apportioning the loss.

Since causal substitutes and causal complements generate similar equilibrium incentives, we concentrate on the case of causal complements. The problem facing the injurer is given by the following:

$$\max_{z,x} \begin{cases} w(z,x) & \text{if } x \geq x^* \text{ and } y < y^*, \\ w(z,x) - \dfrac{c^I(z,x)}{c^I(z,x) + c^V(u,y)} c^I(z,x) c^V(u,y) zu\, D(x,y) \\ \qquad \text{if } (x < x^* \text{ and } y < y^*) \text{ or } (x \geq x^* \text{ and } y \geq y^*), \\ w(z,x) - c^I(z,x) c^V(u,y) zu\, D(x,y) & \text{if } x < x^* \text{ and } y \geq y^*. \end{cases} \tag{18}$$

---

25. Miceli (1997, p. 28) suggests that the task of calculating optimal activity levels is prohibitively costly for courts to undertake. As a consequence, negligence is made conditional only on care.

26. This difficulty is also evident in the mathematical formulation of the activity-level problem. Unlike level-of-care problems, generally modeled as minimization problems, the analysis of care-plus-activity situations is generally reformulated as a maximization problem. This is due to the necessity to account for the private (and social) value of the activity level. If the problem were formulated as a cost-minimization problem, the optimal activity level would always be zero. But corner solutions of this sort would be generally undesirable, since risk-creating activities also create private and social value.

The problem facing the victim is similar: whenever the victim is diligent and the injurer is negligent, the victim receives full compensation for the loss. If the parties are both negligent or both diligent, they share damages, according to the comparative causation principle. If the victim is negligent and the injurer is diligent, the victim bears the total loss without obtaining any compensation from the injurer.

Now consider the behavior of the parties. Note that parties are never induced to take more than socially optimal care, since private marginal benefit of care never exceeds social marginal benefit.

First consider the case in which the injurer chooses his care level while expecting the victim to be negligent. The injurer has two options. He may choose to be negligent, sharing liability with the victim on the basis of comparative causation. Alternatively, the injurer may choose to avoid liability by undertaking due care. The injurer's choice of due care yields only a benefit equal to the difference between no liability and partial liability. Next assume that the injurer chooses his level of care while expecting the victim to be diligent. The injurer may choose a negligent conduct, facing full liability, or he may undertake due care, sharing the loss with the victim on the basis of comparative causation. In this setting, by adopting due care the injurer again cannot avoid liability entirely. The injurer's choice of due care yields only a benefit equal to the difference between full liability and partial liability.

Note that, regardless of the victim's choice of care, the injurer does not fully internalize the full social benefit of his care level. Hence, in comparison to the social optimum, the private incentives to provide care are weakened. This opens up the possibility that less than due care is adopted by the injurer. Unlike the traditional negligence-based regimes, where due care allows the injurer to fully internalize the social benefit of care, diligence strategies are not dominant for the injurer in this case.

Further note that, although not dominant, due care is a possible Nash strategy for the injurer. By reaching the level of due care, a party can capture one of two benefits. In the face of a negligent counterpart, a party can capture the difference between no liability and partial liability. In the face of a diligent counterpart, a party would capture the difference between partial liability and full liability. If these expected gains from due care exceed the additional cost of care, then the party rationally avoids negligence by adopting due care.

362   American Law and Economics Review V6 N2 2004 (345–368)

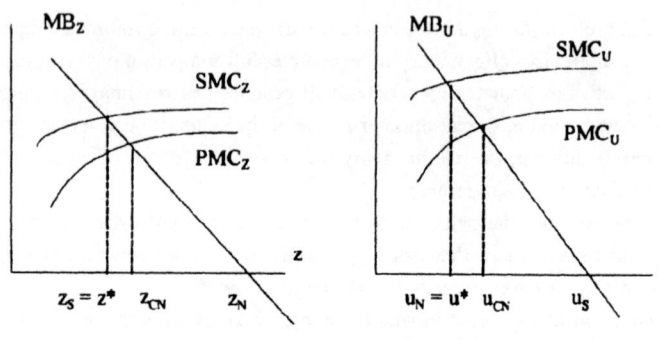

Figure 1. Activity levels in comparative causation regimes.

A similar logic characterizes care strategies of the victim. As a result of the combination of the parties' strategies, multiple equilibria may obtain. Referring to equilibrium levels of care in the regime of comparative causation under negligence as x_{CN} and y_{CN}, we conclude that $x_{CN} \leq x^*$ and $y_{CN} \leq y^*$.

Similar to the pure comparative causation rule, comparative causation under negligence induces parties to carry out their activity levels beyond the socially optimal levels. Denoting the equilibrium activity levels in the regime of comparative causation under negligence as z_{CN} and u_{CN}, we have $z_{CN} > z^*$ and $u_{CN} > u^*$.

As shown in Figure 1, when evaluated against other traditional liability regimes, comparative causation yields an activity level of the injurer that improves upon the activity level under a standard negligence-based regime, $z_{CN} < z_N$, at the expense of the activity level adopted by the victim, $u_{CN} > u_N$. Comparative causation also yields an activity level of the victim that improves upon the activity level in a standard strict liability–based regime, $u_{CN} < u_S$, at the expense of the activity level of the tortfeasor, $z_{CN} > z_S$.

Once again, these results are because, unlike other traditional liability regimes, both parties face positive, albeit not full, expected liability. Absent residual liability, under strict liability with contributory negligence, victims carry out activities until their private optimum is reached: $u_N = u_P$. Likewise, under negligence-based regimes, tortfeasors carry out their activities to the point where private marginal benefit is zero: $z_N = z_P$. Figure 1 compares these points, u_S and z_N, to the activity levels induced by comparative causation, u_{CN} and z_{CN}.

3.3. Summary Results: Comparative Causation at Work

In terms of levels of care, a rule of comparative causation under negligence may induce both victims and tortfeasors to adopt socially optimal levels. This constitutes an improvement over a rule of pure comparative causation, where both parties are induced to adopt suboptimal care levels. In terms of activity levels, both versions of comparative causation fall short of inducing the parties to adopt socially optimal levels.

Difficulties with inducing optimal activity levels for both parties are not unique to comparative causation. As is well known, optimal activity-level incentives are present only for the party that faces the full accident loss in equilibrium. Since it is not possible for both parties to bear the accident loss in equilibrium, most traditional rules fail to provide optimal activity-level incentives for both parties, concentrating such incentives on one or the other party. Comparative causation differs from traditional regimes in this respect, since both parties face positive shares of the accident loss in equilibrium. This results in spreading activity-level incentives between the parties, rather than concentrating such incentives on one or the other party. As a result, in both versions of comparative causation the activity level chosen by one party improves at the expense of the other. Thus, neither version of comparative causation dominates traditional negligence and strict liability rules on both activity-level margins.

Table 1 summarizes the tortfeasor's and victim's equilibrium choices under four regimes: (1) strict liability with contributory negligence, (2) negligence with contributory negligence, (3) pure comparative causation, and (4) comparative causation under negligence. This comparison brings to light the merits and respective limits of alternative loss-sharing rules for bilateral precaution cases.

These summary results provide us with a key for understanding some peculiar features of the comparative causation rule. If applied in conjunction with traditional negligence rules, comparative causation may maintain full incentives for optimal care while spreading the activity level to reduce activity levels between the parties. This is a combination of features that no other liability rule offers, given the fact that under traditional regimes the residual loss is always concentrated on one or the other party in equilibrium.

364   American Law and Economics Review V6 N2 2004 (345–368)

Table 1. Tortfeasor's and victim's equilibrium choices under various liability regimes

	x	y	z	u
Strict Liability with Contributory Negligence	$x_S = x^*$	$y_S = y^*$	$z^* = z_S$	$u^* < u_S$
Negligence with Contributory Negligence	$x_N = x^*$	$y_N = y^*$	$z^* < z_N$	$u^* = u_N$
Pure Comparative Causation	$x_{CS} < x^*$	$y_{CS} < y^*$	$z^* = z_S < z_{CS} < z_N$	$u^* = u_N < u_{CS} < u_S$
Negligence with Comparative Causation	$x_{CN} \leq x^*$	$y_{CN} \leq y^*$	$z^* = z_S < z_{CN} < z_N$	$u^* = u_N < u_{CN} < u_S$

Notes: Superscript (*) refers to the socially optimal case, subscript (_S_) refers to the strict liability with contributory negligence regime, subscript (_N_) refers to negligence-based regimes, subscript (_CS_) refers to the pure comparative causation, and subscript (_CN_) refers to the comparative causation under negligence regime. x = care undertaken by injurer, z = activity level engaged by injurer, y = care undertaken by victim, and u = activity level engaged by victim.

   In both applications, the loss-sharing and resulting dilution of activity-level incentives may or may not increase total net benefits. Further, the creation of such incentives may come at a cost, given the fact that the application of the comparative causation rule under negligence may at times compromise the care incentives. Comparative causation is also likely to exacerbate administrative costs, given the need to ascertain relative causation and the need to adjudicate cases even in situations where neither party is at fault.[27]

   These considerations shed some light on the peculiar historical development of the comparative causation doctrines. In retrospect we can now understand why the early applications of this rule took place in situations involving substantial losses (e.g., the cases of excusable homicide or ship collision found in the seventeenth century). Likewise, we can understand why the rule has continued to thrive in areas of the law where the benefits obtainable from the improved activity level of the parties could justify the increase in adjudication costs (e.g., environmental cases), or where the moderated form of liability produced by the rule was necessitated by concerns of equity or political necessity (e.g., international responsibility of sovereign states).

---

27. The concern for the increase in administrative costs of adjudication have already been voiced by Epstein (1980, pp. 134–37) and Landes and Posner (1980, p. 530), who argued that a simple causation rule should be used for the routine adjudication of tort cases.

Further, spreading activity-level incentives between parties solves the coordination and identification problems that other rules would create due to the well-known problem of reciprocity of cause (Calabresi, 1961; Coase, 1960), when labeling one party as tortfeasor or victim is problematic (e.g., in a maritime collision with no fault and mutual losses). Finally, the loss-spreading result in equilibrium may promote optimal risk allocation among risk-averse agents when insurance is not readily available. Loss-spreading may similarly minimize distortion of incentives deriving from truncated liability when tortfeasors face large potential losses.

4. Conclusion: The Dilemma of Causal Apportionment of the Loss

All bilateral precaution rules struggle with a common dilemma. An increase in care level or a reduction in activity level for one party makes an accident less likely to occur. However, each party's precautions make the accident also less likely for the other party. There is no feasible and cost-effective mechanism in tort law to induce victims and tortfeasors to internalize the benefits and costs of their behavior in all dimensions.

In spite of this common ontological problem, in this article we have shown an important qualitative difference between the workings of traditional liability regimes and the allocation of the loss on the basis of causation. In all traditional liability regimes, one party faces the entire loss in equilibrium. Absent parties' fault, victims bear the entire accident loss if subject to a negligence rule, whereas tortfeasors would bear such full loss under strict liability. This aspect of the traditional liability regimes is at the origin of the historical attempts to formulate alternative criteria of liability that could permit faultless parties to share the accident loss.

The comparative causation principle avoids the imposition of the entire loss on a faultless party. This avoidance poses a different set of problems. In a comparative causation regime, because of the difficulties of identifying socially optimal causation levels and the likely causal contribution of both parties to the accident, the parties share residual liability and expect loss-sharing in equilibrium. The incentives to minimize activity levels follow the allocation of residual liability. Comparative causation consequently yields a dilution of activity-level incentives. In a pure comparative causation, care incentives are likewise diluted.

366   American Law and Economics Review V6 N2 2004 (345–368)

When combined with negligence standards, comparative causation raises the prospect of both parties' adopting efficient care levels yet retains the loss-sharing in equilibrium. Further, such rule spreads the residual incentives to control activity levels between both parties. The overall performance of the rule thus depends on the synergies and complementarities between the parties' activities. As a practical matter, adoption of the comparative causation rule in negligence regimes would likely entail larger administrative costs, given the need to evaluate both negligence and relative causation, and to adjudicate cases that would otherwise not be litigated under traditional rules.

These findings help us understand the limited historical success of comparative causation paradigms. Whenever it is desirable to spread the loss between the parties, comparative causation may be a better legal instrument than most other liability regimes in which damage-sharing is only a threat that cannot be expected in equilibrium. Thus, ex ante comparative causation may appear more appealing when parties are highly risk-averse and when no insurance is available. Additionally, comparative causation paradigms may provide a pragmatic way to allocate liability between faultless parties when the all-or-nothing outcomes of a case are not politically or diplomatically viable. Finally, comparative causation, by spreading the incentives to mitigate activity levels, may decrease net costs in the presence of increasing marginal costs of activity-level reduction. In spite of these attributes, the increase in the administrative costs of adjudication is likely to explain the limited success of comparative causation as a general criterion of tort liability.

References

Calabresi, Guido. 1961. "Some Thoughts on Risk Distribution and the Law of Torts," 70 *Yale Law Journal* 499–553.

——. 1996. Address at the Sixth Annual Meeting of the American Law and Economics Association, Chicago, May 10–11.

Calabresi, Guido, and Jeffrey Cooper. 1996. "New Directions in Tort Law," 30 *Valparaiso University Law Review* 859–84.

Clark, Carla Ann. 1989. "*Howard v. Allstate Insurance Company*—Louisiana's Attempt at Comparative Causation," 49 *Louisiana Law Review* 1163–76.

Coase, Ronald H. 1960. "The Problem of Social Cost," 3 *Journal of Law and Economics* 1–44.

Cooter, Robert D., and Thomas S. Ulen. 1986. "An Economic Case for Comparative Negligence," 81 *New York University Law Review* 1067–110.

Epstein, Richard A. 1980. *Modern Product Liability Law*. Westport, CT: Quorum Books.

Gershonowitz, Alan. 1986. "Comparative Causation as an Alternative to, Not a Part of Comparative Fault in Strict Liability," 30 *St. Louis University Law Journal* 483–515.

Gilles, S. 1992. "Rule-Based Negligence and the Regulation of Activity Levels," 21 *Journal of Legal Studies* 319–63.

Grotius, Hugo. 1625. *De Iure Belli ac Pacis*, (W. Whewell, ed., 1853).

Hondius, E., (ed.) 1999. *Modern Trends in Tort Law*. Dordrecht, The Netherlands: Kluwer.

Hymowitz v. Lilly, 73 N.Y.2d 487 (1989).

Landes, William M., and Posner, Richard A. 1980. "Joint and Multiple Tortfeasors: An Economic Analysis," 9 *Journal of Legal Studies* 517–55.

———. 1983. "Causation in Tort Law: An Economic Approach," 12 *Journal of Legal Studies* 109–34.

———. 1987. *The Economic Structure of Tort Law*. Cambridge, MA: Harvard University Press.

Kaye, David, and Mikel Aickin. 1984. "A Comment on Causal Apportionment," 13 *Journal of Legal Studies* 191–208.

Kruskal, William. 1986. "Terms of Reference: Singular Confusion about Multiple Causation," 15 *Journal of Legal Studies* 427–36.

Martin, Raymond. 1989. *The Past Is within Us: An Empirical Approach to Philosophy of History*. Princeton, NJ: Princeton University Press.

Miceli, Thomas J. 1997. *Economics of the Law*. Oxford: Oxford University Press.

Palmer, Vernon. 1988. "A General Theory of the Inner Structure of Strict Liability: Common Law, Civil Law and Comparative Law," 62 *Tulane Law Review* 1303–1355.

Parisi, Francesco. 1992. *Liability for Negligence and Judicial Discretion*, 2nd ed. (IAS Series). Berkeley: University of California Press.

Parisi, Francesco, and Giampaolo Frezza. 1998. "La Responsabilitá Stocastica," 63 *Responsabilitá Civile e Previdenza* 824–47.

———. 1999. "Rischio e Causalita' nel Concorso di Colpa," 44 *Rivista di diritto civile* 233–271.

Pearl, Judea. 2000. *Causality: Models, Reasoning, and Inference*. Cambridge: Cambridge University Press.

Prentice, Robert A. 1995. "Can the Contributory Negligence Defense Contribute to a Defusing of the Accountant's Liability Crisis?" 13 *Wisconsin International Law Journal* 359–418.

Rizzo, Mario J., and Frank S. Arnold. 1980. "Causal Apportionment in the Law of Torts: an Economic Theory," 80 *Columbia Law Review* 1399–429.

Ribbo, Mario F. and Frank S. Arnold 1986. "Causal Apportionment: Reply to the Critics," 15 *Journal of Legal Studies* 219–26.

Rubinfeld, Daniel L. 1987. "The Efficiency of Comparative Negligence," 16 *Journal of Legal Studies* 375–94.

Schwartz, Gary T. 1978. "Contributory and Comparative Negligence: A Reappraisal," 87 *Yale Law Journal* 697–727.

Shavell, S. 1980b. "Strict Liability versus Negligence," 9 *Journal of Legal Studies* 1–25.

———. 1987. *Economic Analysis of Accident Law.* Cambridge, MA: Harvard University Press.

Sindell v. Abbott Lab., 607 P.2d 924 (Cal. 1980).

Strassfeld, Robert. 1992. "Causal Comparisons," 60   *Fordham Law Review* 913–951.

Twerski, Aaron. 1978. "The Many Faces of Misuse: An Inquiry into the Emerging Doctrine of Comparative Causation," 29 *Mercer Law Review* 403–32.

Wright, Richard W. 1985. "Actual Causation vs. Probabilistic Linkage: The Bane of Economic Analysis," 14 *Journal of Legal Studies* 435–56.

Yoshihsa, Nomi. 1999. "Environmental Liability in Japan," in Ewould Hondius, ed., *Modern Trends in Tort Law.* Dordrecht, The Netherlands: Kluwer.

Yu, Li. 2000. "Book Review: Modern Trends in Tort Law: Dutch and Japanese Law Compared," 6 *Columbia Journal of European Law* 147–48.

[5]

Liability Externalities and Mandatory Choices: Should Doctors Pay Less?*

Robert D. Cooter and Ariel Porat

Abstract

According to legal principles, a driver who negligently breaks a pedestrian's leg should pay the same damages as a doctor who negligently breaks a patient's leg. According to economic principles, however, the driver should pay more than the doctor. Non-negligent drivers impose risk on others without being liable for it. When liability externalities are mainly negative as with driving, liability should increase beyond full compensation to discourage the activity. Unlike pedestrians, patients contract with doctors for treatment and willingly submit to the risk of harm. Imperfections in medical markets cause some kinds of doctors to convey more positive than negative externalities on their patients. Increasing liability for these doctors would discourage an activity that needs encouragement. The argument for decreasing doctors' liability is especially strong when doctors must choose among risky procedures, such as cesarean or vaginal delivery of a baby, which we call a "mandatory choice". Given equal benefits, the doctor ought to choose the least risky alternative. If the doctor negligently chooses a more risky alternative and harm materializes, courts award damages equal to the harm suffered by the patient. Even without the doctor's faulty choice, however, the patient would have been exposed to the least risky alternative. Economic efficiency requires reducing the doctor's liability below the victim's actual harm, which current legal rules usually prohibit. We propose that legislatures give courts the choice of lowering tort damages for doctors in well defined circumstances, and for their mandatory choices in particular, and we suggest some principles for doing so.

*Robert Cooter is Herman Selvin Professor of Law, University of California at Berkeley. Ariel Porat is Alain Poher Professor of Law, Tel Aviv University Faculty of Law and Visiting Professor, University of Chicago Law School (Fall 2006). For helpful comments we wish to thank Jennifer Arlen, Ronen Avraham, Richard Craswell, Mark Geistfeld, Keith Hylton, Barak Medina, Ronen Perry, Mitch Polinsky, Steve Sugarman, Omri Yadlin, the participants in the law and economics workshops at Berkeley and Stanford, and the participants in the conference, "Tort Law and the Modern State", Columbia University School of Law, 15-16 September 2006. We thank Arik Rosen and Jennifer Shakbatur for excellent research assistance.

Cooter and Porat: Liability Externalities and Mandatory Choices

INTRODUCTION

This paper concerns the novel application of some familiar concepts to tort law, as illustrated by three examples:

> *Example 1: Liability externality.* A doctor makes a mistake and negligently breaks his patient's leg. In a separate accident, a driver negligently collides with a pedestrian and breaks her leg. The doctor and driver are both liable for the harm caused by their negligence. The seriousness of injury, pain, treatment, and course of recovery are identical for both victims. According to legal principles, the doctor should pay the same damages as the driver. Should the damages be the same according to economic principles?

Economic principles imply that the driver should pay more than the doctor. *Non*-negligent drivers impose risk on pedestrians without being liable for it, which we call a *liability externality.* Law should discourage activities with negative liability externalities. A tax on these activities will discourage them. Many jurisdictions tax driving, but we know of no jurisdiction that calibrates the tax according to the risk that drivers impose on others.[1] In the absence of a tax on risk, law should increase liability beyond full compensation in order to discourage driving. In general, liability law should adjust damages in light of the externalities that it creates.

Unlike pedestrians and drivers, patients contract with doctors for treatment and willingly submit to the risk of harm. If medical markets worked perfectly, contracts would internalize all marginal costs and benefits, so liability law would not need to encourage or discourage doctoring. In reality, medical markets are imperfect and externalities occur. Imperfections cause some kinds of doctors to convey more positive than negative externalities on their patients. Law should encourage activities with positive externalities. A subsidy on these activities will encourage them. In fact most such activities are not subsidized. Increasing liability for doctors would discourage activities that need encouragement.

Liability law does not need to discourage the activity of doctoring, and it needs to encourage some medical specialties. The following example, however, illustrates that when medical malpractice is proved, the damages often exceed the harm caused by doctors, which discourages doctoring.

> *Example 2: Least Risky Alternative.* An obstetrician must decide whether to deliver a baby by vaginal or cesarean birth. In this difficult case, vaginal birth imposes the unavoidable risk of harm to baby and mother of 200 with

---

[1] The actual amount of the tax is typically too low for internalizing risk. *See* Edlin & Karaca-Mandic, *infra* note 3.

Journal of Tort Law, Vol. 1 [2006], Iss. 1, Art. 2

probability .10 (expected harm of 20), whereas cesarean birth imposes the unavoidable risk of different harm of 300 with probability .10 (expected harm of 30). The obstetrician mistakenly chooses cesarean birth and the harm materialized. A court applies a negligence rule to these facts and finds the obstetrician liable. Should damages equal 300 or 100?

Economic efficiency requires that the obstetrician should be liable for the harm caused by his negligence. Having a baby by vaginal birth risks losing 200 with probability of .10. The obstetrician negligently chose cesarean delivery, which caused risk of losing an additional 100 with probability .10. Legal liability of 100 would make the obstetrician internalize the additional expected loss of 10. Starting with the patient's actual harm of 300, deducing the harm of 200 from vaginal birth yields legal liability of 100.

In general, doctors often choose among risky procedures. The doctor should choose the procedure with largest expected net benefits. When benefits and costs of executing the procedures are similar, the doctor should choose the *least risky alternative*. If the doctor negligently chooses a more risky alternative, his faulty choice causes incremental risk. The practice of the courts, however, is to award damages equal to the harm actually suffered by the patient in most cases. That makes the doctor' expected liability exceed the expected harm caused by the faulty choice. Later we explain why legal rules produce this wrong result in many cases.

Medical professionals allege that high damages for tort liability in the U.S. cause too few doctors to specialize in obstetrics.[2] This allegation implies that

---

[2] Pamela Robinson et al., *The Impact of Medical Legal Risk on Obstetrician Gynecologist Supply*, 105 OBSTETRICS & GYNECOLOGY 1296 (2005); Michelle M. Mello & Carly N. Kelly, *Effects of a Professional Liability Crisis on Residents' Practice Decisions*, 105 OBSTETRICS & GYNECOLOGY 1287 (2005). Some allege that high damages affect not only obstetrics, but also other high-risk specialties as well as the general supply of physicians. *See, e.g.,* Fred J. Hellinger & William E. Encinosa, U.S. Dep't of Health & Human Servs., *The Impact of State Laws Limiting Malpractice Awards on the Geographic Distribution of Physicians* (2003), *available at* http://www.ahrq.gov/research/tortcaps/tortcaps.pdf; Daniel P. Kessler et al., *Impact of Malpractice Reforms on the Supply of Physician Services*, 293 JAMA 2618 (2005). Another recent research claims that caps on damages increase the supply of rural specialist physicians, but do not affect other populations. *See* David A. Matsa, *Does Malpractice Liability Keep the Doctor Away? Evidence from Tort Reform Damage Caps* (2006), *available at* http://ssrn.com/abstract=920846. *See also* U.S. DEP'T OF HEALTH & HUMAN SERVS., ADDRESSING THE NEW HEALTH CARE CRISIS: REFORMING THE MEDICAL LITIGATION SYSTEM TO IMPROVE THE QUALITY OF HEALTH CARE (2003), *available at* http://aspe.hhs.gov/daltcp/reports/medliab.pdf. For an opposite view, questioning the connection between high damages and supply of physicians, see TOM BAKER, THE MEDICAL MALPRACTICE MYTH 140-56 (2005); Patricia M. Danzon et al., *The Effects of Malpractice Litigation on Physicians' Fees and Incomes*, 80 AM. ECON. REV. Papers & Proc. 122 (1990).

Cooter and Porat: Liability Externalities and Mandatory Choices

doctors cannot fully recoup liability through higher fees. Applying this assumption to Example 2, damages of 300 make the obstetrician's practice relatively unprofitable, which would discourage medical students from specializing in obstetrics.

Now we turn from the underlying activity of practicing obstetrics to the choice of procedures. The court in Example 2 can verify whether or not the obstetrician chose the right method of delivery and the court can impose liability for making the wrong choice. In a more common situation described in Example 3, the court cannot verify the right method of delivery in the circumstances. Instead, the court can assess whether the *chosen* method of delivery, right or wrong, was executed negligently or non-negligently. Even the court's assessment of fault in executing the delivery is imperfect and might contain systematic errors, as the next example describes.

> *Example 3: Negligent Execution of a Mandatory Choice.* An obstetrician must decide whether to deliver a baby by vaginal or cesarean birth. The obstetrician's fees and profits are the same. In vaginal delivery the obstetrician makes a mistake with probability .10 that causes harm of 200, and the probability of liability is 1. In cesarean delivery the obstetrician makes a mistake with probability .10 that causes harm of 300, and the probability of liability is .5 According to economic principles, what damages should courts award when harm materializes from negligent cesarean or vaginal delivery?

In Example 3, the court's 50% error in finding liability for negligent cesarean deliveries results in too many of them. To correct this problem, the obstetrician *could* be held liable for 200% of the victim's harm. Instead of liability for more than the victim's harm, a lower damage measure can still cause obstetricians to choose the right method of delivery. To achieve this result, we can equalize the external harm caused by each of the mandatory alternatives. In particular a court can award damages for negligent cesarean delivery at 300 or 100% of victim's harm and for negligent vaginal delivery at 50 or 25% of victim harm. Compared to internalizing the externality, equalizing the externality provides the same incentive to make the efficient mandatory choice and more incentive to engage in the underlying activity.

Examples 1, 2, and 3 illustrate concepts developed in this paper. Part I of this paper develops the general theory of liability externalities as illustrated in Example 1. Part II discusses mandatory choices as illustrated in Examples 2 and 3, including the least harmful alternative and equalizing the externality. Part II also introduces a novel measure of damages for mandatory choices. Part III compares these concepts under uncertainty and identifies some suitable

Journal of Tort Law, Vol. 1 [2006], Iss. 1, Art. 2

circumstances for applying them. When externalities are positive, liability should decrease below the harm caused by the doctor's negligence in order to encourage the underlying activity. We propose that legislatures give courts the choice of lowering tort damages for doctors in well defined circumstances, and for their mandatory choices in particular, and we suggest some principles for doing so. Part IV concludes and briefly discusses other mechanisms to control liability externalities.

I. LIABILITY EXTERNALITIES

According to the standard economic analysis of law, a rule of strict liability with perfect compensation causes injurers to internalize the risk that they impose on others. The precaution and activity levels of injurers, consequently, are efficient. The conclusion is different, however, for a negligence rule. A negligence rule gives actors an incentive to escape liability by satisfying the legal standard of care. Having escaped liability, careful actors engage in too many harmful activities, and they engage in too few beneficial activities.

For drivers, the legal standard concerns how carefully people drive, not how much they drive. Since careful drivers escape liability most of the time, they externalize part of the risk of harming others, which makes them drive too much.[3] For doctors, the legal standard concerns their choice of treatment and their skill in carrying it out. Like drivers, careful doctors satisfy the legal standard and escape liability most of the time. Unlike drivers, escaping liability does not cause careful physicians to doctor too much. Unlike drivers and accident victims, doctors and patients have a contractual relationship and patients agree to submit to the risk that their doctor will accidentally harm them. If the contractual relationships approached the economic ideal of perfect competition, prices would capture all of the benefits and costs. Instead of perfect competition, medical markets have administered prices and quantities. Doctors often create benefits for patients that exceed their fees in total and at the margin.[4]

---

[3] Also negligent drivers drive too much for the same reason, but they pay a higher fraction of the harm they cause relatively to careful driver. Even if drivers create some positive externalities, the negativ: externalities they create are much greater. A careful empirical study concludes that a tax on driving to cover the negative externalities from risk of accident would exceed $2,000 per car in regions with high traffic density. In California the total tax revenue would exceed the sum of the current corporate and personal income tax. *See* Aaron S. Edlin & Pinar Karaca-Mandic, *The Accident Externality from Driving*, 114 J. POL. ECON. 931 (2006).

[4] *See* David S. Bloch & William R. Nelson Jr., *Defining 'Health': Three Visions and their Ramifications*, 1 DePAUL J. HEALTH CARE L. 723, 731 (1997) ("Commentators who consider health a non-marketable good contend that there are elements of health which, though valuable, are unquantifiable, such as hope, compassion, and the extension and preservation of life ... Health's social benefits are not fully realized by the market price it commands"); T.R Marmor et al., *Medical Care and Procompetitive Reform*, 34 VAND. L. REV. 1003, 1009 (1981) ("Improved

Cooter and Porat: Liability Externalities and Mandatory Choices

A negligence rule, however, does not allow careful drivers or doctors to escape liability in all circumstances. Courts sometimes make mistakes in applying the duty of care and hold careful actors liable. Like courts, normally careful actors occasionally make mistakes and harm others. Whether from court or personal error, even normally careful actors bear some of the risk associated with their activity. Higher damages, consequently, reduce the incentive of careful actors to engage in the activity. In the case of drivers, higher damages will increase auto insurance premiums and drivers will respond by driving less and buying fewer cars. In the case of doctors, higher damages will cause them to perform fewer treatments that risk liability and discourage them from specializing in fields with high risk of liability. Lowering damages will decrease these undesirable effects and benefit patients.[5]

Figure 1: Optimal Damages for Drivers and Doctors

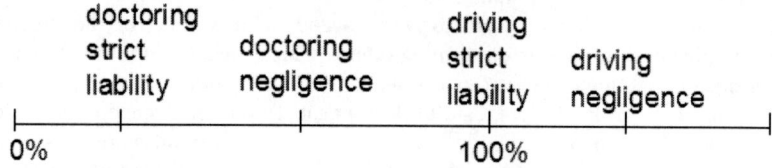

optimal damages as % of actual harm to victim

---

health, the anticipated outcome of medical care, has positive externalities. This makes medical care a merit good, and, unlike many other economic goods, one that should not be allocated solely on the basis of ability to pay"); Stuart Rome, *Medicine and Public Policy: Let Us Look Before We Leap Again*, 41 MD. L. REV. 46, 48 (1981). *See also* Maja Campbell-Eaton, *Antitrust and Certificate of Need: A Doubtful Prognosis*, 69 IOWA L. REV. 1451, 1459 (1984). ("Moreover, health care usually is viewed as a "merit good", with benefits extending beyond its economic value. This view is reinforced by the ethical mandates of the health professions and by a widespread belief that "more is better" in the provision of medical services").

[5] Tom Baker argues that doctors, health care providers, and medical malpractice insurers pay much less than necessary to cover the true social costs of doctors' wrongdoing. *See* BAKER, *supra* note 2. *See also infra* note 22. If the external costs discussed by Baker exceed the external benefits of doctoring, then incentives exist for too many people to become doctors. Our article does not compare the negative and positive liability externalities of doctors in general. Rather, we assume that there are several fields in medicine where the positive externalities exceed the negative externalities. For example, much research supports the argument that positive externalities exceed negative externalities in obstetrics. *See supra* note 2. Liability law biases doctors against specializing in these fields.

Journal of Tort Law, Vol. 1 [2006], Iss. 1, Art. 2

Figure 1 depicts these facts about driving and doctoring. The line in Figure 1 represents optimal damages as a percentage of full compensation. For activities like driving, incentives are optimal under a rule of strict liability when damages equal 100% of the victim's harm. For a negligence rule, however, incentives for drivers' activity are optimal when damages exceed 100% of the victim's actual harm. For activities with positive externalities like some medical specialties, incentives are optimal when damages are less than 100% of the victim's actual harm. For these activities, optimal damages fall as the rule of liability shifts from negligence to strict liability.

Empirical studies show that courts tend to award higher damages in medical malpractice cases than in road accident cases. When researchers controlled for injury severity, amount of reported economic damages, and other factors, malpractice awards remained approximately three times larger than those in automobile cases.[6] Furthermore, in cases of wrongful death, the median award in malpractice trials was $876,000, while the median award in automobile trials was $318,000.[7] This data, however, requires cautious interpretation.[8] Turning from econometrics to raw statistics, plaintiffs have lower success rates[9] and higher

---

[6] AUDREY CHIN & MARK A. PETERSON, DEEP POCKETS, EMPTY POCKETS: WHO WINS IN COOK COUNTY JURY TRIALS 36 (1985) (The median award was $201,000 and the mean was $1,057,000. When outlier awards were excluded, the mean was $432,000. Fully 15% of malpractice awards exceeded $1 million).

[7] Thomas H. Cohen & Steven K. Smith, *Civil Trial Cases and Verdicts in Large Counties, 2001*, BUREAU JUST. STAT. BULL., Apr. 2004, at 1, *available at* http://www.ojp.usdoj.gov/bjs/pub/pdf/ctcvlc01.pdf.

[8] The discrepancy between tort awards overall and malpractice awards is likely due, in large part, to differences in how malpractice cases are selected for trial. *See* Neil Vidmar, *Pap and Circumstance: What Jury Verdict Statistics Can Tell Us About Jury Behavior and the Tort System*, 28 SUFFOLK U. L. REV. 1205, 1212-22 (1994). Other differences could also explain the discrepancy: Automobile cases often involve multiple plaintiffs, the driver and passengers of the second car, but usually a single defendant, the allegedly negligent driver of the first car. Malpractice cases, however, typically involve a single plaintiff, the injured patient, and multiple defendants. Automobile cases may involve contributory negligence, which is not claimed as often in malpractice cases. Medical malpractice lawyers tend to be specialists who carefully screen cases and invest heavily in experts, whereas generalist lawyers who often call few or no experts to litigate automobile cases. *See* FRANK M. MCCLELLAN, MEDICAL MALPRACTICE: LAW TACTICS AND EVIDENCE 45-62 (1993); PAUL C. WEILER, MEDICAL MALPRACTICE ON TRIAL 19-26 (1991). The crux of the matter is that "juries hear very different cases in medical and automobile negligence trials and decide them under different legal standards." Vidmar, *supra*, at 1222.

[9] The overall win rate for medical malpractice plaintiffs (27%) was about half of that found among plaintiffs in all tort trials (52%). *See* Thomas H. Cohen, *Medical Malpractice Trials and Verdicts in Large Counties, 2001*, BUREAU OF JUSTICE STATISTICS CIV. JUST. DATA BRIEF., Apr. 2004, *available at* http://www.ojp.usdoj.gov/bjs/pub/pdf/mmtvlc01.pdf; Cohen & Smith, *supra* note 7, at 1. *See also* NEIL VIDMAR, MEDICAL MALPRACTICE AND THE AMERICAN JURY: CONFRONTING THE MYTHS ABOUT JURY INCOMPETENCE, DEEP POCKETS AND OUTRAGEOUS

Cooter and Porat: Liability Externalities and Mandatory Choices

awards in medical malpractice cases, compared to automobile cases or tort cases in general.[10]

"Externality" usually means costs and benefits conveyed to others that market prices do not capture. When markets fail, liability law often improves the situation by making injurers compensate victims. Sometimes, however, liability law leaves significant costs externalized. We adopt the phrase "liability externality" to mean costs and benefits conveyed to others that market prices do not capture and liability law does not correct. Given liability externalities, adjusting damages can improve incentives. When liability externalities are negative as with driving, increasing damages above full compensation improves incentives for the activity. Conversely, when liability externalities are positive as with doctoring in certain fields, decreasing damages below full compensation improves incentives for the activity.

While decreasing damages improves incentives for the activity, it could distort the incentives for precaution. Thus, if doctors pay, say, 50% of harm, they might take less precaution than required by efficiency. Later we show that medicine involve mandatory choices, and liability lower than 100% will provide efficient incentives for precaution in these cases. In other cases, a tradeoff exists between precautions and activity level, and so improving incentives for activity necessarily worsens incentives for precaution.

DAMAGE AWARDS 39 (1995). For comparison, in automobile negligence trials, plaintiffs prevailed in 61.2% of the trials. Cohen & Smith, *supra.*

[10] In general tort cases, the median verdict, including punitive damages was $51,000. Brian J. Ostrom et al., *A Step above Anecdote: A Profile of the Civil Jury in the 1990's,* 79 JUDICATURE 233, 238 (1996). The mean award was much higher $408,000. The discrepancy between median and mean was produced by some very large awards. When the top and bottom 5% of these outlier awards were excluded, the mean was $ 160,000. Medical malpractice cases, however, had substantially higher awards. *Id. See also* Cohen, *Medical Malpractice Trials, supra* note 10 (showing that the median award of $425,000 in medical malpractice trials was nearly 16 times greater than the overall median award in all tort trials ($27,000)). The RAND corporation studies indicated that even when juries considered injury severity, medical malpractice plaintiffs and products liability plaintiffs received awards several times greater than those received by automobile injury plaintiffs. CHIN & PETERSON, *supra* note 6. Randall Bovbjerg and his colleagues found that the expected awards for automobile cases are only two thirds those for malpractice cases (0.66 as compared to 1.00), or, conversely, malpractice scores half again higher. Randall R. Bovbjerg et al., *Juries and Justice: Are Malpractice and Other Personal Injuries Created Equal?,* 54 LAW & CONTEMP. PROBS. 5, 25 (1991). Almost one out of every four medical malpractice awards exceeded $1 million. In contrast, automobile and premises liability cases had much lower mean and median awards. *See* Neil Vidmar, *The Performance of the American Civil Jury: an Empirical Perspective,* 40 ARIZ. L. REV. 849, 876 (1998). However, punitive damages remain rare in medical malpractice jury trials. From 1992 to 2001, 1% to 4% of plaintiff winners in medical malpractice jury trials received punitive damages. *See* Cohen, *Medical Malpractice Trials, supra* note 10; *see also* Marc Galanter, *Real World Torts: An Antidote to Anecdote,* 55 MD. L. REV. 1093, 1134, 1138 (1996).

Journal of Tort Law, Vol. 1 [2006], Iss. 1, Art. 2

To increase precision, we express the preceding arguments in notation. Consider an activity that benefits other people, and also imposes risks on them. The activity creates benefits of b for other people and imposes risk of harm h on them with probability p. Thus the marginal net benefit to others is b-ph. Because of a market transaction, the actor receives the market price m. Liability law requires the actor to pay damages d with probability q. Thus the actor's expected net benefit equals m-qd. These variables - b, q, d, p, and h - may be interpreted as marginal values.[11] To internalize marginal net benefits, the actor's expected net payoff must equal the net social benefit of the activity to others at the margin:

$$m - qd = b - ph \qquad (1).$$

Solving for d yields the level of damages d* that internalizes social costs:

d*	=	(1/q)	[ph	-	(b-m)]	(2).
		reciprocal	expected		price	
		of enforcement	harm		externality	
		error				

For an application of equation 2, consider defective consumer products. Strict liability implies that most injuries are compensated: q≈p. When consumer products are sold in competitive markets and consumers discount risks due to ignorance, consumers buy the good until the marginal benefit from consumption equals the price: b=m. Thus equation 2 reduces to the proposition that social harms are internalized when manufacturer's liability equals 100% of the actual harm to a consumer: d*=h. This is the standard conclusion of the economic argument for strict liability for defective consumer products.

Now consider automobile accidents. The injurer and victim are usually strangers, so, before the accident, they do not negotiate a price for driving: 0=m. Drivers do not convey benefits to their potential victims: 0=b. Equation (2) reduces to d*=(p/q)h. q represents the probability that a driver involved in an accident is held liable. If drivers were always held liable for involvement in an accident, then q would equal the accident probability p, and optimal damages d* would equal actual harm h. This outcome might occur if drivers were strictly liable for harm to others. Instead of strict liability, drivers face a negligence rule and they expect to escape liability part of the time: q<p. To offset the fall in

---

[11] Thus *p* denotes the change in the probability of an accident from a marginal increase in the activity. For drivers, p is the increase in the probability of an accident from a small increase in driving. For doctors, p is the increase in the probability of an accident from treating another patient.

Cooter and Porat: Liability Externalities and Mandatory Choices

probability of liability, damages must increase above full compensation. Specifically, damages internalize the externality when d=(p/q)h. To illustrate, if drivers expect to be liable 33% of the time, then damages must equal 300% of the actual harm in order to internalize the risk of harm to others.[12]

Unlike drivers, doctors usually have a contractual relationship with an injured patient. The contract may include a price m that encompasses some, but not all, of the benefits to the patient, in which case we have m<b. The unpriced benefit given by b-m is a price externality. According to Equation 2, the price externality causes optimal damages d* to decrease below 100% of the actual harm h. With a negligence rule, doctors are liable for some, but not all, accidents: q<p. This fact, according to Equation 2, causes damages d* to increase above 100% of the actual harm h. The external benefit causes optimal liability to fall, and the external harm causes optimal liability to rise.

To be concrete, assume that the probability p that the treatment harms the patient is .10, and the resulting harm h is 100. Assume that the doctor is found liable in half of the cases where the patient suffers harm, so the doctor's probability of liability q equals .05. Finally, assume that the patient's benefit b exceeds the doctor's fee m by 8. Under these assumptions, equation 2 implies that the doctor's optimal liability d* equals 40% of the actual harm of 100. [13]

II. MANDATORY CHOICES

Providers of services are usually free to choose whether or not to serve a particular client.[14] Once the actor commits to providing the service, however, he subsequently faces mandatory choices in fulfilling his commitment. Mandatory

---

[12] Less care by the injurer increases the probability of an accident. Assume that less care also increases the probability that the victim can prove negligence and recover damages. These assumptions imply Craswell's Paradox: With the multiplier, the optimal sanction is less when wrongdoing is worse. By definition the multiplier equals the reciprocal of the enforcement error, and, by assumption, worse wrongdoing is more likely to be detected, so worse wrongdoing must result in a lower sanction. Richard Craswell, *Deterrence and Damages: The Multiplier Principle and its Alternatives*, 97 MICH. L. REV. 2185 (1999).

[13] By assumption, H=100, p=.10, q=.05, and a-m=8. Thus equation 2 reduces to:

$$d* = \frac{1}{q}(ph - b + m) = \frac{1}{.05}(.10 \times 100 - 8) = 40.$$

[14] Law sometimes requires a professional to provide a service. For example, according to the Emergency Medical Treatment and Active Labor Act, 42 U.S.C. 13955dd (1998), hospitals have an obligation to provide for examination and treatment for emergency medical conditions. For a claim that common law should recognize a duty of 'medical rescue' of doctors and other health care professionals see Kevin Williams, *Medical Samaritans: Is There a Duty to Treat?*, 21 OXFORD J. LEGAL STUD. 393 (2001).

---

choices often arise from a relationship created by contract. For some mandatory choices, each of the alternatives imposes risks on others.[15] We focus on medical services where a doctor must choose among treatments and each one risks harming the patient, such as a choice of how to deliver a baby, whether or not to operate, or whether or not to administer a particular drug. The same problem of mandatory choice with unavoidable risks arises in a fiduciary relationship between, say, a client and his bank, an investor and the firm's board of directors, or a client and his attorney.

Our discussion of Example 2 explained how liability affects the obstetrician's choice between vaginal and cesarean delivery. Figure 2 imbeds this mandatory choice in some decisions that precede and follow it. Before choosing, the obstetrician must prepare to make the choice, which involves examining the patient and ordering tests. Much earlier in the sequence, the medical student must decide whether or not to specialize in obstetrics. Finally, after making the mandatory choice, the obstetrician must carry it out, either carefully or negligently. We will analyze the connection between each of these decisions and liability in tort law.

Figure 2: Acts Preceding and Following a Mandatory Choice

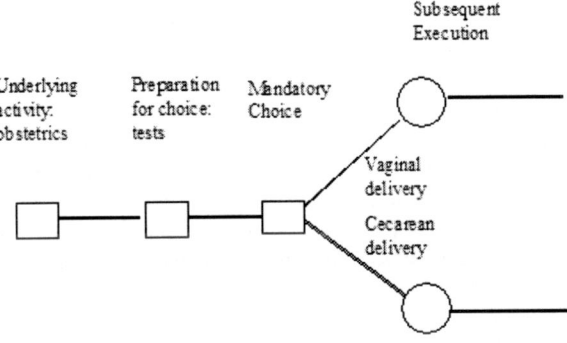

---

[15] Ariel Porat, *The Many Faces of Negligence*, 4 THEORETICAL INQ. L. 105, 121-4 (2003).

A. *The Least Harmful Alternative*

A general principle of tort law holds a person liable for damages equal to the harm caused by his negligence. For mandatory choices, courts apply this principle inconsistently, as we will demonstrate. In Example 2, the actor did not cause the mandatory choice that he must make on behalf of the patient. Given the mandatory choice, risk of harm at the level caused by the least harmful alternative was unavoidable. The actor's faulty choice caused additional risk of harm, which equals the patients' actual risk minus the risk from the least harmful alternative. In Example 2, the additional risk is 30-20=10. In Example 2, the risk associated with the actor's choice materialized and actual harm equaled 300. In setting damages, the court might want to subtract the unavoidable risk from the actual harm, resulting in damages of 280.[16] Or the court might want to subtract the harm of 200 that might have been realized by the non-negligent choice, resulting in damages of 100.

The principles of positive law, however, do not allow the court to subtract anything as long as the risks of the faulty choice and the risks of the least harmful choice do not overlap. To illustrate non-overlapping risks, vaginal delivery is more likely to cause uterine prolepses, whereas cesarean birth carries risks associated with surgery. If the obstetrician wrongfully chooses cesarean delivery and the mother suffers harm in surgery, the principles of positive law do not allow a deduction for avoiding the risk of uterine prolepses.

The principles of economics favor a different conclusion from positive law. The obstetrician's faulty choice increased one risk by 30 and reduced another risk by 20, thus causing additional risk of 10. This is true even though the risks do not overlap. In order to make the doctor internalize the social costs of his wrong choice, he could be held liable for imposing risk of 10, regardless of whether or not the risk materialized. Tort law, however, imposes liability for materialized harm, not for exposure to risk. Harm materializes with probability .10. Liability of 100 for materialized harm has the same incentive effects as liability of 10 for exposure to risk.[17] The socially efficient level of damages for materialized harm equals 100 in this example.

Notice that our rule differs from a rule of probabilistic recovery. A probabilistic recovery principle mandates imposing liability on a defendant for the harm suffered by the plaintiff multiplied by the probability that the harm was

---

[16] An award of 280 is analogical to probabilistic recovery awarded by some courts for lost chances of recovery. *See* ARIEL PORAT & ALEX STEIN, TORT LIABILITY UNDER UNCERTAINTY 73-76, 101-29 (Oxford, 2001).

[17] For simplicity, we also assume that actors are risk-neutral.

Journal of Tort Law, Vol. 1 [2006], Iss. 1, Art. 2

caused by the defendant's wrongdoing.[18] Some courts apply the principle in medical malpractice cases where the doctor's negligence diminished the plaintiff's chances of recovery. Consider the patient who arrives at the hospital with 30% odds of recovery, but because his disease is not diagnosed by the doctor in time, his chances drop to zero. The patient brings a tort action against the doctor. The patient would lose if the preponderance of evidence standard were applied, because the probability that the doctor caused the harm is lower than 50%. The court might apply a probabilistic recovery rule, which would result in the doctor bearing liability for 30% of the patient's harm. [19]

Under a probabilistic recovery rule damages in Example 2 should be 280. The reason is simple: The patient suffered harm of 300. "But for" the doctor's negligence the patient would have suffered either no harm or harm of 200. The probability of the latter is .1. Therefore. 200 x .1 should be deducted from the actual harm of 300 suffered by the patient. Conversely, under our rule, liability should be for 100. Liability for 100—not for 280—will make the doctor internalize the true risk he created by his negligence.

In fact our suggestion is motivated not by the uncertainty of the case (which is the motivation for a probabilistic recovery rule), but by the presence of positive externalities. In Example 2 the doctor's negligent choice caused both negative and positive effects: He increased one risk by 30 (negative externaliy) and he also decreased another risk by 20 (positive externality). Prevailing tort law internalizes the negative effects by imposing liability on the doctor when harm materializes, but the positive effects remains externalized by him. As a result, the doctor bears more than the net risk created by his negligence. We suggest correcting this distortion by crediting the doctor with the positive externalities he created by his negligence and reducing his liability accordingly.

To formalize this argument, let A denote the reasonable choice that risks harm h_a with probability p_a. Let B denote the unreasonable choice that risks harm h_b with probability p_b. The expected harm from the least harmful alternative equals $p_a h_a$, and the expected harm from the chosen alternative equals $p_b h_b$. Deducting the former from the latter yields $p_b h_b - p_a h_a$, which indicates the additional risk from choosing the wrong alternative. Instead of liability for risk, the court imposes liability for realized harm. To find the level of liability for realized harm

---

[18] PORAT & STEIN, *supra* note 16, at 116-29.

[19] In this context, the principle is known as the "lost chances of recovery principle." *See, e.g.,* Herskovits v. Group Health Coop. of Puget Sound, 664 P.2d 474 (Wash. 1983); Perez v. Las Vegas Med. Ctr., 805 P.2d 589, 592 (Nev. 1991). *See also* DAN B. DOBBS, LAW OF REMEDIES 238 (2d ed., 1993). For support for the principle, see J.H. King, *Causation, Valuation, and Chance in Personal Injury Torts Involving Pre-existing Conditions and Future Consequences,* 90 Yale L.J. 1353 (1981). The market share liability doctrine is another application of a probabilistic recovery rule. PORAT & STEIN, *supra* note 16.

Cooter and Porat: Liability Externalities and Mandatory Choices

that is equivalent to liability for additional risk, multiply the preceding difference by $1/p_b$, which yields $h_b - p_a h_a/p_b$.

We have explained that when the risks from a mandatory choice do not overlap, legal principles would not allow subtracting from the victim's actual harm a fraction that reflects the *risk* of the least harmful alternative. When the mandatory choice imposes unavoidable *harm* rather than risk, however, the court has no difficulty subtracting the least harmful alternative when computing damages. To illustrate, modify Example 2 and assume that vaginal delivery causes harm of 200 to mother with certainty, and cesarean delivery causes different harm of 300 to mother with certainty. Courts would note that, but for the actor's negligence, harm would have been 200 rather than 300, so the negligent choice caused harm of 100. When a mandatory choice results in certain harm, the "but for" test of causation requires subtracting the least harmful alternative for victim from victim's actual harm.

The same conclusion applies in another set of circumstances as illustrated by a hypothetical inspired by Example 2. Assume that two alternatives procedures, A or B, benefit the patient equally and cost the doctor the same. Also, procedure A or procedure B risk harm of 200 with probability .1 to patient's *left* leg. Since the risk to the left leg is the same for both procedures, we call it *overlapping*. In addition, procedure B risks harm of 100 with probability .1 to patient's *right* leg. Since the risk to the right leg only occurs with procedure B, we call it *non-overlapping*.

The doctor negligently chooses procedure B and the patient suffers total harm of 300—200 to his left leg and 100 to his right leg. The doctor's negligent choice did not change the overlapping risk to the left leg. The doctor's wrong choice, however, increased the risk to the right leg. Under appropriate application of causation law,[20] liability for making the wrong choice will be imposed on the doctor only for the harm to the right leg. This is true even though the doctor's wrong choice is also a "but for" cause of the harm to the left leg (since but for the doctor's wrong choice the probability of inflicting harm on the patient's left leg was only .1). By this reasoning, doctor's liability equals 100, not 300.

Another variation concerns non-overlapping harm to different people. In Example 2 assume that the additional risk created by cesarean delivery falls on the baby, not the mother, while the risk to mother is identical under both procedures and relates to the same harm. By assumption, the risks to mother by both methods of delivery overlap, while the risks to baby are separate. If the obstetrician delivers by cesarean and harm materializes, mother suffers loss of

---

[20] Guido Calabresi, *Concerning Cause and the Law of Torts: An Essay for Harry Kalven, Jr.*, 43 U. Chi. L. Rev. 69 (1975).

Journal of Tort Law, Vol. 1 [2006], Iss. 1, Art. 2

200 and baby suffers loss of 100. Baby is entitled to damages of 100 while mother is entitled to no damages.[21]

We have explained that computing damages for a negligent mandatory choice requires subtracting from actual harm a fraction that reflects the risk of the least harmful alternative. Legal principles of causation, however, require courts to subtract damages only where harm is certain or overlapping, but not when harm is probabilistic and not overlapping.[22]

Failing to reduce damages has three negative consequences as represented from left to right in Figure 2.

First, it discourages medical students from specializing in obstetrics. Even though in theory doctors could shift the additional liability to their patients, in fact doctors cannot fully recoup liability through higher fees.[23]

---

[21] If vaginal delivery risks harm of 200 with probability .1 to mother, and cesarean delivery risks harm of 300 with probability .1 to baby, and doctor wrongfully choose cesarean and harm materialized, the risks do not overlap and doctor will pay damages of 300, not 100. But this should not come as a surprise to tort law scholars who know that positive externalities to one person (e.g. the mother) do not affect the victim's right to compensation (e.g. the baby). Efficiency would mandate liability of 100 in all such cases.

[22] Arlen and MacLeod argued that doctors' liability should equal the difference between the patient's expected benefits from optimal treatment and the patient's actual benefit from the erroneous treatment that he received. Assuming under-enforcement, that difference should be divided by the probability that the doctor is found liable when negligent. *See* Jennifer Arlen & W. Bentley MacLeod, *Malpractice Liability for Physicians and Managed Care Organizations*, 78 N.Y.U. L. Rev. 1929, 1984-5 (2003). Those authors, however, did not distinguish between certain harms and uncertain risks, overlapping and non-overlapping risk, and risks to same patient or different patients.

The idea developed here with respect to mandatory choices has a wider scope. In general, when a wrongful act creates risks but at the same time reduced other risks, either to the victim or to third parties, liability should be reduced, reflecting the net, rather the gross risks, which the wrongful behavior created. Especially when applied to risks reduced to third parties, the argument invites a strong opposition from corrective justice scholars. *See* Porat, *The Many Faces of Negligence*, *supra* note 15; Ariel Porat, *Offsetting Risks* (on file with authors).

[23] Mello & Kelly, *supra* note 2. Of the inability of doctors to pass higher insurance costs along to patients, see Peter Eisler et al., *Hype Outraces Facts in Malpractice Debate*, USA TODAY, Mar. 5, 2003, *available at* http://www.usatoday.com/news/nation/2003-03-04-malpractice-cover_x.htm (claiming that the cause of this inability is the limitations on reimbursements made by managed care insurers, Medicare and Medicaid). BAKER, *supra* note 2, at 64-65. (admitting that "physicians have little or no ability to raise prices in response to increased costs. When a malpractice insurance crisis hits, the burden falls disproportionately on physicians in high-risk specialties and locations, who cannot raise their prices in response"). It is worth mentioning that medical practice has negative externalities as well due to the fact that many of patients who sustained injury as a result of negligence do not sue. *See id.*; A.R. Localio et al., *Relations Between Malpractice Claims and Adverse Events Due to Negligence: Results of the Harvard Medical Practice Study III*, 325 NEW ENG. J. MED. 245 (1991); David M Studdert et al., *Negligence Care and Malpractice Claiming Behavior in Utah and Colorado*, 38 MED. CARE 250 (2000). Another research by Studdert points to the costly litigation in these cases which might discourage patients from suing. *See* David M.

Cooter and Porat: Liability Externalities and Mandatory Choices

Second, it causes too many tests in preparing to choose a procedure. To illustrate by Example 2, when negligent obstetricians are liable for 300, obstetricians order more tests than if they were liable for 100.[24] In principle, courts could solve the problem by imposing strict liability on obstetricians for the full harm that resulted from either choice. Strict liability would discourage obstetrics by making obstetricians pay much more than the social costs of their activities. Indeed, non-negligent obstetricians would have to pay for the risks caused by the pregnancy of their patients.

Third, it causes obstetricians who face mandatory choices to choose the alternative that reduces the risk of liability and not the risk of harm. This fact might explain the high number of cesarean deliveries compared to vaginal deliveries. In general, when liability for negligence is larger, the incentives of doctors to escape the risk of liability by practicing defensive medicine are stronger.[25]

Studdert et al., *Claims, Errors, and Compensation Payments in Medical Malpractice Litigation*, 354 NEW ENG. J. MED. 2024 (2006). *But see supra* note 6.

[24] The reason for that is the possibility of courts' and doctors' errors in determining whether the doctor satisfied the standard of care.

[25] Lowering the cesarean rate in the United States has been a goal for the past 25 years. *See* U.S. DEP'T OF HEALTH & HUMAN SERVS., NIH PUB. NO. 82-2067, CESAREAN CHILDBIRTH: REPORT OF A CONSENSUS DEVELOPMENT CONFERENCE (1981). It is still highly relevant today, while the total cesarean section rate is 27.5 per 100 births. Actually, cesarean delivery rates in the United States rose from 4.5 per 100 births in 1965 to 24.1 per 100 in 1986. A.R. Localio et al., *Relationship between malpractice claims and cesarean delivery*, 269 JAMA.366 (1993). In response to the growing concerns in the 1980s about the rising cesarean rate, the U.S. Department of Health and Human Services established decreasing the cesarean rate as one of the *Healthy People 2000* objectives. U.S. DEP'T OF HEALTH & HUMAN SERVS., HEALTHY PEOPLE 2000: NATIONAL HEALTH PROMOTION AND DISEASE PREVENTION OBJECTIVES (1990). National efforts to decrease the cesarean rate now focus on low-risk women as defined in the *Healthy People 2010* objectives, while the objective is for a cesarean rate of no more than 15 per 100 births. 2 U.S. DEP'T OF HEALTH & HUMAN SERVS., HEALTHY PEOPLE 2010 §16-9 (2d ed., 2000), *available at* http://www.healthypeople.gov/Document/pdf/Volume2/16MICH.pdf.

A reason for these high rates may be found in the malpractice crisis. Obstetrics experience growing claims rates and now fields more malpractice claims than any other specialty. Roger A. Rosenblatt et al., *Why do Physicians Stop Practicing Obstetrics? The Impact of Malpractice Claims*, 76 OBSTETRICS & GYNECOLOGY 245, 249 (1990). The frequency of claims has increased such that, in 1999, 76.5% of obstetrician-gynecologists surveyed by the American College for Obstetricians and Gynecologists reported being sued at least once. Sarah Domin, *Where Have All the Baby-Doctors Gone? Women's Access to Healthcare in Jeopardy: Obstetrics and the Medical Malpractice Insurance Crisis*, 53 CATH. U. L. REV. 499, 504 (2004).

Fear of being sued if complications arise in a vaginal delivery has contributed to the rising number of cesarean sections. *See* Elizabeth Swire Falker, *The Medical Malpractice Crisis in Obstetrics: A Gestalt Approach to Reform*, 4 CARDOZO WOMEN'S L.J. 1, 15 (1997). Studies examined the impact of malpractice risk on cesarean deliveries and found that a systematic relationship between the rate of cesarean surgical procedures and malpractice claim frequency exists. Michael Daly, *Attacking Defensive Medicine Through The Utilization of Practice*

Journal of Tort Law, Vol. 1 [2006], Iss. 1, Art. 2

The preceding analysis assumed a mandatory choice between two alternatives, but the results change only modestly when there is a mandatory choice among continuous alternatives. Assume that the mandatory choice involves alternatives that run continuously from the least risky alternative to the more risky alternatives. Somewhere along this continuum is the boundary between negligent and non-negligent behavior. As the injurer's behavior approaches this boundary, the risk of injury increases continuously, whereas the expected liability jumps discontinuously at the boundary. The jump occurs so long as the court awards compensation for the victim's actual harm without subtracting damages which reflect the least harmful alternative. This discontinuity in costs has important behavioral consequences described in an earlier literature without the concept of mandatory choices or recognition of non-overlapping risks.[26]

B. *Disgorgement*

Faced with a mandatory choice, a self-interested injurer will choose the alternative whose net benefit is higher for him, even if his choice increases the risks to the victim by more than its net benefit. If injurer must disgorge his savings each time he chooses the more risky alternative, he will have an incentive to choose the less risky alternative. To illustrate, assume that the obstetrician's fee in Example 2 is the same for cesarean and vaginal delivery, but vaginal delivery costs the doctor 1 more than cesarean delivery. The obstetrician thus gains 1 each time he negligently chooses cesarean delivery. If the obstetrician were required to disgorge his gain every time he negligently chooses cesarean delivery, then he

---

Parameters, 16 J. LEGAL MED. 101, 105 (1995). *See also* Antonella Vimercati et al., *Choice of Cesarean Section and Perception of Legal Pressure*, 28 J. PERINATAL MED. 111 (2000) (stating that the perception of legal pressure was directly related to the rate of cesarean section). For an argument that reducing damages could have opposite effects, because when liability is lower doctors tend to perform more unnecessary procedures which are more profitable to them, see Janet Currie & Bentley Macleod, *First Do Not Harm? Reform and Birth Outcomes* (NBER Working Paper Series, Working Paper No. 12478, 2006), *available at* http://papers.ssrn.com/sol3/abstract=926057.

[26] The discontinuity and its behavioral consequences were originally explained in Robert D. Cooter, *Economic Analysis of Punitive Damages*, 56 S. CAL. L. REV. 79 (1982). Cooter later explained that the discontinuity is due to incomplete information by the courts. *See* Robert D. Cooter, *Punitive Damages for Deterrence: When and How Much?*, 40 ALA. L. REV. 1143 (1989). Grady argued against Cooter that courts would not actually hold injurers liable for more harm than they actually caused by negligently untaken precautions. *See* Mark F. Grady, *A New Positive Economic Theory of Negligence*, 92 YALE L.J. 799 (1983). *See also* Marcel Kahan, *On Causation and Incentives to Take Care under the Negligence Rule*, 18 J. LEGAL STUD. 427 (1989); Richard Craswell & John E. Calfee, *Deterrence and Uncertain Legal Standards*, 2 J.L. ECON. & ORG. 279, 295-7 (1986) (advocating liability for incremental damages which is the difference between the social losses inflicted by injurers' activity and the social losses that would have been inflicted had they complied with the legal standard).

would have efficient incentives. If, however, the disgorgement takes place only when the obstetrician negligently chooses cesarean delivery and harm materializes, then deterring wrongdoing requires increasing damages to reflect the obstetrician's gain in the cases where he negligently chooses cesarean delivery and harm did not materialize. In our example, the obstetrician expects to pay damages when harm materializes, which occurs in 10% of cesarean deliveries. Damages of 10 for materialized harm will cause the obstetrician's expected liability to equal his expected gain from negligence, so he expects to disgorge his gain from wrongdoing.

Alternatively, the injurer can cut costs by reducing efforts to verify which alternative is the least risky alternative. Spending less on preparing to choose increases the probability of making the wrong choice. To illustrate, assume that the obstetrician saves 1 by refraining from making costly tests to decide how to deliver the baby, and a lack of test causes the obstetrician to choose the more risky alternative.

We coin the phrase "Disgorgement Damages for Risk of Accidents" ("DDA") to refer to damages that makes the negligent injurer's expected liability equal to his expected gains from negligence. For mandatory choices these gains include the difference between the injurer's costs of executing the two alternative procedures. These gains also include the untaken precautions that should have been taken to prepare to choose. The *DDA* generally equals or exceeds the actual gain in the case where the harm materializes. In the preceding examples, DDA equals the gain multiplied by the reciprocal of the probability of liability.

We will derive this result for a case where the alternative procedures have different costs for the injurer. Let a_A and a_B represent the cost of alternative acts to the actor. Assume that act a_B involves more costs than act a_A. As before, m is the price paid to the actor, q is the probability of liability, and d is damages. Disgorgement damages d_A* equalize the net costs of each act to the actor:

$$[m_B - a_B - q_B d_B] = [m_A - a_A - q_A d*_A].$$

Rearranging terms yields a formula for disgorgement damages:

$$d*_A = \frac{1}{q_A} q_B d_B + \frac{1}{q_A}[(m_A - m_B) + (a_B - a_A)].$$

Under the simplifying assumptions that $d_B=0$ and $m_A=m_B$, the preceding equation reduces to the proposition that damages equal the reciprocal of the probability of harm multiplied by the gain from negligence:

Journal of Tort Law, Vol. 1 [2006], Iss. 1, Art. 2

$$d^*_A = \frac{1}{q_A}(a_B - a_A).$$

$$\underbrace{\phantom{\frac{1}{q_A}(a_B - a_A).}}_{\substack{\textit{gain from}\\ \textit{negligence}}}$$

Since DDA exactly offsets the expected gain from making the wrong choice, DDA is the lowest level of damages that cause self-interested actors to behave non-negligently. Moving from left to right in Figure 2 reveals an advantage and a disadvantage of DDA. For activities with positive externalities, DDA has the advantage of encouraging more of the underlying activity than any alternative damage measure that deters negligence. DDA, however, is likely to give the injurer deficient incentives to prepare for the mandatory choice. The reparations are often non-verifiable, so the gains included in the DDA exclude them. Applied to Example 2, DDA gives the obstetrician the required incentive to choose vaginal delivery, and DDA encourages medical students to become obstetricians, but DDA is likely to give insufficient incentives for testing before deciding on the method of delivery. To illustrate the latter effect by Example 2, under DDA the doctor is likely not to take tests that cost him more than 1, even though the expected harm from making the wrong choice is 10.

Another problem with DDA arises in cases where an ordinarily carefully actor's attention lapses and he causes harm. Under prevailing law a lapse of attention that causes harm is considered negligence and triggers liability. Typically, the injurer gains nothing from lapsing, which implies that DDA equals zero. To avoid DDA of zero, the court would have to find someone liable who saved costs from the doctor's untaken precaution. Thus over-work or inferior working conditions could cause an obstetrician to lapse. Perhaps the doctor's employer overworked the doctor and caused the lapse, or perhaps the doctor's employer provided inferior working conditions that caused the lapse. Courts could apply DDA to the employer's gains from over-working the doctor or providing inferior working conditions.[27]

---

[27] Saul Levmore raised the possibility of using a multiplier in restitution cases but rejected it as impractical. Even though Levmore has not explicitly discussed accidental cases, his analysis can be applied to them. Saul Levmore, *Probabilistic Recoveries, Restitution, and Recurring Wrongs*, 19 J. LEGAL STUD. 691, 713. For a discussion of the possibility of awarding damages at the amount of the injurer's gain, but without suggesting a DDA, see A. Mitchell Polinsky & Stephen Shavell, *Should Liability be Based on the Harm to the Victim or the Gain to the Injurer*, 10 J.L. Econ. & Org. 427 (1994). Laycock posed the question of whether restitution law should be applied to saving of precaution in product liability cases and if yes, in what manner. *See* DOUGLAS LAYCOCK, MODERN AMERICAN REMEDIES: CASES AND MATERIALS 598-600 (3d ed., 2002).

C. *Equalizing Externalities*

Think of liability as having two components: The baseline of liability for harm resulting from the right choice, plus the increase in liability for making the wrong choice. The increase in liability for making the wrong choice is the difference in liability. The difference in liability can be used to control the mandatory choice, and the baseline of liability can be used to control other behaviors: engaging in the underlying activity, preparing to choose and executing the choice. In section A we assumed the baseline to be zero. Now we explore under what circumstance it should be positive.

As we have shown, disgorgement damages (DDA) provide the lowest liability for a mandatory choice that still gives an incentive to make the right choice. As long as the difference in liability for each of the choices equals or exceeds DDA, the actor has incentives to make the right choice. The line labeled "mandatory choice" in Figure 3 depicts the fact that liability at least as large as DDA provides efficient incentives for the mandatory choice.

Figure 3: Damages and Optimal Incentives for Different Choices

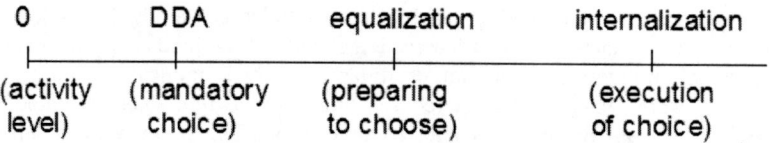

0	DDA	equalization	internalization
(activity level)	(mandatory choice)	(preparing to choose)	(execution of choice)

A mechanical application of the DDA could end up with liability which is higher than liability for the entire harm. That could create a moral hazard. Suppose gains from untaken precautions are 1, probability of harm is .1, and harm, if materialized, is 5 in half of the cases, and 25 in the rest of the cases. Mechanical application of the DDA would impose liability on the injurer for 10, regardless of whether the materialized harm is 25 or 5. That could provide incentives for victims to bring upon themselves harm of 5, and get compensation of 10. *See* Levmore, *supra*. To avoid moral hazard we suggest applying the DDA in a different way: Impose liability according to the ratio between gains and expected harm. In the latter example the ratio between gains and expected harm is 1/3. Therefore, if harm of 5 materializes liability will be for 1.66, and if harm of 25 materializes liability will be for 8.33. The expected liability of the injurer in this example will be exactly 1 and the moral hazard problem completely avoided.

Journal of Tort Law, Vol. 1 [2006], Iss. 1, Art. 2

Now consider how the baseline of liability affects the first choice depicted in Figure 2 - engaging in the underlying activity. The incentive to engage in the underlying activity depends on the resulting level of liability. A higher baseline discourages engaging in the activity, and a lower baseline encourages it. The lowest baseline for damages provides the strongest incentives to engage in the activity. If the activity has more positive than negative externalities, as with specializing in obstetrics, then the most efficient incentives to engage in the underlying activity require the lowest baseline for damages,[28] which is zero.[29] Figure 3 depicts this fact by placing "activity level" at zero on the damages line.

Now consider how liability for the wrong mandatory choice affects the choice that immediately precedes it in Figure 2, which is preparing to choose. The difference in liability determines how much the actor stands to lose from making the wrong choice. When the actor stands to lose more from the wrong choice, he has a stronger incentive to prepare to choose. Damages exceeding DDA are required for efficient incentives to prepare to choose. Specifically, incentives to prepare are efficient when the difference in liability equals the difference in social costs between the alternatives.[30] Figure 3 depicts this fact by placing "equalization" to the right of DDA on the damages line.

We apply these principles to Example 2, where vaginal birth risks harm of 200 with probability .10 (expected harm of 20), and cesarean birth risks harm of 300 with probability .10 (expected harm of 30). For efficient incentives to prepare to choose and to make the right choice, the difference in expected liability must equal the difference in expected harm, which is 10. If liability is imposed for materialized harm and not exposure to risk, the difference in liability must be 100. Assume the *difference* in liability for materialized harm equals 100 – making the wrong choice increases liability by 100 as compared to making the right choice. Now consider the *baseline*, which refers to liability for harm when making the right choice. The baseline could be 200, which implies damages of 200 and 300 for harm from vaginal and cesarean birth, respectively. Or the baseline could be 50, which implies damages of 50 and 150, respectively. Or the baseline could be 0, which implies damages of 0 and 100, respectively. Since the underlying activity in Example 2 has beneficial externalities, damages for making the wrong mandatory choice should be computed by starting with a baseline of 0 and adding the difference in harm to the victim, so liability for materialized harm in cesarean birth should equal 100. This is equivalent to starting with the actual harm of the victim (300) and subtracting the least harmful alternative (200).

---

[28] Note that setting the liability difference and baseline in a discrete choice corresponds to setting the marginal and average liability in a continuous choice.

[29] We assume that the baseline cannot be negative.

[30] *But see* text before the paragrapg which follows note 27, *supra*.

Cooter and Porat: Liability Externalities and Mandatory Choices

We summarize these results in a general principle. The *Equalization Principle* is the principle that the difference in expected social harm between mandatory alternatives should equal the difference in the actor's liability. The Equalization Principle provides socially efficient incentives to prepare to choose and to make the right choice. Since the Equalization Principle concerns the difference in liability and not the baseline, the latter can be adjusted for the best incentives to engage in the underlying activity.

We formalize the Equalization Principle by using the same notation as before, where the mandatory choice is between A and B. The following expressions give the externalities for the two acts:

$$\text{FOR ACT A}: \quad q_A d_A - p_A h_A \quad + \quad b_A - m_A$$

$$\text{FOR ACT B}: q_B d_B - p_B h_B \quad + \quad b_B - m_B.$$

$$\underset{\substack{\textit{liability} \\ \textit{externality}}}{} \qquad \underset{\substack{\textit{price} \\ \textit{externality}}}{}$$

The Equalization Principle requires equating the externality for the two acts:

$$(q_A d_A - p_A h_A) + (b_A - m_A) = (q_B d_B - p_B h_B) + (b_B - m_B) \tag{3}.$$

For an application of equation 3, assume the consumer pays for the benefit he receives, or $b_A = m_A$ and $b_B = m_B$. Equation 3 reduces to:

$$(q_A d_A - p_A h_A) \quad = \quad (q_B d_B - p_B h_B) \tag{3`}.$$

Equation 3` says that the difference between expected liability and social harm for act A equals the difference between expected liability and social harm for act B.

Now we turn to the fourth choice in Figure 2 - execution of a mandatory choice. Expected liability must equal the expected harm of faulty execution in order to provide perfectly efficient incentives for proper execution of the procedure.[31] Figure 3 depicts this fact by placing "execution of choice" at the "internalization" point on the damages line.

To illustrate by Example 3, the obstetrician makes a mistake in executing vaginal delivery with probability .10 that causes harm of 200, and the probability of liability is 1. In cesarean delivery the obstetrician makes a mistake with probability .10 that causes harm of 300, and the probability of liability is .5.

---

[31] Note, however, that this problem could be avoided if execution of the chosen procedure involves a series of mandatory choices. For subsequent mandatory choices, less than 100% liability would suffice for the same reason that it suffices in making the original mandatory choice – the liability difference control, not the baseline.

Journal of Tort Law, Vol. 1 [2006], Iss. 1, Art. 2

Since the probability of liability is .5 for the harm caused by faulty cesarean delivery, the harm is externalized half of the time. To overcome this distortion, set liability equal to 200% of the harm from faulty cesarean delivery. Now the obstetrician is liable for 100% of the expected harm from faulty vaginal or cesarean delivery, as required to internalize the social costs of negligent execution.

Figure 3 summarizes the tradeoffs in incentives for the four choices when setting liability. Incentives for the activity level are best when liability equals zero. We are assuming that the activity has more positive than negative externalities. To provide efficient incentives for making the right mandatory choice, damages must increase at least to the disgorgement level (DDA). Increasing damages to the equalization level will provide efficient incentives for preparing to make the mandatory choice and to make it. To provide incentives for executing the mandatory choice, damages must increase to the internalization level.

III. UNCERTAINTY ABOUT THE RIGHT CHOICE AND APPLICATION

Thus far we have assumed that courts have accurate information about the private and social costs of the relevant acts.[32] In fact courts seldom possess complete information about the alternatives faced by the actors. Even so, courts can often conclude that negligence caused harm. For those cases we propose that in certain areas where positive externalities are high or when mandatory choices are common, legislatures give courts several options for setting damages. Legislatures might authorize courts to award in such areas damages of 25%, 50%, 75%, 100%, 125% or 150% of the plaintiff's harm.

For freely chosen activities, legislatures could allow courts to award damages as guided by the underlying externalities. For driving, liability might equal, say, 150%. When two automobiles collide, part of the damages ideally would be paid to the state.[33] For immunization from diseases, liability might equal, say, 75%.[34]

---

[32] When we applied the Least Harmful Alternative Principle to Example 2, we assumed that courts could verify that the unavoidable risks of vaginal delivery were 20 while the risks of cesarean were 30. When we discussed disgorgement damages for accidents (DDA), we assumed that courts could verify the gains to the doctor from choosing cesarean and the probability of the resulting harm. Similarly, when we applied the Equalization Principle to Example 3 we assumed that courts can verify the risks of negligent execution of each alternative, as well as the level of externality associated with each of the underlying activities.

[33] If a car strikes a pedestrian, damages of, say, 150% will discourage driving and hence correct for the negative externality. This is true regardless of whether or not the pedestrian gets all of the damages. If one car strikes another car, damages of 150% paid to the victim will redistribute money from negligent to non-negligent driver. It will discourage negligent driving and encourage non-negligent driving. The state should take, say, half of the damages in order to discourage non-negligent driving.

Cooter and Porat: Liability Externalities and Mandatory Choices

For mandatory choices with positive externalities in the underlying activity like obstetrics, courts should be allowed to choose damages below 100%. The exact choice should depend on the court's information, and the incentive effects explained in this article. If the actor saved money by untaken precautions, the court might want to give damages that approximate disgorgement for accidents. Application of DDA requires information about the gain of the injurer from untaken precautions and information about the probability of the injurer's liability. In Example 2, DDA requires information on both the doctor's gain from his negligence (which is 1) and the probability of holding him liable when he behaves negligently (which is .10). Disgorgement damages should be low as a percentage of victim's harm, say 25%. Disgorgement damages are especially attractive if the court has little concern with incentives to prepare for the mandatory choice or to execute it.

Alternatively, the court might want to set damages by deducting a fraction that reflects the risk of the least harmful alternative. This approach requires verifying the harm, the risk of the chosen alternative and the risk of the least harmful alternative. When the court cannot verify these two latter values precisely, it might roughly estimate the magnitudes. To illustrate, suppose the court in Example 2 finds out that the risk from cesarean was between 30 and 40, whereas the risk from vaginal delivery was between 10 and 20. The court should reduce damages at least by 25%.[35]

Finally, if the court can verify the extent of the external harm from two alternatives in a mandatory choice, it may want to set damages in order to equalize the externalities. When the court cannot determine the exact expected harm of each alternative, it could use rough estimations. Assume that the court in Example 3 can verify the range of risks associated with cesarean delivery. Instead of exact expected harm of 20, the court verifies that the expected harm is at least 20 and no more than 30. If the rate of externalization of cesarean accidental harms is 50%, courts could safely assume that expected harm of at least 10 was externalized when the doctor chose cesarean. Therefore courts could award damages for the full harm when the doctor chose cesarean, and reduce damages when the doctor chose vaginal delivery. The rate of the reduction should reflect the minimum expected harm that cesarean externalizes. Thus, in our case, if courts could assume that the expected harm of vaginal delivery is, say, also 20 to

---

[34] Since immunization creates benefits also to people who do not take the vaccine, which constitute positive externalities. *See* Steve P. Calandrillo, *Vanishing Vaccinations: Why Are So Many Americans Opting Out of Vaccinating their Children?*, 37 U. MICH. J.L. REFORM 353, 419-20 (2004); Amy B. Monahan, *The Promise and Peril of Ownership Society Health Care Policy*, 80 TUL. L. REV. 777, 833-34 (2006).

[35] The most favorable assumption for the defendant is that the risks associated with cesarean was 40 and for vaginal delivery was 10, thus liability should be for (40-10)/40xH.

Journal of Tort Law, Vol. 1 [2006], Iss. 1, Art. 2

30, they could safely reduce liability for accidental harm caused during vaginal delivery by 33%. That would result in reduction of expected liability for vaginal delivery by no more than 10. Of course, also here the court can reduce damages even further depending on the level of the positive externality of the underlying activity and the risk of eroding incentives to execute the alternative chosen by the doctor.

By using numbers, the preceding discussion suggests a level of precision that courts can seldom achieve. In fact we favor simple rules with modest information requirements that respond to the contours set out in the principles in this paper. As long as the simple rules respond to liability externalities and mandatory choices, many doctors will pay less.

CONCLUSION

Liability externality has various possible remedies. Since Pigou, the standard prescription taxes negative externalities and subsidizes positive externalities.[36] In principle taxes and subsidies are the best solution to externalities whenever private bargains cannot solve the problem. In practice, however, the scope and direction of taxes and subsidies has more to do with interest group politics than with economic efficiency. Given practical limits on controlling externalities by taxes and subsidies, liability law might be adjusted for better results. This is especially true for those externalities that courts can better understand because they arise from the liability system itself, such as the activity level problem.

Several dimensions of liability law could be adjusted in principle: the rule of liability (strict liability versus negligence), the standard of care, the standard and burden of proof, and the level of damages. Recently Jeong-Yoo Kim argued that negligence is generally a better rule than strict liability when the activity involves positive externalities unrelated to the accident. Kim observes that a negligence rule places a smaller burden of liability on the activity, which is desirable when it has positive externalities.[37] Similarly, Keith Hylton argued that a strict liability rule is suitable only when the external costs of the activity exceed the external benefits by a substantial amount, whereas a negligence rule is better when the external costs and external benefits are roughly the same,[38]

---

[36] ARTHUR C. PIGOU, THE ECONOMICS OF WELFARE (London, 1932).

[37] Jeong-Yoo Kim, *Strict Liability Versus Negligence when the Injurer's Activity Involves Positive Externalities*, 22 EUR. J.L. & ECON. 95 (2006). *See also* Mark Geistfeld, *Should Enterprise Liability Replace the Rule of Strict Liability for Abnormally Dangerous Activities?*, 45 UCLA L. REV. 611, 653 (1998) (arguing that with positive externalities strict liability is undesirable as a means of reducing risks relative to negligence).

[38] Keith N. Hylton, *A Missing Markets Theory of Tort Law*, 90 Nw. U. L. REV. 977, 984 (1996). Keith N. Hylton, *Duty in Tort Law: An Economic Approach*, (Boston Univ. Sch. of Law, Working Paper Series, Law & Economics, Working Paper No. 06-04, 2006) *available at*

Cooter and Porat: Liability Externalities and Mandatory Choices

Another possibility is adjusting the legal standard of care under a liability rule. A lower standard of care for activities with positive externalities reduces expected liability and thus increases incentives to engage in the activity, whereas a higher standard of care has the opposite effect. Similarly, increasing the standard of proof reduces the injurer's expected liability and thus increases incentives to engage in the activity, while shifting the burden of proof to the defendant has the opposite effect.

Instead of these possibilities, we focus on adjusting damages to remedy liability externalities. Adjusting damages could be regarded as a supplement or an alternative to the other possibilities. Compared to the alternatives, adjusting damages has distinct advantages. We believe that a full exploration of all the alternatives would conclude that the principles developed in this paper are easier for courts to understand and to apply accurately than the alternatives.

Our suggestions in this Article could be criticized as undermining one of the major goals of tort law, which is compensation. We mention briefly how to defend our focus on incentives rather than compensation. As we demonstrated through the paper, full compensation through tort law is detrimental to potential victims when they benefit from the underlying activity. When excessive liability for child birth discourages doctors from specializing in obstetrics and encourage them engage in defensive medicine, patients ultimately pay much of the price. Given these facts, the potential victims may prefer to provide for compensation by other means than tort law, such as social or private insurance.

http://www.bu.edu/law/faculty/scholarship/workingpapers/abstracts/2006/pdf_files/HyltonK02270 6.pdf.

Published by The Berkeley Electronic Press, 2006   25

Part II
Remedies

[6]

RAND Journal of Economics
Vol. 22, No. 4, Winter 1991

Decoupling liability: optimal incentives for care and litigation

A. Mitchell Polinsky*

and

Yeon-Koo Che**

A "decoupled" liability system is one in which the award to the plaintiff differs from the payment by the defendant. The optimal system of decoupling makes the defendant's payment as high as possible. Such a policy allows the award to the plaintiff to be lowered, thereby reducing the plaintiff's incentive to sue—and hence litigation costs—without sacrificing the defendant's incentive to exercise care. The optimal award to the plaintiff may be less than or greater than the optimal payment by the defendant. The possibility of an out-of-court settlement does not qualitatively affect these results. If the settlement can be monitored, it may be desirable to decouple it as well.

1. Introduction

■ In suits between private individuals, liability is usually "coupled" in the sense that, aside from the parties' litigation costs, a successful plaintiff receives what the defendant pays. This article studies a system of "decoupled" liability—in which the plaintiff is awarded an amount different from what the defendant is made to pay. If the plaintiff is awarded less than what the defendant pays, the government obtains the difference; if the plaintiff is awarded more, the government provides the difference.

Decoupled liability already occurs in certain circumstances. For example, in several states punitive damages are decoupled, with the plaintiff receiving up to 67% of the punitive damage amount paid by the defendant (the percentage depends on the state); the rest goes to the state treasury or to a public compensation fund.[1] Also, decoupled liability has been proposed in the context of private antitrust suits (see footnote 3 below).

The rationale for decoupling liability that will be investigated here is easily explained.

---

* Stanford University and National Bureau of Economic Research.
** University of Wisconsin, Madison.
Research on this article was supported by the John M. Olin Program in Law and Economics at Stanford Law School. Helpful comments were provided by Ian Ayres, Lucian Bebchuk, Keith Hylton, Louis Kaplow, Avery Katz, Saul Levmore, John Lott, Robert Mnookin, Ivan P'ng, Eric Rasmusen, Michael Riordan, Daniel Rubinfeld, Steven Shavell, Warren Schwartz, participants in seminars at Harvard, Stanford, and UCLA, and an anonymous referee.
[1] See Colo. Rev. Stat. sec. 13-21-102 (West 1988); Fla. Stat. sec. 768.73(2)–(4) (West Supp. 1991); and Iowa Code sec. 668A.1(1)–(2) (West 1987).

Consider any level of liability when liability is coupled. This level of liability will determine the incentive of the victim to sue (the higher the award, the greater the incentive) and the incentive of the injurer to take care. The parties' behavior in turn will determine the level of social costs—assumed to be the sum of the injurer's cost of taking care, the victim's expected harm, and the parties' expected litigation costs.[2]

Now consider decoupling liability, starting at the specified level of coupled liability. First raise the amount paid by the injurer, which will cause him to take more care. Then lower the amount awarded to the victim—which will reduce his incentive to sue and thereby cause the injurer to take less care—until the injurer's care is back to its level under coupled liability. Since the level of care is the same under this decoupled system and the original coupled system, so is the injurer's cost of taking care and the victim's expected harm. But since the plaintiff is awarded less under the decoupled system, he will sue less often, and consequently litigation costs will be lower. Thus, starting from any level of coupled liability, there always exists a decoupled system of liability that reduces social costs.

This logic also can be used to establish one of the main results of the article—that in the optimal system of decoupled liability the defendant's payment is as high as possible. For if the payment by the defendant is not at its upper bound, it is possible to raise the defendant's payment and lower the plaintiff's award in such a way that the injurer's care is not affected but the parties' expected litigation costs are lowered.

With the payment by the defendant set at its upper bound, the optimal award to the plaintiff depends on how the plaintiff's award affects the injurer's care (through the plaintiff's incentive to sue) and the parties' litigation costs. It will be shown that the optimal award to the plaintiff may be less than or greater than the optimal payment by the defendant.

To understand why either relationship is possible, consider two limiting cases involving the level of harm. As the level of harm approaches zero, the optimal award to the plaintiff must approach zero; it is not worthwhile to encourage the plaintiff to sue, since the value of inducing the injurer to take care becomes small. In this case, the optimal award to the plaintiff will be less than the optimal payment by the defendant (which is at its upper bound). Conversely, as the level of harm becomes large, suits become more valuable, and it is optimal to continue to raise the award to the plaintiff. In this case, the optimal award to the plaintiff may exceed the optimal payment by the defendant.

Thus far, the discussion has assumed implicitly that all suits result in trials. In practice, however, most cases settle out of court. It will be demonstrated that the possibility of a settlement does not affect the result that the optimal payment by the defendant if the case goes to trial is as high as possible. This is for two reasons. First, as before, by making the defendant's payment as high as possible, the award to the plaintiff—and his incentive to sue—can be lowered. This will reduce either trial costs or settlement costs (which are assumed to be positive). Second, given a suit, by raising the defendant's trial payment and lowering the plaintiff's trial award, the likelihood of a settlement is enhanced because the defendant will be willing to pay more in settlement and the plaintiff will be willing to accept less. Increasing the likelihood of a settlement is beneficial because settlement costs are less than trial costs.

In addition to decoupling the trial outcome, a court sometimes may be able to monitor, and therefore decouple, the settlement. (For instance, in class action suits, settlements often have to be approved by the court.) It will be shown that if suits otherwise would not settle, it is beneficial to be able to decouple settlements because the likelihood of a settlement can thereby be increased. For example, given any decoupled trial outcome, settling can be made more attractive if the settlement amount paid by the defendant to the plaintiff is supplemented by the government.

---

[2] See generally Polinsky and Rubinfeld (1988).

Section 2 introduces the basic model, in which suits are assumed to result in trials, and Section 3 derives the optimal system of decoupling in this context. Sections 4 and 5 extend the model to include settlements. Section 6 contains some concluding remarks.[3]

2. The basic model

■ There is one risk-neutral injurer and many risk-neutral potential victims. The injurer chooses a level of care that affects the probability of an accident. If an accident occurs, one of the potential victims is harmed. The level of harm is fixed and the same for all potential victims. Let

$$c = \text{injurer's level of care,}$$

$$p(c) = \text{probability of an accident } (p' < 0; p'' > 0),$$

$$l = \text{loss if an accident occurs.}$$

Care is measured in units that cost one dollar each, so c also represents the injurer's cost of care.

If the victim sues the injurer, each side bears its own legal costs.[4] The injurer's cost of litigation is fixed. Each potential victim's cost of litigation also is fixed, but is assumed to vary among victims.[5] This variation might be attributed, for example, to differences among individuals in the value of their time or to differences among lawyers in their fees. Let

$$a = \text{potential victim's trial cost } (a > 0),$$

$$f(a) = \text{probability density of } a \ (f(a) > 0 \text{ for all } a > 0),[6]$$

$$b = \text{injurer's trial cost } (b > 0).$$

It is assumed without loss of generality that the victim will prevail at trial if he brings a suit. The plaintiff then receives an award and the defendant makes a payment, which cannot exceed some upper bound. Let

$$x = \text{award to the plaintiff at trial,}$$

$$y = \text{payment by the defendant at trial,}$$

$$m = \text{maximum possible payment of defendant } (y \leq m).$$

The defendant's payment may be bounded for any number of reasons—his limited wealth, considerations of fairness, and so forth. For purposes of our analysis, it does not matter what the bound is.

---

[3] The concept of decoupling liability was first proposed by Schwartz (1980, 1981) in the context of private antitrust enforcement. See also Salop and White (1986) and Polinsky (1986). Although these articles anticipated some of the results demonstrated here, they did not analyze a formal model of decoupling or systematically consider the possibility of settlements.

Several more recent articles concerned with private litigation have mentioned a decoupling-type solution. The discussion that is closest in spirit to the present analysis is by Hylton (1990). He assumes that the award to the victim equals the victim's loss and shows that the optimal payment by the injurer exceeds this amount. See also Katz (1990) and Polinsky and Shavell (1989).

[4] The basic ideas in this article also apply under other rules for allocating legal costs.

[5] Equivalently, there is one potential victim whose litigation cost is uncertain before an accident but known after an accident. (An alternative assumption that would generate similar results is that the level of harm varies among potential victims.)

[6] The assumption that a has positive density for all positive values of a is made mainly for expositional convenience; see footnote 9 below.

If there is an accident, the victim will sue if his trial cost is less than his award at trial: $a < x$.[7] Thus, the probability that a suit will be brought is $F(x)$, where $F(\cdot)$ is the cumulative distribution of a.

The injurer chooses his level of care to minimize the sum of his cost of care, his expected payment at trial, and his expected trial cost:

$$\operatorname*{MIN}_{c} c + p(c)F(x)[y + b]. \tag{1}$$

The social problem is to choose the award to the victim and the payment by the injurer that minimize the sum of the injurer's cost of care, the victim's expected harm, and the parties' expected trial costs:

$$\operatorname*{MIN}_{x,y} c + p(c)\left[l + \int_0^x af(a)da + F(x)b\right], \tag{2}$$

where c is determined by x and y according to (1), and $y \le m$. The optimal values of x and y will be denoted x^* and y^*; it is assumed that x^* is positive and unique.

3. Optimal decoupling in the basic model

■   It will first be shown that the optimal payment by the injurer at trial is as high as possible: $y^* = m$.

This can be proved by contradiction. Suppose that the optimal value of y were $y_0 < m$ and that the optimal value of x were some $x_0 > 0$. Then, if an accident occurs, the sum of the injurer's expected payment at trial and his expected trial cost is $F(x_0)[y_0 + b]$. Now raise y_0 to m and lower x_0 to x_1 such that

$$F(x_0)[y_0 + b] = F(x_1)[m + b]. \tag{3}$$

Since the expected costs borne by the injurer if there is an accident are unchanged, the injurer will choose the same level of care as before. Now observe from (2) that the injurer's cost of care and the victim's expected loss are unaffected, but that because x is lower, both the victim's and the injurer's expected trial cost are reduced. Thus, the original y_0 and x_0 could not have been optimal.

Given $y^* = m$, the optimal award to the victim, x^*, can be determined by minimizing the objective function in (2) just over x, where c now is determined by x from

$$\operatorname*{MIN}_{c} c + p(c)F(x)[m + b]. \tag{4}$$

Let $c(x)$ be the solution to (4). It is easily demonstrated that $c' > 0$ (since raising x raises $F(x)$, the probability of suit).

The first-order condition that determines x^* can be written as

$$-p'c'\left[l + \int_0^x af(a)da + F(x)b\right] = c' + pf(x)[x + b]. \tag{5}$$

The left-hand side of (5) is the marginal benefit of raising x. As x rises, the injurer's care increases and the probability of an accident therefore falls. This reduces the expected harm to the victim and the expected trial cost of both parties (a trial can occur only if an accident occurs). The right-hand side of (5) is the marginal cost of raising x, which consists of the increased care that the injurer is induced to take and the increase in the parties' expected trial costs caused by the greater likelihood that a suit will be brought if there is an accident (the increase in trial costs is $x + b$ because, for the "marginal" suit, $a = x$).

---

[7] There is no loss of generality in assuming that the victim will not sue if $a = x$.

There is no simple relationship between x^* and y^*. The factors that determine x^*—such as the responsiveness of the accident probability to the injurer's choice of care and the magnitude of the parties' trial costs—may have nothing per se to do with the factors that determine y^*—such as the injurer's wealth or considerations of fairness.

In general, x^* may be less than or greater than y^*. To illustrate the former possibility, observe that x^* must approach zero as the victim's loss, l, approaches zero. This can be demonstrated by contradiction. Suppose that x^* is bounded away from zero, say by $\bar{x} > 0$. This implies some minimum level of care, say $\bar{c} > 0$.[8] Thus, social costs at x^* are at least $\bar{c}$. Compare this to social costs when $x = 0$; then, since there are no suits, c is zero and social costs are simply $p(0)l$. But as l approaches zero, these social costs approach zero and become less than $\bar{c}$. Therefore, x^* must also approach zero as l approaches zero, showing that for l low enough, $x^* < y^*$.[9]

By similar reasoning, it can be demonstrated that as l tends to infinity, x^* tends to infinity. As l tends to infinity, the value of taking additional care to reduce the probability of an accident increases without bound. Since $y^* = m$, the only way to induce the defendant to take more care is by raising x so that he will be sued with a higher probability if an accident occurs. Therefore, as l tends to infinity, x^* also must tend to infinity, showing that for l sufficiently large, $x^* > y^*$.[10]

In general, x^* is an increasing function of l. Thus, for accidents with relatively low losses, x^* will be less than y^*, and for accidents with relatively high losses, x^* will be greater than y^*.

4. The extended model

■ Now suppose that after an accident occurs, the plaintiff can make a "take-it-or-leave-it" settlement demand.[11] If it is accepted by the defendant, both parties incur settlement costs (which are assumed to be less than their respective trial costs).[12] If it is rejected, the plaintiff then decides whether to go to trial or to drop the suit. For simplicity, both parties are assumed to have perfect information (including about each other's litigation costs). Let

$$s = \text{plaintiff's settlement demand,}$$

$$\alpha(a) = \text{plaintiff's settlement cost } (0 < \alpha(a) < a),\text{[13]}$$

$$\beta = \text{defendant's settlement cost } (0 < \beta < b).$$

As before, a plaintiff will bring a suit if and only if $a < x$: If a is less than x, the plaintiff would bring a suit if it were to result in a trial; since a settlement must make him at least

---

[8] That $\bar{c}$ must be positive can be proved by contradiction. Suppose $x^* > 0$ and $\bar{c} = 0$. Then social welfare could be improved by setting $x = 0$ (since the level of care would be the same and expected trial costs would be lower). So it must be that $c > 0$ when $x^* > 0$.

[9] If the trial costs of potential victims have a positive lower bound, then x^* would tend to that lower bound as l tends to zero. Assuming this lower bound is less than $y^* = m$, then for l low enough, $x^* < y^*$, as claimed. However, if the lower bound exceeds m, then x^* always would exceed y^*. (Analogous observations apply to the discussion in the next paragraph if the trial costs of victims have an upper bound.)

[10] A potential problem with setting x greater than y is that this may create an incentive for individuals to "fabricate" harms—to claim that an accident has occurred when one has not—in order to obtain the implicit government subsidy equal to $x - y$.

[11] This assumption is not as special as it may appear; results qualitatively similar to those discussed in this article generally would occur if the injurer made a take-it-or-leave-it settlement offer (but see footnote 16 below).

[12] It will be seen that decoupling liability is always socially valuable when settlement costs are positive, whereas if settlement costs are zero, there are some circumstances in which decoupling liability is socially valuable and other circumstances in which it is not needed. The assumption that settlement costs are positive is made both to avoid the additional complexity of having to distinguish between these two sets of circumstances and because it is the more realistic assumption.

[13] For simplicity, $\alpha(a)$ frequently will be written as α. It is assumed that α is increasing in a and that $a - \alpha$ is also increasing in a. These assumptions would be satisfied, for example, if α is a constant fraction of a.

as well off, he also would bring a suit if it were to result in a settlement. If a exceeds x, the plaintiff would not bring a suit if it were to result in a trial. The defendant, knowing this, will reject any settlement demand; and the plaintiff will then drop the suit.

Given a suit, consider whether a settlement is feasible. If the plaintiff goes to trial, his net gain is $x - a$; if he settles, it is $s - \alpha$. Thus, the plaintiff will prefer to settle if $s - \alpha \geq x - a$ or, equivalently, $s \geq x - (a - \alpha)$.[14] If the defendant goes to trial, his total payment is $y + b$, whereas if he settles, it is $s + \beta$. Thus, the defendant will prefer to settle if $s + \beta \leq y + b$ or $s \leq y + (b - \beta)$. Consequently, a settlement will be feasible if

$$x - (a - \alpha) \leq y + (b - \beta). \tag{6}$$

If a settlement is feasible, a settlement will occur and will equal

$$s = y + (b - \beta) \tag{7}$$

because the plaintiff will make his take-it-or-leave-it settlement demand as high as possible. If (6) does not hold, a suit will result in a trial.[15]

Now consider the injurer's choice of care. If a suit results in a trial, the injurer's total payment is $y + b$. If a suit results in a settlement, his total payment is $s + \beta$ or, using (7), $y + b$. (The injurer pays $y + b$ in both cases because the plaintiff's settlement demand makes the injurer indifferent between going to trial and settling.) Thus, the injurer's choice of care is determined by (1).

The social problem is essentially unchanged, except that account must be taken of expected settlement costs.

5. Optimal decoupling in the extended model

■ The principal purpose of this section is to explain why $y^* = m$ even when settlements are possible and why it may be desirable to decouple settlements. Since much of the logic is similar to that used previously, the discussion here will be abbreviated. Formal proofs of the main results are contained in the Appendix.

There are two natural cases to consider, depending on whether the settlement can be observed and decoupled by the court.

□ **Settlements cannot be decoupled.** The reasoning used to show that $y^* = m$ in the basic model carries over with little change. If y is less than m and x is positive, it is possible to raise y and lower x so that the injurer's care is held constant. As before, lowering x is beneficial because it discourages costly suits (now the savings may be in the form of reduced settlement costs rather than reduced trial costs). There is an additional effect, however, in the extended model. For those suits that are still brought, raising y and lowering x leads to more settlements (see (6)). Since settlements are less costly than trials, this effect reinforces the result.

Given $y^* = m$, the optimal choice of x is determined in a way similar to that discussed in the basic model. Also, the earlier observations about the relationship between x^* and y^* carry over essentially unchanged to the extended model.[16]

---

[14] There is no loss of generality in assuming that the plaintiff prefers to settle when $s = x - (a - \alpha)$. An analogous statement applies below to the defendant.

[15] In many recent economic models of litigation, a trial can occur only if the parties have asymmetric information. Here, even though the parties have perfect information, a trial might occur because of the decoupling of liability (when x sufficiently exceeds y).

[16] The question arises whether it is socially desirable to discourage settlements when they cannot be decoupled, since they might undermine the effects of decoupling the trial outcome. Given the assumption that the plaintiff makes a take-it-or-leave-it settlement demand—resulting in a settlement at the upper end of the settlement range—

□ **Settlements can be decoupled.** Now suppose that the court can observe the settlement amount, s, and award an additional amount to the plaintiff and/or make the defendant pay an additional amount. Let

x' = additional award to the victim if there is a settlement,

y' = additional payment by the injurer if there is a settlement.

First note that, if settlements are not decoupled, some suits will result in trials if

$$x - (a - \alpha) > y + (b - \beta) \tag{8}$$

for some a (see (6)), which implies that

$$x > y + (b - \beta). \tag{9}$$

When both the trial outcome and the settlement are decoupled, it is straightforward to show that a settlement will be feasible if

$$x - (a - \alpha) - x' \le y + (b - \beta) - y'. \tag{10}$$

Since (10) is equivalent to

$$x' - y' \ge x - (a - \alpha) - [y + (b - \beta)], \tag{11}$$

any combination of x' and y' such that

$$x' - y' \ge x - [y + (b - \beta)] \tag{12}$$

will satisfy (10) for all values of a and will result in all suits settling.

If (9) holds, (12) implies that $x' - y'$ must be positive and sufficiently large. In other words, to encourage settlements when they otherwise would not occur, the government must decouple settlements in such a way as to provide a net transfer to the parties; this increases the attractiveness of a settlement relative to a trial.

It remains to be shown that it is socially desirable to decouple settlements in this way. Since the plaintiff's settlement demand will equal

$$s = y + (b - \beta) - y' \tag{13}$$

(the right-hand side of (10)), the injurer's total payment as a result of a settlement is $s + \beta + y' = y + b$. (The injurer's total payment does not depend on y' because the payment of y' to the government reduces the settlement amount by y'.) His total payment if the case goes to trial also is $y + b$. Thus, the decoupling of settlements does not affect the injurer's incentive to take care, but it does lower litigation costs.[17]

Assuming x' and y' are chosen to guarantee a settlement, the reasoning used to demonstrate that $y^* = m$ in the basic model applies here too, except that lowering x now saves settlement costs instead of trial costs.

---

it is not desirable to discourage settlements. In essence, this is because the injurer's incentive to take care then is not diminished by a settlement. However, if the defendant were to make a take-it-or-leave-it settlement offer, it might be desirable to discourage settlements if they cannot be decoupled.

[17] There is a potential detrimental effect from decoupling settlements. A victim for whom $a > x$ might nonetheless sue and then settle with the injurer in order for the parties to obtain the net transfer $(x' - y')$ from the government. However, since the injurer knows that such a victim would drop the suit if the injurer rejects the victim's settlement demand, the injurer would have to be *paid* to settle the suit—either by the victim through a "negative" settlement ($s < 0$) or by the government through a "negative" additional payment ($y' < 0$). Consequently, such suits can be forestalled by a policy of decoupling settlements only if the settlement amount is positive and by restricting the additional payment by the injurer to be nonnegative.

6. Concluding remarks

■ **Applicability to a negligence rule.** It has been assumed, implicitly, that the injurer's choice of care does not affect whether he is liable. This assumption corresponds to the rule of strict liability. A natural question is whether the analysis also applies to a negligence rule—under which the injurer is liable only if he does not take some minimum level of care, referred to as the standard of care.

In theory, it would not be necessary to decouple liability under a negligence rule. Given any standard of care, if the level of (coupled) liability for violating the standard is high enough, the injurer will meet the standard. Then the victim will not sue, since he would not prevail. Thus, the first-best level of care could be attained without any litigation costs being incurred.

In practice, however, a negligence rule is likely to lead to some suits because injurers will be found liable sometimes. An injurer may be uncertain about what the standard of care is, and therefore he may choose a level of care that leads to his being found negligent. Conversely, a court or a jury may be uncertain about what level of care was chosen by the injurer, and consequently may find him negligent.

If suits occur under a negligence rule, it is straightforward to see that the analysis of decoupling in this article applies: Whatever level of care results from the best choice of coupled liability under a negligence rule, the same level of care can be achieved with lower litigation costs by decoupling liability.

□ **Relationship to Becker's theory of public enforcement.** Our analysis of decoupling closely parallels the economic theory of public enforcement associated with Becker (1968). Becker concluded that the best system of public enforcement involves using the highest possible fine and a correspondingly low probability of detection, since such a combination can achieve any given amount of deterrence with the lowest investment in detection resources. We concluded that the best system of decoupled liability involves making the defendant's payment as high as possible so that the probability of suit can be lowered, thereby reducing litigation costs. Thus, our analysis of decoupling can be interpreted as a private litigation analogue to Becker's theory of public enforcement.

Becker's theory has been criticized on the grounds that severe fines—as high as an individual's wealth—are hardly ever imposed. An analogous criticism could be leveled against the theory of decoupled liability proposed here. In both contexts, however, there are additional considerations that could be taken into account that would lead to the conclusion that the optimal fine or the optimal payment by the defendant is not as high as possible. For example, if injurers are risk averse, it generally is desirable to reduce the sanction and to increase the probability of its imposition in order to lower risk-bearing costs.

Appendix

■   Statements and proofs of Propositions 1 and 2 follow.

Proposition 1. When settlements are possible but cannot be decoupled, the optimal payment by the defendant at trial is as high as possible: $y^* = m$.

Proof. First define $\hat{a}(x, y) \equiv \min\{\hat{a}(x, y), x\}$, where $\hat{a}(x, y)$ solves for a in

$$x - (a - \alpha(a)) = y + (b - \beta) \tag{A1}$$

if $x > y + (b - \beta)$, and $\hat{a}(x, y) = 0$ otherwise. Since $\hat{a}(x, y)$ is increasing in x and decreasing in y (in the weak sense), so is $\hat{a}$. For a plaintiff with $a < \hat{a}$, a suit resulting in a trial occurs and litigation costs $a + b$ are incurred; for a plaintiff with $\hat{a} \leq a < x$, a suit resulting in a settlement occurs and settlement costs $\alpha + \beta$ are incurred; and for a plaintiff with $a \geq x$, a suit does not occur.

The social problem can be written as

$$\min_{c,x,y} c + p(c)\left[1 + \int_0^x [\alpha(a) + \beta]f(a)da + \int_0^{\hat{a}(x,y)} [a - \alpha(a) + b - \beta]f(a)da \right] \tag{A2}$$

subject to

$$c \; \epsilon \; \text{argmin} \; c + p(c)F(x)[y + b], \tag{A3}$$

$$y \leq m. \tag{A4}$$

To prove that the second constraint (A4) is binding, suppose to the contrary that at the optimal choice (x_0, y_0), $y_0 < m$. Now consider an alternative choice (x_1, y_1) with $y_0 < y_1 \leq m$ and $F(x_1)[y_1 + b] = F(x_0)[y_0 + b]$. Thus, $x_1 < x_0$. It follows from the construction of the new pair (x_1, y_1) that the choice of the level of care c remains unchanged. But the value of the objective function (expected social cost) is lower under the new pair (x_1, y_1), since the first term involving an integral in (A2) is strictly increasing in x, and the second term involving an integral is weakly increasing in x and weakly decreasing in y (since $\bar{a}$ is weakly increasing in x and weakly decreasing in y).

Proposition 2. When settlements are possible and can be decoupled: (i) decoupling settlements is valuable only if some suits otherwise would not settle (i.e., only if $x > y + (b - \beta)$); (ii) when decoupling settlements is valuable, optimal decoupling of settlements requires a minimum net transfer to the parties from the government (at least equal to $x - [y + (b - \beta)] > 0$); (iii) the optimal payment by the defendant at trial is $y^* = m$.

Proof. Let z denote the settlement subsidy to the two parties. (In terms of the notation of Section 5, $z = x' - y'$; the allocation of the subsidy does not matter.) To prove (i) and (ii), it suffices to show that the optimal policy involves a subsidy $z = 0$ if $x \leq y + (b - \beta)$, and $z \geq x - [y + (b - \beta)]$ if $x > y + (b - \beta)$.

Analogously to the proof of Proposition 1, define $\hat{a}(x, y, z) = \min\{\hat{a}(x, y, z), x\}$, where $\hat{a}(x, y, z)$ solves for a in

$$x - (a - \alpha(a)) = y + (b - \beta) + z \tag{A5}$$

if $x > y + (b - \beta)$, and $\hat{a}(x, y, z) = 0$ otherwise. The social problem can be written as

$$\underset{c,x,y,z}{\text{MIN}} \; c + p(c)\left[1 + \int_0^x [\alpha(a) + \beta]f(a)da + \int_0^{\hat{a}(x,y,z)} [a - \alpha(a) + b - \beta]f(a)da \right] \tag{A6}$$

subject to (A3) and (A4). Since $\bar{a}$ is weakly increasing in x and weakly decreasing in y, $y^* = m$ for the same reason as before, proving (iii).

Observe that the choice of the subsidy z does not affect the level of care c chosen by the injurer. Thus, if $x > y + (b - \beta)$, any $z \geq x - [y + (b - \beta)] > 0$ minimizes expected social cost by letting $\hat{a}(x, y, z) = 0$; and if $x \leq y + (b - \beta)$, since $\bar{a} = 0$ anyway, $z = 0$ is optimal (but not uniquely).

References

BECKER, G.S. "Crime and Punishment: An Economic Approach." *Journal of Political Economy,* Vol. 76 (1968), pp. 169–217.

HYLTON, K.N. "The Influence of Litigation Costs on Deterrence Under Strict Liability and Under Negligence." *International Review of Law and Economics,* Vol. 10 (1990), pp. 161–171.

KATZ, A. "The Effect of Frivolous Lawsuits on the Settlement of Litigation." *International Review of Law and Economics,* Vol. 10 (1990), pp. 3–27.

POLINSKY, A.M. "Detrebling versus Decoupling Antitrust Damages: Lessons from the Theory of Enforcement." *Georgetown Law Journal,* Vol. 74 (1986), pp. 1231–1236.

——— AND RUBINFELD, D.L. "The Welfare Implications of Costly Litigation for the Level of Liability." *Journal of Legal Studies,* Vol. 17 (1988), pp. 151–164.

——— AND SHAVELL, S. "Legal Error, Litigation, and the Incentive to Obey the Law." *Journal of Law, Economics, and Organization,* Vol. 5 (1989), pp. 99–108.

SALOP, S.C. AND WHITE, L.J. "Economic Analysis of Private Antitrust Litigation." *Georgetown Law Journal,* Vol. 74 (1986), pp. 1001–1064.

SCHWARTZ, W.F. "An Overview of the Economics of Antitrust Enforcement." *Georgetown Law Journal,* Vol. 68 (1980), pp. 1075–1102.

———. *Private Enforcement of the Antitrust Laws: An Economic Critique.* Washington, D.C.: American Enterprise Institute, 1981.

[7]

RAND Journal of Economics
Vol. 30, No. 1, Spring 1999
pp. 84–105

Contract damages and cooperative investments

Yeon-Koo Che*

and

Tai-Yeong Chung**

We study alternative breach remedies in the presence of specific investments that generate a direct benefit to the investor's trading partner (referred to as "cooperative investments"). We find that (i) expectation damages perform very poorly, inducing no cooperative investment; (ii) privately stipulated liquidated damages can achieve a better, albeit inefficient, outcome; and (iii) the reliance damages perform the best, achieving the efficient outcome if ex post renegotiation is possible. These rankings stand in contrast to those found in the existing literature, but they explain many observed contracting practices.

1. Introduction

■ A principal function of a contract is to coordinate economic activities between two parties who must make relationship-specific investments. It is well known that when parties cannot write a complete contract, they tend to invest too little in specific assets because of the holdup problem.[1] A large literature has been developed to study various aspects of the holdup problem and possible solutions.[2] In particular, the literature on

---

* University of Wisconsin-Madison; yche@facstaff.wisc.edu.

** University of Western Ontario; chung@sscl.uwo.ca.

This article, originally entitled "Incomplete Contracts and Cooperative Investments," was presented at Northwestern, Texas A&M, the Universities of Rochester and Wisconsin, Yale Law School, the 1995 Midwest Mathematical Economics Conference held at the University of Iowa, the 7th World Congress of the Econometric Society held in Tokyo, Japan, the 1996 Canadian Economic Association meeting held at Brock University, the 1996 KAEA meeting held in Pusan, Korea, and the 1997 EARIE conference held in Leuven, Belgium. The authors are grateful to Ian Ayres, Raymond Deneckere, Donald Hausch, Ig Horstmann, William Rogerson, Larry Samuelson, Alan Schwartz, Kathryn Spier, Curtis Taylor, Steve Wiggins, two excellent referees and Editor Michael Riordan for their helpful comments. The research for this article was partially conducted while the first and second authors were visiting the Yale Law School and the University of Rochester, respectively. The authors acknowledge their hospitality and financial support. The first author also acknowledges the support from Wisconsin Alumni Research Foundation.

[1] This statement was originally made by Oliver Williamson (1985) and was subsequently shown formally by Hart and Moore (1988) and Tirole (1986).

[2] The existing literature proposes solutions to the holdup problem that involve asset ownership structures (Grossman and Hart, 1986; Hart and Moore, 1990), legal rules of remedies (Shavell, 1980; Rogerson, 1984), and various incomplete contracting schemes (Chung, 1991; Aghion, Dewatripont, and Rey, 1994; Edlin and Reichelstein, 1996; Hermalin and Katz, 1993; Rogerson, 1992; and Nöldeke and Schmidt, 1995).

contract damages recognizes that the legal rules for assessing damages for a breach of contract can play an important role in remedying the holdup problem (see Shavell (1980) and Rogerson (1984) and the summary of the literature below).

While this latter literature provides very useful policy guidelines to courts by providing unambiguous rankings of different legal remedies, its results are limited by the restriction on the nature of specific investments. Largely, the literature focuses on "selfish investments"—the specific investments that confer direct benefits only to the investor and not to his partner. For instance, it is often assumed that a seller's investment only reduces her cost of performance and that a buyer's investment only increases his benefit from consuming the goods or services provided by a seller.

Specific investments that generate a direct benefit to the investor's trading partner—hereafter referred to as "cooperative investments"—have received little attention.[3] Consider, for instance, an investment that a supplier makes to increase the quality of a good or service procured by the buyer. Many R&D investments that defense contractors undertake for the Department of Defense (DoD), subcontractors' efforts to customize their components to the special needs of manufacturers, and workers' paying attention to their jobs are examples of cooperative investments.[4] (These investments increase the buyer's benefits from trade but do not necessarily reduce the seller's production costs.)

Cooperative investments are becoming increasingly common and important, especially with the growing emphasis on buyer-supplier alliances in industrial purchasing and the increased need for coordination across production stages in modern manufacturing. Such coordination often requires investments of time and resources that have cooperative elements. For example, Asanuma (1989) describes how suppliers customize parts for buyers even when "specific investments . . . have to be incurred to implement such customization" (p. 14). Also, Nishiguchi (1994) reports that suppliers "send engineers to work with [automakers] in design and production. They play innovative roles in . . . gathering information about [the automakers'] long-term product strategies" (p. 138). While both cooperative and selfish investments are difficult to motivate when they are relationship specific and are not directly contractible, they require different contractual arrangements and legal remedies for breach of contracts, as we argue in this article.

Our model features a buyer-seller relationship in which a seller initially makes a specific investment and, after the buyer's benefit from trade is realized, the buyer decides whether or not to accept the seller's performance. Acceptance and rejection respectively lead to trade and no trade, unless the parties renegotiate the buyer's decision. The seller's investment is *cooperative* in that it increases the buyer's benefit (stochastically) without lowering the seller's cost of performance.[5]

---

[3] Hart and Holmström (1987) and MacLeod and Malcomson (1993) consider cases involving such investments. The former recognizes the difficulty of inducing the investments, while the latter suggests a contractual arrangement that specifies the circumstances under which parties exercise their outside options. Our approach is distinguished by not allowing such an arrangement. See also footnote 6.

[4] Hart and Hölmstrom (1987) provide another example involving a coal supplier and an electric utility. The coal supplier chooses the type of mine to be developed. By developing a good seam, the mine may raise the quality of coal supplied. On the other hand, the plant chooses the type of coal-burning boiler to be installed. By investing in a better boiler, the power plant may be able to burn lower-quality coal, thus reducing the seller's costs.

[5] This contracting environment resembles that of the principal-agent literature (see, e.g., Holmström (1979) and Grossman and Hart (1983)). Our model differs from a typical principal-agent model in that the gains from trade, while observable, are not verifiable here, so the sharing contract considered in the principal-agent literature is not feasible. In addition, investment is observable (while not verifiable) in our model, so there is no hidden action problem per se.

Since our focus is on the role of breach remedies, we consider a very simple type of contract: the contract specifies a trade price, p, and a no-trade price (or damages), δ, that the buyer must pay to the seller in the event of his accepting and rejecting the seller's performance, respectively.[6] In all cases, the parties specify their trade price, p. The damages, δ, depend on the legal rules for breach remedies adopted by the court. Specifically, we consider three alternative breach remedies: expectation, liquidated, and reliance damages rules. The expectation damages rule (hereafter, ED rule), which is the default remedy, compensates the victim of breach the profit that the latter would have enjoyed had the contract not been breached. The reliance damages rule (hereafter, RD rule) does not compensate the expectation profits of the victim but does compensate his reliance expenditures (e.g., the expenses that he incurred in anticipation of contract performance). Finally, the liquidated damages rule (hereafter, LD rule) allows the parties to specify any *fixed* monetary damages that the parties mutually agree upon.[7] We compare these alternative breach remedies based on their abilities to overcome the hold-up problem.

Admittedly, these contract forms are very simple and do not cover more sophisticated contracts (that may involve exchange of messages between the parties, for example). Our interest in these simple contract forms is threefold. First, these contract forms are very common in many real circumstances. Standard contracts for house remodelling, book publishing, advertising pilot campaigns, real estate agency services, and government procurement of weapons systems often specify only the amounts of payment to be made for the delivery of contractors' performances. Further, as will be clear, our simple contracts cover other popular contract forms that involve a buyer's acceptance option and a seller's cost reimbursement. Second, the incompleteness of contracts may result from high costs of specifying and verifying contract performances and contingencies. Courts may have developed expertise in verifying standard remedies, but they may have to incur high costs to verify nonstandard remedies. Third, the simple contract forms highlight the roles of breach remedies most clearly and permit a clear comparison with the existing literature on breach remedies, which also restricts its attention to these types of contracts (see Shavell (1980) and Rogerson (1984), for example).[8] Che and Hausch (forthcoming) study cooperative investments with a fully general class of contracts (which allow message games) but do not address legal rules for breach remedies.[9]

Before describing our results, it is useful to review our knowledge about the alternative breach remedies in the selfish-investment setting. Several results are noteworthy. First, the ED rule dominates other court-adopted remedies and performs

---

[6] MacLeod and Malcomson (1993) allow a richer contract design that specifies two different no-trade prices, distinguished by whether the breaching party subsequently trades with a third party. Such an arrangement requires a court to verify the motive of breach, which is often very difficult since a party can engage in a spurious trade with a third party if it turns out to be profitable.

[7] By assuming only fixed damages, the liquidated damages are here defined narrowly. Our definition fits the conventional use of the term "liquidated damages." In principle, one can broadly define the LD rule to include damages that are contingent on any verifiable information. Clearly, this broadly defined LD rule will perform as well as (if not better than) any court-imposed remedy. But such contingent damages are uncommon in reality. See our remark in Section 6.

[8] For a more sophisticated contract, such as one requiring announcement of a message by a party, for example, it is not clear what a breach means and how expectation damages are to be assessed even at the conceptual level.

[9] Che and Hausch (forthcoming) consider a fully general class of contracts, via the revelation principle, which allows for exchange of messages between the parties. They show that contracting is worthless if the parties are unable to commit not to renegotiate the initial contract terms. This result thus extends a similar result established in Proposition 5 here but shows that even contracts requiring announcement of messages by parties will not work in the presence of renegotiation.

reasonably well in various situations (see, for example, Shavell (1980, 1984), Rogerson (1984), Konakayama, Mitsui, and Watanabe (1986), and Edlin (1996)). The ED rule forces a breaching party to internalize the loss imposed on his partner, so it induces the socially efficient breach decision. Furthermore, the breaching party has the right incentive for reliance, although the breached-against party overinvests. Second, an optimally chosen liquidated damages can induce efficient breaching without creating overinvestment (Cooter, 1985; Chung, 1992; and Spier and Whinston, 1995). The optimal LD contract therefore achieves the efficient outcome and is better than the standard court-adopted legal remedies. Third, the RD rule performs worst, since it entails an inefficient breach decision and aggravates the overinvestment problem (of the ED rule). Despite the inefficiency, the RD rule has frequently been used in practice. The RD rule is the *de facto* default remedy in government contracting, for example, as will be argued below. The existing literature explains the common use of the RD rule by citing the difficulty of assessing expectation damages. In this article we provide an alternative rationale for the use of the RD rule.

With cooperative investments, we find results that are drastically different. First, the ED rule performs very poorly in the presence of cooperative investments, inducing a *minimal* (zero) cooperative investment. Since the ED rule compensates the victim of breach (the seller in our context) for the anticipated profit, the seller receives the same payoff regardless of the realized gains from trade, so she has no incentive to increase the gains from trade through the cooperative investment.

Second, the optimal LD contract, whereby the parties stipulate both p and δ, is superior to the ED rule but does not lead to the first-best outcome. The LD contract can create incentives for a cooperative investment by awarding a fixed-sum prize to the seller (investor) whenever the buyer accepts the seller's performance. The awarding of this "trade prize" to the seller means a transfer of trade surplus away from the buyer, which biases his incentive toward breach at the margin. Thus, too little trade occurs. Unlike the case of selfish investments, therefore, the optimal LD contract yields an inefficient outcome, but one that is better than the outcome under the ED rule.

Third, the RD rule outperforms other legal remedies and even the optimal LD contract. Reliance damages serve as a direct investment subsidy which, along with the contractually specified trade prize, leads to a stronger incentive for the investment while creating fewer trade inefficiencies than the optimal LD contract does.

The possibility of *ex post* renegotiation does not alter these results qualitatively. The ED rule continues to perform poorly, again inducing a minimal cooperative investment. The optimal LD contract performs better. As before, the optimal LD contract creates a wedge between the trade and no-trade prices that exceeds the cost of the seller's performance. This wedge leads to an increased probability of renegotiation, which creates some investment incentives for the seller. It turns out that the optimal contract specifies a big enough wedge between the prices so that trade always occurs through renegotiation. The resulting outcome is thus equivalent to the typical spot market outcome that arises when parties initially choose not to contract but *ex post* negotiate the terms of trade. Too little cooperative investment is made in this case.

With *ex post* renegotiation, once again the RD rule performs the best. More important, it yields the first-best outcome. Under the RD rule, the seller can recover the cost of investment as well as part of any renegotiation surplus in the event of breach. This subsidy effect combined with the renegotiation effect is sufficient to overcome the underinvestment problem that arises in the fixed-price contract.

These results, while surprising from the standpoint of the existing literature, explain a number of observed contracting practices when cooperative investments are important. Option contracts, or delivery contingent contracts, are often-observed practices

88 / THE RAND JOURNAL OF ECONOMICS

that are consistent with the optimal fixed-price contract that we identify. Moreover, the superiority of the RD rule explains the prevalence of cost-reimbursement types of schemes and other special features of government contracting, which we shall discuss more in the text. Most of all, our results underscore the difficulty of inducing cooperative investments through contracting. The limited value of contracting may explain the role of organizational design in situations where cooperative investments are important.

The rest of the article is organized as follows. Section 2 illustrates the difficulty of inducing cooperative investments in a simple deterministic model. Section 3 introduces our main model with stochastic gains from trade. Sections 4 and 5 present our main analyses, without and with the possibility of renegotiation. Section 6 concludes.

2. Investment in a deterministic model

■   To contrast cooperative investments with selfish investments, consider a deterministic model in which a buyer and seller trade a good in the second period. Both parties are risk neutral. In the first period, the seller makes a cooperative investment, $e \in \mathcal{R}_+$, that increases the buyer's benefit from trade, $v(e)$ (that is, $v(\cdot)$ is increasing), and a selfish investment, $r \in \mathcal{R}_+$, that reduces her own production costs, $c(r)$ (that is, $c(\cdot)$ is decreasing). Assume that $v(\cdot)$ and $-c(;)$ are strictly concave and continuously differentiable, and that $v(0) > c(0)$, which makes trade beneficial.

The efficient (first-best) investments maximize

$$W(e, r) \equiv v(e) - c(r) - e - r. \tag{1}$$

Assume that the unique solution, (e^*, r^*), has strictly positive components.

Suppose that the parties do not initially write a contract and simply bargain *ex post* to determine terms of trade. Assume that in the bargaining the parties split the surplus, with the seller receiving a share $\alpha \in [0, 1]$. Given investments e and r, total gains from trade are $v(e) - c(r)$. Since the investments are sunk, the seller's *ex post* payoff from the bargaining is $\alpha[v(e) - c(r)]$. In the first period, the seller picks e and r to maximize

$$U(e, r) = \alpha[v(e) - c(r)] - e - r. \tag{2}$$

Unless $\alpha = 1$, the investing party does not appropriate full marginal returns from her investments, so she invests too little (see Edlin and Shannon (1995)). This underinvestment result is precisely due to the hold-up problem that has been emphasized in the transaction-costs economics literature.

Next, suppose that the parties initially write a contract that specifies a fixed-price p at which trade is to occur. Assume that the parties prefer to trade at that price. Under the ED rule, the seller is guaranteed her contract profit: $p - c(r)$, regardless of the buyer's breach decision. Hence, in the first period, the seller picks e and r to maximize

$$U(e, r) = p - c(r) - e - r. \tag{3}$$

Comparison of (3) and (1) reveals that the seller picks the efficient level of selfish investment (i.e., $r = r^*$). The incentives for the cooperative investment are absent, however. Since the objective function is strictly decreasing in e, the seller picks zero cooperative investment (i.e., $e = 0 < e^*$). This example illustrates that the nature of investment has important implications for the performance of a contract. For example, if there were only the cooperative investment, having no contract would be better than entering into such a simple contract based on the ED rule.

Other remedies may provide a better incentive for cooperative investments. In particular, if the parties can design liquidated damages, the efficient investments can be induced in this simple deterministic model. Consider a contract of the form (p, δ_0), where $p = v(e^*)$ and $\delta_0 = 0$, (i.e., the buyer pays nothing to the seller in the event of breach). Given this contract, the buyer will breach if and only if $v(e) - p = v(e) - v(e^*) < -\delta_0 = 0$, or $e < e^*$. Knowing that there will be no sale if $e < e^*$, the seller will invest at efficient levels (e^*, r^*) (since $p - c(r^*) - e^* - r^* = v(e^*) - c(r^*) - e^* - r^* > 0$). This contract works because it rewards the seller only when the buyer is willing to accept the seller's performance, and the price is set so that the buyer is willing to trade only when the seller has invested at the efficient levels.

In our main model with stochastic gains from trade, the simple fixed-price contract can no longer implement the efficient investments. Nonetheless, the idea that the buyer's willingness to trade is used as an investment incentive remains important.

3. The general model

■   Our main model builds on the simple buyer-seller relationship introduced in Section 2. Again, the seller makes a cooperative investment prior to the trade decision. (As usual, the case where the buyer, rather than the seller, invests is completely symmetric.) The buyer's benefit from trade, v, is now a random variable stochastically determined by the amount of the seller's investment, e, measured in dollar expenses.[10] The cost of the seller's performance is deterministic and equal to a known constant, $c > 0$. That is, the seller's investment is *cooperative*, and there are no selfish investments.

The timing of the model, depicted in Figure 1, is as follows. At date 0, the buyer and seller sign a contract. The contract specifies a fixed-price p to be paid by the buyer when he accepts performance from the seller. The damages, δ, are determined by the breach remedy chosen by the court, which could be ED, LD, or RD. In case of the LD rule, the contract specifies δ as well. At date 1, the seller makes a cooperative investment $e \geq 0$. At date 2, the buyer's benefit from the seller's performance, v, is drawn from $[0, V]$ by the distribution function $F(\cdot|e)$. The seller's cost of performance is deterministic and equal to c, where $0 < c < V$. At date 3, the buyer makes a breach decision, by notifying the seller whether he intends to accept her performance or not. Note that the breach decision is *anticipatory* in that it is made prior to the seller's actual performance. At date 4, the contract may be performed or a lawsuit may be brought, depending on the buyer's decision at date 3. If the buyer has not breached, then the contract is performed, in which case the seller performs and the buyer pays the seller p. If the buyer has breached, then the seller can sue to collect damages δ.

Several remarks are in order. First, the buyer is the only breaching party in this model. This assumption is reasonable since only the buyer's payoff is subject to random disturbances. Furthermore, absent renegotiation, the seller will never want to breach when her contract profit is positive (i.e., $p \geq c$), which is the feature of an optimal

---

[10] While we assume, for ease of exposition, that the investment is one-dimensional, many of our results can readily be extended to the multiinvestment environment. See the appendix of our previous version of this article, Che and Chung (1997).

FIGURE 1
THE SEQUENCE OF EVENTS

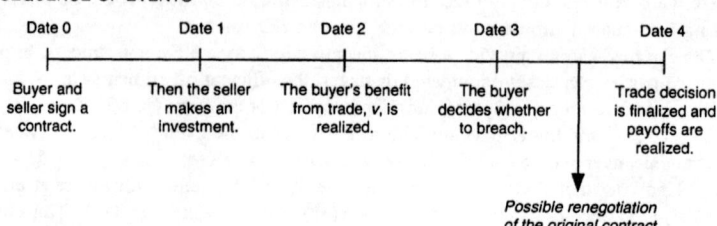

contracting arrangement in all cases.[11] Second, depending on the trading environment, the parties may be able to renegotiate. We consider two different scenarios about renegotiation. In Section 4 we assume that renegotiation is prohibitively costly, so it never arises. Section 5 considers the opposite scenario, in which renegotiation is costless. We assume that renegotiation can occur at any time after date 3 and before the seller actually performs, and that the parties split the surplus from renegotiation at an exogenously given fixed ratio, with the seller receiving a share $\alpha \in [0, 1]$.[12] Under this assumption, the buyer's breach decision at date 3 can be reversed whenever reversing it is mutually beneficial for the parties. A similar timing assumption was made in the models of Edlin and Reichelstein (1996), Segal (forthcoming), and Che and Hausch (forthcoming).

Different breach remedies often require different information to be verifiable. Under the LD rule, the court awards contractually specified damages, δ, upon the buyer's breach, so the court must observe δ and the buyer's breach decision. Under the ED rule, the court must observe the seller's expectation profit, $p - c$, in addition to the buyer's breach decision, whereas under the RD rule it must observe the investment expense, e. It may be an optimistic view of the courts that they can observe all of this information, yet all three remedies are often used in practice. Similar assumptions were made by previous authors such as Shavell (1980) and Rogerson (1984).

The following technical assumptions are made throughout.

Assumption 1. $F(\cdot|\cdot)$ is twice continuously differentiable.

Assumption 2. $F_e(v|e) < 0$ and $F_{ee}(v|e) > 0$ for all v in $(0, V)$ and for all $e \geq 0$.

Assumption 3. $F_e(v|0) = -\infty$ and $F_e(v|\infty) = 0$ for all v in $(0, V)$.

Assumption 2 means that an increase in e moves the distribution in the sense of the first-order stochastic dominance at a decreasing rate, while Assumption 3 ensures an interior solution.

---

[11] When renegotiation is possible, the seller may have an incentive to breach for a strategic reason even when $p \geq c$. We suppress such a possibility by assuming that the buyer can legally compel the seller to the original contract (i.e., specific performance). While such an assumption is restrictive, it has no significant impact on the results. Allowing the seller's strategic breach does not change the subsequent results qualitatively. This latter result is available upon request.

[12] It is possible to specify an underlying bargaining game that corresponds to a constant bargaining share, e.g., a generalized Nash bargaining game or a Rubinstein bargaining game with different discount factors. Our exogenous bargaining specification differs from the view that the parties can manipulate their bargaining power in the renegotiation game (see Hart and Moore (1988), Chung (1991), Aghion, Dewatripont and Rey (1994), and Nöldeke and Schmidt (1995)).

As a benchmark, we first consider the efficient (first-best) outcome. It has two components: (i) the efficient trade decision has trade occur if and only if $v \geq c$, and (ii) the efficient investment level e^*, maximizes the net expected gains from trade, conditional on the efficient trade decision.

$$e^* \in \text{argmax } W(e) \equiv \int_{v \geq c} (v - c) \, dF(v|e) - e. \tag{4}$$

Integrating (4) by parts, the efficient investment level, e^*, is characterized by the following first-order condition:

$$W'(e^*) = -\int_{v \geq c} F_e(v|e^*) \, dv - 1 = 0. \tag{5}$$

By Assumptions 2 and 3, e^* is unique, finite, and strictly positive.

It is also useful to consider the situation where the parties do not contract at date 0, but simply bargain at date 3 to determine the trade price. If the bargaining is efficient, as we assume throughout, then trade will occur if and only if $v \geq c$. Given that the seller receives a share, $\alpha \in [0, 1]$, of *ex post* bargaining surplus, the seller's *ex post* payoff from the bargaining is $\alpha(v - c)$. (The seller's investment e is already sunk, so it does not affect the bargaining outcome.) At date 1, the seller's expected payoff is

$$U(e) = \alpha \int_{v \geq c} (v - c) \, dF(v|e) - e. \tag{6}$$

Upon integration by parts and differentiation, the optimal investment is characterized by

$$U'(e) = -\alpha \int_{v \geq c} F_e(v|e) \, dv - 1 = 0, \tag{7}$$

whenever $e > 0$. Comparison of (5) and (7) reveals that the seller underinvests for all $\alpha < 1$. As before, the underinvestment is attributed to less than full appropriation of the investment returns by the investor. One would expect the parties to improve upon this result by writing a contract, albeit an incomplete and simple one. We turn to this issue next.

4. Contracting when renegotiation is not possible

■ As mentioned in the Introduction, our contracts are distinguished by the manner in which the damages δ are assessed. For now, it is convenient to consider a contracting game with contract terms (p, δ), without being specific about how δ is determined. Defining a "net trade price" $x \equiv p - \delta$, one can use (x, δ) to represent the contract terms, without loss of generality. As will become clear, the net trade price plays a crucial role in determining the performance of a contract.

We apply backward induction, starting with the buyer's breach decision. Given the contract terms, the buyer breaches if and only if his contract loss, $-(v - p)$, exceeds the damages, δ, that he must pay to the seller: i.e., $v - p < -\delta$, or $v < x$. For the

92 / THE RAND JOURNAL OF ECONOMICS

buyer, the net trade price constitutes the true opportunity cost of accepting the performance, since if he accepts the seller's performance, he pays p and saves δ. Rationally
anticipating the buyer's breach decision, the seller invests e to maximize her expected
payoff:

$$U(e, x) = \int_{v<x} \delta \, dF(v|e) + \int_{v\geq x} (p-c) \, dF(v|e) - e = (x-c)[1 - F(x|e)] + \delta - e. \quad (8)$$

Trade occurs with probability $[1 - F(x|e)]$, and when it does, the seller earns additional
profit of $(x - c)$. This net trade profit, $x - c$, can be interpreted as the prize awarded
to the seller for the buyer's not breaching the contract. Since the probability of trade
is increasing in e (see Assumption 2), such a "prize for trade" (i.e., $x - c > 0$) can
induce a positive level of cooperative investment. Absent *ex post* renegotiation, however, the presence of such a trade prize causes the buyer to reject a mutually beneficial
trade when $c < v < x$. The tradeoff between the investment incentive and the trading
efficiency will be the focus of our analysis.

☐ **Expectation damages rule.** The ED rule compensates the victim of breach for
the expected profit she would have earned had the contract been performed. We study
the ED rule for two reasons. First, the ED rule has been used as a default remedy for
breach of contract, so if a contract does not specify remedies for breach, the courts use
the rule to compensate the victim of breach. Second, the existing literature shows that
the ED rule performs reasonably well when cooperative investment is not important,
as mentioned in the Introduction. By contrast, the ED rule fails to provide an incentive
for cooperative investments, as is shown below.

   In our setting the ED rule sets $\delta = p - c$, or $x = c$. Given the ED rule, the trade
decision is efficient because the buyer breaches if and only if $v < c$. Substituting $x = c$
into (8) yields the seller's expected payoff:

$$U^E(e) \equiv p - c - e.$$

Since the payoff is strictly decreasing in e, the seller will make no investment.[13] The
simple intuition is that the ED rule does not reward the seller based on a very important
signal for the cooperative investment—the buyer's breach decision. The buyer's breach
decision is an informative signal for the seller's cooperative investment, since the latter
influences the buyer's benefit from trade. Since the seller receives the same payoff
regardless of the buyer's breach decision under the ED rule, she has no incentive for
the cooperative investment. The social surplus under the ED rule is

$$W^E \equiv W(0) = \int_{v\geq c} (v - c) \, dF(v|0). \quad (9)$$

Because of the poor investment incentive, $W^E < W(e^*)$.

Proposition 1. The ED rule induces the efficient trade decision but zero cooperative
investment.

---

[13] This result is not changed with a Cadillac contract, which effectively makes the investor a breaching
party (see Edlin (1996)). Like the ED contract, a Cadillac contract in our setting induces an efficient trade
decision but no cooperative investment. See Che and Chung (1997) for details.

☐ **Liquidated damages rule.** Under the LD rule, the parties specify (p, δ) or, equivalently, (x, δ). As described earlier, the buyer will breach if and only if $v < x$. Given this breach decision, and the net trade price $x \geq 0$, at date 1 the seller chooses her investment to maximize

$$U^L(e, x) \equiv U(e, x) = (x - c)[1 - F(x|e)] + \delta - e. \tag{10}$$

Since the trade probability, $1 - F(x|e)$, is decreasing in e (see Assumption 2), the seller's expected payoff is strictly decreasing in e, for $x \leq c$. Thus, the seller's choice of cooperative investment is $e^L(x) = 0$, if $x \leq c$. For any $x > c$, $e^L(x)$ is determined implicitly by the first-order condition

$$U_e^L(e, x) = -(x - c)F_e(x|e) - 1 = 0. \tag{11}$$

By Assumptions 2 and 3, $e^L(x)$ is well defined and unique for all $x \geq 0$.
    At date 0, the parties determine the contract terms, (x, δ), to maximize

$$W(e, x) \equiv \int_{v \geq x} (v - c) \, dF(v|e) - e, \tag{12}$$

where $e = e^L(x)$. Note here that the net trade price, x, solely determines the contract performance, which means that δ can be chosen to reflect the relative bargaining power of the parties.
    We now argue that the optimal net trade price, x^L, must exceed the seller's cost of performance, c. To see this, observe first that setting $x = c$ leads to the efficient trade decision but zero cooperative investment (i.e., $e^L(c) = 0$), which is precisely the outcome under the ED rule. Lowering x below c does not help, since the level of investment will remain zero while the trade decision will become inefficient. Next, raise x above c by a small amount. Then, by Assumption 3, $e^L(x)$ will become strictly positive. Consequently, the joint surplus rises stochastically, and its impact is of a first-order magnitude, by Assumption 3. Raising x above c creates trade inefficiencies, as the buyer rejects some mutually beneficial trade opportunities, but the latter effect is of a second-order magnitude because $W_x(e, x) = 0$ at $x = c$ (see (12)). This argument shows that $x^L > c$.[14] It also implies that the optimal LD contract outperforms the ED rule.
    The optimal LD contract institutes a trade prize (i.e., $x^L - c > 0$), since it motivates the seller to increase her cooperative investment. A disadvantage of such a prize is, however, that mutually beneficial trades may not occur when $c < v < x^L$. The higher the prize, the greater the trade inefficiencies. The optimal net trade price, x^L, is therefore chosen to balance the investment incentive and the trade inefficiencies.[15]
    The equilibrium social surplus under liquidated damages is obtained as

----

[14] Without more information on the distribution function, $F(\cdot|\cdot)$, it cannot be determined whether the optimal LD contract induces overinvestment or underinvestment relative to the first-best level. The first-best investment level is not the proper benchmark, however, since the trade decision is distorted. Using the same envelope argument, it can be seen that too little investment is induced, given the (inefficient) trade decision.
    [15] More generally, it is impossible for parties to stipulate a simple damages rule that achieves the first-best outcome unless investment is contractible, or more complex contracts are feasible. In particular, the efficient expectation damages rule, which achieves the first-best outcome in the standard setting with selfish investments, does not work in the presence of cooperative investments.

94 / THE RAND JOURNAL OF ECONOMICS

$$W^L \equiv \max_x W(e^L(x), x) > W(e^L(c), c) = W^E. \tag{13}$$

Proposition 2. The optimal LD contract has $x^L > c$. This optimal contract induces too little trade but a positive level of cooperative investment. The resulting outcome is inefficient but is better than the outcome under the ED rule.

Proof. Since $e^L(x) = 0$ for all $x \leq c$ and $W(0, x)$ is maximized at $x = c$, any $x < c$ is dominated by $x = c$. For the proof, it now suffices to show that $W(e^L(x), x)$ rises strictly when x is raised above $x = c$:

$$\left. \frac{dW(e^L(x), x)}{dx} \right|_{x=c^{+0}} = W_e(0, c)\left. \frac{de^L(x)}{dx} \right|_{x=c^{+0}} + W_x(0, c) > 0,$$

where $d[\cdot]/d[\cdot]|_{x=c^{+0}}$ means the right-hand derivative at $x = c$. The inequality follows because $W_x(0, c) = 0$, $W_e(0, c) = -\int_c^V F_e(v|0)\, dv > 0$, and

$$\left. \frac{de^L(x)}{dx} \right|_{x=c^{+0}} = \left. \frac{-F_e(x|e^L(x)) - (x - c)F_v(x|e^L(x))}{(x - c)F_{ee}(x|e^L(x))} \right|_{x=c^{+0}} = \infty.$$

Q.E.D.

    That x^L completely determines the performance of the contract implies that δ can be set at zero, without loss of generality.[16] One can then interpret the optimal contract as an option contract that gives the buyer an option to accept the seller's performance at date 4 at a predetermined price x^L, with no penalty for refusing the performance. Such an option contract is common, as exemplified by "delivery-contingent contracts" and "purchase upon approval." For instance, advertising agencies often must develop an acceptable pilot campaign before they are paid in full. Real estate agents and other types of brokers typically are not paid until they discover an acceptable match between buyer and seller (see Taylor, 1993). It is a standard practice for a publisher to reserve a right to recover an advance in the event that a book is found unacceptable.[17] One can also interpret the defense profit regulation in the same light. Defense contractors often earn regulated profits when the Department of Defense selects them as suppliers of weapons systems. The prospect of a profitable contractual relationship serves as a prize that induces firms to exert innovation efforts that are otherwise often difficult to motivate (Lichtenberg, 1988; Rogerson 1989).

□   **Reliance damages rule.** Under the RD rule, the breaching party must reimburse the victim of breach for all nonrecoverable reliance expenses—the investment expense, e, in our context. While the ED rule is the default rule, the RD rule is viewed as a more practical substitute, since expectation damages are often difficult to assess. To enforce the RD rule, a court must be able to measure, with reasonable certainty, the amount of expenditure actually incurred by the seller. While this requirement presents

---

[16] If the parties engage in an *ex ante* bargaining to determine the terms of contract, δ may be chosen to split their expected surplus.

[17] Such an acceptability clause was absent in the contract that Joan Collins, a British actress, made with Random House for her novels. Her agent had negotiated a clause that obligated the publisher to pay the actress (a $1.3 million advance payment) for a "complete" manuscript. Later, the publisher found the novels unreadable and sued, but the jury found one of the novels complete and decided in her favor. See "They Just Couldn't Make This Kind of Stuff Up," *Los Angeles Times*, February 14, 1996.

an informational burden for the court, several points are worth noting. First, the common use of the RD rule seems to suggest that the requirement is not unreasonable in many circumstances. For instance, accounting data and expert testimonies often provide good estimates of the investment expenses. The subsequent results rest on the court obtaining only unbiased estimate of the expenses, since the parties make the (investment and breach) decisions based on their *expectation* of the damages. Indeed, the measurement problem is often more severe with the expectation damages.[18] Second, the use of additional information does not guarantee a better performance when the information is not properly incorporated. Indeed, it is well known that the RD rule performs poorly relative to the ED rule in the case of selfish investments (Shavell, 1980; Rogerson, 1984).[19] Third, while individual parties may write contracts that use the additional information better than in the RD rule,[20] the RD rule, whether it is chosen by a court or privately stipulated by the parties, represents an easy way to incorporate the information.

Our interest in the RD rule lies in its common use as a remedy. The RD rule is practically the default remedy in government contracts. The so-called termination for convenience clause gives the government the broad right to terminate a contract without cause and limits the contractor's recovery to costs incurred, profit on work done, and the costs of preparing the termination settlement proposal.[21] Recovery of anticipated profit is precluded (Cibinic and Nash, 1985; Nash and Cibinic, 1980).[22]

Under the RD rule, $\delta = e$, so $x = p - e$. Substituting these into (8) yields the seller's expected payoff function under the RD rule:

$$U^R(e, p - e) = (p - e - c)[1 - F(p - e|e)]. \qquad (14)$$

We assume that $U^R(e, p - e)$ is strictly quasi-concave in e for all p, which ensures that there exists a unique equilibrium investment level. As will be shown below, the equilibrium investment level is zero if $p \leq c$. For any interior solution, it is convenient to describe the first-order condition using x:

$$U_e^R(e, x) = -(x - c)F_e(x|e) + [(x - c)F_v(x|e) + F(x|e)] - 1 = 0. \qquad (15)$$

If $p \leq c$, then $x = p - e \leq c$ for all $e \geq 0$, which implies that $U_e^R(e, x) < 0$. Therefore, the seller makes no investment in this case. Now suppose that $p > c$. If $e = 0$, then $x = p - 0 > c$, so $U_e^R(e, x) > 0$, by Assumption 3. Hence, the equilibrium

---

[18] The ED rule requires estimating anticipated profit on unrealized transactions, which can be quite difficult and subjective. For instance, the expected profit for the seller, $p - c$, may not be readily known if the cost, c, is not realized and it has a random element.

[19] The RD rule induces overinvestment (more so than the ED rule) and an inefficient trade decisions when renegotiation is not possible (Shavell, 1980). When renegotiation is possible, the trade decision becomes efficient, but the overinvestment problem remains worse under the RD rule than under the ED rule (Rogerson, 1984).

[20] For instance, a forcing contract, which would penalize the investor when she does not pick the correct amount of investment, can lead to the first best outcome in our setting. Forcing contracts are not common. A forcing contract may be undesirable if the seller makes both cooperative and selfish investments and only total investment expenses are verifiable, since it will lead the seller to make only selfish investment (and no cooperative investment).

[21] See Federal Acquisition Regulation 49.5 and 52.249 (in Volume 48 of *Code of Federal Regulation*, 1992).

[22] The courts have fashioned a constructive termination doctrine and allowed contracting officers the benefit of the clause in limiting the contractor's recovery, even when they elect not to use the clause. See Cibinic and Nash (1985) and Nash and Cibinic (1980).

96 / THE RAND JOURNAL OF ECONOMICS

investment level must be strictly positive in this case, satisfying (15). While x is not exogenous, it is convenient, for comparison with the other breach remedies, to treat it as such. Let $e^R(x)$ denote the set of e's that satisfy (15) for $x > c$ and $e^R(x) \equiv \{0\}$ for $x \leq c$.[23] Then, any $e \in e^R(x)$ can be induced by $p = x + e$. The two parties' contracting problem is characterized as

$$\max_{x} W^R(x) \equiv \max_{e \in e^R(x)} W(e, x). \qquad (16)$$

We label the optimal net price and the resulting joint surplus x^R and W^R, respectively.

Since $e^R(x) = \{0\}$ for $x \leq c$ and $e > 0$ for $e \in e^R(x)$ for any $x > c$, the argument in the previous section can be used to show that the optimal net trade price, x^R, is strictly greater than c. Next, observe that compared with (12) (i.e., under the LD rule), (15) has additional terms (inside the brackets) that are positive for $x > c$. The second term in the brackets represents a subsidy effect: for each dollar spent for reliance, the seller receives a dollar back whenever the buyer breaches, which occurs if $v < x$, or with probability $F(x|e)$. The first term in the brackets represents the marginal increase in the probability of earning $(x - c)$, which results from the lowering of the threshold value, $x = p - e$, when e is raised slightly. The presence of these additional terms means that the seller has a stronger incentive for investment under the RD rule than under the LD rule, given the same x. Put differently, the RD rule can induce the same level of cooperative investment as the optimal LD contract with a smaller $x - c$, or a smaller degree of trading inefficiencies.

The following proposition formally shows that the RD rule induces a more efficient outcome than the optimal LD contract does.

Proposition 3. The optimal contract under the RD rule induces too little trade, but it leads to a more efficient outcome than the optimal LD contract does.

Proof. That too little trade occurs can be shown in a way analogous to the proof of Proposition 2. To compare the RD rule with the LD rule, let $e^L \equiv e^L(x^L)$ denote the investment level under the optimal LD contract and let

$$\Psi(x) \equiv -(x - c)F_e(x|e^L) + [(x - c)F_v(x|e^L) + F(x|e^L)] - 1.$$

Observe that

$$\Psi(x^L) = -(x^L - c)F_e(x^L|e^L) + [(x^L - c)F_v(x^L|e^L) + F(x^L|e^L)] - 1$$
$$> -(x^L - c)F_e(x^L|e^L) - 1 = 0,$$

and that $\Psi(c) < 0$. Since $\Psi(x)$ is continuous in x, by the intermediate value theorem, there exists $x^0 \in (c, x^L)$ such that $\Psi(x^0) = 0$. Since $U^R_e(e^L, x^0) = \Psi(x^0) = 0$, $e^L \in e^R(x^0)$. That is, the same investment level, e^L, is induced under the RD rule by x^0, or more precisely by $p = x^0 + e^L$. Since $c < x^0 < x^L$, inefficient breach occurs less frequently under the RD rule than under the LD rule. Hence, $W^R(x^0) > W^L$. Since $W^R \geq W^R(x^0)$,

---

[23] $e^R(x)$ is nonempty for all $x \geq 0$. Let $E^R(p)$ denote the unique maximizer of $U(e, p - e)$. Then, for a given $x > c$, there exists $p > c$ such that $x = p - E^R(p) \equiv \xi(p)$. This result holds since $\xi(p) > x$ for sufficiently large p (since $E^R(\cdot)$ is bounded above), $\xi(p) < x$ for p sufficiently close to c, and $\xi(p)$ is continuous (since $E^R(p)$ is continuous by Berge's theorem of maxima). Clearly, $E^R(p)$ at such p must satisfy (15). Thus, $E^R(p) \in e^R(x)$ for such p. Note that $e^R(x)$ may not be a singleton.

the RD rule leads to a more efficient outcome than does the optimal fixed-price contract. *Q.E.D.*

The above result stands in stark contrast to the existing literature that finds the RD rule inferior to the ED rule, let alone the optimal LD contract (Shavell, 1980; Rogerson, 1984). With the cooperative investment, the RD rule outperforms the other contract damages.

The superior performance of the RD rule provides a rationale for a number of observed practices. The termination for convenience clause makes the RD rule virtually the standard remedy for all government procurement contracts in the United States, as mentioned above. A similar arrangement can be found in a cancelled helicopter deal in Canada. The contract calls for the government to reimburse suppliers for work already done, inventory accumulated, and all reasonable costs associated with their involvement in the program.[24] Our result justifies the use of termination for convenience or a similar arrangement, based on their superior incentives for cooperative investment.

Our result is also consistent with the common use of cost-reimbursement type contracts. For instance, the DoD's Independent Research and Development (IR&D) program reimburses a certain fraction of the defense contractors' IR&D expenditures (Lichtenberg, 1988; Rogerson, 1994). This type of direct subsidy can encourage cooperative investment by lowering the cost of investment. Even with the investment subsidy created by the RD rule or a similar contract clause, the "prize for trade" intuition is still important, since $x^R > c$. The subsidy effect augments the prize effect in providing incentives for cooperative investment. If the prize is large enough, the parties may require only a partial reimbursement of the investment cost, as in the DoD's IR&D program.

5. Contracting when renegotiation is possible

■   Under the current judicial system, parties to a contract can always renegotiate their original contract and write a new one. That is, "those who make a contract, may unmake it."[25] In this section we assume that the parties can costlessly renegotiate their prior agreement. The possibility of renegotiation alters our analysis in an important way. Because the parties renegotiate under complete information, it is reasonable to assume that bargaining is efficient. Given this assumption, any *ex post* trading inefficiencies disappear, regardless of the breach remedy in force.

Formally, we assume that renegotiation can occur after date 3 and before the seller actually performs (see Figure 1). In fact, the analysis remains unaffected if the renegotiation can also occur prior to date 3.[26] If the buyer's *anticipatory* breach decision is inefficient, then the renegotiation process can reverse this decision, and the buyer and

---

[24] The former Conservative government in Canada signed a deal to buy 50 new military helicopters. The $4.8 billion deal was cancelled by the new Prime Minister, Jean Chrétien, on the Liberal government's first day in office (*National General News*, November 29, 1993). A similar damages measure is being considered, though not originally specified in the contract, for the cancelled privatization program for the operation of the Pearson Airport in Toronto.

[25] *Beatty v. Guggenheim Exploration Co.*, 122 N.E. 378, 387–88 (N.Y. 1919). One can imagine that parties include a "nonmodification clause" that prevent them from later renegotiating the terms of their original contract, if it is mutually beneficial for them. The courts are reluctant to enforce such a clause, however (see Jolls (1997)).

[26] If the parties can renegotiate after the realization of v but before date 3, they will take the future equilibrium payoffs as their disagreement payoffs, so the equilibrium payoffs will remain the same. The critical assumption is that a renegotiation can occur after the buyer's breach decision. While the timing of renegotiation is ultimately an empirical issue, our current assumption accords well with the fact that many lawsuits are settled out of court.

98 / THE RAND JOURNAL OF ECONOMICS

seller split any resulting surplus at $1 - \alpha$ and α. The buyer's decision to breach the initial contract depends on the anticipated bargaining outcome.

Suppose first that the buyer honors the contract (i.e., notifies the seller of his intention to accept her performance). If trade is efficient, then no renegotiation occurs, and the buyer receives $v - p$. If not ($v < c$), then the parties will renegotiate to cancel the original contract and the buyer will receive $1 - \alpha$ share of the surplus from renegotiation: $(1 - \alpha)(c - v)$. Hence, the buyer's payoff of honoring the contract is

$$v - p + (1 - \alpha)\max\{c - v, 0\}. \tag{17}$$

(Note that renegotiation occurs only when $c > v$.) Now suppose that the buyer announces breach at date 3. Then the seller will sue the buyer. If the case goes to trial, the buyer pays the damages of δ to the seller but saves the contract price of p. Given this trial outcome as a threat point, the parties can negotiate to settle before the case goes to trial. If the breach is efficient ($v \leq c$), the buyer simply pays δ to the seller. If breach is inefficient ($v > c$), the parties reverse the breach and split the surplus. In sum, the buyer's anticipated payoff from announcing breach is

$$-\delta + (1 - \alpha)\max\{v - c, 0\}. \tag{18}$$

(Note that renegotiation occurs when $v > c$ in this case.)

The buyer announces breach if and only if (18) is greater than (17) or, equivalently, v is less than a threshold value,

$$\hat{v}(x) \equiv \min\left\{\frac{x - c}{\alpha} + c, V\right\}. \tag{19}$$

Compared with the scenario of no renegotiation, the threshold value for breach is changed from x to $\hat{v}(x)$. This is because the anticipated renegotiation outcome influences the buyer's breach decision.[27] When the realized benefit exceeds the cost but is small relative to the cost in the sense that $v \in (c, \hat{v}(x))$, the buyer breaches to induce price concession from the seller.

The seller's *ex post* payoff is $p - c + \alpha \max\{c - v, 0\}$ if $v > \hat{v}(x)$, and $\delta + \alpha \max\{v - c, 0\}$ if $v \leq \hat{v}(x)$. The seller's expected net payoff is then

$$U(e, x) = \int_{v < \hat{v}(x)} [\delta + \alpha \max\{v - c, 0\}] \, dF(v \mid e)$$

$$+ \int_{v \geq \hat{v}(x)} [p - c + \alpha \max\{c - v, 0\}] \, dF(v \mid e) - e \tag{20}$$

$$= (x - c)[1 - F(\hat{v}(x) \mid e)] + \alpha \int_c^{\hat{v}(x)} (v - c) \, dF(v \mid e) + \delta - e.$$

---

[27] Rogerson (1984) assumes that the buyer's breach decision is not affected by the renegotiation possibility. That is, the buyer breaches if and only if $v < x$. This result appears to follow from an (implicit) assumption that renegotiation can only occur before the buyer's breach decision. If renegotiation is possible after the buyer's breach decision, then the buyer will rationally account for the renegotiation possibility in his breach decision.

The first term in the right-hand side of (20) is the expected net profit from trade. This term also appears in the corresponding expression with no renegotiation (see (8)). The second term, $\alpha \int_c^{\hat{v}(x)} (v - c) \, dF(v|e)$, is new here and represents the seller's share of the surplus from renegotiation. If a contract (x, δ) induces the seller to invest e, then the joint expected surplus is given by

$$ W(e) = \int_{v \geq c} (v - c) \, dF(v|e) - e. \tag{21} $$

(Recall that the trade decision is efficient because of renegotiation.) The contract terms cannot directly influence the joint surplus, although they can have an indirect effect through the seller's investment.

☐ **Expectation damages rule.** With the ED rule, we have $x^E = c$ and, thus, $\hat{v}(x^E) = c$. The buyer's breach decision is then efficient, so renegotiation never occurs. As when renegotiation is impossible, the seller receives $p - c - e$, regardless of the realized gains from trade. Therefore, the previous results continue to hold: under the ED rule, the seller makes zero investment and the social surplus is given by $W^E = W(0)$.

Proposition 4. The ED rule induces the efficient trade decision but zero cooperative investment.

☐ **Liquidated damages rule.** Suppose that the parties specify both p and δ in their initial contract. Again, it is convenient to focus on (x, δ). At date 0, the parties choose (x, δ) to solve

$$ \max_{x,e} W(e) \qquad \text{subject to} \quad e \in \operatorname*{argmax}_{\tilde{e} \geq 0} U^L(\tilde{e}, x), $$

where the seller's expected payoff, $U^L(e, x)$, is precisely $U(e, x)$ defined in (20). That is,

$$ U^L(e, x) \equiv (x - c)[1 - F(\hat{v}(x)|e)] + \alpha \int_c^{\hat{v}(x)} (v - c) \, dF(v|e) + \delta - e. \tag{22} $$

When renegotiation is possible, setting $x > c$ can create the seller's investment incentive in two different ways. The first is the "prize effect": a positive wedge between net trade price and cost, $x - c$, may serve as a prize that the seller can collect when the buyer does not breach (the first term in (22)). Recall that, without renegotiation, such a wedge generated the incentive for the seller's cooperative investment. The second effect is new here, and is called a "renegotiation effect": the wedge between x and c creates the possibility of inefficient breach that leads to a renegotiation, from which the seller appropriates a share of net trade surplus (the second term in (22)). Internalizing part of the trade surplus motivates the seller to increase her investment.

With renegotiation, only the renegotiation effect is active. The prize effect is inactive, since the seller can command renegotiation surplus even when the buyer breaches, which offsets the prize effect of $x - c > 0$. The seller receives $x - c + \delta$ if $v \geq \hat{v}(x)$, and $\alpha(v - c) + \delta$ if $v < \hat{v}(x)$. At $v = \hat{v}(x)$, the two quantities are exactly the same, since the buyer is indifferent between breaching and not breaching and the total payoff is constant at $v - c$. Thus, the seller has no incentive to increase the probability that

100 / THE RAND JOURNAL OF ECONOMICS

v exceeds $\hat{v}(x)$. The net effect can be seen by collecting the terms of (22) and integrating it by parts.

$$U^L(e, x) = (x - c) + (c - x)F(\hat{v}(x)|e) + \alpha[\hat{v}(x) - c]F(\hat{v}(x)|e)$$

$$- \alpha \int_c^{\hat{v}(x)} F(v|e)\, dv + \delta - e \qquad (23)$$

$$= (x - c) + \alpha\left[\hat{v}(x) - \frac{x - c}{\alpha} + c\right]F(\hat{v}(x)|e) - \alpha \int_c^{\hat{v}(x)} F(v|e)\, dv + \delta - e.$$

The second term in the right-hand side of (23) vanishes if $[x - c]/\alpha + c \leq V$ (see (19)). Otherwise, $\hat{v}(x) = V$, so the second term is independent of e because $F(V|\cdot) = 1$. It follows that the incentive for the cooperative investment can be generated only through the third term (renegotiation effect), which is increasing in e when $x > c$.

The seller's optimal investment, $e^L(x)$, is characterized by

$$U_e^L(e, x) = -\alpha \int_c^{\hat{v}(x)} F_e(v|e)\, dv - 1 = 0 \qquad (24)$$

if $x > c$, and $e^L(x) = 0$ if $x \leq c$. The optimal investment is unique, since $F(v|\cdot)$ is convex for all v from Assumption 2. Since $\hat{v}(x)$ is increasing in x for $x < \alpha V + (1 - \alpha)c$ and constant for $x \geq \alpha V + (1 - \alpha)c$, $e^L(x)$ is increasing for $x < \alpha V + (1 - \alpha)c$ and constant for $x \geq \alpha V + (1 - \alpha)c$.[28] This feature deserves an explanation. In (23), the seller internalizes a fraction of the gains from trade only if the parties renegotiate the initial contract following the buyer's decision to breach inefficiently. Therefore, the seller's increased exposure to renegotiation increases her incentive for the investment. The parties raise the possibility of renegotiation by raising x, since it increases the probability that the buyer breaches inefficiently.

Comparing (24) with (5) reveals that $e^L(x) < (\leq)e^*$ for any x and $\alpha < (\leq)1$. Since the joint expected payoff is increasing in e for all $e < e^*$, the optimal x is the one that maximizes $e^L(x)$. The optimal net trade price, x^L, is any x that is greater than or equal to $\alpha V + (1 - \alpha)c$, which guarantees $\hat{v}(x^L) = V$. With x^L, the buyer always breaches, and then the parties renegotiate to ensure that a trade occurs whenever it is efficient. For any α, the seller's optimal investment, $e^L \equiv e^L(x^L)$, is characterized by

$$U_e^L(e^L, x^L) = -\alpha \int_c^V F_e(v|e^L)\, dv - 1 = 0. \qquad (25)$$

The joint expected surplus generated by the optimal LD contract is denoted by $W^L \equiv W(e^L)$.

Several observations can be made. First, the optimal fixed-price contract yields underinvestment unless the seller has the entire bargaining power. The second and more interesting observation is that (25) coincides with (7), the first-order condition when the parties do not sign an initial contract. That is, the optimal LD contract yields an

---

[28] The result follows since U^L is continuously differentiable and has a positive (respectively, nonnegative) cross partial derivative with respect to (e, x) for $x < \alpha V + (1 - \alpha)c$ (respectively, $x \geq \alpha V + (1 - \alpha)c$). See Edlin and Shannon (1995).

outcome that the parties could have achieved without an initial contract at all! Even without a contract, a voluntary renegotiation between the parties can provide some incentives for cooperative investments, since the seller receives a positive share of the bargaining surplus. When renegotiation is possible, the optimal LD contract fails to create any additional incentive. This irrelevance of contracting is novel with the co-operative investment.[29] This result is in sharp contrast with the selfish-investment set-ting, in which an LD contract (known as "efficient expectation damages") can generate an efficient outcome.

Finally, if parties do write a contract, the resulting equilibrium has the appearance of the classical holdup. Recall that the optimal contract price is so high that the buyer initially refuses to accept the seller's performance, regardless of his valuation. The buyer's refusal triggers a renegotiation that lowers the price downward to a level that ensures an efficient trade decision. What appears to be a holdup here is in fact a process of implementing the optimal contract. Our results are summarized in the following proposition.

Proposition 5. Underinvestment occurs under the optimal LD contract, unless the seller has the entire bargaining power in the renegotiation. The optimal contract induces the buyer to breach the contract with probability one, which is subsequently renegotiated whenever trade is efficient. Contracting is irrelevant in the sense that the parties can achieve the outcome of the optimal fixed-price contract by writing no contract.

Proposition 5 suggests an interesting observation on the value of renegotiation. With selfish investments, an LD contract can implement the first-best outcome, regard-less of the possibility of renegotiation. In that case, therefore, the parties' ability to renegotiate the original contract has no value. With cooperative investments, the value of renegotiation depends on the seller's (investing party's) share, α, of the bargaining surplus. If α is close to one, then the outcome under renegotiation is nearly efficient, so the ability to renegotiate is valuable. If α is close to zero, the outcome under re-negotiation is strictly worse.[30] Therefore, the parties will be better off if they can commit not to renegotiate the original contract, in this case.

□   **Reliance damages rule.** If the seller can be reimbursed at least a fraction of investment expenditure following the buyer's breach, it may be possible to mitigate the underinvestment problem observed in the previous subsection. Not only does such reimbursement improve the incentive for cooperative investment, it can be shown to induce the first-best outcome.

The net trade price, x, is equal to $p - e$ under the RD rule. It is again convenient, for comparison with the other cases, to treat x, rather than p, as the main choice variable. As before, the buyer breaches if and only if $v < \hat{v}(x)$ (defined in (19)), and a renego-tiation corrects an inefficient breach decision. The seller's expected payoff is obtained by substituting $\delta = e$ into (23):

$$U^{\eta}(e, \lambda) = (\lambda - c) + \alpha \left[\hat{v}(\lambda) - \left(\frac{x - c}{\alpha} + c \right) \right] F(\hat{v}(\lambda) | e) - \alpha \int_{c}^{\hat{v}(x)} F(v | e) \, dv. \quad (26)$$

---

[29] Che and Hausch (forthcoming) show that the irrelevance of contracting result holds well beyond the particular contracting and technological environment assumed here, whenever cooperative investments are involved.

[30] When $\alpha = 0$, the outcome under renegotiation can be replicated by a fixed-price contract without renegotiation by setting $x = c$, which is in turn dominated by the optimal LD contract in Proposition 2.

102 / THE RAND JOURNAL OF ECONOMICS

Using $x = p - e$, the first-order condition for the seller's investment decision is obtained as

$$U_e^R(e, x) = F(\hat{v}(x)|e) - \alpha \int_c^{\hat{v}(x)} F_e(v|e) \, dv - 1 = 0, \tag{27}$$

which must hold for any $e > 0$.

If $x \leq c$, then $\hat{v}(x) \leq c$, which implies that $U_e^R(e, x) \leq 0$. Thus, any equilibrium with $x \leq c$ entails zero investment. Now suppose that $x > c$. Then, $\hat{v}(x) > c$, so $U_e^R(e, x) > 0$ at $e = 0$. Thus, in this case the seller will choose a positive investment level that satisfies (27). Since $U^R(e, p - e)$ is strictly concave in e,[31] there exists a unique optimal investment level for the seller for any $p \geq c$. We let $e^R(x)$ denote e that satisfies (27) for $x > c$ and $e^R(x) \equiv 0$ for $x \leq c$.[32] As before, $e^R(x)$ can be implemented by setting $p = x + e^R(x)$ because of the strict concavity of $U^R(e, p - e)$ in e. At date 0, the parties choose x (or a corresponding p) to maximize their joint expected surplus. Their maximized surplus is labelled $W^R \equiv \max_x W(e^R(x))$.

The first two terms in (27) can be explained as follows. The second term, which also appears in the corresponding first-order condition for an LD contract, accounts for the net renegotiation effect. (As before, the prize effect is completely offset at the margin.) The first term accounts for the subsidy effect. When $v < c$, the buyer breaches (and no renegotiation follows), and the seller collects reimbursement of her investment expenses as damages. When $c \leq v \leq \hat{v}(x)$, renegotiation reverses the buyer's breach, but the seller still receives the subsidy indirectly through the improved status quo payoff. Consequently, the subsidy effect arises whenever the buyer breaches, which occurs with probability $F(\hat{v}(x)|e)$. The presence of this subsidy effect implies that the RD rule creates a stronger incentive for a cooperative investment than the optimal LD contract does. In fact, the RD rule implements the first-best outcome, as shown in the next proposition.

Proposition 6. Under the RD rule with the possibility of renegotiation, there exists a contract, specifying p, that implements the first-best outcome. At the optimal contract, the buyer initially defaults more often than under the ED rule, but less often than under the optimal LD contract.

Proof. Define a function of x,

$$\Phi(x) \equiv F(\hat{v}(x)|e^*) - \alpha \int_c^{\hat{v}(x)} F_e(v|e^*) \, dv - 1,$$

where e^* is the efficient investment level defined in (5). Notice that $\Phi(\cdot)$ is continuous, increasing, $\Phi(c) < 0$, and $\Phi(\alpha V + (1 - \alpha)c) > 0$. It thus follows that there exists $x^R \in (c, \alpha V + (1 - \alpha)c)$ such that $\Phi(x^R) = 0$. Then, $e^* = e^R(x^R)$, since

$$U_e^R(e^*, x^R) = \Phi(x^R) = 0 \quad \text{and} \quad U_e^R(\cdot, x^R)$$

---

[31] The second derivative of $U^R(e, p - e)$ with respect to e, $-\hat{v}'(x)F_v(\hat{v}(x)|e) - \alpha \int_c^{\hat{v}(x)} F_{ee}(v|e) \, dv$, is strictly less than zero by Assumption 2.

[32] That there exists a unique optimal investment level for any $p \geq c$ does not necessarily imply that $e^R(x)$ is well defined. One can, however, show that $e^R(x)$ exists and is unique. Note that for all $x > c$, $U_e^R(0, x) \geq 0$ and $U_e^R(\infty, x) < 0$, and $U_e^R(\cdot, x)$ is continuous. Moreover, $U^R(e, x)$ is strictly concave in e. Therefore, $e^R(x)$ exists and is unique.

is decreasing. As noted above, setting $p^* = x^R + e^*$ induces e^*. The second statement immediately follows from the fact that $x^R \in (c, \alpha V + (1 - \alpha)c)$. *Q.E.D.*

This proposition reconfirms the superior performance of cost-reimbursement types of contracting arrangements, such as termination for convenience and investment subsidy programs, and it explains their common use when cooperative investments are important. As in the case of the optimal LD contract, the contracting equilibrium has the appearance of the holdup, since the originally high contract price is negotiated downward after the investment takes place. The holdup phenomenon is often a result of parties' inability to write a complete contract, and it typically yields underinvestment. Interestingly, the appearance of a holdup here serves to achieve the efficient outcome.

6. Conclusion

■   We have examined how alternative breach remedies generate different incentives for cooperative investments. Unlike selfish investments, which benefit the investor whenever the transaction is realized, no such natural source of investment incentive exists for cooperative investments, which makes them much harder to motivate. With cooperative investments, we showed that achieving *ex post* trade efficiency can detract optimal provision of incentives for *ex ante* investments. Rather, the incentive for cooperative investments can only be generated by transferring part of the trade surplus to the investor from her partner—that is, only by distorting the breach decision when renegotiation is impossible. For this reason, the ED rule, which induces an efficient trade decision, performs very poorly, inducing zero cooperative investment. On the other hand, the LD contract, which induces too little trade, performs much better. Finally, the use of the RD rule, or a similar investment subsidy, provides additional incentives for cooperative investments and can significantly improve the performance of contracts. In particular, it leads to the first-best outcome if *ex post* renegotiation is possible.

In practice, most specific investments have elements of both selfish and cooperative investments. In this mixed environment, the performance of the contract damages will depend on the relative importance of each element, so the courts must evaluate the nature of underlying reliance investments in determining a remedy. Since parties to a contract often have better information about the nature of specific investments, it will be desirable to allow parties to stipulate their own contract remedies.[33] Finally, our irrelevance of contracting result suggests the limited value of contracting in the presence of cooperative investments. More precisely, fixed-price contracts have no value in the presence of renegotiation. This result contrasts with the selfish investment case in which a simple fixed-price contract can restore efficiency. The limited value of contracting redirects our attention to property rights and organizational governance as important sources of investment incentives.

References

AGHION, P., DEWATRIPONT, M., AND REY, P. "Renegotiation Design with Unverifiable Information." *Econometrica*, Vol. 62 (1994), pp. 257–282.

AMERICAN LAW INSTITUTE. *Restatement (Second) of the Law of Contracts*. St. Paul, Minn.: American Law Institute Publishers, 1981.

---

[33] Such a damages rule designed by parties is enforceable by the courts: Except for the restrictions imposed by the rule that proscribes the fixing of penalties, parties are free to vary the rules governing damages, subject to the usual limitations on private agreement such as that on unconscionable contracts or terms (American Law Institute, 1981).

104 / THE RAND JOURNAL OF ECONOMICS

ASANUMA, B. "Manufacturer-Supplier Relationships in Japan and the Concept of Relation-Specific Skill." *Journal of the Japanese and International Economies,* Vol. 3 (1989), pp. 1–30.

CHE, Y.-K. AND CHUNG, T.-Y. "Contract Damages and Cooperative Investments." Mimeo, University of Wisconsin, 1997.

——— AND HAUSCH, D. "Cooperative Investments and the Value of Contracting." *American Economic Review,* forthcoming.

CHUNG, T.-Y. "Incomplete Contracts, Specific Investments, and Risk Sharing." *Review of Economic Studies,* Vol. 58 (1991), pp. 1031–1042.

———. "On the Social Optimality of Liquidated Damages Clauses: An Economic Analysis." *Journal of Law, Economics and Organization,* Vol. 8 (1992), pp. 280–305.

CIBINIC, J. JR. AND NASH, R.C. *Administration of Government Contracts,* 2d ed. Washington, D.C.: George Washington University, 1985.

COOTER, R. "Unity in Tort, Contract, and Property: The Model of Precaution." *California Law Review,* Vol. 43 (1985), pp. 1–51.

EDLIN, A.S. "Cadillac Contracts and Up-Front Payments: Efficient Investment Under Expectation Damages." *Journal of Law, Economics and Organization,* Vol. 12 (1996), pp. 98–118.

——— AND REICHELSTEIN, S. "Holdups, Standard Breach Remedies, and Optimal Investment." *American Economic Review,* Vol. 18 (1996), pp. 478–501.

——— AND SHANNON, C. "Strict Monotonicity in Comparative Statics." Department of Economics Working Paper no. 95–238, University of California-Berkeley, 1995.

GROSSMAN, S.J. AND HART, O.D. "An Analysis of the Principal-Agent Problem." *Econometrica,* Vol. 51 (1983), pp. 7–45.

——— AND ———. "Costs and Benefits of Ownership: A Theory of Vertical and Lateral Integration." *Journal of Political Economy,* Vol. 94 (1986), pp. 691–719.

HART, O.D. AND HOLMSTRÖM, B. "Theory of Contracts." In T.F. Bewley, ed., *Advances in Economic Theory: Fifth World Congress.* Cambridge: Cambridge University Press, 1987.

——— AND MOORE, J. "Incomplete Contracts and Renegotiation." *Econometrica,* Vol. 56 (1988), pp. 755–785.

——— AND ———. "Property Rights and the Nature of the Firm." *Journal of Political Economy,* Vol. 98 (1990), pp. 1119–1158.

HERMALIN, B.E. AND KATZ, M.L. "Judicial Modification of Contracts Between Sophisticated Parties: A More Complete View of Incomplete Contracts and Their Breach." *Journal of Law, Economics and Organization,* Vol. 9 (1993), pp. 230–255.

HOLMSTRÖM, B. "Moral Hazard and Observability." *Bell Journal of Economics,* Vol. 10 (1979), pp. 74–91.

JOLLS, C. "Contracts as Bilateral Commitments: A New Perspective on Contract Modification." *Journal of Legal Studies,* Vol. 26 (1997), pp. 203–237.

KONAKAYAMA, A., MITSUI, T., AND WATANABE, S. "Efficient Contracting with Reliance and a Damage Measure." *RAND Journal of Economics,* Vol. 17 (1986), pp. 450–457.

LICHTENBERG, F.R. "The Private R&D Investment Response to Federal Design and Technical Competitions." *American Economic Review,* Vol. 78 (1988), pp. 550–559.

MACLEOD, W.B. AND MALCOMSON, J.M. "Investments, Holdup, and the Form of Market Contracts." *American Economic Review,* Vol. 83 (1993), pp. 811–837.

NASH, R.C. AND CIBINIC, J. JR. *Federal Procurement Law, Volume II: Contract Performance,* 3d ed. Washington, D.C.: George Washington University, 1980.

NISHIGUCHI, T. *Strategic Industrial Sourcing: The Japanese Advantage.* New York: Oxford University Press, 1994.

NÖLDEKE, G. AND SCHMIDT, K.M. "Option Contracts and Renegotiation: A Solution to the Hold-Up Problem." *RAND Journal of Economics,* Vol. 26 (1995), pp. 163–179.

ROGERSON, W.P. "Efficient Reliance and Damages Measures for Breach of Contract." *RAND Journal of Economics,* Vol. 15 (1984), pp. 39–53.

———. "Profit Regulation of Defense Contractors and Prizes for Innovation." *Journal of Political Economy,* Vol. 97 (1989), pp. 1284–1305.

———. "Contractual Solutions to the Hold-Up Problem." *Review of Economic Studies,* Vol. 59 (1992), pp. 777–793.

———. "Economic Incentives and the Defense Procurement Process." *Journal of Economic Perspectives,* Vol. 8 (1994), pp. 65–90.

SEGAL, I. "Complexity and Renegotiation: A Foundation for Incomplete Contracts." *Review of Economic Studies,* forthcoming.

SHAVELL, S. "Damages Measures for Breach of Contract." *Bell Journal of Economics,* Vol. 11 (1980), pp. 466–490.

————. "The Design of Contracts and Remedies for Breach." *Quarterly Journal of Economics,* Vol. 99 (1984), pp. 121–147.

SPIER, K.E. AND WHINSTON, M.D. "On the Efficiency of Privately Stipulated Damages for Breach of Contract: Entry Barriers, Reliance, and Renegotiation." *RAND Journal of Economics,* Vol. 26 (1995), pp. 180–202.

TAYLOR, C.R. "Delivery-Contingent Contracts for Research." *Journal of Law, Economics and Organization,* Vol. 9 (1993), pp. 188–203.

TIROLE, J. "Procurement and Renegotiation." *Journal of Political Economy,* Vol. 94 (1986), pp. 235–259.

WILLIAMSON, O. *The Economic Institutions of Capitalism.* New York: The Free Press, 1985.

[8]

Solomonic Bargaining:

Dividing a Legal Entitlement To Facilitate

Coasean Trade

Ian Ayres[†] and Eric Talley[††]

CONTENTS

   † William K. Townsend Professor of Law, Yale Law School; J.D., Yale Law School; Ph.D. (Economics), Massachusetts Institute of Technology.
   †† J.D., Stanford University Law School; Ph.D. Candidate (Economics), Stanford University. We are grateful to Jennifer Brown, Peter Cramton, Dick Craswell, Bob Ellickson, Lewis Kornhauser, Dean Leuck, Sandy Meiklejohn, Paul Milgrom, Barry Nalebuff, Mitch Polinsky, Jeffrey Rachlinski, Eric Rasmusen, Roberta Romano, Carol Rose, Alan Schwartz, Matthew Spitzer, and Scott Stern for helpful comments. The fundamental insights of Jason Scott Johnston—especially as contained in his excellent manuscript, *Bargaining Under Rules Versus Standards* (June 28, 1994)—have inspired much of the analysis in this Article. Support from the John M. Olin Program in Law and Economics is gratefully acknowledged. We also benefited from comments at a Harvard conference on property and liability rules.

I. INTRODUCTION

It is a common argument in law and economics that divided ownership can create or exacerbate strategic behavior. For instance, when several persons own the land designated for a proposed stadium, individual sellers may "hold out" for a disproportionate share of the gains from trade.[1] Alternatively, when building a public library would benefit multiple residents, individual buyers may "free ride" on the willingness of others to pay for its construction.[2] Such transaction costs of collective action fall under a variety of analytic rubrics, including the "tragedy of the commons" and the theory of "public goods."[3] Nonetheless, each example of market failure shares a common attribute: The division of a single legal entitlement, or of rivalrous entitlements,[4] among joint sellers or joint buyers may prevent socially efficient transactions, particularly when the parties possess private information about their preferences.[5]

This Article explores a different way of dividing an entitlement. Rather than analyzing divisions among buyers or among sellers, we consider the effects of splitting an entitlement *between* the two groups. Our core insight is Solomonic in character: Dividing a legal entitlement between rivalrous users can facilitate efficient trade.[6] More specifically, we show that when two

---

1. *See, e.g.,* ROBERT COOTER & THOMAS ULEN, LAW AND ECONOMICS 192–93 (1988); RICHARD A. POSNER, ECONOMIC ANALYSIS OF LAW 48–49, 55 (3d ed. 1986); George J. Mailath & Andrew Postlewaite, *Asymmetric Information Bargaining Problems with Many Agents,* 57 REV. ECON. STUD. 351 (1990).

2. *See* COOTER & ULEN, *supra* note 1, at 109; POSNER, *supra* note 1, at 55.

3. The contributions to this literature are far too dense and numerous to be mentioned here. For general overviews, however, see WILLIAM J. BAUMOL & ALAN S. BLINDER, ECONOMICS: PRINCIPLES AND POLICY 309–33 (6th ed. 1994); COOTER & ULEN, *supra* note 1, at 88–122; POSNER, *supra* note 1, at 29–77.

4. While it is arbitrary to characterize a particular set of claims either as the division of an individual entitlement or of rivalrous entitlements, we seek to explore rivalries that either party can end by successfully purchasing the other party's claim. For example, an easement and a fee simple subject to an easement might be thought of as separate entitlements or as a division of a single entitlement. *See* Robert C. Ellickson, *Property in Land,* 102 YALE L.J. 1315 (1993). But regardless of their characterization, these claims might be rivalrous if an individual could develop the land more profitably by acquiring ownership of both claims.

5. In his seminal article, Ronald Coase argued that, in the absence of transaction costs, private bargaining will lead to efficient outcomes. *See* Ronald H. Coase, *The Problem of Social Cost,* 3 J.L. & ECON. 1 (1960).

6. The title of this Article is, of course, an allusion to the much-repeated biblical account of King Solomon deciding which of two women claiming parentage of a child was the actual mother. Unable to deduce the truth from claims that the two women made, Solomon requested a sword so that he might slice the baby into two equal pieces, giving half to each party. When only one of the women offered to drop her claim for custody if Solomon spared the child's life, Solomon immediately awarded her custody. *See* 1 *Kings* 3:16–28. This biblical account is suggestive of our results, especially in that Solomon's threat to split the baby induced the revelation of private information, leading ultimately to complete custody by the true mother. Nonetheless, the success of his decision rule is inconsistent with the assumption that both parties know the rules of the legal game (an assumption that we make in this Article). If both women had known what Solomon would do, then it would have been a dominant strategy for each woman to offer to surrender her claim.

Jon Elster has used the Solomonic analogy to argue that divided (probabilistic) entitlements can produce more effective child custody decisions in situations where negotiated settlement is unlikely. JON ELSTER, SOLOMONIC JUDGMENTS: STUDIES IN THE LIMITATIONS OF RATIONALITY 123–74 (1989). For a discussion of the differences between Elster's probabilistic model and ours, see *infra* note 141.

parties have private information about how much they value an entitlement, endowing each party with a partial claim to the entitlement can reduce the incentive to behave strategically during bargaining, thereby enhancing economic efficiency.

Private information is a particularly pernicious form of transaction cost, especially in legal contexts where, for procedural or other reasons, parties must negotiate within "thin" markets.[7] In such contexts, self-interested bargainers have a strong incentive to misrepresent their private valuations so as to capture a larger share of the bargaining "pie." These incentives often lead to predictable opportunistic strategies: Sellers tend to overstate the value they place on the bargained-for item, while buyers tend to understate their desire to purchase it. As a result of such strategic behavior, the parties may fail to detect and exploit a mutually beneficial trade, and even when they can it is usually after considerable and costly delay.

In this Article, we argue that divided entitlements can facilitate trade by inducing claim holders to reveal more information than they would under an undivided entitlement regime. Owners of divided, or "Solomonic," entitlements must bargain more forthrightly than owners of undivided entitlements, because the entitlement division obscures the titular boundary between "buyer" and "seller." More precisely, endowing each bargainer with a share of the underlying entitlement creates the possibility of two different types of Coasean trade: A bargainer might buy the other party's claim, or, alternatively, she might sell her own. During negotiation, each party is likely to be uncertain about whether she will ultimately emerge as a seller or a buyer. This strategic "identity crisis" can strongly mitigate each party's incentive to misrepresent her respective valuation; each party must balance countervailing interests in shading up her valuation, as one would *qua* seller, and shading down her valuation, as one would *qua* buyer. This form of rational ambivalence, we argue, can lead the bargainers to represent their valuations more truthfully.[8]

To illustrate this identity crisis with a traditional type of property division, consider a negotiation between Smith and Jones about who should develop Blackacre as a mall. Assume it is commonly known that Blackacre's most valuable use is as a mall, and that either Smith or Jones is the most efficient developer. But assume also that the parties' private valuations make it unclear who is the more efficient developer. Blackacre is divided so that Smith owns Blackacre in fee simple, subject to an executory interest in Jones that becomes

---

7. *See, e.g.*, ERIC RASMUSEN, GAMES AND INFORMATION: AN INTRODUCTION TO GAME THEORY 227 (1989) (noting that in such thin markets, usual assumptions of efficient competitive markets break down).

8. Within principal-agent literature, this form of rational ambivalence is more often known as "countervailing incentives." The notion of countervailing incentives was first examined in Tracy R. Lewis & David E.M. Sappington, *Countervailing Incentives in Agency Problems*, 49 J. ECON. THEORY 294 (1989); *see also* William Samuelson, *A Comment on the Coase Theorem*, in GAME THEORETIC MODELS OF BARGAINING 321, 324–31 (Alvin Roth ed., 1985) (discussing problems of bargaining inefficiency resulting from parties' self-interest and asymmetric information).

possessory if Blackacre is ever used for any purpose other than a horse buggy factory. Because of the low demand for horse buggies, Blackacre's value as a buggy factory is negligible. Under these circumstances, the mall might only be built if one of the parties agrees to sell her estate in the land to the other.[9] Imagine what would go through Smith's mind in considering how much to offer to purchase Jones' interest. Smith, as a buyer, would want to offer a low price, but the possibility that Smith could become a seller complicates Smith's decision. If Smith offers too low a price, Jones is liable to turn the tables by suggesting that Smith should sell her own claim. In essence, Jones would be saying: "Where did you get that price? If that's all you think Blackacre is worth, I'll buy your claim." Thus, when ownership is so divided, a party's explicit or implicit representation about the entitlement's value might be used by the other side to propose the other type of transaction.[10]

This example illustrates how a particular type of division can facilitate efficient trade. Throughout this Article, we compare bargaining in the shadow of an absolute, undivided entitlement to bargaining in the shadow of a number of such Solomonic divisions.[11] Our analysis, however, revolves around two broad axes of division. The first axis represents the *degree of protection* accorded a given entitlement, and the second axis represents the explicit *ownership structure* of the entitlement.

With respect to the first axis of division, the law may effect a Solomonic division through the degree to which it protects one's ownership interest in the underlying entitlement. Our discussion of this axis centers predominantly on the distinction—first analyzed by Calabresi and Melamed[12]—between "liability rules" (i.e., remedies at law) and "property rules" (i.e., equitable relief). Protecting an "owner" of an entitlement with a liability rule is a type of Solomonic division, because a liability rule endows "nonowners" with an option to take the entitlement nonconsensually and pay the damage amount.[13]

---

9. Even though the value of Blackacre as a buggy factory is negligible, Smith will refuse to fulfill the condition that triggers the executory interest so she can bargain for compensation from Jones.

10. This countervailing effect, however, is not present when one party to the negotiation has an undivided interest in the entitlement: For example, if Jones owns Blackacre in fee simple, then Smith (as buyer) need not worry that Jones will use her low offer as the basis for a counteroffer to purchase Smith's claims, for the simple reason that Smith has nothing to sell.

11. Robert Ellickson has recently characterized absolute entitlements as the "Blackstonian bundle." Ellickson, *supra* note 4, at 1362–63 (citing 2 WILLIAM BLACKSTONE, COMMENTARIES *18–19); *see also* 2 WILLIAM BLACKSTONE, COMMENTARIES *2 (describing right of property as "sole and despotic dominion which one man claims and exercises over the external things of the world, in total exclusion of the right of any other individual in the universe"). Ellickson defines the Blackstonian bundle as ownership by a single individual in perpetuity with absolute rights to exclude would-be entrants, with absolute privileges to use and abuse the land, and with absolute powers to transfer the whole (or any part carved out by use, space, or time). Ellickson, *supra* note 4, at 1362–63. While the fee simple estate is often referred to as if it were such an absolute right, Ellickson stresses that fee simple is "far more nuanced than the pure Blackstonian package." *Id.* at 1363.

12. Guido Calabresi & A. Douglas Melamed, *Property Rules, Liability Rules and Inalienability: One View of the Cathedral*, 85 HARV. L. REV. 1089 (1972).

13. For example, if a farmer's ownership of spark-free land is protected by a "weak" liability rule, then an adjoining railroad would have the option to emit sparks (nonconsensually) onto the land and pay

Property protection, on the other hand, does not represent a division, since the nonowner lacks power to appropriate the underlying entitlement nonconsensually.

We show that liability rules possess an "information-forcing" quality that property rules do not.[14] Under a liability rule regime, a nominal entitlement owner has an incentive to reveal truthfully whether her valuation is above or below the damage amount. We demonstrate that the entitlement owner's choice between two different kinds of Coasean transactions acts as a credible signal whether she has a relatively high or relatively low valuation. This credible signal of valuation decreases the aggregate amount of private information by "partitioning" the entitlement holders into two discrete sets, thereby facilitating more efficient trade. In contrast, property rule protections render such credible signaling impossible.[15]

Our argument that liability rules can catalyze consensual trade challenges various common wisdoms in law and economics. Many scholars have argued that clear property rights are appropriate when transaction costs are low, because property rights encourage people to bargain. For example, Judge Posner has captured the common wisdom by asserting that in "low-transaction-cost settings . . . the law should require the parties to transact in the market; it can do this by making the present owner's property right absolute (or nearly so), so that anyone who thinks the property is worth more *has to negotiate with the owner*."[16] These scholars often assert that property rules are "market-encouraging,"[17] while liability rules are "market-mimicking."[18] Although a

---

damages. The farmer's claims to the land would be partial or incomplete, because her ownership would be subject to the railroad's option to take and pay damages.

A liability rule is usually defined to allow a "nonowner" to take an entitlement nonconsensually from an owner and pay damages that are tailored to "approximat[e] . . . the value of the object to the original owner." *Id.* at 1125. Our analysis, however, focuses on *untailored* liability rules, which require the nonowner to pay a fixed amount of damages upon a taking, regardless of the owner's showing of actual loss. For a definition and discussion of tailoring, see Ian Ayres, *Preliminary Thoughts on Optimal Tailoring of Contractual Rules*, 3 S. CAL. INTERDISCIPLINARY L.J. 1 (1993).

14. While this Article argues that liability rules have information-forcing qualities that can increase efficiency, it does not argue that a randomly chosen liability rule will outperform the optimal property-like assignment. In fact, others have shown that this assertion is demonstrably false. *See* Steven Shavell, Property Rights and the Rule of Liability in a Simple Bargaining Model (1988) (unpublished manuscript, on file with authors). We do assert, however, that it is possible to find a liability rule that will outperform any type of property rule. *See* Eric L. Talley, Property Rights, Liability Rules and Coasean Bargaining Under Incomplete Information (John M. Olin Program in Law and Economics, Working Paper No. 114) (Stanford Law School, Aug. 1994) (formally demonstrating this assertion in mechanism design framework).

15. Even though the property rule itself does not give the parties a method of signaling valuation, other aspects of the law, or prior agreements of the parties themselves, may allow the parties to mitigate the allocational inefficiencies associated with private information. *See generally* Jennifer G. Brown & Ian Ayres, *Economic Rationales for Mediation*, 80 VA. L. REV. 323 (1994) (discussing possibility that various mandatory and voluntary mediation techniques might mitigate adverse selection and moral hazard).

16. POSNER, *supra* note 1, at 49 (emphasis added); *see also* COOTER & ULEN, *supra* note 1, at 100 ("One well-confirmed result in the literature on bargaining is that bargainers are more likely to cooperate when their rights are clear, and less likely to agree when their rights are ambiguous.").

17. Richard Craswell, *Property Rules and Liability Rules in Unconscionability and Related Doctrines*, 60 U. CHI. L. REV. 1, 15 n.28 (1993); Saul Levmore, *Explaining Restitution*, 71 VA. L. REV. 65, 79–81 (1985).

few strands of the law-and-economics literature—particularly the literature on efficient breach of contract—have allowed for parties to bargain in the shadow of liability rules as well as in the shadow of property rules,[19] we are the first to show that liability rules may induce both *more contracting* and *more efficient contracting* than property rules.

Viewing liability rules as market catalysts, rather than substitutes, can also lead to other contradictions of the accepted wisdom in law and economics. For instance, the common assertion that liability rules are market-mimicking has led numerous scholars to conclude that the best liability rules are the ones that carefully "tailor" the damage amount to the plaintiff's valuation.[20] Only in this way, many argue, can a court replicate the terms for which parties would have bargained had they been able to negotiate.[21] Because Calabresi and Melamed were so successful in showing that *tailored* liability rules are appropriate when parties do not have an opportunity to contract, subsequent scholars have overlooked the possibility that *untailored* rules—which fix damages at one size to fit all plaintiffs regardless of plaintiffs' actual valuation—may promote trade when contracting is possible. And, in fact, we find that when parties have the opportunity to contract, untailored liability rules can be more effective in channeling bargainers toward consensual trade, where the parties tailor the terms of trade themselves. Indeed, tailoring legal rules to give parties private information about the consequences of nonconsensual taking can severely undermine the incentives to trade consensually.[22] When dividing entitlements to facilitate trade, courts should therefore avoid tailoring that creates *additional* informational asymmetries that amplify strategic behavior. Untailored liability rules represent a largely missing category of entitlement protection that may facilitate trade without the judicial costs of tailoring.[23]

---

18. David D. Haddock et al., *An Ordinary Economic Rationale for Extraordinary Legal Sanctions*, 78 CAL. L. REV. 1, 21 (1990) ("[I]mitating a market is appropriate only when circumstances make it unreasonable or unnecessary for the parties to rely on a market. In a property violation case, efficient law would not help mimic a missing exchange, but instead would encourage the principals facing other potential exchanges to bargain.").

19. *See* Anthony T. Kronman, *Specific Performance*, 45 U. CHI. L. REV. 351, 353 n.12 (1978); A. Mitchell Polinsky, *On the Choice Between Property Rules and Liability Rules*, 18 ECON. INQUIRY 233 (1980).

20. *E.g.*, COOTER & ULEN, *supra* note 1, at 318; A. MITCHELL POLINSKY, AN INTRODUCTION TO LAW AND ECONOMICS 20 (2d ed. 1989); *cf.* POSNER, *supra* note 1, at 62 n.5 (discussing difficulty of tailoring when damages cannot be ascertained with reasonable accuracy).

21. *See* Haddock et al., *supra* note 18, at 13–17; Kronman, *supra* note 19, at 360–61.

22. This result does not mean, however, that certain (non-probabilistic) rules need to be superior to uncertain rules in promoting Coasean trade. An uncertain ("muddy") rule can promote information revelation, and therefore trade, if the legal consequences of nonconsensual taking are equally uncertain to all bargainers. Indeed, our model of fractional property entitlements shows that legal uncertainty can be more efficient than a certain property rule if the uncertainty is commonly known, as in a coin flip. *See infra* notes 140–42 and accompanying text.

23. *See, e.g.*, Kronman, *supra* note 19, at 360 (suggesting that "it would be very difficult and expensive for a court to acquire the information necessary" to tailor damages). In Section B of Part II, we discuss several contexts in which the consequences of nonconsensual taking come closer to approximating untailored rules that might, according to our thesis, facilitate trade.

The second axis of division we analyze is the actual ownership structure of an entitlement, focusing explicitly on the benefits of ownership that is "fractional" in nature. Following Professor Ellickson's analysis of land divisions, we show that the identity crisis can facilitate trade whenever an entitlement is divided in any of the traditional ways—"by use, space or time."[24] As in the earlier Blackacre example, each of these species of division can facilitate consensual trade by endowing the respective parties with a partial claim to the underlying entitlement. Scholars have previously recognized that blurring the consequences of decision making can mitigate strategic inefficiencies when partners invoke a buy-sell agreement or when children decide how to cut a cake.[25] But we show that a similar countervailing incentive can exist *whenever* parties bargain in the shadow of such fractional ownership structures and hence are uncertain whether they might ultimately buy or sell a Solomonic claim.[26]

In addition to the traditional forms of divided ownership structure, we examine one nontraditional division with similar benefits. Legal uncertainty or ambiguity about who owns property can constitute a probabilistic division in that more than one person has a contingent claim to the enjoyment of the underlying right or privilege. Returning to our Blackacre example, if there is a 50% chance that the court will award Blackacre in fee simple to Jones or Smith, then each party has a probabilistic claim. Bargaining in the shadow of this uncertainty might result again in two different types of transactions: buying the other side's claim or selling one's own claim. Once again, the Solomonic division can make it more difficult for either side to offer a price that diverges from her private valuation: One can easily imagine a conversation in which Smith offers to sell her probabilistic share (relinquish all rights to Blackacre) for an inflated price, and Jones responds, "If you think a 50% chance at Blackacre is worth that much, I'll relinquish my rights to you for that price." Foreseeing the possibility of this response, Smith would inflate her selling price by a lesser amount than if she had unambiguous ownership. Accordingly, we predict that parties with private information may be able to bargain more efficiently when property rights are uncertain. This finding

---

24. Ellickson, *supra* note 4, at 1363. For example, we show that the identity crisis can produce more efficient trade when:
    (1) one party has a part of the acreage and the other party owns the remainder (spacial division);
    (2) one party has a life estate and the other party has the remainder (temporal division); or
    (3) one party has a right to pollute up to a certain level and the other party has a right to enjoin pollution beyond that level (activity-level or use division).
Each of these examples produces a bargaining identity crisis because the entitlement division gives rise to different types of Coasean transactions. *See infra* part III.B–C.

25. For a discussion of these examples, see *infra* note 133 and accompanying text.

26. Our result is reminiscent of Saul Levmore's idea that a property owner will speak more honestly about her value if she is uncertain whether the valuation will be used as an offer to sell. Saul Levmore, *Self-Assessed Valuation Systems for Tort and Other Law*, 68 VA. L. REV. 771 (1982) (discussing strengths and weaknesses of relying on self-assessment to promote accuracy in property tax assessment, tort damage determination, and corporate stock valuation).

contradicts the accepted wisdom that unambiguous property rules encourage contracting.[27] Thus, while Robert Cooter and Tom Ulen merely restate the consensus view in opining that "bargainers are more likely to cooperate when their rights are clear, and less likely to agree when their rights are ambiguous,"[28] we extend the seminal insights of Jason Scott Johnston to show in a rigorous model how ambiguity can induce bargainers to act more cooperatively.[29]

This Article focuses on a specific type of transaction cost: private information. When private information is the predominant form of market failure that impairs the operation of the Coase theorem,[30] Solomonic divisions are likely to facilitate efficient allocations through trade.[31] Consequently,

---

27. *See, e.g.*, Clifford G. Holderness, *A Legal Foundation for Exchange*, 14 J. LEGAL STUD. 321, 344 (1985) (arguing that "a unique definition and assignment [of property rights] is essential to a well-ordered system [of social interactions]"); Thomas W. Merrill, *Trespass, Nuisance, and the Costs of Determining Property Rights*, 14 J. LEGAL STUD. 13, 14 (1985) ("[W]hen the costs of transacting are low, the legal system will gravitate toward rules that determine entitlements at a low cost—such as the strict liability rule of trespass."); Carol M. Rose, *Crystals and Mud in Property Law*, 40 STAN. L. REV. 577, 590 (1988) (discussing several articles claiming that "precise entitlements facilitate the efficient allocation of goods; they allow us to identify right-holders and to organize trades with them until all goods arrive in the hands of those who value them most"); *see also* Craswell, *supra* note 17, at 15; Levmore, *supra* note 17, at 79–81 (explaining how denial of restitution to intervening providers encourages complex market of many active buyers and sellers).

28. COOTER & ULEN, *supra* note 1, at 100. Cooter and Ulen cite to Elizabeth Hoffman & Matthew L. Spitzer, *The Coase Theorem: Some Experimental Tests*, 25 J.L. & ECON. 73 (1982), and Elizabeth Hoffman & Matthew L. Spitzer, *Experimental Tests of the Coase Theorem with Large Bargaining Groups*, 15 J. LEGAL STUD. 149 (1986). While these articles by Hoffman and Spitzer explore the effects of bargaining *after* an entitlement is allocated (so that there is no legal ambiguity at the time of bargaining), we explore the effects of bargaining *before* legal uncertainty is resolved.

29. Johnston was the first to see how uncertain ownership of an entitlement could improve bargaining efficiency. *See* Jason Scott Johnston, Bargaining Under Rules Versus Standards (June 28, 1994) (unpublished manuscript, on file with authors). Our analysis in Part III shows more directly how the parties' uncertainty about who will be the buyer and who will be the seller causes this increased efficiency. We also show how the same type of identity crisis might improve negotiations over a number of other types of divided entitlement allocations. *See infra* part III.

Our conclusion that legal uncertainty can promote more efficient negotiation also qualifies the traditional view that adjudicators should strive for accuracy (as long as accurate decision making is not too costly). *See* Louis Kaplow, *The Value of Accuracy in Adjudication: An Economic Analysis*, 23 J. LEGAL STUD. 307 (1994). We find that decision makers might eschew accuracy even if making accurate court decisions were costless.

30. Private information is a major source of negotiation inefficiency: Buyers and sellers frequently attempt to capitalize on private knowledge by misrepresenting their respective valuations or by shading their contractual offers.

31. The law does not ordinarily penalize strategic misrepresentations of valuation. Although the law of fraud traditionally regulates misrepresentations of fact, courts almost never rescind contracts because representations of the parties' own valuation were proven to be false. Courts often cannot verify private knowledge of how one values a particular entitlement. Some jurisdictions have treated such representations as being beyond the purview of fraud law by finding as a matter of law that these facts are not "material." *See* Ian Ayres & F. Clayton Miller, *"I'll Sell It to You at Cost": Legal Methods To Promote Retail Markup Disclosure*, 84 NW. U. L. REV. 1047, 1049–51 (1990) (stating various ways in which courts have declined to penalize sellers for misrepresenting their costs); *see also* MODEL RULES OF PROFESSIONAL CONDUCT Rule 4.1 cmt. 2 (1983) ("Under generally accepted conventions in negotiation, certain types of statements ordinarily are not taken as statements of material fact. Estimates of price or value placed on the subject of a transaction and a party's intentions as to an acceptable settlement of a claim are in this category . . . ."). When sellers inflate their asking price or when buyers understate what they are willing to pay, the entitlement may not end up with the highest-valuing owner.

Solomonic entitlements may not always facilitate trade if other transaction costs are primarily responsible for Coasean inefficiency.[32] In such cases, Solomonic divisions may even exacerbate such inefficiencies by impeding competition, exacerbating hold-up problems, or weakening investment incentives.[33] These contraindications make clear why undivided property rules are still efficient in many settings. And, in fact, an overarching "Coasean" theme of our analysis is that the type of transaction cost matters: It is inadequate to think of "transaction costs" as some sort of composite good whose components imply similar policies. Nevertheless, this Article shows that claims about the efficiency of property rules cannot be justified by the common, unqualified assertion that property rules encourage trade.

The Article is divided into three parts. Part II describes the information-forcing effect of liability rules and shows how conditioning either liability or damages on private information can exacerbate the inefficiencies of bargaining under asymmetric information. Part III explores the identity crisis that can be created by other types of entitlement divisions, including probabilistic, physical, temporal, and activity-level divisions. Part IV discusses some limiting principles and examines the legal implications of our analysis.

II. THE INFORMATION-FORCING EFFECT OF UNTAILORED LIABILITY RULES

More than twenty years ago, Guido Calabresi and Douglas Melamed saw that, as a descriptive matter, the legal system protects entitlements in two qualitatively distinct manners.[34] In some contexts, the law attempts to impose sanctions that are severe enough to deter all nonconsensual takings.[35] The protection of entitlements with such severe sanctions is what Calabresi and Melamed called "property" rules. In other contexts, the law requires nonconsensual takers to pay an amount of damages that is set not to deter all

---

32. For example, if there is a fixed cost of writing a contract (representing the only impediment to transferring entitlements to their highest valuer), then Solomonic entitlements will not induce more efficient contracting. See also COOTER & ULEN, supra note 1, at 101 (providing useful typology of transaction costs).

33. See infra part IV.A.

34. Calabresi & Melamed, supra note 12, at 1092.

35. Calabresi and Melamed did not focus on the mechanism of deterrence: "An entitlement is protected by a property rule to the extent that someone who wishes to remove the entitlement from its holder must buy it from him in a voluntary transaction in which the value of the entitlement is agreed upon by the seller." Id. While they did not dwell on what aspect of a legal rule would force the would-be taker to the bargaining table, it is axiomatic that rational takers will be deterred from nonconsensual taking if the sanction is greater than any possible benefit. Still, the authors did emphasize that nonlegal sanctions may play an important part in deterring nonconsensual taking. Id. at 1093; see also ROBERT C. ELLICKSON, ORDER WITHOUT LAW (1991). Subsequent authors, however, have explicitly seen that legal, and possibly nonlegal, reactions to nonconsensual takings create a property rule. See Haddock et al., supra note 18, at 13 (defining property rule damages as amount that "would reduce to zero the expected gain available to the defendant from the injurious activity, leaving no incentive for him to attempt the activity in the first place").

takings but rather to compensate the entitlement holder for the loss of the entitlement.[36] The protection of entitlements with these less severe sanctions is what Calabresi and Melamed called "liability" rules.[37] Restraining orders, specific performance clauses, and certain types of punitive sanctions represent "property" protections, while expectation damages, the Takings Clause of the Fifth Amendment, and compulsory licenses are examples of "liability" protections.[38]

This descriptive distinction between property rules and liability rules has led some scholars to suggest that the normative choice of the appropriate form of protection is really between contracting costs and litigation costs. The "folklore" among law-and-economics academics is that property rules induce negotiation and contracting, while liability rules induce nonconsensual taking, subsequent litigation, and judicially determined prices.[39] The folklore instructs efficiency-minded lawmakers to choose the form of protection that minimizes these costs.

While this dichotomy between contracting costs and litigation costs has considerable power,[40] it ignores the fact that liability rules can themselves

---

36. A liability rule obtains "[w]henever someone may destroy the initial entitlement if he is willing to pay an objectively determined value for it." Calabresi & Melamed, *supra* note 12, at 1092; *see also id.* at 1125 ("Liability rules represent only an approximation of the value of the object to its original owner . . . .").

37. *Id.* at 1105–06. Calabresi and Melamed also analyzed "inalienability" rules. *Id.* at 1111–15. The precise definition of an "inalienable" right is somewhat murky, but common definitions focus on non-salability, non-transferability, non-relinquishability, or non-losability. *See* Margaret J. Radin, *Market-Inalienability*, 100 HARV. L. REV. 1849, 1849–50 (1987); Susan Rose-Ackerman, *Inalienability and the Theory of Property Rights*, 85 COLUM. L. REV. 931 (1985). In this Article, we confine our attention to legal rights that are readily "commodifiable" in that they are salable under legally valid contracts. This is by no means a complete description of legal rights; rather, it catalogues only the set of legal rights that can be readily subjected to economic analysis. For many other legal entitlements, there are frequently philosophical problems with commensurability between individuals' rights. *See generally* Cass R. Sunstein, *Incommensurability and Valuation in Law*, 92 MICH. L. REV. 779, 780 (1994) (noting that "efforts to insist on a single kind of valuation and to make goods commensurable, while designed to aid in human reasoning, actually make such reasoning inferior to what it is when it is working well").

38. For a discussion of the distinction between property and liability rules in contract remedies, see, e.g., Kronman, *supra* note 19, at 352.

39. *See, e.g.*, COOTER & ULEN, *supra* note 1, at 107 (explaining that injunctive relief is optimal when "bargaining is likely to be successful"); POLINSKY, *supra* note 20, at 19 (noting that under "intermediate" levels of entitlement, in which entitlement holders are protected by liability amount, there is no negotiation); POSNER, *supra* note 1, at 55–56 (arguing that when bilateral monopoly problems exist, liability rules are efficient because they prescribe terms of exchange); Calabresi & Melamed, *supra* note 12, at 1125 (noting that because liability rules force transactions at "approximate" prices, it is "obvious" that property rules are often more desirable than liability rules); Craswell, *supra* note 17, at 8–9 (noting that property rules are more efficient when courts wish to "induce the parties to negotiate," because liability rules tend to "select[] a price on behalf of the parties"); Haddock et al., *supra* note 18, at 16 (arguing that liability rules allow potential defendants simply to take from potential plaintiffs and pay liability amount rather than negotiate with plaintiffs as they would do under property rules); Robert Merges, Intellectual Property Rights and Bargaining Breakdown: The Case of Improvement Inventions and Blocking Patents 30–31 (1994) (unpublished manuscript, on file with authors) (arguing against compulsory licenses in "new use" patents—a type of liability rule—because such rules "allow[] *courts*, not the parties themselves, to set the terms of exchange").

40. It is true, for example, that there should be no litigation for nonconsensual taking when entitlements are protected by property rules, assuming rational decision making and no mistaken or

induce a great deal of contracting.[41] The vast majority of potential "disputes" settle even before one of the parties files suit. Moreover, of those suits filed, the lion's share settle before trial, even when the damages in tort or contract serve a compensatory, rather than deterrent, purpose.[42] Even when liability rule damages are not sufficient to deter nonconsensual takings, the Coase theorem predicts that the parties may still have incentives to engage in consensual transactions.[43]

This Part moves beyond the traditional argument that liability rules are market-mimicking substitutes for consensual trade, arguing that liability rules may actually *facilitate* trade by reducing the effective amount of private information. Indeed, when an entitlement is protected by a liability rule, the entitlement holder may wish to engage in two very different types of consensual transactions: The entitlement holder may wish to (1) "bribe" a potential taker not to take the entitlement; or (2) "sell" her entitlement at a price less than the liability rule damage amount.[44] The fundamental insight of this Part is that under a liability regime, only those entitlement holders who value the entitlement more than the liability award will be interested in entering the first type of bargain, and only those entitlement holders who value the entitlement less than the liability award will be interested in the second type of transaction.

---

accidental takings. The goal of minimizing the costs of protection would need to account for how the form of protection affected incentives to create or develop the entitlement. Systematic undercompensation for entitlement holders under a liability rule regime would undermine the entitlement holders' incentive to create or develop the entitlement. We discuss these important forms of inefficiency *infra* part IV.A.1.

41. Oliver Williamson's monumental work on transaction cost economics underscores the notion that it is insufficient simply to examine the initial allocation of entitlements to infer their ultimate allocation. Consequently, he argues that the appropriate approach is to assume that bargaining is always possible, or even likely, after allocation of initial property rights:

> Transaction cost economics maintains that it is impossible to concentrate all of the relevant bargaining action at the *ex ante* contracting stage. Instead, *bargaining is pervasive*—on which account the institutions of private ordering and the study of contracting in its entirety take on critical economic significance. The behavioral attributes of human agents, whereby conditions of bounded rationality and opportunism are joined, and the complex attributes of transactions . . . are responsible for that condition.

OLIVER E. WILLIAMSON, THE ECONOMIC INSTITUTIONS OF CAPITALISM 29 (1985). The law-and-economics literature has addressed this issue only sporadically, predominantly in the literature on "efficient breach." *See* COOTER & ULEN, *supra* note 1, at 290; *see also infra* note 208 and accompanying text.

42. Among federal cases filed, less than five percent go to trial. *See, e.g.,* H. LAURENCE ROSS, SETTLED OUT OF COURT: THE SOCIAL PROCESS OF INSURANCE CLAIMS ADJUSTMENTS 217 (1970). Many of these pretrial negotiations, however, occur after a taking, as in the run-of-the-mill tort case. But many contractual entitlements to performance that are protected merely by a liability rule are renegotiated prior to the promisor's taking of the entitlement through breach.

43. ROBERT E. SCOTT & DOUGLAS L. LESLIE, CONTRACT LAW AND THEORY 98–103 (1988); *see also* Johnston, *supra* note 29, at 6 (noting this phenomenon); Eric L. Talley, Note, *Contract Renegotiation, Mechanism Design, and the Liquidated Damages Rule*, 46 STAN. L. REV. 1195, 1218–42 (1994) (noting phenomenon within "mechanism design" framework, but without using explicit bargaining procedure); Zvika Neeman, Property Rights and Efficiency in Public-Good Mechanisms Under Asymmetric Information (1993) (unpublished manuscript, on file with authors).

44. Contrary to intuition, the owner may be willing to sell her entitlement for less than the liability amount, especially if the liability amount is sufficiently high so that the nominal owner believes that in the absence of such a sale, the potential defendant will not be willing to take and pay the liability amount.

Thus, despite the fact that strategic misrepresentations are normally endemic to bargaining, the entitlement holder bargaining under a liability rule does not act strategically when signaling her preferred *type* of transaction. We show that:

> *Under a liability rule, the type of offer that an entitlement holder makes credibly signals whether her valuation is above or below the liability amount.*

An offer to bribe signals that the entitlement holder's valuation is greater than the damage amount, while an offer to sell signals that her valuation is less than the damage amount. By simply listening to the type of offer, the potential taker can infer the entitlement holder's relative valuation.

Ordinarily, bargainers can put little faith in the other side's representation concerning valuation. The adage "talk is cheap" (meaning unreliable) seems to apply. Here, however, liability rules induce entitlement holders to engage in a credible form of "cheap talk" to communicate whether their valuations are above or below the liability amount.[45] Property rules, in contrast, allow for only one type of Coasean bargain, and thus do not induce this type of information revelation.

Using an instructive example in Section A and then an explicit game-theoretic model in Section B, we begin by analyzing "untailored" liability rules, which require payment of a fixed damage amount whenever an entitlement is taken nonconsensually. Section C then explores how "tailoring" the liability rule affects bargaining. We examine two particular types of judicial tailoring: tailoring the amount of *damages* (usually to the plaintiff's valuation) and tailoring the assessment of *liability* (usually to the defendant's valuation). Somewhat surprisingly, we find that certain tailored liability rules can significantly *reduce* parties' respective incentives to bargain truthfully.

A. *Information Revelation in the Shadow of Liability and Property Rules*

This Section examines how property and liability rules differentially affect the parties' incentives to reveal information. To motivate the analysis, consider the potential trade of an entitlement between two people: a potential "plaintiff," who ostensibly owns the original entitlement, and a potential "defendant," who

---

45. This argument is related to other results in the "cheap talk" bargaining literature, which note that although bargaining parties formally "compete" with one another in capturing gains from trade, they often have mutual incentives to signal to one another whether conditions are "good" or "bad" for trade to occur. *See, e.g.,* Joseph Farrell & Robert Gibbons, *Cheap Talk Can Matter in Bargaining,* 48 J. ECON. THEORY 221 (1989) (discussing possible gains created by allowing bargaining parties to signal whether they are "keen" or "not keen" on reaching bargaining agreement); Jason Scott Johnston, Cheap Talk, Sunk Costs, and Contractual Liability in Preliminary Negotiation (Apr. 1994) (unpublished manuscript, on file with authors) (modeling role that "cheap talk" can play in facilitating negotiations).

threatens to take the entitlement nonconsensually.[46] Suppose that the plaintiff and the defendant each know their own private valuations of the entitlement but not that of the other party. For concreteness, we assume that each party's valuation can take on any value between $0 and $100. These assumptions produce a canonical example of negotiation under asymmetric information.[47] The parties' private information makes it unclear whether there are gains to trade and if so, what would be a mutually agreeable price.

We begin by analyzing bargaining in the shadow of untailored rules, which force a defendant who takes nonconsensually to pay a fixed, or untailored, damage amount. Although courts often attempt to tailor damages to equal the plaintiff's lost value (which we have assumed to vary between $0 and $100), there are several contexts in which the damages are sufficiently untailored—i.e., they sufficiently diverge from the plaintiff's actual valuation—to give plaintiffs an incentive to signal whether their valuation is above or below the expected court award.[48]

---

46. It is important to note here that the nominal identities of the parties are only of empirical, and not theoretical, significance. In the paradigmatic civil suit, the plaintiff typically accuses the defendant of appropriating her entitlement, and therefore seeks compensatory or injunctive relief. A popular example of such an action pits plaintiff residents against a defendant smoke-billowing factory, as in Boomer v. Atlantic Cement Co., 257 N.E.2d 870 (N.Y. 1970) (awarding plaintiffs property-like injunctive relief against defendant cement company).

Nevertheless, there have been a number of cases in which the identities of the parties were reversed. For instance, the equally popular case of Spur Industries, Inc. v. Del E. Webb Development Co., 494 P.2d 700 (Ariz. 1972), established the right of a residential development to enjoin the operation of a stinky cattle feedlot, but only if the development compensated the feedlot for lost profits. The holding in this case arguably gives a plaintiff (e.g., the development) the option of appropriating a defendant's entitlement in exchange for compensating the defendant (e.g., the feedlot) for reasonable damages pursuant to the taking. This option is essentially a liability right. Similarly, in patent law, the paradigmatic case pits a patentee plaintiff against an infringing (i.e., "taking") defendant. *See infra* part IV.C.1. It is just as frequent for a potentially infringing user to bring suit under the Declaratory Judgment Act, 28 U.S.C. § 2201 (1988), to litigate the question of infringement; in these suits, the identities of the plaintiff and the defendant are the opposite of those in the paradigmatic case.

47. The assumption of uniformly distributed valuations is consistent with a myriad of other analyses that study bargaining under private information. *See, e.g.,* Kalyan Chatterjee & William Samuelson, *Bargaining Under Incomplete Information,* 31 OPERATIONS RES. 835 (1983); John Kennan & Robert Wilson, *Bargaining with Private Information,* 31 J. ECON. LITERATURE 45 (1993).

48. Such contexts include:

   (1) Liquidated damages. The assumption of constant damages is reasonable if we want to assess negotiation to modify a contract when there is a fixed liquidated damages amount. In this context, the promisee would be the entitlement holder who would have an incentive to say whether she valued performance more or less than the liquidated damages amount.

   (2) Unverifiable damages. If the plaintiff will not be able to prove to a court the exact amount of harm (the damages are not *ex post* observable), the court will only be able to set damages on the basis of verifiable evidence. The untailored assumption also captures a class of cases that are observationally equivalent to the judge: where both sides know that a certain amount of damages is provable, but both sides also know that plaintiff's valuation may be more or less than this amount. For example, if damages for breach of a promise to perform are limited to diminution of market value, it is possible that the plaintiff has a subjective valuation that is greater or lower than the likely judicial award. *See, e.g.,* Jacob & Youngs v. Kent, 129 N.E. 889 (N.Y. 1921) (holding that damages for using incorrect brand of pipe in building were equal to difference in market value).

The magnitude of the untailored damages determines whether the plaintiff's entitlement receives property or liability protection. Specifically, if the damages are greater than $100 (the highest valuation of any potential defendant), then the plaintiff's entitlement is "property-like" in nature: With such relatively high damages, potential takers would be deterred from nonconsensual takings, and the entitlement would be transferred only by consensual agreement. Damages less than $100 would not, however, deter all defendants from taking and would provide only a weaker form of liability protection. Protecting the plaintiff's entitlement by a liability rule is an example of dividing the possible claims to the entitlement between the parties.

Under a property rule, the plaintiff owns an undivided entitlement because she has the only legally cognizable claims. In contrast, under a liability rule, the defendant in effect has a "call option"—i.e., an option to buy the entitlement for the damage amount.[49] Under such a regime, the plaintiff owns the entitlement subject to the defendant's decision whether to exercise this liability call option.

Here, we explore the parties' incentives to disclose information when negotiating under either a property rule of $100 damages or a liability rule of $50 damages.[50] It is well known that bargainers have an incentive to

---

This list is not exhaustive. Several other legal rules produce a similar effect. For example, the doctrine of "conditional privilege" (or "incomplete privilege") creates an untailored liability rule: The privilege allows a shipowner, during a storm, to use someone else's dock nonconsensually and pay compensation equal to the rental value of the dock, plus damages for any loss inflicted during the storm. *See* RICHARD A. EPSTEIN, BARGAINING WITH THE STATE 54–58 (1993) (discussing "conditional privilege" doctrine).

The copyright statute provides for compulsory licenses at specified royalties for musical recordings, songs played on jukeboxes, certain cable television transmissions, and certain uses of copyrighted works by public television. Robert P. Merges, Contracting into Liability Rules: Institutions Supporting Transactions in Intellectual Property Rights 24–25 (1994) (unpublished manuscript, on file with authors). These compulsory licenses also represent classic untailored liability rules. Although it is safe to say that most liability rules are at least partially tailored, one purpose of this Article is to suggest that lawmakers and academics have not paid sufficient attention to untailored liability rules as a policy alternative. *But cf.* AMERICAN LAW INST., ENTERPRISE RESPONSIBILITY FOR PERSONAL INJURY 223 (1991) (suggesting use of relatively untailored schedule of damages in awards for pain and suffering).

49. In finance, a "call option" is a right to purchase a financial instrument (such as a stock) at a prespecified price (called the "strike price" or "exercise price") at some future date. In this context, the plaintiff holds a "long" position with regard to the entitlement, but a "short" position with regard to this call option. *See* RICHARD A. BREALEY & STEWART C. MYERS, PRINCIPLES OF CORPORATE FINANCE 485 (4th ed. 1991).

50. Setting the liability amount at $50 corresponds not only to the mean valuation of all plaintiffs, but also to the mean valuation of plaintiffs who go to trial in equilibrium. *See infra* text accompanying notes 137–53. We confine our attention to these two damage amounts for expositional purposes only. The Appendix shows the effect of other damage amounts on bargaining. *See infra* app. at pp. 1104–13. Our analysis supports Coleman and Kraus' claim that the type of protection determines the content (and value) of each party's entitlement. Jules L. Coleman & Jody Kraus, *Rethinking the Theory of Legal Rights*, 95 YALE L.J. 1335 (1986).

We also assume that after a taking, or after contractual allocation of the entitlement, the ownership is protected by a property rule. So, for example, if the defendant takes nonconsensually and pays the plaintiff $50, we assume that the plaintiff does not have an option to retake the entitlement—or, more precisely, that the legal consequences of such a retaking are so dire that plaintiffs would never retake. This assumption that the defendant's call option is protected by a property rule is not foreordained. Ellickson has suggested that in nuisance actions, defendants have an option to pollute and pay damages, but that this option itself should be protected merely by a liability rule—the plaintiff should have an option to take back

misrepresent their valuations: Sellers tend to overstate their true valuation, and buyers tend to understate their true valuation. When the plaintiff's entitlement is protected by a property rule, the parties know that the plaintiff owns an undivided claim and therefore *must* bargain as a seller, while the defendant owns nothing and therefore *must* bargain as a buyer. Plaintiffs accordingly will offer to sell the entitlement for some amount more than their valuation, and defendants will offer to buy the entitlement for some amount less than their valuation. The strategic inefficiency created by the parties' private information is an example of what economists call "adverse selection."[51]

When the plaintiff's entitlement is protected by a liability rule, however, the parties can enter into two different types of Coasean trade:

COASEAN BARGAIN #1	The *plaintiff bribes the defendant* not to take the entitlement.
COASEAN BARGAIN #2	The *defendant buys the plaintiff's* entitlement.

TABLE 1. *Liability Rules Create Two Types of Coasean Transactions*

Under the first Coasean bargain, *the plaintiff buys the defendant's call option.* For example, as shown in Figure 1, a plaintiff (with a $90 valuation) might pay a defendant (with a $60 valuation) $15 not to exercise his call option and take nonconsensually. In the absence of the bargain, the defendant would take; after a taking and payment of the $50 damages, the plaintiff and defendant would end up with $50 and $10, respectively.[52] But the $15 Coasean bribe not to take is Pareto-superior—increasing the plaintiff's and defendant's payoffs to $75 and $15, respectively.[53]

---

the right to stop pollution nonconsensually by paying some prescribed amount. Robert C. Ellickson, *Alternatives to Zoning: Covenants, Nuisance Rules, and Fines as Land Use Controls,* 40 U. CHI. L. REV. 681, 738–48 (1973).

51. *See* Brown & Ayres, *supra* note 15, at 331–35; *see also infra* part IV.A.1 (discussing how attempts to remedy adverse selection caused by private information may exacerbate problems of underinvestment).

52. The defendant would have a net payoff of $10, because she would own an undivided claim to the entitlement, worth $60, but would have paid the damage amount of $50. Even though the plaintiff would value an undivided claim to the entitlement at $90, she only owns a divided or partial claim, because her ownership is subject to the defendant's call option.

53. The plaintiff gains an undivided interest in the entitlement, worth $90, but needs to pay $15. The defendant gains the $15 bribe. The explicit numbers given in the text are only illustrative. The driving force behind this example is that the parties' valuations are privately held. If the parties' information were part of the public domain, then it would be common knowledge who should receive the entitlement, and the only real decision for the parties would be how to divide the gains from trade. Assuming they can "coordinate" on a division, the Coase theorem would hold. It is in this frictionless context that the system of legal entitlement becomes "irrelevant" under the "perfect information" version of the Coase theorem. *See* COOTER & ULEN, *supra* note 1, at 101 n.11.

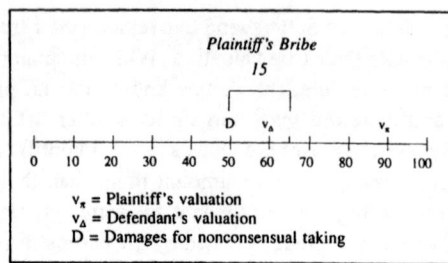

FIGURE 1. *Example of Plaintiff's Incentive To Bribe Defendant Not To Take*

Under the second Coasean bargain, *the defendant buys the plaintiff's entitlement.* As shown in Figure 2, a defendant (with a $30 valuation) might pay a plaintiff (with a $10 valuation) $25 for the entitlement. In the absence of the bargain, the defendant would not take the entitlement, even though it was the higher valuer, and the plaintiff's and the defendant's payoffs would be $10 and $0, respectively. In response, the plaintiff might agree to "renegotiate" the liability term downward, so as to induce the defendant to take. In this case, a $25 Coasean agreement is again Pareto-superior to autarky, raising both the plaintiff's and the defendant's payoffs to $25 and $5, respectively.

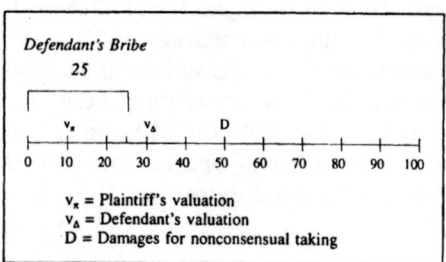

FIGURE 2. *Example of Defendant's Incentive To Buy Plaintiff's Entitlement*

This second Coasean bargain is analogous to the sale of an entitlement protected by a property rule. Under a liability rule regime, however, the contract price will never be more than the damage amount: Even if the plaintiff knows that the defendant has a $90 valuation for the entitlement, the plaintiff will never be able to extract a price higher than $50, because defendants will never consent to pay more than $50 for what they can take nonconsensually for $50.

It is important to note that the possibility of entering into two different types of Coasean bargains generally does not mitigate the *defendant's* incentives to misrepresent his valuation. High-valuing defendants, who will exercise their call option in the absence of bargaining, might feign a low valuation in order to purchase the entitlement from plaintiffs for even less than the $50 exercise price. Low-valuing defendants, on the other hand, who have no intention of exercising the call option, might feign a high valuation so that plaintiffs would bribe them not to exercise their option.

The possibility of entering into two different types of Coasean bargains, however, *does* dramatically affect the *plaintiff's* incentives to reveal information. Under liability rule protection, only plaintiffs who value the entitlement more than the damage amount would have an incentive to express interest in purchasing the defendant's call option (Coasean bargain #1). A low-valuing plaintiff (with, say, a $40 valuation) would have no reason to pay a defendant not to take the entitlement. Indeed, absent bargaining, the low-valuing plaintiff stands to make a windfall should the defendant take nonconsensually and pay the $50 damage.

An analogous argument illustrates that only plaintiffs who value the entitlement less than the damage amount would have an incentive to express interest in selling their entitlement (Coasean bargain #2). A high-valuing plaintiff (with, say, a $65 valuation) would never agree to sell the entitlement for less than $50 and would never be able to sell it for more than $50. Put simply, a plaintiff's type of offer credibly signals whether her valuation is above or below the liability amount: High-valuing plaintiffs will never offer to sell their entitlement for less than $50, while low-valuing plaintiffs will never offer to bribe the defendant not to take.

As a result of this incentive structure under a liability rule, high-valuing and low-valuing plaintiffs willingly "partition" themselves into two sets. As shown in Figure 2, only plaintiffs to the left of the damage amount would be interested in selling their entitlement, and only plaintiffs to the right of the damage amount would be interested in buying the defendant's call option.

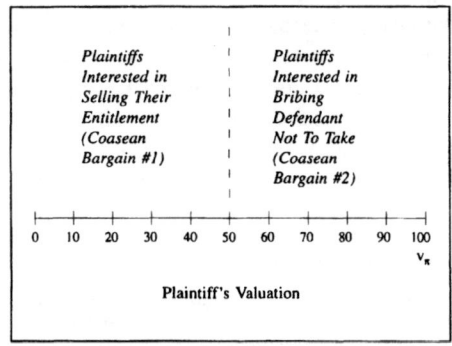

FIGURE 3. *The Damage Amount Partitions Plaintiffs into Two Groups*

This partitioning is an example of self-selection, because the plaintiffs have individual, private incentives to separate themselves into two groups. A defendant can infer whether the plaintiff's valuation is greater or less than the liability amount simply by inquiring which type of transaction the party prefers.[54]

Liability rules have an "information-forcing" characteristic not shared by property rules.[55] With "property-like" damages (i.e., $100 or more), plaintiffs are still willing to signal whether their private valuations are greater than or less than the damage amount; however, because the damage amount is so high, the plaintiffs cannot partition themselves into two groups.[56]

The willingness of plaintiffs to self-select in this fashion is consistent with the normal strategic incentives of sellers to overstate and buyers to understate their respective valuations. Thus, the plaintiff at times will have a seller's incentive to overstate her valuation and at other times will have a buyer's incentive to understate her valuation. The plaintiff's normal incentive to overstate as a seller or to understate as a buyer, however, is severely constrained by the defendant's ownership of the liability rule call option, because under a liability regime the plaintiff must choose between buying or selling one of the divided entitlements.

As a potential seller of the entitlement, a plaintiff wishes to overstate her private valuation. But a low-valuing plaintiff gains nothing from misrepresenting her valuation as larger than the damage amount, because a defendant would never buy for $60 what she could take nonconsensually for $50. The defendant's ownership of the liability rule call option thus acts as an upper bound on the ability of a low-valuing plaintiff to overstate her valuation: Low-valuing plaintiffs will still attempt to overstate their valuations, but since they have less "room to lie," their misrepresentations will never exceed the damage amount.[57]

Similarly, as a potential buyer of the defendant's call option, the high-valuing plaintiff wishes to understate her valuation, so as to reduce the size of the bribe necessary to stop the defendant from taking nonconsensually. Nonetheless, there is a natural limit to how much the plaintiff can understate her valuation: A plaintiff offering to buy the defendant's option—that is, offering to bribe the defendant not to take—cannot credibly claim that her valuation is less than the damage amount, because defendants know that

---

54. Such a simple device is in fact what we use to model the bargaining game. *See infra* text accompanying notes 78–83.

55. Default rules can also be chosen to induce parties to reveal information to each other or to the courts by penalizing silent parties with unwanted terms. *See* Ian Ayres & Robert Gertner, *Filling Gaps in Incomplete Contracts: An Economic Theory of Default Rules*, 99 YALE L.J. 87, 97–100 (1989).

56. Because plaintiffs' valuation never exceeds $100, no plaintiff would want to bribe the defendant not to take.

57. The plaintiff would love to be able to extract some of the valuation from a high-valuing defendant, but the defendant's call option eliminates the plaintiff's ability to bargain for a higher selling price.

plaintiffs with such low valuations would have no reason to pay to stop a nonconsensual taking. The defendant's ownership of the liability call option, therefore, places a lower bound on the amount by which a high-valuing plaintiff can understate her valuation.

The damage amount under a liability rule thus serves as both a *ceiling* to overstatements and a *floor* to understatements by the plaintiff choosing whether to make offers to buy the defendant's call option or to sell her own entitlement.[58] Property rule regimes cannot produce this type of partitioning, because the plaintiff would only be interested in *selling* her entitlement, and the high damage amount does not constrain the incentive of the plaintiff (*qua* seller) to overstate her valuation.

The willingness of entitlement holders to engage in credible signaling during Coasean bargaining is not a fragile result of a specific game-theoretic model. It does not depend on particular bargaining rules. It does not depend on particular assumptions about how the parties' valuations are distributed; indeed, the plaintiff need not know the defendant's distribution of valuations. And, most important, it generally does not depend on the plaintiff's beliefs about the defendant's behavior: Regardless of the defendant's strategy,[59] a high-valuing plaintiff will not offer to sell the entitlement for less than the damage amount, and a low-valuing plaintiff will not offer to buy the defendant's call option. Self-selection of plaintiffs is an "iterated" dominant strategy.[60]

---

58. The defendant does not face the same upper and lower bounds on her misrepresentation. As a potential seller of her call option, the defendant has an incentive to overstate her valuation (of the option), and thus even low-valuing sellers might claim high valuations. As a potential buyer of the entitlement, the defendant has an incentive to understate her valuation (of the entitlement), so that even high-valuing defendants will have an incentive to claim low valuation.

59. One requirement that we do place on the defendant, however, is that he be somewhat rational and avoid behaving in a way that is clearly not in his interests relative to his payoffs absent bargaining. For instance, it cannot be the case that the defendant will offer the plaintiff $1 million for the entitlement when the most the defendant could lose by taking nonconsensually is $50.

60. *See* DREW FUDENBERG & JEAN TIROLE, GAME THEORY 45–57 (1991) (defining iterated dominance).

The only assumptions that are crucial to this "no misrepresentation" result are that (1) the damage amount must be common knowledge, and (2) the defendant's own valuation of the entitlement must not depend on his beliefs about the plaintiff's valuation. If either of these assumptions fails, a plaintiff may affirmatively misrepresent whether her valuation is greater or less than the damage amount to manipulate the defendant's choice about whether to take the entitlement nonconsensually. For example, in many litigation contexts, both parties are trying to value an entitlement where the parties' valuations are both uncertain and correlated. In this setting, a liability rule might not reveal information, because a high-valuing plaintiff may not want to increase the chance that the defendant will want to take, and a low-valuing plaintiff may not want to decrease the chance of a taking. *See infra* part IV.A.3.

In the precise parlance of game theory, partitioning is a rationalizable strategy. Essentially, rationalizability builds on the assumption that it is common knowledge that no player will behave in a way that is clearly against her interests. Such an assumption allows one to narrow down the number of transactions that rational parties would make in an iterative way. Thus, as applied to our model, it is common knowledge that no plaintiff would accept a settlement offer from a defendant that was lower than what the plaintiff could expect through litigation. In turn, a defendant can deduce the types of offers that the plaintiff might accept. Among these "acceptable" offers, we can be sure that no rational defendant would make an acceptable offer that would, if accepted, make the defendant worse off. Finally, knowing

Although our conclusion is robust that plaintiffs' type of offer credibly signals whether their valuations are higher or lower than the damage amount, several factors can mitigate the practical importance of this conclusion. First, liability rules do not produce an incentive to produce precise information; plaintiffs separate themselves into only two groups. Second, liability rules can exacerbate defendants' incentive to misrepresent valuation,[61] so that liability rules are most likely to mitigate informational inefficiencies when the plaintiff's private information is the primary impediment to efficient trade.[62] Third, various costs of contracting can deter entitlement holders from making *any* Coasean offer. While those plaintiffs who do make serious Coasean offers signal whether they are high-valuing or low-valuing, some subset of plaintiffs may remain silent. Finally, although this partitioning result clearly holds for all types of damages awards, it may fail to have efficiency-enhancing qualities when the legal rules become more tailored.[63]

B. *A Formal Model of Untailored Liability and Property Rules*

To illustrate the implications of the intuition presented above, we now show in an explicit model how the information-forcing effect of liability rules can produce more efficient Coasean trade than a property rule regime. The structure of the Coasean bargaining game is the following. There are two players, a potential plaintiff (denoted "π") and a potential defendant (denoted "Δ"). Each of these parties places a privately known value on the right to conduct her activities free from interference by the other's activities. For instance, recall the example from the Introduction in which Smith and Jones are bargaining over land development: Each party privately knows how much she values developing the land, but only one of them can do it. While there are numerous such hypothetical examples,[64] assume for now that the competing

---

what types of serious offers she can expect, a plaintiff will have no incentive to lie about whether her valuation is above or below the liability amount. Rationalizability is the Bayesian cousin of iterated dominance. In fact, for strategic situations with two players, the notions of rationalizability and iterated dominance coincide. *See* FUDENBERG & TIROLE, *supra*, at 48–53 (explaining concept and noting that rationalizability is "weak" restriction on behavior).

61. For example, under a property rule, a $20 defendant might represent that he only has a $10 valuation in an attempt to purchase the plaintiff's entitlement cheaply. Under a liability rule, however, the same defendant might falsely claim to have a $70 entitlement in an attempt to sell his worthless call option at an inflated price.

62. For example, if the plaintiff has a contractual entitlement as a buyer to the seller's manufacture of a certain machine, it may be that the seller's valuation is more readily observable than the plaintiff's valuation, for the simple reason that the seller's cost or resale option may be more accessible. If the defendant's private valuation is the more important cause of informational inefficiency, then a reverse liability rule may be appropriate. *See infra* part II.B.4.

63. In a later section, we will show how various forms of tailoring can undermine the information-forcing quality of liability rules. *See infra* part II.C.

64. To take a quintessential Coasean example, the potential plaintiff may represent a farmer who wishes to grow corn free from the potential hazards of sparks from a passing train, and the potential defendant may represent a railroad company that wishes to run its train across tracks that run alongside the farmer's land. Alternatively, in a contracts setting, the potential plaintiff may represent a promisee who is

uses are completely incompatible—if one party enjoys the entitlement, the other cannot.[65]

1. *Defining the Game*

As before, to capture the essence of bargaining under incomplete information, suppose that each party knows the value *she* places on the legal entitlement, but is unsure of the other party's valuation. Explicitly, assume that the plaintiff's privately known valuation, v_π, takes on a realization between $0 and $100 with equal probability—the so-called "uniform distribution."[66] The defendant's private valuation, v_Δ, on the other hand, takes on only two equally probable values, $40 and $60. Our assumption that plaintiffs have a wider range of valuations than defendants makes the plaintiff's private information an important cause of Coasean inefficiency and allows us to focus on the potential benefits of inducing the plaintiff to reveal information.[67]

Absent agreement, the defendant may "take" from the plaintiff,[68] but in return he must pay the plaintiff a fixed damage amount of $D.[69] As argued above, the size of the damage amount determines whether the plaintiff's entitlement is protected by a liability rule or a property rule.[70] Damages of $100 represent a property rule, because this damage amount would deter both types of defendant from nonconsensual taking;[71] damages of $50 represent a liability rule—which, absent bargaining, allows nonconsensual takings.[72]

---

awaiting performance from the potential defendant, who in turn values breaching his duties under contract.

65. In Part III, we analyze the case in which an entitlement is divisible into activity levels, thus allowing both parties to utilize the resource in part. To focus on the role of liability rules, however, this Section assumes that the outcome is binary—only one party can receive the entitlement.

66. More explicitly, v_π is a continuous random variable with probability *density* of $1/100$ for each value of v_π. The term "probability" is used in the text only for stylistic reasons, since for a continuous random variable the probability that it takes on an exact value is zero.

67. The plaintiff's revelation is more important because the variance of the defendant's valuation is less than the variance of the plaintiff's valuation, so that the pooling of defendants is less significant than the pooling of plaintiffs. As discussed *infra* part II.B.4, if the defendant's private information is the major cause of inefficiency, then reverse liability rules may enhance allocational efficiency relative to a property rule.

68. Assume for simplicity that there are only two possible activity levels: Either the defendant "takes" (e.g., the rail company runs its train by the farmer's land), or the defendant does not take (e.g., the train does not run, and the farmer conducts her activities unimpeded). For a discussion of settings where the level of taking is a continuous variable, see *infra* part III.B.

69. We begin by assuming that plaintiffs are "observationally equivalent" to both the defendant and the court, and the damage amount thus is not "tailored" to vary with a plaintiff's actual damages. Later in this Section, we analyze the effects of awarding to the plaintiff a more "tailored" liability amount that equals her actual damages v_π, see *infra* part II.C.1, and awarding damages to the plaintiff only if the court determines that $v_\Delta < X$, where X is the negligence standard, see *infra* part II.C.2.

70. *See supra* notes 35–36 and accompanying text.

71. For this particular specification, any damage amount greater than $60 would represent a property rule, which would deter nonconsensual takings. *See infra* app. at pp. 1106–09.

72. Table 2 below describes the "noncooperative" expected payoffs for the defendant and the plaintiff (i.e., the payoffs that the parties could expect absent bargaining) when damages equal $50 or $100. As shown in the table, under the liability rule when D equals $50, only the high-valuing defendant takes absent bargaining. In this situation, the plaintiff's expected payoff is the average of her private valuation v_π (which

As discussed above, liability rules can give rise to two types of bargains. When D = $50, a defendant whose valuation is $40 may be interested in "buying" the right to take from a low-valuing plaintiff at a price less than the judicially determined $50 exercise price. Conversely, a $60 defendant might attempt to sell his option to take for $50.

To illustrate explicit bargaining under liability rules and property rules, we adopt the following stylized bargaining procedure.[73] In the first stage of the game, the plaintiff tells the defendant whether she is interested in buying the defendant's call option or in selling her entitlement. Thus, the plaintiff must solicit one of two different types of offers from the defendant: She can say "I would like to bribe you not to take my entitlement" (i.e., Coasean bargain #1), or she can say "I would like to sell my entitlement" (i.e., Coasean bargain #2). In the second stage of the game—after this proclamation by the plaintiff—the defendant makes a single all-or-nothing offer: The defendant can either offer to sell his call option (i.e., agree not to take nonconsensually) for some price, or the defendant can offer to buy the plaintiff's entitlement.[74] Thus, the

---

she would earn if the defendant were a low valuer) and the $50 damages (which she would get if the defendant were a high valuer).

Damage Amount	D = $50	D = $100
Type of Entitlement Protection	Liability Rule	Property Rule
Defendant's Behavior	Only high-valuing defendants take	Defendants never take
Plaintiff's Expected Noncooperative Payoff	$(50 + v_\pi)/2$	v_π
Defendant's Expected Noncooperative Payoff	0 if $v_\Delta = 40$; 10 if $v_\Delta = 60$	0

TABLE 2. *Expected Noncooperative Payoffs Under Liability and Property Rules*

In the Appendix, we more generally analyze liability-like rules based on damage amounts ranging between $40 and $60. *See infra* app. at pp. 1110–13. The Appendix also shows that damage amounts less than $40 effectively allocate the entitlement to the defendant, because all defendants will take absent bargaining, though such amounts will mandate a small compensatory payment. *See infra* app. at p. 1109.

73. This model assumes that the parties use a single bargaining procedure to govern their Coasean negotiations, regardless of the legal environment that they face. Assuming a consistent bargaining procedure allows us to extract conclusions that must be due to the change in legal environment rather than a change in bargaining procedures. On the other hand, by clinging to a single bargaining game, we do not address the prospect that the parties' procedure might be environment-dependent, and that as the legal rule changes, so will the bargaining "game." Coauthor Talley has addressed this prospect in another paper and has found that our results recur even when the parties choose bargaining procedures that are socially "optimal" for every legal environment. *See* Talley, *supra* note 14, at 35–39.

74. Giving the defendant the power to make an all-or-nothing offer allocates a great amount of market power to the defendant. *See* Ian Ayres & Robert Gertner, *Strategic Contractual Inefficiency and the Optimal Choice of Legal Rules*, 101 YALE L.J. 729, 735–46 (1992) (exploring inefficiencies that arise from strategic bargaining when one party to contract has private information and other side has some market power). For example, if the defendant knew the plaintiff's type, the defendant could capture all the gains from trade by simply demanding a price that was just lower than the plaintiff's valuation. Giving the

The Yale Law Journal   [Vol. 104: 1027

defendant's offer, must specify what is being traded—the plaintiff's entitlement or the defendant's option—and the price. In the third stage of the game, the plaintiff, upon hearing the defendant's offer, accepts or rejects this offer, and the trade occurs if the offer is accepted.[75] Because the defendant's offer, however, is "take-it-or-leave-it," a rejection by the plaintiff ends the bargaining, and in the final possible stage of the game,[76] the defendant chooses whether to take the entitlement nonconsensually and pay the damage amount,[77] or to abstain from taking and leave the entitlement with the plaintiff.

2. Deriving the Equilibrium

The equilibrium bargaining strategies and outcomes of the above bargaining game depend on the type of entitlement protection. Thus, we analyze property rule damages (of D = $100) and liability rule damages (of D = $50) separately.[78] Before proceeding, however, it is useful to derive as benchmarks the expected payoffs both (1) when Coasean bargaining is perfectly efficient, and (2) when bargaining is not allowed—a situation that we shall call "legally mandated autarky."[79] Under the first scenario, in which Coasean negotiations succeeded in costlessly allocating the entitlement to the highest valuer, the parties would have an expected surplus of $63 to divide.[80] Under the second benchmark of legally mandated autarky, the expected joint

---

defendant this all-or-nothing offer also reduces the relative importance of the defendant's private information, thereby allowing the model to focus on the strategic inefficiency of the buyer's information. Because liability rules can exacerbate misrepresentations by defendants, this type of divided entitlement is likely to facilitate trade only when the plaintiff's private valuation is the impediment to efficient negotiations.

75. Thus, if the plaintiff agrees to sell her entitlement, she transfers the entitlement to the defendant in exchange for the agreed purchase price; if the plaintiff agrees to buy the defendant's option, the plaintiff retains the entitlement, but pays the defendant the agreed bribe.

76. Of course, players only reach this stage of the game if the plaintiff rejects the defendant's offer. The explicit game tree is depicted in the Appendix. *See infra* text accompanying notes 246–47.

77. We assume that the plaintiff can costlessly sue and collect damages. Including litigation costs in the model can result in even higher rates of Coasean trade, because the parties have a joint incentive to avoid the costs of litigation. This incentive only holds true for liability rules, under which the parties still have credible threats to take and/or sue. *See* Talley, *supra* note 14, at 32–35.

78. Thus, we examine only two "snapshots" of the value of the damage amount (D), which more generally could take on any positive value.

79. The notion of "legally mandated autarky" is closely related to what Calabresi and Melamed called "inalienability" rules. *See* Calabresi & Melamed, *supra* note 12, at 1106. If one defines "autarky" as the absence of trade, then legally mandated autarky is analogous to what Radin has called a rule of "nonsalability." Radin, *supra* note 37, at 1854; *see also* Rose-Ackerman, *supra* note 37, at 933–37 (noting that non-salability is but one manifestation of inalienability rules).

80. Even though the average valuation of each plaintiff and each defendant is $50, the average *highest* valuation of a plaintiff *and* a defendant is $63, because, intuitively, there are two chances to draw a party with a valuation greater than $50. In statistics terminology, the expected $63 is an "ordered statistic." *See, e.g.*, SHELDON ROSS, A FIRST COURSE IN PROBABILITY 224–25 (3d ed. 1984). For an explanation of the calculation of the $63, see *infra* app. at p. 1104.

welfare in a property regime is $50,[81] while the expected joint welfare in a liability regime is $55.[82] The ability of liability rules to increase the expected social welfare when bargaining is impossible resonates with the insights of Calabresi and Melamed: When transaction costs are prohibitively high, liability rules can enhance allocational efficiency by allowing high-valuing defendants to take and pay damages. It is a different question, however, whether this result holds when Coasean bargains are made in the presence of asymmetric information, which adds some (though not prohibitive) friction to bilateral bargaining.[83]

a. *Bargaining Under an Undivided Property Rule*

Under an undivided property rule, the defendant would never want to exercise his option to take and pay $100. Because the defendant has no credible threat of taking, he has nothing to "sell" to the plaintiff. The plaintiff, therefore, would never offer to bribe the defendant not to take the entitlement. Accordingly, in the first stage of the game under a property rule, the plaintiff signals only an interest in selling her entitlement to the defendant (i.e., Coasean bargain #2).

The defendant will make a take-it-or-leave-it offer to purchase the plaintiff's entitlement for a price that maximizes the defendant's expected profits, given his uncertainty about the plaintiff's valuation. As usual, the defendant as a buyer has an incentive to offer less than his valuation. A lower offer benefits the defendant if the plaintiff accepts, but reduces the chance of acceptance. In the Appendix, we show that the defendant whose valuation is $40 will bid $20 and the defendant whose valuation is $60 will bid $30 to buy the entitlement.[84] Plaintiffs with valuations below the contract offers will accept and those with valuations above the contract offers will reject.

This bargaining equilibrium is depicted in Figure 4.

---

81. Under this type of property regime, both consensual and nonconsensual takings by defendants would be deterred, so the entitlement would simply remain with the plaintiff, who would have an expected valuation of $50.

82. If contracting were prohibited but the defendant had an option to take the entitlement nonconsensually for $50, only defendants with $60 valuations would take, so that 50% of the time a $60 valuer would own the entitlement and 50% of the time the entitlement would remain with a random plaintiff who would have an expected valuation of $50. The expected value is thus: $(.5)\$60 + (.5)\$50 = \$55$.

83. As noted above, the folk wisdom on this point is that the existence of "some" transaction costs will likely mean that property rules are more efficient, since such rules give parties the incentive to set their own price for a taking; liability rules, on the other hand, usually are unable to overcome small transaction costs, so the parties must use the court-determined price for exchange. *See supra* notes 16–18 and accompanying text.

84. *See infra* app. at p. 1108.

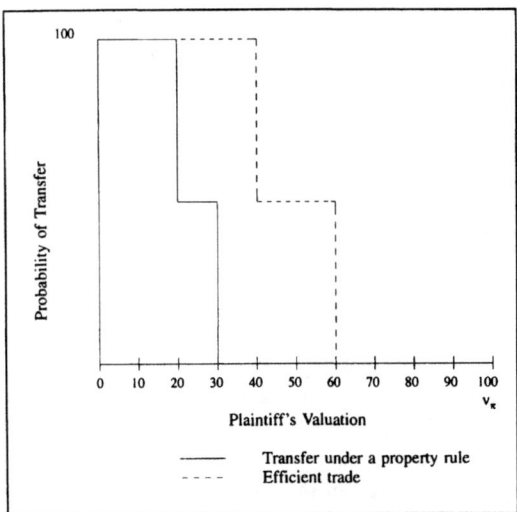

FIGURE 4. *Probability that Entitlement Will Be Transferred from Different Plaintiff Types Under a Property Rule*

The horizontal axis depicts the various plaintiff valuations and the vertical axis depicts the probability that the entitlement will be transferred (by sale or taking) to the defendant. As shown in Figure 4, 100% of plaintiffs with valuations less than $20 will sell their entitlement, because these plaintiffs will accept both the $20 and $30 offers from both types of defendants; there is a 50% chance that plaintiffs with valuations between $20 and $30 will sell their entitlement, because these plaintiffs will reject the $20 offers (from $40 defendants) and accept the $30 offers (from $60 defendants). Plaintiffs with valuations above $30 will never sell because they value the entitlement more than either type of the defendants' take-it-or-leave-it offer. The figure also illustrates the inefficiency of this equilibrium outcome by showing (with dotted lines) the efficient level of trade. For example, 100% of plaintiffs with valuations less than $40 should sell their entitlement to higher-valuing defendants, yet in the figure only 50% of plaintiffs with valuations between $20 and $30 sell and no plaintiffs with valuations between $30 and $40 are willing to sell.[85]

---

85. Efficient trade would also induce 50% of plaintiffs with valuations between $40 and $60 to sell to those defendants with $60 valuations. Under a property rule, however, none of these transactions takes place; the plaintiff's private information is a but-for cause of this inefficiency. If the seller knew the plaintiff's valuation, the higher-valuing seller would offer to buy the entitlement at a price just below the plaintiff's valuation, thereby inducing allocational efficiency.

Under a property rule, the parties' strategic interactions produce an expected surplus of approximately $59.75.[86] Thus, Coasean bargaining with imperfect information does not guarantee efficiency under a property rule; the parties' expected payoffs are some $3.25 less than the "first-best" level of $63.[87] There are, however, significant gains from Coasean trade: As discussed above, the parties' expected payoffs under a liability rule *without* Coasean trade were only $55—so (as is well understood[88]) protecting an entitlement with a property rule and allowing the parties to bargain can enhance allocational efficiency. If one were to assume that bargaining is infeasible under a liability rule, the property protection would, after bargaining, produce an expected surplus that is $4.75 higher than "autarky" under a liability rule. The traditional analysis of liability and property rules is flawed, however, in that (at least implicitly) it only compares the expected gains from a liability rule *without* trade to the gains from a property rule *with* trade. In contrast to this rather popular comparison, we show below that protecting an entitlement with a liability rule—because of the information-forcing effect—can enhance Coasean bargaining even more.

b. *Bargaining Under a Liability Rule*

When the damage amount D is equal to $50, in the absence of agreement the $60 defendant will take, and the $40 defendant will abstain from taking. Under a liability rule, then, the defendant's threat to take is credible *if and only if* the defendant's private valuation is $60. At first blush, one might intuit that the intermediate level of damages merely adds another dimension of private information to bargaining—for only the defendant knows whether his ostensible threat to take is credible—so that the bargaining outcome would be more inefficient than bargaining under a property rule. It turns out, however, that the information-forcing character of liability rules has a much stronger efficiency-enhancing effect that can facilitate Coasean exchanges.

When the damage amount is $50, the bargaining game delineated above has a number of potential equilibria. All of these equilibria, however, exhibit the information-forcing characteristic that plaintiffs never have an incentive to misrepresent their valuations.[89] Moreover, the most "plausible" of these

---

86. As one would suspect, plaintiffs endowed with an (undivided) entitlement protected by a property rule garner the bulk of this expected value. As shown below in Table 5, the plaintiffs on average garner $53.25, and the defendant earns $6.50. *See infra* part II.B.3. The $40 defendant's expected payoff is $4, and the $60 defendant's is $9. The plaintiff's expected payoff will be $v_π$ if her valuation exceeds $30; $(v_π/2 + $30)$ if her valuation is between $20 and $30; and $25 if her valuation is less than $20.

87. *See supra* note 80 and accompanying text.

88. *See supra* notes 27–28 and accompanying text.

89. A number of plaintiffs with intermediate valuations, however, will be indifferent between expressing interest in the two types of Coasean trade, because these plaintiffs know that in equilibrium they will not be able to reach agreement with defendants exploiting their take-it-or-leave-it market power. The valuation of these plaintiffs is not sufficiently different from the damage amount to make trade worthwhile.

equilibria produce expected payoffs that exceed the expected $59.75 surplus produced by bargaining under a property rule. Table 3 reports the representative strategies of just such an equilibrium:[90]

STAGES OF THE GAME	EQUILIBRIUM STRATEGY
PLAINTIFF'S REPORT OF INTEREST:	• If a plaintiff's valuation v_π is less than $50, she reports interest in selling her entitlement. • If a plaintiff's valuation v_π exceeds $50, she reports interest in buying defendant's option to take.
DEFENDANT'S OFFER:	• If plaintiff reported interest in selling her entitlement, *both* types of defendant offer to buy the entitlement for $32.50. • If plaintiff reported interest in buying defendant's option to take, *both* types of defendant offer to sell their option to take for $17.50.
PLAINTIFF'S ACCEPTANCE DECISION:	• A plaintiff, who has reported interest in selling her entitlement, will accept the defendant's $32.50 bid if and only if her valuation is less than $15. • A plaintiff, who has reported interest in buying defendant's option to take, will accept the defendant's $17.50 demand if and only if her valuation is greater than $85.
DEFENDANT'S TAKING DECISION:	• After a rejected offer, the defendant will take the entitlement (and pay plaintiff $50) if and only if $v_\Delta = $60.

TABLE 3. *Representative Strategy Profiles in Equilibrium*

In this equilibrium,[91] the plaintiff's willingness to reveal some informa-

---

These intermediate-valuing plaintiffs will drop out of any bargaining game if communication costs increase even an infinitesimal amount. Thus, in many real-world settings, we would expect plaintiffs to partition themselves into three groups: High valuers would seek to bribe defendants, low valuers would seek to be bribed, and intermediate valuers would remain silent.

90. The Appendix contains a derivation of this equilibrium for liability rule values of D between $40 and $60. *See infra* app. at pp. 1110–13.

91. Unlike the D = $100 game, the D = $50 does not have a unique Bayesian perfect equilibrium. There are a number of equilibrium "refinements," however, that allow one to dismiss certain equilibria as "implausible" because they require threats of deviation by players who are unlikely to want to deviate. Using one such refinement known as "divinity," we can narrow the plausible equilibrium outcomes of this game precisely to those described in the text. For more on the notion of equilibrium refinements, see Jeffrey S. Banks & Joel Sobel, *Equilibrium Selection in Signaling Games*, 55 ECONOMETRICA 647 (1987)

tion about her valuation (by expressing an interest in purchasing the defendant's option or selling her own entitlement) can facilitate Coasean trade: Only plaintiffs with valuations greater than $50 will say, "I am interested in bribing you not to take my entitlement," and only plaintiffs with valuations less than $50 will say, "I am interested in selling you my entitlement." This self-selection, or partitioning phenomenon, can increase the likelihood of an efficient transaction, because it effectively gives the parties less "room" to misrepresent their private valuations in bargaining.[92]

As discussed above, however, liability rules can amplify defendants' incentives to misrepresent their valuations: Even though liability rules induce plaintiffs to act less strategically, they may induce defendants to act more strategically. In particular, as shown in Table 3, the liability rule induces the different types of defendants to formulate identical offers. In game-theoretic terms, the liability rules cause the defendants to "pool."[93] No matter whether the plaintiff expresses interest in buying (the defendant's call option) or in selling (her own entitlement), one "type" of defendant will always find it optimal to *mimic* the behavior of the other type of defendant so as not to reveal his true intention about taking.[94]

Because of the defendant's mimicking behavior, the plaintiff will be unsure whether a bid/offer has issued from a "contender" or a "pretender." For

---

(discussing divinity as such); In-Koo Cho & David M. Kreps, *Signaling Games and Stable Equilibria*, 102 Q.J. ECON. 179 (1987) (discussing less restrictive refinements).

92. The existence of the "cheap talk" signaling phase in our model is, as one might expect, crucial to our results. When we take away the ability of the plaintiff to signal, bargaining under liability rules no longer leads to more efficient outcomes than under property rules. Indeed, while liability rules create the possibility for two types of bargaining, the signaling phase of the game is what allows the parties to coordinate the type of transaction. Removing signaling lowers the probability of consensual trade to zero. Thus, a $50 liability rule without signaling by the plaintiff results in the equivalent of autarky, which produces an expected social welfare of $55. Conversely, a property rule does not suffer from such a coordination failure, and it thereby produces consensual trade, resulting in an expected social surplus of $59.75.

93. Recall that under the property rule, the different types of defendants did not pool because they offered to buy at different prices.

94. While the precise derivations of defendants' equilibrium bids are in the Appendix, we can sketch some of the intuitions here. Consider the case where a plaintiff values her entitlement less than the $50 and has so signaled to the defendant. The only possible transaction of interest to the plaintiff involves selling her entitlement to a $40 defendant who otherwise would not take. But the plaintiff will only be able to make such a transaction at a price less than $40, because low-valuing defendants will not offer to purchase an entitlement for a price greater than $40.

At the same time, this brand of transaction is extremely attractive to high-valuing defendants. Even though these defendants would take in the absence of successful bargaining, by taking they would have to pay $50. If, however, the high-valuing defendant could convincingly "mask" herself as a low-valuing defendant, she might be able to buy the entitlement at an even lower price than the $50 damage amount. As such, the high-valuing defendant will find it profitable to feign a low valuation so as to "fool" the plaintiff into reducing the price of taking. Such a defendant, then, must mimic the bid of a low-valuing defendant, for if she reveals herself to be a high-valuing defendant, the plaintiff will surely reject any bid, knowing that a $50 damages payment is forthcoming. This is why both types of defendants "pool" to bid $32.50 for the plaintiff's entitlement in Table 3.

A similar type of strategic mimicking occurs in the other situation, when a plaintiff has signaled a preference for the "bribe" transaction. Here, conversely, the low-valuing defendants mimic the behavior of the high-valuing defendants.

example, when a low-valuing plaintiff hears a defendant's $32.50 offer to buy the entitlement, the plaintiff will know there is a 50% chance that the defendant has a $60 valuation (and intends to take the entitlement for $50 should the plaintiff reject the offer). Accordingly, a low-valuing plaintiff will be reluctant to sell her entitlement *unless* the sales price sufficiently exceeds her valuation to compensate her for the (50%) possibility that she is facing a $60 defendant who will pay $50 if she rejects the offer. Thus, even though the low-valuing plaintiffs receive all-or-nothing offers to buy for $32.50, only plaintiffs who value the entitlement at less than $15 choose to sell. A plaintiff whose valuation is $15 is indifferent between accepting and rejecting the defendant's $32.50 offer to sell because rejecting yields a 50% chance of $50 and a 50% chance of $15, which equals an expected value of $32.50.

The willingness of plaintiffs to accept only contractual offers that are higher than their valuations can help discipline the $40 defendant to make a more competitive offer. In choosing an offering price to purchase the plaintiff's entitlement, the low-valuing ($40) defendant knows that the high-valuing ($60) defendant will mimic his bid. The $40 defendant recognizes that because of this mimicking, the plaintiff will be less willing to accept that bid *ceteris paribus*. This heightened scrutiny can help to discipline the $40 defendant to raise his bid closer to his actual valuation. The $32.50 offer to purchase thus represents the price that maximizes the $40 defendant's expected payoff (given the $60 defendant's mimicking and the plaintiff's reluctance that the mimicking engenders). A similar analysis explains the defendants' $17.50 offers not to take.[95]

The plaintiffs' reluctance to trade with pooling defendants reduces the information-forcing effect of liability rules. Plaintiffs with intermediate valuations (between $15 and $85) know that they will not accept any pooled-defendant offers and thus have a weaker incentive to signal their relative valuations. Indeed, if reporting an interest in a particular type of Coasean trade costs an arbitrarily small amount, then plaintiffs with these intermediate valuations would remain silent and only the 30% of plaintiffs with relatively extreme valuations (i.e., with valuations greater than $85 or less than $15) would signal their types. Defendant pooling might therefore easily induce silence among plaintiffs with intermediate valuations, but it does not give plaintiffs with intermediate valuations an affirmative incentive to misrepresent

---

95. In both cases, the plaintiff demands a payoff that is at least $17.50 greater than the worst-case outcome. A plaintiff with a valuation of $15 is worried that the defendant will not take in the absence of bargaining, but still demands a payoff of $32.50 ($17.50 higher) to sell her entitlement. A plaintiff with a valuation of $85 is worried that the defendant will take in the absence of bargaining (which would give the plaintiff only $50), but this plaintiff still demands a net payoff of $67.50 (which again is $17.50 higher) and accordingly is unwilling to pay a bribe of more than $17.50 (because $85 minus the $17.50 bribe not to take produces the required net payoff of $67.50). The willingness of $40 defendants to mimic the $60 defendants' $17.50 offers not to take thus causes high-valuing plaintiffs to bribe only when their private valuations are sufficiently high (greater than $85).

that their valuation is above or below the damage amount. Moreover, this example shows that liability rules induce affirmative disclosure among those plaintiffs for whom Coasean trade has the highest return.

This equilibrium for bargaining under a $50 liability rule is depicted in Figure 5. As in Figure 4, the horizontal axis depicts the various plaintiff valuations, and the vertical axis depicts the probability that the entitlement will ultimately be enjoyed by the defendant, through either a purchase or nonconsensual taking.

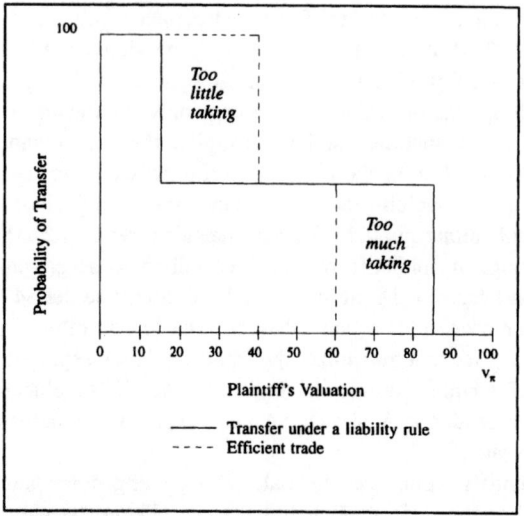

FIGURE 5. *Probability that Entitlement Will Be Transferred from Different Plaintiff Types Under a Liability Rule*

Under the $50 liability rule, there is a 100% chance that plaintiffs with valuations of less than $15 will sell their entitlements because these plaintiffs will accept the $32.50 offer that both types of defendants will make to buy the entitlement. There is a 50% chance that plaintiffs with valuations between $15 and $85 will have their entitlements taken nonconsensually (by $60 defendants). Plaintiffs with valuations between $15 and $50 will reject defendants' offers to buy for $32.50, and plaintiffs with valuations between $50 and $85 will reject defendants' offers to sell their options to take for $17.50. Finally, plaintiffs with valuations above $85 will acquire an undivided ownership in the entitlement.

As before, Figure 5 shows why bargaining under a liability rule does not eliminate strategic inefficiency. By comparing these equilibrium probabilities of transfer under a liability rule to the efficient level of trade (indicated with dotted lines), we can identify two areas of inefficiency: (1) plaintiffs with valuations between $15 and $40 should always sell their rights to higher-valuing buyers, but these plaintiffs refuse to accept any pooled offers to buy their entitlements—so that only 50% of the entitlements are taken nonconsensually by defendants (with $60 valuations); and (2) plaintiffs with valuations between $60 and $85 should always retain the entitlement, but these plaintiffs refuse to accept the pooled offers to sell the liability call option—so that 50% of the entitlements are taken nonconsensually by lower-valuing, $60 defendants.

3. *Liability Rules Can Facilitate Coasean Trade*

As is obvious from the above example, bargaining under a liability rule does not necessarily result in a "first-best" outcome. Nevertheless, bargaining under a liability rule may be more efficient than bargaining under a property rule. Table 4 shows for both property and liability rules the equilibrium proportion of defendants who will:

- enter into one of the two types of Coasean agreements;
- take nonconsensually; and
- refrain from contracting or taking.

	PROPERTY RULES			LIABILITY RULES		
	%	EXPECTED JOINT PAYOFFS	CONTRIBUTION TO TOTAL INEFFICIENCY	%	EXPECTED JOINT PAYOFFS	CONTRIBUTION TO TOTAL INEFFICIENCY
COASEAN TRADE	25%	$52.00	$0.00	30%	$71.25	$0.00
NONCONSEN- SUAL TAKING	0%	$0.00	$0.00	35%	$60.00	$1.56
NEITHER TRADE NOR TAKING	75%	$62.33	$3.25	35%	$50.00	$1.56
EXPECTED TOTAL	100%	$59.75	$3.25	100%	$59.88	$3.12

TABLE 4. *Equilibrium Trade and Taking Under Property and Liability Rules*

Table 4 shows how liability rules facilitate Coasean trade. Under a property rule only 25% of the bargainers reach Coasean agreement, but under a liability rule this figure rises to 30%.[96] The table also shows that expected payoffs for

---

96. As shown in Figure 4, under a property rule 25% of bargainers reach agreement, because all plaintiffs with valuations under $20 trade (20% of all bargains) and half of plaintiffs with valuations

those reaching a Coasean agreement are significantly higher under a liability rule ($71.25) than under a property rule ($52.00).[97] Even though liability rules induce excessive nonconsensual takings by some defendants (giving rise to an inefficiency of $1.56),[98] bargaining under the liability rule is more efficient because it raises the probability of Coasean trade (where the entitlement always ends up in the hands of the highest valuer) and dramatically reduces the failure of goods to pass to higher-valuing defendants due to the defendants' failure to contract or take. Under a property rule, 75% of plaintiffs fail to contract and no taking occurs; under a liability rule this figure is reduced to 35%. The liability rule equilibrium reduces the inefficiency from this autarkic category by more than half (from $3.25 to $1.56).

The net impact of these effects is that under a liability rule, the expected joint payoffs ($59.88)[99] are higher than those produced by bargaining under a property rule ($59.75).[100] Liability rules are more efficient because they induce more trade.[101] By effectively forcing the plaintiffs to reveal

---

between $20 and $30 trade (5% of all bargainers). As shown in Figure 5, under a liability rule 30% of bargainers reach agreement because all plaintiffs with valuations less than $15 trade (15% of all bargainers) and all plaintiffs with valuations more than $85 trade (15% of all bargainers).

97. Under a liability rule, half of the trades will allow plaintiffs with an average value of $92.50 (between $85 and $100) to retain the entitlement, and half of the trades allow defendants with an average value of $50 ($40 or $60) to acquire the entitlement—so the expected payoff will be (.5)$92.50 + (.5)$50 = $71.25. Under a property rule, 40% of trades allow a $40 defendant to acquire the entitlement and 60% of the trades allow a $60 defendant to acquire the entitlement—so the expected payoffs will be (.4)$40 + (.6)$60 = $52.

98. In the liability rule equilibrium, this excessive taking was caused by $60 dollar defendants who would inefficiently take from plaintiffs with valuations ranging from $60 to $85.

99. For the exact calculations, see *infra* app. at p. 1113.

100. Although in this example the liability rule only increases the expected surplus from the property rule by $0.12, alternative assumptions about the distribution of plaintiff and defendant types could easily produce a greater differential. For example, if the defendant's two valuation types were $20 and $80, then an intermediate liability rule could produce an expected surplus $3.00 higher than what a property rule would produce. In this case, the liability rule would mitigate 75% of the inefficiency that would otherwise exist under a property rule.

The amount of improvement is of course capped by the size of the surplus available under first-best trade, which in Table 5 equals $63, but the improvement is not limited to an amount less than "transaction costs." First, in this model, transaction costs are not easily monetized because of the amount of private information that induces the inefficiency. Second, even when the dollar costs of contracting inhibit Coasean bargaining, the amount of inefficiency may be greater than the contracting costs. *See* Ayres & Gertner, *supra* note 74.

101. In the absence of bargaining (a situation that we have labeled "autarky"), a $50 liability rule dominates a property rule in terms of expected joint payoff. Kaplow and Shavell have persuasively shown that liability rules already have a "head start" on property rules under autarky because nonconsensual takings will tend to transfer the entitlement to a higher-valuing owner, and that it is not surprising that this liability rule advantage *persists* in circumstances when bargaining is possible. Louis Kaplow & Steven Shavell, *Property Rules Versus Liability Rules* (1994) (unpublished manuscript, on file with authors). While Kaplow and Shavell are clearly correct about the autarkic headstart of liability rules, the information-forcing property of liability rules may provide an independent reason that liability rules can dominate property rules when bargaining is possible. Two phenomena support this belief. First, as the next Section makes clear, an attempt by the court to "tailor" its damages to the plaintiff's private valuation can actually decrease joint welfare. *See infra* part II.C.1. If the persistence of the autarky advantage were the sole cause of the liability rule advantage with bargaining, one would expect that bargaining under a tailored liability rule could do no worse than bargaining under the untailored rule studied here (the opposite is in fact the case). Second, coauthor Talley has found that introducing litigation costs into the model can induce "first best" bargaining

The Yale Law Journal

information about their valuations, liability rules mitigate the inefficiencies of bargaining under private information.[102]

This efficiency-enhancing quality of liability rules stands at odds with the law-and-economics "folk wisdom" on how to induce bargaining. Most scholars have assumed that the law can best ensure efficient Coasean bargaining by maximizing the size of the potential "bargaining pie"—i.e., the range of

---

under a liability rule (again because the parties bargain more forthrightly). *See* Talley, *supra* note 14, at 29–33. Property rules, on the other hand, are unable to induce first best bargaining, with or without litigation costs. Once again, if the predominant value of liability rules were their ability to facilitate nonconsensual transfer to higher-valuing owners, then we would expect that increasing the cost of nonconsensual transfer (via litigation costs) would decrease (rather than increase) the expected payoffs. Clearly, the benefit must be substantially driven by bargaining.

102. The distributional consequences of the various rules are also somewhat interesting. Table 5 compares the relative efficiency and distributional consequences of four different entitlement regimes.

LEGAL BARGAINING REGIME	EXPECTED JOINT PAYOFF	EXPECTED PLAINTIFF PAYOFF	EXPECTED DEFENDANT PAYOFF
"FIRST-BEST" ALLOCATION	$63.00		
BARGAINING UNDER LIABILITY RULE	$59.875	$51.125	$8.75
BARGAINING UNDER PROPERTY RULE	$59.75	$53.25	$6.50
AUTARKY UNDER LIABILITY RULE	$55.00	$50.00	$5.00
AUTARKY UNDER PROPERTY RULE	$50.00	$50.00	$0.00

TABLE 5. *Expected Payoffs Under Four Legal Regimes*

The above table confirms that plaintiffs, *on average*, favor a property rule, while defendants, *on average*, favor a liability rule. This result is consistent with the intuition about the distributional consequences of these rules. Once both parties learn their respective valuations, however, neither plaintiffs nor defendants are unanimous in their preference. Even though a property rule would seem to disfavor defendants in general, low-valuing defendants actually prefer a property rule. Since a property rule does not induce defendant "pooling" or "mimicking," plaintiffs do not scrutinize the bids they receive from low-valuing defendants as closely. Indeed, low-valuing defendants receive a larger payoff from the property rule ($4.00) than they do under the liability rule ($3.75), while high-valuing defendants do better under liability rules ($13.75) than under property rules ($9.00). Conversely, all plaintiffs whose private valuations are less than $50 favor liability rules over property rules.

Because of this heterogeneous ordering of preferences both among and between litigants, it is unlikely that the parties would be able to agree on one rule over another. If, however, the parties were able to bargain about which rule to implement *before they became aware of their private valuations*, and if side payments were allowed, then it is a straightforward Coasean proposition that the parties would settle on a divided entitlement rather than a property rule. This Coasean conclusion is valid in such a situation because the parties do not have any private information when they bargain over the legal rule. This possibility may explain why contracting parties often wish to liquidate damages in a contractual term before they learn their private information, for a liquidated damages term is nothing more than a simple liability call option as modeled here. It might also explain why courts often invalidate stipulated terms that appear penalty-like in nature. For a more extensive analysis of this point, see generally Talley, *supra* note 43.

potential prices that might be agreed upon by the parties.[103] In contrast, our model finds that liability rules can increase social welfare by forcing people to bargain over smaller, discrete bargaining ranges. A $50 liability rule actually bifurcates one large bargaining range (under a property rule between $0 and $100) into two smaller bargaining ranges,[104] yet *increases* expected social welfare. This quality of liability rules exposes the fundamental flaw in the "maximize the pie" recipe for characterizing efficient legal rules. Such a recipe mistakenly assumes that the amount of strategic behavior *remains constant* regardless of the size of the underlying bargaining pie. To the contrary, the above model illustrates that even though liability rules force parties to agree to a price within a narrower bargaining range, these rules can have an *even greater* effect of stemming the amount of strategic behavior by inducing entitlement holders to reveal some of their information.[105]

---

103. *See, e.g.,* Merges, *supra* note 39, at 22–28.

104. Under a property rule, the possible prices from a Coasean transaction can range from $0 to $100. Under a liability rule, however, regardless of which Coasean transaction the entitlement holder signals, the potential prices range only between $0 and $50.

105. As noted earlier, our results are robust amid variations in our assumptions about the structure of information and the bargaining rules. *See supra* notes 57–60. For instance, the defendant's valuation need not take on symmetric values around $50, nor need it have symmetric 1/2 probabilities. Moreover, our results are robust even in environments where the parties vary their bargaining procedure when the legal environment changes. *See supra* note 73.

In their text on game theory and the law, Baird, Gertner, and Picker explore a bargaining environment similar to ours in analyzing the potential effects of a specific performance remedy in the classic case of Peevyhouse v. Garland Coal & Mining Co., 382 P.2d 109 (Okla. 1963) (holding that when cost of specific performance of contract calling for land restoration would substantially outweigh enhanced value of land after reclamation, plaintiff is not entitled to specific performance). Their analysis underscores the importance of "exit options" in determining the outcome of bilateral bargaining. *See* DOUGLAS BAIRD ET AL., GAME THEORY AND THE LAW 224–32 (1991). In their example, a taking of sorts—breach of contract—has already occurred. Garland has refused to perform its promise to restore the Peevyhouses' land after strip mining. The Peevyhouses, as the aggrieved party, are conjectured to have a right to specific performance should bargaining fail, and thus they may "exit" from negotiations and force Garland to restore the land at any time during negotiations. The authors examine a situation where there are two "types" of plaintiffs: a high-valuing type who places a subjective value of $800,000 on land restoration, and a low-valuing type who values such reclamation at only $200,000. The cost of restoration is commonly known in their model to be $1,000,000. *Id.* at 224–26.

The authors find that the existence of this specific performance option can lead to inefficient outcomes if the Peevyhouses have private information. High-valuing Peevyhouses will choose to exit the negotiations since their offers (not to seek specific performance in exchange for compensation) are indistinguishable from mimicking "bluffs" issued by low-valuing Peevyhouses. If the probability of a low-valuing Peevyhouse is sufficiently high, Garland will likely reject any bids by the Peevyhouses of $800,000 or more, thinking that the bid is more likely than not a bluff. As such, Garland is willing to let the high-valuing Peevyhouses exit even though their exiting and exercising the specific performance remedy results in inefficiency. *Id.* at 229–31.

Their results are consistent with our finding that an absolute property right vested in one party can often lead to allocational inefficiencies. Indeed, the specific performance entitlement is a type of property rule: The Peevyhouses have the ability to "take" from Garland for zero compensation. Our discussion in the Appendix of the case where D = $0 conducts just such an analysis. *See infra* app. at p. 1109. Both our model and theirs find that property rules can create inefficient failures to transfer the property right through negotiations.

While Baird, Gertner, and Picker do not formally analyze bargaining with incomplete information under a "liability rule," our model could easily incorporate such a rule. Consider, for instance, a rule that allows the Peevyhouses to force restoration of their land, but only for an exercise price of $500,000. In such a case, just as in our model, the low-valuing Peevyhouses would not exercise such an option, while

4. *Reverse Liability Rules and Compensated Injunctions*

Throughout the above analysis, we have assumed that the defining characteristic of a liability rule is that it gives the defendant a call option to take. There are, however, other types of liability regimes that can be given alternative option interpretations. Indeed, it is plausible to think of situations in which the option on whether a taking occurs lies with the "aggrieved" party. A reverse liability rule is just such a situation. This rule would give the *plaintiff* the right to force a taking at the prescribed liability amount. Effectively, then, while a "run-of-the-mill" liability rule places a *call option* in the hands of the defendant, the reverse liability rule places a *put option* in the hands of the plaintiff.[106]

As it turns out, reversing the option right produces a truth-telling result similar to what an ordinary liability rule produces, but it affects the opposite party. Consider, for example, a reverse liability rule that endows the plaintiff with the right to force a sale to the defendant at a price of $50. Analogous to the previous case, there are two types of Coasean bargains. In the first type,

---

the high-valuing Peevyhouses would.

To "map" our model onto theirs completely, however, we would need to relax the assumption that "no restoration" is the efficient decision. Indeed, the assumption that the cost of restoration ($1,000,000) exceeds any realistic valuation of the Peevyhouses ($200,000 or $800,000) ensures that the first-best allocational decision is common knowledge in their model. Therefore, Garland always prefers the type of Coasean bargain in which it bribes Peevyhouse not to take. Selling its liability entitlement for an amount less than $500,000 is never attractive to such a high-valuing Garland, as this would only increase the probability of a taking *and* increase Garland's net loss in the event of such a taking. The analogue of our model, in contrast, allows for Peevyhouse's privately known valuation to vary between $0 and $1,000,000. When Garland's valuation varies in this manner, it creates an incentive for the high- and low-valuing Garlands to separate themselves through credible signaling, thus giving our "partitioning" result. This example illustrates the notion that liability rules can increase efficiency when there is private information on the non-optionholder's side (i.e., Garland).

106. The difference between a liability rule and a reverse liability rule can be illustrated by the facts of *Boomer v. Atlantic Cement Co.*, 257 N.E.2d 870 (N.Y. 1970), which involved a cement plant's polluting of neighboring homes. The court's decision implemented a traditional liability rule: The neighbors had a right not to be exposed to pollution, but this right was subject to the cement plant's option to pollute and pay court-determined damages. One could imagine a court, possibly on alternative facts, finding that it would be so difficult to determine whether the cement plant was polluting that the court would give the neighbors not only the right not to be exposed to pollution, but also the option to sell this right to the cement plant for the same court-determined damage amount. This remedy would protect the neighbors from surreptitious pollution that could not be legally proven to violate the neighbors' original entitlement. Giving the neighbors the pollution entitlement plus this put option constitutes a reverse liability rule. Under *Boomer's* liability holding, the cement plant has the right to decide whether to pay court-determined damages for the right to pollute. Under a reverse liability rule, the neighbors have the right to decide whether they will be paid court-determined damages to give the cement plant the right to pollute.

Madeline Morris was the first to use this put-call analogy to examine ordinary and reverse liability rules. *E.g.*, Madeline Morris, *The Structure of Entitlements*, 78 CORNELL L. REV. 822, 851–56 (1993). While reverse liability rules are much less common than ordinary rules, there are instances within American law in which the plaintiff likely has a limited put option. A possible example of this notion is the so-called "forced sale" doctrine in contract law. Under U.C.C. § 2-709, a seller aggrieved by a buyer's material breach may have the option of forcing the buyer to purchase contracted goods at the specified price. Note, however, that this remedy is limited to the case of unique or damaged goods—i.e., goods that cannot easily be resold. *See* U.C.C. § 2-709 (1993). Examples of legally imposed liability rules include "[g]un buy-out offers by police departments and soft-drink container deposit redemption laws." *See* Morris, *supra*, at 855.

a low-valuing defendant might bribe the plaintiff not to exercise her option.[107] In the second type, a high-valuing defendant might purchase the plaintiff's entitlement.[108]

Under a reverse liability rule, the possibility of these two transactions now eliminates the *defendant's* incentive to misrepresent whether his valuation is above or below the damage amount. While plaintiffs might have some incentive to lie,[109] a defendant's type of offer credibly signals his valuation: Low-valuing defendants would never offer to purchase the entitlement for more than $50, and high-valuing defendants would never want to bribe the plaintiff to abstain from exercising the put option.[110]

Defendants can also be induced to partition themselves if they are given the entitlement and plaintiffs are given the call option to take nonconsensually and pay damages. This allocation corresponds to the famous "category 4" of Calabresi and Melamed—which would permit the plaintiff to enjoin the defendant's conduct, but only if she compensated the defendant for the defendant's losses caused by the injunction.[111] Lawmakers and jurists largely overlooked this form of "compensated injunction" until the Arizona Supreme Court in *Spur Industries v. Del E. Webb Development Co.* required, as a condition for granting a nuisance injunction against a preexisting feedlot, that

---

107. For example, suppose the plaintiff's valuation is $30 and the defendant's valuation is $10. Absent bargaining, the plaintiff will exercise the put option and will receive a payoff of $50, leaving the defendant with a payoff of minus $40. This result is clearly inefficient, since the aggregate social surplus ($10) is lower than what would emerge if the plaintiff abstained from exercising her option ($30). One can imagine a Coasean bargain in which the defendant pays (bribes) the plaintiff $25 to abstain from taking (i.e., the defendant purchases the plaintiff's put option). Such a bribe would reduce the defendant's loss from $40 to $25, and it would increase the plaintiff's payoff to $55.

108. This transaction might occur if the high-valuing defendant did not expect the plaintiff to force a sale. For instance, going back to the situation where the exercise price on the plaintiff's option is $50, suppose that the plaintiff valued the entitlement at $60 and the defendant valued it at $80. Absent bargaining, the plaintiff clearly would not choose to exercise her option. This inaction would result in an aggregate surplus of $60—again inefficient. If, however, the defendant offered to purchase the plaintiff's entitlement for, say, $65, the plaintiff, after accepting, would be better off (as would the defendant), and aggregate welfare would increase to $80.

It is interesting to note here that, contrary to our example of regular liability rules, the two transactions both entail the defendant's purchasing something from (i.e., bribing) the plaintiff. The bribes, however, are for two distinct actions that the plaintiff might take (exercising or not exercising). This observation suggests that what is important under a liability rule is *not* the possibility that the parties might be on either *side* of a transaction, but rather the possibility that a liability rule would create two qualitatively distinct *types* of transactions that the parties might pursue.

109. Indeed, low-valuing plaintiffs would sometimes offer to sell for more than $50, and high-valuing plaintiffs would sometimes propose a bribe not to exercise the put option.

110. As a worst-case scenario, the low-valuing defendant would be forced to purchase the entitlement for $50, should the plaintiff exercise the put. Since this forced transaction would give the defendant a negative payoff to begin with, it makes little sense for the low-valuing defendant to pay *even more* to receive the entitlement. Since the low-valuing defendant would therefore never enter into such a transaction, such a defendant is always willing to signal credibly that his valuation is less than $50.

A high-valuing defendant, on the other hand, will receive a windfall if the plaintiff exercises the put option and therefore has no incentive to purchase the put option from the plaintiff. Hence, the only transaction that appeals to the high-valuing defendant involves purchasing the entitlement from the plaintiff.

111. Calabresi & Melamed, *supra* note 12, at 1115–23.

the plaintiff pay for the feedlot's costs "of moving or shutting down."[112] Our earlier argument suggests that if the costs of the injunction are untailored—so that the defendant feedlot's costs might be higher or lower than the court-ordered compensation—then the defendant feedlot could credibly signal whether its damages were higher or lower than the court award by offering either to bribe the plaintiff not to seek an injunction or to agree to stop polluting for a price less than the court award. Compensated injunctions induce defendant partitioning by merely switching the roles of plaintiff and defendant. The defendant is given the entitlement, but its ownership is subject to the plaintiff's option to take the entitlement and pay compensating damages.

This analysis suggests that there are two liability rule methods of inducing defendants to partition themselves: reverse liability rules and compensated injunction rules. A fundamental equation from finance theory, called the "put-call parity formula," shows the precise relationship between these two types of liability rules. The put-call parity formula establishes the relative value of put and call options written with identical exercise prices on the same underlying entitlement as follows:

Value of entitlement + Value of put = Value of call + Value of exercise price.[113]

This put-call parity formula can easily be restated in terms of the reverse liability and compensated injunction rules. Under a reverse liability rule, the plaintiff owns both the entitlement and a put option to sell the entitlement at fixed exercise price—so that the value of the plaintiff's claims under a reverse liability rule should equal the left-hand sum of the put-call parity formula. Under a compensated injunction rule, the plaintiff owns only a call option to take the entitlement and pay the fixed exercise price. Accordingly, it is possible to rewrite the parity formula as follows:

Value of reverse liability rule = Value of compensated injunction rule + Value of exercise price.

Restated in this manner, it is easy to see that the plaintiff's payoffs under a reverse liability rule will exceed her payoffs under a compensated injunction by exactly the amount of the untailored damages. As a first approximation, the only difference between the two types of liability rules is that a reverse liability rule transfers the value of the exercise price from the defendant to the plaintiff.[114]

---

112. 494 P.2d 700, 708 (Ariz. 1972). Ellickson originally coined the term "compensated injunction." *See* Ellickson, *supra* note 50, at 738 & n.202.

113. For greater elaboration of the put-call parity formula, see JOHN HULL, OPTIONS, FUTURES, AND OTHER DERIVATIVE SECURITIES 110–16 (1989).

114. In the absence of bargaining, the payoffs under the two rules differ by exactly the amount of this transfer. In the presence of bargaining, the expected payoffs of all types differ by this amount.

This discussion of reverse liability and compensated injunction rules illustrates that various permutations of liability rule options will induce either the plaintiff or the defendant to reveal information about her valuation. Just as traditional liability rules can induce plaintiff partitioning, we have shown that both reverse liability and compensated injunction rules can induce defendant partitioning. Thus, these latter rules are more likely to be appropriate when the defendant's private information about his valuation predominates in Coasean negotiations.[115]

C. *The Perverse Effects of Tailoring Liability*

In the previous sections, we illustrated the information-forcing effect of dividing the claims to an entitlement by giving a defendant (the potential taker) an option to take nonconsensually and pay a fixed liability amount. Here, we ask a slightly different but equally important question: How does the court's ability to "tailor" a remedy to the specific litigants' characteristics affect this result?

At first, we expected that greater accuracy by the court in tailoring either its liability determinations or the amount of damages would produce more efficient outcomes;[116] after all, by tailoring its decisions to the specific circumstances of a legal dispute, the court would be able to induce more efficient taking when bargaining failed.[117] We were wrong. Tailoring can exacerbate strategic impediments to bargaining because tailoring gives the parties private information about the legal consequences of nonconsensual taking. For instance, if the court were to match the level of damages to the precise magnitude of the plaintiff's injury (v_π in our example), the plaintiff would know more than the defendant about the legal consequences of a nonconsensual taking. Though the defendant would still own a call option, he would not know its exercise price.

---

115. It would also be possible to construct an alternative liability scheme that induced plaintiff partitioning by endowing the defendant with both the entitlement and a put option to sell the entitlement to the plaintiff for a fixed price. This scheme would be equivalent to a reverse liability rule, but the identities of the plaintiff and the defendant would be switched so that in the pollution context, the polluter would have a right to pollute and an option to sell its right to pollute to its downwind neighbor for a fixed amount of money.

116. This belief, as a default proposition, seems almost axiomatic in the law-and-economics literature. *See, e.g.,* STEVEN SHAVELL, ECONOMIC ANALYSIS OF ACCIDENT LAW 127 (1987) ("It has been implicit all along that if liable parties pay for the actual level of losses they cause, they will be led to act optimally under liability rules."); *see* POSNER, *supra* note 1, at 62 n.5 (noting that property rules are likely to predominate over liability rules if courts cannot compute damages with reasonable accuracy); *see also* A. Mitchell Polinsky, *Resolving Nuisance Disputes: The Simple Economics of Injunctive and Damage Remedies,* 32 STAN. L. REV. 1075, 1112 (1980) (discussing optimality of property rules when court cannot observe parties' valuations).

117. This rationale is consistent with what Cooter has referred to as the "Normative Hobbes Theorem: Structure the law to minimize the harm caused by failures in private agreements." COOTER & ULEN, *supra* note 1, at 99.

In this Section, we argue that the added dimension of private information that tailoring introduces can seriously hamper the bargaining process. Exact tailoring of *damages* gives the plaintiff a form of "perfect insurance" against bargaining breakdown because the plaintiff's noncooperative payoff is unaffected by the defendant's decision to take nonconsensually. Conversely, if the court were to fix its *liability* determination in a contingent fashion, making the defendant liable (under a negligence-like standard) if his private valuation was subsequently found to be insufficient to justify the taking, the defendant would have private information about whether the court would eventually find him liable. As such, if the defendant knew that he would satisfy the negligence standard, he would now have perfect insurance against bargaining breakdown. In this Section, we consider each of these possibilities within the bargaining framework defined above to show that tailoring can reduce the incentives for plaintiffs under a liability rule to partition themselves affirmatively into high- and low-valuing groups. We stress, however, that even with tailored legal rules, we would never expect to see a low-valuing plaintiff make (or accept) an offer to bribe a defendant not to take the entitlement, and we would never expect to see a high-valuing plaintiff make (or accept) an offer to sell her entitlement for less than the damage amount. Therefore, while tailoring may induce a larger range of plaintiffs to refrain from trade, it is still true that any observed offers by a plaintiff credibly signal information about her relative valuation.

1. *Tailored Damages*

Suppose that instead of awarding the plaintiff an untailored damage amount as in our analysis above, the court was able to "pierce" the plaintiff's private information at trial, awarding her actual damages of v_π.[118] As mentioned above, tailoring the amount of damages gives the plaintiff private information about the consequences of a taking. The defendant has an option to take, but is unsure of the exercise price. This type of uncertainty often exists in contractual settings. For example, a consumer who has promised to purchase a new automobile from a dealership may know that the dealership will be liable for lost profits if she breaches the contract and thus takes the seller's contractual entitlement, but the consumer as a potential defendant usually does not know the size of the dealer's profits.[119]

---

118. This is still the case with strict liability. We briefly discuss a "tailored" damages award under a negligence regime below. *See infra* part II.C.2.

When bargaining is not allowed, such a tailored damages award yields an expected social surplus of $55, just as would intermediate fixed damages with no bargaining. The expected damages award $E(v_\pi) = 50. Hence, in the absence of bargaining, the defendant will take only if $v_\Delta \geq 50, and thus the $60 defendant will be the only type to take.

119. *See, e.g.,* Victor P. Goldberg, *An Economic Analysis of the Lost-Volume Retail Seller,* 57 S. CAL. L. REV. 283, 295–96 (1984); *see also* Ian Ayres, *Fair Driving: Gender and Race Discrimination in Retail*

Tailoring the amount of liability reduces plaintiffs' incentive to reveal information. A plaintiff can no longer credibly signal whether her valuation is greater or less than the damage amount because tailoring makes the damage amount equal each plaintiff's valuation. This kind of tailoring thus decreases plaintiffs' incentives to engage in Coasean negotiations. In particular, because the tailored damages perfectly compensate a plaintiff for a nonconsensual taking, the plaintiff has nothing to gain from discouraging such a taking.

Plaintiffs with valuations greater than $60 know that they will never be able to sell their entitlements to defendants (whose highest value is $60), and because tailoring provides "taking insurance" they never have an incentive to pay defendants not to take. Accordingly, there is a large class of plaintiffs with relatively high valuations who are indifferent between expressing interest in the two types of bargaining because they know that they will never come to terms with a defendant.

As shown in the Appendix, this model of tailored damages produces a unique equilibrium outcome in which there is much less Coasean trade.[120] Under an untailored liability rule, 30% of plaintiffs succeed in reaching a pre-taking agreement, but under a tailored liability rule only 10% of the plaintiffs trade. In this equilibrium the $60 defendants abstain from bargaining and take nonconsensually, and the $40 defendants buy the entitlement (for $20) from plaintiffs with valuations less than $20. In equilibrium, plaintiffs with valuations of less than $20 have an affirmative incentive to express an interest in selling their entitlement, but tailoring destroys the incentive of all other plaintiffs to bargain because they know *ex ante* that they will not come to terms with either type of defendant. Accordingly, plaintiffs with valuations greater than $20 simply refrain from bargaining if expressing an interest costs even an infinitesimal amount.

Since tailoring eliminates plaintiffs' incentives to bribe defendants not to take, it exacerbates the number of inefficient nonconsensual takings. As shown in Figure 6, under an untailored liability rule, plaintiffs with valuations greater than $85 deterred inefficient takings by bribing defendants not to take. Under a tailored liability rule, however, high-valuing plaintiffs have no incentive to stop these inefficient takings, and the $60 defendants rationally choose not to make serious offers.[121]

Figure 6 also shows that tailoring the liability rule induces more entitlement sales from low-valuing plaintiffs to $40 defendants. Under an

---

Car Negotiations, 104 HARV. L. REV. 817, 818 (1991) (showing that market competition did not eliminate racial and gender discrimination in retail car market).

120. *See infra* app. at pp. 1114–15. Because a large class of plaintiffs is indifferent between expressing interest in a particular kind of Coasean bargain, there are many equilibrium strategies that can produce this unique outcome.

121. The Appendix shows that $60 defendants would rather simply take and pay an expected damage amount of $50 than bargain. *See id.*

untailored rule, low-valuing plaintiffs are reluctant to accept offers to sell their entitlements because they know that half of the offers come from $60 defendants who will take nonconsensually and pay $50. This reluctance causes only plaintiffs with valuations of less than $15 to accept offers from plaintiffs to buy at $32.50. In contrast, under a tailored rule, the plaintiffs know that only $40 defendants will make offers to buy and that these defendants will not take nonconsensually if bargaining fails. Hence, under a tailored rule, the $20 offer (made by a $40 defendant) will be accepted by any plaintiffs with lower valuations.

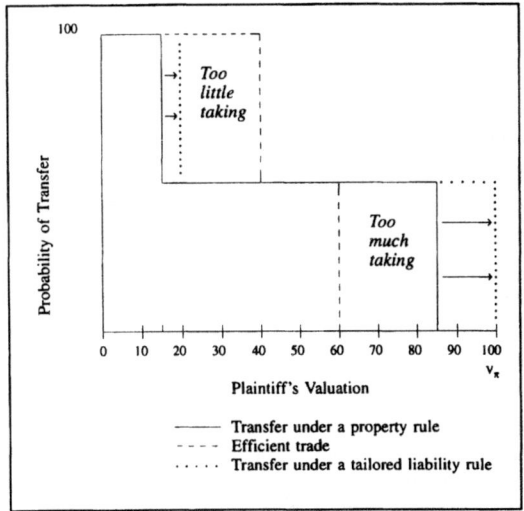

FIGURE 6. *Effect of Tailoring Damages on the Probability of Transfer*

Tailoring thus encourages plaintiffs to engage in one type of Coasean bargain (selling their entitlement), but eliminates their opportunity to engage in the other type of bargain (bribing the defendant not to take). These two effects are not merely offsetting. The expected surplus under a tailored liability rule ($58)[122] is less than that produced under *either* a property rule ($59.75) or the untailored liability rule ($59.88). Moreover, tailoring induces more nonconsensual takings. Under untailored liability regimes, 35% of the negotiations end with nonconsensual takings, as opposed to 50% under tailored liability regimes. Thus, untailored rules are likely to save on court costs both

---

122. $60 with probability 1/2 (i.e., when the $60 plaintiff obtains); if the $40 plaintiff emerges (again with probability 1/2), there is a $40 social surplus 20% of the time and a $60 surplus the other 80% of the time. The $60 comes from the expected value of v_π given v_π>20. *See supra* note 102, tbl. 5.

by reducing the number of decisions and by reducing the costs per decision.[123] In sum, tailoring decreases trade, increases nonconsensual taking, and decreases welfare. These findings highlight the unique benefits of untailored liability rules. Scholars arguing in favor of property rules have seen that the equitable impulse to tailor damages *ex post* may impede efficient negotiation[124]—after all, property damages are typically not tailored to make the plaintiff whole—but the academy has failed to see that untailored liability rules can predominate over both property rules or tailored forms of liability protection.[125]

2. *Tailored Liability (a.k.a. The Negligence Standard)*

Another way that courts can institute tailored awards is not by tailoring the damage amount, but by tailoring the determination of liability. The most common manifestation of such an approach is the familiar negligence standard that Judge Hand articulated in the classic *United States v. Carroll Towing Co.*[126] Under such a standard, the defendant must pay damages to the plaintiff if the court finds that the defendant acted "unreasonably." An important indication of reasonableness is whether the defendant's benefit from taking outweighs the plaintiff's expected cost. Accordingly, we consider a permutation of the model in which the defendant is liable only if the value he gains through taking (v_A) is less than the plaintiff's expected damages at the time of the taking.[127] In the current example, since the plaintiff's damages are distributed uniformly between $0 and $100, the negligence standard is $50. Thus, under this standard, the $40 defendant will be judged negligent when he takes, but the $60 defendant who takes will be judged to have acted reasonably and hence will incur no liability. To concentrate on the element of tailored liability rather than tailored damages, let us assume for now that the court imposes fixed damages of $50 if it finds the defendant negligent.[128] In our earlier discussions, the defendant was strictly liable for any nonconsensual taking; here, however, the court conditions—i.e., tailors—the determination of

---

123. Talley has shown in a formal model that with litigation costs, untailored rules can produce even more negotiations. Talley, *supra* note 43, at 1229–33. The intuition behind this argument is that when litigation costs are a "credible threat," they can act as an effective "tax" on strategic behavior. The prospect of bearing this tax reduces each party's marginal incentive to misrepresent her valuation.

124. Haddock et al., *supra* note 18, at 8–9.

125. *But see* Kathryn E. Spier, *Settlement Bargaining and the Design of Damage Awards*, 10 J.L. ECON. & ORGANIZATION 84, 85 (1994) (finding that untailored rules produce more bargaining than tailored rules and can be more efficient when litigation costs are small).

126. 159 F.2d 169, 173 (2d Cir. 1947).

127. Note that this efficiency criterion is a manifestation of Judge Hand's now famous $PL \geq B$ criterion for negligence, where here $P = 1$, $L = E(v_\pi)$, and $B = v_A$. *See* POSNER, *supra* note 1, at 147–49.

128. As it turns out, even if the court tailored the damage amount to equal the plaintiff's actual damages, v_π, the outcome would be exactly the same from an efficiency standpoint. *See infra* app. at pp. 1114–15. Moreover, the results presented below do not change qualitatively when the fixed liability amount takes on other values.

liability to the facts of the case. The negligence standard gives the defendants private information about who owns the entitlement. The $60 defendants know that they own the property, and the $40 defendants know that they have no legal claim to the property. Crucially, however, a plaintiff, in bargaining with a particular defendant, does not know whether she has a legal claim in the entitlement.

There are, once again, two potential types of transactions that might occur under a negligence standard: First, a high-valuing plaintiff might bribe the non-negligent $60 defendant to abstain from taking; second, a low-valuing plaintiff might sell her entitlement to a $40 defendant, who, absent negotiation, would never take. As it turns out, however, using a negligence standard to tailor the issue of liability destroys the parties' ability to engage in the first type of transaction. Even though a high-valuing plaintiff would want to bribe $60 defendants, the plaintiff cannot determine whether it is bribing a $40 or $60 defendant. Indeed, the $40 defendant will pretend to be a $60 defendant in an attempt to sell what he does not have—a credible threat to take. The plaintiff's uncertainty about whether she is bribing a low-valuing or high-valuing defendant reduces the amount that the plaintiff is willing to pay as a bribe. For example, even the highest-valuing plaintiff would only be willing to pay a $50 bribe.[129] Because a $60 defendant is never liable, however, such a defendant would not offer to sell his right to take for less than $60. As with tailored damage amounts, the tailored negligence standard eliminates plaintiffs' ability to bribe defendants not to take.

In fact, the Appendix shows that tailoring the issue of liability in this negligence model produces the same unique equilibrium outcome as the tailored damages model in the previous Section: Because plaintiffs will never bribe defendants not to take, the $60 defendants will abstain from serious bargaining and simply take nonconsensually; $40 defendants buy the entitlement for $20 from those plaintiffs whose valuations are less than $20.

Tailoring once again decreases a plaintiff's incentive to reveal her type. Although plaintiffs with valuations less than $20 still have an affirmative incentive to express an interest in selling their entitlement, those 80% of plaintiffs with valuations higher than $20 know that in equilibrium they will not be able to engage in either type of Coasean trade. The tailoring of legal consequences under the negligence standard accordingly makes high-valuing plaintiffs indifferent between expressing an interest in the two types of trade. As with tailored damages, high-valuing plaintiffs do not have an *affirmative* incentive to express an interest in selling their entitlement, but they become indifferent to making this implicit misrepresentation. And if there were any cost to expressing an initial interest, 80% of plaintiffs would remain silent.

---

129. The plaintiff whose valuation is v_x will accept that offer if and only if her net gain from the bribe (v_x-σ) exceeds his expected payoff absent negotiation ($v_x/2$).

Both tailoring damages and tailoring liability give one of the bargainers private information about the consequences of nonconsensual taking: When the amount of damages is tailored, the plaintiff has private information about the exercise price of defendant's call option. When the class of defendants who are liable is tailored under a negligence standard, the defendant has private information about who owns the entitlement. Bargainers with private information have a strong incentive to extract an "informational rent" by demanding more favorable terms. In this context, tailoring the consequences of nonconsensual taking causes the parties to change their demands concerning Coasean bribes not to take: Tailored damages rules give the high-valuing plaintiffs additional information and therefore reduce their willingness to pay a bribe (to $0 because the plaintiff would be made whole by any nonconsensual taking); tailored liability rules give the $60 defendants additional information and therefore increase the bribe that they demand, because these defendants incur no liability if they take. In both cases, tailoring amplifies the informational asymmetry and undermines plaintiffs' ability to make efficient Coasean bribes.[130]

Many commentators have suggested that, as a normative issue,

- liability rules are preferable only when transaction costs make contracting prohibitively expensive; and,

- when invoked, liability rules should be tailored to replicate the transactions that parties would have made.[131]

This Section has cast doubt on both of these assertions. We have shown that liability rules can induce more Coasean agreements than property rules and thus might be used even when transaction costs are not prohibitively high. But we have also shown that tailoring legal rules to be contingent on private information can exacerbate bargaining inefficiency. This Section thus not only

---

130. A rule that tailors both liability and damages—incorporating both a $50 negligence standard and imposing liability in the amount of v_x—produces the same equilibrium outcome. Under this doubly tailored scheme, the $60 defendant, as before, is never negligent and values his position at $60. The $40 defendant is always negligent and expects to pay $E(v_x) = \$50$ if he takes noncooperatively. Thus, his reservation utility is 0. Finally, the plaintiff's reservation value reflects an uncompensated taking half of the time and no taking the other half of the time, thus giving $v_x/2$. As discussed in the Appendix, even though there are a number of equilibrium strategy profiles under this legal rule, the only differences in strategy occur with plaintiff types who are never destined to make a bargain; thus, the bargaining *outcome* will be the same for all these equilibria. See *infra* app. at pp. 1114–15.

131. See, e.g., COOTER & ULEN, *supra* note 1, at 107 (supporting first proposition); POSNER, *supra* note 1, at 55–57, 62 n.5. Judge Posner also argues that transaction costs are much more likely to be large with numerous parties. *Id.* at 55. The implication of this position is that property rights are more likely to be socially optimal in the case of bilateral monopolies (as long as the bilateral monopolies themselves do not have a large number of parties involved). In this Article, we argue that this view overlooks the problems of information costs, which can cut the other way: When markets are "thin," information costs are often an extremely pernicious form of transaction costs. In such situations, liability rules have efficiency-enhancing qualities.

expands the classes of cases where liability rules might be appropriate, but also challenges the accepted notion that liability rules should be tailored to replicate the transactions that the parties would otherwise make.[132]

III. "FRACTIONAL" PROPERTY ENTITLEMENTS AND COASEAN IDENTITY CRISES

Up to this point, we have shown that dividing an entitlement by protecting it with a liability rule may be more efficient because entitlement holders may have an incentive to signal whether they value the entitlement more or less than the damage amount. Varying the degree of protection, however, is not the only theoretical axis for Solomonic division. This Part focuses on how specific ownership structures can also facilitate Coasean bargaining through four different types of fractional divisions along probabilistic, temporal, physical, and activity-level dimensions. We argue that these fractional ownership structures can also curb or even eliminate the strategic inefficiencies attributed to bargaining under private information.

The intuition behind the efficiency of fractional property rights is similar to the rationale for dividing ownership in a traditional partnership buy-sell agreement. Partnerships (and close corporations) with two owners often have dissolution provisions that force the instigating owner to name a firm value and then let the other owner choose whether to buy (the other owner's share) or sell (its own share of the firm). Because the party naming the value does not know whether it is the seller or the buyer, it is less likely to misrepresent its valuation. In fact, Peter Cramton, Robert Gibbon, and Paul Klemperer have shown that as long as the ownership shares of the firm are divided fairly evenly, the buy-sell agreement can induce efficient dissolution.[133]

---

132. This result is similar to the finding that contractual default rules that fail to replicate the provisions that the parties would have made can induce the parties to reveal information and bargain more efficiently. *See* Ayres & Gertner, *supra* note 55, at 91.

133. *See* Peter Cramton et al., *Dissolving a Partnership Efficiently*, 55 ECONOMETRICA 615 (1987). This result depends, *inter alia*, on sufficient liquidity among the partners, so that all can choose whether to buy if the named price is too low.

This kind of identity crisis is also present in one traditional method of dividing a dessert between two children: One child cuts, and the other child chooses which piece to take. Because the cutting child knows that the choosing child will pick the larger piece, the dominant cutting strategy is to divide the cake evenly. *See, e.g.*, ROGER FISHER & WILLIAM URY, GETTING TO YES: NEGOTIATING AGREEMENT WITHOUT GIVING IN 86–87 (Bruce Patton ed., 2d ed. 1991). Notice that in this cake-cutting example, however, the identity crisis is used to ensure an equitable division and not an efficient allocation: Even if the one child values the entire cake more than the other, this decision rule will lead to an even division of the cake. (Allocational efficiency only results if the children have identical diminishing marginal utilities for cake).

Another common example of how the identity crisis ensures allocational efficiency arises in informal gambling arrangements: Two friends who want to bet on a sporting event agree that one person will choose the point spread, and the other person will then choose which side of the bet to take. Again, because the person choosing the point spread does not know whether she is offering to buy or to sell, she has a strong incentive to state her actual expectation.

As discussed in Part II, academics have long recognized that private valuations can significantly inhibit efficient trade as sellers "shade up" and buyers "shade down" their private valuations.[134] This Part shows that, just as in a buy-sell agreement, the mere existence of private information need not always result in inefficient behavior, and the consequent loss of potential gains to trade, when bargaining occurs in the shadow of "fractional" property rights. In particular, we show that partial entitlements tend to mitigate the adverse incentive for individuals to bargain deceptively, because the attendant ownership structure creates ambiguity *a priori* about who ultimately will be the buyer and the seller.[135] As a consequence of this ambiguity, the players are uncertain about whether they should overstate or understate their valuations during bargaining. The parties' respective "identity crisis"—not knowing whether they will end up as buyers or sellers—can induce them to distort their true valuations less than they would if one party owned an undivided, or fee simple, property interest in the underlying asset. The identity crisis that these partial property rights create, we argue, can result in substantial efficiency gains, and even in "first best" outcomes.

A. *Probabilistic Divisions*

We first examine the effect of allocating property rights probabilistically. A probabilistic property rule randomly awards one of the litigants an undivided property right according to some publicly known probability distribution. Such a situation might occur when there is underlying uncertainty about the court's opinion in a case of first impression, or when a legal rule reflects contingent

---

134. *See* Kalyan Chatterjee & William Samuelson, *Bargaining Under Incomplete Information*, 31 OPERATIONS RES. 835 (1983); Roger Myerson & Mark Satterthwaite, *Efficient Mechanisms for Bilateral Trading*, 29 J. ECON. THEORY 265 (1983).

135. The results in this Section are presaged by the seminal work of Johnston, *supra* note 29; *see* Cramton et al., *supra* note 133; *see also* Talley, *supra* note 43 (applying variation of this notion explicitly to renegotiation of liquidated damages clauses). Johnston's work on this topic uses a model of one-sided incomplete information (with the plaintiff), and a two-period skimming model that is derived from Drew Fudenberg & Jean Tirole, *Sequential Bargaining with Incomplete Information*, 50 REV. ECON. STUD. 221 (1983). Johnston compares three types of property rules: one in which the property rule is clearly assigned *ex ante*; another in which the property right assignment depends on a judicial balancing test *ex post*; and a final one in which the judicial balancing test is "imprecise" (in a rather precise way). He finds that the last entitlement system is the only one (under certain conditions) that supports equilibria entailing efficient Coasean transactions (e.g., the defendant "buys" the entitlement only when it is efficient for him to do so). *See* Johnston, *supra* note 29.

Johnston clearly identifies the "countervailing incentives" effect that divided entitlements might have, which produces the possibility that either party can be a buyer or a seller. *Id.* at 6–7. Yet while his model partially illustrates this fundamental insight, it allows only for "buy offers" from the defendant; the rules of his game do not allow offers to sell. Our model diverges from his in allowing either party to "purchase" the other party's share of the underlying legal asset.

Our model also differs from Johnston's approach in one other major way. While he concentrates on the beneficial role of "*ex post* balancing" as a source of efficiency enhancing, we broaden the application of this analysis to include legal entitlements that are "partial" in nature, but that need not be reduced to "*ex post* balancing." In fact, the rules we analyze here are completely clear from the *ex ante* stage.

"standards" rather than rules.[136] Litigation, as is well recognized, can also involve significant uncertainty about court outcomes.[137] We show in this Section that such probabilistic entitlements can create a "countervailing effect" upon bargainers' respective incentives to lie: The bargainers still would like to shade their representations of value,[138] but uncertain ownership dampens the degree of misrepresentation that occurs.[139]

As in the canonical example given earlier, we suppose that both parties' private valuations (v_π and v_A) vary between \$0 and \$100 with uniform probability density. Absent a negotiated agreement, the court randomly awards undivided ownership of the entitlement; this assignment is injunctive in nature. For simplicity, suppose the court flips the analogue of a "loaded coin"[140] to determine ownership: The plaintiff receives the entitlement with probability q, and the defendant receives the entitlement with probability (1-q), where q is some number between 0 and 1.[141] Note that when q = 0, it is common knowledge that the court will award the defendant an undivided interest in the entitlement, and when q = 1, the plaintiff has clear ownership. This loaded coin analogy has a natural legal interpretation: Increasingly large values of q correspond to greater degrees of "pro-plaintiff" bias among the courts determining property entitlements.[142]

Before moving on, it is important to note that the probability distribution that the court uses is *common knowledge* to both parties. The negligence

---

136. Johnston explicitly discusses the differences in bargaining behavior under rules versus standards. Johnston, *supra* note 29, at 9–28. For a description of his results in relation to ours, see *supra* note 135.

137. *See, e.g.,* COOTER & ULEN, *supra* note 1, at 490–91.

138. With liability rules, the parties knew which way to shade, but the existence of the liability call option created a ceiling to the plaintiff's overstatement of her valuation of the entitlement and a floor to the plaintiff's understatement of her valuation of the call option.

139. *See* Brown & Ayres, *supra* note 15, at 347 (showing that commitment to break off bargaining creates countervailing incentive in "solicit offer" mediation game); Johnston, *supra* note 29, at 8; *see also* Merges, *supra* note 39, at 25–28 (arguing that probabilistic use of "reverse doctrine of equivalents" in patent law can induce settlement).

140. The exact nature of the coin's bias—i.e., that we get "heads" with probability q and "tails" with probability (1-q)—must be common knowledge.

141. Jon Elster has similarly suggested that courts might use a coin toss to resolve child custody disputes between divorcing parents who are both found to be fit. ELSTER, *supra* note 6, at 163. In contrast to our theory, Elster's proposal of probabilistic custody awards is not made to promote bargaining, but because the divorcing couple cannot reach consensual agreement, and because the court cannot rationally divine which parent would better serve the interests of the children. *Id.* at 134–50. Indeed, Elster argues that even when an optimal procedure for awarding custody exists, divorcing couples are unlikely to agree to use it:

> [The optimal procedure] could be derived on the basis of (a) the threat point, (b) the utilities associated with the pure outcomes and (c) the particular solution concept adopted. Each of these, however, would lend itself to strategic or nonstrategic posturing or misrepresentation. . . . [The parties] might exaggerate the extent to which they would suffer if their preferred outcome were not chosen.

Id. at 169. Elster does not explore, however, the possibility that probabilistic court determination might induce more consensual resolution prior to trial.

142. Also, note that we can think of q as a long-run frequency that the parties view as a probability. Thus, q might simply refer to a lack of uniformity among jurisdictions, or, more appropriately, among judges within one jurisdiction. In general, then, this type of probabilistic entitlement gives the plaintiff an "inside" option of qv_π, and the defendant an exit option of $(1-q)v_A$.

standard also created uncertainty about who owned the legal entitlement, but under a tailored liability rule, the defendant had private information about whether its taking would give rise to any liability. Here, by contrast, the court's probabilistic division of the underlying asset is publicly known.[143]

Given this probabilistic legal "shadow," we can stylize a bargaining game that will illustrate how probabilistic entitlements can induce more truthful representations. The bargaining game is a type of "double auction" that is fairly familiar in the bargaining literature.[144] It begins with each party simultaneously submitting a "report" of her valuation (which need not be truthful[145]), which the court will use—along with the report of the other party—to determine (1) who ultimately receives absolute ownership, and (2) the price of purchasing the other party's probabilistic share in the underlying asset. Each of the parties' reports thus represents an offer to be bound by certain terms of trade if the other side submits a mirror-image offer: Each of the offerors agrees to sell all claims to the entitlement if her reported valuation is lower, and she agrees to buy if her reported offer is higher.[146] *Crucial to this analysis is that when the parties submit their bids, each is uncertain about whether her report will ultimately represent an offer to buy or to sell.*[147] The party submitting the highest bid becomes the "buyer" of the entitlement and receives the entitlement in full, but in return she must pay the "seller" a purchase price for the entitlement. We assume that the price is calculated by "splitting the difference" between the two reports (i.e., averaging them), and then *discounting* that amount by the seller's initial probabilistic share in the

---

143. This conclusion is consistent with Johnston's finding that "*ex post* balancing" becomes more efficient when judicial error is introduced. *See* Johnston, *supra* note 29, at 8.

Our assumption that the bargainers' assessment of adjudication is the same also diverges from many litigation models that predict settlement unless the litigants are overly optimistic about their prospects in court. *See, e.g.,* POSNER, *supra* note 1, at 436; John P. Gould, *The Economics of Legal Conflicts*, 2 J. LEGAL STUD. 279, 285–88 (1973). In those models, the likelihood of agreement turns only on the degree of agreement about the plaintiff's prospect of winning at trial, not on the agreed probability level. Thus, in a world where the parties have private assessments about the likely amount of damages, the optimism model predicts that if the parties agree on the probability of a plaintiff trial victory, the likelihood of settlement should not depend on whether this agreed probability is 50% or 100%. Allowing the parties to negotiate before a taking, however, changes this result. This Section shows that a 50% probability might increase the likelihood of a consensual resolution, compared to non-probabilistic allocation.

144. *See* Chatterjee & Samuelson, *supra* note 134, at 837–38; Kennan & Wilson, *supra* note 47, at 88.

145. This procedure is closely related to examples of "bargaining mechanisms" analyzed elsewhere. *See, e.g.,* Myerson & Satterthwaite, *supra* note 134; Talley, *supra* note 43; Kathryn Spier, Optimal Mechanisms for Pretrial Bargaining (1989) (unpublished manuscript, on file with authors).

146. The use of an analogous simultaneous-offers mechanism can be found in Brown & Ayres, *supra* note 15. While the exchange of these simultaneous incomplete offers restricts the parties to a highly stylized form of bargaining, the beneficial countervailing effect of obscuring the buyer's and seller's identities carries over to other bargaining games. For example, Cramton, Gibbons, and Klemperer note that the efficiency results of our stylized game carry over to more generalized rules, such as not "splitting the difference" between the parties' bids, but rather using a weighted average with weight k between 0 and 1 (often called a "k + 1 price auction"). Cramton et al., *supra* note 133, at 624–25.

147. Note that this uncertainty is not always present, such as when q = 0 or 1, or when v_x or v_Δ is on an extreme. The presence of this uncertainty for at least *some* player types, however, is what generates our identity crisis result.

property right. Thus, assume for example that q = 1/2 (thus giving each party an equal chance at winning in court), and that the plaintiff submits a report of $50 while the defendant bids $30; the above rules mandate that the plaintiff shall receive an undivided ownership interest, but that she must compensate the defendant with $20 in return.[148]

Calculating the equilibrium strategies of this game is somewhat technical, and we therefore relegate it to the Appendix.[149] The core result is that the plaintiff will buy the defendant's probabilistic claim to the entitlement if and only if:

$$v_\pi \geq v_\Delta + 25 - 50q.$$

In all other cases, the defendant will buy the plaintiff's probabilistic claim. From the above expression, it is possible to "describe" the extent of inefficiency for any probabilistic division (i.e., any value of q). First, notice that when the plaintiff has no chance of winning in court (q = 0), she will "purchase" the entitlement from the defendant only when v_π exceeds v_Δ by 25. Symmetrically, when q = 1—corresponding to absolute plaintiff bias—the defendant will purchase only when v_Δ exceeds v_π by $25.[150] In both cases, this $25 bid-ask spread prevents plaintiffs and defendants from consummating transactions that could improve social efficiency. The total social surplus in this case is equal to $64.06. When the plaintiff and the defendant each have a 50% chance of winning in court (q = 1/2), however, the plaintiff purchases the defendant's probabilistic claim if and only if the plaintiff has a high valuation ($v_\pi \geq v_\Delta$); this is *precisely* the condition for efficiency—i.e., that the party valuing the legal entitlement the most should possess it. As Figure 7 illustrates, the probabilistic division of q = 1/2 maximizes expected social welfare, which in this case is equal to its first-best level of $66.67.[151]

---

148. This $20 amount is simply the average of the bids ($40) multiplied by the probability of the defendant prevailing in court (or 1/2).

149. *See infra* app. at pp. 1116–17. The equilibrium derived in the Appendix is the unique *symmetric* and *monotone equilibrium*. By "symmetric," we mean the equilibria that entail identical strategies for the two same-type players when they are in similar positions. For instance, a symmetric equilibrium mandates that a plaintiff with valuation of $25 when q = 1/4 should have the same strategy as a defendant with valuation of $25 when q = 3/4. By monotone, we mean that the equilibrium strategies imply that both players' reports should increase (weakly) as their private valuations increase. There are a number of asymmetric and nonmonotonic equilibria of this game, but the intuitive appeal of the symmetric equilibrium leads us to believe that it is the most plausible. *See* Chatterjee & Samuelson, *supra* note 134, at 849–50.

150. This result is well recognized in Brown & Ayres, *supra* note 15, at 342; Chatterjee & Samuelson, *supra* note 134, at 839–42.

151. The equations from which these figures are calculated are provided *infra* app. at pp. 1116–17.

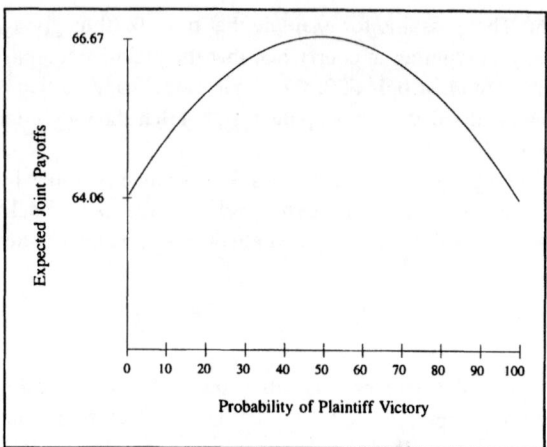

FIGURE 7. *Effect of Varying the Plaintiff's Fractional Entitlement on Expected Joint Payoffs*

The identity-crisis intuition for the efficiency effect of probabilistic divisions is different from the information-forcing intuition for liability rules discussed in Part II. Under a liability rule regime, even though there are two types of Coasean bargains, each plaintiff is interested in only one of the two types. We showed in Part II that plaintiffs credibly signal whether their valuation is above or below the damage amount by expressing an interest in one of the two types of trade. The willingness of plaintiffs to so signal enhances efficiency by (1) eliminating some of the private information, and (2) bounding the range of offers and bids that the defendant can propose, thereby decreasing the defendant's "room to lie" (even though he still has the incentive to lie). In contrast, probabilistic entitlements, along with other forms of fractional entitlements, do not necessarily induce either party to "self-select" into discrete groups, nor does such an entitlement system constrain either party's "room" to exaggerate her valuation. Rather, the identity crisis—uncertainty about whether a bargainer will ultimately become a buyer or a seller—reduces both parties' *incentives* to lie.[152]

---

152. This assertion does not imply that the parties do not distort their valuations at all. Indeed, when q = 1/2, *low*-valuing parties will perceive themselves as likely sellers and thus will slightly overstate their private valuations. Conversely, *high*-valuing parties will perceive themselves as likely sellers and will slightly understate their valuations.

For instance, consider the optimal report of the plaintiff π in this game:

$$r_\pi^*(v_\pi) = \tfrac{2}{3}v_\pi + \tfrac{25}{3} + \tfrac{50q}{3}$$

When q = 1/2, it is easy to confirm that $v_\pi < r_\pi^*(v_\pi)$ whenever $v_\pi < 50$, and $v_\pi > r_\pi^*(v_\pi)$ whenever $v_\pi > 50$. When $v_\pi = 50$, the plaintiff tells the truth. Even with some lying, first-best efficiency is possible. *See* Cramton et al., *supra* note 133, at 624.

Although probabilistic entitlements have a strong efficiency advantage, they bring a number of significant procedural and philosophical disadvantages. While we discuss most of these at length later, one disadvantage stands out in particular. Sustaining a probabilistic property rights system forces the courts to eschew rulelike decision making so as to preserve the random outcomes that induce Coasean efficiency. As many have noted, however, legal standards often evolve inexorably toward rules.[153] Indeed, the legal system's use of analogy and precedent is inconsistent with a decision-making process that ultimately resembles a flip of a coin. On the other hand, the committing of legal decision making to juries operating under vague instructions, or even unarticulated demands for equity, might be seen as an existing mechanism that resists the pull toward predictability.

B. *Activity-Level Divisions*[154]

Thus far, we have assumed for simplicity that the defendant's act of taking is binary, or "all-or-nothing," in nature. Either the defendant breaches, or he does not; either the factory pollutes, or it does not; either the product infringes, or it does not. In many real-world applications, however, the defendant may be able to appropriate only a *portion* of the plaintiff's enjoyment of the underlying legal asset.

Examples of such "activity-level" rules abound. In a tort context, for example, a factory that wishes to dump one ton of waste into a river may be endowed with a property right to dump up to one-half a ton. This reduced activity level may rule out certain uses of the river by the surrounding community, such as drinking, but it may not be so damaging as to rule out other uses, such as fishing or lawn watering. Thus, the factory dumping hampers, but does not destroy, the community's enjoyment of the river. In a criminal law environment, speed limits endow drivers with a property right to drive up to sixty-five miles per hour on the highway, but those who drive too fast above the limit may be subject to punitive fines that serve injunctive purposes.[155]

These activity-level limitations that give another user the right to enjoin represent another manifestation of divided entitlements. In the pollution example, the factory owns a property interest in the first one-half ton of

---

153. *E.g.*, Johnston, *supra* note 29; Louis Kaplow, *Rules vs. Standards: An Economic Analysis*, 42 DUKE L.J. 557, 578–79 (1992). *But see* Rose, *supra* note 27, at 580–90 (illustrating how several laws of property oscillate back and forth between rules and standards).

154. This Section is inspired by Mitchell Polinsky's early insights into Coasean negotiations. *See, e.g.*, Polinsky, *supra* note 19; Polinsky, *supra* note 116.

155. While not all states impose punitive sanctions on speeders, coauthor Talley's empirical observations while driving between California and New Mexico indicate that this phenomenon is prevalent in Arizona. Note, however, that for ordinary speeding fines, the entitlement system is more like the liability rule system analyzed above.

pollution rights, and the residents own the right to enjoin all pollution beyond this amount. This entitlement division once again gives rise to two different types of bargains: The factory may purchase the right to increase the amount of pollution, or the residents may bribe the factory to produce less.[156]

It turns out that we can analyze activity-level limitations by using the previous Section's model of probabilistic assignments. To adopt the tort example as an illustrative device, consider a factory that needs to dispose of one ton of industrial waste. Suppose that the factory would pay up to v_Δ to be able to dump its ton of waste into a local river,[157] and that this valuation is privately known, distributed uniformly between $0 and $100. Suppose a downstream landowner values the unpolluted river at v_π, again privately known and identically distributed.[158] For simplicity, we assume that payoffs to the factory and downstream landowner will be proportional to the percentage of a ton that is released—e.g., if the factory were to dump one-fourth of a ton into the river, the factory's payoff would be $v_\Delta/4$ and the landowner's payoff would be $3v_\pi/4$.[159]

An undivided property entitlement would endow either the factory or the landowner with unperturbed use of the stream. Under a limited activity-level rule, however, courts might only allow the factory to dump some fraction of the ton of its waste material into the river free of charge and unimpeded by the downstream landowner; beyond that fraction, the landowner is protected by injunctive relief. This limited activity-level rule would allow the factory to bargain for the right to pollute more or allow the downstream landowner to bargain to restrict the factory's right to pollute.

Under these assumptions, activity-level limitations are isomorphic to the probabilistic allocations described above. If we interpret q as the fraction of the ton that the community can enjoin absent a negotiated outcome (rather than a probability), then a double auction procedure will produce the same

---

156. The speed limit example is less clearly a divided entitlement because (except in Chicago) it is difficult to negotiate with representatives of the state for the right to drive faster.

157. One might interpret v_Δ in this case to represent the amount that the factory knows it would have to pay to dispose of the waste outside the locality.

158. We assume that pollution affects only a single downstream landowner or that the residents of the downstream community have devised a procedural mechanism to overcome free-rider problems. Recall from the Introduction that the division of entitlements *among* parties is not the focus of this Article. Rather, we are concerned with the division of entitlements *between* parties. A number of economists, however, have proposed "pivot mechanisms" that allow for efficient decisions regarding public-good provision. *See, e.g.,* DAVID M. KREPS, A COURSE IN MICROECONOMIC THEORY 704–14 (1991).

159. Implicit in these figures is the assumption of a constant marginal effect of pollution on both parties' payoffs. Hence, for each infinitesimal amount of pollution in the lake, dq, the factory benefits by $v_\Delta dq$ and the community is injured by $v_\pi dq$. In this formulation, the optimal level of pollution is 0 if $v_\Delta < v_\pi$, 1 if $v_\Delta > v_\pi$, and indeterminate if $v_\Delta = v_\pi$. This example is limited in its generality, since it implies that the optimal outcome is generically binary. In fact, such a constant-returns utility structure is not often likely to hold in practice. We conjecture that it is possible to use a slightly different model in which the first-best level of pollution is somewhere on the interior, and that such a model would have the same properties as that discussed in the text.

equilibrium strategies.[160] As before, if either party held an undivided interest in the control of the stream, there would be a $25 bid-ask spread between the buyer and the seller of the right, a spread that would confound efficient Coasean exchanges. Consequently, the best that the legal system can do in this bargaining scheme is to endow the factory with a property right to dump up to one-half ton of waste into the river, and to allow the community to enjoin the dumping of any more than that half ton.

The above example of an activity-level division underscores our assertion that the "identity crisis" phenomenon studied above can occur in non-probabilistic contexts. Indeed, it is possible for an activity-level division to crystalize into a rulelike form through time without adversely affecting the "identity crisis" phenomenon that promotes Coasean efficiency. At least for legal rights that can be taken in part, a system of partial property rights is feasible and exists in various legal contexts.

C. *Temporal and Physical Divisions*

Some entitlements can also be divided temporally or physically. In property and contract law, for example, title to land or a piece of capital equipment is often divided into a term of years held by one party and a remainder interest held by another.[161] Another example is the relationship between an original patentee and an inventor of a "new use" for the patentee's invention, in which the original patentee has monopoly rights over her original invention until expiration, upon which the new use entrant can pursue the distribution, use, and sale of her innovative addition unimpeded.[162] Physical partitions of complementary parcels of land are even more easily accomplished and any joint tenant or tenant in common has a legal right to seek such a partition.

The model used above to examine probabilistic and activity-level divisions maps directly into this situation as well, with only minor alterations. We illustrate this possibility with an example of temporally divided claims to a piece of property. Suppose that the parties' respective entitlement valuations (denoted before as v_π and v_Δ) represent their payoffs *per period* (rather than their aggregate payoff), and that these valuations are distributed uniformly and

---

160. Given q (which we note must be between 0 and 1), the community's reservation payoff is equal to q times its private valuation, and the factory's payoff equals (1-q) times its private valuation. Since these reservation payoffs are identical to those corresponding to a q-probability assignment of the entitlement to the plaintiff (and a probability assignment of (1-q) to the defendant), the equilibrium strategies must be the same as in the previous Section.

161. Consider, for instance, a fee simple determinable held by A until B reaches her 25th birthday, with the remainder to B.

162. *See, e.g.*, Merges, *supra* note 39, at 5–10 (describing how patent entitlements are divided between original "pioneer" and subsequent "improver" of invention); *infra* part IV.C.1. Note that in the pre-expiration period, the original patentee cannot extend the use of the invention to the entrant's new use if the entrant has patent protection over such a use.

independently between \$0 and \$10 (rather than between \$0 and \$100 as before). Absent bargaining, the plaintiff has title to the asset for a certain period of time (call this number t), with the remainder going to the defendant in perpetuity.[163] At an illustrative discount rate of 10%, it is straightforward to show that in present value, each party's privately known payoff from permanent ownership lies uniformly between \$0 and \$100, just as in our previous example.[164]

The length of the plaintiff's claim to the asset determines, in a sense, what proportion of the asset the plaintiff owns. For example, because of discounting, either the plaintiff or the defendant should be indifferent between receiving a claim to the first 6.93 years or receiving a claim to all subsequent years (in perpetuity).[165] Thus, this temporal division effectively divides the asset between them equally and is analogous to the optimal division of setting q = 1/2 in the probabilistic entitlement model. By varying the term of years from zero to infinity, the entitlement may be partitioned in the same way that probabilistic and activity limitations allowed the entitlement proportions to vary. If the plaintiff and the defendant have different per period valuations, then it will be efficient for the higher valuer to buy the other side's claim to the asset. As in the earlier examples, it turns out that with a 6.93-year partition, the bargaining game outlined in the probabilistic entitlement section will again produce first-best efficiency.

This Part has illustrated numerous ways for efficiency-minded lawmakers to divide an entitlement "fractionally": Probabilistic, activity-level, physical,

---

163. The order or exact partitioning of the terms of ownership are not particularly relevant so long as they are mutually exclusive and exhaustive through time, and so long as the parties' enjoyment is not rivalrous through time. For instance, it would be unwise to award a lumber company a term-of-years property interest over an old-growth forest, with the remainder to the spotted owl. The lumber company's initial exploitation of the natural resources would have a profound effect on the enjoyment that the spotted owl might receive after the term expires.

164. The present discounted value of permanent ownership for a party with valuation v_i is equal to:

$$PDV_i(v_i, r) = \int_{t=0}^{\infty} v_i e^{-rt} dt$$

where r denotes the interest rate. Substituting $r = 1/10$ into the above expression and integrating, the above expression becomes:

$$PDV_i(v_i, r) = \int_{t=0}^{\infty} v_i e^{-t/10} dt = 10 v_i.$$

Since v_i is assumed to be between \$0 and \$10 with equal probability, the party's present value of permanent ownership must lie between \$0 and \$100, again with equal probability.

165. Consider a division set at t^* years. The entitlement holder will value her term-of-years entitlement at exactly half of a fee simple entitlement when and only when:

$$\int_0^{t^*} v_i e^{-t/10} dt = \frac{1}{2} \cdot \int_0^{\infty} v_i e^{-t/10} dt,$$

which occurs at $t^* = (10)\ln(2) = 6.93$.

and temporal divisions can create an identity crisis that enhances bargaining efficiency. While liability rules channel high- and low-valuing plaintiffs to different types of Coasean bargains, and thereby constrain their "room" to lie, fractional property rights make it difficult for the parties to choose between the different types of Coasean trade, and thereby constrain their incentives to lie. The next Part draws out the implications of these results and also points to limiting principles.

IV. CHOOSING AMONG ENTITLEMENT FORMS

The previous two Parts have illustrated that divided entitlements can enhance welfare by promoting greater revelation of information during bargaining. The ability of liability rules to induce self-selection among entitlement holders and the ability of fractional property rights to create a valuable countervailing incentive for both parties can promote more efficient trade than undivided property protection. Nevertheless, these illustrations alone are of limited guidance to legal policymakers who not only must decide which type of entitlement structure to implement, but also must consider the panoply of other factors that a stylized model inevitably fails to consider. Below, we respond to this shortcoming by adding some relational "flesh" to our theoretical observations.

This Part begins by analyzing the choice between divided and undivided entitlement allocations. In particular, we identify four factors that militate against the efficiency of divided entitlements and suggest that the presence of any one of these factors might undermine the efficiency of divided entitlements in promoting pre-taking trade. Then, assuming that the conditions are ripe for entitlement division, this Part proceeds to examine which type of division is most likely to promote efficient trade.

Before proceeding, however, we remind the reader of an important caveat: Our analysis is restricted to how "efficiency-minded" lawmakers might pursue the narrow goal of maximizing gains from trade. Lawmakers might respond to a myriad of other legitimate policy goals that we do not address explicitly in this Part.[166] Nevertheless, while there is often a conflict between efficiency and equity,[167] divided entitlements can actually further *both* goals. In addition to enhancing efficiency, Solomonic entitlements also tend to equalize, at least among the bargainers, the distribution of wealth (in comparison with undivided entitlements allocated to individuals).

---

166. For instance, we have assumed throughout that underlying legal rights are "commodifiable" and "commensurable." *See supra* note 37. If they are not, the notion of efficient trade tends to lose its meaning.

167. *See, e.g.*, Richard A. Posner, *Essay: The Efficiency and the Efficacy of Title VII*, 136 U. PA. L. REV. 513, 515–16 (1987) (dismissing argument that Title VII is efficient and pointing to its equity objectives).

A. *Divided vs. Undivided Entitlements: Four Factors Militating Against the Use of Entitlement Division*

While the earlier analysis illustrates *how* divided entitlements might facilitate Coasean trade, we do not conclude that efficiency-minded lawmakers should uniformly reject the "undivided" species of property rules approximated by "fee simple" ownership and forms of strong legal protection. While promoting Coasean trade can be determinative in the choice of entitlement form, this Section identifies other aspects of efficiency that Solomonic allocations might impair. As an initial matter, the structural impediments to pre-taking negotiations might be so great that the facilitating effects of liability rules or partial property rules are not sufficient to induce any bargaining. For example, the class of potential automobile tortfeasors is so large and amorphous that it would be impractical to imagine any sort of legal reform inducing pre-taking negotiation. Thus, dividing entitlements to facilitate Coasean trade will only be appropriate when the transactional barriers to trade can at least be surmounted.[168]

Yet even when this condition is satisfied, so that divided entitlements could potentially mitigate the inefficiencies of bargainers' private valuations, other factors might still make undivided entitlements more efficient. In particular, this Section explores how a Solomonic entitlement can itself exacerbate these alternative forms of transaction costs. We also show how variations on the information structure underlying bargaining and tailored divisions can undermine the incentives that Solomonic bargainers might otherwise have to reveal information. Explicitly, we consider three such exceptions:

   (1) *Solomonic entitlements can induce underinvestment.* Divided entitlements can undermine the incentives of any individual to develop an entitlement. For example, under a liability rule regime, the nominal owner might have an inefficiently weak incentive to make asset-specific investments, if she is only likely to recoup a proportion of the benefits in later bargaining.[169]

   (2) *Solomonic entitlements can exacerbate the hold-up problem.* If lawmakers misidentify those parties who might have the highest

---

168. Even if it is inadvisable to use divided entitlements to promote trade, we might still have independent reasons for using them. Insurmountable transaction costs also undermine one of the primary rationales for property rules (i.e., the contractual channeling of goods to the highest-valuing owner). Thus, one of the central insights of Calabresi and Melamed is that when such transaction costs are prohibitively high, liability rules or activity-level limitations might be appropriate. Calabresi & Melamed, *supra* note 12.

169. *See, e.g.*, Benjamin Klein et al., *Vertical Integration, Appropriable Rents, and the Competitive Contracting Process*, 21 J.L. & ECON. 297, 307–24 (1978) (discussing lack of incentive to invest in firm-specific assets when contracting, instead of vertical integration, is employed to secure such assets).

valuations—by (a) allocating Solomonic claims to people who are commonly known to have low valuations, or (b) failing to allocate claims to people who are commonly known to have potentially the highest valuations—then this entitlement division can induce collective-action inefficiency.[170] The holdout problem of multiple parties selling parcels to a single large user, discussed above, is a classic example of this inefficiency.[171]

(3) *Solomonic entitlements can impede competition.* When a potential seller owns an undivided interest in an entitlement, competition among several potential buyers can mitigate the strategic inefficiencies created by the seller's and buyers' private information. Dividing Solomonic claims among the potential buyers can impede this competitive effect. For example, we will show that if each buyer has an option to take the entitlement, a high-valuing seller may be unwilling to bribe all of the potential buyers not to take. Accordingly, divided entitlements are most likely to facilitate trade when the two Solomonic claim holders are bargaining to capture gains of trade that are idiosyncratic to their relationship.[172] Idiosyncratic gains from trade are often present, for example, when people try to renegotiate a contractual obligation[173] or when merchants have made relation-specific investments.[174] More prosaically, Solomonic entitlements might facilitate capturing these "idiosyncratic gains of trade" whenever it is clear that two people are the most efficient trading partners, but it is not clear whether gains from trade exist.[175]

1. *The Underinvestment Trade-Off*

This Article has shown that dividing an entitlement between two bargainers can mitigate the inefficiency caused by the bargainers' private

---

170. For instance, the FCC traditionally utilized random lotteries—a form of divided entitlement—to allocate rights to new bandwidths in the broadcast spectrum. Because FCC regulations allowed all applicants to enter the lottery, the FCC was bombarded with hundreds of thousands of applications, many from parties that intended only to speculate in the market. The FCC's inability to discriminate between speculators and bona fide prospective owners forced it to spread the ownership shares so thinly that Coasean bargaining was virtually impossible. The FCC has now adopted an auction system to allocate these rights. *See* John McMillan, *Selling Spectrum Rights,* J. ECON. PERSP., Summer 1994, at 145.

171. *See supra* note 1 and accompanying text.

172. In economics terminology, the two negotiators have a "bilateral monopoly" over the creation of these potential gains from trade. POSNER, *supra* note 1, at 55–58.

173. When covering is unavailable, the buyer and seller often can enhance gains of trade by renegotiating an original contract's terms of performance.

174. *See* WILLIAMSON, *supra* note 41, at 54–56.

175. For example, it might be clear that only one of two neighboring landowners is the most valuable owner on a particular easement, but it might not be clear who has the higher valuation.

valuations. The contractual inefficiency caused by such private information is often called "adverse selection."[176] Although adverse selection represents an important cause of inefficiency in bargaining, it is not the only cause. Indeed, contracts often cannot specify types of behavior that increase the expected gains from trade. If courts are unable to observe certain types of hidden behavior, a contractual provision will not be able to mandate efficient performance. In economic terms, these aspects of performance that contract law cannot regulate are often termed "non-contractible,"[177] and the failure to regulate these aspects gives rise to "moral hazard."[178] Moral hazard—i.e., the inability to control individual behavior contractually—can lead to dramatic departures from efficiency.[179]

Attempts to remedy adverse selection often exacerbate moral hazard.[180] This Article's findings provide no exception. In particular, Solomonic entitlements may give bargainers suboptimal prebargaining incentives to make value-enhancing investments. For example, the nominal owner of land is less likely to make efficient improvements on her land if her ownership is protected by an untailored liability rule or a fractional property rule. Divided claims to a single resource can thus lead to a tragedy of the commons, as the multiple claimants engage in the moral hazard of overuse, in not accounting for the effect of their use on other claimants.[181] Even though it would be in the parties' joint interest to develop the asset efficiently, in many contexts the parties do not have a realistic opportunity to bargain before important investment decisions are made, and individual investors cannot be confident that they will receive adequate compensation in subsequent bargaining for prior (marginal) investments.[182] Thus, policymakers often face a trade-off in choosing legal rules to constrain the twin evils. This fundamental tension between adverse selection and moral hazard limits the applicability of Solomonic entitlements, because in many contexts Solomonic entitlements will

---

176. PAUL MILGROM & JOHN ROBERTS, ECONOMICS, ORGANIZATION AND MANAGEMENT 149 (1992). Adverse selection is often referred to as the problem of "hidden type" or "hidden preferences." *See* Brown & Ayres, *supra* note 15, at 327–28. The term was inspired by the disproportionate tendency for sick persons to obtain insurance. *Id.* at 328 n.14.

177. *See, e.g.,* Ayres & Gertner, *supra* note 74, at 741.

178. The term "moral hazard" originated in the insurance context from the tendency of insured people to take more risk. *See* Brown & Ayres, *supra* note 15, at 328 n.14.

179. *Id.* at 328.

180. *See* Robert H. Gertner & Geoffrey P. Miller, Settlement Escrows 14–33 (Chicago Law & Economics Working Paper No. 25 (2d Series)) (The University of Chicago Law School, 1994) (arguing that settlement escrow may mitigate adverse selection inefficiency but exacerbate moral hazard in claiming activity).

181. *See, e.g.,* POSNER, *supra* note 1, at 63–66; Garrett Hardin, *The Tragedy of the Commons,* 162 SCIENCE 1243 (1968).

182. Tailored liability rules have similar drawbacks. Interestingly, however, their shortcomings stem from inefficient *overinvestment* rather than underinvestment. Under tailored liability rules, for instance, the plaintiff is always insured against a taking by the defendant. As such, the plaintiff may have an excessive incentive to make reliance expenditures. *See, e.g.,* Steven Shavell, *Damage Measures for Breach of Contract,* 11 BELL J. ECON. 466, 472 (1980).

produce moral hazard inefficiencies that dwarf any reduction in adverse-selection inefficiency. Allocating an undivided property right to the resource is often the optimal solution.[183]

Nevertheless, the potential for moral-hazard inefficiency is not ubiquitous in equally virulent forms. Divided entitlements are less likely to be efficient when moral-hazard inefficiency is a primary concern, but may still be appropriate when adverse selection is the primary impediment to efficiency. Moreover, to the extent that Solomonic allocations encourage the migration of assets to the highest-valuing user, these allocations can enhance the investment decisions that take place *after* Coasean trade. By producing less efficient bargaining, undivided property rules can lead to less efficient *postbargaining* investments, because if bargaining fails to transfer an asset to the highest valuer, the lower-valuing owner is likely to have a suboptimal incentive to develop the asset after the negotiation. Accordingly, the tension between moral hazard and adverse selection in this context represents a tension between inducing efficient precontractual and postcontractual investment choices.[184]

2. The Hold-Up Problem

Lawmakers attempting to implement a Solomonic regime also face a serious "identification" problem. Solomonic negotiations can help a defined set of participating bargainers discover who among them has the highest valuation, but lawmakers may have difficulty determining who the appropriate participants are in this negotiation. This identification problem can give rise to problems of both over- and underinclusiveness. Overinclusiveness arises when Solomonic claims are given to individuals who clearly are not the highest valuers; this can exacerbate bargaining inefficiency, because these claimants have a strong incentive to hold up the negotiations of the serious contenders. When a partial entitlement is given to a person who is not the efficient owner, she will only be a seller, and her traditional incentive to seek an inflated price can impede negotiation among the class of potential ultimate owners. This hold-up problem is exemplified by the difficulty of consensually purchasing a group of adjoining properties to build a stadium or other public projects. An analogous problem of underinclusion results when potentially efficient owners

---

183. *See, e.g.*, Carol Rose, *The Comedy of the Commons: Custom, Commerce, and Inherently Public Property*, 53 U. CHI. L. REV. 711, 720–21 (1986). To take the fact pattern from *Spur v. Del Webb* as an illustration, it is conceivable to think that the feedlot owner, knowing that its entitlement was subject to a liability option of the growing retirement village, failed to make certain land improvements that would have increased the profitability of the land. Interestingly, however, the investment decision may go the other way if the landowner was protected by a tailored liability right awarding him "expectation-like" damages. In such a case, it is well documented that parties have the incentive to incur too many reliance expenditures. *See* Shavell, *supra* note 182, at 472. These forgone profits, incurred until the point at which Del Webb is clearly identified as the competing user, represent a bona fide and significant economic cost.

184. MILGROM & ROBERTS, *supra* note 176, at 143–47 (describing adverse selection and moral hazard).

are not given Solomonic claims. These excluded bargainers have the traditional incentives to understate their offers. Thus, inartful (over- or underinclusive) conferral of divided entitlements to people who are clearly inefficient owners induces costly transactions as those with low valuations are forced to sell their claims. The potential Coasean benefits of divided entitlements only occur if the partial owners have something real to negotiate about—i.e., if there is uncertainty about who should be the ultimate owner.[185]

Restricting the class of partial owners to the set of potentially highest valuers will be impossible in some contexts. Nevertheless, lawmakers or private parties themselves may be able to identify parties who ultimately may become the highest valuers. For example, the partial ownership interests of partners often coincide with the class of persons who, because of their idiosyncratic knowledge of the business, are most likely to be the highest valuers of the firm. It is instructive that the partners often choose to adopt buy-sell agreements that are strikingly analogous to the bidding mechanism outlined above in our fractional property rights model.[186]

Moreover, even if a divided entitlement scheme "misses" the highest valuer when casting its endowment net, this errant assignment may not, compared to undivided entitlement schemes, create onerous efficiency losses. First, even if the partial property claimants do not include the highest valuer, the Solomonic negotiation will at least facilitate allocating the entitlement to the highest valuer in the Solomonic group. Under an undivided scheme, an errant assignment would frequently entail greater inefficiencies. Second, some contexts naturally suggest a well-defined set of potential owners that may help lawmakers mitigate the problems of over- and underinclusion. A limited set of adjoining landowners, for example, might sufficiently define the set of potentially highest valuers with regard to local omissions or easements for a view.[187]

---

185. When this uncertainty is not present, lawmakers could do at least as well by simply allocating the property to the higher valuer. *See, e.g.,* Polinsky, *supra* note 116, at 1111–12.

186. *See supra* part III.

187. At least in some circumstances, allocating partial ownership to a party who is commonly known to have a low valuation, and who would thus be a seller, can still facilitate Coasean trade. For example, consider a house owned by "Low" but subject to an untailored liability rule so that A has an option to buy nonconsensually for $100,000. This liability rule division might facilitate A's negotiations with another potential purchaser, B, because the liability rule allows A to signal credibly a high cost, thereby reducing the amount of Coasean inefficiency from this third-party transaction.

On the other hand, various scholars have explored the proposition that such liability amounts, when high, represent a mechanism for exacting anticompetitive monopoly rents from B, the third party. *See, e.g.,* Phillippe Aghion & Patrick Bolton, *Contracts as a Barrier to Entry,* 77 AM. ECON. REV. 388 (1987).

3. *The Disabling Effects of Correlated Valuations and Tailored Rules*

Besides giving rise to underinvestment and hold-up problems, divided entitlements may sometimes be incapable of inducing bargainers to reveal their private valuations. In this Subsection, we briefly address how structural variations on this model—correlated valuations of the bargainers or tailored legal rules—can undermine the information-inducing quality of Solomonic entitlements.

Both of our earlier models showed that Solomonic entitlement facilitated Coasean trade when the bargainers had "independent valuations." The valuations were independent because one side's knowledge of her own valuation gave her no information about the other side's valuation. In many real-world contexts, however, the bargainers' valuations are often correlated, and one party frequently has better information about her valuation than does the other. For example, in litigation over a taking that has occurred, the plaintiff and the defendant are both trying to estimate the likely monetary outcome at trial. Litigants' valuations are usually correlated, because if one side believes the case is "worth a lot," the other side, at least after discovery, is likely to come to the same conclusion.

Correlated valuations with asymmetric information can create an additional impediment to inducing the revelation of information, because credibly revealing that one has a high valuation will often lead the other side to increase her own valuation and thus narrow the bargaining range.[188] For example, a buyer's revelation of value always tells the seller the maximum that she might demand. When their valuations are correlated, however, a buyer's revelation may also raise the minimum price that the seller is willing to accept. With correlated valuations, then, a buyer may be even more reluctant to reveal her valuation. With correlated valuations, each party has an additional strategic reason to misrepresent her respective valuation: to mislead the other side about her own valuation.

For example, consider again our analysis of bargaining under a liability rule regime. If we instead assume that the plaintiff's and the defendant's valuations are correlated, but that defendants have only an imprecise, initial signal about their valuation, then defendants would rationally try to infer their valuation more precisely from the bargaining behavior of the plaintiff. In this circumstance, plaintiffs might strategically try to misrepresent their valuation, to mislead defendants about the defendants' own valuation. In the earlier

---

188. While economic models can easily capture the process of updating one's own valuation based on rational inferences of the other side's valuation, psychologists have also explored more extreme adjustments referred to as "reactive devaluations." Lee Ross, *Reactive Devaluation in Negotiation and Conflict Resolution, in* BARRIERS TO THE NEGOTIATED RESOLUTION OF CONFLICT (Kenneth Arrow et al. eds., forthcoming 1995) [hereinafter BARRIERS TO RESOLUTION].

liability model, we asserted that low-valuing plaintiffs would never have an incentive to make a serious offer to bribe defendants not to take.[189] It is possible, however, that if defendants have imprecise but correlated valuations, a low-valuing plaintiff might cleverly try to bribe the defendant not to exercise her liability call option. The plaintiff would hope that the defendant would reject the offer, wrongly believing that she (the plaintiff, and thus the defendant as well) had a high valuation, then exercise the option.[190] In the future, we hope to explore this conjecture formally, since it represents the only instance when a plaintiff might have an affirmative strategic incentive to misrepresent whether her valuation was above or below the liability amount.[191] For now, it is sufficient to see that correlated valuations and one-sided information can make the bargainers reluctant to reveal information and thus reduce the potential benefit of Solomonic bargaining.[192]

Correlated valuations, however, are not the only factor that can increase the disincentives to reveal information. As argued above, tailoring legal consequences so that they are contingent on private information can deter parties from revealing the information. For example, giving the plaintiff private information about the size of the liability rule's exercise price by making the damages payment relate to the plaintiff's actual loss in value undermines the plaintiff's otherwise strong incentive to reveal whether her valuation is high or low.[193]

To the extent that equity constrains lawmakers to tailor legal rules to make *ex post* consequences turn on *ex ante* privately held information, divided tailored entitlements are likely to produce relatively less efficient pre-taking negotiations. For example, it may be difficult for a judge to implement an untailored rule such as a $50 liability amount when, by the time of trial, sufficient information has revealed that the defendant actually valued

---

189. *See supra* part II. Similarly, we asserted that high-valuing plaintiffs would never make a serious offer to sell their entitlement for less than the liability amount.

190. Similarly, a high-valuing plaintiff might strategically offer to sell the entitlement for a low price, again hoping that the defendant would reject the offer but mistakenly choose not to take.

191. Though we do not rule out the possibility that information structures such as the one described in the text can render property rules more efficient than liability rules, we conjecture that the more likely result from this information structure is of the type obtained in the so-called "no-trade" papers in finance. *See, e.g.,* Paul Milgrom & Nancy Stokey, *Information, Trade and Common Knowledge,* 26 J. ECON. THEORY 17 (1982). Essentially, when one party has superior information about the value of the underlying asset, her willingness either to purchase or to sell that asset is a signal to the other, uninformed party that such a transaction would be unwise. Thus, in such environments, we conjecture that autarky might reign regardless of the underlying rule. Interestingly, then, because autarky under liability rules tends to dominate autarky under property rules, *see supra* part II, the existence of correlated information need not prove fatal to the relative wisdom of liability rules.

192. Note, however, that when the players' types are correlated, but each knows her own valuation with precision, both liability rules and property rules are likely to tend toward efficiency as the amount of correlation increases. *See, e.g.,* R. Preston McAfee & Philip J. Reny, *Correlated Information and Mechanism Design,* 60 ECONOMETRICA 395 (1992) (discussing ability of correlated information to induce first-best bargaining).

193. Similarly, giving the defendant private information about who owns the entitlement deterred plaintiffs from partitioning themselves into high- and low-valuing groups.

ownership at $75, and that the plaintiff's lost value was $100. While our theory predicts that courts would adjudicate fewer cases under an untailored liability rule than under a tailored liability rule, it is neither practically nor theoretically possible to continue seeing a limited number of such cases in litigation.[194]

B. *Choosing Among Divided Entitlements*

While the last Section identified conditions under which divided entitlements might induce additional inefficiencies, these potential pitfalls still may not outweigh the Coasean benefits of Solomonic entitlements. At least theoretically, we have shown that a number of different types of divided entitlements can enhance pre-taking negotiations, each for different reasons. Assuming *arguendo*, then, that divided entitlements are beneficial overall, this Section explores which of the various divisions is most likely to be efficient.

A striking result of Part III was that bargaining under fractional property rights could achieve first-best efficiency. The expected payoffs in these models were higher than those in Solomonic bargaining under liability rules (even though liability rule divisions still produced higher gains than undivided property rules). As an initial matter, it seems that fractional property divisions would dominate liability rules as a mechanism for facilitating Coasean trade.

The information-forcing quality of untailored liability rules, however, is much more robust than the beneficial identity crisis that fractional property rules create. We were only able to demonstrate first-best efficiency in an extremely stylized bargaining game with simultaneous offers. While some of the Solomonic benefits of fractional property rules undoubtedly are present in related procedures, the information-forcing quality of liability rules depends on fewer assumptions. Most important, we showed that a plaintiff owning an entitlement protected by a property rule would never offer the "misrepresentative" type of Coasean bargain, regardless of the defendant's expected strategy.[195] Our showing that liability rules make truth telling an

---

194. *See generally* Gillian K. Hadfield, *Bias in the Evolution of Legal Rules*, 80 GEO. L.J. 583 (1992) (noting that judges often make decisions that are optimal for the particular case in front of them but not for the population in general).

Our models also have implications for the "rules" versus "standards" debate. For these purposes we adopt Louis Kaplow's cogent definition that: "[T]he only distinction between rules and standards is the extent to which efforts to give content to the law are undertaken before or after individuals act." Kaplow, *supra* note 153, at 560. Under this definition, all of our untailored laws are rulelike; even the probabilistic allocations are rulelike in that there is nothing for the parties to learn about the law before the court's application. Our focus on tailored rules, which make legal consequences contingent on parties' private information, suggests that under Kaplow's scheme a law might be "rulelike" from the perspective of the informed party, but it may be "standardlike" from the perspective of the uninformed party, who will try to infer its content prior to trial. Our assertion is that this asymmetry creates impediments to Coasean trade in particular.

195. As noted above, we need to limit the parties from certain types of extremely irrational play. *See supra* note 59–60 and accompanying text.

iterated dominant strategy suggests that the benefits of liability rules may be much less fragile than fractional property rules equilibria.

Moreover, certain types of partial property divisions may be difficult to implement. Activity-level divisions may not be possible where the competing uses are qualitatively incompatible. For instance, it may be impossible to divide the right to various trees in the Oregon old-growth forests between Union Pacific and the Rocky Mountain spotted owl. Temporal divisions may not be possible either, especially when the activity of the first user of the entitlement is likely to render the resource useless for the next in right.[196]

The feasibility of probabilistic property divisions raises particularly interesting legal issues. For example, the common law process itself may make it difficult to sustain the beneficial effects of probabilistic determinations, since precedents tend to further define the consequences of nonconsensual taking. Although we traditionally conceive of the process of announcing precedent as a public good redounding to the benefit of others, our model perversely suggests that reducing uncertainty may, at least with regard to its effect on pre-taking negotiations, be a public bad.[197] While it is not our goal to apologize for the diverse types of legal uncertainty, the probabilistic entitlement model might force us to reexamine a host of procedures that may have this unintended benefit. For example, cloaking decisions in the opinionless determination of idiosyncratic juries or the unarticulated demands of equity may produce unintended benefits in pretrial bargaining.[198]

In general, the optimal way to divide an entitlement will turn on how the particular divisions interact with the various limiting factors outlined above. For example, Solomonic entitlements may be particularly effective when legal rules respond to the "identification" problem by excluding inefficient owners from the bargaining process. Liability rule divisions tend to do just this: If the state mistakenly grants a probabilistic property right to an individual who is clearly not one of the efficient owners, that individual may inhibit efficient trade by holding up the efficient owner for an inefficient sale price. If, however, the state mistakenly grants a liability call option to someone who

---

196. Consider a situation in which each of the competing uses leaves the property unusable for anything else for a long time. The underlying legal entitlement might be the ownership of a plot of land in the desert, while the two potential owners are a farmer, who plans to excavate irrigation ditches to grow alfalfa, and a scientific R&D venture that wishes to study the effects of toxic chemical spills in "pristine" desert climates. If one attempted to divide the title to the land temporally, it would be difficult to find a split such that use by the first party would not render the plot useless to the remainderperson.

·197. This perspective contrasts with the argument put forth in Owen M. Fiss' much-cited article, *Against Settlement*, 93 YALE L.J. 1073, 1073–78 (1984), that litigants might inefficiently ignore the *positive* externality of precedent when deciding to settle. Our probabilistic property model, in contrast, suggests that precedent may also produce a *negative* externality that litigants may ignore in failing to settle.

198. This list is far from exhaustive. Indeed, the probabilistic entitlement model might provide an unwitting efficiency rationale for various "abstention" doctrines (such as *Pullman* and *Colorado River* abstentions) that avoid resolution by federal courts of ambiguities in state law. *See, e.g.*, PETER W. LOW & JOHN C. JEFFRIES, JR., FEDERAL COURTS AND THE LAW OF FEDERAL-STATE RELATIONS 554–63, 574–83 (3d ed. 1994).

clearly values the property less than the option's exercise price—i.e., the damage amount—then the class of potentially efficient owners can simply ignore any demands from this inefficient owner, because her threat to take nonconsensually is not credible. Thus, liability rule divisions may better allow private parties to limit the problem of overinclusiveness that results from mistaken allocations.

The choice of entitlement division might also reflect appropriate responses to other limiting factors analyzed above. For example, while probabilistic divisions might be hard to sustain over time, liability rules may be less susceptible to *ex post* tailoring: Even if courts feel compelled to tailor the amount of liability to plaintiff's actual loss, the prospect of a probabilistic determination of whether the defendant will be liable may be sufficient to induce more efficient pre-taking negotiation.[199]

C. *Specific Legal Applications*

This Section analyzes some potential legal applications of our theoretical findings. We focus first on intellectual property law, and then more briefly on impossibility and mistake doctrines and legal "dissolutions" of concurrent ownership.

1. *Intellectual Property and Compulsory Licenses*

An area of modern legal practice where entitlement allocation is of paramount importance is the law of intellectual property. Indeed, this field is one of the few in which new property rights emerge on a daily basis, especially within the patent and copyright process. Moreover, the prevalence of patent and copyright licensing is testimony to the pervasiveness of bargaining in the shadow of the extant legal entitlement schemes.

Intellectual property often entails a significant amount of thin-market bargaining. In patent law, a nontrivial amount of bargaining occurs between parties possessing "blocking" patents.[200] For instance, consider the case where an individual has patented a pioneering invention, and a second individual then patents a "new use" that incorporates the pioneering technology. It may be quite profitable for the second individual to market

---

199. As noted above, the choice between liability and reverse liability rules could turn in part on which party's private information is the greatest impediment to Coasean trade. The party with the *least* amount of private information should receive a liability call or put option so as to exploit maximally the "partitioning" of the opposite party. Thus, reverse liability rules are appropriate when inducing defendant partitioning is the primary concern, while liability rules are appropriate when inducing plaintiff partitioning is the primary concern. For example, in a competitive market, a seller's cost of performance may be readily inferred from the market price, so endowing the seller as promisor/defendant with a liability call option (to breach and pay damages) may induce better Coasean trade.

200. This Subsection draws heavily upon Merges, *supra* note 39.

products that use this improvement patent, but because U.S. patent law grants property protection to the pioneer patent,[201] the improver cannot market her invention without first negotiating a licensing agreement with the incumbent.

This situation, though seemingly stylized, is not uncommon. An oft-cited example is the stalemate in the early-twentieth-century negotiations between the Marconi Wireless & Telegraph Company and AT&T over patents in radio technology.[202] Marconi, the pioneer, owned a series of patents disclosing an oscillating radio diode, which was then a fundamental component of transmission technology. AT&T, on the other hand, was a licensee to a radical improvement, disclosed in the "de Forest" patents for an oscillating triode, which incorporated Marconi's pioneering technology. After a court had established Marconi's dominant status, thus giving it a property right over its diode technology,[203] the parties attempted to negotiate a licensing agreement to merge their respective technologies. Their bargaining efforts, replete with strategic behavior, were largely unsuccessful. In fact, the parties did not reach an agreement for nearly ten years, and even then it was largely motivated by the government's creation of RCA. Many have estimated that the impasse squandered an annual surplus in the tens of millions of dollars and delayed numerous other advances in radio technology.

The property-like protection that patent law gives to innovators may well have contributed to the deadlock in the Marconi–de Forest negotiations. Our analysis suggests that, at least in analogous circumstances, a liability-like regime might induce more efficient allocations by facilitating truthful revelation more rapidly, thereby minimizing costly delay. Such a system would likely take the form of a "compulsory licensing" scheme, giving the improver an option to infringe the pioneer's patent in exchange for a fee determined by a licensing tribunal. Current U.S. patent law generally eschews such approaches, except for *sui generis* patents in nuclear power and environmental engineering technologies. In various Asian and European nations, however, compulsory licensing exists for just such a pioneer/improver circumstance.[204]

A number of groups have long opposed compulsory patent licensing in the United States, the most vocal of which is (perhaps not surprisingly) patent attorneys. Among academics, however, common objections to such schemes include arguments that licensing tribunals are notoriously bad at correctly

---

201. *See, e.g.*, 35 U.S.C. § 283 (1988).

202. For an extensive analysis of the radio history, see GEORGE H. DOUGLAS, THE EARLY DAYS OF RADIO BROADCASTING (1987).

203. *See* Marconi Wireless & Tel. Co. v. DeForest Am. Co., 236 F. 942 (S.D.N.Y. 1916), *aff'd*, 243 F. 560 (2d Cir. 1917).

204. *See* Gianna Julian-Arnold, *International Compulsory Licensing: The Rationales and the Reality*, 33 IDEA 349 (1987) (noting that blocking patents are one of three most common conditions for compulsory licensing abroad). Countries that have compulsory licensing provisions in such instances include Australia, China, France, Japan, the Netherlands, New Zealand, and Switzerland. *See* Merges, *supra* note 39, at 34–36 & nn.57–59.

"pricing" the licensing fees.[205] As our arguments illustrate, however, these arguments may lose their force when one allows for bargaining in the shadow of the compulsory licensing regime. Indeed, the inability of a court to tailor a damages award and the existence of litigation costs can often improve the ability of the parties to reach a consensual, efficient agreement on their own terms, not those dictated by the underlying liability rule.[206] Moreover, restricting the compulsory licensing to the pioneer/improver context might be a rational way for government to respond to the identification problem—because the two parties involved in the initial innovation may, at least as a first approximation, be the most efficient developers as well.

2. *Mistake, Impossibility, Frustration, and Bargaining over Efficient Breach*

Another set of potential applications for our results arises in the contract doctrines of mutual mistake, impossibility, and frustration. While formally distinct, all of these doctrines address situations in which the "state of the world" at the time of contractual performance differs vastly from what the parties had anticipated during their initial contract bargaining. In such instances, it is often no longer clear whether continued performance of the contract would be efficient, as the promisor may value breaching more than the promisee values performance. Moreover, in the absence of any excuse doctrines, should an adversely affected party breach, the typical damages measures may be wholly out of phase with the underlying state of the world, thereby giving one party an "effective" property right.[207] Thus, when such an unanticipated contingency occurs, there is a strong argument for inducing the parties to reconsider jointly, through renegotiation, the prudence of continued performance. Private information can often impede this renegotiation process, however, so structuring the law to lubricate the bargaining—via Solomonic divisions—may be one mechanism for encouraging efficient breach.[208]

---

205. *See, e.g.*, Merges, *supra* note 39, at 30–32.

206. There is some soft empirical support for this proposition as well. Despite the compulsory licensing schemes in these countries, Merges reports an unusually low incidence of royalty proceedings, suggesting that the parties are largely successful at bargaining around the default liability rule. *See id.* at 35.

207. *See supra* text accompanying notes 48–49 (discussing how misaligned or "extreme" damage amount can give rise to property-like rule). One can see how such a situation might come about in, say, the classic frustration case of Krell v. Henry, 2 K.B. 740 (C.A. 1903), in which the frustration doctrine was used to nullify a subletting agreement for property overlooking the planned route of a royal processional. Reliance or expectation damages may well have given the lessor an effective property right over performance.

208. That efficient breach of contract is an important goal of contract law is virtually indisputable. *See* COOTER & ULEN, *supra* note 1, at 290.

Consider, for instance, the doctrine of mutual mistake first articulated in the classic and still-popular case of *Sherwood v. Walker*.[209] The dispute in *Walker* centered on whether a contract for the sale of a cow should be nullified upon the discovery by the parties that the cow—which was mutually thought to be infertile—was in fact pregnant. Reversing the trial court's enforcement of the contract, the Michigan Supreme Court found that when the "nature" of the contracted exchange changes dramatically, either party has a legitimate right to refuse performance and seek nullification. Interestingly, however, both the *Walker* court and many courts since have applied the mistake doctrine somewhat randomly.[210] The Restatement does not substantially help to resolve the line-drawing ambiguities. Section 152 states that nullification under the mistake doctrine is warranted so long as there is a failure of a "basic assumption," and so long as the adversely affected party does not "bear[] the risk" of mistake.[211] Both of these standards are decidedly unclear, as is the notion of what types of mistake are mutual.[212] These ambiguities have led a number of commentators to conclude that the standards governing the mistake doctrine are "confused beyond reconciliation."[213]

The current legal standards for excuse are suggestive of our analysis in two ways. First, given the lack of clear standards governing the mistake doctrine, the legal landscape arguably gives rise to a particular type of Solomonic division studied above: probabilistic property rights. Indeed, if courts must operate within a hazy set of irreconcilable legal standards when applying the mistake doctrine, then their ultimate decisions may fall victim to arbitrariness and randomness. To the extent that this randomness approximates a legal "coin flip" over the entitlement, the parties may see themselves each as owning a probabilistic or fractional share of the respective rights over breach or performance. This muddy default legal rule may thereby engender more efficient renegotiation of the contract than would occur if the impossibility doctrine were more crystalline.

Second, the failure of a "basic assumption" requirement may help to solve the identification problem of overinclusiveness by limiting the court's effective coin flipping to circumstances in which it is no longer clear whether the promisee values performance more than the promisor. The legal rule may prohibit promisors—whose *ex ante* assent signals that they value their performance less than the promisee—from opportunistically holding up

---

209. 33 N.W. 919 (Mich. 1887).

210. *See* Eric Rasmusen & Ian Ayres, *Mutual Mistake and Unilateral Mistake in Contract Law*, 22 J. LEGAL STUD. 309, 312 (1993) (noting that "courts are left puzzled about when to void for mistake," and citing continued puzzlement in current casebooks). Even Judge Morse in *Walker* noted the difficulty in line drawing: "I know that this is a close question, and the dividing line between the adjudicated cases is not easily discerned." Sherwood v. Walker, 33 N.W. at 923.

211. RESTATEMENT (SECOND) OF CONTRACTS § 152 (1981).

212. Rasmusen & Ayres, *supra* note 210, at 311–12.

213. *E.g.*, ARTHUR ROSETT, CONTRACT LAW AND ITS APPLICATION 669 (5th ed. 1994).

promisees. The occurrence of some unexpected event, however, may so undermine the court's confidence that there are gains of trade at any price, that the legal system may wish to use probabilistic discharge to encourage more efficient renegotiations. A similar analysis may apply to the doctrines of impossibility and frustration, where the unanticipated state of the world was not caused by mistaken impressions during contracting, but by dramatic and unanticipated changes in the world after execution of the contract. In these situations as well, a probabilistic application of excuse doctrine may facilitate efficient renegotiation.[214]

The current legal standards, however, may not effectively respond to the identification problem of underinclusiveness.[215] While the "basic assumption" requirement may be sufficient to establish that either the promisor or the promisee may have the *higher* valuation, this requirement is not sufficient to establish that one of the two bargainers has the *highest* valuation among a larger class of potential owners. For example, in *Sherwood v. Walker*, a third party might have been the efficient owner of the pregnant cow. Inducing Solomonic bargaining between the two litigants is less likely to be efficient if potentially efficient owners are not given a Solomonic share. This reasoning suggests that the probabilistic rescission might only be appropriate when there are idiosyncratic gains from trade—say, because of deal-specific investments—that create conditions of "bilateral monopoly."[216]

3. *Concurrent Ownership and Dissolutions*

The legal rules governing concurrent ownership[217] of property may also promote Solomonic bargaining. While concurrent ownership normally arises in ongoing, cooperative relationships (especially tenancy by the entirety, which is an artifact of marriage), the law by necessity must respond to rivalrous claims of use by concurrent owners. Solomonic entitlements may be especially appropriate in these contexts because the intimate relationship that gave rise to the concurrent ownership may also cause the concurrent owners to place an idiosyncratic, above-market value on the property. For example, two spouses may subjectively value their summer home, where they reared their children, much more than potential third-party buyers, and yet it might be unclear which

---

214. *See* Rasmusen & Ayres, *supra* note 210, at 310–14. This list of renegotiation-facilitating contractual doctrines is not exhaustive. *See, e.g.*, Talley, *supra* note 43 (discussing rule against penalty enforcement as another form of bargain-inducing device).

215. This paragraph incorporates a probing question by Richard Epstein and thoughtful comments by Richard Craswell.

216. When there is a competitive market for the promised performance, certain rescission will not lead to inefficiency if the original seller after rescission can simply sell to the highest bidder.

217. There are three traditional forms of concurrent ownership of property: tenancy in common, joint tenancy, and tenancy by the entirety. *See* A. JAMES CASNER & W. BARTON LEACH, CASES AND TEXT ON PROPERTY 251–55 (3d ed. 1984).

spouse values the home more, since at all prior times their use of the house was nonrivalrous.

The common law has developed a number of ways of resolving conflicting claims of concurrent owners. Most basically, a tenant in common or a joint tenant often can obtain a physical partition of the property. We have already shown that a physical division of property can create an identity crisis, because at the outset of negotiations a claimant would not know whether she would ultimately sell her share or buy the other party's share. The mere option of obtaining a physical partition can have the same effect as an actual physical division, because each party would know that in the absence of an agreement on buying or selling this partition option, an actual physical partition would be the ultimate result. Indeed, the prospect of judicial partitioning may induce even more bargaining than an existing partition, since the parties will be uncertain, *ex ante*, about who will get what parts. If the court might benightedly divide the land in a way that reduces its use to each of the claimants, then the parties would have even more incentives to resolve the dispute themselves.

Courts have also forced a tenant in common to compensate her co-owners for disproportionate use of concurrently owned property.[218] Such rulings effectively create liability rule options: A tenant may take the benefit of certain uses, but only if she compensates her cotenant. To the extent that the court's determination of the damages deviates from the cotenant's valuation, our analysis in Part II suggests that this legal rule will induce cotenants to disclose whether their valuation is above or below the damage amount. Accordingly, this legal rule may effectuate Solomonic negotiations.

*   *   *

The analysis in this Part is far from exhaustive. Its primary purpose is to illustrate that Solomonic allocations should neither predominate in all legal categories nor define a null set. Nonetheless, the fact that there are many divisions that may promote more efficient Coasean bargaining than clear property rules calls into question many "settled" notions about the

---

218. McKnight v. Basilides, 143 P.2d 307, 315 (Wash. 1943) ("No practical or reasonable argument can be advanced for allowing one in possession to reap a financial benefit by occupying property owned in common without paying for his personal use of that part of the property owned by his cotenants.").

law[219]—including blanket condemnation of entitlement allocations that are indeterminate or weakly protected.

V. CONCLUSION

Emerging academic disciplines frequently use "extreme cases" as instructional benchmarks. Law and economics is no exception. Over the last thirty-five years, law and economics has produced two fundamental insights about the relationship between legal entitlements and consensual trade, each stemming from diametric assumptions about the world.[220] First, Coase showed that when transacting is costless, the choice between property and liability rules does not affect the attainment of efficiency.[221] Second, Calabresi and Melamed followed by showing that when transaction costs make consensual transfer prohibitively expensive, liability rules, which allow for nonnegotiated transfer, are likely to dominate property rules.[222]

This Article has ventured further into the economic purgatory between the findings of Coase and of Calabresi and Melamed.[223] In this intermediate region, where transaction costs are positive but not prohibitive, law-and-

---

219. For example, it is possible that the current departures from the absolute priority rule represent a move toward a divided entitlement scheme for a firm's assets, which can lead to more efficient taking negotiations. *See generally* Douglas G. Baird & Thomas H. Jackson, *Bargaining After the Fall and the Contours of the Absolute Priority Rule*, 55 U. CHI. L. REV. 738 (1988) (documenting this movement).

Our analysis might also provide an additional rationale for Easterbrook and Fischel's argument that courts should require target managers to be passive in response to hostile takeover attempts. *See* Frank H. Easterbrook & Daniel R. Fischel, *The Proper Role of a Target's Management in Responding to a Tender Offer*, 94 VA. L. REV. 1161 (1981). Haddock, Macey, and McChesney persuasively criticized this target passivity requirement by explicitly arguing that the entitlements of target shareholders should be protected by a property rule instead of the Easterbrook-Fischel liability rule (which in essence would give raiders a call option to take over the firm). David D. Haddock et al., *Property Rights in Assets and Resistance to Tender Offers*, 73 VA. L. REV. 701 (1987). Our analysis suggests that analogizing the passivity proposal to a liability rule does not doom its application. To the contrary, target passivity might induce target managers to reveal whether they believe the company is worth more than the tender offer—at least if the targets were allowed to bribe the hostile bidder to cease and desist. *See* Jonathan R. Macey & Fred S. McChesney, *A Theoretical Analysis of Corporate Greenmail*, 95 YALE L.J. 13 (1985).

220. Interestingly, the evolution of the economics of competition follows a similar track, with initial concentration on the polar environments of perfect competition and monopoly. Only recently have models of oligopoly and monopolistic competition breached the more realistic middle ground between these polar benchmarks.

221. *See* Coase, *supra* note 5. Though Coase never articulated this proposition verbatim in that article, most scholars have attributed it to him since. *See, e.g.*, COOTER & ULEN, *supra* note 1, at 105 & n.15; Calabresi & Melamed, *supra* note 12, at 1094 (attributing to Coase the notion that "[in] the absence of transaction costs, Pareto optimality or economic efficiency will occur regardless of the initial entitlement").

222. Just as Coase did not explicitly articulate the Coase theorem, *see supra* note 221, Calabresi and Melamed left it to others to state explicitly this fundamental implication of their analysis. *See* POSNER, *supra* note 1; Haddock et al., *supra* note 18; Kronman, *supra* note 19.

223. The insights of this Article fit nicely with the seminal insights of Robert Cooter, *The Cost of Coase*, 11 J. LEGAL STUD. 1 (1982). Cooter hypothesized that the normative task of the law was to find an optimal trade-off between "Coasean" concerns about lubricating consensual trade, and "Hobbesian" concerns about allocating legal entitlements when trade collapses. *See id.* at 19–20. Liability rules have often been perceived as serving the second of these goals quite well but generally failing to serve the first. Our analysis, however, illustrates that these two concerns need not conflict. Liability rules can, at least in dealing with private information, serve *both* objectives better than property rules.

economics scholars have firmly favored the use of undivided entitlements—i.e., clear, fee simple allocations protected by property rules—to "force" parties to negotiate.[224] But the near-universal acceptance of this proposition by academics (including ourselves until recently) is a little puzzling. If liability rules can promote efficient contracting in a world without transaction costs, why was it clear that property rules should dominate when transaction costs increase slightly?[225] At a minimum, this Article shows that the preference for undivided property rules in low-transaction-cost settings should no longer rest on the naive notion that property rules are superior at channeling people toward efficient Coasean trade. We have shown that a host of Solomonic entitlement divisions—including liability rules and fractional property entitlements—can induce pre-taking negotiations superior to those of undivided property rules.[226]

Two distinct families of entitlement division can engender more truthful bargaining. Fractional ownership structures might induce honest bargaining by obscuring the titular boundary between buyer and seller during a negotiation. For example, if a court is equally likely to rule that either a factory or a neighboring laundry is entitled to control the amount of factory pollution, then the factory may be unsure whether it should try to buy the laundry's right to

---

224. *See supra* notes 27–28 and accompanying text.

225. Louis Kaplow and Steven Shavell ask the same question, but focus on a different margin—decreases in transaction costs from a prohibitively high level. In their discussion of harmful externalities, they assert:

> [T]he liability rule is superior when there is no bargaining. That is, before any bargaining occurs, at the beginning of the "race" between the types of rule, the liability rule is ahead of the property rules. Hence, we would expect that after imperfect bargaining occurs, the liability rule should remain ahead of the property rules. This would be true unless bargaining were for some reason to result in mutually beneficial agreements substantially more often under the property rules than under the liability rule.

Kaplow & Shavell, *supra* note 101, at 25–26. This explanation correctly identifies how, *ceteris paribus*, liability rules can mitigate the consequences of failed bargaining. Following Cooter, this might be characterized as a "Hobbesian" rationale for liability rules. *See supra* note 223. In this Article, we have tried to expose a "Coasean" rationale for liability rules as well: By inducing bargainers to reveal information, liability rules may "result in mutually beneficial agreements substantially more often" than property rules. Thus, liability rules may be more able than property rules to serve the joint purpose of lubricating bilateral negotiations and mitigating the consequences of failed bargaining.

The failure of the academy to ask the question in the text may lie, in part, in the fact that Calabresi and Melamed succeeded too well in showing that liability rules were appropriate for high transaction cost contexts, and also because most Coasean bargaining examples were explained in terms of property rights. *But cf.* SCOTT & LESLIE, *supra* note 43, at 101–03 (discussing Coasean bargaining around gap-filling legal rules). While the law-and-economics community knows the Coase theorem by heart, legal scholars have largely ignored how the Coasean impulse to internalize externalities would affect liability rules and other forms of entitlement divisions. *See generally* John J. Donohue III, *Opting for the British Rule, or If Posner and Shavell Can't Remember the Coase Theorem, Who Will?*, 104 HARV. L. REV. 1093 (1991) (arguing that Coasean implications have been overlooked in other areas as well).

226. Ellickson has cogently shown why the law has placed immutable constraints on the "excessive decomposition" of bundles. *See* Ellickson, *supra* note 4, at 1374 ("A landowner can reveal incapacity not just by swinging an axe at an antique armoire but also by splintering rights in a fee simple bundle into bits that are far less valuable than the pre-splintered whole."). Our Article, however, suggests that the law might also worry about excessive *composition* of entitlement claims.

stop the pollution, or to sell its own right to pollute.[227] A similar characterization holds for the laundry. Because of this "identity crisis," the bargainers will not know whether they should strategically inflate their offers (*qua* sellers) or deflate their offers (*qua* buyers). As a consequence, the parties may distort their offers less, so more efficient trade can occur.

Additionally, liability rules have an information-forcing quality that has heretofore gone unnoticed: They can induce entitlement holders to signal credible information about their valuation. Under a liability rule, high-valuing owners never offer to sell their entitlement, and low-valuing owners never offer to bribe potential appropriators not to take. Consequently, the type of transaction that the owner willingly offers credibly signals her relative valuation.[228] Liability rules thus can cause entitlement holders to partition themselves into two valuation groups,[229] thereby reducing the aggregate amount of private information and increasing Coasean efficiency. We showed that this result is remarkably robust, in that the owner's incentive to reveal her relative valuation is independent of either side's behavior[230] or specific assumptions about the form of the bargaining game.

The academy's failure to view liability rules as catalysts (rather than substitutes) for bargaining has led it not only to misprescribe *when* such rules are appropriate, but also to misprescribe what *type* of liability rules are optimal. Numerous scholars have argued that liability rules should be tailored to replicate the transaction the individual litigants might have made had they bargained.[231] We have demonstrated, however, that when private information is the dominant transaction cost, tailored rules can actually impede efficient bargaining by making bargainers more reluctant to reveal information. Tailored damages give the plaintiff added information about the default "price" for a taking, while tailored liability gives the defendant added information about whether such damages will ever be assessed. This additional dimension of private information actually forecloses the possibility that both species of

---

227. *See* Johnston, *supra* note 29, at 6–7.

228. For instance, if an entitlement-holding plaintiff makes the statement, "I am interested in selling you my entitlement," the defendant knows that only a low-valuing plaintiff could have made such a statement. Conversely, if the plaintiff makes the statement: "I am interested in buying your option to take," the defendant knows that only a high-valuing plaintiff could have made such a statement. *See supra* part II.B.3.

In Part II, we also showed that reverse liability rules can analogously induce potential takers ("defendants" model) to reveal whether their valuations are greater than or less than the damage amount. *See supra* part II.B.4.

229. If it is costly to make Coasean offers, entitlement holders will often partition themselves into three groups: high-valuing owners, who will offer defendants a bribe not to take; low-valuing owners, who will offer to sell their entitlement for a price below the damage amount; and intermediate-valuing owners, who will refrain from either type of bargaining. For a more thorough description of intermediate-valuing owners, see *supra* note 89.

230. For a slight caveat to this assertion, see *supra* note 60.

231. *See, e.g.*, POSNER, *supra* note 1, at 62 n.5 (noting that when courts assess damages inaccurately, liability rules may not be beneficial vis-à-vis property rules); Calabresi & Melamed, *supra* note 12, at 1125 (pointing out that liability rules "approximat[e] . . . the value of the object to its original owner").

Coasean bargains will occur under liability rules.[232] Thus, while tailored liability rules may be appropriate when transaction costs make bargaining impracticable, lawmakers choosing liability rules to facilitate trade should be careful not to make the legal rule contingent on the parties' private information.

The ability of Solomonic entitlements such as untailored liability rules to facilitate Coasean trade is starkly at odds with the accepted wisdom that property rules are "market-encouraging" when transaction costs are low.[233] Property rules and liability rules may thus run neck and neck in a Coasean horse race, even when transaction costs are low;[234] and when private information is the major source of inefficiency, liability rules and other divided entitlement forms may hold the lead.[235]

While our arguments favoring divided entitlements arise from an economic concern about the ways that private information can impede negotiation,[236] these arguments also dovetail nicely with theories of psychological barriers to negotiation. Several experiments have shown that people tend to value an object more once they identify the property as their own, and that this "endowment" or "framing" effect is independent of any attachments that might develop over time.[237] For example, in an oft-cited experiment, Daniel Kahneman, Jack Knetsch, and Richard Thaler explored subjects' willingness to buy or sell a coffee mug. The authors gave one group (the "buyers") the opportunity to "buy" a mug instead of giving them monetary compensation for participating in the experiment. They gave the other group (the "sellers") an initial "endowment" of the mug as a gift at the beginning of the experiment, then gave them the chance to sell their newly acquired property.[238] The authors found that the sellers' valuations were more than double the buyers'

---

232. Indeed, as we showed in Part II, tailoring of either damages or liability in our model reduces to zero the probability that the plaintiff would buy the defendant's call option. *See supra* text accompanying notes 116–31.

233. *See, e.g.,* Levmore, *supra* note 17, at 83–84.

234. We demonstrated these results in models with a precise definition of transaction costs. Instead of artificially assuming a fixed cost of contracting, *see, e.g.,* Ayres & Gertner, *supra* note 74, at 732–33, the models in this Article highlight the real-world inefficiencies caused by bargainers' private information.

235. Even when transaction costs are low, the choice of the efficient entitlement form may be significant. The amounts of social inefficiency are not bounded above by the costs of contracting. *See id.*

236. For an analogous exploration of the adverse selection inefficiency in bargaining, see Brown & Ayres, *supra* note 15, at 331–35.

237. *See, e.g.,* David Kahneman & Amos Tversky, *Advances in Prospect Theory: Cumulative Uncertainty,* 9 J. RISK & UNCERTAINTY (forthcoming 1994); David Kahneman & Amos Tversky, *Conflict Resolution: A Cognitive Perspective, in* BARRIERS TO RESOLUTION, *supra* note 188.

238. Daniel Kahneman et al., *Experimental Tests of the Endowment Effect and the Coase Theorem,* 98 J. POL. ECON. 1325 (1990) [hereinafter Kahneman et al., *Experimental Tests*]; *see also* Daniel Kahneman et al., *The Endowment Effect, Loss Aversion, and Status Quo Bias,* J. ECON. PERSP., Winter 1991, at 193, 194–97 (1991) (describing this and similar experiments); George Loewenstein & Samuel Issacharoff, *Source Dependence in the Valuation of Objects,* 7 J. BEHAVIORAL DECISION MAKING 157 (1994) (finding that means by which people obtain objects impacts valuation of their property); Amos Tversky & Daniel Kahneman, *Loss Aversion in Riskless Choice: A Reference Dependent Model,* 106 Q.J. ECON. 1039 (1991).

1102   The Yale Law Journal   [Vol. 104: 1027

valuations, even though the experiment presented the subjects with an identical economic choice.[239] This type of framing effect can impede trade by narrowing the set of mutually acceptable prices.[240] But divided entitlements may mitigate such cognitive barriers: As emphasized above, probabilistic entitlements obscure the identity of the buyer and the seller, so we might predict that this entitlement division would reduce, or even eliminate, ownership bias. Similarly, if the parties understood that in a liability rule regime, the nominal owner's claim was subject to another's call option, then the adverse cognitive effects might be less severe.[241]

Our conclusion that uncertain and weakly protected entitlements might produce more efficient trade than undivided property rights runs counter to deeply held but possibly unexamined beliefs. For a large range of applications, undivided property rules remain the most efficient scheme; yet our analysis suggests that the justification for undivided property rules cannot reside in the simple (*a priori*) assertion that undivided entitlements promote more efficient trade. Undivided entitlements sometimes may be preferable for a number of traditional reasons: As many commentators have seen, property regimes may produce superior incentives to create and develop wealth. Or, as suggested above, undivided claims may be appropriate because Solomonic regimes cannot adequately identify and exclude low-valuing claimants who would hold up beneficial trade.[242] Our earlier list of contraindicators is not exhaustive.[243] Nevertheless, the ubiquitous claim that strong property regimes promote trade, and are therefore most effective at eliciting the parties' revealed

---

239. *See* Kahneman et al., *Experimental Tests, supra* note 238, at 1338.

240. The endowment effect as a barrier to trade may not be inconsistent with efficiency if the divergent preferences of the endowed and unendowed bargainers are taken at face value. *See* Daniel S. Levy & David Friedman, *The Revenge of the Redwoods?: Reconsidering Property Rights and the Economic Allocation of Natural Resources*, 61 U. CHI. L. REV. 493, 506–15 (1994) (describing circumstances in which endowment bias may be consistent with rational decision making).

241. Divided entitlements, however, are unlikely to facilitate value-enhancing trade if the costs of negotiation, or "toll costs," are the sole impediment to Coasean efficiency. Divided entitlements, such as liability rules, may be efficient if toll costs are sufficiently high, but divided entitlements are not likely to produce more consensual trade than property rules when there is no informational or psychological barrier to trade.

242. Solomonic regimes may be particularly difficult to sustain over time. The teleological rationale for Solomonic entitlements is reunification of the entitlement in the hands of the highest valuer. Solomonic divisions therefore are intended to be transitory allocations. After Solomonic negotiations produce undivided entitlements, subsequent events may create uncertainty about who is the highest valuer. It may be difficult for a Solomonic regime to divide an entitlement repeatedly among ensuing generations of potential owners, and the prospect of continual reallocations may undermine initial bargainers' incentives to purchase.

243. Undivided property rule allocations might foster competition among multiple sellers or buyers. For example, technical economic models have explored the effects on bargaining outcomes of an increase in the number of parties. *See, e.g.,* Thomas A. Gresik & Mark A. Satterthwaite, *The Rate at Which a Simple Market Converges to Efficiency as the Number of Traders Increases: An Asymptotic Result for Optimal Trading Mechanisms*, 48 J. ECON. THEORY 304 (1989); Robert Wilson, *Incentive Efficiency of Double Auctions*, 53 ECONOMETRICA 1101 (1985). But there are many contexts in which two (or a small set of) parties have bilateral (or multilateral) control over the allocation of idiosyncratic gains from trade. Moreover, divided entitlement allocations may not be inconsistent with competition. For example, giving a buyer call options on multiple sellers may facilitate competition, in part by destabilizing seller collusion.

preference, does not withstand close analysis. The Coasean impulse to bargain transcends many entitlement structures and may even be strongest when claims are divided among the class of potentially efficient owners.

APPENDIX

A. *Derivation of Liability Rule Results*

This portion of the Appendix derives the equilibrium outcomes of the stylized bargaining game considered in Part II. Recalling our notation, let v_π denote the plaintiff's valuation, and let v_Δ denote the defendant's valuation. v_π is assumed to be distributed uniformly on [0,100], while v_Δ is a discrete and independent random variable, distributed on [40,60] with equal (1/2) probabilities. As an evaluative measuring stick, consider the expected social welfare associated with a "first-best" allocation (ESW^{fb}), in which the highest valuer always receives the entitlement:[244]

$$ESW^{fb} = \frac{1}{2}[\$40 \cdot Pr\{v_\pi < \$40\} + E\{v_\pi|v_\pi \geq \$40\} \cdot Pr\{v_\pi \geq \$40\}]$$
$$+ \frac{1}{2}[\$60 \cdot Pr\{v_\pi < \$60\} + E\{v_\pi|v_\pi \geq \$60\} \cdot Pr\{v_\pi \geq \$60\}].$$

Given the assumed distributions, it is straightforward to calculate the value of ESW^{fb} to be \$63.00.

We consider a game of bargaining under incomplete information that has the following rules. In the first stage of the game, the plaintiff is allowed to send a "signal" to the defendant indicating which type of transaction she would like to enter. The plaintiff can either signal "Mβ" (or "make me a buy offer for my entitlement"), or she can send the signal "Mσ" (or "make me a sell offer on your call option"). After hearing the signal, the defendant makes the requested type of offer: Either he offers to buy the plaintiff's entitlement for some amount β, or he offers to sell the plaintiff his option position for some demanded amount σ.[245] This is a take-it-or-leave-it offer.

Upon hearing either offer, the plaintiff may either accept it (A_i) or reject it (R_i), where i = β,σ. If the plaintiff who signaled Mβ accepts the defendant's buy offer β, then the plaintiff receives a payoff of β (she sells her entitlement but gets the offered price \$$\beta$), and the defendant gets a payoff of v_Δ-β (he enjoys undivided interest in the entitlement, but must pay \$$\beta$). Conversely, if the M$\beta$ signaling plaintiff rejects, then the players enter the "noncooperative" litigation game that they would play in the absence of bargaining: The defendant can play "Take" or "No Take," corresponding to a decision whether

---

244. Note that since $v_\pi \sim U[0,100]$, the density of v_π must be 1/100 over that interval.

245. Though we constrain the defendant to make the requested type of offer, the truth of the plaintiff's signal would actually be enough to induce the defendant to make that type of offer even if the rules did not constrain him. It is therefore quite simple to transform this game into a true "cheap talk" model. In their recent manuscript, Kaplow and Shavell assert a model where such pre-bid signaling is not permitted. Their model therefore does not detect any bargaining-facilitating effects of liability rules, stressing instead the "Hobbesian"—or autarkic—rationale for liability rules. *See* Kaplow & Shavell, *supra* note 101, at 28 n.31 ("[W]e expect the liability rule to be superior to property rules because, under a liability rule there is a lessor need for the parties to engage in bargaining.").

or not, upon bargaining breakdown, he will induce a nonconsensual transfer of the entitlement. If the defendant decides not to take, then the plaintiff enjoys her private valuation v_π, while the defendant gets nothing. Conversely, if the defendant does take, the plaintiff can play either "Suit" or "No Suit." If the plaintiff files suit, she is assumed to win with probability one (i.e., there is no judicial "error" as such) and collect the $D in damages. A similar description follows the path subsequent to a plaintiff signal of "Mσ."

As Harsanyi has shown,[246] because this is a game of incomplete information, it can be modeled as a game of imperfect information through the introduction of a "nature" player (player number 0 in the text) who initially chooses the player types (v_π, v_Δ). A course representation of the extensive form of the bargaining game is contained in Figure A1.

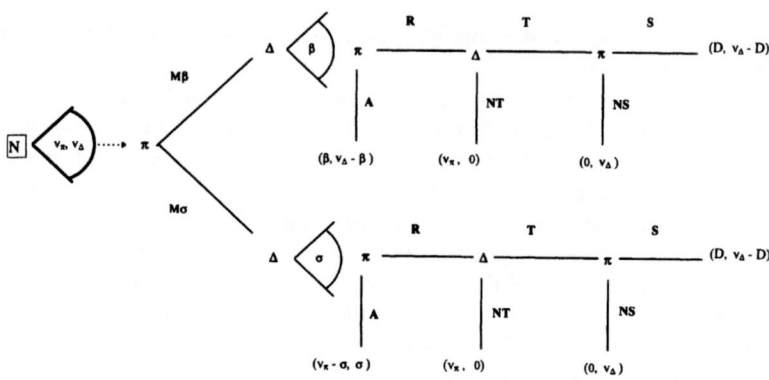

FIGURE A1. *Extensive Form Representation of Bargaining Game for Liability and Property Rules*

Note that this representation is "course" because it shows only a representative branch of the "continuation game" after nature has chosen the player types. There is in actuality a continuum of those branches. Moreover, because each player is aware only of her type, neither is completely certain which branch she is in (though each can rule out certain branches). This means that this

---

246. *See* John C. Harsanyi, *Games with Incomplete Information Played by "Bayesian" Players, I-III,* 14 MGMT. SCI. 159 (1967).

game has no singleton information sets, as is usually the case in signaling games.[247]

Upon inspection of this game, it is immediately clear that, should the game progress to the right-most decision node, a rational plaintiff will always file suit no matter what the size of the liability amount, so long as $D \geq 0$, which we henceforth assume. Thus, any perfect Bayesian equilibrium (PBE) must call for the plaintiff to play "Suit" on or off the equilibrium path. Working backward, it becomes apparent that the defendant's decision whether to "take" depends on whether his valuation is above or below the liability amount D. There are thus three relevant intervals for D: $D \leq \$40$, $\$40 < D \leq \$60$, and $D > \$60$. Although the text compares only damage amounts of \$100 and \$50, for clarity we analyze all the relevant cases below *ad seriatim*. Before proceeding, however, the reader should note that when $D > \$60$, the liability rule effectively reproduces a pro-plaintiff property right, since no defendant would take absent a consensual transaction. Conversely, when $D < \$40$, the law gives a theoretical equivalent of a property right to the defendant (albeit combined with a type of lump-sum transfer to the plaintiff).[248]

In each case, we will establish our main assertion: that rational plaintiffs for whom $v_\pi \leq D$ never have an incentive to play Mσ (which would signal a desire to bribe the defendant not to take), and plaintiffs for whom $v_\pi > D$ never have an incentive to play Mβ (which would signal a desire to transfer entitlement to the defendant consensually). We use the notion of "rationalizability"—the Bayesian cousin of iterated strict dominance—to make this point. We will then calculate the equilibrium strategies under each case.

Case (a): $D > \$60$

PROPOSITION 1A: When $D > \$60$, all perfect Bayesian outcomes of the above signaling game are supported by a "partitioning" strategy of the plaintiff types, where the plaintiff signals Mβ if $v_\pi \leq D$ and signals Mσ if $v_\pi > D$.

The proof of this proposition is as follows. We first note that any perfect Bayesian equilibrium must involve "rationalizable" strategies—i.e., strategies that survive iterated removal of irrational actions.[249] (Note that for two-player

---

247. Because of the technical difficulty in doing so, we have not attempted to represent the players' information sets in the above diagram. Nevertheless, they must be considered as a component of any signaling equilibrium.

248. Noting this point again is important, since it exposes the fact that a "true" liability rule (in a strategic sense) depends on the defendant's value as well as the plaintiff's. It is therefore somewhat uninstructive to think of liability rules and bargaining solely in terms of damage amounts that depend only on plaintiffs' valuations.

249. *See* B. Douglas Bernheim, *Rationalizable Strategic Behavior*, 52 ECONOMETRICA 1007, 1016 (1984); David G. Pearce, *Rationalizable Strategic Behavior and the Problem of Perfection*, 52 ECONOMETRICA 1029, 1035 (1984).

games like this one, rationalizability is equivalent to iterated strict dominance). We therefore consider the set of rationalizable strategies in the game depicted above for $D > \$60$.

When D exceeds \$60, no rational defendant would ever play "Take" should the game proceed that far. Indeed, so doing would induce the plaintiff to sue with probability one (as we noted above), thereby giving the defendant a negative payoff. Thus, the parties know that absent a negotiated solution, the plaintiff's payoff must be v_π and the defendant's payoff will be 0 (regardless of his type).

Given this structure of "reservation utilities," we now work back to the bargaining stages. Consider first the branches of the game where the defendant offers to buy the plaintiff's entitlement for $\$\beta$. A plaintiff will accept this bid only if it exceeds her reservation utility v_π. Since the plaintiff's valuation, however, can take on any value between \$0 and \$100, acceptance is always a rationalizable action with positive probability. Iterating back, the defendant realizes that the plaintiff could rationally accept any positive bid with at least some probability. But under no circumstances will the defendant be willing to bid more than \$60 for the plaintiff's entitlement (the largest valuation the defendant could have). Thus, the interval between \$0 and \$60 represents the range of rationalizable defendant buy offers β. Iterating back once more, it is clear that plaintiffs for whom $v_\pi > \$60$ will never receive an acceptable bid by the defendant (and they thus will receive only their reservation value v_π, since no bargains are possible). Plaintiffs whose valuations are less than \$60, however, stand to increase their payoffs above their reservation value of v_π by reporting $M\beta$.

Now consider branches in the game where the defendant offers to sell his call option to the plaintiff for an amount σ. Notice that when $D > \$60$ the plaintiff knows that the defendant will never exercise the call option in equilibrium. Thus, the defendant really has nothing to sell, and acceptance of the defendant's demand is rationalizable only when $\sigma = \$0$. This leaves the defendant in this branch indifferent between selling for \$0 and making a frivolous offer (anything greater than zero). Thus, all offers by the defendant are equally rationalizable here, and all have the same outcome—the plaintiff gets her reservation utility v_π, and the defendant gets a zero payoff.

Finally, consider the plaintiff's choice whether to play $M\beta$ or $M\sigma$. As we have stated above, plaintiffs for whom $v_\pi \leq \$60$ stand to increase their payoffs (above v_π) by reporting $M\beta$. Thus, for these plaintiffs this strategy is the only rationalizable strategy and must be part of any perfect Bayesian equilibrium. On the other hand, all plaintiffs for whom $v_\pi > \$60$ know that reaching nontrivial consensual transactions of either kind is impossible. They therefore resign themselves to receiving v_π in equilibrium. As such, these "high" plaintiffs are indifferent between reporting $M\beta$ and $M\sigma$. Moreover, the defendant is unaffected by their ultimate decision, since he knows that his market consists only of plaintiffs for whom $v_\pi \leq \$60$.

This establishes our assertion from the text (at least for $D > \$60$) that plaintiffs whose valuation is less than the liability amount D have no affirmative incentive to signal anything other than $M\beta$, and those whose valuation exceeds the damage amount have no affirmative incentive to signal anything other than $M\sigma$. It also completes the proof of the proposition. To determine the perfect Bayesian equilibrium *outcomes* of this game, one can concentrate solely on equilibria where the plaintiff signals $M\beta$ if and only if $v_\pi \leq D$ and $M\sigma$ if and only if $v_\pi > D$. Although this constraint truncates the set of equilibrium strategy profiles of the game, it prunes only those strategy profiles that are "outcome irrelevant," in that it coerces a particular signal only from indifferent players who were destined not to consummate any Coasean bargains in the first place. Similar reasoning applies to the other two relevant intervals of D.

Imposing this behavior on the plaintiff types, then, it is extremely straightforward to calculate the equilibrium strategies and outcomes for $D > \$60$. It turns out that in this case there is a unique perfect Bayesian outcome (albeit supported by a number of strategy profiles). A representative profile looks like the following. Any defendant who receives the signal $M\sigma$ replies with a "nonserious" bid of $\sigma = \sigma^* > \$0$, which the plaintiff rejects, giving the players respective payoffs of v_π and 0. Conversely, when the defendant receives a signal of $M\beta$, he sets his buy offer β at the point that maximizes his continuation payoff. Noting that a plaintiff will accept any bid β that is greater than her reservation value v_π, the defendant maximizes the following:

$$Max_{\beta \in [0, v_\pi]} \ Pr\{v_\pi \leq \beta | v_\pi \leq D\} \cdot [v_\Delta - \beta] + Pr\{v_\pi > \beta | v_\pi \leq D\} \cdot 0.$$

Using the fact that $v_\pi \sim U[0,100]$, the first-order conditions of this maximization problem imply that the optimal bid function, $\beta^*(v_\Delta)$, is given by

$$\beta^*(v_\Delta) = \frac{v_\Delta}{2},$$

for $v_\Delta = \$40, \$60$, which is the typical result obtained in a panoply of take-it-or-leave-it games with a distinct buyer and seller. In fact, this result is what we would expect for $D > \$60$, since such an entitlement is effectively a pro-plaintiff property rule. The above equation immediately produces the result given in Part II of the text for a "property rule" protection for the plaintiff; i.e., a $60 defendant bids $30 for the plaintiff's entitlement, while a $40 defendant bids $20. As one can see, this is a partially "separating" equilibrium in which defendants completely reveal their private information through their bid. The expected social welfare (ESW$^{D>60}$) associated with this strategy profile, as well as all other perfect Bayesian profiles, is $59.75.

Case (b): D ≤ $40

Just as in the previous case, this case supports our partitioning hypothesis. Because of the similarity in the approach to the case of D > $60, however, we state the following proposition without proof.

> PROPOSITION 1B: When D ≤ $40, all perfect Bayesian outcomes of the above signaling game are supported by a "partitioning" strategy of the plaintiff types, where the plaintiff signals Mβ if $v_\pi \leq D$ and signals Mσ if $v_\pi > D$.

In contrast to the previous example, when D ≤ $40 it is common knowledge that, absent a negotiated agreement, the defendant will take with probability one. Thus, the reservation utilities for the plaintiff and defendant are $D and $(v$_A$-D), respectively. Once again assuming this partitioning behavior on behalf of the plaintiff, it is straightforward to calculate the equilibrium outcomes of this game. A representative strategy profile looks like the following. Any defendant who receives a signal of Mβ replies with a "nonserious" buy offer of β = β** < $D, which the plaintiff promptly rejects (since she knows that she can get $D through litigation), and the parties each receive their respective reservation values. If the defendant receives the signal of Mσ, however, he sets his sell offer σ at the point that maximizes his continuation payoff. Noting that a plaintiff will accept any offer σ that ensures that her postpurchase payoff (v$_\pi$-σ) is greater than her reservation value $D, the defendant maximizes the following:

$$Max_{\sigma \in [0, v_A]} \; Pr\{v_\pi - \sigma \geq D | v_\pi \geq D\} \cdot \sigma \; + \; Pr\{v_\pi - \sigma < D | v_\pi \geq D\} \cdot [v_A - D].$$

The first-order conditions of this maximization problem imply that the optimal ask function, σ**(v$_A$), is given by

$$\sigma^{**}(v_A) = \frac{(v_A + 100)}{2} - D,$$

for v$_A$ = $40, $60. The above equation immediately produces the result given in Part II of the text for "property rule" protection for the defendant, a case not discussed explicitly in the text. Note that this equilibrium is also separating, since the different types of defendants make different sell offers. The expected social welfare (ESW$^{D≤40}$) associated with this strategy profile, as well as all other perfect Bayesian profiles, is $59.75, just like the earlier case.

Case (c): $40 < D ≤ $60.

As in the previous two cases, this interval also supports our partitioning hypothesis. And once again, because of the similarity in the approach to the case of D > $60, we state the following proposition without proof:

> PROPOSITION 1C: When $40 < D ≤ $60, all perfect Bayesian outcomes of the above signaling game are supported by a "partitioning" strategy of the plaintiff types, where the plaintiff signals Mβ if $v_\pi ≤ D$ and signals Mσ if $v_\pi > D$.

This is probably the most interesting of the three cases, since absent negotiation, the defendant types are destined to take different actions. Low-valuing defendants will not take while high-valuing defendants will take and pay the liability amount. This gives $40 defendants and $60 defendants reservation utilities of $0 and $(60-D), respectively. The plaintiff's reservation value, as given in Part II of the text, is $(v_\pi/2 + D/2)$.

We can now calculate the equilibrium outcome for this intermediate range of damage amounts. Since this game has no equilibria involving mixed strategies by the defendant in making buy offers β or sell offers σ,[250] we concentrate on characterizing a possible pure strategy equilibrium.

Unlike the previous two cases, there are now two nontrivial types of transactions that can occur. These transactions, labeled Coasean bargains #1 and #2 in the text, take the following forms. In the first, the defendant offers to sell his call option to the plaintiff at a price of σ. The plaintiff is interested in such a transaction, however, only if she thinks she is buying out the position of a $60 defendant; for the $40 defendant does not present a threat to take, and therefore has nothing to sell. Consequently, if the defendant ever submits a sell offer that reveals him to be a $40 defendant, the plaintiff will surely reject that offer. Note further, however, that the $40 defendant would *like* to have his sell offer accepted by the plaintiff, as acceptance would give him a payoff of σ rather than a sure payoff of $0 should no agreement be reached.

In a similar vein, the second type of Coasean bargain entails the defendant offering to buy the plaintiff's entitlement for a price of β, which is less than the liability amount of $D. The plaintiff is interested in such a transaction, however, only if she thinks she is selling to a $40 defendant, who otherwise would not take; the $60 defendant is not an attractive trading partner for this type of transaction, since negotiation failure would result in a nonconsensual taking by this defendant, but would garner the plaintiff a payoff of $D—more than any rationalizable value of β. Consequently, if the defendant ever submits

---

250. We do not attempt to prove this here. A more rigorous analysis appears in a separate piece by coauthor Talley that also takes a more general approach to bargaining in the shadow of default entitlements. *See* Talley, *supra* note 14, at 7–13.

a buy offer that reveals him to be a $60 defendant, the plaintiff will surely reject that offer. Once again, however, the $60 defendant would *like* to have his bid accepted by the plaintiff, as acceptance would lower the price that he would otherwise have to pay for a nonconsensual taking (since $\beta \leq D$). Given the above reasoning, we immediately arrive at the following corollary:

> COROLLARY 1: For $D \in (40,60]$, all pure strategy perfect Bayesian equilibria of bargaining game Γ involve complete pooling among the defendant types in choosing β and σ.

The above corollary allows us to limit our attention to equilibria of Γ in which the optimal bidding strategies for each defendant type are equal (i.e., $\beta^{**}(40) = \beta^{**}(60) \equiv \beta^{**}$) and the optimal sell offers of each defendant type are equal (i.e., $\sigma^{**}(40) = \sigma^{**}(60) \equiv \sigma^{**}$).

While the above results allow us to parse down significantly the various types of equilibria in this game, it turns out that the concept of Bayesian perfection is not capable of narrowing down the class of equilibria beyond the reach of Proposition 1a and Corollary 1. Indeed, for every hypothetical PBE involving pooled strategies σ^{**} and β^{**}, the sustainability of that equilibrium depends on the reaction of the plaintiff to *deviations* from the pooled offering strategies.[251] In the previous two cases, the plaintiff's reactions were easy to gauge, since she did not care which type of defendant issued a bid or ask; beliefs were irrelevant. In this case, however, the plaintiff has a vested interest in knowing whether a deviating offer was issued by a high- or low-valuing defendant. Because the concept of PBE does not specify an off-equilibrium belief structure, one cannot pin down a unique PBE. Thus, we have:

> COROLLARY 2: For $D \in (40,60]$, there is a continuum of pure strategy perfect Bayesian equilibria of bargaining game Γ involving pooled offers of σ^{**} and β^{**}.

Unfortunately, even some of the immediately obvious refinements to the PBE concept do not yield unique equilibria. The belief restrictions of sequential equilibrium[252] and even the added restriction of equilibrium domination[253] are insufficient to establish unique equilibrium.

The stronger refinement notion of "divinity,"[254] however, is immensely helpful, and it turns out that imposing the requirements of divinity allows us to pin down a single equilibrium outcome. In fact, this equilibrium outcome has an intuitively appealing form:

---

251. Clearly, along the equilibrium path, the plaintiff places a 1/2 probability that β^{**} or σ^{**} is sent by a $40 defendant.

252. *See* David M. Kreps & Robert Wilson, *Sequential Equilibria*, 50 ECONOMETRICA 863 (1982).

253. *See generally* Cho & Kreps, *supra* note 91.

254. *See generally* Banks & Sobel, *supra* note 91.

PROPOSITION 2: For D ∈ (40,60], there is a unique divine equilibrium outcome involving pooled pure strategy offers, σ^{**} and β^{**}, that correspond to the most-preferred PBE strategy of the high- and low-valuing defendants, respectively.[255]

Proposition 2 provides a convenient recipe for calculating the equilibrium offers of the defendant types. More important, Proposition 2 is extremely intuitive. As noted above, each of the two possible Coasean transactions will entail one bona fide offeror type (the $60 defendant in the case of sell offers σ, and the $40 defendant in the case of buy offers β), and one "pretender" who mimics the bona fide type's behavior. Proposition 2 states that the unique divine equilibrium of this game allows the $60 defendant to make his most-preferred sell offer σ, given that the $40 defendant will mimic that offer; and it allows the $40 defendant to make his most-preferred buy offer β, given that the $60 defendant will mimic that offer. This equilibrium coincides with a slightly different strategic situation in which the bona fide offeror in each case specifies his price first, and is then copied by the "pretender."[256]

Thus, consider the "optimal" offers for the bona fide type under each branch of the game Γ. Suppose first that the plaintiff signals Mβ, indicating that her valuation is below D, and that she is interested in perhaps selling her entitlement for $\beta \leq D$. By Corollaries 1 and 2, we know that the equilibrium must involve a pooled bid β from both types of defendants. Upon receiving this bid, the plaintiff knows that rejecting it will give her an expected payoff of $(v_\pi + D)/2$, and thus the probability that she accepts this bid is given by

$$Pr\{\pi \ accepts \ \beta\} = Pr\{\beta \geq \frac{(v_\pi + D)}{2} \mid v_\pi \leq D\} = \frac{2\beta - D}{D}.$$

Accordingly, the pooled bid that maximizes the expected return of the "bona fide" bidder type ($v_\Delta = \$40$) is the value of β that solves

$$Max_{\beta \in [0,40]} [\frac{2\beta - D}{D}] \cdot [40 - \beta].$$

As is easily confirmed, the first-order conditions of this maximization problem imply that the equilibrium pooled bid of the defendant is

$$\beta^{**} = 20 + \frac{D}{4},$$

which is equal to $32.50 when D = $50, the result given in the text.

A similar analysis applies to deriving the pooled equilibrium sell offer σ^{**}. Here, we find that the optimal offer for the "bona fide" $60 defendant is

---

255. The proof of this Proposition is omitted.

256. The driving force behind this equilibrium is the fact that off-equilibrium beliefs are such that any rationalizable deviation from the equilibrium behavior induces a belief that it came from either type with a 1/2 probability.

$$\sigma^{**} = 55 - \frac{3D}{4},$$

which is equal to $17.50 when D = $50, as given in the text.

Piecing the three regions together, we can plot the relationship between expected social welfare and information costs.

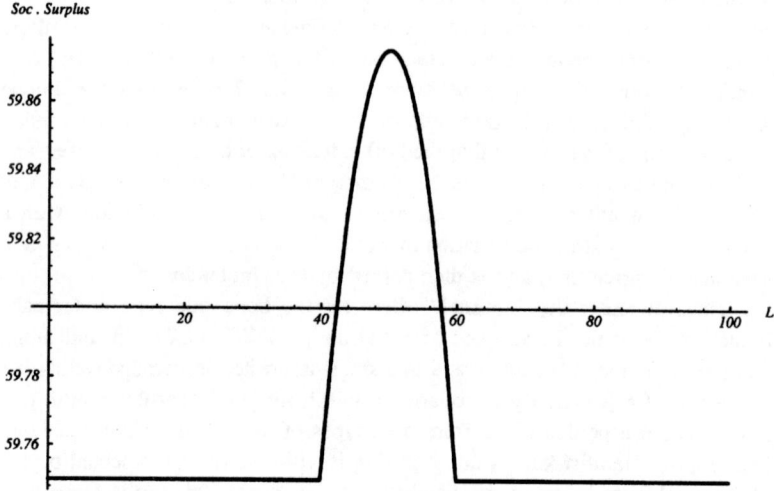

FIGURE A2. *Expected Social Welfare for Different Damage Amounts*

From Figure A2, one can see that social welfare has a "single-peaked" quality, in which welfare does not depend on D for all values of D that are less than $40 or greater than $60. These all represent "property-like" protections, since they ensure, respectively, that the defendant will always take, or that the defendant will never take absent a consensual transfer. For damage amounts that are more intermediate in nature, however (i.e., between $40 and $60), the welfare function is parabolic in shape, and its global maximum occurs at D = $50. Here, expected social welfare is equal to $59.875. Thus, expected social welfare increases continuously from the same value as property-like rights to a maximum at the mean valuation for the parties ($50).

B. *The Perverse Effects of Tailoring*

Below, we briefly show how the above model can be used to derive the results from the Section on "tailored" liability rules.[257] We consider tailored negligence and liability separately.

1. *Tailored Damages*

Suppose that instead of a fixed liability amount, the court awarded the plaintiff her valuation v_π. The defendant, on the other hand, will take only if his valuation v_Δ exceeds the expectation of the plaintiff's damages (or $50). Thus, the $40 defendant expects a payoff of $0 absent bargaining, while the $60 defendant expects a payoff of $10 (= $60-$50) absent bargaining.

Tailored damages effectively give the plaintiff a form of "perfect insurance" against a taking by the defendant. As such, the plaintiff will never wish to pay a positive amount to discourage a taking by the defendant. Indeed, paying the defendant not to take could only earn the plaintiff her private valuation less the cost of the bribe. Thus, it is rationalizable for all types of plaintiff to play Mβ in the first stage of the game.

Assuming, then, that all plaintiffs play Mβ, let us construct the (unique) perfect Bayesian outcome of the bargaining game within this legal environment. Because the plaintiff is guaranteed her private valuation, she is unconcerned whether the defendant's bid, β, reveals that the defendant is high- or low-valuing. The only factor influencing π's decision is whether the bid exceeds her private valuation v_π.

The $40 defendant (who as noted receives nothing absent bargaining) will set his bid so as to maximize his expected net revenue:

$$Max_{\beta \geq 0} \frac{\beta}{100} \cdot [40-\beta],$$

which is maximized at $\beta = $20.

The $60 defendant, on the other hand, faces a more complex decision. As mentioned above, absent bargaining, the $60 defendant will take, willingly bearing the expected $50 liability payment. If the $60 defendant makes a bid to buy the plaintiff's entitlement, however, then the defendant ultimately might decide not to take for one of two reasons. Either (1) the plaintiff will have accepted the defendant's bid β, or (2) the plaintiff will have rejected his bid, but his "updated" assessment of the type of plaintiff he faces induces him to abstain from taking. Thus, the $60 defendant chooses β to maximize the following:

---

257. *See supra* part II.C.

$$Max_{\beta \geq 0} \frac{\beta}{100} \cdot [60 - \beta] + \frac{100 - \beta}{100} [Max\{0, 60 - E\{v_\pi | v_\pi > \beta\}\}],$$

or, equivalently,

$$Max_{\beta \geq 0} \frac{\beta}{100} \cdot [60 - \beta] + \frac{100 - \beta}{100} [Max\{0, 10 - \beta/2\}].$$

Analyzing the cases of $\beta \leq \$20$ and $\beta > \$40$ separately, we find that there are two local maxima of this objective function, but that the global maximum occurs at $\beta = 0$—a nonserious bid. We thus have the result outlined in the text for tailored damages. The expected social surplus in this case is \$58 ($= (.5)\$60 + .5[(.2)\$40 + (.8)\$60]$).

2. *Tailored Liability*

Consider now the case of tailored liability, in which the court imposes damages of \$50 on a defendant whenever he is found to be negligent (*i.e.*, $v_\Delta < E\{v_\pi\}$). In such a situation, the \$60 defendant is never found to be negligent, and therefore always takes absent bargaining, paying no damages. The \$40 defendant, on the other hand, is always found to be negligent, and thus never takes absent bargaining. Consequently, the plaintiff's expected payoff absent bargaining is $v_\pi/2$ (i.e., 0 and v_π, each with probability 1/2).

When the plaintiff plays Mβ in the first round, she may expect serious offers only from the \$40 defendant. Indeed, the \$60 defendant is in a similar situation to the plaintiff in the previous Section: He receives his valuation regardless of whether a transaction is made. Upon playing Mβ, then the plaintiff proceeds as if she is facing a \$40 defendant. Thus, the \$40 defendant will enter a bid of \$20 (just as before), with the \$60 defendant once again entering a frivolous bid of \$0.

On the other hand, should the plaintiff play Mσ, then the \$60 defendant might be interested in such a transaction. The \$60 defendant, however, will offer to sell his right to take for no less than \$60. Clearly, there is a potential here for a Coasean improvement. Unfortunately, when the plaintiff plays Mσ, the \$40 defendant has the incentive to mimic the behavior of the \$60 defendant. Consequently, the plaintiff hearing a sale offer of σ will only accept it if her postcontractual payoff, $v_\pi - \sigma$, exceeds her expected reservation utility, $v_\pi/2$. Equivalently, it is easily verified that no plaintiff whose valuation is at most \$100 is willing to accept any sell demand in excess of \$50. Since the only bona fide seller in this situation is the \$60 defendant, then *no such transactions are ever made*. We can thus conclude that the only types of plaintiffs who are not indifferent between Mβ and Mσ are those for whom $v_\pi \leq \$20$. We therefore have the same equilibrium outcome we had in the case of tailored damages. Once again, the expected social surplus is \$58.

C. Derivation of Fractional Property Rule Results[258]

This Section derives the results from the fraction model of Part III. Recall from the text that the reservation utilities of the two players are qv_π for the plaintiff and $(1-q)v_\Delta$ for the defendant. Further, recall that the allocation and pricing rule associated with reports of r_π and r_Δ as described in the text is as follows: If $r_\pi \geq r_\Delta$, then π receives the injunctive right, but must pay Δ a price of

$$(1-q) \cdot (\tfrac{r_\pi + r_\Delta}{2}).$$

Conversely, if $r_\Delta > r_\pi$, then Δ receives the injunctive right, but must pay π an price of

$$(q) \cdot (\tfrac{r_\pi + r_\Delta}{2}).$$

In equilibrium, suppose that the players adopt a reporting strategy $r_i(v_i)$, where $i = \pi, \Delta$. Let $g_\pi(.)$ and $g_\Delta(.)$ represent the density of r_π and r_Δ, respectively, with $G_\pi(.)$ and $G_\Delta(.)$ representing the respective cumulative distribution functions, and r-upper bar and r-lower bar representing the supremum and infimum of the equilibrium bids. The plaintiff's net gain in making his report r_π is given by

$$R_\pi(r_\pi|v_\pi) = \int_{\underline{r}_\pi}^{\overline{r}_\Delta} [\tfrac{q}{2}(r_\pi + r_\Delta) - qv_\pi]dG_\Delta(r_\Delta) + \int_{\underline{r}_\Delta}^{r_\pi} [(1-q)v_\pi - \tfrac{(1-q)}{2}(r_\pi + r_\Delta)]dG_\Delta(r_\Delta).$$

Similarly, the defendant's net gain in making her report r_Δ is given by

$$R_\Delta(r_\Delta|v_\Delta) = \int_{\underline{r}_\pi}^{r_\Delta} [qv_\Delta - \tfrac{q}{2}(r_\pi + r_\Delta)]dG_\pi(r_\pi) + \int_{r_\Delta}^{\overline{r}_\pi} [\tfrac{(1-q)}{2}(r_\pi + r_\Delta) - (1-q)v_\Delta]dG_\pi(r_\pi).$$

The first-order conditions associated with maximizing the above functions are, respectively:

---

258. The analysis below follows Chatterjee & Samuelson, *supra* note 134, and Cramton et al., *supra* note 133.

$$(v_\pi - r_\pi)g_\Delta(r_\pi) + \frac{q}{2} - \frac{1}{2}G_\Delta(r_\pi) = 0,$$

$$(v_\Delta - r_\Delta)g_\pi(r_\Delta) + \frac{(1-q)}{2} - \frac{1}{2}G_\pi(r_\Delta) = 0.$$

It is possible to solve these differential equations, though not uniquely,[259] and arrive at the following equilibrium strategies:

$$r_\pi^*(v_\pi) = \frac{2}{3}v_\pi + \frac{25}{3} + \frac{50q}{3},$$

$$r_\Delta^*(v_\Delta) = \frac{2}{3}v_\Delta + 25 - \frac{50q}{3}.$$

Using these optimal reports for the parties, we can conclude that π receives the entitlement if and only if

$$r_\pi^*(v_\pi) \geq r_\Delta^*(v_\Delta),$$

or, equivalently, when

$$v_\pi \geq v_\Delta + 25 - 50q.$$

This is the equation given in the text.

---

259. *See* Chatterjee & Samuelson, *supra* note 134, at 842.

[9]

VOLUME 109　　　　FEBRUARY 1996　　　　NUMBER 4

HARVARD LAW REVIEW

ARTICLE

PROPERTY RULES VERSUS LIABILITY RULES: AN ECONOMIC ANALYSIS

Louis Kaplow and Steven Shavell

TABLE OF CONTENTS

PROPERTY RULES VERSUS LIABILITY RULES: AN ECONOMIC ANALYSIS

*Louis Kaplow and Steven Shavell**

*Should property rights be protected absolutely — by property rules —
or instead by the requirement that infringing parties pay for harm done
— that is, by liability rules? In this Article, we present a systematic
economic analysis of this fundamental question. Our primary object is to
explain why liability rules are often employed to protect individuals
against harmful externalities (such as pollution and automobile accidents), whereas property rules are generally relied upon to protect individuals from having their possessions taken from them, thereby ensuring
a basic incident of ownership.*

*In the course of our analysis, we suggest that a variety of commonly
held beliefs about property and liability rules are in error, and we also
derive results bearing on legal policy. Notably, we show that, for controlling some important externalities, liability rules (and pollution taxes) are
superior to property rules (including many forms of regulation) even when
damages must be set using only limited information about harm.*

I. INTRODUCTION

The state has at its disposal two fundamental ways of protecting property rights. On one hand, it may adopt *property rules*, under which it guarantees property right assignments against infringement through the threatened use of its police powers. On the other hand, the state may employ *liability rules*, under which it merely discourages violations by requiring transgressors to pay victims for harms suffered.

In this Article, we offer a systematic economic analysis of the relative desirability of property and liability rules.[1] A major objective of

---

* Professors, Harvard Law School, and Research Associates, National Bureau of Economic Research. We wish to thank Ian Ayres, David Charny, Richard Craswell, Robert Ellickson, William Fisher, Victor Goldberg, Eric Kramer, Frank Michelman, A. Mitchell Polinsky, Richard Posner, Carol Rose, Stewart Schwab, Warren Schwartz, Robert Stavins, Eric Talley, and workshop participants for comments; Jennifer Shields and Matthew Stowe for research assistance; and the John M. Olin Center for Law, Economics, and Business at Harvard Law School for research support.

[1] The leading article on the subject is Guido Calabresi & A. Douglas Melamed, *Property Rules, Liability Rules, and Inalienability: One View of the Cathedral*, 85 HARV. L. REV. 1089 (1972). Our Article does not examine rules prohibiting alienation, as did Calabresi and Melamed's, *see id.* at 1111–15, because such rules are not generally employed in the contexts we examine and are usually used for reasons different from those we consider. For a discussion of rules prohibiting alienation, see generally Susan Rose-Ackerman, *Inalienability and the Theory of Property Rights*, 85 COLUM. L. REV. 931 (1985). Other prominent articles that study property and liability rules from an economic perspective include Robert C. Ellickson, *Alternatives to Zoning: Covenants, Nuisance Rules, and Fines as Land Use Controls*, 40 U. CHI. L. REV. 681 (1973); A. Mitchell Polinsky, *Controlling Externalities and Protecting Entitlements: Property Right, Liability*

the Article is to explain why possessory interests in things are generally protected by property rules, whereas interests in not suffering from harmful externalities are often, though not always, protected only by liability rules.[2]

To amplify, if I have rightful possession of some thing — such as an automobile or a home — another person ordinarily cannot take it without my permission.[3] He cannot make a unilateral decision to borrow my automobile and pay me for my trouble, or invite himself into my home and simply pay me for the intrusion. Indeed, the inability of others to appropriate my things lies at the core of the notions of "ownership" and "property."

If, however, I am exposed to the risk of harm generated by another party's conduct, I may be protected primarily by a liability rule. Liability rule protection applies to much polluting behavior and to many of the great multitude of acts governed by the law of unintentional torts. We are permitted to engage in such acts — from hunting to driving to construction — even though they create risks of harm and thus constitute probabilistic invasions of property interests, but we are often obligated to pay damages for any harm that we cause. To be sure, not all harmful externalities are regulated by liability rules. Notably, a person's right to be free from loud noises, noxious odors, and certain other nuisances may be ensured by his power to have harmful

---

Rule, and Tax-Subsidy Approaches, 8 J. LEGAL STUD. 1 (1979) [hereinafter Polinsky, *Controlling Externalities*]; A. Mitchell Polinsky, *Resolving Nuisance Disputes: The Simple Economics of Injunctive and Damage Remedies*, 32 STAN. L. REV. 1075 (1980) [hereinafter Polinsky, *Resolving Nuisance Disputes*]; and Frank I. Michelman, *Pollution as a Tort: A Non-Accidental Perspective on Calabresi's Costs*, 80 YALE L.J. 647, 667–83 (1971) (book review). *See also* Darryl Biggar, *A Model of Punitive Damages in Tort*, 15 INT'L REV. L. & ECON. 1 (1995) (addressing related issues in the context of punitive damages in tort).

Several articles have been written about contract law analogs to the choice between property and liability rules. *See, e.g.,* Anthony T. Kronman, *Specific Performance*, 45 U. CHI. L. REV. 351 (1978) (analyzing the choice between specific performance, a property-like protection of the promisee, and damages for breach, a liability rule); Alan Schwartz, *The Case for Specific Performance*, 89 YALE L.J. 271 (1979) (same); Richard Craswell, *Property Rules and Liability Rules in Unconscionability and Related Doctrines*, 60 U. CHI. L. REV. 1 (1993) (analyzing whether the remedy for unconscionable contracts should be voiding the agreement, affording property-rule-like protection to the "victim," or supplying terms that a court believes reasonable, a liability-rule-like approach). Our Article does not consider the contractual context (although our analysis may have some bearing on contract law).

[2] As will become evident, by the protection of possessory interests in things, we refer to the prevention of the unwanted transfer of possession of a physical object to a taker. By harmful externalities, we mean adverse outcomes that occur as a byproduct of an injurer's activity, a familiar instance being pollution caused by a firm's operations. We will presume in most of the analysis that the distinction between the taking of things (violation of possessory interests) and harmful externalities is easily made. We discuss in section III.G possible difficulties in making the distinction and why our analysis is still informative when difficulties in classification arise.

[3] Of course, possessory rights are in fact often insecure; theft of one sort or another is frequently a serious problem. The social intent, however, is ordinarily for possessory rights to be inviolate, and for ease of exposition, this Article will usually analyze them as such. *But see infra* p. 757 (addressing the incomplete enforcement of property rights).

behavior enjoined (although some nuisances are controlled by liability rules).[4]

Somewhat surprisingly, this pattern of legal protection — definite and uncontroversial use of property rules to guarantee possessory interests, yet frequent, albeit not exclusive, use of liability rules in the domain of harmful externalities — has not been carefully evaluated heretofore.[5] Moreover, as we will discuss, arguments that commentators have advanced in support of liability rules for the control of externalities would seem to apply as well in the context of possessory interests.[6] This observation suggests that something is missing from their arguments, assuming that property rule protection of possessory interests is appropriate. We will discuss the problems with these arguments and adduce factors that justify the use of liability rules to regulate harmful externalities but that favor property rules to protect possessory interests.

In the course of our analysis, we will resolve important issues that have received substantial attention in the literature on property and liability rules. For example, when there is only limited information about harm, such as in the case of pollution, prior work emphasizes that liability rules will not function perfectly but does not indicate whether property rules would be superior.[7] However, we demonstrate

---

[4] *See, e.g.,* ROGER A. CUNNINGHAM, WILLIAM B. STOEBUCK & DALE A. WHITMAN, THE LAW OF PROPERTY 417–18, 421–22 (2d ed. 1993); JOSEPH W. SINGER, PROPERTY LAW § 3.4, at 321–24 (1993); 4 RESTATEMENT (SECOND) OF TORTS §§ 821F, 826 (1977); *see also* Boomer v. Atlantic Cement Co., 257 N.E.2d 870, 874–75 (N.Y. 1970) (holding that a cement plant producing air pollutants should pay damages instead of being subject to an injunction); Ellickson, *supra* note 1, at 719–22 (suggesting that the historical weakness of nuisance law in confining relief to property rules was partly responsible for the belief that zoning was necessary); Thomas W. Merrill, *Trespass, Nuisance, and the Costs of Determining Property Rights,* 14 J. LEGAL STUD. 13, 14–20 (1985) (discussing the domains of trespass and nuisance, which have different standards of liability and may provide different remedies); Note, *Efficient Land Use and the Internalization of Beneficial Spillovers: An Economic and Legal Analysis,* 31 STAN. L. REV. 457, 464–65 (1979) (describing the historical movement from property rules protecting victims, to property rules protecting injurers, and finally to liability rules).

[5] Most prior literature (such as that cited in note 1) focuses on harmful externalities. Calabresi and Melamed, however, briefly address the question why property rules are used to guarantee possessory interests. More precisely, they pose the question why the sanction for robbers should not be the value of the thing taken — that is, why a liability rule should not be employed. *See* Calabresi & Melamed, *supra* note 1, at 1124–25. The main answer they supply, *see id.* at 1126–27, is essentially that described in the text to follow, *see infra* p. 718, which we conclude is erroneous. (We discuss their specific argument further in note 6.)

[6] For example, the chief argument that Calabresi and Melamed advance in favor of a liability rule for nuisance when bargaining is difficult seems to imply that thieves should be subject to a liability rule for taking things when the owners cannot be contacted. *See* Calabresi & Melamed, *supra* note 1, at 1125–27. At the same time, the doubts that Calabresi and Melamed express about the efficiency of liability rules for theft — due to the difficulty of evaluating victims' losses, *see id.* at 1125–26 — would seem to be equally serious with respect to nuisances.

[7] One of the main concerns of a recent article by James Krier and Stewart Schwab is that the existing literature is inadequate because it has not resolved this ambiguity. *See* James E. Krier & Stewart J. Schwab, *Property Rules and Liability Rules: The Cathedral in Another Light,*

that, even though liability rules perform imperfectly when information about harm is limited, they remain superior to property rules. This conclusion has strong implications for the assessment of current and proposed schemes of environmental regulation.[8]

In addition, we will cast doubt on the belief that property rules are best when transaction costs are low — assertedly because the use of property rules will induce parties to bargain and reach desirable outcomes — whereas liability rules are best when transaction costs are high — supposedly because the use of liability rules will induce injurers to act desirably, mimicking the outcomes that would otherwise have been reached through bargaining.[9] We find that this belief is often contradicted: when transaction costs are low, parties will tend to bargain under liability rules as well as under property rules and may reach outcomes superior to those reached under property rules;[10] and when transaction costs are high and bargaining is impossible, property rules may lead to better outcomes than do liability rules.[11]

Our analysis is divided into two Parts: Part II deals with harmful externalities; Part III addresses the taking of things.[12] (We formally prove a number of the arguments made in these Parts in an Appendix to this Article.) Let us begin by briefly describing for each context what we consider to be the present understanding of the virtues of property versus liability rules and how we extend or modify the conventional wisdom.

---

70 N.Y.U. L. REV. 440, 447–64 (1995). They correctly observe that Calabresi and Melamed's article, cited above in note 1, is difficult to interpret on the issue, and that Polinsky's writing, cited above in note 1, calls into question the desirability of liability rules when harm is difficult to evaluate, but that much subsequent work seems to assume the desirability of liability rules without addressing the problem of imperfect information about harm.

[8] *See infra* section II.E.1.

[9] *See, e.g.,* RICHARD A. POSNER, ECONOMIC ANALYSIS OF LAW § 3.7, at 56–57, § 3.9, at 70 (4th ed. 1992); Calabresi & Melamed, *supra* note 1, at 1125–27 (discussed in note 6); Krier & Schwab, *supra* note 7, at 447–53 (presenting the conventional wisdom for purposes of subsequent criticism); *see also* Craswell, *supra* note 1, at 1–15 (adopting the conventional view on transaction costs and liability rules in the contract context, and noting the acceptance of the view by others); David D. Haddock, Fred S. McChesney & Menahem Spiegel, *An Ordinary Economic Rationale for Extraordinary Legal Sanctions,* 78 CAL. L. REV. 1, 13–36 (1990) (arguing for the "extraordinary" sanction of punitive damages in tort actions and liquidated damages beyond actual loss in contract claims — property rule protection — to force bargaining in certain circumstances); Merrill, *supra* note 4, at 14, 25–26 (arguing that a legal system seeking efficiency will tend to use the law of trespass when transaction costs are low and the law of nuisance, with a balancing test to assign the entitlement — which sometimes implies only a right to the payment of damages — when transaction costs are high).

[10] *See infra* section II.B.2. This general point is also a theme of Polinsky, *Resolving Nuisance Disputes,* cited above in note 1, at 1090–91, 1093–95, 1101–02, 1104–05, and of an article written contemporaneously, but independently, of ours, Ian Ayres & Eric Talley, *Solomonic Bargaining: Dividing a Legal Entitlement to Facilitate Coasean Trade,* 104 YALE L.J. 1027 (1995). *See infra* note 19 (discussing Polinsky's and Ayres and Talley's conclusions).

[11] *See infra* section III.A.2.

[12] On the distinction between the two contexts, see note 2 and section III.G.

Harmful Externalities. When the problem of harmful externalities arises, it is often the case that the involved parties cannot practically bargain with one another, so that the resolution of difficulties will be determined directly by the choice of legal rules. In this context, the commonly held view in the literature is that liability rules are superior to property rules, assuming that courts can accurately determine the extent of harm.[13] In a classic example, a firm that is liable for pollution-caused harm will behave desirably: it will prevent pollution if and only if its prevention cost is less than the harm caused, simply because the firm will have to pay for any harm done. By contrast, if victims are protected by a property rule, firms will be forced to prevent pollution even when their prevention costs exceed the harms that would result — an undesirable outcome.[14]

However, some of the literature suggests that liability rules may be inferior to property rules if courts would have difficulty ascertaining the actual level of harm.[15] If courts underestimate harm, a liable firm might pollute even though its prevention cost is less than the true level of harm, whereas under a property rule protecting victims, the firm would not pollute.

This latter belief we believe to be mistaken. We demonstrate that *even when courts are uncertain about the magnitude of harm, liability rules are superior to property rules*. Specifically, we show that if a court sets damages equal to its best estimate of harm — the average harm for cases characterized by the facts the court observes[16] — the outcome under the liability rule will be superior, on average, to the outcome under property rules. To explain, let us compare the liability rule to a property rule protecting victims.[17] These two rules result in the same outcome — no pollution — when prevention costs are below average harm, for then firms will be induced to prevent pollution under the liability rule. The rules differ when prevention costs are high — in excess of average harm — for then firms will pollute under the liability rule. But in this case, it is desirable for firms not to prevent pollution because harm, *on average*, is lower than the high prevention costs. (To be sure, it will *sometimes* be true that actual harm

---

[13] *See, e.g.*, POSNER, *supra* note 9, § 3.9, at 70 & n.5; Calabresi & Melamed, *supra* note 1, at 1108, 1119–21; Krier & Schwab, *supra* note 7, at 452–53 & n.44 (describing this view — without the caveat that harm can be accurately determined — as "virtual dogma" and citing authorities); Polinsky, *Resolving Nuisance Disputes, supra* note 1, at 1076 & n.7 (noting several commentators' views).

[14] Or, if firms' rights to pollute are protected by a property rule — that is, if they are freely permitted to pollute — they will generate pollution even when their prevention costs are less than the harm caused by their activity.

[15] *See, e.g.*, POSNER, *supra* note 9, § 3.9, at 70 n.5; Calabresi & Melamed, *supra* note 1, at 1125–27; Krier & Schwab, *supra* note 7, at 453–64.

[16] We discuss possible difficulties in estimating average harm in sections II.A.2 and II.A.3.

[17] Analysis of a property rule protecting injurers is analogous.

is greater than a firm's high prevention costs, but on average that will not be so.)

Our conclusion about the superiority of the liability rule might not follow, though, if courts were systematically to underestimate harm in setting damages, rather than to use estimates of harm that are correct on average. We discuss grounds for such an assumption but suggest that courts should be able to take corrective steps, so that a liability rule will retain its superiority.

We next compare property and liability rules when transaction costs are low, in which case parties can bargain with each other about potential externalities. As Coase emphasized, if there are no obstacles to the consummation of mutually beneficial bargains, it will make no difference what the legal regime is; thus, it will be irrelevant whether property rules or liability rules apply.[18] For instance, even if a firm cannot choose to pollute and pay court-ordered damages because victims are protected by a property rule, the firm will pay victims for permission to pollute when its prevention cost is high. But what if bargaining is not always successful because parties sometimes misgauge what each other is willing to pay or accept? In this case, no unambiguous conclusion can be drawn: either property rules or liability rules could be better, depending on rather subtle particulars of the situation.[19]

We then examine several factors — apart from the ability to bargain — that are of possible relevance to the choice between property and liability rules. One is victim behavior, specifically concerning victims' ability to mitigate harm.[20] Although the state can provide victims some incentives to reduce harm by using liability rules accompanied by defenses, the factor of victim behavior lends appeal to the property rule entitling injurers to cause harm or to modified liability rules under which injurers pay compensation to the state. Under these rules, victims are left uncompensated for injuries they suffer,

---

[18] *See* R.H. Coase, *The Problem of Social Cost*, 3 J.L. & ECON. 1, 2–15 (1960). The application of Coase's general conclusions to the context of property rules and liability rules is made, for example, in Polinsky, *Resolving Nuisance Disputes*, cited above in note 1, at 1088–92, which shows that property rules and liability rules each lead to efficient outcomes when bargaining is perfect.

[19] Polinsky also reached the conclusion that it is indeterminate whether property or liability rules are superior when bargaining is imperfect (although he did not analyze a formal model of bargaining with asymmetric information). *See, e.g.*, Polinsky, *Resolving Nuisance Disputes*, *supra* note 1, at 1079–80. Ayres and Talley devote much of their article to exploring the relative performance of property and liability rules when bargaining is imperfect. *See* Ayres & Talley, *supra* note 10. They do not emphasize the theoretical ambiguity about the relative performance of property versus liability rules. Instead, they stress that under liability rules, problems of asymmetric information are likely to be less severe than under property rules. We believe their view to be misleading. For further discussion, see note 71 and Appendix section I.B.2, comment c, below.

[20] The point that victims as well as injurers may be able to prevent harm was emphasized by Coase. *See* Coase, *supra* note 18, at 2, 12–13.

thereby creating incentives to avoid harm. Another factor that we investigate is the judgment-proof problem: injurers may not have enough wealth to pay for the harm done. When wealth is inadequate, a liability rule may be ineffective in inducing injurers to prevent harm, such as when a company whose assets are under a million dollars operates a highly dangerous chemical process that could kill thousands. In the face of this problem, we indicate that property rule protection of victims may become desirable. An additional factor that we discuss is administrative costs. We do not find that this factor leads to a systematic preference for either type of rule, although in particular circumstances it may be determinative. Finally, we consider risk aversion, effects on the distribution of income, and notions of entitlement, and we suggest that these factors have little relevance for the choice between property and liability rules.

The overall conclusion that we draw from our analysis is that *there is a prima facie case favoring liability rules over property rules for controlling harmful externalities, but property rule protection may become desirable on account of one or more of the factors mentioned above.* We illustrate our analysis by considering briefly the problems of industrial pollution, automobile accidents, and nuisance. We also explain that our analysis applies in important respects to the choice among conventional private remedies, regulation, corrective taxes, and marketable pollution rights.

The Taking of Things. Part III of the Article concerns the question whether things that an individual has in his or her possession should be protected by means of a liability rule rather than a property rule. That is, we ask: what would be wrong with a regime under which a person would be free to take a thing away from its possessor and pay an amount equal to a court's assessment of its value?

This basic question has not been considered by other writers in a sustained manner. One does, however, often find summary expression of the belief that use of a property rule to bar outright appropriation of things is desirable because it forces a person who wants something to bargain for it with its possessor.[21] The belief derives from the idea that, through the requirement of bargaining, we can be reasonably confident that property will change hands when and only when the change is efficient. For example, bargaining can ensure that my car will be transferred to another person when and only when he values it more highly than I do. This argument, however, is *not* one that supports property rules over liability rules in any obvious way. If we believe that bargaining will result in the achievement of mutually beneficial transfers when they exist, that will be so under a liability rule as well as under a property rule. If Jack can take my car if he

---

[21] *See, e.g.,* POSNER, *supra* note 9, § 3.9, at 70; Calabresi & Melamed, *supra* note 1, at 1124–27 (discussed in note 6).

pays damages of $10,000, but in fact I value the car more highly than he does, I could still bargain with Jack, paying him to refrain. (This is, of course, an application of the Coase Theorem.[22])

How then can one justify the use of property rules for protection of property rights in things? We develop a number of arguments that rationalize this fundamental characteristic of property law.[23] First, we explain that under a liability rule, bargaining might be rendered effectively impossible. Under a liability rule, we presume that *anyone* would enjoy the right to take my car. Thus, even though I would be willing to pay Jack not to take my car if it were inadequately valued by the courts, there would be no point in paying him to desist — for Jill, or someone else, could come along and take it the next day. Consequently, I would not pay Jack to forbear, and not being paid, he would in fact take my car.

Another problem with a regime of liability rules is what we call reciprocal takings: if Jack takes my car and the liability award is less than the car's value to me, I would want to take my car back from Jack. In a regime of liability for takings,[24] I could do this. The inevitable result would be tugs-of-war, altercations, frictions of some type. A pure system of liability rule protection would become unworkable.

If the problems of reciprocal takings and the effective impossibility of bargaining are put to the side, it might seem that the liability rule with damages equal to the average value of a thing taken would be attractive, by the logic we offer in favor of liability rules in the case of harmful externalities. But that logic, it turns out, does not extend to the case at hand, for reasons that are subtle and best deferred.[25]

Still another problem affecting the performance of liability rules concerns ex ante incentives: the behavior of parties prior to takings. To the degree that things might be undervalued by courts, potential victims of takings may take measures to protect their things (such as installing special locks on their cars) or may curtail productive activities, and potential acquirers may make investments to accomplish takings (such as obtaining devices to counter the locks). Such effects on behavior are socially counterproductive, akin to those engendered by the problem of theft. This waste is a further disadvantage of liability rules.

After discussing these arguments and considering administrative costs and several other factors, we conclude that *there is a strong theo-*

---

[22] *See* Coase, *supra* note 18, at 2–15.

[23] The order in which we consider the arguments here is somewhat different from that in Part III.

[24] A pure regime of liability for the taking of things provides that anyone may take another's thing, subject to the payment of damages. Once Jack takes my car, he becomes the possessor and I become a prospective taker, who is permitted under a liability rule to take what is now Jack's car. We discuss this issue further in section III.D.

[25] *See infra* section III.A.2.

retical case favoring the use of property rules for protection of posses-
sory rights in things, in contrast to our more qualified conclusion
favoring liability rules with regard to harmful externalities.

II. HARMFUL EXTERNALITIES

Our task here is to compare property rules and liability rules as
methods of controlling harmful externalities. To do this, we make several simplifying assumptions in our basic analysis: that there is a single
potential injurer and a single potential victim, and that the injurer can
prevent harm by making an expenditure (such as installing a smoke
arrestor).[26]

We will suppose that a *property rule* involves two elements: the
grant of an entitlement to either the victim or the injurer and absolute
protection of that entitlement. Specifically, if the victim has the entitlement to be free from harm, the injurer is precluded from causing
harm. We might imagine, for instance, that an injurer would suffer
such a stringent sanction if he caused harm that he would not dare to
cause it, or that the state would directly prevent the injurer from acting to cause harm (for example, by closing down a plant that did not
stop polluting). Similarly, if the injurer possesses the entitlement to
cause harm, the victim cannot stop him from doing so.[27]

We will presume that under a *liability rule*, the injurer is permitted to cause harm but must compensate the victim for the harm, or
the court's[28] best estimate of it.[29] That the measure of damages under

---

[26] Our conclusions, and the logic behind them, would not be altered in an essential way if we
were to assume that the injurer only reduced, rather than eliminated, the risk of harm or its
magnitude by taking a precaution, or if the injurer could alter harm by changing his level of
activity. However, our conclusions are affected by consideration of *victims'* behavior. *See infra*
section II.C.

[27] The characterization of a property rule as a choice of who should enjoy an entitlement,
coupled with its absolute protection, is emphasized in Calabresi and Melamed, cited above in note
1, at 1090–93.

In the analysis here, we take an entitlement to be complete. More generally, an entitlement
could be partial; for example, the victim could have the right to be free from more than x units of
harm. Partial entitlements are emphasized in Polinsky, *Controlling Externalities*, cited above in
note 1. We discuss partial entitlements below at pages 749–50 and 753–54.

[28] Throughout the article, we will use the word "court" as shorthand for a decisionmaker.
Thus, by the "court's" estimate, we mean to include the possibilities that damages are determined
by a jury, an arbitrator, an expert agency, and so forth.

[29] We assume for simplicity that liability is strict, but discuss the negligence rule in section
II.E.2. Also, we do not consider in the text Calabresi and Melamed's "fourth rule," now commonly referred to as the "reverse" liability rule, under which the victim has the right to prevent
harm, but must pay the injurer his cost of doing so. *See* Calabresi & Melamed, *supra* note 1, at
1116–17; Spur Indus. v. Del E. Webb Dev. Co., 494 P.2d 700, 708 (Ariz. 1972). The analysis of a
reverse liability rule would be similar to that of a conventional liability rule. We briefly comment
on reverse liability rules below in notes 37, 89, 92, 93, and 142, and in Appendix section I.A.2,
comment c. Finally, we note that what is sometimes referred to as a conditional injunction, *see*
Edward Rabin, *Nuisance Law: Rethinking Fundamental Assumptions*, 63 VA. L. REV. 1299, 1300
(1977) — an injunction that the injurer can dissolve upon the payment of damages — is tanta-

the liability rule is assumed to equal harm or its approximation is consistent with practice and makes our exposition easier. Also, were we to allow damages to be any quantum, then "liability" rules and property rules would no longer be distinct: a liability rule with very high damages is equivalent to property rule protection of victims, and a liability rule with damages of zero is equivalent to property rule protection of injurers. Later, however, we do discuss the class of liability rules in which damages may be set at any level.[30]

Finally, in most of the analysis, we take the social goal to be the minimization of the sum of harm and prevention costs. In section II.D, though, we also discuss administrative costs, the bearing of risk by the risk averse, distributional objectives, and notions of entitlement.

Let us now proceed to the analysis, beginning with the case in which parties do not bargain with one another, then addressing the situation in which they do, and subsequently examining the various other factors relevant to the performance of property and liability rules. Finally, we apply our analysis in a number of important legal domains.

A. Parties Do Not Bargain with Each Other[31]

Victims and injurers often will not bargain with each other because of the costs of doing so, their ignorance of each others' identities, or other familiar reasons.[32] The case in which bargaining is unlikely is of great practical significance, as it describes most settings in which industrial pollution is generated as well as the context of automobile accidents.

If parties do not bargain with each other, the legal rule will directly determine whether or not harm occurs. Under a property rule, there will be harm when the injurer has the entitlement to cause harm,[33] whereas under the liability rule, there will be harm when the injurer chooses to cause it and pay damages. We now consider whether the liability rule or a property rule is better.

1. State's Information Is Perfect. — Suppose initially that the state has perfect information about harm and prevention costs. Then

---

mount to a liability rule (except for the way it addresses the judgment-proof problem, *see infra* section II.D.1).

[30] *See infra* section II.E.4.

[31] Many of the arguments in this section and the next are developed formally in our Appendix.

[32] *See, e.g.,* Coase, *supra* note 18, at 15–18.

[33] It might be asked how property rights are enforced given our assumption that parties do not bargain. If a victim enjoys property rule protection but cannot bargain with an injurer because the two are not in contact with each other, how do we imagine that the victim's property rights are enforced? The answer is that we envision that the state would impose such a severe sanction on the injurer were he to cause harm without permission that the injurer would be deterred from doing so.

it is clear that property rules and the liability rule are equivalent because, under each, the optimal outcome is achieved.[34] Under property rules, the state can assign the entitlement to obtain the optimal result: the state grants the entitlement to the victim if harm exceeds prevention cost and to the injurer otherwise. Under the liability rule, the state sets damages equal to the harm; thus the injurer causes harm if and only if prevention cost exceeds harm.

2. *State's Information Is Imperfect.* — Next, suppose that the state's information is imperfect. In particular, assume first that the state does not know the injurer's prevention cost but can determine harm to the victim. In this case, the liability rule is superior to property rules. Under property rules, the state will not know to whom to assign the entitlement because it will not know whether the prevention cost exceeds harm. If harm is $1000 but the state does not know whether the prevention cost is $800 or $1200, the state may make one of two mistakes: giving the victim the right to be free from harm when in fact the prevention cost is $1200 (so that it would be socially desirable for harm to occur), or giving the injurer the right to cause harm when the prevention cost is only $800 (so that it would be desirable for the injurer to prevent harm). Inevitably, the state will make mistakes in assigning entitlements to parties when its information about the injurer's prevention cost is imperfect.

Under the liability rule, however, the socially optimal outcome will always occur.[35] Faced with damages of $1000 for harm, the injurer will cause harm if and only if his prevention cost (which he knows[36]) is $1200; if his prevention cost is $800, he will prevent rather than cause harm. In other words, *the virtue of the liability rule is that it allows the state to harness the information that the injurer naturally possesses about his prevention cost.* When the state does not have that information, this virtue is important.[37]

The foregoing argument in favor of the liability rule — that the state can harness injurers' knowledge about their prevention costs —

---

[34] When we state that such outcomes are equivalent, keep in mind that we are examining the social objective of maximizing value (efficiency). The outcomes obviously may differ with respect to what the parties pay or receive, an issue that we consider in section II.D.4.

[35] *See, e.g.*, Polinsky, *Resolving Nuisance Disputes, supra* note 1, at 1100–02, 1111–12.

[36] We assume throughout that injurers know their own prevention costs. Although this is certainly a plausible assumption, we note that injurers will sometimes be unaware of prevention costs, particularly with regard to the development or use of new technology. Even here, however, injurers' information will usually be better than the state's — in which case the benefit we identify with the use of the liability rule (that it takes advantage of injurers' superior knowledge about prevention costs) will still exist.

[37] An analogous argument shows the desirability of the reverse liability rule when the state lacks information about harm but possesses information about prevention cost. Under the reverse liability rule, a victim who wants to be free from harm pays the injurer's prevention cost (which the court knows). Thus, the victim will elect to be free from harm if and only if harm exceeds prevention cost, and the state thereby harnesses the victim's information about harm.

also applies in the general case in which the state's information about harm as well as about prevention cost is imperfect. Typically, a court will observe some information about actual harm, but this information will be incomplete: there will be more than one possible level of harm that could give rise to the facts that the court observes. Suppose that the court sets damages equal to its best estimate of harm — that is, equal to the average harm for the class of cases consistent with what is observed. For example, damages might be set at $1000, even though in fact there are three equally probable levels of harm: $500, $1000, and $1500.[38] We now show that this liability rule — with damages equal to the average level of harm — is superior on average to property rules.

Under the liability rule, if the prevention cost is $800, the injurer would prevent harm to avoid paying damages of $1000. This result is desirable because the average harm is $1000. (On average, $200 is saved by preventing harm.) If the prevention cost is $1200, the injurer would cause harm, which is the desirable result because only $1000 of harm is generated on average.

By contrast, under property rules, outcomes will involve greater social cost on average. Suppose first that the state awards the entitlement to victims,[39] so that no harm occurs. The outcome will differ from that reached under the liability rule only when the prevention cost is $1200. In this case, under the liability rule, harm occurs, and on average it is $1000 — the average of $500, $1000, and $1500. But under the property rule, the injurer spends $1200 in all events. Because $1200 exceeds $1000, average social costs are higher under the property rule. Of course, social costs *sometimes* would be higher under the liability rule than under the property rule. This would occur if the true harm were $1500. On average, however, social costs are higher under the property rule, because the average harm is $1000. Thus, the liability rule is superior on average.

Now suppose that the state confers the entitlement on injurers. They will cause harm, so the outcome will differ from that reached under the liability rule only when the prevention cost is $800. Average harm under the property rule will be $1000, which exceeds the $800 spent by injurers to avoid the harm under the liability rule, so again the liability rule will be superior.

If the reader reflects on this example, he or she will see that the inherent advantage of the liability rule in the situation in which the state can ascertain harm continues to apply when the state must estimate harm. Namely, under the liability rule, the state is able to make

---

[38] At the end of this subsection, we comment on how damages would be set if the court did not have all the data necessary to compute the mean level of harm.

[39] The choice of entitlement must be the same in all cases because the state is assumed not to know the prevention cost or the harm in any particular case.

implicit use of injurers' information about prevention costs, because injurers know their *actual* prevention cost,[40] which they compare to average harm. By contrast, under property rules, the state does not compare actual prevention cost to average harm on a case-by-case basis because the state does not know actual prevention cost. Rather, the state makes the decision whether harm should be prevented using information only about *average* prevention cost, and its decision applies on a uniform basis.

The argument we have made is not particular to the example: we prove the general superiority of liability rules in the mathematical Appendix to this Article.[41] Specifically, we show the following conclusion:[42] in the case of harmful externalities in which parties do not bargain with each other, *the rule of liability, with damages equal to average harm, is superior on average to property rules, regardless of how imperfect the state's information is about harm or prevention cost.*[43] This conclusion may appear to depend upon the assumption that the court knows the full distribution of harm so that it can compute the average, as in our example, whereas in reality the court's information often will be insufficient for it to do so. But as long as the court sets damages equal to its best estimate of the average, the logic of our argument favoring liability rules is essentially unaffected.[44]

---

[40] *See supra* note 36.

[41] *See infra* Appendix section I.A.2.

[42] Some readers may wonder how our argument that a liability rule is necessarily superior can be reconciled with arguments such as Martin Weitzman's claim that it is indeterminate whether pollution taxes (a form of liability rule) or regulation of the amount of pollution (a form of property rule) will prove to be more efficient. *See* Martin L. Weitzman, *Prices vs. Quantities*, 41 REV. ECON. STUD. 477 (1974). As we explain in the Appendix in section I.A.2, comment e, Weitzman assumes what we believe to be unreasonable limits on how pollution taxes are implemented, limits that entail knowingly using taxes unequal to average harm.

[43] In demonstrating this result, we suppose that the distribution of harm is statistically independent of the distribution of prevention costs. This assumption seems natural to make because, for example, one would not expect a firm's cost of controlling emissions per unit to be correlated with a victim's susceptibility to disease. It is true, though, that a firm's *total* prevention cost and a victim's *total* harm will be correlated because both will rise with the quantity of the firm's emissions. But if, as seems reasonable, the quantity of emissions is assumed to be observable by courts, *see infra* section II.E.1, courts can vary the legal rule and damages with the quantity of emissions. Hence, what is relevant is the distributions of harm and of prevention costs given a particular quantity, and these distributions are plausibly independent.

In any case, if the assumption of independence is relaxed, it is possible that a property rule would be superior to a liability rule. See section III.A.2 and Appendix Part II for further discussion. Finally, we note that, if the quantity of emissions were not observable, the only feasible property regime of a conventional type would involve banning or permitting all pollution, both of which are likely to be very inefficient outcomes. (It may be possible to impose some direct limits, however, such as by forbidding factories to operate in an area or requiring the use of a particular technology. *See* Weitzman, *supra* note 42, at 479 n.3.)

[44] To amplify, suppose that a court does not know the distribution of harm that applies in a particular context — which in our example in the text is $500, $1000, and $1500. Nonetheless, the court's less precise knowledge will always be reflected by *some* probability distribution. *See* HOWARD RAIFFA, DECISION ANALYSIS 104–05 (1968). For instance, consider a case in which the

In fact, the conclusion we demonstrate in the Appendix is even stronger. We show that under the liability rule, *the optimal magnitude of damages is average harm.*[45] In other words, not only is the liability rule with damages set equal to average harm superior to property rules, but also there is no measure of damages — such as a higher level — that would make the liability rule function better. The explanation for this result is that it is socially desirable for the injurer to weigh the average social harm caused by failing to prevent harm when making his decision about a precaution.[46]

    3. *Concerns About the Use of Liability Rules When the State's Information Is Imperfect.* — With the above conclusions in mind, let us turn to the suggestions that we mentioned in the Introduction, to the effect that when harm is uncertain, liability rules might not function well, and property rules, particularly a rule providing protection to the victim, may be superior. In subsection (a), we consider the difficulty in estimating harm in the absence of systematic bias, and in subsection (b), we allow for the possibility of systematic underestimation of harm.

    (a) The Possibility That Difficulty in Estimating Harm Favors Property Rule Protection of Victims. — One frequently heard argument favoring property rule protection of victims is exemplified by the following: "We don't know how injurious the effect of pollution ultimately will be. It might cause only an occasional rash, but it might also be strongly carcinogenic. Because we don't want to face the risk of great harm, we should not employ the liability rule — we should be

---

court is unsure whether the situation it confronts is of one type or another. The court imagines that there are two possibilities: one is described by the $500, $1000, $1500 distribution (the mean is $1000); the other is described by an $800, $1600, $2400 distribution (again, with each outcome equally likely, so the mean is $1600). Further, suppose that the court's best guess is that each of these descriptions is equally likely to be accurate. In this case, the situation is equivalent to one in which the distribution of possible harms is $500, $800, $1000, $1500, $1600, $2400, each with probability 1/6. Because the mean of this distribution is $1300, our argument implies that the liability rule with damages equal to $1300 is superior to either property rule. The sense behind the optimality of damages of $1300 is that, when there are two possible, equally likely distributions of harm, the average taken over all possible outcomes is indeed $1300.

  [45] *See infra* Appendix section I.A.2. Were other factors admitted, like litigation costs, optimal damages would differ. *See* A. Mitchell Polinsky & Daniel L. Rubinfeld, *The Welfare Implications of Costly Litigation for the Level of Liability*, 17 J. LEGAL STUD. 151 (1988); A. Mitchell Polinsky & Steven Shavell, *Enforcement Costs and the Optimal Magnitude and Probability of Fines*, 35 J.L. & ECON. 133 (1992).

  [46] The reader should bear in mind that we are assuming that the court cannot observe the actual harm in particular cases, so it must use a single, fixed number as the measure of damages. Subject to this constraint, we are saying that the best number for it to use is average harm. For further discussion of liability rules with the level of damages considered to be a variable, see section II.E.4.

conservative and accord victims property rule protection, the right to clean air."[47]

This argument overlooks the important point that, under the liability rule, there will not tend to be much pollution if the risk of cancer is serious, for damages will then be high precisely because average harm will be high.[48] Thus, a property rule protecting victims will result in a different outcome from that reached under the liability rule only when the cost of preventing pollution is so great that it surpasses even the high average harm. This, however, is a circumstance in which prevention of pollution would be socially undesirable.

The foregoing point might be criticized on the ground that a court may not possess all the data necessary to estimate average harm, so that the court cannot even formulate a proper damage award. In this case, the use of property rules appears to have the virtue that courts need not estimate harm. But this view is specious. It ignores the fact that a court must make some estimate of harm in selecting which property rule to apply: to decide whether it is victims or injurers who are to be accorded property rule protection, courts must determine whether the harm or the prevention cost is greater, which requires that the court estimate both.[49] Whatever the court's estimate of harm is, the same estimate can be used to set damages under a liability rule. And, as we have explained at length, this rule will be superior to a property rule based on the same information (essentially because errors in estimating harm plague both rules but errors in estimating prevention costs hinder only property rules).

One could nevertheless object that it would appear arbitrary for courts to award damages on the basis of rough judgments and intui-

---

[47] This argument, which we believe to be part of the folk wisdom on the subject, is one we have heard often, including in response to our preceding analysis.

[48] Moreover, it should be realized that it is always possible to raise the level of protection of victims under a liability rule by setting damages above average harm, but this is not socially desirable on average — recall our conclusion at page 727 that the optimal level of damages equals average harm.

Additionally, note that our premise is that the courts cannot accurately determine harm in particular cases. When courts can ascertain harm on a case-specific basis (for example, because suits are brought only after cases of cancer eventuate), the liability rule will automatically result in damages equal to harm and in behavior superior to that under a property rule.

[49] In some contexts (for example, comparing the height of adjacent trees), it is possible to determine which of two things is larger without having to quantify either separately. But the harm caused by externalities (say, the seriousness of a disease caused by an emission) and the costs of reducing it (for example, changing production technology) are not immediately comparable, so it is necessary to quantify each. (How precise an estimate is appropriate is a subject we explore further in the text and notes that follow.)

It also would not be necessary to quantify harm and prevention costs separately if the two were directly correlated. In this Part, however, we assume that there is no correlation. *See supra* note 43. We later show that, when there is a correlation, property rules might indeed be better. *See infra* section III.A.2.

tion. But all findings of fact, to varying degrees, involve guesswork.[50] Moreover, as just noted, recourse to property rules hardly enables courts to avoid estimating harm. At most, the use of property rules enables courts to shield their guesswork about harm from view. Even further, the use of property rules requires courts to make some estimate of prevention costs, so the actual guesswork involved is necessarily greater than under liability rules.

Another reason why the use of rough estimates under a liability rule should not be disturbing is that property rules can be understood as liability rules that use inferior estimates. Recall that under property rules the court implicitly sets damages equal either to zero (when the rule permits injurers to act freely) or to infinity (when the rule protects victims).[51] These levels of damages — zero or infinity — may be regarded as guesses about harm, and are ones that are, by definition, worse than the court's best estimate of actual harm, however rough and uncertain that estimate may be.[52]

(b) The Possibility That Systematic Underestimation of Harm Favors Property Rule Protection of Victims. — A different criticism of liability rules concerns the possibility that a court might set damages systematically below average harm. The liability rule might then be inferior to property rule protection of victims because excessive harm will occur under the liability rule.[53] (We say "might" for two reasons: (1) the underestimation must be large for the liability rule to be inferior; and (2) a court that significantly underestimates harm might mistakenly assign a property right entitlement to the injurer, an even worse outcome than that reached under a liability rule with damages that are too low.) This possibility leads us to consider why in fact damages might be too low.

We do suspect that damages are too low when there are components of loss that are hard to estimate, including idiosyncratic elements

---

[50] Our argument assumes that guesses are not systematically biased even if imprecise. (For example, the height of a single, randomly selected American is an unbiased estimate of the average height of Americans, even though it would not be a very reliable estimate.) We consider systematic bias below in subsection (b).

[51] *See supra* pp. 723–24.

[52] There remains the question of how accurate damages *should* be under liability rules. Although the need to state a specific figure may motivate courts to expend more effort to achieve greater precision, our argument in the text is that courts will do better under liability rules than under property rules even if they do not expend additional effort. Moreover, additional precision will often be of little value with regard to affecting behavior, particularly when injurers cannot predict courts' errors in advance. *See* Louis Kaplow & Steven Shavell, *Accuracy in the Assessment of Damages*, 39 J.L. & ECON. (forthcoming April 1996) (on file with the Harvard Law School Library).

[53] *Cf.* Polinsky, *Resolving Nuisance Disputes, supra* note 1, at 1103–06 (discussing the problem for the case in which bargaining is possible, but imperfect).

of harm.[54] For example, when a person's home is destroyed, courts normally limit damages to market value even though the person might have attached special additional value to the home. When individuals are killed, courts ordinarily base damages on lost income, even though this determination ignores the value of individuals to themselves as well as to family and friends. When environmental harms involve losses that are hard to measure from market data (such as the death of animals, like sea otters, without clear commercial value), damages calculated under standard tort principles may understate true social losses. If damages understate average harm significantly, then a property rule protecting victims might be superior to a liability rule. We might, for example, want to protect an environmentally important area by forbidding factories from operating nearby if this activity would expose the area to a substantial risk of harm.

But such a proposal raises the allied question: if damages do not approximate average harm, can the legal system remedy this problem? In principle, we believe that the problem can be solved, but perhaps only if the process by which damages are calculated is altered. To amplify, the reason that courts exclude certain components of loss is that, in contrast to market-related losses, they are "speculative" and thus cannot be "objectively determined."[55] Further, we presume that were these categories of loss allowed in damage calculations, much dispute between the parties would ensue because damages would have an open-ended quality. This contest would tend to consume the courts' and the parties' time and resources. One might therefore attempt to explain the exclusion of such categories of loss from damage calculations as being the lesser of two evils — an inadequate level of damages (implying inadequate deterrence) being better than excessive administrative costs.

Yet if the administrative costs of fully determining harm according to customary procedures would be problematic for our legal system, courts could employ streamlined methods — for example, disallowing introduction of all but the most limited evidence — to arrive at estimates of harm including now-omitted components. As long as these estimates are not systematically biased, average damages will equal average harm, and our argument about the superiority of the liability rule will remain valid.[56] (Recall our observation that courts could set

---

[54] *See* Calabresi & Melamed, *supra* note 1, at 1108; Ellickson, *supra* note 1, at 735–37; Polinsky, *Resolving Nuisance Disputes, supra* note 1, at 1103 & n.48. Damages also may be systematically low if not all victims sue. Note, however, that imperfect enforcement may also pose problems for property rules.

[55] *See, e.g.*, Bigelow v. RKO Radio Pictures, Inc., 327 U.S. 251, 264 (1946) ("[T]he jury may not render a verdict based on speculation or guesswork."); Krier & Schwab, *supra* note 7, at 457–58; sources cited *supra* note 54.

[56] *See* Kaplow & Shavell, *supra* note 52.

damages using the same crude estimate of harm that they would have employed in assigning the entitlement under a property rule.)

Going further, courts could employ predetermined tables for estimating losses (for example, so much for a sea otter, so much for a life). The table entries might be calculated on some reasonable basis with information furnished by experts. The use of tables would reduce, potentially to nothing, the cost on a per-case basis of including a presently excluded component of loss.[57] The argument that there is a systematic tendency to underestimate loss would then not apply, and the argument in favor of liability rules would be strengthened.[58]

B. Parties Bargain with Each Other

In some situations, victims and injurers will have an opportunity to bargain with each other relatively cheaply, such as when a single injurer and a single victim are neighbors. To understand this case, we will suppose that parties can bargain costlessly with each other before the injurer decides whether to cause harm.[59] In this situation, the choice between property and liability rules should diminish in importance because, if the rule chosen would lead to a suboptimal result, the parties could in principle make a mutually desirable agreement incorporating the optimal result, harm or no harm, as the case may be. This observation is an application of the Coase Theorem.[60]

To elaborate, we must make an explicit assumption about the nature of bargaining. We consider a simple model of bargaining: one party makes a take-it-or-leave-it offer or demand to the other. In this model (as well as in more general models), mutually beneficial agreements are always made if parties have perfect information about each other. But if parties do not have perfect information about each other, a party may misgauge another and make a demand or offer that

---

[57] *See* Randall R. Bovbjerg, Frank A. Sloan & James F. Blumstein, *Valuing Life and Limb in Tort: Scheduling "Pain and Suffering,"* 83 Nw. U. L. REV. 908, 928–30 (1989); Ellickson, *supra* note 1, at 736–37, 739–40 (advocating schedules for the subjective value of homes in the nuisance context to avoid undervaluation while limiting administrative costs); Kaplow & Shavell, *supra* note 52 (manuscript at 16–18); Frederick S. Levin, *Pain and Suffering Guidelines: A Cure for Damages Measurement "Anomie,"* 22 U. MICH. J.L. REFORM 303, 319–22 (1989).

[58] In the latter part of this subsection, we have discussed how courts can remedy the problem of systematic underestimation of harm by altering their methods of damage assessment. But it might be objected that this is for some reason infeasible and, as a consequence, that the legislature should protect victims through use of a property rule. If the legislature could do that, however, we wonder why it could not instead require that courts employ damage tables. (Fear that courts would circumvent the legislature's damage tables is no more plausible than a concern that courts would be unfaithful in enforcing the legislature's property rule.)

[59] For discussion of costly bargaining, see section II.D.2.

[60] *See* Coase, *supra* note 18, at 2–15.

would be refused, so that mutually beneficial agreements might not be made.[61]

    1. Bargaining Is Always Successful. — Consider first the case in which parties always strike mutually beneficial bargains because they have perfect information about each other.[62] In this case, *there is no difference between property and liability rules*: bargains leading to an optimal result will always be made. If, under either type of rule, an optimal outcome otherwise would not occur, it must be possible to lower total costs by agreeing to the optimal outcome; thus, with an appropriate payment by one side to the other, both sides can be made better off.

    For example, suppose that a property rule under which the victim has the right to be free from harm applies but that this allocation is suboptimal because harm would be $1000 and prevention cost would be $1200. Then a mutually beneficial agreement by which the injurer would be allowed to cause harm exists: any payment by the injurer to the victim between $1000 and $1200 would be acceptable to both the injurer and the victim. If, for concreteness, we assume that the victim makes a demand, then he would ask for an amount between these two figures, and an agreement would be made; in fact, he would ask for (just under) the maximum amount, $1200.[63] The victim would not ask for more than $1200 (to avoid preventing an agreement) because, by assumption, he knows the injurer's prevention cost.

    Let us consider one more example, in which harm is $1500, the prevention cost is $1200, and a liability rule in which damages are incorrectly estimated to be $1000 applies. The injurer would choose to cause harm in the absence of bargaining. With bargaining, the victim would make an offer to induce the injurer not to cause harm; any

---

[61] *See, e.g.*, Joseph Farrell, *Information and the Coase Theorem*, 1 ECON. PERSP. 113, 115 (1987) (discussing how the applicability of the Coase Theorem depends upon the nature of bargaining).

[62] *See* Alvin E. Roth & J. Keith Murnighan, *The Role of Information in Bargaining: An Experimental Study*, 50 ECONOMETRICA 1123, 1124–37 (1982) (offering evidence that parties usually come to an agreement when each knows the other's willingness to pay).

[63] If the victim asked for $1200, the injurer would be indifferent about whether to make an agreement, so the victim might demand slightly less, say $1199.99. In the discussion to follow, we assume for convenience that injurers who are indifferent will accept victims' offers.

We note, however, the existence of studies suggesting that, in contexts such as the present one, the party receiving the offer might reject it, against his own self-interest, if the offeror insists on too large a share of the surplus. *See, e.g.*, Lawrence M. Kahn & J. Keith Murnighan, *A General Experiment on Bargaining in Demand Games with Outside Options*, 83 AM. ECON. REV. 1260 (1993); Richard H. Thaler, *Anomalies: The Ultimatum Game*, J. ECON. PERSP., Fall 1988, at 195. The implication is that gains might be shared differently, but this does not directly influence our argument. An insistence on the sharing of gains may, however, introduce asymmetric information into the bargaining process (because the offeror may be unsure of when the offeree would reject an offer), which would make the analysis of the next subsection relevant.

offer between $200 and $500 would be mutually beneficial to them,[64] and the victim would choose $200.

These examples illustrate that when bargaining always succeeds, the outcome reached will always be optimal. Consequently, the choice between property and liability rules does not affect the achievement of optimality.

2. *Bargaining Is Not Always Successful.* — Now let us examine the case in which bargaining does not always lead to a mutually beneficial outcome. As we said, this problem occurs when a party, misconceiving the other's true position, offers too little or asks for too much, in which case his offer or demand will be rejected. For example, consider again the case in which the victim enjoys the property right not to be injured and harm would be $1000. Now assume that the victim is uncertain about the injurer's prevention cost: some injurers' costs are $1200, others' costs are $2000, and the victim does not know which type of injurer he confronts. In this case, if the victim demands $2000 for allowing the injurer to cause harm and the injurer happens to be one whose prevention cost is $1200, the injurer will refuse the demand. Further, the victim would find it rational to ask for $2000 if the probability that the injurer's prevention cost is $2000 is sufficiently high (over 20%): the extra $800 he obtains from those willing to pay $2000 rather than $1200 will more than compensate for the rejections and loss of $200 (receipt of $1200 net of harm of $1000) from those only willing to pay $1200.[65] More generally, parties will often find it rational to ask for an amount exceeding the maximum the other party might be willing to pay, even though that strategy will lead to some rejected offers.[66]

---

[64] The victim would be willing to pay up to $500, for if the injurer caused harm, then the victim's net loss, after collecting damages of $1000, would be $500. The injurer would want at least $200 because this amount would reduce his cost to $1000 after he bears the prevention cost of $1200, and $1000 is what he would pay if he caused harm.

[65] If the fraction of injurers whose prevention cost is $2000 is f and the victim asks for $2000, then the likelihood of acceptance will be f, and the victim's expected gain will be ($2000–$1000)f = 1000f$. (The $1000 is subtracted because the victim suffers harm if and only if his demand is accepted.) If the victim demands $1200, then both types of injurers will accept, so the expected gain will be $1200–$1000 = $200. Therefore, a $2000 demand is profitable for the victim if and only if 1000f$ > $200, which is to say, if and only if f exceeds .2.

[66] This proposition is true independently of the particular model of bargaining. For example, in models with repeated rounds of bargaining, the problem of failure to make a mutually beneficial agreement remains, because during such rounds parties can bluff, dissimulate, and engage in other strategies through their offers, demands, and statements. As long as there is uncertainty about some factor affecting the other party's willingness to make an agreement, a rational party may make a demand or offer that the other will turn out to refuse. *See* Roger B. Myerson & Mark A. Satterthwaite, *Efficient Mechanisms for Bilateral Trading*, 29 J. ECON. THEORY 265 (1983); John Sutton, *Non-Cooperative Bargaining Theory: An Introduction*, 53 REV. ECON. STUD. 709 (1986) (literature survey).

However, William Samuelson emphasizes that, if an entitlement is auctioned in a particular way between the parties rather than allocated through bargaining, the problems associated with

How does the chance that bargaining may not lead to mutually beneficial agreements bear on the comparison between property and liability rules? When parties bargain in the face of asymmetric information, does the liability rule remain superior to property rules — or does it become equivalent or inferior? *There is no unambiguous conclusion: examples can be constructed in which either the liability rule is superior to property rules or the reverse is true.*[67]

We present such examples in the Appendix,[68] but it is useful for us to state here our assumptions and exactly what we show. We assume that there is a population of injurers whose prevention costs vary and a population of victims who differ in the harms they might suffer. Each injurer knows only the distribution of harms among victims, each victim knows only the distribution of prevention costs among injurers, and courts know only the distributions of prevention costs and of harms. Given the legal rule, the victim makes a single offer or demand, which the injurer either accepts or rejects. The offer or demand is that which maximizes the expected gain of the victim. To evaluate a legal rule, we compute the average social costs under the rule. Our examples demonstrate that these average social costs could be lower either under a liability rule with damages equal to average harm or under a property rule.[69]

Although we cannot say that the liability rule is necessarily superior to property rules when imperfect bargaining occurs, there is an argument suggesting that the liability rule tends to be superior. This argument is based upon the liability rule's superiority in the absence of bargaining. That is, before any bargaining occurs, at the beginning of the "race" between the two types of rule, the liability rule is ahead of the property rules. Hence, one might expect that, after imperfect bargaining occurs, the liability rule will remain ahead of the property rules, although not as far ahead. (More precisely, one might expect this outcome because, when bargaining is entirely successful, liability

---

asymmetric information and bargaining can be overcome. *See* William Samuelson, *A Comment on the Coase Theorem, in* GAME-THEORETIC MODELS OF BARGAINING 321, 331–35 (Alvin E. Roth ed., 1985). Yet, as Samuelson acknowledges, the auctions he discusses are often not useful because they would require the initial holder of an entitlement to share too much of the auction proceeds with others. Holders of entitlements might therefore not agree to participate in the auctions (and, if the law required participation, incentives to acquire and improve property would be adversely affected). *See id.* at 336–37.

[67] This indeterminacy was first shown in Steven Shavell, Property Rights and the Rule of Liability in a Simple Bargaining Model (July 1988) (unpublished manuscript, on file with the Harvard Law School Library).

[68] *See infra* Appendix section I.B.2, cmts. a, b.

[69] Ayres and Talley consider a model similar to ours. The main difference in their model concerns the bargaining regime that they choose to study. They assume that the victim does not make a single offer or demand; instead, he makes a preliminary statement about his willingness to pay or his demand, and then the injurer replies with a single offer or demand. *See* Ayres & Talley, *supra* note 10, at 1047–50. For further discussion of their model, see Appendix section I.B.2, comment c.

and property rules are equivalent.) The liability rule will remain ahead of property rules unless bargaining is, for some reason, substantially more successful under property rules than under the liability rule (a possibility to which we will return).[70]

Another way to express the foregoing point is to observe that the advantage of the liability rule over property rules in the absence of bargaining rests upon two elements: that an efficient outcome is more likely under the liability rule and that, when the outcome is inefficient, the extent of inefficiency tends to be less. Because an efficient outcome is more likely under the liability rule, bargaining need not take place as often, so the prospect that bargaining will fail is irrelevant in a greater range of cases. And because the extent of initial inefficiency tends to be less under the liability rule, the failure of bargaining will be less serious when it does occur. Both factors lend credence to the conjecture that the liability rule will tend to be superior to property rules when bargaining is not always successful.[71]

---

[70] We remind the reader that, under the liability rule we have been discussing, damages equal average harm. It should be observed, however, that the optimal liability rule is likely to involve a different level of damages. Whereas the optimal level of damages in the absence of bargaining is the average harm, *see supra* p. 727; *infra* Appendix section I.A.2, we would not suppose that the optimal level of damages in the presence of bargaining, given its complexities, would remain equal to average harm. We have no reason to believe, however, that the optimal level of damages would systematically be either above or below the average harm.

We note that it is possible for fairly extreme damages to be optimal. This is demonstrated by our examples in Appendix section I.B.2, comments a and b. When fairly extreme damages (for example, damages of $.01) are optimal, we would interpret the liability rule to be a property rule (for example, to be a rule protecting the injurer if optimal damages are $.01).

[71] Ayres and Talley, cited above in note 10, suggest that liability rules are likely to be superior to property rules when there is imperfect bargaining. But the reason they furnish for this conclusion is different from that given here. They believe that *the liability rule facilitates bargaining* as compared to property rules. We see no systematic reason for this to be so; indeed, the numerical example they examine supports our view, not theirs! (For further discussion of their argument, see Appendix section I.B.2, comment c, and Louis Kaplow & Steven Shavell, *Do Liability Rules Facilitate Bargaining? A Reply to Ayres and Talley*, 105 YALE L.J. 221 (1995).) The argument in the text is that the liability rule may tend to be superior to property rules mainly because, *under the liability rule, there is less need for parties to engage in bargaining, and inefficiency in the absence of bargaining will tend to be only moderate.* We do not argue (as they do) that the liability rule is superior because, *when* parties engage in bargaining, they are systematically more likely to achieve an agreement than under property rules. (Indeed, as discussed in the text to follow, the opposite tendency is plausible.)

Ayres and Talley also make a separate point: that bargaining under the liability rule actually will be impeded if courts assess harm accurately because this accuracy effectively introduces asymmetry of information between victims and injurers. *See* Ayres & Talley, *supra* note 10, at 1065–69. This general point is correct and was initially developed in similar contexts by Kathryn E. Spier, *Settlement Bargaining and the Design of Damage Awards*, 10 J.L. ECON. & ORGANIZATION 84 (1994) [hereinafter Spier, *Settlement Bargaining*], and JASON S. JOHNSTON, BARGAINING UNDER RULES VERSUS STANDARDS (University of Pa. Inst. for Law and Economics Discussion Paper No. 165, 1994). *Cf.* Kathryn E. Spier, *Incomplete Contracts and Signalling*, 23 RAND J. ECON. 432 (1992) (concerning contract renegotiation). In the present context, suppose that victims know their levels of harm and anticipate receiving damages equal to true harm from courts, but that injurers do not know victims' levels of harm. Then bargains will tend not to be struck

In light of this advantage of the liability rule, the reader may wonder why we conclude that it is formally indeterminate which type of rule is superior given imperfect bargaining and why we were able to construct examples illustrating this point.[72] The reason that the liability rule does not necessarily perform better is that bargaining may not be equally successful under the two types of rules. Indeed, just because property rules are behind in the race with the liability rule before any bargaining occurs — that is, just because the parties have more to gain from bargaining successfully — they will be more likely to conclude beneficial bargains. In addition, because imperfect bargaining involves subtle and complex elements, it is hard to predict the effect of this or that starting point for bargaining — here, a property rule or a liability rule. (For example, if most inefficiency may be eliminated under both rules when bargaining occurs, it may be a matter of happenstance whether slightly more inefficiency remains under one type of rule or another.) The only conclusion that can safely be offered is that the choice between property and liability rules is less likely to be important when parties can bargain than when they cannot.[73]

---

between victims and injurers: the only offer a victim would accept would be for more than his true loss, yet injurers would know that victims would accept only such offers and thus would not want to make offers that victims would accept. (We do note, however, that victims may have an incentive and the ability to reveal their true harm to injurers, which would eliminate the problem of asymmetric information.) By contrast, if courts only estimate harm, then both victims and injurers may have similar knowledge of the damage amount in advance, thus reducing the asymmetry of information and allowing for the conclusion of some bargains.

We also mention that, aside from the foregoing point, courts should not seek to ascertain harm with accuracy if (as was just assumed) injurers do not know the harm victims would suffer. In that circumstance, accuracy will not improve injurers' incentives to reduce harm but will involve added costs for the legal system. On this theme, see Kaplow and Shavell, cited above in note 52, and, for a qualification, see Spier, *Settlement Bargaining*, cited above.

[72] See *infra* Appendix section I.B.2, cmts. a, b. In a separate paper, Eric Talley demonstrates that a liability rule with a properly chosen level of damages is always superior to property rules. See ERIC L. TALLEY, PROPERTY RIGHTS, LIABILITY RULES, AND COASEAN BARGAINING UNDER INCOMPLETE INFORMATION 17–26 (John M. Olin Program in Law and Economics, Stanford Law School, Working Paper No. 114, 1994). This result might appear to be inconsistent with our conclusion that whether a property rule or the liability rule is superior is indeterminate, but it is not, because it is derived under a particular set of assumptions. Among other things, Talley's demonstration assumes that an "optimal mechanism" (which need not be the bargaining process that the parties actually would employ) governs the outcome of bargaining. See *infra* note 219. Moreover, Talley shows only that there exists *some level of damages* such that the liability rule with these damages will be superior to a property rule, not that a liability rule with damages equal to or near the average harm will be superior. Thus, according to his analysis, the liability rule that is superior to a property rule might be a liability rule with damages of $.01, but we would view that rule as tantamount to a property rule (favoring injurers). See *supra* note 70.

[73] In the numerical examples we report in Appendix section I.B.2, comments a and b, the difference between the inefficiencies resulting under property and liability rules in the case of imperfect bargaining is usually quite small relative to the difference in the case without bargaining.

C. Victims' Behavior

Until this point in our analysis, we have not mentioned the important role victims may play with respect to harmful externalities. Victims sometimes make choices that expose themselves to harm, such as electing to locate near a polluter. And, if exposed to harm, victims also are frequently able to mitigate or prevent it, for instance by installing air purifiers to temper the ill effects of pollution. Victims' ability to reduce or avoid harm means that it may be socially advantageous for them to do so. If victims can cheaply locate away from a factory, the factory need not undertake expensive precautions to prevent harm; if victims can install air purifiers at lower expense than the factory would bear for smoke scrubbers, then victims should do so.

The role of victim behavior in preventing harms suggests three implications for our conclusions. (For simplicity, we confine our consideration here to the situation in which bargaining is not possible.[74]) First, the liability rule loses some of its appeal because, by compensating victims for their losses, it dulls their incentives to avoid or prevent harm.[75] Courts can ameliorate this problem by denying or limiting payments to victims who fail to take action to avoid or mitigate harm, as is accomplished through the defense of contributory negligence and the principle of mitigation of damages. Arguably, these are imperfect tools for controlling victims' behavior because courts' information about what victims could have done and what various actions would have cost will often be inadequate.[76] However, a legal rule compelling injurers to make payments to the state rather than to victims would solve the problem of inadequate victim incentives.[77]

Second, the case for property rule protection of victims (such as it is) also becomes weaker because it similarly dilutes victims' incen-

---

[74] If bargaining occurs and is always successful, it may involve agreements about victim as well as injurer behavior. Then, as before, the choice of legal rule will not affect social welfare. If bargaining is imperfect, the effects to be noted in the text will be relevant but less important than in the absence of bargaining because of the possibility of successful bargaining. We note, however, that the likelihood of successful bargaining, especially about victims' location decisions, may be small because it may require injurers to identify and bargain with all potential victims before they make their location decisions.

[75] *See, e.g.*, Coase, *supra* note 18, at 42.

[76] The problem, in part, is that defenses will only incorporate variables that the court can observe; this is the argument in Steven Shavell, *Strict Liability Versus Negligence*, 9 J. LEGAL STUD. 1 (1980), that defenses typically take into account levels of "care" but not levels of "activity."

[77] Examples include fines, pollution taxes, *see infra* note 121, and "decoupling," under which a portion of what injurers pay goes to the government rather than to victims, *see* A. Mitchell Polinsky & Yeon-Koo Che, *Decoupling Liability: Optimal Incentives for Care and Litigation*, 22 RAND J. ECON. 562 (1991).

tives.[78] Again, as with liability rules, the law may seek to circumvent the incentive problem in the property rule context, notably through the doctrine of "coming to the nuisance"[79] and by limiting the right to an injunction to those circumstances in which the victim could not have prevented the harm.[80] However, these approaches are not cure-alls.

Third, property rule protection of injurers' right to cause harm may become appealing: under this regime, victims will plainly have strong incentives to avoid exposure to harm and to reduce harm if exposed. (We say "may" because the improvement in victims' incentives comes at the price of a dilution of injurers' incentives.)

In sum, consideration of victims' incentives to avoid or reduce harm diminishes the attractiveness of the conventional liability rule, lends no support to property rule protection of victims, and may enhance the appeal of both property rule protection of injurers and modification of liability rules to require that damages be paid to the state rather than to victims.

D. Additional Considerations

1. Judgment-Proof Injurers. — In evaluating the liability rule, we have assumed that injurers are able to pay damages for harm done. In reality, however, their ability to pay may not be sufficient to cover a court award. For example, a firm that causes many deaths through the release of toxic substances may not have the assets necessary to pay damages.

Under a liability rule, a general consequence of a party's limited wealth is the dilution of its incentive to reduce harm.[81] For example,

---

[78] In the absence of bargaining (as is assumed in the text), victims do not suffer losses under the property rule because injurers are prevented from causing harm. Thus, victims do nothing to reduce harm. Victims also do nothing to reduce harm under the liability rule (in the absence of defenses concerning victims' behavior), for they are fully compensated for any losses suffered. Thus, victims' behavior under both rules is the same.

When there is bargaining, however, the situation is more complicated, and the property rule and the liability rule are not generally equivalent with regard to victims' behavior. A case of interest, *see supra* note 74, is the one in which victims have already made their location decisions (or other decisions affecting exposure to harm), so that bargaining concerns only injurers' behavior. Here, under property rule protection, victims can generally extract some part of any surplus to be had from agreements with injurers allowing them to cause harm. By contrast, under the liability rule, injurers do not surrender any surplus when they cause harm; injurers merely compensate victims for their losses. Victims' ability under property rule protection to extract surplus from injurers when they suffer harm does two things: it creates incentives for them to expose themselves to harm ex ante (relative to their incentives under the liability rule), but it also creates some incentives for them to reduce the magnitude of harm because doing so would increase the surplus they can later obtain through bargaining.

[79] *See* Donald Wittman, *First Come, First Served: An Economic Analysis of "Coming to the Nuisance,"* 9 J. LEGAL STUD. 557 (1980).

[80] *See* Ellickson, *supra* note 1, at 758–61 (criticizing nuisance doctrine for failing to allow sufficient defenses addressed to plaintiffs' failure to minimize damages).

[81] *See* Steven Shavell, *The Judgment Proof Problem,* 6 INT'L REV. L. & ECON. 45 (1986).

a firm with assets of only $1 million might well decide against spending $200,000 to reduce the risk of a $20 million accident by 10%: such an expenditure would reduce the firm's expected pay-out by only 10% × $1 million, or $100,000. But the expenditure would be eminently desirable from a social standpoint because it reduces expected harm by 10% × $20 million, or $2 million. More generally, the greater the difference between the assets of a party and the harm it could cause, the more its liability-related incentives to take precautions will be compromised.

An answer to these incentive problems under the liability rule is for the state to employ property rule protection of victims.[82] If victims enjoy this protection, then in principle they can prevent harm regardless of how little wealth the injurer may have. A potential victim of a $20 million accident can enjoin the firm with assets of only $1 million from continuing its dangerous operations.[83] Property rule protection of victims will be superior to the use of the liability rule when the drawback of the liability rule — the inadequacy of injurer incentives due to the judgment-proof problem — is more important than the disadvantage of property rule protection — the possibility that injurers will be forced to spend excessively to prevent harm.

Alternatively, it may be possible to retain the advantages of the liability rule in some contexts by requiring injurers to pay in advance for *expected* harm rather than to pay for *actual* harm after it occurs. Because the expected harm — the harm discounted by the probability that it will occur — will often be much lower than the actual harm, it may be within the capacity of an otherwise judgment-proof injurer to pay.[84] Another response to the judgment-proof problem would be to retain the liability rule while requiring potential injurers to demon-

---

[82] One may interpret property rule protection of victims to include not only granting victims the right to enjoin harmful operations of firms, but also imposing common safety regulations. A requirement that a firm install a safety device is a species of guarantee against harm for the victim. The general point that safety regulation becomes attractive relative to liability rules when the judgment-proof problem is important is advanced in Steven Shavell, *Liability for Harm Versus Regulation of Safety*, 13 J. LEGAL STUD. 357, 360 (1984).

[83] A qualification to this statement is that the legal system sometimes employs monetary sanctions (such as criminal fines) to enforce property rules. In such cases, a party's lack of assets might hamper enforcement. In this situation, however, the state could also use its police powers to enforce property rule protection (for example, by closing down a firm). Also, the state might resort to imprisonment as a further sanction.

[84] Consider a firm with assets of $1 million that could cause a $10 million accident, and assume that the cost of a safety device that would reduce the risk of the accident from 5% to 4% is $60,000. The device is socially worthwhile because it reduces expected accident losses by 1% × $10 million = $100,000. If the firm must pay in advance for expected harm, its bill would fall from $500,000 to $400,000 if it installs the device, so it will do so, saving $40,000. The judgment-proof problem does not affect the firm because it has sufficient assets to pay in advance for expected harm. But if the firm faces liability only when harm occurs, it will not spend $60,000 to install the device: if it does so, its expected liability will drop from 5% × $1 million = $50,000 to 4% × $1 million = $40,000, or by only $10,000.

strate their ability to pay prior to causing harm (for example, by posting bonds or acquiring insurance).[85]

2. *Administrative Costs.*— Now let us consider the issue of the administrative costs surrounding the use of property and liability rules. These costs consist of the public and private costs associated with settled or litigated lawsuits and the costs of bargaining to avoid the suboptimal outcome a rule would produce.

(a) *Litigation and Settlement.*[86] — Suppose that courts were able to apply property and liability rules perfectly and that parties were able to predict exactly what courts would do. Then, under property rules, no litigation would arise — and consequently no administrative costs would be incurred — because parties would know who possesses the entitlement. By contrast, the liability rule would generate positive administrative costs because all injurers would have to pay damages to victims. Even though all such cases would be settled immediately because parties would know the amounts of damages that courts would eventually award, effecting the transfers would involve some expenses. Hence, the liability rule would involve greater administrative costs than property rules.[87]

In reality, legal outcomes are uncertain. In this case, it is unclear whether property rules or the liability rule is administratively cheaper. Uncertainty implies that, under both types of rule, some litigation will arise (because parties may disagree about possible trial outcomes) and that settlement will involve positive costs (which will mirror trial costs to some degree).[88] Would trial and settlement costs be higher under property rules or under the liability rule? Under property rules, courts

---

[85] *See* Ellickson, *supra* note 1, at 741 (noting that the judgment-proof problem could be addressed by requiring plaintiffs to demonstrate defendants' inability to pay as a condition to injunctive relief; in many nuisance cases, the defendant is a landowner who, by definition, has assets).

[86] A more complete analysis than that contained in this subsection would account for the effect of litigation and settlement costs on behavior (and bargaining) and would explain how the optimal level of damages under a liability rule should reflect such costs. For more information, refer to the sources cited above in note 45.

[87] *But see* Ellickson, *supra* note 1, at 762–71 (suggesting that specialized nuisance boards could reduce the administrative costs of damages assessment under a liability rule); *id.* at 772 (indicating that collective systems, such as fines and regulatory taxes, would be administratively more efficient for pervasive harms).

[88] *See id.* at 739 (arguing that the task of assigning property entitlements under nuisance law is expensive and introduces uncertainty). Ellickson makes the interesting observation that bargaining costs may be higher under property rules because, due to asymmetric information, parties will invest resources in determining each other's reservation prices, whereas, under a liability rule, the "collective rules on damages would establish targets for appropriate settlements and would considerably narrow the range of disagreements to be negotiated." *Id.* at 744. With liability rules, however, there will remain an incentive (albeit less of an incentive) to determine the other party's reservation price when damage awards do not equal actual harm, as in asymmetric information settings. Ellickson's observation is also applicable to bargaining in instances in which no lawsuit will be brought.

need to consider two variables — prevention cost and harm — whereas under the liability rule, only harm is relevant.[89] Property rules might appear to have an offsetting benefit because, to apply them, courts need only rank the variables to ascertain who ought to have the entitlement,[90] whereas under the liability rule, courts are compelled to derive a specific estimate of harm. But, as we have discussed in section II.A.3.(a), courts may in principle use the same estimate of harm employed under a property rule (in deciding whether the victim or injurer should have the entitlement) to set damages under a liability rule; a more accurate estimate of harm under a liability rule would be appropriate only if the further benefit with regard to behavior were greater than the incremental administrative cost.[91]

In sum, taking into account both the problem of effecting transfers and that of resolving uncertainty, we cannot determine a priori whether property or liability rules would involve lower litigation and settlement costs.

(b) Bargaining to Avoid Undesirable Outcomes. — Bargaining costs will tend to be higher under property rules than under the liability rule. The reason is that the liability rule tends to produce the efficient result more often than property rules do (assuming that the state's information is imperfect). As a result, bargaining to avoid a suboptimal result will occur less often under the liability rule.

(c) Overall comparison. — It is apparent from the preceding discussion that the administrative cost comparison depends upon the particulars of the situation. Nonetheless, we can indicate circumstances in which each type of rule has an administrative cost advantage.

The liability rule will probably generate lower administrative costs than will property rules if it is difficult to determine an injurer's prevention cost but the extent of harm is readily apparent.[92] In this instance, little bargaining will occur under the liability rule, and cases that arise when injurers cause harm — whenever prevention cost exceeds harm — will be settled quickly. By contrast, under property rule protection of, say, victims, injurers will need to bargain for permission to cause harm whenever prevention cost exceeds harm. To complete the argument, we observe that bargaining expenses under the property rule plausibly exceed settlement expenses under the liability rule. (Under the liability rule, the only issue before the parties is the

---

[89] If courts employed a reverse liability rule instead, they would have to determine prevention cost rather than harm. In some instances, this may be cheaper. *See* Calabresi & Melamed, *supra* note 1, at 1120–21.

[90] However, if the property rule entitlement were intermediate — permitting some level of pollution rather than permitting or prohibiting all pollution — the precise values of prevention cost and harm would be relevant.

[91] *See supra* pp. 729–30 & note 52.

[92] If prevention cost but not harm is easily estimated, both rules would entail significant bargaining and litigation costs. But a reverse liability rule would be administratively cheaper.

extent of harm, which we are assuming to be apparent. Under the property rule, the parties need to agree on the division of the surplus — the difference between prevention cost and harm — which in these circumstances may be difficult.) We also note that, when ascertaining prevention cost is difficult, the parties may be uncertain about who would receive the property rule entitlement. This uncertainty might compound bargaining costs and also produce costly litigation.

In other circumstances, property rules can be cheaper than the liability rule. For instance, suppose that the state can easily assign property rights to injurers because prevention costs are usually very high relative to harm. In this case, under the property rule, neither litigation nor bargaining will be likely to occur. Under the liability rule,[93] however, there will be many cases and associated costs (at least those associated with settlement) because prevention cost usually exceeds harm.[94]

3. *Risk Aversion.* — We have not yet commented on the protection of risk-averse parties (mainly individuals and small businesses[95]) against risk. We do not believe, however, that issues of risk-bearing are of much importance to the choice between property and liability rules, due to the widespread availability of insurance on reasonably competitive terms. Risk-averse victims should often be able to insure against inadequate liability awards, or against harms they would suffer when injurers enjoy the property rule entitlement to cause harm. Furthermore, the fact that parties do not insure — because they are not

---

[93] The text refers to the ordinary liability rule, under which injurers pay damages to victims. In the instance described in the text, in which committing the harmful act is almost always efficient, a reverse liability rule might be attractive. Administrative costs would be incurred only when victims were willing to pay injurers not to act; this would be infrequent and, when it occurred, would involve a more efficient outcome.

[94] A property rule may have an administrative cost advantage even if property rights cannot be cheaply assigned in a manner that is usually correct. Consider a more general case in which efficient bargains are always struck, but there is some fixed cost of reaching agreement (the costs of getting together, drafting agreements, and making payments). Then, agreements that produce small efficiency gains (less than the bargaining cost) would not be made, and all agreements that are made would come at a cost. In this case, it can be demonstrated that, if the distribution of possible harm is symmetric (that is, if harm is just as likely to be a given amount above average as it is to be the same amount below average), the optimal level of damages continues to equal average harm. Because bargaining is less necessary under the liability rule, bargaining costs are less important, so the liability rule continues to be more efficient than a property rule. Now, consider the administrative costs of litigation. Suppose that there is no litigation under a property rule (if the rule is clear, parties may simply follow it) but that the costs of paying damages under the liability rule just equal the fixed cost of reaching ex ante bargains. Then it can be shown that the property rule would tend to be superior. The frequency of bargains under the property rule would be less than the combined frequency of bargaining and litigation under the liability rule, so total administrative costs would be lower under the former.

[95] Publicly traded businesses should be operated in an approximately risk-neutral manner because their owners are able to diversify their portfolios. This means that they would want each of their holdings to be operated roughly so as to maximize its expected value, without particular regard to risk. *See* ROBERT C. CLARK, CORPORATE LAW § 11.3, at 476–77, § 15.7, at 658 (1986).

able to purchase coverage at a price they consider attractive — need not constitute an argument for state provision of implicit insurance coverage through legal rules. If market-provided insurance is expensive, that will usually reflect real costs in its supply: moral hazard, fraudulent claims, or the effort required to assess harm. In such cases, legal rules should not generally be adjusted on account of risk-bearing unless courts can address the problems leading to expensive insurance better than insurance companies can.[96]

Even if insurance were generally unavailable, it is not readily apparent whether risk-bearing considerations would favor property or liability rules. First, both property rule protection of victims and liability rules shield victims from risk.[97] Second, whatever may be the differences between the risks associated with property and liability rules, we cannot determine whether one rule is more desirable than the other without knowing whether victims or injurers are generally more in need of protection against risk. Although we may be able to form a judgment about this factor in particular contexts,[98] we cannot do so in general.

4. *Income Distribution.* — Concern about the distribution of income has no bearing on the choice between property and liability rules. Income redistribution can be accomplished more efficiently through the use of the income tax and transfer arms of government than through the selection of legal rules to serve distributional goals. If legal rules are chosen in part for distributional reasons, the goal of efficiency will sometimes be compromised, whereas distributional changes can be effected through modification of income taxes and transfers without sacrificing efficiency in the use of legal rules.[99] Moreover, legal rules are usually imprecise instruments for accomplishing distributional change because the groups affected by a rule tend to

---

[96] If, however, insurance markets fail due to adverse selection, it is possible that legal solutions would increase welfare, although the problem of how to accomplish this tends to be complex. *See, e.g.*, B.G. Dahlby, *Adverse Selection and Pareto Improvements Through Compulsory Insurance*, 37 PUB. CHOICE 547 (1981).

[97] One may note subtle differences. An imperfect liability rule may over- or undercompensate victims, whereas a property rule protecting victims would perfectly insure them in the absence of bargaining. However, a property rule protecting victims may induce bargaining, through which victims are overcompensated because they will receive some of the surplus generated by their agreements.

[98] For instance, we would say that victims are more in need of protection against risk if they are poor people living near a polluting factory owned by a large corporation but less in need of protection if they are wealthy individuals living near polluting farms owned by poor farmers.

[99] For development of the argument that legal rules should not be used to redistribute income because the income tax and transfer system is superior, see Steven Shavell, *A Note on Efficiency vs. Distributional Equity in Legal Rulemaking: Should Distributional Equity Matter Given Optimal Income Taxation?*, 71 AM. ECON. REV. 414 (1981), and Louis Kaplow and Steven Shavell, *Why the Legal System Is Less Efficient Than the Income Tax in Redistributing Income*, 23 J. LEGAL STUD. 667 (1994).

be heterogeneous in their need for money or their ability to pay.[100] For example, the incomes of both pollution victims and polluters (that is, polluting firms' owners, workers, and consumers) will vary greatly;[101] also, it is not clear which group would be relatively favored by the use of property or liability rules because the effects would depend upon how the property entitlement was assigned. In addition, a change in a legal rule affects only a fraction of any income class, whereas the income tax and transfer system affects virtually everyone.[102]

   5. Notions of Entitlement. — Notions of entitlement — noninstrumental justifications for rights — are often advanced in arguments about property and the law, and we briefly address them here. We should say, however, that our discussion is tentative, in no small part because we are unaware of a sustained, coherent statement and application of entitlement arguments to our subject.[103]

   What is the implication of a belief in entitlements for the choice between property rules and liability rules? By definition, property rule protection of a potential victim's entitlement protects it absolutely, whereas use of a liability rule may result in violation of the entitlement and possible undercompensation for its breach (if damages are sometimes too low). Thus, property rule protection of victims' entitlements to be free from harm appears superior to liability rule protec-

---

[100] *See* A. MITCHELL POLINSKY, AN INTRODUCTION TO LAW AND ECONOMICS 125–27 (2d ed. 1989).

[101] Recall the example in note 98.

[102] The general preference for redistribution through direct means has often been noted. *See, e.g.*, Ellickson, *supra* note 1, at 683 (noting that most economists prefer direct transfer payments to indirect redistribution). But some of the important investigations of property versus liability rules have suggested that distribution should be taken into account. Both of Polinsky's articles on the subject, cited in note 1 above, devote substantial attention to the issue. In these articles, he does not regard the use of the income tax system as an adequate solution to distributional objectives because of the adverse incentive effects of redistributive taxation. *See, e.g.*, Polinsky, *Resolving Nuisance Disputes, supra* note 1, at 1083–85, 1096. But, as explained in the articles cited above in note 99, departing from efficient legal rules to further distributive objectives causes the *same* adverse incentive effects as does redistributive taxation and *also* produces additional inefficiency; thus, only the income tax system should be employed to achieve distributional goals. (We note that Polinsky has subsequently expressed more skepticism about the desirability of using the legal system to redistribute income. *See* POLINSKY, *supra* note 100, at 7–10, 119–27, 144 n.87.)

   Calabresi and Melamed also believe distributional factors to be important in the choice of legal rules. *See* Calabresi & Melamed, *supra* note 1, at 1098–1101. Their exposition is somewhat difficult to interpret, however, as they include many possible considerations under the rubric of "distribution." *See id.* at 1102–05. We understand their conception of distribution to include the following elements: (1) distributive justice directed at equality of income or wealth (the subject under present discussion); (2) natural law or corrective justice, concerned with entitlement (discussed in the next subsection); and (3) a possibly related concern for "merit goods" (such as education or bodily integrity) to which citizens might deserve an inalienable entitlement (which we believe to be inapposite in most contexts that we consider, unless interpreted as variations of the entitlement arguments discussed in the next subsection). *See id.*

[103] The closest example is Calabresi and Melamed's discussion of distributional factors. *See supra* note 102.

tion. But this same property rule violates any entitlements that potential injurers might have. A landowner, for example, might have an entitlement to burn leaves or to raise pigs, and this entitlement would be violated if he were forced to stop in order to protect his neighbor's entitlement to clean air or to odor-free air. Protection of the entitlement of the injurer, therefore, requires his possession of the property right to harm the victim. (And if he does not possess this right, it would appear, at the least, that a liability rule should govern, which would permit him to act and pay damages rather than be denied the opportunity.)

In consequence, consideration of the notion of entitlement does not generally point in favor of a property rule protecting victims, a property rule protecting injurers, or the liability rule — because victims' and injurers' entitlements compete with each other. Thus, it is necessary to invoke some justificatory theory to decide who should possess which entitlements and when.

One justification would derive from an underlying conception of natural rights. To make such a justification plausible, we would have to identify the origin of natural rights, which involves articulating a normative theory that is not connected to individuals' welfare (for a welfare-based theory is already captured by our original analysis). But if, by assumption, no person cares about a natural right per se — that is, independently of its utilitarian value — why should it be given any weight?[104]

A second possible justification for why an entitlement should go to a particular person may emerge from a belief that, when a person uses property, a species of psychological bond to the property is formed. Violating a person's entitlement to his property would cause disutility by breaking the bond. This conception of the basis of entitlement raises such empirical questions as how long it takes for the bond to form, what the nature of the bond is for a corporation rather than for a person, and so forth. In any event, to the extent that psychological bonds underlie entitlements, one can, and presumably ought to, analyze the breaking of the bonds as components of harm (analogous to pain and suffering) in the type of utilitarian analysis that we have undertaken; separate treatment is not required. Indeed, our analysis of possible underestimation of harm emphasized that all elements of disutility should be reflected in damages.[105]

A third source of justification of entitlements is that a legal rule itself confers an entitlement on a person. In other words, ownership of

---

[104] This is, of course, the time-honored question that utilitarians have put to anti-utilitarians. The question is particularly significant in the present context, for individuals may (and often do) sell their entitlements if their valuations are less than others' valuations.

[105] *See supra* section II.A.3.(b); *see also infra* section III.A.2 (making the same claim when addressing the taking of things).

a thing gives a person a set of entitlements with respect to it. But this idea is vulnerable to an obvious criticism: it renders circular any claims that the law should be this or that way in order to protect a person's entitlement.

A fourth justification of entitlements concerns distributive justice. In the preceding subsection, we explained why the general notion of distributive justice does not affect our analysis. Some commentators, however, have sought to justify distributive outcomes in specific cases by appealing to particularistic norms of corrective justice.[106] But difficulties remain in identifying the basis for these norms, in justifying them independently of parties' desires, and in distinguishing them from general theories of distributive justice.[107]

---

[106] Accounts of corrective justice include JULES L. COLEMAN, RISKS AND WRONGS (1992); Richard A. Epstein, *Nuisance Law: Corrective Justice and Its Utilitarian Constraints*, 8 J. LEGAL STUD. 49 (1979); George P. Fletcher, *Fairness and Utility in Tort Theory*, 85 HARV. L. REV. 537 (1972); and Ernest J. Weinrib, *The Gains and Losses of Corrective Justice*, 44 DUKE L.J. 277 (1994).

[107] Before proceeding to discuss some of this work, we pause to note that it is not clear the extent to which corrective justice is advanced as a prescriptive theory rather than as a descriptive one. *Compare* Jules L. Coleman, *The Practice of Corrective Justice*, 37 ARIZ. L. REV. 15, 18 (1995) ("Most legal theorists who have been interested in corrective justice have been interested in it insofar as it might figure in an account, explanation or interpretation of various legal practices . . . .") *with id.* at 20 ("[L]egal theorists who invoke the concept of corrective justice mean to treat it as a substantive moral ideal . . . .").

We find peculiar the argument that a person deserves a particular payment from another person in a particular type of case when general distributive norms might call for the payment received to be taxed away (and, similarly, when the norms might call for the person making the payment to enjoy an income tax benefit to restore him to his correct level of income). To be sure, one could argue that the payment is nonetheless meaningful to the parties themselves, but then corrective justice is merely a component of preferences; its existence would be an empirical question, and if the preference exists, a utilitarian analysis would already include it. *See generally* George P. Fletcher, *Corrective Justice for Moderns*, 106 HARV. L. REV. 1658, 1666–69 (1993) (book review) (criticizing COLEMAN, cited above in note 106, for failing to offer a successful account of corrective justice that is independent of general distributive concerns); Stephen R. Perry, *Comment on Coleman: Corrective Justice*, 67 IND. L.J. 381 (1992) (making a similar critique of Coleman's views).

We are not alone in finding it difficult to ascertain clearly the various claims of corrective justice: "There are a number of quite different accounts of corrective justice [involving obligations of reparations between parties], but it has proven surprisingly difficult to specify the circumstances under which correlative rights and obligations of reparation arise and to say why they are justified." Stephen R. Perry, *The Moral Foundations of Tort Law*, 77 IOWA L. REV. 449, 450 (1992). Perry emphasizes the problem that corrective-justice claims, as others have formulated them, may dissolve into general distributive claims. *See id.* at 451–52. He sketches his own account, in which corrective and distributive justice are not wholly distinct. *See id.* at 496–513. In his scheme, he asserts that an obligation of reparation arises when there is culpable fault or when there is "outcome-responsibility" that "at a certain point" is "publicly acknowledged" as sufficiently equivalent. *Id.* at 510. The location of that point is not a "matter[ ] capable of rational demonstration," but "depend[s] on a sense of appropriateness that emerges from considered reflection on the normative implications of outcome-responsibility, where the outcomes in question are harmful interferences with human well-being." *Id.* The basis for overriding general distributive preferences or failing to advance the parties' interests as they perceive them (which would be necessary for Perry's theory to have independent significance) is not identified.

In the end, therefore, we find the notion of entitlement — as we understand its possible meanings — unclear and unhelpful for analysis.[108]

E. Examples

Having completed our analysis of property versus liability rules in the context of externalities, we now briefly discuss several examples of the use of these rules to illustrate our arguments. We follow the examples with a comment on the distinction between property and liability rules.

1. Industrial Pollution.[109] — The problem of industrial pollution has become increasingly important over the years as the volume of discharges released into the environment has grown and as our knowledge of its consequences has developed. Pollution control is achieved predominantly through direct regulation,[110] which is to say, through property rule protection.[111] Still, liability rules are utilized to some extent. Also, closely related to liability rules, tradeable pollution rights

---

[108] Our list of additional considerations does not include the so-called "offer-asking" problem associated with the possibility that the price that an individual would demand to give up an entitlement may exceed the price that he would pay to acquire it. *See* Don L. Coursey, John L. Hovis & William D. Schulze, *The Disparity Between Willingness to Accept and Willingness to Pay Measures of Value*, 102 Q.J. ECON. 679 (1987); W. Michael Hanemann, *Willingness to Pay and Willingness to Accept: How Much Can They Differ?*, 81 AM. ECON. REV. 635 (1991); Daniel Kahneman, Jack L. Knetsch & Richard H. Thaler, *Experimental Tests of the Endowment Effect and the Coase Theorem*, 98 J. POL. ECON. 1325 (1990). (For discussions of the offer-asking problem in the context of critiquing the economic analysis of law, see Mark Kelman, *Consumption Theory, Production Theory, and Ideology in the Coase Theorem*, 52 S. CAL. L. REV. 669 (1979); and Duncan Kennedy, *Cost-Benefit Analysis of Entitlement Problems: A Critique*, 33 STAN. L. REV. 387 (1981).) We do not believe, however, that this possibility raises issues separate from those we have already considered. Specifically, consider the most plausible sources of differences in offer and asking prices. One source is a wealth effect (individuals with an entitlement are thereby wealthier than those who do not have it). In such a case, it is possible that an outcome in favor of either party is efficient because efficiency is conditional on the distribution of wealth, which is affected by the assignment of the entitlement. As we discuss above in subsection 4, however, distributional goals should be pursued independently, using taxes and transfer payments. Other plausible sources of offer-asking differences are psychological factors (such as a feeling of attachment) and the effect of the law itself on parties' valuations; these factors were considered in the text. Regardless of the cause of an offer-asking difference, we are inclined to believe that, once the cause is identified, the appropriate implications for the analysis, if any, will be apparent.

[109] For statements of the standard economic analysis of pollution remedies (but ones that do not emphasize the categories of property and liability rules), see WILLIAM J. BAUMOL & WALLACE E. OATES, ECONOMICS, ENVIRONMENTAL POLICY, AND THE QUALITY OF LIFE (1979); HARVEY S. ROSEN, PUBLIC FINANCE 100–07 (3d ed. 1992); and JOSEPH E. STIGLITZ, ECONOMICS OF THE PUBLIC SECTOR 184–97 (1986).

[110] *See, e.g.*, Clean Water Act, 33 U.S.C. §§ 1311–1314 (1988 & Supp. V 1993); Clean Air Act, 42 U.S.C. §§ 7407–7410 (1988 & Supp. V 1993).

[111] The main difference between regulation and property rule protection is that private parties enforce the latter at their option, whereas the government enforces regulation. This difference, however, does not affect our analysis.

have begun to be employed,[112] and the possible imposition of pollution taxes has been widely discussed.[113]

Bargaining appears to have relatively little importance in the context of industrial pollution because, as is often stated, victims of pollution are unlikely to bargain with those responsible for it. One reason is that the victims of many types of pollution are numerous, making coordination among them difficult, in part because individual victims will want to rely on other victims to bargain on their behalf.[114] A further obstacle to bargaining is that each victim's expected harm from a particular generator of pollution may be small, so that individual victims may have weak incentives to bargain with that party.[115]

Our analysis suggests, of course, that when bargaining is improbable, liability rules tend to be superior to property rules. This conclusion raises questions about the observed degree of reliance on property rule protection and regulation. We note, however, that the legal rule that is actually applied is neither of the simple property rules that we studied, namely the rule protecting victims against any amount of pollution and the rule allowing firms to pollute without bound. Either rule would be extremely inefficient. What we find in reality are regulations that divide entitlements, that allow firms to pollute within prescribed limits, or that impose technological requirements — restrictions

---

[112] *See* Robert W. Hahn & Gordon L. Hester, *Where Did All the Markets Go? An Analysis of EPA's Emissions Trading Program*, 6 YALE J. ON REG. 109 (1989). For a discussion of the provisions of the 1990 Clean Air Act Amendments that authorize tradeable pollution rights, see PETER S. MENELL & RICHARD B. STEWART, ENVIRONMENTAL LAW AND POLICY 408–12 (1994). For an overview of the recent movement toward the use of economic incentives in federal pollution control policy, see Richard H. Pildes & Cass R. Sunstein, *Reinventing the Regulatory State*, 62 U. CHI. L. REV. 1, 112–25 (1995). In addition, California has a system of tradeable pollution rights. *See* CAL. HEALTH & SAFETY CODE § 44256 (West 1995); John P. Dwyer, *The Use of Market Incentives in Controlling Air Pollution: California's Marketable Permits Program*, 20 ECOLOGY L.Q. 103, 113 (1993) (stating that through the tradeable rights program "the Los Angeles Basin will become an experimental laboratory for the rest of the nation"). For analyses of tradeable rights, see J.H. DALES, POLLUTION, PROPERTY & PRICES (1968); T.H. TIETENBERG, EMISSIONS TRADING: AN EXERCISE IN REFORMING POLLUTION POLICY (1985); Bruce A. Ackerman & Richard B. Stewart, *Reforming Environmental Law*, 37 STAN. L. REV. 1333, 1341–51 (1985); and Robert N. Stavins, *Transaction Costs and Tradeable Permits*, 29 J. ENVTL. ECON. & MGMT. 133 (1995).

[113] *See, e.g.*, ROSEN, *supra* note 109, at 100–07; STIGLITZ, *supra* note 109, at 185–94; Adam Chase, *The Efficiency Benefits of "Green Taxes": A Tribute to Senator John Heinz*, 11 UCLA J. ENVTL. L. & POL'Y 1, 9–18 (1992) (arguing that pollution taxes are more efficient and provide better incentives than direct regulation).

[114] *See, e.g.*, Calabresi & Melamed, *supra* note 1, at 1119 (discussing the collective-action problem).

[115] *Cf.* Ellickson, *supra* note 1, at 772–79 (proposing adjustments in the legal rules governing pervasive nuisances, which may impose minor costs on individual plaintiffs but substantial harm in the aggregate).

that one hopes reflect to some degree the harmfulness of pollution and the costs of its prevention.[116]

Nonetheless, we believe that significantly greater use of liability rules should be made. The primary advantage of liability rules, recall, is that firms facing liability are allowed to decide for themselves whether and how much to pollute, on the basis of their knowledge of the costs of pollution prevention and of the extra profits they can make by expanding production. Because courts and regulators frequently cannot discover this information in practice, they will sometimes make poor decisions when they prescribe particular behavior or a particular level of permissible pollution.[117] Thus, only under liability rules is society able to make use of firms' superior knowledge of the costs of pollution control.[118]

Moreover, the criticism that a liability rule should not be employed because harm from pollution cannot be adequately measured is invalid. We have demonstrated that the use of a liability rule under which damages are set equal to estimated harm is superior to the use of property rules, and thus to pollution regulation. Indeed, the criticism overlooks the point that difficulties in assessing harm pose as great a problem for regulation as for the use of a liability rule: under regulation, the state must use its knowledge of harm (as well as of prevention costs) in deciding how much pollution to permit.[119]

Another implication of our analysis is that pollution taxes are preferable to the system of tradeable pollution rights that is in partial use

---

[116] *See* statutes cited *supra* note 110. Nominally, many pollution regulations may have been set without the use of cost-benefit analysis. *See* Ackerman & Stewart, *supra* note 112, at 1334-40 (discussing the costs of present failure to use cost-effective means of reducing pollution). For example, the Clean Air Act does not include cost as a factor in standard-setting. *See* Union Elec. Co. v. EPA, 427 U.S. 246, 265 (1976) (holding that "economic or technological infeasibility" is precluded from consideration). Similar limitations exist in the Clean Water Act. *See* Reynolds Metals Co. v. EPA, 760 F.2d 549, 565 (4th Cir. 1985) (stating that balancing of costs and benefits is not required with respect to the "best available technology" standard); Association of Pac. Fisheries v. EPA, 615 F.2d 794, 805 (9th Cir. 1980) (stating that costs must be "wholly disproportionate to potential effluent reduction" before the EPA may take them into account). It is not clear, however, that existing rules are as extreme as would be implied by such formulations or that existing rules are fully enforced. *See* MENELL & STEWART, *supra* note 112, at 374.

[117] Apparently, a significant error of this type may have occurred in the design of the Clean Air Act Amendments of 1990. *See* Jeff Bailey, *Electric Utilities Are Overcomplying with Clean Air Act*, WALL ST. J., Nov. 15, 1995, at B8.

[118] *See* BAUMOL & OATES, *supra* note 109, at 241; STIGLITZ, *supra* note 109, at 192-93.

[119] In some instances, it also may be difficult to measure the quantity of emissions. In such cases, liability rules (including pollution taxes) and property rules that regulate the amount of pollution (including tradeable permit schemes) would be excessively costly or infeasible. *See supra* note 43. But regulation of plant location, technology, or other observable characteristics would be possible.

today.[120] Pollution taxes are essentially a form of liability rule,[121] whereas the tradeable-rights system has property-rule-like elements. To be sure, tradeable pollution rights have an advantage over conventional regulation of the amount of pollution each firm may generate. Under tradeable rights, firms that find it relatively cheap to prevent pollution do not buy the rights, but rather proceed to prevent pollution, while firms that find it quite expensive to prevent pollution tend to buy pollution rights and proceed to pollute. As a result, the induced *distribution of pollution among firms* is socially desirable. But the *total quantity of pollution* is fixed by the government when it decides on the quantity of tradeable rights. In setting the quantity, the government must use its own estimate of pollution control costs.[122] Only if the government's estimate is accurate will the price that emerges in a market for tradeable pollution rights equal the best estimate of harm. As we have stressed, however, the government's estimates of costs are likely to be inaccurate, so the price of tradeable rights is likely to be incorrect.[123] Thus, firms will not decide how much to pollute on the appropriate basis; the result is that the total quantity of pollution will not be determined as it ought to be. By contrast, if the government employs pollution taxes in the way economists generally recommend — setting the tax equal to expected harm — the total quantity of pollution will be approximately efficient.[124]

We further believe that pollution taxes offer certain advantages over conventional liability. As we discussed above, liability-related incentives are dulled if firms do not have the assets to pay for the harms that they might cause. This disadvantage is often relevant in the context of pollution — for example, with regard to the possibility of large-scale release of radioactive waste. Moreover, the problem of tracing harm to injurers means that damages have to be inflated for proper incentives to exist under the liability system, thereby making the judg-

---

120 As we will explain in the text to follow, the belief that a tradeable rights system is preferable to a pollution tax because it is easier to set the quantity of pollution rights than the rate of the pollution tax, *see, e.g.*, James E. Krier, *Marketable Pollution Allowances*, 25 U. TOL. L. REV. 449, 452–54 (1994), is wrong.

121 The main difference between pollution taxes and a conventional liability rule is that victims do not receive tax receipts as payments for harms suffered. This difference is not important for what we have to say in this subsection — although it obviously does improve victims' incentives relative to what they are under conventional liability rules, as discussed in section II.C.

122 We emphasize that control costs include not only the costs of existing technology, but also the costs of developing new technologies and of reducing output, which may be even more difficult for the government to ascertain.

123 See the example cited above in note 117.

124 Instead of imposing pollution taxes, the government might sell pollution rights for a price equal to expected harm. The results under these two regimes would be the same. Such pollution rights differ from the ones under discussion in the text because the quantity of these rights would be determined by firms' willingness to purchase the rights at a price equal to expected harm, rather than by the government. *See* Robert Cooter, *Prices and Sanctions*, 84 COLUM. L. REV. 1523, 1535–36 (1984).

ment-proof problem more serious.[125] The use of pollution taxes rather than ex post liability would alleviate the judgment-proof problem because pollution taxes are set equal to *expected* harm, not actual harm. Hence, the magnitude of the taxes is lower, perhaps much lower, than the magnitude of possible liability. Taxes, therefore, would create proper incentives for some firms with insufficient assets to be adequately deterred by the prospect of liability.[126] We also note that a system of pollution taxes would avoid the administrative costs of determining damages suffered by individual victims and the adverse effect of compensation on victims' incentives.[127]

2. *Automobile Accidents.* — Driving behavior provides a standard example of an activity creating harmful externalities that cannot be resolved through bargaining. The individuals who drive do not know whom they might injure in an accident, and bargaining between each potential injurer and every potential victim is manifestly impossible. As a result, liability rules should, according to our analysis, be superior to property rules. Two particular features of the current means used to control driving behavior seem worth noting. First, although liability rules are widely employed to control driving behavior, so is regulation to a significant extent. Second, the form of liability applied in the automobile accident context, the negligence rule, is different from the form we have discussed, strict liability. Nevertheless, as we now explain, both of these features of the control of driving behavior are roughly consistent with our analysis.

The regulations governing driving behavior are the traffic laws: speed limits, requirements to obey stop signs and traffic signals, and so forth. The general disadvantage of regulations — that they will be inefficient because of the state's lack of knowledge — may not be too important in the case of traffic laws. These laws are often minimal in character and are based on common experience; thus, compliance may result in relatively little loss of social welfare. (Further, as we explain in the next paragraph, when there are gains to be made from noncompliance, noncompliance may occur.) In addition, an important benefit of traffic regulations is that they address the judgment-proof problem.

---

[125] Suppose that a firm that dumps pollutants at night faces a one-in-three chance of being caught. Then, if the harm that the pollutants cause is $1 million, damages would have to be $3 million when the firm is caught in order for incentives to be appropriate. The firm thus needs to have assets of at least $3 million, rather than only $1 million, to be adequately motivated to prevent harm under the liability approach.

[126] For instance, a firm that discharged a pollutant that has a 1% chance of causing harm of $10 million would have inadequate incentives under a liability rule if its assets were only $2 million. If the firm paid a tax, however, the proper amount of the tax would be 1% × $10 million or $100,000, an amount it could afford to pay. (If it could not pay the tax — perhaps in advance — it might then be forbidden from polluting.) Hence, the firm's incentives under the tax would be adequate. *See* Steven Shavell, *The Optimal Structure of Law Enforcement*, 36 J.L. & ECON. 255, 285 (1993); *supra* note 84.

[127] *See supra* note 121.

Many drivers do not have assets nearly sufficient to pay for the harm they might cause, even after existing levels of liability insurance coverage are taken into account. Thus, it is desirable that they be required to obey regulations.

We also note that traffic regulations are sometimes not so much commands that must be obeyed as they are, or closely resemble, liability rules.[128] In particular, sanctions for failure to comply with traffic regulations often are not prohibitive; that is, they are not sufficient to induce nearly perfect compliance. Rather, sanctions are frequently moderate and might be better viewed as approximating harm in an expected sense. (For example, like the pollution taxes discussed in the preceding subsection, traffic fines might be seen as a tax on behavior that has the potential to cause harm.) This liability-rule-like feature of regulation is socially desirable for the usual reason that liability is attractive: it allows injurers latitude to act in harm-producing ways when the cost of not doing so is high. For instance, some drivers will have important reasons to double park (perhaps they will otherwise be late for an important meeting), and they will choose to do so because the expected fine they will pay for double parking is not prohibitively large.

Let us turn now to the issue of the form of liability. As we mentioned, it is the negligence rule that is actually applied in the context of automobile accidents, whereas our analysis focused on the strict liability rule. On reflection, one may view the negligence rule as a hybrid of a property rule granting a partial entitlement to cause harm and a liability rule (strict liability): provided that an injurer exercises due care, he effectively acquires a property rule entitlement to cause harm; only if he fails to take due care does he become liable for harm.[129] Our concern is to evaluate the advantages and disadvantages of the property-rule-like feature of the negligence rule.

This characteristic of the negligence rule — no liability if due care is taken — obviously provides injurers with an incentive to exercise due care. But like any property regime, it poses the following problem: when the rule assigning rights (here, the due care level) fails to reflect actual danger and prevention costs, undesirable behavior results. In addition, the property-rule-like aspect of the negligence rule is incomplete in the kind of injurer behavior it controls: injurers do not have incentives to reduce harm through moderating their level of driving or through taking other actions that the negligence rule does not encompass. Under strict liability, by contrast, injurers would have

---

[128] We discuss the general point that what is nominally a property rule may in fact approximate a liability rule in section II.E.4.

[129] *Cf.* Polinsky, *Resolving Nuisance Disputes, supra* note 1, at 1087 (discussing intermediate mixed entitlements in the pollution context).

incentives to take care whenever care is appropriate, and they would also have incentives to reduce their level of driving to mitigate risk.[130]

But the property-rule-like element of the negligence rule may have an administrative cost advantage relative to strict liability: when injurers clearly are not negligent, victims will tend not to file suit under the negligence rule, but victims will bring such suits under strict liability. In addition, negligence determinations in the domain of automobile accidents are often based upon simple rules, such as the traffic laws themselves; this also conserves administrative costs.[131] Finally, the negligence rule better preserves victims' incentives to avoid harm (although defenses to strict liability can address this problem to some extent).

    3. Nuisance. — Nuisances range from common disturbances (exemplified by noisy parties, dogs that roam around making pests of themselves, and compost heaps that produce foul odors) to more serious problems (such as a factory's discharge of wastes onto a neighboring farm).[132] Frequently, if not typically, these negative-externality-creating actions could be discussed by the involved parties, who are often few in number (perhaps just two). Thus, we suspect that in the nuisance context, bargaining can often help to solve problems if they are not addressed well by legal rules. Accordingly, although liability rules tend to be superior to property rules in controlling other harmful externalities, the legal approach adopted for the resolution of nuisances may matter less than in many other situations.

The legal approach that is traditionally employed for nuisances is a property rule regime. If a disturbance is sufficiently bothersome, then the victim is accorded the right to enjoin it; otherwise, he is denied the injunctive right and the injurer can continue his actions without having to pay damages.[133] If noisy parties are judged to be too disturbing, injunctions against them will be granted; but if they are not

---

[130] *See* Shavell, *supra* note 76. Needless to say, a general comparison of strict liability and negligence rules would involve factors in addition to those we discuss.

[131] Although victims will sue less often under a negligence rule than under strict liability, litigation costs will be greater under a negligence regime. The arguments in the text suggest that the frequency effect will be large and the cost differential of diminished significance (relative to many negligence inquiries), but ultimately the question whether the negligence rule is indeed cheaper is an empirical one.

[132] Many would include pollution in the category of nuisance. *See, e.g.,* Polinsky, *Resolving Nuisance Disputes, supra* note 1, at 1075. We find it convenient, however, to distinguish industrial pollution, the subject of subsection 1, for which there are usually large numbers of victims and bargaining is impossible, from nuisances, in which bargaining often will be feasible. Indeed, in the article just cited, Polinsky limits his attention to cases in which there are only two parties or in which many parties have a common representative. *See id.* at 1075–76; *see also* Ellickson, *supra* note 1, at 761–79 (advocating different approaches for localized nuisances and those causing pervasive harm).

[133] For a discussion of the law and exceptions to the property rule, see the sources cited above in note 4.

so judged, they can be held and damages need not be paid. How, if at all, can the use of property rules be justified for nuisance?

Administrative cost considerations provide a plausible rationale for property rules in the context of modest, quotidian nuisances like noisy parties.[134] As noted above, if property rule assignments of entitlements tend to resemble optimal assignments, then property rules involve low administrative costs. Under liability rules, however, administrative costs will be borne whenever harm optimally occurs, because damages will be paid. In the area of common nuisances, this difference may matter. Determining when a gathering is too disturbing may be reasonably easy, so that festivities will not usually generate litigation: only parties that are not overly disturbing will be held, and no one will try to enjoin these parties because they know they will be unsuccessful; conversely, parties that would be overly noisy will tend not to be held, because individuals would realize that such parties would be stopped.

Under the liability rule, however, either of two inferior outcomes might well occur. On one hand, the cost of litigation might discourage victims of noisy parties from suing for damages,[135] thus converting the rule into a de facto property rule favoring injurers. On the other hand, victims might be willing to bring suits. In this case, approximately the same number and types of parties will be held as under the property rule in question. But when parties are held, damages will often be paid for the disturbances created, and thus administrative costs will tend to be higher. Of course, to the extent that property-rule decisions are difficult for courts to make in an approximately optimal manner, the force of our argument is reduced because of the costs that would be incurred in bargaining and litigation.

With regard to serious nuisances, the liability rule might be superior to property rules. The issue of administrative costs is relatively unimportant for nuisances of substantial magnitude (certainly by comparison to the context of common nuisances). As we explained previously, the liability rule might be superior to property rules when bargaining is imperfect due to asymmetric information. If there were also other impediments to bargaining, it is likely that the liability rule would be attractive.[136]

---

[134] Another factor that we advanced for property rule protection of victims is the judgment-proof problem. *See supra* section II.D.1. But this does not seem to be relevant for the common nuisance. It is doubtful that people who hold noisy parties or allow their dogs to roam would be unable to pay for any harm done. For many serious nuisances, however, this factor may favor property rule protection of victims (or posting of bonds, and the like).

[135] By contrast, under the property rule, a victim of a noisy party can often initiate legal action merely by calling the police.

[136] Robert Ellickson, in his important investigation of land use controls, offers similar arguments for preferring a regime that relies much more heavily on nuisance law than on zoning to regulate conflicts among neighbors' activities. *See* Ellickson, *supra* note 1. He criticizes zoning as

4. *Comment on the Distinction Between Property Rules and Liability Rules.* — We have proceeded, for the most part, under the assumption that property and liability rules are distinct: under property rules, a person's entitlement is guaranteed, whereas under the liability rule, the injurer is permitted to harm the victim as long as he pays damages equal to harm. As we briefly noted at the beginning of this Part,[137] however, one can conceive of the two property rules and the liability rule that we studied as all being, in fact, liability rules with different levels of damages: the property rule protecting injurers corresponds to a liability rule with zero damages; the conventional liability rule that we emphasized is the rule with damages equal to courts' best estimate of harm; and the property rule protecting victims mirrors a liability rule with extremely high, or infinite, damages.

Viewing property rules and the conventional liability rule as members of a continuum of liability rules that differ merely in their level of damages has relevance for the conceptual analysis and for the understanding of particular legal rules. The primary conceptual point is that the fully optimal liability rule may, in principle, be one with any level of damages. Thus, the fully optimal rule may be neither one with extreme damages (that is, a property rule) nor one with damages equal to harm (that is, the conventional liability rule). In this regard, we should remind the reader that, in the simple situation of section II.A, in which injurers and victims do not bargain, we in fact demonstrated that the conventional liability rule is optimal — that is to say, superior to a liability rule with any other level of damages. However, in other situations, such as those for which a property rule might be superior to the conventional liability rule, the property rule might not be fully optimal; instead, some liability rule with other than extreme damages might be best. For example, we said in section II.C that, because payment of damages equal to harm may dilute victims' incentives to avoid harm, property rule protection of injurers might be superior to the conventional liability rule. Here, the fully optimal rule arguably would not be property rule protection of injurers, but rather a liability rule with damages less than harm.[138]

---

a species of inalienable property rule; for example, if an area is zoned exclusively for residential use, a store may not pay the neighbors who would be disturbed for permission to build in a strategic location. *See id.* at 691–711. Moreover, motivated by a concern that not all bargaining will be successful, Ellickson advocates a liability rule (or reverse liability rule) to regulate nuisances. *See id.* at 738–48; *see also* Rabin, *supra* note 29 (advocating liability rules in the nuisance context). Ellickson also discusses how the administration of nuisance law might be changed to address a range of important land use conflicts in a more administratively efficient manner than conventional private litigation. *See* Ellickson, *supra* note 1, at 762–71.

[137] *See supra* p. 724.

[138] Such a rule would possess some of the advantages of conventional liability — it would harness the information injurers have about prevention costs — and would still provide victims with some incentive to avoid harm.

When we consider how property and liability rules are actually applied, we also see that the view that they lie on a continuum is descriptively helpful, because the rules often turn out to be different from both true property rules and the liability rule with damages equal to harm. We pointed out, for example, that what appears to be property rule protection of victims of automobile accidents is in fact far from absolute; much prohibited driving behavior (such as speeding or double parking) is only nominally proscribed, and the expected sanction for an offense may not be very high and may even approximate expected harm. We also noted earlier that damages paid by liable parties may fall systematically short of harm; damages may also exceed harm, notably if they include a punitive element.

Although the view that property rules and conventional liability rules lie on a continuum is helpful, we found it expositionally convenient to consider only the conventional liability rule and the property rules in our analysis above, and we will do the same in Part III.

III. THE TAKING OF THINGS

In this Part, we turn from the subject of harmful externalities to that of protecting possessory interests in things,[139] that is, preventing them from being taken.[140] Under the *property rule*, no one may take a thing from its present possessor. More precisely, this is the property rule when the possessory entitlement resides with the present possessor, and that is what we will usually mean by a property rule; however, we briefly mention the alternative property rule of granting the entitlement to a taker.[141] Under the *liability rule*, a person is permitted to take a thing from its possessor but must then pay damages equal to its court-estimated value.[142] Of course, in reality a property rule protecting possessors generally prevails; use of a liability rule is exceptional.[143]

---

[139] Although we do not address an individual's possessory interest in himself, an interest that also receives property rule protection, we note that many of the arguments developed in this Part would apply in that context.

[140] We discuss the nature of the distinction between the taking of things and harmful externalities in section III.G. For now, it suffices for the reader to interpret the taking of a thing primarily as an instance in which a person brings into his own possession a physical object that had been in another person's possession.

[141] As will be clear to the reader, the property rule with the entitlement granted to the taker will usually have all the undesirable features of the liability rule, but to an even greater extent. Thus, we do not consider this version of property rule in most of our discussion.

[142] As in the case of harmful externalities, there is the possibility of a reverse liability rule. *See supra* note 29. Under it, the possessor is permitted to prevent the taker from appropriating his thing if he pays the taker damages equal to its estimated value to the taker. We do not consider this reverse rule here, because it will be evident that in the present context the reverse rule will generally be inferior to the standard liability rule.

[143] The main examples of liability rules for the taking of things are the government's right of eminent domain, which allows the state to take private property in exchange for payment of just

We will assume that legal rules are used to promote the social objective of maximizing the value of things, which means channeling things to the parties who place the highest value on them. But the social goal will be appropriately modified when we go beyond the basic analysis to consider additional factors.

We now analyze property and liability rule protection of possessory interests, beginning with the situation in which parties do not bargain with each other and then considering the case in which they do. Afterwards, we will examine several other issues, including how the choice of rule affects the feasibility of bargaining, the problem of reciprocal takings, and efforts to avoid or to carry out takings.

We believe that our analysis will explain why property rule protection is superior to liability rule protection of possessory interests, which is to say, the analysis rationalizes observed practice. That is, *we will provide justifications for a fundamental aspect of ownership: that the owner of a thing has the right to prevent others from taking it from him, even if they are willing to pay damages.* In the course of our demonstration of this point and at the end of this Part, we will reconcile this view with our sharply different conclusion in the previous Part that liability rules are often superior in controlling harmful externalities.

---

compensation, and the right of private parties to violate possessory interests in cases involving emergencies, *see, e.g.,* Ploof v. Putnam, 71 A. 188 (Vt. 1908) (discussing the right to moor one's boat at another's dock in a storm); Vincent v. Lake Erie Transp. Co., 124 N.W. 221 (Minn. 1910) (discussing the obligation to pay damages caused by mooring one's boat to another's dock during a storm).

The subject of eminent domain has received extensive attention in academic literature. *See, e.g.,* POSNER, *supra* note 9, § 3.7, at 56–61; Lawrence Blume & Daniel L. Rubinfeld, *Compensation for Takings: An Economic Analysis*, 72 CAL. L. REV. 569 (1984); Louis Kaplow, *An Economic Analysis of Legal Transitions*, 99 HARV. L. REV. 509 *passim* (1986); Frank I. Michelman, *Property, Utility, and Fairness: Comments on the Ethical Foundations of "Just Compensation" Law*, 80 HARV. L. REV. 1165 (1967). Eminent domain is usually viewed independently, rather than as part of the subject of property versus liability rules. *See infra* note 189. Nonetheless, some authors have cited this example in the present context. *See, e.g.,* Calabresi & Melamed, *supra* note 1, at 1106–08.

Because the classic taking involves the government's converting land from private to public possession, our analysis suggests that a property rule protecting the private possessor is best. Indeed, most property the government acquires is purchased, rather than forcibly taken. (Consider defense procurement and an endless variety of routine purchases, as well as many acquisitions of land.) The best (and most familiar) justification for takings arises when there is a need to assemble particular parcels, such as for a road — a situation in which holdout problems can be serious. *See, e.g.,* POSNER, *supra* note 9, § 3.7, at 56–57; Calabresi & Melamed, *supra* note 1, at 1106–07. Takings are commonly employed for this purpose. We note that the relevant analysis differs for government takings because it is not obvious that the government will be motivated in the same way as private actors. For some discussion of the relevant institutional differences, see Kaplow, cited above, at 566–76 and 602–06.

A. *Parties Do Not Bargain with Each Other*[144]

We consider first the situation in which the party who initially possesses a thing, whom we will for simplicity call the owner,[145] is unable to bargain with a potential appropriator, whom we will call a taker. Although this situation might be thought atypical — we expect the taker would usually have the opportunity to bargain with the owner — it is possible. For example, someone may want to take my boat to go fishing when I am not around the pier. Moreover, the case of no bargaining is worth analyzing because it provides a baseline for evaluating outcomes when bargaining is possible.

1. State's Information Is Perfect. — If the court has perfect information about the values of a thing both to the owner and to the taker,[146] then (as in the case of externalities) it makes no difference whether a property or liability rule is employed. The property rule assignment of an entitlement will be to the owner if he values a thing more highly than the taker; otherwise the entitlement will be awarded to the taker.[147] Under the liability rule, the taker will take the thing if and only if he values it more highly than the owner, because damages will equal the true value to the owner. Thus, under either type of rule, the thing will be, or come to be, possessed by the party who values it more highly.[148]

2. State's Information Is Imperfect. — If the court does not have perfect information about value, as will typically be true in cases of interest, it must estimate value. Let us consider the following assumptions about value and the court's knowledge.[149] First, suppose that things have a significant *common value*, that is, a component of value

---

[144] The analysis in this section is presented formally in the Appendix, Part II.

[145] Even though owners do enjoy property rule protection of their possessory interests, and this is the very practice that we are trying to explain, we trust that our usage will not cause confusion. We also note that owners are not the only ones who in fact enjoy possessory rights. For example, renters, with interests derived from owners, also enjoy such rights.

[146] It will be easy for courts to determine value in the case of fungible goods that are regularly traded on markets and in contexts in which there is no situational value (in contrast to the example described below in which a laptop computer is needed at a particular place and time, *see infra* p. 760). Another situation in which courts may be able to ascertain value tolerably well is in the case of an emergency: it may be apparent in such exceptional circumstances that the taker's value exceeds the owner's.

[147] Interestingly, it is just in the case of emergency situations, *see supra* notes 143, 146, that exceptions to property rule protection of possessors are sometimes made. (We also mention that some of the problems we identify later in this Part are less likely to be important in many emergency situations: a single taker may be identifiable, and the probability of the emergency may be small enough to have little adverse effect on possessors' incentives. Defining emergencies too broadly, however, would give rise to most of the liability rule's defects.)

[148] We remind the reader that in this section we consider only the efficient ex post possession of things, without factoring in ex ante incentives, which are considered in section III.E.

[149] How the assumptions and the argument here relate to the analysis of the parallel situation in the case of harmful externalities is discussed on page 763 and in the Appendix at section II.B, comment b.

that is the same for both the owner and any taker. For example, a boat or a home will have certain characteristics that all will evaluate similarly, such as the speed and operating characteristics of the boat or the number of rooms in the home.

Second, assume that things also have *idiosyncratic value* to individuals. Idiosyncratic value derives from characteristics of a thing that different individuals evaluate differently, such as the design of a home.[150] Assume also that the average idiosyncratic value to owners exceeds the average idiosyncratic value to takers. One justification for this assumption is, of course, that owners often obtain (or choose to retain) things precisely because they place greater idiosyncratic value on them than others do. For example, I may purchase my home just because it has higher idiosyncratic value for me than for others: I may particularly like its design, setting, or location.

Another important justification for the assumption that idiosyncratic value for owners is higher than it is for takers concerns a thing's *situational value*. For example, consider the owner of a laptop computer who has brought it to a conference for the purpose of taking notes. On average, such an individual will place a higher value on using it at the conference than would a random person, or another attendee who did not make the effort to bring a laptop.[151]

The assumption that idiosyncratic value is higher for owners means that it will be socially desirable on average for things not to be taken, but rather for them to remain in the possession of their owners. It will on average be optimal for a boat or for a home to remain in the possession of the present owner because he places a higher idiosyncratic value on it than a possible taker, and it will on average be optimal for those who bring laptop computers to conferences to retain possession of their computers during the conferences. Of course, this assumption does not imply that it will always be optimal for things not to be taken; there will be some occasions when things ought to change hands, when the idiosyncratic value to the taker exceeds that to the owner.

We now examine the choice among legal rules. An immediate consequence of the assumption that value is higher on average for owners is that, as between property rule protection of owners and property rule protection of takers, the former is preferable.

Now consider property rule protection of owners versus the liability rule. Under property rule protection, the situation is simple: there are no takings. The disadvantage of this result is that when a taking would be desirable, it will not transpire. (Recall that in this section

---

[150] *See, e.g.*, Ellickson, *supra* note 1, at 735–36.

[151] Note here that the higher idiosyncratic value to the owner does not arise from any special value the computer may have had to him when he purchased it. Rather, the idiosyncratic value at issue here is dependent upon the particular time and place.

we are assuming that no bargaining occurs.) How important this problem is depends on the likelihood that the idiosyncratic value of a taker exceeds that of an owner. The higher is the distribution of idiosyncratic values of owners relative to that of takers, the less important is the problem.

Under the liability rule, we presume that damages are set equal to the average value of owners, that is, owners' average common value plus their average idiosyncratic value. Inevitably, therefore, damages will sometimes be too high and sometimes too low. When takers expect courts' estimates of common value to be too high, takings will be rare,[152] so that the result will be close to that achieved under the property rule. By contrast, when takers expect courts' estimates of common value to be too low, it is likely that takers will take things; this result will be socially undesirable. Thus, the possibility of error (even when there is no systematic bias, as we have assumed that damages equal owners' average values) implies that the liability rule may be inferior to a property rule protecting owners. We now explain why this disadvantage of the liability rule will tend to be worse than the disadvantage of a property rule.[153]

Suppose, for example, that the common value associated with the use of a laptop computer during conferences varies between $0 and $200, depending on the type of conference, and is $100 for the average conference. Courts are able to determine the average common value but are unable to identify at which conferences laptops are more or less valuable. In addition, assume that the average idiosyncratic value of those who bring computers to conferences is $25 and that most of these idiosyncratic values are in the neighborhood of $25, whereas for other individuals, who do not bring computers, the average and usual idiosyncratic value is $5. Thus, the idiosyncratic value to a person who brings a computer to a conference virtually always exceeds that of a possible taker.[154]

Under these assumptions, almost any taking of a computer at a conference will be undesirable. Accordingly, property rule protection of owners to prevent takings will be socially preferable. It will prevent all takings. By contrast, under the liability rule, there may well be many takings. To explain, damages under the liability rule will be

---

[152] The reason is that takers' actual common values will be less than courts' estimates and that takers' idiosyncratic values will usually be less than courts' estimates of owners' average idiosyncratic value.

[153] If damages were systematically too low, the disadvantage of liability rules would be much greater. For discussion of why courts' values will tend to be systematically too low, see section II.A.3.(b). As we note there, however, it may be possible to correct systematic errors.

[154] This assumption is made for simplicity and to dramatize our point. It will be clear from the example that our point about the inferiority of the liability rule would hold as well if the distributions of owners' and takers' idiosyncratic value were to overlap more substantially. *See infra* Appendix section II.B, cmt. c (supplying examples).

the $100 average common value plus the $25 average idiosyncratic value to owners, or $125. Consequently, whenever a conference is of a type such that the common value is above the $125 damage amount, all potential takers, aware that their value exceeds the level of damages,[155] will take computers, a very undesirable outcome.[156]

It should be evident from the logic of this example and what we have said about it that *property rule protection of owners is superior to use of the liability rule if the distribution of idiosyncratic values of owners lies sufficiently above that of takers and if courts also err sufficiently in estimating common values.* The essential reason is that the problem under the liability rule of socially undesirable takings — when damages are too low because the common value is high — will dominate in importance the problem under property rule protection that desirable takings will not occur. Setting damages above the court's best estimate — in the limit, a property rule — avoids a potentially significant problem of excessive takings while discouraging few desirable takings.[157] (This conclusion follows when there is no systematic bias in setting damages, which are sometimes too high and sometimes too low. The problem of excessive takings under the liability rule would be exacerbated if courts were systematically to ignore idiosyncratic value.[158] In the preceding example, if courts were to ignore idiosyncratic value, damages would be only $100, and takings would occur more often than we said.)

---

[155] It seems plausible that those attending a specialized conference in their field would know when taking notes was particularly valuable while, at the same time, they would understand that a court might be unable to appreciate the above-average value of the information provided.

[156] When the common value is less than $125 but exceeds $100, there will still be a tendency for undesirable takings. (If the idiosyncratic values of potential takers are concentrated around $5, the takers will want to take whenever the common value plus $5 exceeds damages, which is to say whenever the common value is at least $120.)

[157] However, we should consider briefly whether a liability rule with damages different from average value might perform better than the liability rule with damages equal to average value. If damages exceed average value — say, damages equal the highest possible common value plus the mean idiosyncratic value to owners — those few takings that would occur would constitute efficient transfers, on average. The reason is that, with damages this high, no one would take unless his idiosyncratic value exceeded the mean idiosyncratic value of owners. (In addition, such high damages would reduce or even eliminate most of the other problems we describe below because owners would usually benefit when a taking occurs.) We mention, however, that the range of possible common values can be quite large. (Just what is the highest possible common value of having a laptop computer with which to take notes at a conference?) Thus, such a liability rule would approximate property rule protection. Also, although raising damages removes most of the inefficiency caused by a liability rule, in most instances it would also eliminate most of the benefits of the rule (as efficient takings would become rare). Thus, in general it is not clear that a liability rule will become preferable as damages are raised. Finally, as we observed in note 3, actual property rights are presently not in fact perfectly protected. As a result, even if some small gain were possible from relaxing property rule protection from an absolute level, it is not clear that lesser protection than currently exists would be justified. *See also infra* Appendix section II.B, cmt. c (discussing numerical examples).

[158] *See supra* pp. 730–31.

Finally, let us observe that there is no contradiction between the conclusion drawn here that the liability rule may well be inferior to property rule protection and our conclusion in the externality context that the liability rule is superior to property rule protection. The resolution of the seemingly opposed conclusions is presented in the Appendix.[159] For the moment, we note that the crucial difference between the model studied in the externality context and that examined here, from a theoretical perspective, is as follows. In the case of externalities, we assume that the prevention cost and the harm to victims are independent of each other (for example, that an injurer's cost of preventing pollution is independent of a victim's susceptibility to disease).[160] In the present context, however, the two variables analogous to prevention cost and harm are not independent: the value of a thing to its owner and the value of the same thing to the taker are dependent because they both include the thing's common value.[161]

B. Parties Bargain with Each Other

We now consider the more usual situation in which owners and potential takers are assumed to be able to bargain with one another. (In this section, we set aside the problems identified in sections III.C and III.D that might render bargaining infeasible under a liability rule.)

1. Bargaining Is Always Successful. — If parties always will make mutually beneficial transfers when such transfers are possible, *then property rule protection and a liability rule are equivalent.*[162] Under property rule protection, a transfer will occur if and only if a potential taker values the thing more highly than does the owner. Under a liability rule, this statement will also be true. In particular, even if low damages would lead a potential taker to take when the owner values the thing more highly than does the taker, no taking would occur. For example, suppose that the value of a thing to the

---

[159] *See infra* Appendix section II.B, cmt. b.

[160] *See supra* note 43.

[161] It can be shown that, if the common value were zero in the present case, then the liability rule would be superior to property rule protection of owners. This consequence follows because damages would thereby equal the average of owners' idiosyncratic values; hence, when a taking occurred, it would be socially desirable on average because it would occur only when the taker's idiosyncratic value exceeded the average owner's idiosyncratic value. *See infra* Appendix section II.B, cmt. b.

We also note that raising damages above owners' average values (in the limit, a property rule) causes little inefficiency due to the deterrence of desirable takings, because owners' idiosyncratic values are usually higher than those of takers. By contrast, in the externalities context, raising damages above average harm is more likely to produce inefficiency by discouraging desirable activity than to avoid inefficiency that otherwise occurs as a result of failing to deter injurers who should be deterred.

[162] We abstract from the costs of entering into agreements and of litigation. For a discussion of these elements, see section III.F.

taker is $400, damages are $300, and the value to the owner is $500. The taker would have an incentive to take, but the owner would be willing to pay the taker up to $200 not to do so, and the taker would accept any amount over $100; hence, the two parties would reach an agreement whereby the owner retains the thing. If and only if the taker values the thing more highly than does the owner would a transfer result under the liability rule.

   2. *Bargaining Is Not Always Successful.* — If bargaining does not always lead to a mutually beneficial outcome — because a party may ask for too much, misconceiving the other's true position — either property rule protection or a liability rule might be superior. Observe that under either type of property rule, not all mutually beneficial sales will be consummated, because of asymmetry of information. The owner, for example, might ask too much of the taker even though the taker does in fact value the thing more highly than does the owner. Furthermore, the problem of failure to conclude mutually beneficial bargains might be either more or less serious under property rule protection than under the liability rule. Thus, it may be that either rule is better (as was true in the case of externalities).

   Still, we suspect that property rule protection will tend to be superior to the liability rule. Under the liability rule, recall that takers will often have an incentive to take when courts underestimate the common value of things, even though takings will usually be undesirable because owners generally have higher valuations. Thus, in order to maintain the socially desirable status quo, owners will frequently need to bribe takers not to take. However, in some percentage of these instances, bargaining will fail, and, usually undesirably, the things will be taken. By contrast, under property rule protection, bargaining will never be needed to prevent an undesirable taking. Bargaining will be needed for socially desirable outcomes only when a taker places a higher value on a good than does an owner, which will tend to be infrequent. Thus, even if bargaining sometimes fails under a property rule, the adverse consequences should be limited.[163]

   3. *Conventional View of the Advantage of Property Rule Protection.* — We mentioned in the Introduction that there exists in the folklore, and to some extent in writings, an idea that property rule protection of things is good because it forces someone who wants something to bargain for it, and presumably he will tend to obtain it if and only if he values it more highly than does the owner.[164] We find this reason for favoring property rule protection to be misleading. As

---

[163] As in the case of harmful externalities, *see supra* section II.B.2, which rule is better is indeterminate. However, when the property rule almost always produces an efficient outcome without bargaining as in the present context, it seems plausible that the property rule's advantage will remain when imperfect bargaining is introduced.

[164] *See supra* note 9 and accompanying text.

we have stressed, under a liability rule, a potential taker will also tend to obtain a thing if and only if he values it more highly than does the owner. When damages do not equal owners' valuations, bargaining may be necessary, as under property rule protection. In particular, if, under a liability rule, a taker would decide to take a thing, and the owner wished to pay him not to do so because the owner places a higher value on the thing, the taker will very much have reason to bargain for a payment from the owner.

To be sure, we did suggest that if bargaining is imperfect, due to asymmetry of information, property rule protection may tend to be superior to a liability rule. However, this preference is *not* because property rule protection is needed to induce takers to bargain. Rather, it is because property rule protection leads to a lesser need for bargaining and thus to a lesser chance of failure to conclude a necessary agreement.[165]

C. A Fundamental Problem with Bargaining Under a Liability Rule

1. The Impediment. — Our discussion of property versus liability rules in the preceding section on bargaining presumed implicitly that bargaining is feasible when parties are in proximity to each other and that the bargaining process is not itself costly. However, as we mentioned in the Introduction, *a fundamental obstacle impedes bargaining under the liability rule but not under property rule protection.* The difficulty with bargaining under the liability rule arises when courts set damages too low — for instance, when damages for taking a car are $10,000 but its common value is $12,000.[166] In such a situation, there would often be a *multiplicity of potential takers*: anyone who happens to be about and who places a value on the car exceeding damages would want to take the car. Moreover, individuals would be attracted to places where cars might be undervalued, raising the likely number of potential takers.

Consider the situation of an owner and a *particular* potential taker who values the car less highly than does the owner (but above the level of damages). The owner would like to bargain with the taker and pay him not to take the car. However, it would be irrational for

---

[165] We should also note that these points apply if one imagines anarchy (rather than liability rule protection) to be the alternative to property rule protection. Under anarchy, when a taker could take and not pay any damages, there could also be bargaining and bribes not to take things, and so forth. The problems noted in the sections to follow, however, would be even more serious.

[166] Our argument assumes that parties can anticipate when damages will be too low, in this case $10,000. We observe that this assumption can hold when damages on average are unbiased — sometimes they are too high and sometimes they are too low — which is what we assume throughout. If damages were systematically too low, our argument would hold in a greater fraction of cases and perhaps in all cases.

the owner to pay *this* taker not to take the car, for he would subsequently have to pay *another* potential taker not to take the car, and then another and another.[167] Therefore, the potential taker will tend to take the car even though the owner values it more highly. The general point, in other words, is that when courts err and set damages too low, bargaining by owners will be effectively infeasible, and socially undesirable takings will occur.

By contrast, property rule protection of owners involves no similar barrier to bargaining. Although there may be many potential buyers, the owner need not trade with any of them, and he can choose with whom he wants to bargain and possibly consummate a trade. Thus, no undesirable trades will occur. Furthermore, if there are no asymmetries of information between the owner and possible buyers, all socially desirable transfers will occur.

Our conclusion from the present argument is that a property rule enjoys a strong advantage over the liability rule, assuming, as is plausible, that the probability of underestimation of owners' values would be substantial under a liability regime. We emphasize that this conclusion does not depend upon the assumption that there is systematic underestimation of owners' values under a liability rule. Even when one assumes that courts' estimates are on average correct, but are sometimes too high and sometimes too low, the liability rule will be inferior because the occasions in which damages are too low will involve the multiple-taker problem we have identified. (When damages are too high, there will be few takings, so the liability rule in such instances will be similar to a property rule.)

Finally, we note that the identified problem with the liability rule does not seem as important in the externality context. Specifically, suppose that damages are underestimated and that the victim, say a person bothered by noise from his neighbor, contemplates paying the neighbor to desist. It will be worth the victim's effort to make a bargain with this neighbor if there are few other neighbors who would also make noise and cause the same disturbance to the victim, which we think will often be the case. More generally, we suspect that frequently there will not be many parties who would cause the same harm to a victim, so that the victim would indeed find it worthwhile to bargain with a particular injurer.[168] When there are multiple injurers in the externality context, however, we do believe that bargaining will frequently break down. However, the typical reason for break-

---

[167] This argument also suggests the possibility that a potential taker would worry that the car would later be taken from *him*, thereby diminishing his desire to take the car. One can understand this complication as a variation on another problem with the liability rule — that of reciprocal takings — which we address next, in section III.D.

[168] A reason for the difference between the two contexts involves common value: many people will wish to take my car if it will be undervalued, but those who enjoy noisy parties will not wish to relocate their festivities in order to disturb my peace and quiet.

down will involve the free-rider problem that arises when there is a multiplicity of victims (as when pollution victims free ride on each others' efforts to bribe polluters) rather than the difficulty created by a multiplicity of injurers, as analyzed in this section.[169]

2. *Contrast to the Conventional View of the Advantage of Property Rule Protection.* — In the present section, we have identified a reason to prefer property rule protection that is altogether different from the conventional reason, which holds that property protection fosters the bargaining process between a prospective acquirer and an owner. The advantage of property rule protection that we have discussed is not that it encourages prospective *takers* to bargain. (They would be happy to bargain under the liability rule.) Rather, the advantage is that property protection gives *owners* an incentive to bargain that they would not have under the liability rule, because under the liability rule, an owner's payment to a taker to step aside would be wasted on account of other prospective takers waiting in the wings.

D. *Reciprocal Takings*

Another difficulty with the liability rule arises when damages are too low:[170] if a person takes a thing from the owner, the owner will want to retrieve it from the taker. Suppose that, under the liability rule, damages would be only $75 for taking something worth at least $100 to its owner and to many others. Then if someone takes the thing, which is likely, the owner would wish to take it right back (returning to the taker the $75 that the owner received as damages).[171] Moreover, this behavior could continue, and it may come to involve additional parties. Such *reciprocal takings* are problematic because they will lead inevitably to destructive contests to retain or to take control of things, and thus to the use of force. Indeed, the issue of reciprocal takings seems to us so serious as to make a true liability rule system unworkable.

The only apparent solution to the problem of reciprocal takings lies in a mixed system that would employ a liability rule for the initial taking combined with property rule protection of the taker's posses-

---

[169] Suppose, though, that in the externality context there is only a single victim and multiple injurers, say a single victim of multiple polluters. In such circumstances, bargaining may or may not be inhibited for the reason discussed in this subsection. There will tend not to be a problem with bargaining if each additional unit of pollution causes additional harm. In this case, the victim would benefit from striking a bargain with a particular polluter, for if that polluter alone desists, the victim will suffer from less pollution. If, however, pollution from any one polluter would cause a complete loss for the victim (consider the situation of a company that bottles spring water claimed to be pristine, in which any amount of pollution would make the product of little value), the victim would not benefit from making an agreement with only a particular polluter. If even a single polluter does not agree to prevent harm, the victim will suffer his full loss.

[170] As discussed in note 166, we do not assume that damages are systematically too low but do assume that parties can anticipate when damages will be too low.

[171] *See* Rabin, *supra* note 29, at 1333.

sory right afterwards. But this type of regime has two problems. First, if one must choose between property rule protection of those who create or acquire things and those who take them, it seems clear that the former choice generally would be superior because it would produce better incentives, as will be discussed in section III.E. Second, this mixed system seems unworkable. Notably, a single party would have to be selected and given the right to take; otherwise, destructive competition might arise among potential takers. The problems the courts would face in selecting this fortunate taker are daunting.[172]

Finally, let us note that the analog of the problem of reciprocal takings does not arise in the case of harmful externalities. If pollution harms a victim, he can ordinarily do nothing to reverse his harm (he cannot cause an effluent to flow back to the polluter). Once harmful externalities occur, they cannot be undone, unlike the taking of a thing.

However, a problem of "reciprocal action" could arise before harm occurs if a victim tried to prevent an injurer from causing harm and the injurer tried to thwart the victim. Yet the law tends to prevent such problems of reciprocal action. For instance, if a factory is subject to a liability rule and a potential victim were to attempt to enter the factory's premises and interfere with its operations, he could be stopped or prosecuted for a crime. The legal system can adopt this solution to potential problems of reciprocal action because it can naturally distinguish between the victim of harm and the injurer.[173]

E. Incentives of Owners to Avoid Losses and Incentives of Others to Take Property

An additional factor that works against the liability rule is the effort that owners may make to avoid having their property taken by others and the effort that potential takers may exert to take things. Owners and potential takers will engage in such activity under a liability rule, and the more so the greater the probability that damages would be less than the value of things to owners.[174] When damages

---

[172] Imagine the difficulties courts would have were they to hold hearings at which anyone wishing to take a thing would be allowed to attend. Alternatively, suppose that the policy were to grant the right to take to the first person to appear, in which case there would be unproductive races to be first.

[173] Notice that the legal system might adopt the analogous remedy to the problem of reciprocal takings under a liability rule, namely, by giving property rule protection either to the taker or to the owner. But if the law gave property rule protection to the taker (that is, if the law gave the taker the freedom to act), we would face the problem of having to distinguish just one taker from among many potential takers, as we discussed above. If, instead, the legal system gave property rule protection to the owner (the right to be free from takings), it would thereby have adopted the property rule.

[174] In making this claim, we are assuming, as in the preceding sections, that owners and potential takers are able to anticipate circumstances in which damage awards will be below the

are expected to be too low, owners will do things to prevent takings, such as hiding or locking up assets. Moreover, owners will change their investments in things (fail to make improvements to things likely to be taken) and their patterns of purchase (decide against acquiring things that can easily be taken). Potential takers will invest effort in looking for things because such takings amount to bargain purchases.[175]

Efforts to protect and to take property are economically sterile — a social waste — and thus constitute a disadvantage of a liability rule.[176] Changes in investment, purchase, and use decisions constitute an additional source of inefficiency under a liability rule. Of course, these effects also constitute the well-known disadvantages of theft.[177] In fact, the difference between the disadvantages of theft and the disadvantages under a liability rule in cases in which damages are underestimated is only one of degree.[178]

By contrast to the situation under a liability rule, under property rule protection of owners no wasteful effort will be expended either to avoid takings or to take things. (This assumes, as we have throughout, that property rules are perfectly enforced.[179])

We note that the qualitative character of owners' behavior in the present context often differs from that of victims in the context of harmful externalities. In the externality context, it is best if victims are uncompensated, so that they have an incentive to mitigate harm.[180] But in the context of the taking of things, owners are creators of value, so that it is best for them to be fully compensated: this preserves the proper incentives for them to raise the value of their things and not to expend resources to protect their things from being taken.

---

value of things. *See supra* note 166. Circumstances in which the parties expect damages to exceed the value of things will not influence the behavior of owners: they will not try to prevent a taking if they would make a profit from it. Such circumstances would not tempt a taker either.

[175] *Cf.* Haddock, McChesney & Spiegel, *supra* note 9, at 16–17 (making an analogous point when damages undercompensate for a possessor's market opportunities).

[176] Note that bargaining will not generally solve the sorts of problems described here because adverse effects will arise before parties bargain. *Cf. supra* note 74 (discussing the issue in the externalities context). Indeed, individuals will protect their property to avoid having to bribe a prospective taker, because some surplus will typically be lost by such a bribe compared to the circumstance in which no taking is possible in the first place. Moreover, the problem of multiple takers identified in section III.C would arise even if ex ante bargaining were possible.

[177] *See* Steven Shavell, *Individual Precautions to Prevent Theft: Private Versus Socially Optimal Behavior*, 11 INT'L REV. L. & ECON. 123 (1991).

[178] One may conceive of legalized theft as a liability system in which damages for a taking are zero, whereas we have emphasized problems that exist as long as there is a probability of underestimation of value.

[179] *See supra* note 3.

[180] *See supra* section II.C.

F. Other Considerations

We comment here on several remaining considerations: the judgment-proof problem, administrative costs, risk aversion, income distribution, and entitlement. We can be brief because of our discussion in section II.D.

The judgment-proof problem would plainly be a count against the liability rule if it meant that a party could take and retain a thing despite being unable to pay a judgment.[181] But we think the more natural interpretation of how a liability rule would function is that a taker would not be able to take (or keep) a thing if he could not pay the judgment. If so, the judgment-proof problem would not be important.[182]

The major administrative costs under property rules are those involved in effecting transfers, which may involve bargaining, but need not (consider sales on organized markets). Under the liability rule, administrative costs will be incurred whenever there is a taking; these costs might or might not exceed those of a sale in a property rule regime, depending on the character of the legal system and typical expenses of settlement. But our conjecture is that even settlement costs would tend to exceed those of concluding a sale. In addition, when takers anticipate that damages will be underestimated, bargaining (if feasible[183]) might frequently take place between owner and taker to induce the latter to refrain. The costs of such bargaining would tend to make a liability rule administratively more expensive than a property rule.[184]

With respect to the risk aversion of owners,[185] we observe that they are well insulated from risk under property rule protection,[186] whereas they are not fully shielded under a liability rule, assuming that there is uncertainty as to the magnitude of damages. But the risk of inadequate damages could, in principle, be insured.

---

[181] *See* Calabresi & Melamed, *supra* note 1, at 1125 n.69.

[182] Problems would, however, arise if the thing were harmed, such as when a car is stripped. The judgment-proof problem is of a different nature in the externality context for two reasons. First, the harm from externalities cannot be undone (in the way that a thing taken can be returned). Second, the harm can more readily exceed the assets of the injurer.

[183] For bargaining to be feasible under liability rules, the multiplicity of takers problem and the reciprocal takings problem discussed in sections III.C and III.D must somehow be overcome. That is, we are implicitly assuming some qualified form of liability regime in which a particular taker is allowed to take but is then himself protected by a property rule.

[184] As we have discussed, bargaining merely to preserve the status quo — retention of things by their owners — may be frequent under a liability rule because of the possibility that damages would be less than the value of things.

[185] Parallel comments to ours may be made with respect to the risk aversion of potential takers.

[186] Some risk remains, as owners may be unsure of the surplus they will gain from a sale. (Also, values may change over time. This risk, however, is not directly affected by the choice of legal rule.)

As for the distribution of income, we note that property rule protection favors owners over takers. Under property rule protection, when owners sell things, they tend to receive more than the value they place on them; they are generally able to extract some of buyers' surplus. Under the liability rule, owners' valuation is all that they are in principle awarded, and when damages are too low, they will suffer undercompensated takings or pay bribes to others to refrain from taking things. Consequently, were one to assume that owners generally possess more wealth than takers, property rule protection would favor richer individuals. But even if true, this result should not be considered a disadvantage of property rule protection. As we said before, the income tax and transfer system is superior to legal rules as a means of meeting distributional objectives.

Finally, for the sorts of reasons advanced previously, we do not believe that notions of entitlement are likely to have independent relevance in the choice of rules. We do suspect, however, that most who are concerned about supporting security of entitlements would favor a property rule protecting possessors over a liability rule.[187]

G. Comment on the Distinction Between the Taking of Things and Harmful Externalities

We have divided our analysis in this Article between the taking of things and harmful externalities, and we have generally assumed that the scope of each context was self-evident. We have interpreted the taking of a thing to be an instance in which possessory rights in a physical object are transferred from one individual to another and in which the object generally has a component of value common to the two individuals. And we have defined a harmful externality to be an event adverse to a victim arising when an injurer takes some action from which he benefits and which only incidentally causes the adverse event.

We note, however, that not all cases can easily be placed within one category or the other. For example, suppose that when an apartment building is erected in front of a hotel, it blocks the hotel's view of the ocean.[188] Should this be considered a taking of a thing even though no one takes possession of a tangible object? (Note that the view will have a common component of value, as it will be desirable both to those who live in the building and to those who stay in the

---

[187] This preference is particularly clear for libertarians. In the context of externalities, however, application of a libertarian approach is more difficult for the sorts of reasons identified by Coase with regard to joint causation by victims and injurers. *See* Coase, *supra* note 18, at 2, 8–15.

[188] *Cf.* Fontainebleau Hotel Corp. v. Forty-Five Twenty-Five, Inc., 114 So. 2d 357 (Fla. Dist. Ct. App. 1959) (concerning a shadow cast on the neighboring hotel's pool), *cert. denied*, 117 So. 2d 842 (Fla. 1960).

hotel.) Or should it be considered a harmful externality? (Note that the blocking of the hotel's view may have been a consequence incidental to the construction of the apartment building.)

Moreover, the distinction between externalities and the taking of things appears to be subject to linguistic manipulation. A harmful externality can often be described as the taking of a thing; for example, a firm that pollutes someone's air can be said to have taken clean air or an easement from the victim. Similarly, the taking of a thing can be described as the doing of harm to a victim.

Ambiguity about how to categorize a situation does not, however, make our analysis or our conclusions problematic.[189] The main reason is that we have identified the assumptions underlying our conclusions, rather than having relied simply on our categorization of situations as involving either harmful externalities or the taking of things.

For example, when we examined whether use of a liability rule (with damages equal to average harm) would result in an efficient allocation of resources in the absence of bargaining, we explained in sections II.A and III.A that our conclusions ultimately depend on whether the victim's harm is independent of the injurer's benefit or is not (that is, whether the two have a common value). Hence, when considering the blocking of the hotel's view by the apartment building, we can say that the use of a liability rule may not result in a more efficient allocation of the resource of ocean views because an ocean view has common value to the different parties. In this respect, the analysis of the situation involving the blocking of ocean views is closer to our analysis of the taking of things.[190] However, unlike in our analysis of the taking of things, reciprocal takings are no problem here because the hotel can hardly take the ocean view back from the apartment building. In this regard, therefore, the situation is more like one involving harmful externalities. It is unnecessary for us to say whether, on the whole, we consider the situation involving the blocking of views to be a harmful externality or instead the taking of a

---

[189] The problems with the distinction between harmful externalities and the taking of things are reminiscent of the difficulty the Supreme Court has had distinguishing between governmental takings for which just compensation is required by the Fifth Amendment (a liability rule) and regulation for which no compensation is required (a property rule entitling the injurer to act freely). *See* Jeremy Paul, *The Hidden Structure of Takings Law*, 64 S. CAL. L. REV. 1393 (1991); Joseph L. Sax, *Takings, Private Property and Public Rights*, 81 YALE L.J. 149 (1971). We note, however, that our use of the distinction is different from the Court's. When determining whether government compensation is constitutionally required, the legal result follows directly from the categorization, but courts have not been clear or consistent about the rationales underlying the distinction. We explain in the text to follow how our analysis addresses this problem.

[190] We note, however, that unless one is willing to assume that those who arrive first generally value things more highly than do subsequent takers, it need not follow that original possessors — the hotel in this instance — would be expected on average to have higher idiosyncratic values.

thing. We can profit well enough from our analysis by drawing on its elements as described in Parts II and III.[191]

In any case, we emphasize that the distinction between harmful externalities and the taking of things is useful, even if imperfect. The distinction often is readily made in important contexts, such as industrial pollution, automobile accidents, and transfers of things — indeed, in most of the cases explored in prior literature. Moreover, even if the distinction sometimes blurs, most situations that we would say are harmful externalities have a set of characteristics (independence of injurer benefit and victim harm, no problem of reciprocal takings, and so forth) different from the set of characteristics describing the taking of things. Finally, analysis of the two sets of characteristics points to very different conclusions: the distinction is analytically useful. Thus, we believe that the distinction is a constructive addition to prior literature, in which commentators have often mixed the two contexts in the presentation of arguments.

IV. Conclusion

Having completed our analysis of the question whether liability or property rules enjoy an advantage, let us take brief stock of our conclusions. In the examination of harmful externalities, we showed that in the absence of bargaining between victims and injurers, a liability rule with damages equal to estimated harm is unambiguously superior to property rules even though actual harm in a given case may be difficult to determine.[192] This result is significant in light of the important contexts, like those of automobile accidents and industrial pollution, in which parties are practically unable to bargain because potential victims are strangers to injurers or are too numerous. When we then considered additional factors, we found that some (the possibility of bargaining, administrative costs) did not systematically favor either type of rule, whereas others (the judgment-proof problem, victim behavior) lent appeal to forms of property rule protection or modifications of a conventional liability rule. Thus, we can point to circumstances in which property rule protection might be desirable, even though the liability rule enjoys an underlying advantage.

Our analysis of possessory interests in things differed in substantial respects from that of externalities, as did our conclusions. We emphasized that, contrary to traditional thinking, property rule protection of

---

[191] In addition to distinctions based on common value and reciprocal takings, we also identified differences between the contexts with respect to the problem of multiple potential takers in section III.C, victims' ex ante incentives in section III.E, and the judgment-proof problem in note 182.

[192] This assumes that there is no systematic bias in damage awards. We discussed in section II.A.3.(b) the possibility that damages might be too low, and offered possible solutions to this problem.

possessory interests is not unique in inducing prospective takers to bargain for transfers; that could happen under a liability rule as well. However, we did develop a number of arguments disfavoring the liability rule. In particular, we discussed the tendency toward excessive takings when bargaining is not possible, the reluctance of owners to bargain (even when feasible) due to the multiplicity of potential takers, the problem of reciprocal takings, and the creation of wasteful incentives to protect and take property. Together, these arguments furnish a powerful theoretical case against the liability rule and, we believe, justify one of the most basic incidents of ownership: the right of the owner of a thing to prevent others from taking it. Most observers have probably felt that this property right is best explained on account of its superiority to the alternative of anarchy,[193] but this misses the significant possibility of permitting takings upon the payment of damages.[194] Rationalizing this basic incident of ownership against the alternative of liability rules is an essential part of the justification of a private property regime.

We hope that our analysis will clarify conceptual understanding of property rules versus liability rules — especially to make apparent that the functions and desirability of property and liability rules are substantially different in the contexts of harmful externalities and of individuals' possessory interests in things. We also hope that some of our conclusions will be helpful for policymaking, especially with assessments of the desirability of liability rules and pollution taxes when the calculation of harm is difficult.

---

[193] For a comprehensive synthesis of the economic costs and benefits of forms of property ownership of land, see Robert C. Ellickson, *Property in Land*, 102 YALE L.J. 1315 (1993).

[194] We comment on Calabresi and Melamed's brief discussion of the issue in notes 5 and 6 above. We also note that a liability rule has long been considered a serious alternative to property rule protection in the context of eminent domain. *See supra* notes 143, 189.

APPENDIX

I. HARMFUL EXTERNALITIES

There is a population of risk-neutral victims and of risk-neutral injurers. An injurer may act in a way that causes harm h to a victim or may prevent harm by incurring a cost c. The harm that a particular victim might suffer is assumed to be fixed, but harm varies among victims according to positive density g(h), with cumulative distribution function G(h). Similarly, the prevention cost c that each injurer might incur is taken to be fixed, but c is assumed to vary among injurers according to positive density f(c), with cumulative distribution function F(c). The variables h and c are assumed to be independent.[195] An injurer knows his c but not necessarily the victim's h, and a victim knows his h but not necessarily the injurer's c. The state may or may not know h or c, as will be specified. There may or may not be bargaining between victims and injurers.

The social objective is minimization of total expected social costs: harm plus prevention cost. Thus, it is socially optimal for an injurer to prevent harm if and only if $c \leq h$. (For convenience, we say that when $c = h$ it is optimal to prevent harm.)

We consider two types of legal rule. Under *property rules*, the state, given its information, either assigns to the victim the entitlement to be free from harm or assigns to the injurer the entitlement to cause harm. If the victim has the entitlement, the injurer cannot harm him (without his permission). If the injurer has the entitlement, the victim cannot prevent the injurer from causing harm.

Under the *liability rule*, an injurer is permitted to harm the victim but must pay him non-negative damages d. Although in principle damages could be set at any level, we will focus primarily on the case in which d equals h, when the state can observe h, or when it cannot, the case in which d equals the mean (expected value) of h, E(h). This is because, as was noted in the text, damages are intended to equal harm. We note also that $d = 0$ corresponds to property rule protection of the injurer (for the injurer can cause harm and not pay damages) and $d = \infty$ (or any d exceeding the highest possible value of c) corresponds to property rule protection of the victim (for the injurer effectively would never cause harm without bargaining).

We now compare property and liability rules in two cases: when there is no bargaining between a victim and an injurer and when there is bargaining.

---

[195] We discuss this assumption further in this Appendix at section I.A.2, comment d.

A. No Bargaining

    1. *State's Information Is Perfect.* — In this case, we have:
PROPOSITION 1. *Assume that there is no bargaining between victims
and injurers. If the state has perfect information about harm h and
prevention cost c, property rules and the liability rule with d = h are
equivalent.*

    To demonstrate this, observe that under property rules, the first-
best outcome can be achieved: because the state knows c and h, the
state can assign the entitlement to victims when $c \leq h$ (so harm will
not occur) and to injurers when $c > h$ (so harm will occur). Also, the
first-best outcome can be achieved under the liability rule with $d = h$,
for then an injurer will prevent harm if and only if $c \leq h$.

    2. *State's Information Is Imperfect.* — We assume here that the
state knows only the distributions of h and c, and we have:
PROPOSITION 2. *Assume that there is no bargaining between victims
and injurers. If the state knows only the distributions of harm h and
prevention cost c, then (a) the liability rule with d = E(h) is superior
to property rules. Also, (b) the liability rule with d = E(h) is superior
to the liability rule with any other d.*

    Under property rules, because the state does not observe c or h, it
must assign the entitlement in the same way for all parties. If it assigns the entitlement to victims, injurers must prevent harm so that
social costs will be $E(c)$; and if it assigns the entitlement to injurers,
social costs will be $E(h)$. Hence, social costs will equal $\min(E(c), E(h))$,
and the state will assign the entitlement to victims if and only if
$E(c) \leq E(h)$. Under the liability rule with $d = E(h)$, an injurer will
incur c and prevent harm if and only if $c \leq E(h)$, so that expected
social costs will be

    (1) $\int_0^{E(h)} cf(c)dc + \int_{E(h)}^{\infty} E(h)f(c)dc.$

Now (1) is strictly less than $E(h)$, for the first term is strictly less than
$\int_0^{E(h)} E(h)f(c)dc$ because, when c is in the range between o and $E(h)$,
$c < E(h)$. Also, (1) is strictly less than $E(c)$, for the second term is
strictly less than $\int_{E(h)}^{\infty} cf(c)dc$ because, when c is in the range between
$E(h)$ and ∞, $c > E(h)$. Hence, (1) is less than $\min(E(c), E(h))$, so we
have demonstrated (a).

    With respect to (b), since an injurer will prevent harm if and only
if $c \leq d$, expected social costs given d are

    (2) $\int_0^d cf(c)dc + \int_d^{\infty} E(h)f(c)dc.$

The socially best d minimizes (2). Setting the derivative of (2) with
respect to d equal to zero, we obtain the first-order condition,
$df(d) - E(h)f(d) = o$, which implies that $d = E(h)$, confirming (b).

    Comments. (a) Part (a) of the proposition actually follows from part
(b). This is because, as we remarked above, the property rules corre-

spond to liability rules with d = o or d = ∞, yet we showed in (b) that the optimal d is E(h). Furthermore, one of the property rules will be the *worst* possible rule (and the other property rule will tend to be poor) because social costs are strictly decreasing as d increases from o to E(h), and social costs are strictly increasing as d rises from E(h).[196]

(b) If the state has imperfect information about prevention cost c but can observe harm h, then the liability rule not only is superior to the property rule, but also allows achievement of the first-best outcome. Under the property rule, if the state assigns the entitlement to the injurer, social costs are E(c), and if to the victim they are h; hence the state assigns the entitlement to the injurer if and only if E(c) ≤ h. In either case, the outcome will sometimes deviate from the first-best result. But under the liability rule, the outcome will always be first-best, since when d = h, injurers prevent harm if and only if c ≤ h.

(c) If the state has imperfect information about h but can observe c perfectly, property rules and the liability rule are equivalent. Under property rules, the state will assign the entitlement to the victim if and only if E(h) ≥ c. Under the liability rule, since d = E(h), the same outcome will occur. But a reverse liability rule, under which victims pay c to prevent harm, would be superior to either property rule.

(d) The assumption that c and h are independent was used when we wrote E(h) in the integrands in (1) and (2), for that presumed that the mean harm, conditional on c being larger than E(h) or d, was just E(h). We have discussed the plausibility of this assumption previously.[197]

When c and h are not independent, the liability rule may not be superior to property rules. To illustrate, consider a discrete example in which there are two equally possible pairs of (c, h), namely (o, o) and (100, 110). If victims have the property entitlement, the first-best outcome results for c ≤ h in each case, and expected social costs are 50 (that is, 50% × 100). Under the liability rule, however, d = 55 (for this is average harm), so that the injurer will cause harm when c = 100, and expected social costs are thus 55 (that is, 50% × 110). The reason for this result is that, although the injurer makes his decision on the basis of average harm, it turns out that the injurers who have high prevention costs are also the ones who cause high amounts of harm. Our model for the taking of things in section II.B of this Appendix is another illustration of how the lack of independence between c and h

---

[196] This is true because the derivative of (2) is f(d)(d − E(h)).

[197] As noted earlier, this assumption is plausible because we think that the way in which, say, pollution could be prevented would have little to do with the harm that it might cause, which would be determined by the character of the thing or the environment exposed to the pollution. *See supra* note 43. We also noted a caveat in the case in which both harm and cost depend on the quantity of an externality and the quantity cannot be observed.

can change the result that the liability rule is more efficient than property rules.

(e) Our conclusion that a liability rule — which as we discuss in section II.E.1 includes the use of pollution taxes — is optimal in the externality context may appear to be inconsistent with arguments such as Martin Weitzman's claim that either price or quantity regulation may be optimal.[198] Weitzman's argument that quantity regulation may be desirable depends on two assumptions. First, he assumes that the level of harm may be a nonlinear (and in fact sharply increasing) function of the quantity of pollution; thus, the optimal price or tax depends on the quantity of pollution. (If there is a single level of harm, as in our model, a price approach will clearly be optimal.[199]) But second, he assumes that a *single* price (a specific pollution tax rate, or damage level per unit of effluent) must be set *once and for all*; that is, it cannot be adjusted upward if the level of pollution is higher than expected (in which case the harm per unit of pollution is higher) or downward if the level of pollution is lower than expected.

We find the second assumption to be an unnecessary and unrealistic restriction, simply because it is not administratively difficult to change a price, tax rate, or damage level.[200] In addition, pollution regulators might announce a tax *schedule* at the outset, indicating the tax due as a function of the amount of pollution.[201] Alternatively, if they used a permit scheme of the sort we describe in note 124, they could

---

[198] *See* Weitzman, *supra* note 42.

[199] *See* Marc J. Roberts & Michael Spence, *Effluent Charges and Licenses Under Uncertainty,* 5 J. PUB. ECON. 193, 202 (1976).

[200] Weitzman motivates his restrictive assumption with examples involving emergencies. *See* Weitzman, *supra* note 42, at 478 n.1, 486. But these contexts are not typical of the problem of regulating harmful externalities. Marc Roberts and Michael Spence motivate restrictions on the ability to adjust prices by arguing that much investment in pollution control takes substantial time to plan and complete. *See* Roberts & Spence, *supra* note 199, at 193. But this does not prevent adjusting prices or announcing quantity-dependent prices. Rather, it suggests that firms' responses to price adjustments would not be immediate. But instant responses presumably are no more feasible when injurers are ordered not to pollute more than a stated quantity. Roberts and Spence seem to envision an initial announcement of a fixed level of pollution, in force for years; there could, however, also be an initial announcement of a pricing scheme under which prices depend on the total quantity of pollution, as we describe in the text to follow.

[201] *See* STIGLITZ, *supra* note 109, at 193–94. Roberts and Spence propose a scheme under which prices (the pollution tax) need not be constant. In their appendix, they show that by allowing the price schedule to adjust gradually with the quantity, the first-best scheme can be implemented. *See* Roberts & Spence, *supra* note 199, at 204–08. (In their model, harm is known with certainty; our analysis shows that if harm were uncertain, the pricing scheme would still be best, although not first best.)

We believe that the debate about whether one should regulate price or quantity misstates the issue. When harm varies with output, the optimal scheme is a *quantity-dependent price*. Such a pricing scheme allows the regulator to make use of injurers' information about prevention costs. If one simply sets quantities, this information is not used. (One could use this information by adjusting quantities in the manner described in note 124, which amounts to setting a price-dependent quantity, a scheme essentially equivalent to the quantity-dependent pricing mechanism.)

associate fees with permits or vary the quantity of permits (such as by selling more or repurchasing some) to ensure that the net price polluters paid was equal to expected harm at the observed level of pollution.

B.   Bargaining[202]

We assume here that a victim makes a single demand (or offer) x to an injurer, who accepts or rejects it; x may correspond to payments received by the victim and/or to payments made by him — we will discuss the interpretation of x below. (We adopt the assumption that the victim makes the demand for concreteness and simplicity; for the most part, it does not affect the qualitative nature of our analysis.[203])

   1.   Parties Have Perfect Information About Each Other — Bargaining Is Always Successful. — Suppose first that parties have perfect information about each other, that a victim knows the injurer's c, and that an injurer knows the victim's h. In this case, bargaining will always result in a mutually optimal agreement when one exists, so that we have:

PROPOSITION 3. *Assume that victims and injurers bargain and that they have perfect information about each other. Then a property rule and a liability rule with any level of damages d are equivalent and optimal — regardless of whether the state has perfect information about c and h.*

Suppose that a property rule in which the victim has the entitlement to be free from harm applies. One possibility is that $c \leq h$. In this case, the victim will make no demand of the injurer, for the injurer would pay at most c to be allowed to cause harm, but the victim would want at least h. The other possibility is that $c > h$. In this case, the victim will make the highest demand that the injurer would accept, a demand of c, for the injurer to be allowed to cause harm; the injurer will barely accept this demand and the victim will be better off (because he will make a profit of $c - h$).[204] Thus, the outcome will be optimal after possible bargaining whether or not the entitlement is

---

[202] This section is based on Shavell, cited above in note 67.

[203] We note, however, that if injurers instead of victims made offers, the analysis would be more complicated in the case in which information is imperfect and the liability rule applies. In that case, there would be a "signalling" phenomenon: the injurer's offer would convey information about his prevention cost; this information would be used by the victim in responding, as it would tell him something about the injurer's reaction (whether the injurer would cause harm and pay damages if the parties did not reach an agreement). Under our assumption, by contrast, the analysis is simpler because the victim makes the offer and the injurer either agrees or reacts. For further discussion, see Appendix section I.B.2, comment c.

[204] Note the role of perfect information. The victim can determine the highest demand that the injurer will accept, c, because the victim knows c. In this case, only the victim's information matters, but that is because, for concreteness, we assumed that the victim makes a single offer or demand; had we assumed that the injurer makes the offer or demand, his information would matter.

given to the individual who values it most. Essentially, the same logic shows that the outcome will be optimal if the entitlement is assigned to the injurer or if a liability rule is employed, regardless of the relationship of d to c and h. For instance, suppose that the liability rule applies and that $h > c > d$. Here the injurer would cause harm and pay d in the absence of bargaining because $c > d$, even though this is not optimal. However, the victim would offer to pay the injurer $c - d$, the minimum the injurer would accept not to cause harm (for if the injurer causes harm, he pays d, and if he accepts the offer, he spends c but receives $c - d$, so he loses d on net); the injurer would barely accept, and the victim would be better off (he spends $c - d$, rather than suffering h and receiving d, for a net loss of $h - d$).

Comments. (a) As we stressed in the text, it is important to realize that bargaining results in the optimal outcome under the liability rule just as it does under property rules.

(b) That an optimal outcome results regardless of the legal rule (and regardless of the quality of information possessed by the state) is a classic illustration of the Coase Theorem.[205]

2. Parties Have Imperfect Information About Each Other — Bargaining Is Not Always Successful. — Now suppose that the parties have only imperfect information about each other; each knows only the distribution of the other's value. Also, suppose that the state knows only the distributions of c and h. For simplicity, we assume that both c and h are distributed on the unit interval and have positive density there; it will be obvious that this assumption is inessential.

We first characterize the nature of bargaining under property and liability rules.

PROPOSITION 4. *Assume that victims and injurers bargain and that their information is imperfect; they know only the distributions of each others' values. Also, the court knows only the distributions of harm h and prevention cost c. Then the behavior of the parties is as illustrated in Figure 1:*

(a) Under the property rule in which victims are entitled to be free from harm, a victim, who would suffer harm h, makes a demand of $x_v(h) > h$ (see (5)), which he must be paid if harm is done; the injurer accepts this demand, pays $x_v(h)$, and causes harm if and only if $c > x_v(h)$.

(b) Under the property rule in which injurers are entitled to cause harm, a victim, who would suffer harm h, makes an offer of $x_i(h) < h$ (see (8)), which he will pay to avoid harm; the injurer accepts this offer, collects $x_i(h)$, and refrains from causing harm if and only if $c < x_i(h)$.

(c) Under the liability rule, the nature of a victim's offer or demand $x_l(h)$ depends on whether h is below or above d. When h is

---

[205] *See* Coase, *supra* note 18, at 2–15.

FIGURE 1

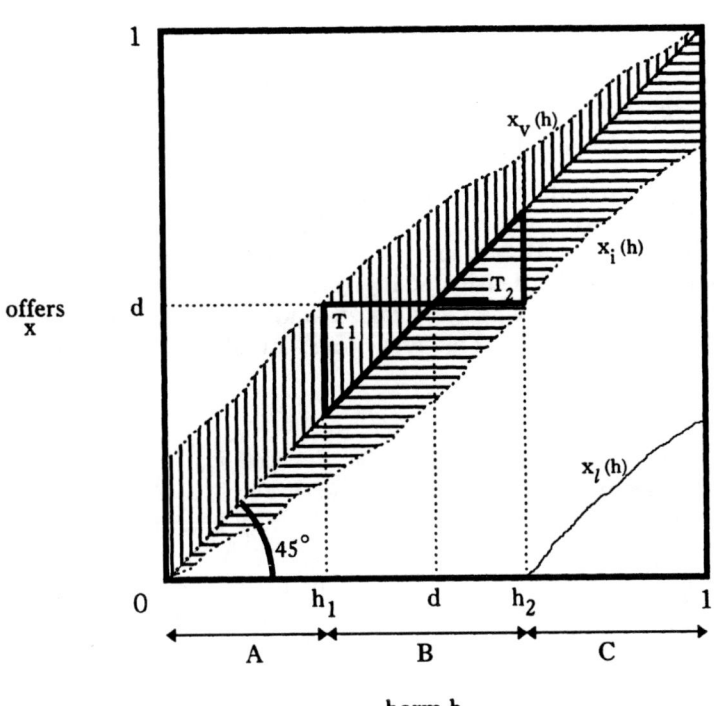

harm h

sufficiently below d (that is, when $h \leq h_t$), a victim will demand $x_l(h) < d$, which the injurer can pay (rather than d) if he causes harm; the injurer will pay and cause harm if and only if $c > x_l(h)$ (if $d < c < x_l(h)$, the injurer will reject the demand and still cause harm). Further, it turns out that $x_l(h)$ coincides with $x_v(h)$. For intermediate values of h (that is, when $h_t < h < h_2$), a victim will offer d (or equivalently, make no offer). When h is sufficiently above d (that is, when $h \geq h_2$), a victim will offer $x_l(h)$ to the injurer for him not to cause harm; the injurer will agree, collect $x_l(h)$, and not cause harm if and only if $c < x_l(h) + d$; and it turns out that $x_l(h) = x_i(h) - d$.

We demonstrate the claims in turn.

(a) We suppose first that victims possess the entitlement to be free from harm under a property rule. Under this regime, a victim will make a demand x such that, if the injurer pays x to the victim, the injurer may cause harm. Because the injurer will pay x if and only if his prevention cost c exceeds x[206] and $1 - F(x)$ is the probability of that event, the victim's expected payoff as a function of x is

(3) $(1 - F(x))(x - h)$.

The victim will select x to maximize (3). We can restrict attention to x in $[0,1]$ (since $x > 1$ is equivalent to $x = 1$, which all injurers would refuse). The derivative of (3) with respect to x is

(4) $1 - F(x) - f(x)(x - h)$.

Note that $1 - F(x)$ is the expected marginal benefit to the victim of raising his demand by a dollar (since $1 - F(x)$ is the probability that the offer will be accepted) and that $f(x)(x - h)$ is the marginal cost of so doing (since $f(x)$ is the density of injurers who will just decide not to accept the demand of x when x is raised, and $x - h$ is what is lost if a demand is not accepted). The first-order condition determining x is[207]

(5) $x = h + (1 - F(x))/f(x)$.

The graph of demands as a function of h, denoted $x_v(h)$ (the subscript v standing for victims' rights), is shown in Figure 1. The Figure is justified by the following: (i) The optimal x for any h must be positive since (4) evaluated at $x = 0$ is positive; (ii) If x is in $(0,1)$, then (5) holds, so that $x > h$ and $x_v(h)$ is increasing in h;[208] and (iii) $x = 1$ if and only if $h = 1$. In particular, if $h = 1$, then clearly $x < 1$ would not be chosen; and if $x = 1$, (4) must be non-negative, that is, $f(1)(1 - h) \leq 0$, implying that $h = 1$.

(b) We suppose next that injurers possess the entitlement to cause harm under a property rule. Here, the victim will make an offer to pay x to the injurer for him not to cause harm; if the injurer accepts and collects x, then he will have to spend c to prevent harm. Since the injurer will accept if and only if $c < x$, the victim will choose x to minimize

(6) $F(x)x + (1 - F(x))h$.

As before, we can restrict attention to x in $[0,1]$. The derivative of (6) with respect to x is

(7) $F(x) + f(x)(x - h)$,

so that the first-order condition determining x is

(8) $x = h - F(x)/f(x)$,

---

[206] If $c = x$, the injurer will of course be indifferent between paying x and causing harm and incurring c and preventing harm. For concreteness, however, we assume that the injurer will not cause harm when $c = x$, and we make similar assumptions below without further comment.

[207] Here and below, we assume that the second-order condition sufficient for a global maximum holds.

[208] This can be verified by totally differentiating (5), using the second-order condition, and solving for $x_v'(h)$.

and the graph of offers as a function of h, $x_i(h)$ (the subscript i standing for injurers' rights), is shown in Figure 1, which can be justified analogously to that of $x_v(h)$.

(c) Now we suppose that injurers are liable for harm done and that the damages d that they have to pay for causing harm are known both to them and to victims. If $h < d$, the victim may offer to accept as damages an amount x that is less than d, but greater than h, for this will increase the probability that the injurer will cause harm and pay the victim more than h.[209] If the victim offers such an amount x, then the injurer will accept if and only if $c > x$. Hence, the victim will choose x to maximize (3), subject to $x \leq d$. Therefore, for $x < d$, the graph of victims' offers $x_l(h)$ (the subscript *l* standing for liability) coincides with the graph of $x_v(h)$ when the latter does not exceed d (that is, for $h < h_l$); otherwise, the victim's offer equals d, or equivalently, he makes no offer. Similarly, if $h > d$, the victim will offer to pay an amount x to the injurer for him not to cause harm, for if the injurer causes harm, the victim will suffer a loss of $h - d$. The injurer will accept an offer if and only if $c - x \leq d$, or if $c \leq x + d$. Hence, the victim will choose x to minimize

(9) $F(x + d)x + (1 - F(x + d))(h - d)$.

The derivative of (9) with respect to x is

(10) $F(x + d) + f(x + d)(x + d - h)$,

yielding the first-order condition

(11) $x + d = h - F(x + d)/f(x + d)$.

This equation has the same form as (8), with $x + d$ here playing the role of x in (8). Hence, if $x_i(h)$ solves (8), $x_i(h) - d$ will solve (11). Thus, as long as $x_i(h) \geq d$ (that is, for $h > h_2$) — so that $x_i(h) - d$ is non-negative — we have $x_l(h) = x_i(h) - d$; when $x_i(h) < d$ (that is, for $h < h_2$), $x_l(h) = 0$, or equivalently, no offer is made. Finally, if $h = d$, the victim makes no offer (or equivalently, an offer of d).

From the last three paragraphs, it follows that the graph of $x_l(h)$ can be understood from Figure 1 for damages of d. In region A, the victim's offer and the outcome are the same as if he has a property right to be free from harm; in region B, no offers are made, and the injurer commits the act if and only if c exceeds d; in region C, the victim offers $x_i(h) - d$, and the injurer commits the act exactly when he would under a property rule under which he has the entitlement. We now compare social costs under property and liability rules.

---

[209] The victim cannot ask for more than d since the injurer can always cause the harm and pay only d. And, obviously, a victim with $h < d$ would never offer to pay the injurer not to engage in his activity. Thus, the only possible type of offer or demand is that under consideration.

PROPOSITION 5. *Assume that victims and injurers bargain and that their information is imperfect; they know only the distributions of each others' values. Also, the court knows only the distributions of harm h and prevention cost c. Then either the liability rule with damages d equal to E(h) or a property rule could be superior — the liability rule and property rules cannot be unambiguously ranked.*

The argument behind this claim is most easily made graphically, using Figure 1 to describe the inefficiencies that occur under the different rules.

Under the property rule in which victims have the entitlement, the vertically shaded area shows the c and h for which there is inefficiency, because an injurer with c above the 45° line but below x_v will not accept the offer from the victim but ought to cause harm. Thus, the inefficiency is the integral of $x_v(h) - c$ over the vertically shaded region.[210] Similarly, under the property rule in which injurers possess the entitlement, the inefficiency is the integral of $c - x_i(h)$ over the horizontally shaded region. The state is assumed to choose optimally who will receive the entitlement, so that inefficiency is minimized.

Under the liability rule, the inefficiency in region A corresponds to the vertically shaded area, and the inefficiency in region C corresponds to the horizontally shaded area. In region B, the inefficiency corresponds to the triangles T_1 and T_2. Note that T_1 is contained in the region between x_v and the 45° line, so that for h in the left part of B, the liability rule is superior to the property rule with the entitlement protecting victims. Likewise, for h in the right part of B, the liability rule is superior to the property rule with the entitlement protecting injurers.

The liability rule will be superior to property rules if and only if the inefficiency under the liability rule is smaller than that under property rules (when the entitlement under the latter is given to minimize the inefficiency). It is apparent from Figure 1 that either property rules or the liability rule could be superior to the other. Specifically, suppose that the distribution of h is concentrated in B about d.[211] (Note that the Figure applies regardless of the distribution of h, for the functions $x_v(h)$, $x_i(h)$, and $x_l(h)$ depend only on the distribution of c.) Then it is clear from the Figure that the inefficiency under the liability rule (corresponding to the parts of T_1 and T_2 near d) is less than the inefficiency either under x_v or under x_i; thus, the liability rule is superior to either property rule.

Suppose, on the other hand, that the distribution of h lies virtually all outside the region B.[212] Then the liability rule must be inferior to a property rule. To explain, suppose for concreteness that it is optimal

---

[210] That is, the deviation from first-best welfare is: $\int_0^I [\int\int_h^{x_v(h)} (x_v(h)-c)f(c)dc]g(h)dh$.

[211] This assumption is obviously consistent with d = E(h).

[212] This assumption is also consistent with d = E(h).

for victims to enjoy the entitlement. Then the liability rule is equivalent to victims' having the entitlement for h in region A and is equivalent to injurers' having the entitlement for h in region C. But in region C, the inefficiency with x_v is less than that with x_i, so that the liability rule is inferior to the property rule protecting victims.

Comments. (a) To illustrate that the liability rule with d = E(h) may be superior to property rules, suppose that injurers' costs c are uniformly distributed on the interval [0,1] but that victims' harms are concentrated toward the center, in particular, that h is uniformly distributed on [¼,¾]. Then it can be demonstrated that the liability rule with d = ½ is superior to either of the property rules.[213] Indeed, d = ½ is the optimal level of damages, and the further d is from ½, the lower is welfare. (This is the same result that holds when there is no bargaining, as stated in Proposition 2(b).)

To illustrate that a property rule may be superior to the liability rule with d = E(h), suppose that harm is concentrated away from E(h); specifically, assume that h is 0 or 1, each with probability ½.[214] In this instance, a property rule (in fact, either property rule) is superior to the liability rule with d = ½. Moreover, it can be shown that a property rule is superior to a liability rule with any d in (0,1), and d = ½ is the worst possible value of d.

(b) We have also investigated the performance of property and liability rules in the case of triangularly distributed c and h. (The density of a triangular distribution on [0,1] rises linearly from zero to a peak and then falls linearly to zero; thus, such a distribution allows for probability mass to be highest around a central value.) In the symmetric case, in which both densities have peaks at ½, both property rules are superior to the liability rule with d = ½. More precisely, social costs are lowest (and are constant) for d in the range [0,⅓] and [⅔,1], and social costs increase for d between these ranges, reaching a maximum at d = ½. If either of the distributions is highly skewed, then the optimal d is extreme, approximating zero or one. The triangular-distribution example thus raises questions about the argument that liability rules tend to remain superior when bargaining is imperfect.

(c) We briefly note how our conclusions relate to those reached in recent work by Ian Ayres and Eric Talley.[215] (For a more complete

---

[213] For this illustration and others that follow in the Appendix, our method consisted of two steps: (1) deriving expressions for all the relevant terms (such as victims' offers for various values of harm, social costs due to rejected offers); and (2) solving the expressions for social costs by using a computer.

[214] This corresponds to any case in which there are only two types of victims, one type suffering greater harm than the other.

[215] *See* Ayres & Talley, *supra* note 10.

discussion, the reader should see our reply to their article.[216]) Ayres and Talley consider a model of bargaining similar to ours, but one in which victims first make a statement to injurers, and then injurers make offers or demands. In the single numerical example that they solve, they find that the liability rule with $d = E(h)$ is superior to either property rule. This is, of course, consistent with our conclusion. They do not, however, illustrate the possibility that property rules may be superior to the liability rule. (In their original example in which injurers' benefits are uniformly distributed, which they discuss but do not solve,[217] it turns out that property rules and the liability rule perform equally well.)

Their article emphasizes, but never demonstrates, that liability rules enjoy a systematic advantage over property rules. They contend that liability rules are advantageous because they facilitate bargaining more than property rules do, but we do not understand why this should be so. Indeed, the very example they solve contradicts this hypothesis: under the liability rule, bargaining increases welfare by only 4.875, whereas under the property rule (with the victim having the entitlement), bargaining increases welfare by twice as much, 9.75.

We have noted the possibility that the liability rule with $d = E(h)$ may have some advantage over property rules. The reason is that, in the absence of bargaining, the liability rule is definitely superior to property rules, so that the liability rule might retain its advantage in the presence of bargaining. In the example that Ayres and Talley consider, this argument indeed explains the superiority of the liability rule in the presence of bargaining. Social welfare under the liability rule in the absence of bargaining is 55, whereas, under the property rule, it is only 50. The liability rule retains a slight advantage after bargaining: bargaining results in a greater increase in welfare under the property rule, but not quite enough to pass the liability rule.

In a separate paper, Talley demonstrates that a liability rule with a properly chosen d is always superior to property rules.[218] This result might appear to be inconsistent with our conclusions, but it is not, because it is derived under a particular set of assumptions.[219] Given our arguments, it is, of course, no surprise that there exist assumptions

---

[216] *See* Kaplow & Shavell, *supra* note 71. (In our reply, we also comment on their response to us.)

[217] *See* Ayres & Talley, *supra* note 10, at 1039–47.

[218] *See* TALLEY, *supra* note 72, at 17–26.

[219] One assumption that may be unfamiliar to the reader is Talley's use of the "optimal mechanism" for bargaining. The optimal mechanism is optimal in the sense that it is what would be imposed by a utilitarian dictator, who wished to maximize the sum of the parties' welfare. It is well understood by game theorists that there is no clear basis for interpreting the optimal mechanism as what the parties themselves would choose to adopt, and thus there is no clear basis for interpreting outcomes under the optimal mechanism as those that would actually obtain. *See, e.g.,* DREW FUDENBERG & JEAN TIROLE, GAME THEORY 284, 289–90 (1991).

under which a liability rule with some d is superior to property rules; indeed, we have shown this as well. Moreover, we emphasize (as mentioned in note 72) that Talley's analysis does not show that the optimal liability rule is more than trivially different from a property rule (for example, optimal damages might be $.01, in which case the liability rule resembles a property rule giving the entitlement to injurers).

II. The Taking of Things

There is a population of risk-neutral owners of things and of risk-neutral takers;[220] each owner faces a single taker.[221] The value of a thing to a person is the sum of two values: a *common value* and an *idiosyncratic value*. The common value of a thing is the same for all individuals. (As explained in the text, it derives from some feature of the thing that all individuals value in the same way, such as a car's gas mileage.) The common value, denoted v, varies from one object (or situation) to another as described by the density z(v). The idiosyncratic value of a thing arises from aspects of it that people value differently (the color of a car may be liked by some but not others). The idiosyncratic value of a thing to its owner is x and to a potential taker, y. The densities of x and y will be denoted g(x) and f(y). We assume that x, y, and v are independent of each other. We also suppose that owners, on average, attach a higher idiosyncratic value to things than do takers: E(x) > E(y). We discussed the justification for the latter assumption in section III.A.2 of the Article. The total value of a thing to its owner is v + x and to a taker, v + y.

Each person knows v and his own idiosyncratic value. The state may or may not know v, x, and y.

The social objective is maximization of the expected value of things.[222] It is socially desirable for an owner to possess a thing if and only if v + x ≥ v + y, that is, if and only if x ≥ y; otherwise, the taker should have the thing.

We consider the property rule and the liability rule. Under the *property rule*, the state, given its information, assigns the entitlement to possess the thing either to the owner or to the taker. Under the *liability rule*, a taker is permitted to take the thing but must pay nonnegative damages d. We will focus on the case in which d equals the value to the owner, v + x, if the state can observe this, or if not, when d equals the mean of v + x.

---

[220] We call the party that faces an owner a "taker" even though that party may not in fact take a thing and thus might better be called a "potential taker."

[221] We emphasized in section III.C of the Article the importance of the possibility that multiple potential takers might face a particular owner, but here we abstract from this possibility.

[222] Thus, we abstract from incentives to protect and to take things and from other issues discussed in the Article.

We now compare property and liability rules for the case in which the owner and taker do not bargain. (The case in which there is bargaining was informally described in the text.)

A.   State's Information Is Perfect

Here we have:

PROPOSITION 6. *Assume that owners and takers do not bargain. If the state has perfect information about parties' values, the property rule and the liability rule with d = v + x are equivalent and optimal.*

Under the property rule, the state can achieve the first-best outcome by assigning the entitlement to owners if and only if $y \leq x$. Also, the state can achieve the first-best outcome under the liability rule with $d = v + x$, for then a taker will refrain from taking the thing if and only if $v + y \leq d = v + x$, or if and only if $y \leq x$.

B.   State's Information Is Imperfect

Let us assume here that the state has imperfect information about the common value and the idiosyncratic values; it knows only their distributions. Then we have:

PROPOSITION 7. *Assume that owners and takers do not bargain. If the state knows only the distributions of parties' values, then:*

(a) The property rule with the entitlement given to owners is superior to the property rule with the entitlement given to takers.

(b) The property rule with the entitlement given to owners may be superior to the liability rule with d = E(v) + E(x). A sufficient condition for superiority of the property rule is that the support of the distribution of y lies below E(x).

With regard to (a), if owners have the entitlement, the expected value is $E(v) + E(x)$, and if takers have it, the expected value is $E(v) + E(y)$. Because $E(x) > E(y)$, the state should grant the owners the entitlement.

With regard to (b), observe that a taker will take a thing when $v + y > E(v) + E(x)$, or when

(12) $y > E(v) - v + E(x)$.

Now there will be a difference between the outcome under the liability rule and that reached under the property rule if and only if the taker takes — that is, when (12) holds. Further, when the taker takes, the expected difference in values between the taker and the owner is $y - E(x)$. Hence, the difference in social welfare under the liability rule is equal to

(13) $\int_0^\infty [\int_{E(v)-v+E(x)}^\infty (y - E(x))f(y)dy]z(v)dv$.

If (13) is negative, the liability rule is inferior to the property rule. If the support of y lies below E(x), then y − E(x) is always negative, so that (13) must be negative.

Comments. (a) The interpretation of (12) and (13) bears comment. From (12), it is clear that if v is higher than its estimated value E(v), then there may be takings even though y, the taker's idiosyncratic value, is "low"; the higher is v relative to E(v), the lower may be the y for which a taker would take. Further, the more likely it is that takings will occur when y is low (less than E(x)), the more negative the contribution to (13) will be, and the less well the liability rule will perform. What makes takings likely even when y is low is the variability in v, which means that there is a substantial probability that v > E(v). Because much of the probability mass of the distribution of y lies below E(x), the probability is substantial that, when there is a taking, it will tend to reduce social welfare.

(b) Note that the liability rule may be inferior to the property rule even though damages equal the expected value of the object to the owner, which is analogous to the victim's harm in the externality context. The contrast with the externality context arises because here the total values of the two parties are correlated: both total values include v. If v is zero or if there is no variation in v — which eliminates the correlation — it is readily shown that the liability rule (with d = E(x)) is superior to the property rule with entitlement to the owner.[223] Thus, the present result is consistent with the result in the externality context. (Recall also comment d in section I.A.2 of the Appendix showing that, in the externality context, relaxing the independence assumption altered the conclusion.)

(c) To illustrate our argument, we provide some numerical examples. All distributions are uniform on the intervals described in the table below. The final column displays the ratio of the social costs imposed by the liability rule from inducing undesirable takings to the social benefits from inducing desirable takings. A ratio that exceeds one indicates that the property rule is superior.

COMMON VALUE (v)	IDIOSYNCRATIC VALUE OWNERS' (x)	IDIOSYNCRATIC VALUE TAKERS' (y)	COSTS/BENEFITS OF LIABILITY RULE
[90,110]	[0,10]	[0,5]	5.571
[90,110]	[0,10]	[0,8]	1.313
[95,105]	[0,10]	[0,6]	2.111
[95,105]	[0,10]	[0,8]	0.792

The property rule is clearly superior unless, as in the final example, the range of the common value is small (here, within 5% of its mean) and

---

[223] In (13), the lower limit of the second integral becomes E(x), so y − E(x) is positive for all y in (E(x),∞).

the average takers' idiosyncratic value (4) is almost as high as the average owners' idiosyncratic value (5). (Shrinking the range of the common value alone would be sufficient to induce a preference for the liability rule, as explained in the preceding comment.)

The above analysis assumes that damages equal the average common value, 100, plus the average owners' idiosyncratic value, 5, for a total of 105. Higher damages clearly are optimal. In the third example, for instance, if damages were 110, takings would be rare: only takers with idiosyncratic values above 5 would take (for the highest possible common value is 105 and damages are 110) and they would take infrequently (a necessary condition is that the common value exceed 104). Such takings would, on average, be desirable, because the taker's value would, on average, exceed the owner's value. (See our discussion in note 157.) We would, however, interpret such a rule as more like a property rule than a liability rule: even though damages are not infinite, they are high enough to deter virtually all takings.

[10]

Unifying Remedies: Property Rules, Liability Rules, and Startling Rules

Saul Levmore[†]

Imagine that *B* complains about pollution spewing forth from a factory owned by her neighbor, *A*. A generation of law students has now learned that *B*'s possible remedies traverse the boundaries normally drawn between legal subject areas, much as the previous generation of lawyers learned to lower the divide between law and equity. The educational watershed was surely Calabresi and Melamed's justly celebrated article of twenty-five years ago, suggesting a grand theory of remedies and concentrating on what it called property rules and tort liability rules.[1] By focusing on (and moving between) property rights, damage awards, and private bargains around these rights and awards, Calabresi and Melamed vaporized the inherited barriers between private law rights and remedies.

In retrospect, that article is at least as interesting for what it missed as for what it wrought. Readers of law reviews know that a good deal of attention had been paid to the question of when judges should assign property rights or liability awards, and Calabresi and Melamed can be said to have anticipated and initiated that inquiry—which I largely avoid in the present Essay.[2] Some readers also know that Calabresi and Melamed might be described as having produced something less than a grand theory of remedies—if "grand" implies completeness—because subsequent innovators have shown remedies not anticipated twenty-five years ago. My aim here is, first, to learn about

---

† Brokaw Professor and Albert Clark Tate, Jr. Professor of Law, University of Virginia. I am grateful for comments received from Laura Brodbeck, Jody Kraus, Daryl Levinson, Jeffrey Standen, and George Triantis, and for many conversations with Bill Stuntz.

1. *See* Guido Calabresi & A. Douglas Melamed, *Property Rules, Liability Rules, and Inalienability: One View of the Cathedral*, 85 HARV. L. REV. 1089 (1972).

2. Doubt has been raised about Calabresi and Melamed's analysis of when courts ought to prefer various remedies. *See* Ian Ayres & Eric Talley, *Solomonic Bargaining: Dividing a Legal Entitlement to Facilitate Coasean Trade*, 104 YALE L.J. 1027 (1995) (disputing claim that property rules best encourage bargaining and arguing that liability rules and other "divided entitlements" have information-forcing qualities that lead to efficient outcomes); Louis Kaplow & Steven Shavell, *Do Liability Rules Facilitate Bargaining? A Reply to Ayres and Talley*, 105 YALE L.J. 221 (1995) (challenging themes in Ayres and Talley's article); Louis Kaplow & Steven Shavell, *Property Rules Versus Liability Rules: An Economic Analysis*, 109 HARV. L. REV. 713 (1996) (arguing that liability rules are preferable to property rules for minimizing externalities even in cases where damages are difficult to determine). In the present Essay, I primarily explore the gamut of remedies rather than the question of when different remedies ought to be used, although I do on occasion cross the line into normative territory. *See infra* Section III.A.

remedies by exploring the nature of these renovations to the Calabresi-Melamed framework, and second, to build on this framework in a way that yields substantial payoffs. I explore ways in which rights, remedies, and bargains can be combined to serve a variety of new tasks even while carrying on traditional efficiency, fairness, and redistributive functions. One particular finding is that rules that startle because they break a sensible convention—not asking those in the right to pay when they are wronged—can serve the interesting function of encouraging honest claims in the first place. The larger practical goal is to develop a more unified theory of remedies by showing how substantive and procedural considerations might be integrated.

Part I reviews the Calabresi-Melamed framework with a focus on the gaps it left unfilled. I explore in some detail a startling recent addition to the property and liability rules literature, authored by Professors Krier and Schwab. Calabresi and Melamed attracted attention, in large part, because they "found" a new and startling remedy in front of their readers' collective eyes; when *A*'s behavior is a nuisance to *B*, a court might give *B* the power to enjoin *A*, but it might require *B* to pay *A*. Something about this split decision captivated most audiences even as it infuriated others, who found it too unusual to be of note. Krier and Schwab deepened the wedge by suggesting that there may be occasions when courts should decide that *A* can choose to stop and collect damages (that *B* would have suffered had *A* not stopped) from *B*. Part II identifies the singularly startling quality found in this work and, by implication, in their predecessors' work a quarter century earlier. Part III argues that the real contribution of the more recent work to the development of a unified theory of remedies may be something quite unanticipated. Along the way, I develop some ideas about the arrows of time associated with various remedies and about the content of (surprisingly ambiguous) familiar remedies. Finally, in a way that might be said to echo Calabresi and Melamed's work, I suggest that the more complete framework we can construct today reveals yet more rules that may be of some use to courts.

I. PROPERTY RIGHTS AND LIABILITY RULES ONCE MORE

A. *The Four-Rule Framework*

Calabresi and Melamed were plainly not seeking to specify all of the remedial choices available to courts. Their exploration did include criminal law,[3] and was therefore not limited to tort damages ("liability rules") and to (the issuance or denial of) injunctions regarding property rights ("property rules"); it

---

3. There was no attempt, however, to discuss choices among remedies normally found in criminal law. *See* Calabresi & Melamed, *supra* note 1, at 1124–27 (discussing nature of criminal sanctions as property rules and suggesting reasons why liability rules would not be appropriate).

did not, however, include remedies for breach of contract, burdensome unconstitutional statutes, or violations of international law. It is somewhat more difficult to specify the terrain that Calabresi and Melamed did intend to cover in their work. It seems a bit circular (and insufficiently appreciative of the genius of their framework) to take them almost at their word and say that their target included (only) all the disputes we normally think of as contained in property and tort law.[4] Not only is property an elastic and ill-defined subject, but some of the value of the Calabresi-Melamed framework lies in its ability to illuminate fields outside of traditional property and tort law.[5] Nevertheless, inasmuch as the implicit collaborative goal of all who write on this matter is to develop a more complete framework, or a grander theory of remedies, it seems useful to take aim at the same target as one's predecessors. It may well be the case that an expanded set of remedies also covers a greater range of disputes, but I begin by returning to the very dispute Calabresi and Melamed brought on stage, a conflict among neighbors regarding an alleged nuisance.

By way of quick review, imagine that *B*'s injuries could be avoided by *A* shutting down its neighboring factory or, perhaps, installing a much taller smokestack to redirect its wastes.[6] Calabresi and Melamed organized the remedial world we know by describing three possible "rules," and then observing that their description suggested the emergence of a fourth, previously unappreciated remedial possibility. Rule 1: *B* might successfully enjoin *A* from operating (or from operating without the more formidable smokestack). *A* might, of course, negotiate with *B* after losing in court in this manner but, with this Rule 1, the court will have established the starting point for such bargains.[7] Rule 2: *A* can be required to pay damages for injuries that *B* has absorbed.[8] Rule 3: *A* can be permitted to continue as before—the inverse of Rule 1. After describing these three rules, Calabresi and Melamed sought to demonstrate the value of this categorization by suggesting that the inverse of Rule 2 might also

---

4. *See id.* at 1089 ("Only rarely are Property and Torts approached from a unified perspective.").

5. *See, e.g.,* Saul Levmore, *Love It or Leave It: Property Rules, Liability Rules, and Exclusivity of Remedies in Partnership and Marriage,* LAW & CONTEMP. PROBS., Spring 1995, at 221 (applying Calabresi-Melamed framework to remedies available in partnership law).

6. Thus, we might imagine that *A*'s factory earns $10,000 per year and injures *B* to the tune of $5000 a year, but that these damages could be reduced to $3000 by investing the equivalent of $1500 per year in a taller smokestack. *B* is presented as a single resident in this example and in the text, but it should be noted that although this simplification is troubling for arguments about the relative desirability of property and liability rules, the present Essay has other aims.

7. Calabresi and Melamed's emphasis on such Coasean bargaining might be understood as implicitly expanding the scope of their framework to include contract law and its remedies because the impact of these bargains around property and liability rules will depend on remedies for breach of contract.

8. Continuing with the example from note 6, *supra, A* would pay *B* $2000 per year (subject to a statute of limitations or other procedural constraint) for the past injuries suffered because the incremental damages caused by the absence of the efficient smokestack amount to $5000-$3000=$2000. *See* SAUL LEVMORE, FOUNDATIONS OF TORT LAW 99 (1994) (posing question regarding valuation of incremental damages in a negligent accident example). If these numbers are hard to come by, courts might be expected to assess "full" damages of $5000. If *A* makes no changes, then *A* can expect to pay the same next year, so that with these numbers we can expect *A* to invest in the taller smokestack.

2152   The Yale Law Journal   [Vol. 106: 2149

be used even though it was apparently unknown. The scheme was thus rounded out with Rule 4: *B* stops *A* but compensates *A* for *A*'s damages (such as relocation costs).[9]

TABLE 1. SUMMARY OF CALABRESI-MELAMED FRAMEWORK

RULE	DESCRIPTION	FRAMEWORK BUILDER	COMMENTS
1	*B* stops *A*	Calabresi-Melamed (C-M)	Classic injunction or "property rule"
2	*A* pays *B*	C-M	Classic damages or "liability rule"
3	*A* can continue as before	C-M	Reverse of Rule 1; *B* loses to *A*'s property right
4	*B* stops *A*, but pays *A*'s damages	C-M and Atwood; see note 9	Analogous to eminent domain, but likely to involve low damages; see note 9

Every reader of this Essay already knows that this four-rule framework revealed the ability of courts to choose among endowments, whether in the form of property rights (as in Rules 1 and 3) or liability rules (as in Rules 2 and 4), in order to balance considerations of fairness and efficiency. One strategy or the other might be favored because of the likelihood of judicial error in assessing costs and benefits, because of intuitions about parties' (and judges') abilities to overcome collective action and strategic behavior problems and other transaction

---

9. In this particular example, begun note 6, *supra*, *B* might pay *A* the $1500 (efficient) avoidance cost. I have argued elsewhere that in most nuisance cases these damages are unlikely to be high because the property right assignment normally follows changes that have benefitted the "loser" in financial terms. Thus, in *Spur Industries v. Del E. Webb Development Co.*, 494 P.2d 700 (Ariz. 1972) (en banc), it is likely that the defendant's property value increased because of the encroaching residences. Defendants would of course be happier with a "double recovery" of property appreciation and the ability to sell the right to operate as before (Rule 3), but it is likely that even the prospect of single, extralegal recovery makes most potential defendants in these circumstances happy to see approaching residential development. For other examples of this sort of implicit compensation, see Richard A. Epstein, *The Ubiquity of the Benefit Principle*, 67 S. CAL. L. REV. 1369, 1386–87, 1399–402 (1994). Such implicit compensation can also be found in *Mohr v. Williams*, 104 N.W. 12 (Minn. 1905), in which the patient-plaintiff received a nominal damage award representing her actual damages for an unauthorized surgical procedure, less a "fee" to the defendant-physician for nonetheless beneficial services rendered. Note, however, that at the time *Spur Industries* itself was resolved, the Sun City residents had a suit pending against Spur for damages. Del Webb paid Spur to abate and relocate and Spur cross-complained against Del Webb, saying that it should be indemnified for damages that might be owed to the residents. The Arizona Supreme Court agreed that Del Webb might be liable, but the residents' case was settled. *See* JESSE DUKEMINIER & JAMES E. KRIER, PROPERTY 986 n.10 (3d ed. 1993).

As is well known, Calabresi and Melamed (along with an earlier commentator, *see* James R. Atwood, Note, *An Economic Analysis of Land Use Conflicts*, 21 STAN. L. REV. 293, 315 (1969)) correctly anticipated at least one nuisance decision using Rule 4, namely *Spur Industries*. Arguably, they also described another area of law with many more applications. *See* Levmore, *supra* note 5, at 238 (characterizing doctrine of wrongful dissolution in partnership law as example of *B* stopping *A* but paying *A*'s damages from cessation).

costs associated with bargaining, because of the likely redistributive or wealth consequences for bargaining itself, and because of sensibilities about the question of whether ex post payments legitimate (or grudgingly compensate) forced private transfers.[10] My focus here, however, is on the framework itself, and on the range of possible rules or remedies that may be found.

It may be useful to comment on the role of Rule 4 (*B* stops *A* but compensates *A*) in the Calabresi-Melamed framework, because of both its notoriety over the last twenty-five years and its importance in the discussion below.[11] One of the novel characteristics of the Calabresi-Melamed work was its trans-substantive character. Other scholars had enumerated, classified, compared, and even invented remedies, but the new approach was radical in its sweep across takings law, property rights, and tort damages with as broad (and confident) a brush as had been seen before. Conventional readers required a payoff from this reconceptualization. Rule 4 provided a kind of evidence that a new view of the cathedral would, as the exquisite title promised, reveal something not seen before. Another novelty was that the Calabresi-Melamed work showed that law and economics was something more than a taste for markets (and prices) and the worship of efficiency. Indeed, the article might be credited with making private law scholarship and judging respectable, economically sophisticated, and politically correct ventures. Judges could use property and liability rules to do what they thought efficient, fair, and even sensitive to concerns about wealth distribution. Rule 4 was instrumental in this regard inasmuch as it offered a remedy that shut down one party's operation in the interest of efficiency but then required compensation of the apparent winner. This sort of "separation" of remedial tools promised maneuvering space for judges.

B. *Other Property and Liability Rules*

1. *Filling in the Gaps*

One example of the genius of the early law and economics movement was its ability to conceptualize Rule 4 where thousands of lawyers had not seen it

---

10. *See* Calabresi & Melamed, *supra* note 1, at 1106–10. Note that the judicial "error" associated with assessing damages may be virtually inevitable, or simply not designed to provide full compensation, so that it is possible to think of liability rules as less "complete" remedies than property rules. *Compare* Jeffrey Standen, *The Fallacy of Full Compensation*, 73 WASH. U. L.Q. 145 (1995) (analyzing and providing justification for incomplete remedies), *with* Jules L. Coleman & Jody Kraus, *Rethinking the Theory of Legal Rights*, 95 YALE L.J. 1335 (1986) (discussing differences in concepts of compensation that flow from different definitions of rights).

11. Calabresi and Melamed themselves emphasized this aspect of their contribution, and correctly so. *See* Calabresi & Melamed, *supra* note 1, at 1128 ("The framework we have employed may be applied in many different areas of the law. We think its application facilitated perceiving and defining an additional resolution of the problem of pollution. As such we believe the painting to be well worth the oils.").

before.[12] It was perhaps easier for later commentators, empowered by the Calabresi-Melamed framework, to find other rules that were omitted twenty-five years ago. The best known of these additions is probably the idea that a court may sometimes wish to do something between Rule 1 (*B* can enjoin *A*) and Rule 2 (*A* pays *B*'s damages). For instance, a court could enjoin *A* from engaging in some level of operation, or from operating with a smokestack below some specified height, but then promise (or award) damages for injuries sustained by *B* when *A* operates within the specified parameters. We might refer to this remedy as Rule 1P, where P suggests either the author of this idea, Mitch Polinsky, or its poetic "partial property rule" character.[13] Calabresi and Melamed might well have anticipated Rule 1P but thought of it as a mixture of their first two rules. Calabresi had, for example, spent many years thinking about negligence and strict liability, but he did not bother to split (the straightforward liability) Rule 2 in two, presumably so as not to weigh down the four-rule framework.[14]

Somewhat similarly, Rule 1 (*B* can enjoin *A*) comes in a variety of intriguing forms not explored twenty-five years ago. Calabresi and Melamed's references to property rules appear to conceive of those rules as including lesser liability remedies,[15] so that their version of Rule 1 not only gives *B* the right

---

12. It seems fair to give credit to the movement, rather than to the obvious powers of these particular authors, because another, earlier author also came to Rule 4, albeit from a different direction. *See* Atwood, *supra* note 9.

13. *See* A. Mitchell Polinsky, *Resolving Nuisance Disputes: The Simple Economics of Injunctive and Damage Remedies*, 32 STAN. L. REV. 1075, 1087 (1980) (arguing that entitlements need not be absolute). It has also been suggested that there could be a system of "comparative nuisance," similar to comparative negligence. *See* Jeff L. Lewin, *Comparative Nuisance*, 50 U. PITT. L. REV. 1009 (1989). In such a system, damage awards could be apportioned based on fairness, efficiency, and relative levels of causation. *See id.* at 1035–37. Lewin also suggests that injunctions could be awarded on a comparative basis, by requiring a successful plaintiff to compensate an enjoined defendant for an amount that corresponds to the plaintiff's comparative fault. Thus, in a comparative nuisance system, we might expect to see more Rule 4-type decisions. *See id.* at 1046–47.

14. There is Rule 2N, under which defendant pays damages when negligently causing harm, and Rule 2S, representing strict liability, requiring defendant to pay damages when causing injury. On the spectrum of remedies, Rule 2S would occupy a space closer to Rule 1, in that it gives a "property right to damages" to plaintiffs. Most damages arising out of contract are of the Rule 2S type, but Rule 2S is sometimes used to penalize wrongdoing. This is so even in the context of contract remedies, because the remedy of rescission is limited to certain cases, including ones in which there is evidence of fraud, unilateral mistake known to the other party, and duress. Rescission may therefore be a version of Rule 2 or 2N damages. *See* DOUGLAS LAYCOCK, MODERN AMERICAN REMEDIES: CASES AND MATERIALS 580 (2d ed. 1994). In any event, Calabresi was no stranger to any of this. *See* Guido Calabresi & Jon T. Hirschoff, *Toward a Test for Strict Liability in Torts*, 81 YALE L.J. 1055 (1972).

15. *See* Calabresi and Melamed, *supra* note 1, at 1116 ("Missing is a fourth rule representing an entitlement in Taney to pollute, but an entitlement which is protected only by a liability rule."). It should be noted, however, that the cases cited as Rule 1 examples by Calabresi and Melamed do *not* include damage awards. They cite *Ensign v. Walls*, 34 N.W.2d 549 (Mich. 1948), in which the court enjoined annoying dog breeding, as well as a case enjoining the production of chemical odors that later generated a successful suit for past damages, *see* Capurro v. Galaxy Chem. Co., 2 Envtl. L. Rep. (Envtl. L. Inst.) 20386 (Md. Cir. Ct. 1972). *See also* Pendoley v. Ferreira, 187 N.E.2d 142, 146–47 (Mass. 1963) (enjoining operation of piggery and awarding past damages); Morgan v. High Penn Oil Co., 77 S.E.2d 682, 690 (N.C. 1953) (enjoining owner and operator of oil refinery and awarding damages to neighbors); Quinn v. American Spiral Spring & Mfg. Co., 141 A. 855, 858 (Pa. 1928) (awarding past damages to resident living

to stop *A* but also anticipates that *B* can collect from *A* for past injuries resulting from the activity that *B* succeeds in halting.[16] Lawyers are familiar with injunctions that are forward-looking only,[17] and many of these do not even glance back in the reparative sense,[18] but again Calabresi and Melamed can be applauded for their elegance. Resting in between their Rules 1 and 2, we can picture the occasional use of other rules, useful when judges are disinclined to award past damages for reasons of fairness or even efficiency.[19] Rule 1 (*B* can

---

adjacent to manufacturing plant and enjoining plant from keeping noisiest machines on side of building closest to plaintiff's house).

16. This assumption is somewhat problematic, because statutes of limitations are an obstacle to plaintiffs' awards for past damages, but not (at least explicitly) for injunctive relief. Also, combined injunctions and damage awards suggest a blurring of the distinction between the roles of judges and juries. Such a decision also spans the old divide between law and equity, although courts of equity did decide legal issues, despite apparent res judicata problems, even if the grounds for equitable relief no longer existed. *See, e.g.,* Shaw v. Owen, 90 So. 2d 179, 181 (Miss. 1956) (stating that courts of equity may and will decide issues of law to "award" by single comprehensive decree "all appropriate remedies"). Finally, it should be said that the mixing of the past with the future, through the novel device of using payments of money to remedy future harms, may serve to confuse things even as it opens new possibilities.

Much as I am reading Calabresi-Melamed as emphasizing one version of Rule 1 (*B* enjoins *A* and collects past damages) but acknowledging through citations the possibility of a variation (Rule 1F: *B* stops *A* and does not collect for the past), so too Rule 2 (*A* pays *B*) is set out as giving *A* license to continue as before by paying the price set out by the tort system but apparently recognizing the possibility of a court's terminating the license and converting Rule 2 to Rule 1, by "sanctioning" *A* if it continues to be "tortious." We might think of this version as Rule 2C: *A* pays *B*, but if *A* continues *A* might be told to stop. The label refers to the convertibility of the damage rule (into a property rule) as well as to the idea that a liability rule has some content that is not quite captured by the immediate remedy it provides. *See supra* note 10 and accompanying text. After writing this Essay, I was fortunate to see Dale A. Nance, Guidance Rules and Enforcement Rules: A Better View of the Cathedral (1996) (unpublished manuscript, on file with author), which emphasizes the distinction between the enforcement and guidance qualities of rules. Rule 2C is a version of Rule 2, but might be listed best between Rule 1 and Rule 2 inasmuch as it recognizes that the remedy of Rule 2 may signal the coming imposition of Rule 1 if *A*'s offending behavior continues.

17. We might call this Rule 1F. An obvious example would be cases involving prison overcrowding, in which courts are highly unlikely to grant successful plaintiffs damages for the past. *See, e.g.,* Hutto v. Finney, 437 U.S. 678 (1978) (affirming order that conditions of confinement in Arkansas prisons be improved). Examples also exist in nuisance. *See, e.g.,* Ohio River Sand Co. v. Commonwealth, 467 S.W.2d 347 (Ky. 1971) (enjoining industrial company that polluted atmosphere and waters and awarding plaintiff one dollar in nominal damages); Dolata v. Berthelet Fuel & Supply Co., 36 N.W.2d 97 (Wis. 1949) (enjoining fuel company from blowing coal dust onto neighboring properties, but awarding no damages because "evidence is insufficient to sustain any definite amounts").

18. Some injunctions are thus forward- and backward-looking in that they repair past wrongs while taking steps to prevent continuing wrongs, such as antitrust violations and flawed election procedures. *See generally* OWEN M. FISS, THE CIVIL RIGHTS INJUNCTION 7 (1978); Douglas Laycock, *The Death of the Irreparable Injury Rule,* 103 HARV. L. REV. 687, 771 (1990).

19. One such rule (perhaps a subtle form of Rule 1F (*B* stops *A* but gets nothing for the past)) could be used in cases where injunctions serve as a form of compromise, perhaps because damages are considered too speculative to assess. A good example is *Champion Spark Plug Co. v. Sanders,* 331 U.S. 125 (1947), in which the court required the seller of reconditioned Champion spark plugs to label such plugs clearly as "repaired" or "used," but did not award damages because the "likelihood of damage to petitioner or profit to respondents due to any misrepresentation seem[ed] slight." *Id.* at 131–32. Rule 1E is also possible: Plaintiff might be awarded an injunction plus defendant's past enrichment, rather than her own past damages. This might also be considered a form of compromise, since such a remedy would normally be less generous to plaintiff than Rule 1 (*B* stops *A* and by implication collects for past damages). I have found no cases in which a court could easily have determined and awarded damages and instead chose for reasons of fairness or equity to award past enrichment. However, numerous examples can be found in which courts award past enrichment because monetary damages are impossible or difficult to determine. A celebrated example is *Edwards v. Lee's Administrator,* 96 S.W.2d 1028 (Ky. 1936), in which two neighbors owned the land above a cave containing onyx formations. Edwards owned the land containing the entrance to the

enjoin *A*) can thus be seen as set out at one end of the remedy spectrum, with Rule 3 (*A* can continue as before without paying *B*) at the other end; Rule 2 (*A* pays *B*'s damages) and Rule 4 (*B* stops *A* but compensates *A*) are appropriate intermediate locations to have specified because they accommodate liability rules in simple fashion. The other rules that I have mentioned and alluded to were, perhaps, left as exercises to test the combinatorial skills of us mortal readers.[20]

TABLE 2. EXPANDED SET OF ANTI-NUISANCE RULES

RULE	DESCRIPTION	SOURCE	COMMENTS
1	*B* stops *A* (and collects for past injuries)	C-M's apparent Rule 1	Injunction with likelihood of damage collection
1F	*B* stops *A* but does not collect for past injuries		See notes 16–19
1P	*B* stops *A* up to a point, and *A* pays the damages associated with its permitted operation	Polinsky; see note 13	Partial property rule
2C	*A* pays *B*, but may be stopped later on	Hints in Coleman & Kraus, Nance	See notes 10, 16
2S	*A* pays *B* even if not negligent	Partition of Rule 2	Strict liability rule; see note 14
2N	Negligent *A* pays *B*	Partition of Rule 2	Negligence liability rule; see note 14

One last example of this expansive view of the four-rule framework concerns the absence of restitutionary remedies. Surely a judge could have the polluting factory, *A*, disgorge its enrichment from "unjustly" failing to invest in the efficient precautions that were available to it.[21] Missing, therefore, is Rule

cave and admitted the public for a charge, taking them into the portion owned by Lee. The court awarded Lee an accounting of profits for the trespass, as well as an injunction prohibiting Edwards from further trespass on those lands. "The law, in seeking an adequate remedy for the wrong, has been forced to adopt profits received, rather than damages sustained, as a basis of recovery." *Id.* at 1032; *see infra* notes 21–27 and accompanying text.

For discussion of another, perhaps implicit, rule, see the discussion of Rule 2C in note 16, *supra*: *A* pays *B* but may be more strongly encouraged to stop if underlying behavior continues.

20. One rule not mentioned is general average contribution in admiralty law, which (put simply) provides that in emergencies at sea, all the interests in a vessel and its cargo share the cost of sacrifice in proportion to the value. *See* GRANT GILMORE & CHARLES L. BLACK, LAW OF ADMIRALTY §§ 5-1 to 5-2 (2d ed. 1975).

21. Continuing with the example from note 6, *supra*, *A* could pay the $1500 per year that represents the avoided cost of the efficient taller smokestack. There are problems with this rule, but we might imagine cases where the legal system would add a small penalty in order to make sure that *A* is not indifferent between precaution-taking and injury-inflicting, and where there is reason to think that no complex premium is needed to compensate for the probability that although *A*'s behavior is antisocial, *B*'s claim does not regularly materialize. *See* Saul Levmore, *Probabilistic Recoveries, Restitution, and Recurring Wrongs*, 19 J. LEGAL STUD. 691 (1990) (explaining normal preference for tort damages over restitution).

TABLE 3. RESTITUTION-INSPIRED EXPANSION OF ANTI-NUISANCE REMEDIES

RULE	DESCRIPTION	SOURCE	COMMENTS
1	*B* stops *A*	C-M	
1E	*B* stops *A* and *A* disgorges earlier wrongful gains	C-M combined with restitution	See notes 19–23 and accompanying text
2	*A* pays *B*'s damages	C-M	
2E	*A* pays *B* its own unjust enrichment	Familiar alternative (outside of nuisance law) to Rule 2	See note 21 and accompanying text

2E, where *A* pays over its wrongful enrichment to *B*, as well as Rule 1E,[22] where *A* is enjoined as to the future and also expected to disgorge from the past.[23] We have come to expect such rules to be attractive only where *B*'s damages are significantly more difficult to measure than *A*'s unjustly saved avoidance costs[24] (or, perhaps, where these gains are a source of punitive damages),[25] but a unified theory of remedies would presumably account for these tools. Again, it is a matter of taste whether one prefers the simplicity of a four-rule framework or the completeness that more rules might have offered. It would be wrong to describe Calabresi and Melamed as having "missed" these other remedies. The brooding presence of these remedies would have been fairly obvious,[26] and their consequences fall within the range of the four-rule viewfinder.[27]

Note that there is also the possibility of combining restitution with strict liability rather than with negligence or wrongfulness. There are therefore at least two versions of what the text calls Rule 2E.

There are also at least three different types of restitution in which the amount that the wrongdoer must restore to the plaintiff represents either its profits, the value of the used item in its next best use, or its full value. For a discussion of this tangential matter, see Peter K. Huber, *Mistaken Transfers and Profitable Infringement on Property Rights: An Economic Analysis*, 49 LA. L. REV. 71, 103–08 (1988).

22. *See supra* note 19.

23. One advantage of such a rule is that it might overcome the historical disinclination to leave damage remedies to juries because the damage remedy was a matter of law rather than of equity. *See supra* note 16.

24. *See, e.g.*, Olwell v. Nye & Nissen Co., 173 P.2d 652 (Wash. 1946) (holding that owner of egg-washing machine wrongfully used by defendant, but that otherwise would have been idle, receives profit derived by defendant from use of machine).

25. *See, e.g.*, Sturm, Ruger & Co. v. Day, 594 P.2d 38, 50 (Alaska 1979) (Burke, J., dissenting in part) (describing use of cost of company's untaken precaution as amount of punitive damages); Grimshaw v. Ford Motor Co., 174 Cal. Rptr. 348, 388–89 (Ct. App. 1981) (citing defendant's net worth and previous year's income as evidence that punitive damage award was not excessive).

26. Put differently, Rules 1E and 2E might be of interest to a reader who seeks a unified theory of remedies, but they are neither startling in the manner of Rule 4 nor critical in the construction of a remedies framework.

27. Similarly, although Calabresi and Melamed do incorporate some of takings law, *see* Calabresi & Melamed, *supra* note 1, at 1106, they ignore sovereign immunity, which might be thought of as creating a Rule 3G: *A* can continue as before if *A* is the government. Note that 3G can be more powerful than 3. In *Miller v. Schoene*, 276 U.S. 272 (1928), for instance, a state government was able to eradicate ornamental cedar trees (hosting parasites) that threatened nearby apple orchards without compensating the cedar owners. If the apple growers had simply gone to court alleging a private nuisance, they might have

2. *Arrows of Time*

I have already suggested that a unified theory of remedies might pay more attention (than earlier work did) to purposeful slices of the spectrum of time. An injunction regarding property rights might (or might not) be purely prospective, so that there would be no damages for past inflictions.[28] Similarly, while liability rules are generally backward-looking—albeit accompanied by the implicit threat of repeated, future damage claims if the actionable behavior continues[29]—it is easy to imagine a forward-only liability rule.[30] This sort of rule might be appealing either where the defendant seems culpable only once put on notice or where a kind of comparative negligence regime is best instituted through these slices of time (as opposed to slices of aggregate damages).[31]

Putting aside the capacity of a liability rule to be as forward-looking and as fine-like as any property rule, it is apparent that in most cases the convenient

---

been able to stop further planting of cedars, but I doubt that a court would have required the uncompensated destruction of existing cedars. This is not the place to explore the relationship among legislative, judicial, and private interventions, so I leave for another day the question of whether sovereign immunity is best thought of as an escape from a liability rule or as a property rule in favor of the government. Note, however, that governmental action, as in *Miller*, raises another version of the question about the relationship between judicial declarations and past damages. *See supra* notes 16–18. It is surprisingly difficult to divine whether the *Miller* court would have anticipated that after its decision the apple growers could collect for past damages suffered at the hands of the cedar-based parasite.

28. Rule 1 (*B* stops *A* and by implication collects for past damages) can thus be contrasted with the forward-looking only Rule 1F, which is most closely analogous to conventional legislation. The contrast illuminates the intuition that Rule 1 includes damages for the past because it is often thought that a remedy for past injuries is necessary to ensure that meritorious claims are brought in the first place. To some extent, it seems that "purely prospective" remedies are the work of legislatures or administrative agencies, but of course judges can use declaratory judgments (which themselves will generate future damage recoveries in the event of violations) and injunctions with contempt sanctions to do much the same. *See* Douglas Laycock, *The Triumph of Equity*, LAW & CONTEMP. PROBS., Summer 1993, at 53, 79; *see also* United States v. Brotherhood of R.R. Trainmen, 95 F. Supp. 1019 (D.D.C. 1951) (ordering fine for civil contempt, where fine corresponded to plaintiff's loss from defendant's violation of injunction). *See generally* OWEN M. FISS, INJUNCTIONS 703–74 (1972) (analyzing details and implications of enforcing injunctions through contempt proceedings).

29. An example of a case explicitly granting damages for the future is *Boomer v. Atlantic Cement Co.*, 257 N.E.2d 870 (N.Y. 1970), in which the court denied an injunction, but awarded permanent damages to the neighbors of a dust-blowing cement plant. We can also imagine a liability rule that is explicitly limited to the past, either because future behavior is enjoined or because circumstances have changed such that future injuries would not be regarded as wrongfully caused. Instances of such a backward-looking Rule 2B include *Allison v. Smith*, 695 P.2d 791 (Colo. Ct. App. 1984), which held that weekend cabin owners could enjoin their neighbors from storing scrap metal and other "obnoxious debris" on their property, and awarded the owners $5000 in damages; *Edwards v. Lee's Administrator*, 96 S.W.2d 1028 (Ky. 1936) (discussed *supra* note 19); and *Morgan v. High Penn Oil Co.*, 77 S.E.2d 682 (N.C. 1953), which held that oil refinery emissions of noxious gases were actionable by neighboring trailer park and restaurant owner and remanded for a hearing on the facts.

30. I might label it 2F. If Rule 1F is analogous to legislation prohibiting certain behavior, Rule 2F can be compared to legislatively imposed fines for certain behavior. Again, lawyers tend to think that fine-setting is a job for legislators. *See supra* note 27.

31. Instances of such a rule in the case law are difficult to find, but *Champion Spark Plug Co. v. Sanders*, 331 U.S. 125 (1947), and *Boomer*, 257 N.E.2d 870, can be seen as Rule 2F (*A* pays *B* for future damages only) cases. In *Champion*, we can imagine that although the court held that an accounting of profits was not required and that an injunction "will satisfy the equities of the case," 331 U.S. at 132, future violations of the injunction might have been expected to lead to damages awards for Champion, *see id.* at 131–32.

means of anticipatory judicial intervention is through injunctive, or property, rules. Given that Calabresi and Melamed classified along the property-liability axis, it is noteworthy but perhaps not terribly remarkable that there is also a time axis (primarily in the sense that legal intervention can be anticipatory or ex post) to be added, so that a liability rule can be forward- or backward-looking (or both) and a property rule, while forward-looking by nature, can include damages for the past.[32]

TABLE 4. EXPANSIONS BASED ON DIRECTION OF REMEDY AND OTHER EXPECTATIONS

RULE	DESCRIPTION	SOURCE	COMMENTS
1	B stops A (and collects for past injuries)	C-M's apparent Rule 1	Injunction with likelihood of damage collection
1F	B stops A but does not collect for past injuries		See notes 16–19
2C	A pays B, but may be stopped later on	Hints in Coleman & Kraus, Nance	See notes 10, 16
General Average Contribution	Nonnegligent A shares in B's loss if part of same community		See note 20
2B	A pays only for past injuries to B		See note 29
2F	A pays only for future damages to B	Legislative practice	See notes 30–31 and accompanying text
2X	A pays what B might have extracted in a bargain if B had property right to sell	Farber	More generous damages than Rule 2; see note 48

If the original Calabresi-Melamed framework had been built around forward-looking and backward-looking rules, a later observer could just as easily slice in another direction by introducing the property-liability axis.[33] The emphasis on

---

32. *See supra* notes 16–17, 29 and accompanying text (suggesting that Calabresi-Melamed's version of Rule 1 was probably meant to include past damages, but calling Rule 1F (*B* stops *A* but does not collect for past damages) a version that does not). Note that an injunction can verge on a call for future damages because the penalty for civil contempt can amount to nothing more than modest damages. *See supra* note 31.

33. For example, a framework built on the time axis might have offered: (1) remedies that look forward only; and (2) remedies that look both forward and backward. The introduction of (3), remedies that look backward only, might then have been as startling as Calabresi and Melamed's Rule 4 (*B* stops *A* but compensates *A*), because most awards for past damages at least implicitly suggest that further antisocial activity will result in future successful suits by one's neighbors. Forward-looking only remedies could come in at least four varieties, corresponding to Calabresi and Melamed's property and liability rules, as could dual-direction, forward- and backward-looking rules. Exclusively backward-looking rules, however, would make sense only in the form of liability rules, because injunctions regarding past behavior are more the stuff of morality plays than of law.

property rules and liability rules spawned a literature on transaction costs and default rules,[34] while an earlier focus on the timing of intervention and the direction of the intervention (whether forward or backward or both) would have encouraged the law and economics literature to explore both the division of labor between judges and legislatures,[35] and isomorphically perhaps, the ripeness doctrine[36] and the question of private standing where there is public harm.

3. *Krier and Schwab's Startling Extension*

In 1994, Jim Krier and Stewart Schwab imaginatively suggested a rule under which *A* can stop (itself) and then collect *B*'s damages—that is, those damages that will now not be borne by *B* because *A* has stopped.[37] Krier and Schwab

---

34. *See, e.g.,* sources cited *supra* note 2.

35. Legislatures are often said to be in the business of forward-looking rulemaking, while judges decide actual cases or controversies that have already matured. Note that the judge-legislature choice has become a topic in the public choice literature. *See, e.g.,* Einer Elhauge, *Does Interest Group Theory Justify More Intrusive Judicial Review?,* 101 YALE L.J. 31 (1991) (comparing interest group problems found in litigation and judicial intervention with those found in legislative decisionmaking).

36. Put differently, it is not easy to explain why *B* has some chance of gaining an injunction against the operation of *A*'s factory next door, while *B* has little chance of such anticipatory relief from another neighbor who reliably drives too fast down the block each day. It is possible that the role of fines in the administrative state is more central than it at first appears, in that the system may count on *B*'s ability to convince a police officer to observe *A*'s behavior and issue a summons at very low cost both to the legal system and to *B*. It is also possible that the explanation lies in some complicated combination of considerations regarding error costs, measurement costs (which may be much the same thing as the irreparable injury rule), and the comparative advantages of juries, judges, and legislatures. Similarly, many claims dismissed for lack of ripeness may be understood as addressing the roles of juries and legislatures (rather than the suitability of later damage suits against the same court). *See, e.g.,* Nicholson v. Connecticut Half-Way House, Inc., 218 A.2d 383 (Conn. 1966) (overturning injunction against start of operations of halfway house for parolees).

37. Note that this is different from Rule 1E described above; Rule 1E entitles *B* to stop *A* and receive *A*'s untaken past precaution cost as a kind of restitution paid by the wrongdoer to the aggrieved party. Krier and Schwab give *A* an option that, when exercised, works to stop *A* in return for *B*'s payment of *B*'s forgone damages. *See* James E. Krier & Stewart J. Schwab, *Property Rules and Liability Rules: The Cathedral in Another Light,* 70 N.Y.U. L. REV. 440, 471 (1995). The Krier-Schwab notion is thus closer to Rule 4 (*B* stops *A* but compensates *A*) than to Rule 1E, in that *B* pays, but its real interest derives from some combination of offering *A* an option and linking liability to *B*'s "gain" rather than *A*'s past gain (as in Rule 1E) or *A*'s cost of compliance (Rule 4).

The idea of giving *A* an option, or even an option leading to a reverse "sale," did not originate with Krier and Schwab. It has strong roots in the idea of self-assessed taxes and damages, and it has been grafted onto the nuisance literature in Madeline Morris, *The Structure of Entitlements,* 78 CORNELL L. REV. 822, 854–56 (1993), which described put options as examples of reverse liability rules, in which the "in-kind" holder has both an exclusive veto power and the right to a forced compensated transfer. *See also* Ayres & Talley, *supra* note 2. For an expanded discussion of such put options and the way these options might be auctioned, see Ian Ayres & J.M. Balkin, *Legal Entitlements as Auctions: Property Rules, Liability Rules, and Beyond,* 106 YALE L.J. 703, 729–33 (1996). Similarly, the idea of expanding Calabresi-Melamed by taking advantage of the notion that there is a range over which *A* and *B* can bargain is older than Krier-Schwab and Morris. For one example of an emphasis on the range and indefinite number of potential initial bargaining points, see WILLIAM A. FISCHEL, THE ECONOMICS OF ZONING LAWS: A PROPERTY RIGHTS APPROACH TO AMERICAN LAND USE CONTROLS 113–14 (1985). Krier-Schwab, Morris, and Ayres-Talley were working contemporaneously with these twists and tools.

Krier and Schwab may startle readers who come to their work last (although my own startle reflex was surely enhanced by the fact that I read Krier-Schwab in a draft form before I encountered the pieces by Morris and Ayres-Talley) by referring neither to a prenegotiated option price (familiar in the world of options, but less interesting in nuisance and other conflicts) nor to an up-front offer (as suggested in Morris,

frame this as a choice put in *A*'s hands in order to exploit the fact that *A* is sometimes best situated to decide whether the socially preferred result is to cease or to continue operations.[38] This choice thus sometimes devolves into Rule 3 (*A* may continue as before with no payments required), because *A* may choose to continue (perhaps because her gains from continuing exceed *B*'s damage claim despite the court's contrary estimate), and sometimes into what I will call Rule 5. It is useful to emphasize that when *A* stops and collects, it is the complainant's enrichment that is extracted.[39] Plainly, the availability of Rule 5 must come as something of a surprise to *A*, and perhaps to *B* as well. If *A* knew that a judge would respond to any complaint by *B* with this Rule 5, then *A* would have a perverse incentive to create nuisances in order to collect from *B*. Indeed, as we will see, an element of the strategy implicit in Rule 5 is to encourage parties to be wary of judges' discretion and to gamble, if it can be called that, on the likelihood that a court will impose one remedy or another.

The more general strategy is to "subsidize" behavior that is sought from *A* rather than to "tax" *A* for the costs it externally imposes. When *A* is offered the choice between Rule 3 (continuing its operation as before) and Rule 5 (*A* stops and collects *B*'s gain from the cessation), *A* may essentially be paid to stop being a nuisance. The Calabresi-Melamed framework emphasized bargaining from initial positions imposed by (or expected of) courts, and Krier and Schwab can be seen as following this lead by suggesting yet another bargain that might have taken place between *A* and *B* in a world where *A* was armed with the property right to do as it pleased. I will suggest below that the most useful—but perhaps unambitious—way to think of these rules is to note that while Rule 4 (*B* stops *A* but compensates *A*) asks for the minimum amount *A* would require in order to take the precaution in question, Rule 5 can be understood as asking for the maximum amount *B* would pay.

The four-rule framework advances and manipulates the familiar idea that most sticks have corresponding carrots, so that both regulatory strategies and private bargains will usually come in pairs. In a somewhat obscure footnote,

---

supra, at 855 (describing police offer of twenty-five to fifty dollars to induce those possessing guns to turn them in)) but rather to a judicial decision that sometimes turns *B*'s complaint into an option available to *A*. Put differently, we normally think of bargains, including privately offered options, as making both parties better off, but Krier-Schwab elevate the possibility, as discussed *infra* in Section II.B, of doing no such thing. In any event, the present Essay suggests that we sometimes remove the option element from the "reverse liability" rule. *See infra* text accompanying note 69.

38. *A* is sometimes the best chooser because it has the best information about its own avoidance costs, and frequently is free of the collective action problems that might plague *B*, the neighbor.

39. As indicated, the Krier-Schwab idea is to be able to offer *A* a choice between Rules 3 (*A* "wins" in the sense of being allowed to continue as before with no payments required) and 5 (*A* chooses to stop in order to collect *B*'s "forgone" damages). It is unlikely that we would ever want to make Rule 5 mandatory, although the option has been mistakenly suggested elsewhere. *See* Levmore, *supra* note 5, at 234 n.42. *A* will shy away from Rule 5 when *A*'s gains from continuing exceed even the high level of payment captured in *B*'s damage allegations. In these situations we will be especially happy that we did not shut *A* down. If, for some reason (such as strategic pleading), *B*'s actual damages exceed *B*'s alleged damages, *B* may be able to pay *A* more than the Rule 5 amount in order to get *A* to stop.

2162   The Yale Law Journal   [Vol. 106: 2149

Krier and Schwab shuffle and deal another such pair by suggesting a rule under which *A* must choose between cessation and turning over its own enrichment.[40] Rule 5 looked to the objector's (*B*'s) enrichment, but now we look for the defendant's (*A*'s) gains from continuing as before. A court might decide that *A* can choose either to undertake a specific precaution such as building a taller smokestack (or stopping altogether), and neither pay nor collect, or to go on as before by paying *B* the amount determined in court to be *A*'s (untaken) precaution cost.[41] I will call this Rule 5CE because the defendant can choose to continue and disgorge its own enrichment, although I should emphasize that what is suggested is really giving *A* the power to choose between Rule 5CE and Rule 1 (*A* is stopped).[42] Krier and Schwab hint that the choice between offering Rule 5 (*A* stops itself but collects *B*'s alleged gain from this cessation) and Rule 5CE (*A* chooses to continue, rather than to stop and perhaps pay for the past, and *A* pays over its gain from continuing as before) might depend on a judge's assessment as to which party is the best decisionmaker.[43] But both rules just sketched seem to suppose that *A* is a good decisionmaker; one asks *A* to absorb the cost of continuing while the other asks *A* if it is willing to absorb the opportunity cost of forgone income associated with stopping. The strategy has a self-assessment component to it, but that is not a topic I wish to dwell on here.[44]

---

40. *See* Krier & Schwab, *supra* note 37, at 473 n.92. Note that Krier and Schwab seem at first to be setting out a mandatory rule that *A* must stop, but they go on to say that *A* holds a "trump" and can simply avoid rather than pay the costs of avoidance.

41. Note that the restitution in Rule 5CE draws on *A*'s gain from continuing, while that found in Rule 5 points to *B*'s gain from *A* not continuing. Rules 5 and 5CE are thus unrelated, or at least more distant relatives than other numerical pairs set out here; in Rule 5, *A* both stops and collects *B*'s enrichment, while in Rule 5CE, *A* both continues and pays based on its own enrichment. Returning to our hypothetical factory and neighbor, *see supra* notes 6, 8, in Rule 5 the enrichment to be collected is what *B* gains from *A*'s cessation, which is *B*'s (incremental) loss in the event that *A* continues, or $2000. But in Rule 5CE the enrichment to be paid derives from the unspent avoidance, or cessation, costs and is $1500.

42. Assume now that *A* claims that the better smokestack, *see supra* text accompanying note 41, costs $3000, and *B*'s incremental injury from the absence of this precaution is still $2000. If the judge suspects that *A*'s true avoidance costs are $1500, then following Rule 5CE the judge might offer *A* a choice between stopping (or improving the smokestack, and owing past damages under Rule 1) and continuing without the new smokestack—but then paying $3000, the alleged gain from not taking the precaution that the judge suspects is efficient.

43. I do not mean that a judge would offer *A* a choice between Rules 5 and 5CE. Unless the measurement problem is out of control, Rule 5 will always be vastly more attractive to *A*. The "choice" is the judge's; *A* can be offered a choice between Rule 5 and continuing as before, which is to say between Rules 5 and 3, or *A* can be offered a choice between 5CE and stopping, which is to say between Rules 5CE and 1.

44. *See* Saul Levmore, *Self-Assessed Valuation Systems for Tort and Other Law*, 68 VA. L. REV. 771 (1982) (discussing value and advantages of self-assessment as tool for overcoming valuation problems).

RULE	DESCRIPTION	SOURCE	COMMENTS
2E	A pays its unjust enrichment	Well-known alternative to C-M's Rule 2	1E could do the same with injunction plus restitutionary payment arising out of past injuries
3	A can continue as before	C-M	Reverse of Rule 1; B fails in court
4	B stops A, but pays A (at least A's relocation costs)	C-M and Atwood	Analogous to private eminent domain but likely to involve low damages
5	A stops and collects B's ("unsuffered") gain from this cessation; A can instead elect to continue as before (Rule 3)	Krier-Schwab's (K-S) "double reverse twist" modified	K-S have court determine B's enrichment, A choosing whether to stop and accept this amount; the present Essay converts this to a claims-control tool such that A collects what B claimed she would have suffered
5CE	A chooses to continue as before but then must pay its enrichment in being allowed to do so	K-S	See notes 40–43 and accompanying text; see also text accompanying note 69 on modifying this rule to encourage accurate claims by A

II. UNDERSTANDING THE STARTLE REFLEX

A. *Dissecting Krier-Schwab*

Krier and Schwab cite no cases applying or anticipating their idea, and I have suggested elsewhere that there may be reasons (other than a lack of judicial and lawyerly imagination) for the emptiness of this set.[45] Nevertheless, it may be useful in systematizing remedies to identify the novelty of Krier-Schwab and to see whether this contribution can be further generalized.

One possibility is that the novelty of Rule 5 (A stops itself but collects B's alleged gain from this cessation) is that it can fall outside the range contemplated by Calabresi-Melamed. B will normally be disappointed with a Rule 3 decision (allowing A to continue) and increasingly pleased[46] with Rule 4 (B stops A but compensates A), Rule 2 (A pays B's damages), and Rule 1 (A is stopped and normally owes damages). Technically speaking, it is of course the case that all of these rules understate B's victory, if it is that, because after any one of these

---

45. *See* Levmore, *supra* note 5, at 234; *infra* notes 52–58 and accompanying text.
46. This is more or less the case anyway. There are imaginable situations in which B's preferences would not be represented by this ordering. For example, B may place a higher premium on A's stopping and would therefore prefer Rule 4 to Rule 2.

rules is imposed, *A* may bargain with *B* and leave *B* (as well as *A*) better off than the initial judicial decision.[47] Similarly, Rule 3 (*A* can continue as before) may leave *A* even better off than it first appears. Still, a fair reading of Calabresi-Melamed may be that Rules 1 (*B* stops *A*) and 3 (*A* can continue) define the two ends of the decision spectrum available to judges in civil cases of a certain (not quite specified) kind. Rules 2 (*A* pays *B*) and 4 (*B* stops *A* but compensates *A*) seem to offer compromises, or intermediate positions, through the introduction of the liability tool. In any event, the Krier-Schwab innovation (Rule 5's offer to *A* that it can stop and collect *B*'s gain from this cessation) gives *A* a bigger victory than the four-rule framework appears to have anticipated. Under their approach, *A* can still choose Rule 3, which is to say that *A* can continue as before or entertain offers from *B* (who may want to pay *A* to stop), but *A* is obviously better off with the ability to choose between Rule 3 and Rule 5, which allows *A* to stop *and* to collect handsomely (in the amount of *B*'s gain from *A*'s cessation).

If, as just intimated, Krier-Schwab have simply leveraged four rules into something of a larger shape, then their creation might play a role in developing a comprehensive list of remedies—but it would hardly present the cathedral in a new light. Thus, the introduction of punitive damages would also have made *A* or *B* better or worse off than did the "extreme" property rules, 1 (*A* is stopped) and 3 (*A* may continue); however, the absence of punitive damages from the four-rule framework surely demonstrates nothing more than that Calabresi and Melamed sought elegance rather than completeness. Much as we would hardly have been startled by a suggestion that the four-rule framework be extended to include punitive damages, the novelty of the Krier-Schwab work cannot derive from its generating a remedy more extreme than those found in the first four rules.

Somewhat similarly, the striking character of Rule 5 probably does not come from its clever use of *B*'s unsuffered damages. These damages reflect one of two possible sources of payment based on restitution, while Rule 5CE (*A* chooses to continue and pay over its gain from continuing as before) draws on the other source. Once again, it would be disappointing if the true root of the novelty resided in the introduction of something that Calabresi-Melamed and a generation of readers compressed rather than failed to comprehend. I have already suggested in Part I that the four-rule framework ignores many possible

---

47. To be sure, that improvement may be anticipated by the judge. Note in this regard that Calabresi-Melamed and the discussion in the present Essay ignore remedies that might be described as anciently empathetic or internalizing, such as noxal surrender (goring ox is itself handed over to successful plaintiff) or talionic liability (eye for an eye). These remedies must generally have been "avoided" by bargains reached in their shadow, but their character might well have expanded the range of likely bargaining outcomes (beyond the range enclosed in modern times by the Calabresi-Melamed rules) and left the victim better off than before. But this is not the place to advance the cause of comparative study; it is merely useful to see that a theory of remedies that sought to specify all known and conceivable remedies would be as long as the history of legal experimentation and imagination.

rules that can appear fair and efficient but that feature restitution rather than damages as their centerpiece. To the extent that the Krier-Schwab innovation camouflages the introduction of a tool from the restitution family, where a taste for elegance held it offstage before, the startling reaction comes from a sleight of hand.[48] In any event, if restitution is the key, then Krier and Schwab themselves missed many other, more useful rules than the ones they sketch.[49]

Finally, the character of the Krier-Schwab innovation is not captured either by what they emphasize as the "choosing function"[50] they seek to encourage or by the observation that the winner in terms of property rights can be the loser in terms of payments. It is true of course that *A* might be best situated to decide whether or not it is socially efficient to continue as before, so that giving *A* a choice between stopping and continuing can be sensible, but the original Rule 2 (*A* pays *B*'s damages) was explicitly designed (by the father of least cost avoidance analysis) to perform just such a choosing, or least cost avoiding, function. If *B*'s complaint about *A*'s nuisance-making leads to a liability rule in *B*'s favor, then whatever the intended arrow of time,[51] Calabresi-Melamed plainly thought that an advantage of such a liability rule was that *A* would sometimes decide to cease or modify its operation in order to avoid paying future damages. Rule 2 (*A* pays *B*) thus assigned to *A* the choosing function even (or especially) in the absence of easy bargaining between the parties. As for the separation of objectives or tools, Rule 4 (*B* stops *A* but compensates *A*) already demonstrated the idea of making one party stop but another pay.[52] The same move would not startle us twice.

In the end, I think that what is startling about the Krier-Schwab idea is quite different from what is promising and systemically interesting about it. Its initial

---

48. Put differently, if Calabresi and Melamed had offered a six-rule framework with restitution included, then Krier and Schwab's innovation would still have been outside the range contemplated by Calabresi-Melamed, but it would have seemed more an interesting recombination or piece of leveraging.

Note the possibility of a compromise rule, calling for damages to be paid by *A* but in the more generous amount that *B* might have been willing to accept if *B* had been assigned a property right as in Rule 1. Such a rule contains an element of restitution because it extracts some of *A*'s gain. This rule is advanced in Daniel A. Farber, *Reassessing* Boomer: *Justice, Efficiency, and Nuisance Law, in* PROPERTY LAW AND LEGAL EDUCATION: ESSAYS IN HONOR OF JOHN E. CRIBBET 7 (Peter Hay & Michael H. Hoeflich eds., 1988). Farber is attracted to Rule 1 or (where more feasible) to this compromise Rule 2X (*A* pays what *B* might have extracted in a bargain had Rule 1 been in effect), because of a sense that in cases of egregious nuisance, *A* comes close to "stealing" *B*'s prior entitlements. *See id.* at 13–19.

49. *See supra* notes 17, 21–27 and accompanying text.

50. That is, they emphasize that the party with the best information that can make decisions most cheaply should be the party to choose whether the behavior should be stopped or continued. This means that in "double reverse twist" cases, as they describe what I have called Rule 5 (*A* stops itself and collects *B*'s gain from the cessation), the party that does the choosing (the polluter) is not the same party that pays (the neighbors). *See* Krier & Schwab, *supra* note 37, at 471. For a general discussion of whether these remedies should be chosen by plaintiffs or courts, see DAN B. DOBBS, HANDBOOK ON THE LAW OF REMEDIES 13–23 (1973).

51. *See supra* Subsection I.B.2.

52. It might be said that Rule 5 (*A* stops and collects *B*'s gain) innovates with its use of the idea of separating functions and using a subsidy because Rule 4 separated functions but used a tax. I would not have thought that this distinction could be so impressive. Moreover, it is arguable that the payment in Rule 4, while described as a liability rule, is just as easily called a subsidy.

impact has little to do with the choosing functions if only because it is Rule 5 (*A* stops itself and collects *B*'s gain from such cessation), rather than the choice between Rule 5 and Rule 3 (*A* continues), that is captivating. Instead, my sense is that we are too accustomed to entertaining the restitution tool only (and even then infrequently) where the loser's enrichment is "unjust." Rule 5's unbundling of the property right and liability results, such that one party stops doing business as usual while the *other* disgorges, is surprising because the disgorger is apparently neither wrongful nor unjust. The rule is about just enrichment rather than unjust enrichment. Viewed from a different perspective, albeit perhaps by process of elimination, what startles is that the degree of separation (between the property right and liability rule winners) is sufficient to make it plausible that the objecting party, *B*, will be left worse off than before. It happens that this feature, discussed presently in the next Section, is precisely what threatens to make the Krier-Schwab innovation self-destructive or at least rare (in a way that I think its authors did not fully anticipate), if only because *B* will no longer want to bring suits as the likelihood that her own complaints will make her worse off increases.

B. *Penalizing the Victim*

If a judge follows Krier-Schwab and allows the defendant, *A*, to continue on as before or instead choose to stop but then collect *B*'s (projected but not yet suffered) damages, *B* may well be sorry that she brought her complaint. It is not just that legal fees will have been wasted either when *B* loses, in the manner of Rule 3, and the injunction against *A* is denied, or when *A* opts for Rule 5 (*A* stops and collects *B*'s gain from this cessation) so that *B* gets what she asked for in harm-preventing terms, but only by paying her full reservation price.[53] The problem from *B*'s perspective is that *B* might not have been willing to pay this amount in order to stop *A*. Armed with the legal right to be free of pollution, *B* might have demanded $100,000, for example, before allowing *A* to send effluents her way, so that *B*'s damages from *A*'s operation can fairly be said to amount to $100,000; but this does not mean that *B* could or would pay this amount to stop *A*, if the law requires *B* to pay in order to change the status quo of *A*'s operation. The wealth effect of the property right might itself cause *B* to spend something less than $100,000 on clean air. This well-known offer-asking differential, or endowment effect, may often be small enough to ignore,[54] but inasmuch as every penny of *B*'s potential gain from

---

53. That is, *B* would have been willing to pay up to $2000 to be free of *A*'s pollution in the example considered *supra* in notes 6, 8, 41. However, *A* would have been willing to sell the right to pollute for as little as $1500.

54. For a discussion of the endowment effect, see Mark Kelman, *Consumption Theory, Production Theory, and Ideology in the Coase Theorem*, 52 S. CAL. L. REV. 669, 673 (1979); and Duncan Kennedy, *Cost-Benefit Analysis of Entitlement Problems: A Critique*, 33 STAN. L. REV. 387, 401–22 (1981).

A's cessation is here sought, the problem is likely to be present and significant in most instances.[55] There is something of an analogy here to the annoying insistence of a teacher that a student's request for the regrading of an exam will be entertained only on the condition that the student bear the risk that, when the exam is reviewed, it may be determined that the grade should be decreased rather than increased.[56]

A subtle (or even subconscious) comprehension of this problem may well be at the heart of what is startling about the Krier-Schwab innovation. *B* complains that *A*'s smokestack configuration causes *B* $100,000 in harm, and the shocking suggestion is that *A* can go on as before or choose to shut down (or alter the smokestack) and collect $100,000 from *B*. Even readers who are unfamiliar with the offer-asking literature may intuit that *B* is not indifferent, but is now worse off than before. None of the other rules threatens *B* in this manner.[57] Indeed, the companion rule, 5CE, introduced by Krier-Schwab as theoretically isomorphic to Rule 5, does not seem at all startling. It will be recalled that this companion rule also draws on the restitution idea as it offers *A* the choice between stopping (Rule 1) and continuing at the cost of paying (to *B*) *A*'s own gains from continuing rather than stopping (Rule 5CE). The fact that this proposal does not seem nearly as interesting as its partner, Rule 5 (*A* stops and collects *B*'s gain from cessation), suggests again that it is neither the choosing function nor the restitutionary quality that generates surprise, but rather the fact that only in Rule 5 is it the case that *B* can emerge worse off than before.[58]

It goes almost without saying that Rule 5 (*A* stops itself and collects *B*'s gain from this cessation) must be deployed cautiously. As noted earlier, there is the moral hazard that *A* will engage in an activity in order to induce a

---

55. A sloppy correction would be to redraft Rule 5 to provide either that *B* can be forced by *A* to disgorge some percentage of *B*'s gain from *A*'s cessation, or that the court should take the offer-asking differential into account in assessing the payment required of *B*.

56. The analogy to the offer-asking problem can be improved by noting that to make the regrading risk symmetrical and perhaps less obnoxious or self-serving, the teacher might lose something (or the student might be doubly rewarded) if the review proves the student correct. Tony Waters was gracious enough to point out the analogy to the British practice with respect to criminal appeals: A court reviewing a criminal sentence can raise as well as lower the penalty, while criminal defendants in U.S. courts have less to lose from complaining. This contrast makes certain assumptions about the government's behavior in cross-appealing and it also raises interesting and more general questions about the link between allowable responses to appeals (broadly understood) and rules of standing (as in who can appeal and how often), but I leave these interesting positive and normative matters for another day.

57. Again, I leave out legal fees, because it might be suggested that the British Rule threatens *B* in this manner and yet such a rule would, without startling, make a list of possible remedies more comprehensive.

58. The surprise may also come from the separation of the choosing function from the paying function because Rule 5 reflects that separation while Rule 5CE (*A* chooses and *A* pays) does not and Rule 4 entails not choosing and paying (because *A* is offered no choice) but the separation of stopping from paying. But I suggested earlier that it was Rule 5 and not the choice (between Rules 5 and 3) that startled. A judicial decision *requiring* *A* to stop and collect *B*'s (unsuffered) damages (subject to *B*'s ability to bargain around this decision) would startle, I think, without this separation.

complaint and then profit from stopping and collecting.[59] The possibility that a judge will use Rule 3 (*A* may continue as before) presents much less of an encouragement for *A*'s strategic, inefficient location; not only is the potential payment from *B* greater in Rule 5, but also with Rule 3, *B* can simply decline to offer to pay *A*, so that *A* will lose out if it has located simply to extract payment from *B*. In contrast, Rule 5 forces *B* to pay at *A*'s insistence and, therefore, poses more of a moral hazard problem. Put differently, if Rule 5 is in each judge's portfolio, then there is the risk that *B* will be truly harmed by an antisocial, inefficient *A*, but will nevertheless decline to object for fear that she will trigger a Rule 5 decision and be yet worse off. *B* must think that there is a substantial chance of victory in the form of the judicial imposition of Rule 1 (*A* is stopped), Rule 2 (*A* pays *B*), or any of a number of other rules in order to complain about *A*'s wrong.

III. UNIFYING SUBSTANTIVE AND LITIGATION-CONTROLLING REMEDIES

A. *Deterring Excessive Claims*

In retrospect, an interesting way to describe the expansion of the four-rule framework over the last twenty-five years is that from an initial shape designed around the three most common patterns of judicial decisions, the framework has been stretched to cover the entire bargaining range. Given the default (and alienable) character of most of these "rules," it is almost surprising that the stretching has gone so slowly unless the thinking has been that default rules should rarely amount to corner solutions.[60] Rule 5 (*A* stops and collects *B*'s gain from the cessation) extracts from *B* all that she could possibly want to pay to stop *A*, while Rule 5CE (*A* continues but pays its gain from doing so) calls for the most *A* would be willing to pay in order to be allowed to continue rather than stop.[61] If a judge's goal is to generate efficient and fair default rules, taking into account the likelihood and outcomes of private bargains following the case-by-case issuance of judicial decisions or default positions,[62] it may be hard to see why Rule 5 or 5CE would ever be selected.[63] Indeed, this probably explains both why Krier and Schwab use

---

59. Note that this is true even if Rule 5 is redrafted to award but a fraction of *B*'s claimed damages. *See supra* text accompanying note 54 (describing potentially limited impact of offer-asking problem).

60. We generally expect the result of bargaining between parties to produce some type of compromise solution; that Rule 5 would be the result of a bargain therefore strikes us as counterintuitive. Again, it seems unlikely that *B* would accept Rule 5 in a bargaining context, as it may leave her worse off than under the status quo.

61. Perhaps we should think of each rule as demanding payment of one dollar less than what has been described in the text (and by Krier-Schwab) in order to make it seem plausible that the chooser might actually select either of the proffered options.

62. I include bargains reached in the shadow of judicial decisions, but based on the parties' understanding of what is likely to happen to them if their case is taken to court.

63. Hard, but not impossible. There may be times when Rule 5 makes sense, for instance, because *A*'s

each of these options only as an element of a choice offered to the better decisionmaker, and why Calabresi and Melamed might not wish that they had set out these options twenty-five years ago (instead of, or in addition to, the straightforward victory and loss for *A* represented by Rules 1 and 3, respectively) as a way of defining the end points of the decisionmaking (and bargaining) spectrum.

There is, however, potential value to Rule 5—and to other rules as well—that is easy to miss. It will seem at first that if *A* chooses to stop and extract *B*'s "gain," rather than to continue as before, then it is often pointless or dangerous for the legal system to incur the transaction costs of the assessment of damages and transfer from *B*. *A* has revealed that its avoidance costs are less than *B*'s damages, and the same choosing function could have been assigned through Rule 2 (*A* pays *B*'s damages); the threat of damages would have caused *A* to stop and it would normally seem unjust—and risky in moral hazard terms[64]—for the antisocial *A* to collect from the victim, *B*.[65] But if we modify the Krier-Schwab idea so that, instead of asking the court to assess *B*'s would-be damages, we insert into Rule 5 *B*'s *alleged* damages, then we can appreciate the value of offering *A* a choice between Rule 3 (*A* can continue) and Rule 5 (*A* stops and collects *B*'s gain from the cessation). This choice combines some least cost avoidance, or "choosing," with a novel check on *B*'s allegations. Rule 5 can serve to control *B*'s temptation to overstate her damages in an attempt to convince the court that Rule 1 (*A* is stopped) or Rule 2 (*A* pays *B*), for example, is appropriate.[66] *B* will recognize that an overstatement can lead to disaster because if a judge uses Rule 5, then *B* will need to pay the amount stated as if *B* gains that amount from the decision to stop *A*. The occasional use of Rule 5—or giving *A* the choice between Rules 3 (*A* can continue) and 5 (*A* stops itself and collects *B*'s gain from the cessation)—will encourage *B* to be careful in her allegations about the facts that are most in her control. The beauty of this particular incentive for better self-assessment or litigation behavior is that there is no additional threat to

---

avoidance costs are surely less than *B*'s damages, and there is an intuition that *A* should be paid something more than *A*'s own avoidance costs.

64. At the very least, there is the danger that *A* will set up the antisocial activity near *B* in order to induce a complaint and possibly profit from a decision following Rule 5. Of course, the day after collecting *B*'s damages, *A* will simply go elsewhere or perhaps not operate anywhere at all. In that case, perhaps the moral hazard only arises where the court has incorrectly and overgenerously computed *A*'s avoidance costs. On the other hand, inaccurate assessments may be inevitable.

65. However, Rule 5 may be attractive where *A* is the more sympathetic party or *B*'s claim is difficult to verify.

66. Again, Rule 5 will be most useful where the judge has little or no information and where the judge is not known to overuse this approach. There are, to be sure, other means of encouraging accurate self-assessments, beginning with occasional independent inquiries by courts (and penalties for exaggerations), but this sort of further expansion of the range of remedies is beyond the scope of this Essay. The information-forcing component of this Essay could be seen as expanding on the discussion in Ayres & Talley, *supra* note 2, at 1062–65.

efficiency when it is misapplied.[67] Judges can use this rule when they sense that *B* has overstated her potential damages from *A*'s operations.[68] Even if this is a misassessment, however, *A* will still perform the choosing function and continue its operation as before only when *B*'s damages are less than *A*'s avoidance costs. The rule is thus information-forcing in the important sense that it controls *B*'s incentive to overassess potential damages. Put differently and less optimistically, there is something to offset the moral hazard (and offer-asking) problem associated with Rule 5: The gains from more accurate allegations by *B* may sometimes exceed the costs associated with creating conflicts where none would have materialized in the absence of the availability of Rule 5.

Inasmuch as it too is based on what might be thought of as maximum hypothetical restitution, Rule 5CE (*A* continues but pays its gain from doing so) shares this ability to deter excessive claims but with respect to *A* rather than *B*—and only if *A* is not given a choice between remedies. The possibility that a judge will require *A* to continue as before but disgorge its alleged avoidance costs (now saved because Rule 1 (*A* is stopped) was not selected) will encourage *A* not to overstate its avoidance costs. *A* may press for Rule 3 (*A* can continue), for example, by trying to convince the court that its avoidance costs are truly high while *B*'s damages are low, but the threat of Rule 5CE can control the temptation to overstate one's avoidance costs. Moreover, if the court errs in its estimate that *A* has exaggerated, the social harm is limited because *A* is, after all, permitted under 5CE to continue operating as before. Finally, the worst outcomes in efficiency terms are avoided, as usual, so long as the parties manage to bargain. If, for example, *A* has greatly overstated its avoidance costs and the court responds with 5CE, then *A* can offer to stop in return for *B*'s agreeing to accept something less than the alleged avoidance costs that *A* has been told to pay. The point is that *A* cannot simply avoid this obligation by now choosing to stop.[69]

B. *Combining Substantive and Procedural Remedies*

The original four-rule framework did not ignore the realities of litigation and factfinding. Its authors suggested that a judge's choice among remedies

---

67. This assumes that *B* can cheaply ascertain her own actual damages. Note that the incentive to engage in some combination of self-assessment and appraisal of what courts and adversaries will think and do is analogous to that provided by a variety of well-known schemes in systems with and without a background rule of fee-shifting. For example, Rule 68 of the Federal Rules of Civil Procedure, FED. R. CIV. P. 68, aims to encourage offers of settlement and the acceptance of reasonable offers by attaching a cost to continued litigation following what appears ex post to have been a reasonable offer of settlement.

68. Of course, they can also use it when considerations of fairness recommend it; I have already suggested that such situations will be extremely rare.

69. This is contrary to Krier and Schwab's version of this rule, in which the polluter is the chooser and the avoidance costs are those that are determined by the court. Note that for simplicity's sake I am assuming that *A* knows well its own avoidance costs.

might be based on the judge's degree of confidence about the relative magnitude of damages and benefits, as well as the likelihood of collective action problems or other impediments to bargaining.[70] The capacity of courts to assess these things, both systematically and in case-by-case terms, was plainly understood to enter the calculus of selecting among remedies. Nor was this a new way of thinking, for the field of remedies had been long accustomed to integrating substantive remedies with factfinding considerations. For example, the "irreparable injury" mantra, invoked by a court confident enough to issue ex ante injunctive relief, and therefore inclined to say that ex post damages would not make the plaintiffs whole, reflects the very same thinking about property rules versus liability rules.[71] Somewhat similarly, the additional procedural burdens placed on plaintiffs who seek preliminary injunctions reflect serious thinking about substantive decisions (and errors) and procedural rules.[72] Nevertheless, there is a tendency in thinking about rights and remedies to exile or hold constant some "procedural" considerations. Thus, discussions about remedies take the plaintiff's burden of persuasion as given, with no attention paid to the possibility that the choice between damages and injunctive relief, for example, might be linked to this burden (or to switching it).[73] More provocatively, the choice between negligence and strict liability, or, for that matter, between damages and injunctions, might be linked to the acceptability of contingency fees.[74] Similarly, the choice between partial and full property rules might be tied to the terms of fee-shifting rules.[75] We are not yet accustomed to thinking about these kinds of substantive-procedural connections. It is common to recognize such things as the ability of courts to shift legal costs and to levy penalties for inappropriate discovery behavior when attempting to construct a complete list of remedies, but it is uncommon to integrate these items in a way that illuminates the choices among more "substantive" remedies. I have tried to suggest that with modest effort such unification is possible and worthwhile. I suspect that the next twenty-five years

---

70. *See* Calabresi & Melamed, *supra* note 1, at 1122.

71. Doug Laycock has suggested that the irreparable injury rule actually does very little work in explaining cases. *See, e.g.*, Laycock, *supra* note 28, at 54–55 ("When I say that the irreparable injury rule is dead, I do not mean that judges no longer talk about it in opinions. Rather, I mean that the rule is always satisfied, so that it never constrains a court's decision in any case where the choice of remedy matters.").

72. Thus, plaintiffs may be required to post a bond before seeking a preliminary injunction. The bond assures defendants of compensation in the event that they are injured by a preliminary injunction that was wrongfully granted. *See* FED. R. CIV. P. 65, 65.1.

73. Thus virtually every rule in the expanded Calabresi-Melamed framework could be further subdivided with alterations in the burden of proof.

74. It is apparent that the plaintiff's attorney, working on a contingency fee basis, will prefer to win liability awards rather than property "rights." This preference may in turn affect the ideal use of these rules by judges.

75. The idea is that if partial victories avoid penalties for refusing settlements or cost-shifting in systems built around a fee-shifting, or British, rule, then there is likely to be some feedback as to the appropriateness of the substantive rule itself.

will see great strides on this front, with the links between substantive and procedural rules more clearly understood than they are today.

IV. CONCLUSION

The exploration of links between remedies and procedures and the development of new rules (of the kind introduced here and in the earlier works to which I have referred) reinvigorate the Calabresi-Melamed framework. These research paths will guarantee, I predict, the continuing place of the Calabresi and Melamed article as one of the most cited and important law review articles of all time, and as one of a very few pieces that influenced a generation of scholars at the same time that it educated students new to the law. One particular advance suggested here is that, when we explore that which is most startling about the property and liability rules literature and recognize the importance (and availability) of information-forcing rules, we can expand the scope of the original four-rule framework with more reconceptualization than added complexity. Calabresi and Melamed's success in linking rights and remedies and in creating an elegant framework capable of accommodating many remedies can be extended to introduce tools that control strategic litigation. And the limits of the bargaining range reveal specific—and even startling—tools that can control strategic litigation without much risk of inefficient results.

APPENDIX: SUMMARY OF REMEDIES

RULE	DESCRIPTION
1	*B* stops *A* and collects for past injuries
1E	*B* stops *A* and *A* disgorges earlier wrongful gains
1F	*B* stops *A* but does not collect for past injuries
1P	*B* stops *A* up to a point, and *A* pays damages associated with its lawful operation
2C	*A* pays *B*, but may be stopped later on
General Average Contribution	Nonnegligent *A* shares in *B*'s loss if part of same community
2S	*A* pays *B* even if not negligent
2 or 2N	Negligent *A* pays *B*
2E	*A* pays *B* its own unjust enrichment
2B	*A* pays only for past injuries to *B*
2F	*A* pays only for future damages to *B*
2X	*A* pays what *B* might have extracted if *B* had property right to sell
3	*A* can continue as before
4	*B* stops *A* but pays *A* (at least *A*'s relocation costs)
5	*A* stops and collects *B*'s gain from this cessation; *A* could opt for Rule 3
5CE	*A* chooses to continue but pays its own enrichment from doing so

[11]

PLIABILITY RULES

Abraham Bell* and Gideon Parchomovsky**

TABLE OF CONTENTS

---

* S.J.D. candidate, Harvard Law School. A.B. 1989, J.D. 1993, University of Chicago.

** Assistant Professor of Law, University of Pennsylvania Law School. L.L.B. 1993, Hebrew University of Jerusalem; LL.M. 1995, University of California, Berkeley; J.S.D. 1998, Yale. — Ed.

This Article greatly benefited from comments and criticisms by Ian Ayres, Hanina Ben Menahem, Yemima Ben Menahem, Hanoch Dagan, Brad Daniels, Kirsten Edwards, Bob Ellickson, Assaf Hamdani, Israel Gilead, Alon Harel, Fred Schauer, Steve Shavell, Peter Siegelman, Benjamin Zipursky, and participants in the Law and Economics and Faculty Seminars of the Fordham Law School, Hebrew University of Jerusalem's Faculty of Law and the University of San Diego Law School, as well as from Michael Pereira's excellent research assistance. We are grateful for the financial support of the John M. Olin Center for Law, Economics, and Business at Harvard Law School. Finally, we acknowledge our intellectual debt to the teachings of Guido Calabresi and Douglas Melamed, whose work has so enriched our scholarship.

INTRODUCTION

In 1543, the Polish astronomer, Nicolas Copernicus, determined the heliocentric design of the solar system.[1] Copernicus was motivated in large part by the conviction that Claudius Ptolemy's geocentric astronomical model, which dominated scientific thought at that time, was too incoherent, complex, and convoluted to be true.[2] Hence, Copernicus made a point of making his model coherent, simple, and elegant. Nearly three and a half centuries later, at the height of the impressionist movement, the French painter Claude Monet set out to depict the Ruen Cathedral in a series of twenty paintings,[3] each presenting the cathedral in a different light. Monet's goal was to demonstrate how his object of study may be perceived by observers differently depending on the circumstances of the observation. In the spirit of these two projects, in 1972, Guido Calabresi and Douglas Melamed resolved to craft a comprehensive, yet elegant,[4] model for

---

1. *See* JACOB BRONOWSKI & BRUCE MAZLISH, THE WESTERN INTELLECTUAL TRADITION 113 (1960). For the purpose of historic accuracy, it is important to note that 1543 was the year in which Copernicus published his REVOLUTIONS OF THE HEAVENLY BODIES. It is highly likely that Copernicus completed his account well before 1543, but was afraid that his views would offend the religious establishment of his time. Thus, Copernicus delayed the publication of his book until 1543, the year of his death, and rumor has it that he died holding the first printed copy of the book in his hands. *Id.*

2. *Id.* at 112-15.

3. *See* KARIN SAGNER-DÜCHTING, CLAUDE MONET, 1840-1926, at 172-73 (1998).

4. *See* Guido Calabresi, *Remarks: The Simple Virtues of the Cathedral*, 106 YALE L.J. 2201, 2202 (1997) [hereinafter Calabresi, *Remarks*] (stating that the Calabresi-Melamedian framework was intended to be simple and elegant); Saul Levmore, *Unifying Remedies: Property Rules, Liability Rules, and Startling Rules*, 106 YALE L.J. 2149, 2155 (1997) (commending Calabresi and Melamed for the elegance of their model).

organizing the universe of legal entitlements.[5] The article's impact has been profound and enduring.[6]

In their path-breaking article, *Property Rules, Liability Rules, and Inalienability: One View of the Cathedral,*[7] Calabresi and Melamed established a new way of conceptualizing legal rights and duties. Departing from traditional jurisprudential notions, Calabresi and Melamed introduced the concepts of "property rules" and "liability rules" as the ordering principles of the legal system, and then analyzed their virtues and vices as means of protecting legal entitlements. Property rule protection forces potential takers to secure the consent of the entitlement owner, and thus allows the owner to determine the price of her entitlement. Liability rule protection, by contrast, allows potential takers to avail themselves of other people's entitlements as long as they are willing to pay a collectively determined price that is usually set by a court, a legislator, or an administrative agency.[8]

Having introduced the distinction between property rules and liability rules, Calabresi and Melamed ventured to explain how these rules should be employed to promote economic efficiency. Their normative insight was that property rules should be favored over liability

---

5. Guido Calabresi & A. Douglas Melamed, *Property Rules, Liability Rules, and Inalienability: One View of the Cathedral*, 85 HARV. L. REV. 1089 (1972). Following convention, we will call the article *The Cathedral*.

6. Virtually all citation studies list Calabresi and Melamed's article as one of the top thirty most-cited articles. *See, e.g.*, Fred R. Shapiro, *The Most-Cited Law Review Articles*, 73 CAL. L. REV. 1540 (1985); Fred R. Shapiro, *The Most-Cited Law Review Articles Revisited*, 71 CHI.-KENT L. REV. 751 (1996). According to Shapiro's citation studies, *The Cathedral* ranked twenty-second in 1985, and climbed up to number eleven in 1996. A different study by Krier and Schwab ranks *The Cathedral* as the fourteenth most cited article. *See* James E. Krier & Stewart J. Schwab, *The Cathedral at Twenty Five: Citations and Impressions*, 106 YALE L.J. 2121, 2140 (1997) [hereinafter Krier & Schwab, *Citations and Impressions*].

It bears emphasis, however, that no citation study can capture the full impact of *The Cathedral*. In our experience, very few scholarly works have affected legal thought as did *The Cathedral*. Our impression is consistent with the findings of Krier and Schwab, who report that "Calabresi and Melamed's contribution to the literature has had a significant and ongoing, even increasing, influence." *Id.* at 2130. They, too, note that "evidence of the importance of their work is found in the many anthologies, casebooks, and textbooks that reproduce [the work] in whole or in part or otherwise discuss or refer to it." *Id.* Furthermore, the framework devised by Calabresi and Melamed is taught and discussed in property and tort law classes, and is often extended to other legal fields. *See* Levmore, *supra* note 4, at 2151 (noting that "some of the value of the Calabresi-Melamed framework lies in its ability to illuminate fields outside of traditional property and tort law"); *accord* Krier & Schwab, *Citations and Impressions, supra* at 2130 (noting that "Calabresi and Melamed's article figures regularly in books on subjects like Property, Torts, and Contracts").

7. 85 HARV. L. REV. 1089 (1972).

8. In principle, the price of the use may be determined by any third party. For example, two parties may contractually agree to accept any price X would set for the entitlement. The determination may occur either ex ante, before the taking occurs, or ex post, following the taking.

As the title of their article suggests, Calabresi and Melamed also discussed a third type of protection: inalienability rules. An entitlement protected by an inalienability rule cannot be transferred at any price.

rules when transaction costs are low, and parties can cost-effectively bargain with one another. When, on the other hand, transaction costs are high, and voluntary bargaining cannot be expected, liability rules should be employed.

In the vast literature that followed,[9] commentators have attempted to refine, revamp, and, at times, challenge the Calabresi-Melamedian analysis. In particular, attempts have been made to distinguish between various types of transaction costs, and then examine which type of rules is better suited to combat each particular cost. Yet, the analytical structure devised by Calabresi and Melamed, and in particular, the foundational distinction between property and liability rules, has been accepted by virtually all the commentators — supporters and critics alike. The Calabresi-Melamedian typology has been widely understood to exhaust all possible ways of protecting legal entitlements, and the binary system they devised has dominated legal thought and scholarship. Almost thirty years after its publication, *The Cathedral* is experiencing a renaissance as increasing numbers of preeminent scholars flock to reevaluate and improve upon Calabresi and Melamed's classic.[10] This Article shares the same ambition.

We contend that, while the Calabresi-Melamedian framework presents a solid basis for understanding legal entitlements,[11] a more com-

---

9. *See, e.g.,* Ian Ayres & Paul M. Goldbart, *Optimal Delegation and Decoupling in the Design of Liability Rules,* 100 MICH. L. REV. 1 (2001); Richard Craswell, *Property Rules and Liability Rules in Unconscionability and Related Doctrines,* 60 U. CHI. L. REV. 1 (1993); Robert C. Ellickson, *Alternatives to Zoning: Covenants, Nuisance Rules, and Fines as Land Use Controls,* 40 U. CHI. L. REV. 681 (1973); Ward Farnsworth, *Do Parties to Nuisance Cases Bargain After Judgment? A Glimpse Inside the Cathedral,* 66 U. CHI. L. REV. 373 (1999); Zohar Goshen, *Controlling Strategic Voting: Property Rule or Liability Rule?,* 70 S. CAL. L. REV. 741 (1997); Louis Kaplow & Steven Shavell, *Property Rules Versus Liability Rules: An Economic Analysis,* 109 HARV. L. REV. 713 (1996); Daphna Lewinsohn-Zamir, *The Choice Between Property Rules and Liability Rules Revisited: Critical Observations from Behavioral Studies,* 80 TEXAS L. REV. 219 (2001); Robert P. Merges, *Contracting into Liability Rules: Intellectual Property Rights and Collective Rights Organizations,* 84 CAL. L. REV. 1293 (1996); Thomas W. Merrill & Henry E. Smith, *What Happened to Property in Law and Economics?,* 111 YALE L.J. 357 (2001); Dale A. Nance, *Guidance Rules and Enforcement Rules: A Better View of the Cathedral,* 83 VA. L. REV. 837 (1997); A. Mitchell Polinsky, *Resolving Nuisance Disputes: The Simple Economics of Injunctive and Damage Remedies,* 32 STAN. L. REV. 1075 (1980); Susan Rose-Ackerman, *Inalienability and the Theory of Property Rights,* 85 COLUM. L. REV. 931 (1985); Symposium, *Property Rules, Liability Rules and Inalienability: A Twenty-Five Year Retrospective,* 106 YALE L.J. 2081 (1997). This list is intended to be illustrative; it is far from being exhaustive. We discuss many other articles in the text and in subsequent footnotes.

10. See sources cited *supra* note 9.

11. A brief caveat is in order here. It is very possible that Calabresi and Melamed noticed other ways to protect legal entitlements, but decided, for the sake of simplicity and elegance, to discuss only property, liability, and inalienability rules in their celebrated article. As Calabresi illuminated in a recent symposium that marked the twenty-fifth anniversary of *The Cathedral,* crucial distinctions and nuances "were left out because I *had* to make [the article] simple so that people would understand it." Calabresi, *Remarks, supra* note 4, at 2202. It is safe to assert, however, that *The Cathedral* does not discuss, or even mention, pliability rules and the important functions they serve in the legal system.

plete analysis must probe beyond the ostensible dichotomy between property and liability rules. We seek to add another level to Calabresi and Melamed's analysis, to capture fully the protection of entitlements in our legal system.

By looking at their cathedral frozen in a moment in time — as in a single one of Monet's paintings — Calabresi and Melamed have overlooked the importance of examining the cathedral over the course of time, as did Monet's series. More concretely, by focusing their attention on *static* property and liability rules, Calabresi and Melamed have obscured the possibility of protecting legal entitlements by means of *dynamic* rules that we call "pliability rules."[12]

Pliability, or pliable, rules are contingent rules that provide an entitlement owner with property rule or liability rule protection as long as some specified condition obtains; however, once the relevant condition changes, a different rule protects the entitlement — either liability or property, as the circumstances dictate. Pliability rules, in other words, are dynamic rules, while property and liability rules are static. This can be seen by revisiting the famous case of *Boomer v. Atlantic Cement Co.*[13] In *Boomer*, homeowners near a manufacturing plant of Atlantic Cement complained that the plant's pollution gave rise to an actionable nuisance, and they sought an injunction that would close down the plant. The court, however, decided to permit the plant to continue operations, subject to its payment of permanent damages to the homeowners. Calabresi and Melamed viewed the case as presenting a choice between enforcing property rule protection, as the homeowners demanded, or liability rule protection, as the court eventually ruled. Calabresi and Melamed believed these to be the two basic options[14] because they — like the theorists that followed them — focused on discrete moments of legal protection in isolation. In reality, though, the court could have chosen a pliability rule. For example, the court might have allowed Atlantic Cement to pay damages and continue operating for five years to avoid immediate and massive layoffs at the plant, but also decree that at the end of the five years, the injunction would become absolute to enable homeowners' quiet and clean use of their realty.[15] This pliable rule — a five-year liability rule, followed by

---

12. The term "pliability rule" owes its origin to Peter Siegelman, who suggested it in a conversation with one of the authors.

13. 257 N.E.2d 870 (N.Y. 1970).

14. Calabresi and Melamed allowed for four options: property rule protection in the hands of either the homeowner or plant, and liability rule protection for either the homeowner or plant.

15. As we discuss later, pliability rules can come in many forms, and may involve any number of different combinations of property and liability rules. *See infra* Part II.

indefinite property rule protection — would permit the court to combine the features of liability and property rules over the course of time.

While the term "pliability rule" is original, this mode of legal entitlement has long existed in our legal system. The legal protection of share ownership in mergers is a classic example of a positive pliability rule. Consider the case of a corporate takeover succeeded by a freeze-out. The minority shareholders can either accept the price offered by the acquirer or exercise their appraisal right, in which case a court will determine the appropriate compensation. In either case, the minority shareholders lose the ability to refuse to part with their shares. In other words, their initial property rule protection changes into a liability rule. As in other liability rules, the price they will receive is not determined by them; it is set by a third party.

Likewise, a real property owner may lose her property right if she allows adverse possessors to take hold of her land and use it openly for a statutorily specified period. The property rule protection of the landowner is conditional since it depends on her vigilance in safeguarding her land against potential takers. Failure to perform this duty erases the original protection of the land and transfers it to the adverse possessor. Adverse possession thus creates a "title shifting pliability rule," that is, a combination of property rules in which the triggering of a condition transfers property rule protection from the original entitlement holder to another.

Another pervasive kind of pliability rule in the law is "the zero order pliability rule." In fact, zero order pliability rules are the organizing principle of much of our intellectual property law. In zero order pliability rules, property rule protection is succeeded by a no liability rule. Specifically, upon a triggering event, the initial entitlement holder loses the ability to exercise property rule protection, such as the right to exclude, over her property. Instead the entitlement holder must allow all comers to use the property free of charge — that is, with zero order liability. Importantly, the subject item has not been abandoned. Notwithstanding the zero order liability, no third party may gain a superior right to that of the original entitlement holder. Rather, zero order pliability rules create anti-exclusion, or open access regimes. Consider, for example, a patent. A patent confers upon the patentee property rule protection for twenty years, but, upon the expiration of that term, the nature of protection changes from a property rule to a zero order liability rule since she can no longer refuse others the right to use her patent.[16] Copyright law provides a similar example.

---

16. To be sure, it is possible to think of other ways of characterizing patent protection. For instance, it is possible to view it as a property rule limited in time. Alternatively, it is possible to classify patent protection as a property rule protection to the patentee followed by a property rule protection to the user. We do not dispute that both of these alternative characterizations are plausible. Both, however, obfuscate the possibility of viewing patent

These examples, and others, show the attractiveness of pliability rules. Pliability rules combine two separate rules; with the passage between the two stages of rule protection triggered by a preset condition. Owing to their amalgamated nature, pliability rules are capable of combining the respective strengths of property and liability rules while avoiding their respective weaknesses. Pliability rules allow decisionmakers to avoid the all-or-nothing decision of creating property rule or liability rule protection. Instead, decisionmakers may build flexibility into the rule, setting conditions that switch from a stronger to a weaker protection of entitlements (or vice versa) when economic efficiency or fairness considerations so require. As a result, pliability rules present decision makers with a wide array of options that are unavailable to them in the Calabresi-Melamedian bipolar world of property and liability rules.

This Article has three goals: the first conceptual, the second descriptive, and the last normative. Conceptually, we demonstrate that pliability rules fall in a distinct category of rule protection, and that they must be recognized alongside their more familiar counterparts — property and liability rules. Descriptively, we show that, although this fact may have eluded Calabresi and Melamed,[17] pliability rules are widely used in our legal system. Furthermore, we devise a typology of pliability rules to illuminate the myriad options the use of such rules presents to policy makers. Normatively, we argue that in many cases pliability rules can promote economic efficiency, and fairness, better than either property rules or liability rules. The two main legal fields we use to substantiate these claims are property and intellectual property, but we also show that pliability rules are present in other legal areas, such as antitrust and corporate law.

---

protection as a continuum starting with property rule protection, which endures for twenty years, and then shifts into a zero order liability rule. Thinking of patent protection as a "zero order pliability rule" is helpful as it sensitizes one to the possibility of "positive pliability rules," i.e., pliability rules which set the liability amount above zero. Furthermore, it is important to recall that patent and copyright differ from traditional property rights because they are limited in time; standard property rights, on the other hand, may exist in perpetuity. Thus, it is useful to distinguish the theoretical characterization of the protection accorded by the Patent and Copyright Acts from that accorded to regular property entitlements. For these reasons, we propose that patent and copyright protection should be thought of as zero order pliability rules.

The idea of equating no-liability with zero-liability protection draws on a famous insight of Ian Ayres and Robert Gertner, who, in characterizing U.C.C. § 2-201, provided that a contract failing to specify quantity is enforceable as a "zero-quantity default." They justify the "zero-quantity default" by noting "it is cheaper for the parties to establish the quantity term beforehand than for the courts to determine after the fact what the parties would have wanted." Ian Ayres & Robert Gertner, *Filling Gaps in Incomplete Contracts: An Economic Theory of Default Rules*, 99 YALE L.J. 87, 96 (1989).

17. *See* Levmore, *supra* note 4, at 2157 (noting that because Calabresi and Melamed sought elegance as opposed to comprehensiveness, it would be wrong to describe them as having "missed" remedies not explicitly discussed in their article).

Structurally, the Article consists of three parts. In Part I, we review Calabresi and Melamed's seminal article, as well as its predecessors and progeny. In Part II, we present the concept of pliability rules. We identify the many areas of law in which pliability rules are already in use, and discuss how the use of pliability rules serves to promote efficiency and fairness. Among the instances of pliability rule protection we discuss are those used in eminent domain, copyright, antitrust, and corporate law, as well as the doctrine of adverse possession. Finally, in Part III, we draw on the analysis in Part II to suggest how policymakers may use pliability rules in the future to enhance social utility. Here, we show how a pliability analysis can reshape key doctrines of property and intellectual property law. We then venture even further and demonstrate how the use of pliability rules can be used to overcome anticommons problems that plague the integrity of such vulnerable social units as Native American tribes and rural African-American communities. We conclude by discussing the potential of a pliability analysis to revolutionize the doctrine of eminent domain.

I.   THE EVOLUTION OF ENTITLEMENT THEORY

A.   *Coase and the Problem of Social Cost*

To fully appreciate the contribution of Calabresi and Melamed, it is necessary to begin with Ronald Coase's seminal article *The Problem of Social Cost*.[18] Importantly, Coase was not interested in the assignment of legal entitlements per se, but rather in the problem of externalities — the costs and benefits of one's activity on third parties that are not captured by the price system. The paradigmatic manifestation of the externalities problem that concerned Coase and his contemporaries was industrial pollution.[19] Coase's primary aim was to challenge the Pigouvian theory that government intervention in the form of taxation was necessary to remedy the problem of social cost. Specifically, Pigou had proposed that the government levy a tax on polluters in the amount of the social harm they cause in order to force them to consider this cost in their production decisions.[20] By contrast to Pigou, and the other theorists of his time, who focused exclusively on the

---

18. Ronald H. Coase, *The Problem of Social Cost*, 3 J.L. & ECON. 1 (1960).

19. *See* Henry E. Smith, *Ambiguous Quality Changes from Taxes and Legal Rules*, 67 U. CHI. L. REV. 647, 684 n.87 (2000) (noting that "[i]n his critique of Pigouvian taxes, Coase proposed that property rights could internalize pollution externalities"); *cf.* Carol M. Rose, *The Shadow of the Cathedral*, 106 YALE L.J. 2175, 2189 (1997) [hereinafter Rose, *Shadow of the Cathedral*] (noting that Calabresi and Melamed cited "air pollution and noise (including the ubiquitous *Boomer*) as examples of negative 'externalities' "). For a more recent treatment of industrial pollution using the Calabresi-Melamedian framework, see Kaplow & Shavell, *supra* note 9, at 748-52.

20. *See* ARTHUR C. PIGOU, THE ECONOMICS OF WELFARE 159 (2d ed. 1925); ARTHUR C. PIGOU, WEALTH AND WELFARE (1912).

polluter, Coase observed that pollution — as well as all other externalities — are reciprocal in nature. Coase was the first to notice that, in principle, not only the wrongdoer but also the victim can eliminate the harm. If pollution from a nearby factory prevents residents from hanging their laundry outdoors, the harm can be eliminated in one of two ways: the factory can install smokescreens on its chimneys or the residents can purchase electric dryers.[21]

Realizing the reciprocal nature of the externalities problem enabled Coase to notice an important connection between contracts and torts. More specifically, it enabled Coase to see that private bargaining may substitute for regulatory intervention as a means of controlling social harms. From there, the Coase theorem was very much in sight, but it took another ingenious step to get there.

To demonstrate the flaw in Pigou's analysis, Coase conjured up a frictionless world in which transacting is costless.[22] He then showed that, in such a world, private bargaining would always yield the economically efficient outcome regardless of the initial allocation of legal entitlements or liabilities.[23] Coase recognized the need for clear delineation and assignment of legal entitlements as a prerequisite for bargaining even in his zero transaction cost world.[24] But once this task is accomplished, no other legal rules are necessary since private bargaining would override any legal norm and result in efficient resource

---

21. *See* A. MITCHELL POLINSKY, AN INTRODUCTION TO LAW AND ECONOMICS 11-14 (2d ed. 1989).

22. *Cf.* R.H. COASE, THE FIRM, THE MARKET, AND THE LAW 174 (1988) ("The world of zero transaction costs has often been described as a Coasian world. Nothing could be further from the truth. It is the world of modern economic theory, one which I was hoping to persuade economists to leave.").

23. This formulation has come to be known as the "strong version," or the "invariance version" of the Coase Theorem. *See* Thomas S. Ulen, *Flogging a Dead Pig: Professor Posin on the Coase Theorem*, 38 WAYNE L. REV. 91 (1991). A "weaker" version of the Coase Theorem maintains that in a world without transaction costs the allocation of entitlements would not influence the total value of output, but it might affect the use of resources and the pattern of output. *See* Robert D. Cooter, *The Coase Theorem, in* THE NEW PALGRAVE: A DICTIONARY OF ECONOMICS (1987). It is debatable whether either version of the Coase theorem actually holds. Famously, Robert Cooter has pointed out that even in a world with zero transaction costs, strategic bargaining may thwart efficient allocation of resources. *See* Robert Cooter, *The Cost of Coase*, 11 J. LEGAL STUD. 1, 23 (1982). A different concern has been raised by Clifford Holderness, who proposes that the strong version only holds true when entitlements are granted to closed groups, but not when they are given to open groups that allow entry. *See* Clifford G. Holderness, *The Assignment of Rights, Entry Effects, and the Allocation of Resources*, 18 J. LEGAL STUD. 181 (1989). *But see* Henry E. Smith, Two Dimensions of Property Rights (Mar. 31, 2001) (unpublished manuscript, *cited in* Merrill & Smith, *supra* note 9, at 368 n.45) (suggesting that "[i]f transaction costs were truly zero . . . bargaining could costlessly close all classes"). It should be emphasized that the Coase theorem does not guarantee efficiency in positive transaction cost settings. *See* Dierdre McCloskey, *Other Things Equal: The So-Called Coase Theorem*, 24 E. ECON. J. 367 (1998).

24. Coase, *supra* note 18, at 8. *But see* Steven N.S. Cheung, *The Transaction Costs Paradigm*, 37 ECON. INQ. 514, 518-20 (1998) (questioning the need for a well-defined system of entitlement in a world with zero transaction costs).

allocation. If clean air were more valuable than the activity causing the pollution, residents would pay plants to shut down; if the opposite were true, industrial companies would pay residents to relocate.[25] Private ordering would rule; law could be shunted aside.

The transition to the real world, in the second part of the article, thrust law back to the fore. The introduction of positive transaction costs forced Coase to address the significance of legal rules, as well as of the courts administering them. Once the assumption of zero transaction costs is abandoned, Coase's analysis, although still illuminating, loses some of its analytical rigor. Coase's general prescription is that in a world with positive transaction costs, courts should assign property rights in a manner that maximizes the value of production.[26] In assessing the ability of the courts to reach efficient outcomes in particular cases, Coase reviewed a host of nuisance decisions. Although he failed to trace any economic theorizing in the decisions, and worse, he found the reasoning employed by the courts odd and irrelevant,[27] Coase concluded, somewhat surprisingly, that courts are conscious of the economic consequences of their decisions. Thus, at the end of the day, Coase was willing to entrust the courts with the challenging task of allocating legal entitlements efficiently.

Coase, however, did not provide the courts with any meaningful guidance as to how to perform this task. All he had to say was that, insofar as this is at all possible, courts should consult economic considerations in making their decisions without creating too much uncertainty about the legal position itself . . . ."[28] This proposal exposes an

---

25. An obvious problem with this conclusion, as well as with the Coase theorem in general, is that it ignores wealth effects. *See* Richard Craswell, *Passing on the Costs of Legal Rules: Efficiency and Distribution in Buyer-Seller Relationships*, 43 STAN. L. REV. 361, 385-91 (1991) (noting that Coase's model overlooks cognitive biases, such as wealth and framing effects); *see also* Ian Ayres & Jack Balkin, *Legal Entitlements as Auctions: Property Rules, Liability Rules, and Beyond*, 106 YALE L.J. 703, 718 n.52 (1998) (explaining that "wealth effects are produced by budget constraints on our ability to pay"). Although residents affected by the pollution may value the right to live pollution-free more highly than the activity generating the pollution, they may not have sufficient resources to pay the plants, causing the problem to shut down. If transactors do not possess sufficient funds, assuming away transaction costs would not help bring about efficient allocation of resources. *See* Herbert Hovenkamp, *Marginal Utility and the Coase Theorem*, 75 CORNELL L. REV. 783, 797-808 (1990) (noting that wealth effects are more common than is sometimes thought); William M. Landes, *Copyright, Borrowed Images, and Appropriation Art: An Economic Approach*, 9 GEO. MASON L. REV. 1, 21 (2000) (listing the absence of transaction costs and wealth effects as two preconditions for effective operation of the Coase theorem). *But see* Russell Korobkin, Note, *Policymaking and the Offer/Asking Price Gap: Toward a Theory of Efficient Entitlement Allocation*, 46 STAN. L. REV. 663, 679-82 (1994) (disputing Hovenkamp's wealth effect claims); *cf.* Christine Jolls, Cass R. Sunstein & Richard Thaler, *A Behavioral Approach to Law and Economics*, 50 STAN. L. REV. 1471, 1483 (1998) (observing that "even when transaction costs and wealth effects are known to be zero, initial entitlements alter the final allocation of resources").

26. *See* Coase, *supra* note 18, at 15-16.

27. *See id.* at 15.

28. *Id.* at 19.

inherent tension in Coase's analysis. On the one hand, Coase's article calls for a clear delimitation of legal rights in order to encourage private bargaining. On the other hand, its reliance on the courts injects a considerable degree of uncertainty into the legal system as it necessitates extensive use of judicial discretion to promote efficiency in particular cases. More importantly, perhaps, the two perspectives developed in Coase's article — the contractarian and the judicial — are in potential conflict when transaction costs are positive. The more courts exercise judicial restraint by deferring to private bargaining, the stronger the incentive to bargain privately. Conversely, when courts take an interventionist approach to private ordering, the incentive to bargain privately over efficient allocation of resources is significantly undermined. Yet, Coase did not suggest how this tension can be resolved, or which perspective, the contractarian or the judicial, should take precedence in cases of conflict. Ultimately, Coase advanced neither a theory, nor a list of factors, to help the courts in performing their charge; he trusted them, based on past performance, albeit a very mediocre one, to succeed in the future.

Despite these drawbacks, Coase's analysis is illuminating and it has been extremely influential. It would not be an exaggeration to state that Coase's discussion of transaction costs blazed the trail for all subsequent law and economics scholars. In particular, Coase's focus on contractual arrangements has elevated private bargaining to unprecedented heights, turning it into the primary focus of law and economics scholarship. Yet, Coase's analysis by itself did not aptly explain the role of legal norms in promoting efficiency; nor did it provide a positive account of how exactly, if at all, the law protects entitlements in the real world. Moreover, Coase did not discuss how entitlements should be protected after the initial allocation. These tasks were reserved for Calabresi and Melamed.

B. *The Calabresian-Melamedian Framework*

Unlike Coase, whose primary goal was to determine the role of government intervention in the regulation of harmful activities, Calabresi and Melamed's goal was to analyze the role of law in the assignment and protection of entitlements. Specifically, Calabresi and Melamed sought to shed light on the ways in which the legal system does, and ought to, protect rights. Yet, Coase's insights had a palpable influence on Calabresi and Melamed. His contractarian perspective and the careful attention to transaction costs informed much of Calabresi and Melamed's normative analysis. Due to their different focus and superior mastery of law, however, Calabresi and Melamed ventured far beyond Coase's legal insights and developed a new conceptualization of the law.

In *The Cathedral*, Calabresi and Melamed made three important contributions to legal theory. The first was conceptual. Calabresi and Melamed were the first to realize that a theory of entitlement allocation must address two questions, not one. One question is how to assign the entitlement initially between the contending parties. The other is how to protect the initial assignment.[29] In addressing the former question, Calabresi and Melamed did not advance a simple answer, or even a single principle according to which entitlements should be assigned. Instead, they proposed that in assigning entitlements, society should consider three broad types of considerations: economic efficiency, distributional preferences, and other justice reasons.[30] Calabresi and Melamed discussed and explored all three concerns, and, in contrast to Coase, they did not single out one value the courts should maximize. Rather, they advocated a careful weighing of the various criteria they listed as a basis for entitlement allocation in particular cases.[31]

Calabresi and Melamed's second important contribution was descriptive. In analyzing how the law protects entitlements, Calabresi and Melamed divided the universe of legal remedies into three modalities of protection: property rules, liability rules, and inalienability rules.[32] They defined the three modalities as follows. Property rule protection confers upon the entitlement holder the exclusive power to determine the price nonholders would have to pay for using the protected asset or right.[33] Thus, all transfers of entitlements protected by a property rule must be consensual; all attempts to transfer the entitlement nonconsensually would be met with an injunction. Liability rule protection, by contrast, gives the nonholder the power to take the entitlement without the consent of the entitlement holder and pay a price to be determined by a third party, typically a court or the legislature. The entitlement holder would not be able to enjoin third parties from taking her entitlement; instead, she would have to settle for damages.[34]

---

29. Calabresi & Melamed, *supra* note 5, at 1089-93.

30. *Id.* at 1093-95. Calabresi and Melamed recognized that it is hard to pour content into the term "justice reasons." *Id.* at 1102. Furthermore, they admitted that, broadly defined, distributional considerations can subsume all other justice reasons. *Id.* at 1104. Yet, they suggested that it is preferable to think of considerations such as equality, caste preferences, and other idiosyncratic preferences, separately from traditional distributional considerations. *Id.* at 1098.

31. *Id.* at 1093-1105. *See generally* GUIDO CALABRESI, THE COSTS OF ACCIDENTS 24-33 (1970) (discussing economic efficiency, distributional preferences, and other justice considerations as bases for entitlement allocation).

32. Calabresi & Melamed, *supra* note 5, at 1092, 1105-06.

33. *Id.* at 1092, 1105.

34. *Id.* at 1092, 1106-10. Coleman and Kraus have criticized the idea of liability rule protection for being at odds with the classic view of rights as domains of freedom and personal autonomy. *See* Jules Coleman & Jody Kraus, *Rethinking the Theory of Legal Rights,*

Finally, inalienability rules bar all transfers of the entitlement, whether consensual or nonconsensual.[35]

Moreover, Calabresi and Melamed noticed the existence of what Carol Rose later called "bilateral symmetry;"[36] namely, that property and liability rule protection may be accorded to either of the parties to the conflict.[37] This insight enabled Calabresi and Melamed to craft their famous four-rule menu, which captures the remedial choices available to courts. To illustrate the operation of the four different rules, it would be helpful to return to the pollution dispute example. Assume, first, that society decides to favor the residents' interest in clean air. In this case, a court can vindicate the residents' right to live pollution-free either by enjoining the polluting activity (rule 1), or by conditioning the continuance of the pollution on the payment of damages to the victims (rule 2). Conversely, if society assigns the initial entitlement to the factory owner, the court can vindicate her right to pollute by permitting her to pollute with impunity (rule 3), or by conditioning the abatement of the pollution on the payment of damages to the factory owner (rule 4). The four-rule framework and the taxonomy developed by Calabresi and Melamed to describe the different rules have become staples in legal scholarship and teaching.[38]

Calabresi and Melamed's third important contribution was normative. In analyzing how the legal system should protect entitlements, Calabresi and Melamed successfully synthesized the contractarian and

---

95 YALE L.J. 1335, 1339 (1995). Furthermore, Coleman and Kraus have noted that the protection accorded changes the nature of the entitlement. *Id.* at 1346.

35. Calabresi & Melamed, *supra* note 5, at 1092. Later in the article, Calabresi and Melamed broadened the definition of inalienability rules to include not only outright prohibition on transfers, but also weaker forms of regulatory oversight. *Id.* at 1111. According to Calabresi and Melamed, inalienability rule protection may be appropriate when changes in the initial assignment have untoward effects on third parties, or for paternalistic or distributional reasons. *Id.* at 1111-15.

36. Rose, *Shadow of the Cathedral, supra* note 19, at 2177.

37. Calabresi & Melamed, *supra* note 5, at 1115-17; *see also* James E. Krier & Stewart J. Schwab, *Property Rules and Liability Rules: The Cathedral in Another Light*, 70 N.Y.U. L. REV. 440, 444 (1995) [hereinafter Krier & Schwab, *The Cathedral in Another Light*] (mapping the symmetrical relation in a two-by-two matrix).

38. It is noteworthy that at the time *The Cathedral* was authored, rules 1 through 3 were well known, but rule 4 was not. Indeed, at the time, there were no cases in which rule 4 was employed. Fortunately for Calabresi and Melamed, the year *The Cathedral* was published, the Arizona Supreme Court, in *Spur Industries Inc. v. Dell E. Webb Development Co.*, 494 P.2d 700, 708 (Ariz. 1972), enjoined the operator of a feedlot from continuing its operation, but ordered that a developer representing residents indemnify the tortfeasor for the cost of moving or shutting down. Although it was believed that Calabresi and Melamed were the first to unveil rule 4, it was, in fact, suggested several years earlier by James Atwood in a student note in the *Stanford Law Review*. *See* James R. Atwood, Note, *An Economic Analysis of Land Use Conflicts*, 21 STAN. L. REV. 293, 315 (1969); *see also* Calabresi, *Remarks, supra* note 4, at 2204 (attributing the "discovery" of rule 4 to Atwood). Yet, it is indisputable that rule 4 has become famous thanks to its inclusion in the Calabresian-Melamedian framework.

judicial perspective raised by Coase.[39] They proposed that property rules be employed when transaction costs are low, when there are only a few parties to the dispute, and when the parties to the dispute are readily identifiable.[40] When these conditions obtain, there is no need for legal intervention since the private transacting would lead to an efficient allocation of resources. Liability rules, on the other hand, should be used in the presence of high transaction costs, which prevent the parties from easily identifying and bargaining with one another.[41]

Calabresi and Melamed's normative analysis has solidified the dominance of private ordering over public ordering. Private ordering, through transacting, should take precedence over legal intervention. It is only when we suspect that private bargaining might be ineffective that we should resort to legal intervention. Otherwise, the law should merely provide the backdrop against which private bargaining takes place. The centrality of private bargaining to Calabresi and Melamed is most evident in their discussion of the criminal law. The role Calabresi and Melamed assign to the criminal law is not to protect individual rights and personal security, but rather, to deter "attempts to convert property rules into liability rules."[42]

However, the strong emphasis on bargaining, the potential weakness of Calabresian-Melamedian framework, was also the source of its appeal and success. This focus enabled Calabresi and Melamed to propose a revolutionary way of thinking about the law. Moreover, it enabled them to keep their analysis coherent and elegant. Yet, Calabresi and Melamed's analysis was not at all one-dimensional; nor did it only seek to maximize economic efficiency. Another laudable aspect of Calabresi and Melamed's analysis was the call for the incorporation of fairness-based considerations into entitlement theory. Unfortunately, this aspect of the article has not attracted nearly as much attention as the efficiency analysis. In fact, it was largely ignored by subsequent commentators.[43]

---

39. Calabresi & Melamed, *supra* note 5, at 1108-10.

40. *Id.* at 1125-27.

41. *See id.; see also* RICHARD A. POSNER, ECONOMIC ANALYSIS OF LAW 56-57, 70 (4th ed. 1992) (discussing the "conventional wisdom" favoring property rules where transaction costs are low, and liability rules where transaction costs are high); Krier & Schwab, *The Cathedral in Another Light, supra* note 37, at 447-53 (presenting the "conventional wisdom" for later critique); *cf.* Kaplow & Shavell, *supra* note 9, at 718 (noting that their findings contradict the "conventional wisdom").

42. Calabresi & Melamed, *supra* note 5, at 1126. *Cf.* HANOCH DAGAN, UNJUST ENRICHMENT 15 (1997). Dagan argues that the choice between property rules and liability rules embodies a choice between well-being and control, with liability rules protecting the former and property rules protecting the latter. Thus, "the choice between the two rules requires a choice of the substantive content of the entitlement itself." *Id.* (footnote omitted).

43. We seek to redress this omission in Part III, *infra*.

C.   Subsequent Contributions

As one could expect, *The Cathedral* has not met with universal acceptance. Subsequent scholars have challenged both the descriptive and the normative claims of the article.[44] The normative challenges have targeted Calabresi and Melamed's prescriptions as to how property and liability rules should be applied to enhance economic efficiency. The descriptive challenges have focused on the accuracy and comprehensiveness of Calabresi and Melamed's portrayal of the legal system.[45] We commence by reviewing the normative challenges and then turn to the descriptive ones.

1.   *Normative Challenges*

a. Ayres and Talley's Solomonic Entitlements. Following Calabresi and Melamed, the accepted lore was that property rules outperform liability rules when disputes involve a small number of parties and the costs of identifying the relevant parties are low. In such settings, the employment of property rules was presumed to induce successful private bargaining and consequently efficient allocation of resources.[46] Ayres and Talley called this view into question. They contended that liability rules might be superior to property rules in settings in which property rules were believed to work best: thin markets.[47] To reach this somewhat counterintuitive claim, Ayres and Talley recharacterized two important components in the Calabresi-Melamedian framework: liability rules and transaction costs.

Ayres and Talley began their account by pointing out that the use of liability rules divides entitlements into an option to buy the subject

---

44. A comprehensive review of all the challenges is beyond the scope of this Article. Naturally, we focus on the challenges that are most relevant to our discussion. We do not suggest that the challenges we discuss are necessarily the most important or powerful ones.

45. Admittedly, this distinction involves a degree of imprecision. Some of the challenges we label normative also contain descriptive insights, and vice versa. Yet, this distinction helps organize the subsequent literature in a sensible fashion.

46. *See supra* text accompanying note 41.

47. *See* Ian Ayres & Eric Talley, *Solomonic Bargaining: Dividing a Legal Entitlement to Facilitate Coasean Trade*, 104 YALE L.J. 1027, 1030-33 (1995). In parallel with Ayres and Talley, Johnston reached a similar finding. *See* Jason S. Johnston, *Bargaining Under Rules Versus Standards*, 11 J.L. ECON. & ORG. 256 (1995). Johnston demonstrated that when certain conditions obtain, contingent ex post entitlements may produce more efficient bargaining than clear ex ante entitlements. An important implication of this observation is that blurry balancing tests and even judicial error are more socially desirable than previously thought. In a subsequent article, Johnston and Croson adduced experimental results that offer support of the theoretic predictions of Johnston's model. *See* Rachel Croson & Jason S. Johnston, *Experimental Results on Bargaining Under Alternative Property Rights Regimes*, 16 J.L. ECON. & ORG. 50 (2000). In the text, we focus on Ayres and Talley simply because they framed their analysis in property versus liability rule terms, whereas Johnston's main prism is that of rules versus standards.

of the entitlement[48] and a right subject to the option.[49] Moreover, they insightfully observed that this division creates a unique opportunity for "Solomonic bargaining" between the holders of the divided entitlement. Because the partition of the entitlement permits two-way trading, rather than one, liability rules could generate more private bargaining than property rules. If the option-holder values the subject of the entitlement more highly than the right holder, she would exercise her option and buy the right. Conversely, if the right holder values the underlying asset more highly, she would "bribe" the option holder not to exercise the option.[50] Each party to a liability rule dispute is simultaneously a potential buyer and a potential seller. By contrast, property rules create only one seller and one buyer; no alternating is possible.

But what about transaction costs? Even if liability rules have the potent:al to generate more trades, this advantage may be lost in the presence of transaction costs. To overcome this challenge, Ayres and Talley modified traditional transaction cost analysis. They noted that in thin markets the main obstacle to private bargaining is not the cost of locating and assembling the affected parties, which preoccupied Calabresi and Melamed, but rather, strategic bargaining.[51] In such an environment, where price is not readily determinable, each negotiator has an incentive to posture in order to secure a larger share of the bargaining surplus. Consequently, the challenge for legal rules is to facilitate exchange by countering the predisposition to bargain strategically. Liability rules accomplish just that. By dividing entitlements, liability rules put the bargainers in an "identity crisis," with neither of them knowing whether she would wind up buying or selling. Asking too much, or offering too little, runs the risk of the other party selecting to sell for the quoted price instead of buying, or buy for the quoted price instead of selling.[52] Moreover, dividing the entitlement lowers the stakes for each bargainer, thus further reducing the incentive to bargain dishonestly.[53]

---

48. That is, a "call option."

49. *See* Ayres & Talley, *supra* note 47, at 1031.

50. *See id.* at 1038.

51. *See id.* at 1030; *see also* Robert Cooter, *The Cost of Coase,* 11 J. LEGAL STUD. 1, 23 (1982) (pointing out that disagreements as to how to divide the contractual surplus may prevent successful Coasean bargaining); John Kennan & Robert Wilson, *Bargaining with Private Information,* 31 J. ECON. LITERATURE 45, 46 (1993) (hypothesizing that differences in private information are a primary cause of bargaining delays).

52. *See* Ayres & Talley, *supra* note 47, at 1030. This "identity crisis" is strongest when entitlements are divided evenly. *See, e.g.,* Peter Cramton et al., *Dissolving a Partnership Efficiently,* 55 ECONOMETRICA 615 (1987).

53. *See* Rose, *Shadow of the Cathedral, supra* note 19, at 2184.

Finally, Ayres and Talley have illuminated the information-revealing aspect of liability rules. They proposed that the values the parties place on the whole entitlement may be discerned from their bargaining tactics. Assume, for example, that the option holder seeks to exercise her option. A high-value right holder would offer to pay the option holder not to exercise. Conversely, a low-value right holder would not attempt to stave off the exercise of the option, and may even approach the option-holder with an offer to sell. Thus, the Solomonic bargaining generated by liability rules partitions the holders of the divided entitlement into higher- and lower-value bidders, thereby divulging private information and facilitating trade.[54]

b. Kaplow and Shavell. A different refinement to the Calabresi-Melamedian framework has been proposed by Kaplow and Shavell.[55] Like Ayres and Talley, Kaplow and Shavell have called for a more expansive use of liability rules, albeit for different reasons. Furthermore, unlike Ayres and Talley who disregarded property rules, Kaplow and Shavell redefined the proper role of property rules in protecting entitlements.

At the core of Kaplow and Shavell's analysis lie two analytical distinctions which enabled them to compartmentalize the universe of entitlement disputes into a two-by-two matrix. The first distinction is between "externalities disputes" and "possessory disputes." A paradigmatic example of the former is industrial pollution, or noise. A typical example of the latter is a dispute over an item of personal property, such as a laptop computer. The second, and more familiar, distinction is between high transaction cost and low transaction cost settings.

Kaplow and Shavell proposed that property rules are superior to liability rules in the context of possessory disputes irrespective of whether transaction costs are high or low. This is because liability rule protection of possessory interests raises two problems: reciprocal takings and sequential taking.[56] If A's possession of her laptop computer is protected by a liability rule, and the damage amount is set too low,[57] B would take A's laptop and pay the damage award. This, in turn, would prompt A to take back the laptop and pay B, and so a vicious

---

54. *See id.* at 2184-85; *see also* Ayres & Talley, *supra* note 47, at 1039-47. Ayres and Talley acknowledged that negotiators would continue to misrepresent their true valuations in the hope of extracting a larger share of the bargaining surplus. They pointed out, however, that the liability amount restricts the ability of the parties to exaggerate. Or, as they put it, the expected damage award "serves as both a *ceiling* to overstatements and a *floor* to understatements." *Id.* at 1046.

55. *See* Kaplow & Shavell, *supra* note 9.

56. *Id.* at 722, 765-67.

57. If the damage award is too high, the distinction between liability rule protection and property rule protection loses its significance. *See id.* at 724 (observing that "a liability rule with very high damages is equivalent to a property rule protection of victims").

cycle of reciprocal takings would ensue. Even worse, other parties, such as, C and D, may choose to take the laptop and pay, spearheading an infinite series of sequential takings. Instead of negotiating in the shadow of liability rules, as Ayres and Talley would have them, the contending parties would repeatedly take from one another.[58]

In externalities cases, the choice of legal rules depends on the magnitude of transaction costs. Reiterating Coase's main insight, Kaplow and Shavell conclude that when transaction costs are low, the choice of legal rule does not matter. In this instance, property rules and liability rules would perform equally well since parties can bargain to achieve the optimal allocation of resources. When transaction costs are high, liability rules have the edge. When private bargaining is impossible, the court must allocate the right to the higher value user. If the court chooses to employ property rule protection, it must know both the damage to the victim and the prevention cost to the polluter. By contrast, the use of liability rules requires the court to know only one variable: the damage to the victim. Once the court sets the liability amount correctly, the polluter, who knows the cost of prevention, has a choice to make. If the cost of prevention exceeds the damage amount, she would continue with the polluting activity and pay damages. If the cost of prevention is lower than the expected liability, she would invest in preventive measures and abate the pollution. Thus, liability rules minimize information costs. According to Kaplow and Shavell, it is for this reason that liability rules should be favored over property rules when transaction costs are high, and not because of the impossibility of bargaining, as Calabresi and Melamed suggested.[59]

c. Krier and Schwab. The final challenge to the Calabresi-Melamedian framework differs dramatically from the two previously discussed. In a marked departure from the conventional view among law and economics scholars, Krier and Schwab questioned the presumed superiority of liability rules in high transaction costs settings. They noted that the conventional view that liability rules outperform property rules when transacting is prohibitively costly rests on a tacit assumption that courts can assess damages with reasonable accuracy in such situations. Yet, following Polinsky,[60] Krier and Schwab pointed out that this key assumption has never been substantiated.[61] Krier and

---

58. Ian Ayres and Jack Balkin, however, have pointed out that this problem could be avoided if each taking were accompanied by an incremental price increase. More generally, they note that liability rules are essentially truncated auctions. Thus, they propose that entitlements be auctioned off between the contending parties with the highest bidder ultimately receiving the entitlement. *See* Ayres & Balkin, *supra* note 25, at 707-716.

59. *See* Kaplow & Shavell, *supra* note 9, at 719, 726-27; *see also* Rose, *Shadow of the Cathedral, supra* note 19, at 2191.

60. *See* Polinsky, *supra* note 9, at 1111.

61. *See* Krier & Schwab, *The Cathedral in Another Light, supra* note 37, at 453-54.

Schwab attributed this omission to the failure of scholars to recognize the existence of assessment costs — the transaction costs of the judicial process — and, more generally, to engage in comparative institutional analysis.[62]

In addressing these omissions, Krier and Schwab found that the presumed superiority of liability rules in high transaction costs settings is illusory. Krier and Schwab contended that although private bargaining over damages is costly when transaction costs are high, the cost of judicial assessment of damages may be higher still. Hence, it is impossible to determine in the abstract which mode is superior.[63] Moreover, they suggested that there is a positive correlation between factors that give rise to high transaction costs and those creating high assessment costs.[64] For example, bargaining is likely to be ineffective in disputes involving multiple parties and in bilateral monopoly cases. But so is judicial assessment of damages. Consider, for example, the case of *Boomer v. Atlantic Cement Co.*[65] In *Boomer*, the presence of multiple victims, which gave rise to high transaction costs and potential holdout problems, thwarted the possibility of a voluntary agreement between the cement plant and the residents. The same fact, however, made judicial determination of damages extremely difficult.[66] This example may be generalized: the involvement of multiple parties and the lack of readily ascertainable market prices make accurate assessment of damage virtually impossible.[67] Thus, the very factors that undermine efficient bargaining also frustrate the ability of courts to determine damages with reasonable precision.

Furthermore, because courts routinely grant objective damages and ignore subjective, or idiosyncratic, harms, damage awards tend to be undercompensatory; victims' losses are rarely fully redressed in litigation.[68] At the end of the day, therefore, Krier and Schwab posit that there is no inherent reason to assume that liability rules would better enhance economic efficiency when transaction costs are high.[69]

---

62. *See id.* at 454, 475-77.

63. *See id.* at 454-55.

64. *See id.* at 459-61.

65. 257 N.E.2d 870 (N.Y. 1970).

66. For discussion, see NEIL K. KOMESAR, IMPERFECT ALTERNATIVES: CHOOSING INSTITUTIONS IN LAW, ECONOMICS, AND PUBLIC POLICY 14-28 (1994) (discussing the assessment problem in the *Boomer* case); Daniel A. Farber, *Reassessing* Boomer: *Justice, Efficiency, and Nuisance Law, in* PROPERTY LAW AND LEGAL EDUCATION: ESSAYS IN HONOR OF JOHN E. CRIBBET 7, 11-12 (Peter Hay & Michael H. Hoeflich eds., 1989) (pointing out that Atlantic's total liability "ultimately came to $710,000, some four times the amount mentioned in the Court of Appeals decision denying injunctive relief").

67. *See* Krier & Schwab, *The Cathedral in Another Light, supra* note 37, at 460-62.

68. *See id.* at 457-59.

69. It bears emphasis, however, that Krier and Schwab have not positively shown that property rules would outperform liability rules in high-transaction-costs settings. Their

2. Descriptive Challenges

a. Put Protection. Combining the Calabresi-Melamedian frame-work with option theory, several scholars have noticed an interesting extension to Calabresi and Melamed's analysis of liability rules. Spe-cifically, they observed that while Calabresi and Melamed treated li-ability rules strictly as call options, i.e., options to "buy" entitlements from their holders, entitlements may also be protected with put op-tions.[70] The mirror image of calls, put options bestow upon the enti-tlement holder the power to sell the entitlement to the other party to the dispute, for example the polluter, for a certain exercise price. Hence, it can be said that put option protection grants to "the initial entitlement holder everything that she would have under a property rule plus a put option."[71]

The choice between "calls" and "puts" has important distributional consequences. Puts increase the expected payoff of the entitlement holder relative to calls and standard property rule protection.[72] Moreover, put option protection reduces the risk to which entitlement

---

analysis only suggests that Calabresi and Melamed's conclusion that liability rules better en-hance efficiency in the face of high transaction costs may be incorrect due to Calabresi and Melamed's omission of comparative institutional analysis.

70. *See, e.g.,* Ian Ayres, *Protecting Property with Puts,* 32 VAL. U. L. REV. 793, 798 (1998) (noting that a put option, or "forced purchase" rule, gives the entitlement holder the option to force the nonentitlement holder to purchase); Madeline Morris, *The Structure of Entitlements,* 78 CORNELL L. REV. 822, 854-56 (1993) (describing put options as examples of reverse liability rules in which the entitlement holder has the right to a forced compensated transfer); *cf.* Ayres & Balkin, *supra* note 25 (describing various mechanisms for auctioning put options). *But see* Richard A. Epstein, *Protecting Property Rights with Legal Remedies: A Common Sense Reply to Professor Ayres,* 32 VAL. U. L. REV. 833 (1998) (challenging the efforts of Ian Ayres and others to apply financial economics to elaborate on Calabresi and Melamed's original two-by-two matrix).

71. *See* Ayres, *supra* note 70, at 799. Correspondingly, the nonentitlement holder against whom the put option may be exercised has less than nothing, since she may be forced to buy an entitlement against her will. *Id.*

72. *See id.* at 804-13. Ayres points out that in addition to changing the division of the bargaining surplus between the parties, put protection also affects the bid/ask difference. He notes that "[f]or both cognitive and wealth effects reasons, it is often the case that a particu-lar person will demand a higher price when selling an entitlement than she would be willing to pay if forced to buy." *Id.* at 809-10; *see also* Levmore, *supra* note 4, at 2166 (describing the offer-asking differential, or "endowment effect").

On the "endowment effect," see generally Daniel Kahneman et al., *Experimental Tests of the Endowment Effect and the Coase Theorem,* 98 J. POL. ECON. 1325 (1990) (concluding that endowment effects are not easily altered by experience); Daniel Kahneman et al., *The Endowment Effect, Loss Aversion, and Status Quo Bias,* 5 J. ECON. PERSP. 193, 194 (1991) (defining the "endowment effect" as a behavior in which "people often demand much more to give up an object than they would be willing to pay to acquire it"); Richard Thaler, *Toward a Positive Theory of Consumer Choice,* J. ECON. BEHAV. & ORG. 1 (1980) (exam-ining ways in which consumers deviate from rational economic models). On the impact of the endowment effect on legal policymaking, see Elizabeth Hoffman & Matthew L. Spitzer, *Willingness to Pay vs. Willingness to Accept: Legal and Economic Implications,* 71 WASH. U. L.Q. 59 (1993); Russell Korobkin, Note, *Policymaking and the Offer/Asking Price Gap: To-ward a Theory of Efficient Entitlement Allocation,* 46 STAN. L. REV. 663 (1994).

holders are exposed. Call options vest the power to exercise in the nonentitlement holder. Put options, by contrast, grant the decision-making power to the entitlement holder. Consequently, put option protection provides the greatest incentive to property owners to invest in their assets, and the strongest deterrent to potential takers.[73]

Although put option protection is an important theoretical possibility, it is rarely used in reality.[74] Richard Epstein, for example, suggested that puts "are never imposed as a matter of law on strangers, but are the outgrowth of consensual transactions over organized markets."[75] In response to this claim, Ian Ayres showed that the reach of put option protection extends to certain nonconsensual settings, such as conversion, and trespass disputes. Even Ayres, however, conceded Epstein's basic point: that the common law does not employ puts *in rem*, but rather, as limited *in personam* rights in certain bilateral monopoly situations.[76]

   b. "Startle" or "Startling" Rules.[77] Aside from the possibility of put option protection, several scholars have observed various other extensions to the Calabresi-Melamedian four rule framework. The scholarly interest in the possibility of additional rules has been rekindled by Krier and Schwab's "discovery" of a new rule, which they entitled "rule 5."[78] Krier and Schwab proposed that in certain instances the transgressor should be permitted to choose to abate the tortious activity and collect the victim's gains occasioned by this decision. Under this rule, A, who causes a nuisance to B, gets the discretion to stop at

---

73. *See* Ayres, *supra* note 70, at 807.

74. *See, e.g.*, Richard A. Epstein, *A Clear View of the Cathedral: The Dominance of Property Rules*, 106 YALE L.J. 2091, 2093 (1997) (noting that certain financial arrangements, such as puts, are "common enough in financial markets, but are rarely encountered in the world of legally created remedies"). Even Morris, who was the first to observe the possibility of put option protection, found only two real world examples of this type of protection: "[g]un buy-out offers by police department, and soft drink container deposit redemption laws." *See* Morris, *supra* note 70, at 855.

75. Epstein, *supra* note 74, at 2093.

76. *See* Ayres, *supra* note 70, at 814 n.63. It should be noted that some of the put protection examples identified by Ayres do not clearly fall under his own definition of the term. For instance, Ayres characterizes the famous case of *Pile v. Pedrick*, 31 A. 646 (Pa. 1895), as granting the plaintiffs, the victims of the encroachment, put option protection. In fact, the court merely permitted the plaintiff to choose between injunction and damages, and the plaintiff ultimately preferred the former, i.e., property rule protection. Since true put option protection would give the plaintiffs more than a simple property rule, the plaintiffs' choice seems quite odd. It is possible, then, that the court was not offering the plaintiff put option protection, but rather, a choice between property rule protection and a call option protection to the defendant-transgressor. This is not to say that Ayres' construction of the case is necessarily incorrect. However, without knowing what exactly the damage award was in this case, it is impossible to say with certainty that the court employed put option protection.

77. The term "startling rule" owes its origin to Levmore.

78. *See* Krier & Schwab, *The Cathedral in Another Light*, *supra* note 37, at 470-71. It is widely agreed that the original startling rule was Calabresi and Melamed's rule 4. *See* Levmore, *supra* note 4, at 2150.

her choice, and collect damages from B in the amount of the benefit B receives as a consequence or to continue the nuisance and receive nothing.[79] Krier and Schwab's proposal reportedly "infuriated [certain scholars] who found it too unusual to be of note."[80] But it captivated the minds of most others,[81] despite the fact that Krier and Schwab were unable to find any judicial authority employing or foreshadowing their insight, and the obvious risk of strategic abuse of this remedy by tortfeasors.[82] Importantly, Krier and Schwab's insight, debatable as it might be, demonstrated that other rules may be hiding in the wings of Calabresi and Melamed's four basic rules.

Indeed, three years later, Saul Levmore, in an analytical *tour de force*, derived as many as sixteen variants from Calabresi and Melamed's original four.[83] To accomplish this feat, Levmore divided the four basic rules according to various familiar legal distinctions. For example, in the context of liability rules, Levmore proposed that a court might order compensation only if the injurer was negligent, but not otherwise.[84] Furthermore, drawing on the distinction between torts and unjust enrichment, Levmore noted that in determining the proper compensation award, a court could choose between the victim's loss and the injurer's gain.[85] Levmore also observed that instead of awarding compensation for *both* past and future injuries, a court may compensate the victim for *either* past *or* future injuries.[86] In the same vein, in the context of property rules, a court may award the victim an injunction, but deny her damages for past injuries. Or, if the court wishes to increase the victim's compensation, it may enjoin the harmful activity and award the victim the injurer's past gain.

Inspired by the unveiling of rule 5, Levmore also sought to uncover several "startling rules" of his own. Ultimately, Levmore found one such rule, which he dubbed "Rule 5CE."[87] Drawing on rule 5, Levmore proposed a rule that would permit the injurer to continue

---

79. Ian Ayres correctly noted that rule 5 is essentially an example of put option protection. *See* Ayres, *supra* note 70, at 801.

80. Levmore, *supra* note 4, at 2150.

81. *See id.*

82. *See* Levmore, *supra* note 4, at 2161 (noting that "[i]f A knew that a judge would respond to any complaint by B with this rule 5, then A would have a perverse incentive to create nuisances in order to collect from B").

83. A full review of all of Levmore's variants is beyond the scope of this Article. For a table summarizing the sixteen different rules, see Levmore, *supra* note 4, at 2173.

84. *Id.* at 2156. In a different variant, Levmore proposed that if the injurer was not negligent she would share in the victim's loss if they both belong to the same community. *Id.* at 2159.

85. *Id.* at 2157.

86. *Id.* at 2159.

87. *Id.* at 2162.

with the harmful activity, but would force her to pay all her gains from choosing to do so to the victim.[88] However, Levmore himself admitted that "it may be hard to see why Rule 5 or 5CE would ever be selected [by a court]."[89]

c. Summary and Evaluation. The Cathedral and its progeny have had a profound impact on entitlement theory as well as our understanding of the legal system as a whole. The focus on transaction costs, the defining characteristic of this body of literature, has transformed traditional understandings of property, contract, and tort. Several changes are worth noting.

First, the focus on transacting has reduced the status of property rights from near-absolute rights that denote individual autonomy and security to fungible bargaining chips. From a right that granted to its holder the power to exclude others,[90] property has become no more than a contractual lever. And, from a right that could only in rare cases be taken for a public use,[91] property has become an up-for-grabs right, open to all potential takers. The familiar "no-trespassing" sign was replaced with an "all welcome" one.

Second, the entitlement literature has largely changed the internal hierarchy between property and contract. Traditionally, property was deemed a keynote right,[92] and contract as a subservient right, designed to enable property owners to transfer their property. The right to transfer, represented by contract, was just one stick in the bundle of rights property confers upon its holder.[93] The entitlement literature has turned this relationship around, placing contract at the core of our legal system, and property at the fringes. Under the new conceptualization, property merely facilitates contracting by defining the initial bargaining positions of the parties.

---

88. *Id.*

89. *Id.* at 2168.

90. *See, e.g.*, Kaiser Aetna v. United States, 444 U.S. 164, 176 (1979) (" '[T]he right to exclude others' is 'one of the most essential sticks in the bundle of rights that are commonly characterized as property.' "); Thomas W. Merrill, *Property and the Right to Exclude*, 77 NEB. L. REV. 730, 730 (2000) (positing that "the right to exclude others is more than just 'one of the most essential' constituents of property — it is the sine qua non").

91. *See* U.S. CONST. amend. V ("[N]or shall private property be taken for public use, without just compensation.").

92. *See* Carol M. Rose, *Property as the Keystone Right?*, 71 NOTRE DAME L. REV. 329 (1999) [hereinafter Rose, *Keystone Right*] (reviewing and critically examining the various sources of the view of property as a keynote right).

93. *See* STEPHEN R. MUNZER, A THEORY OF PROPERTY 40-50 (1990) (suggesting that the right to transfer the "stick" distinguishes property rights from personal rights); J.E. Penner, *The "Bundle of Rights" Picture of Property*, 43 UCLA L. REV. 711, 747 (arguing that "the right to transfer property is an inherent feature of property rights"); *cf.* Merrill & Smith, *supra* note 9, at 365 (observing that for some writers influenced by the legal realism of the 1920s and 1930s, "the bundle-of-rights concept simply meant that property could be reduced to recognizable collections of functional attributes, such as the right . . . to transfer").

Third, the economic analysis of entitlements has stripped property of one of its defining characteristics, its *in rem* nature.[94] By contrast to *in personam* contractual rights that are binding only on the parties to the contract, property rights are binding upon the rest of the world.[95] Yet, owing to the tendency to model disputes as two party conflicts, the economic literature on entitlements has obliterated this important difference. As Thomas Merrill and Henry Smith have observed, "most modern economic accounts endow property with no distinctive character at all." Property rights are "simply . . . little empty boxes filled with a miscellany of use rights that operate in the background of a world consisting of nothing but in personam obligations."[96]

Fourth, the virtually exclusive focus on facilitating transactions has pushed to the corner the traditional utilitarian justifications of property, most notably the need to incentivize owners to invest in resources.[97] For this reason, property regimes overwhelmingly employ property rules as the default regime.[98] As Carol Rose explained, this property rule favoritism is not accidental. Strong, undivided, and sharply defined property rights not only facilitate contracting but also "encourage individual investment, planning and effort" by giving actors "a clearer sense of what they are getting."[99] Moreover, the transactional focus has marginalized another key role of property law —

94. Merrill & Smith, *supra* note 9, at 360 (noting that "[p]roperty rights historically have been regarded as *in rem*"); Thomas W. Merrill & Henry E. Smith, *The Property/Contract Interface*, 101 COLUM. L. REV. 773, 777 (2001) (noting that "[p]roperty rights are in rem — they bind the 'rest of the world' ").

95. *See* Wesley Newcomb Hohfeld, *Fundamental Legal Conceptions as Applied in Judicial Reasoning*, 26 YALE L.J. 710 (1917) (discussing the difference between *in personam* rights, which avail against one or a few persons, and *in rem* rights, which avail against a large and indefinite class of people).

96. Merrill & Smith, *supra* note 9, at 385.

97. *See* JEREMY BENTHAM, THEORY OF LEGISLATION 111-13 (4th ed. 1882) (positing that property is the basis of an expectation of advantages). Examples of modern law and economics scholars of this view include: RICHARD POSNER, ECONOMIC ANALYSIS OF LAW (4th ed. 1998), JESSE DUKEMINIER & JAMES E. KRIER, PROPERTY 53 (4th ed. 1998) (noting that "[u]tilitarian theory is, without doubt, the dominant view of property today . . . especially among those working in law and economics"); Harold Demsetz, *Toward a Theory of Property Rights*, 57 AM. ECON. REV. 347 (1967) (providing a utilitarian account of the emergence of property rights); Robert C. Ellickson, *Property in Land*, 102 YALE L.J. 1315 (1993) (comparing private and group land ownership, and noting that a change in land regimes is efficient when it reduces the sum of transaction costs and deadweight losses); and Rose, *Shadow of the Cathedral*, *supra* note 19, at 2182, 2187.

98. *See* Rose, *Shadow of the Cathedral*, *supra* note 19, at 2187; Epstein, *supra* note 74, at 2096-2105 (discussing the dominance of property rules in property law).

99. Rose, *Shadow of the Cathedral*, *supra* note 19, at 2187.

striking the balance between exclusivity and access,[100] and in some cases, between monopoly and competition.[101]

Finally, Calabresi and Melamed's call to consider distributive and other justice considerations in determining the allocation of entitlements has been all but ignored by subsequent law and economics scholars. Although Calabresi and Melamed put the various considerations on equal footing, economic efficiency somehow eclipsed the two other values.

II. Enter Pliability Rules

In this Part, we introduce the concept of pliability rules.[102] Metaphorically speaking, Calabresi and Melamed viewed the law as a three-level structure, with inalienability rules at the ground level, property rules at the first floor, and liability rules at the second. While we adopt Calabresi and Melamed's three basic categories, we show that their metaphor is incomplete. It fails to capture the dynamism of the legal system, which allows for the changing of entitlements over time. In other words, it neglects to account for connections within the structure and the ability to move around in it. We propose that pliability rules should be viewed as the stairways between the floors, and the corridors and doorways connecting rooms on those floors. In other words, we contend that the set of entitlements described by the metaphor should include not only the rule in isolation, but also their

---

100. *See, e.g.,* Laura Underkuffler, *On Property: An Essay,* 100 YALE L.J. 127, 129, 144-45 (1991) (positing that property embodies an inherent tension between the individual and the collective.); *cf.* Neil Weinstock Netanel, *Copyright and a Democratic Civil Society,* 106 YALE L.J. 283, 364 (1996) (suggesting, in the context of copyright, that the challenge facing decisionmakers is to structure the law so that it strikes a "careful balance between exclusivity and access").

101. *See* RICHARD A. EPSTEIN, TAKINGS: PRIVATE PROPERTY AND THE POWER OF EMINENT DOMAIN (1989); *cf.* J.H. Reichman, *Intellectual Property in International Trade: Opportunities and Risks of a GATT Connection,* 22 VAND. J. TRANSNAT'L L. 747, 867 (1989) (suggesting that progress in international intellectual property relations has been based "on a process of consensus that enabled all participants to determine the desired balance between monopoly and competition"); Deborah Tussey, *From Fan Sites to Filesharing: Personal Use in Cyberspace,* 35 GA. L. REV. 1129, 1171 n.141 (2001) (noting, in the intellectual property context, that "utilitarianism seeks to balance creators' incentives against the public right of access, providing monopoly incentives only to the extent necessary to induce creation").

102. As Ian Ayres cautioned, originality is tricky to claim. Indeed, it is possible that Calabresi and Melamed saw the possibility of mixing property and liability rule protection. It is likely that Levmore saw this option, but never developed it, when he mentioned the possibility of less than perfect property rule protection. And clearly, Merrill noticed, and even discussed, the possibility of incorporating a similar mode of protection into the doctrines of adverse possession and prescriptive easements. *See* Thomas W. Merrill, *Property Rules, Liability Rules, and Adverse Possession,* 79 Nw. U. L. REV. 1122 (1984). However, Merrill's discussion was limited to that context, and was primarily normative. Merrill never went beyond adverse possession. He did not explore the descriptive prevalence of pliability rules in other legal areas, nor did he propose the use of pliability rules in other settings.

interconnections. Calabresi and Melamed's model is static; ours is dynamic.

Our three-fold project in this Part is to demonstrate the conceptual distinctiveness of pliability rules, show the descriptive pervasiveness of such rules, and to expound the various goals pliability rule protection serves. Our conceptual discussion focuses on demonstrating the distinctiveness of the category of pliability rules, and the importance of pliability rules for extending Calabresi and Melamed's analysis.

As should be clear by the large number of examples presented in this Part, we contend that lawmakers have preceded the academy to pliability rules; pliability rules are already widely used. Our descriptive exposition covers various legal areas, with a major focus on property and intellectual property law, as well as antitrust law and corporate law. We show that in certain instances pliability rules enhance economic efficiency, while in others they promote fairness and distributive concerns.

Our normative aim here is to show that, due to their amalgamated nature, pliability rules provide a unique policy tool for a variety of circumstances, such as the need to accommodate competing societal interests such as efficiency and equity, and monopoly power and competition. By combining property and liability rule protection, pliability rules merge the respective strengths of the two modalities. We generalize our normative discussion in the next Part; here, our aim is to show the gains achieved by each of the examples of pliability rule we cite.

A. *Property + Liability = Pliability*

1. *Pliability and Grue*

Pliability rules are amalgamated rules. They combine their familiar cousins — property rules and liability rules — in numerous combinations. Among the many legal fields employing pliability rules are corporate law, intellectual property, eminent domain, and antitrust, as well as several areas of law not discussed in this Part, such as bankruptcy. However, pliability rules are much more than a rearrangement of familiar materials.

To illustrate the importance of pliability rules, we turn to an analogy provided by the philosopher Nelson Goodman. In his *Fact, Fiction and Forecast*, Goodman sought to illustrate a problem with inductive reasoning by hypothesizing an imaginary color called "grue."[103] An item that is colored "grue" looks green to anyone who observes it prior to a given time — for example, the year 2003. Thereafter, the grue item appears blue. Goodman notes that before the year 2003,

---

103. NELSON GOODMAN, FACT, FICTION AND FORECAST 74 *et seq.* (2d ed. 1965).

anyone examining the grue-colored item would be unable to tell whether she was looking at something that was green or something that was grue. Anyone hearing an item described as "green" before 2003, or as "blue" afterwards, would not know whether the described item were actually green or blue, on the one hand, or grue, on the other. This, says Goodman, demonstrates a characteristic failure of induction. While green, blue and grue are all ontologically distinct — each has its own distinct color characteristic — the observer can never induce whether she has seen grue or either green or blue. Induction, notes Goodman, fails to distinguish between items that appear the same, but are ontologically different.

Pliability rules are distinct from property and liability rules, as grue is from green and blue. While a pliability rule may appear as a property or liability rule at any given point in time, it is nevertheless ontologically distinct. Unlike a property or liability rule, a pliability rule contains within itself its own conditions for change. A person who observes property rule or liability rule protection at a given point in time, and assumes that the property rule or liability rule protection encapsulates the true legal protection of an object, may be making a critical error. If the entitlement holder actually enjoys pliability rule protection over the object, describing the protection as property rule or liability rule protection would constitute an ontological error. In this sense, a pliability analysis is thus the opposite of what Louis Kaplow labeled a "transitional" analysis — the analysis of how entitlements should be treated in the face of "the existence of uncertainty concerning [a] future government policy [transition] prior to the government action."[104] Pliability rules provide entitlement holders with certainty concerning future changes in the rules protecting their entitlements, and, therefore, a truer appreciation of the nature of protection they enjoy at present.

Importantly, given that pliability rules have distinct properties and a unique identity and course, they create a different set of incentives. Property rules are generally thought to encourage greater investment than liability rules, since the entitlement holder may prevent involuntary loss of the object. Pliability rules fall somewhere in the middle, depending on the particular combination of property rules and liability rules. Also, certain pliability rules offer the additional advantage of self-regulation as they allow the entitlement holder to affect the nature of the protection she enjoys. We illustrate these important features of pliability rules in the discussion and examples later in this Part.

Nelson Goodman's discussion of grue provides a metaphor for another key feature of our analysis of pliability rules. Goodman does not

---

104. Louis Kaplow, *An Economic Analysis of Legal Transitions*, 99 HARV. L. REV. 509, 512 (1986).

suffice with grue's ontological distinctiveness; ultimately, Goodman rejects the importance of grue on pragmatic grounds, noting that grue is not a significant category in the real world. Thus, for the existence of pliability rules to be noteworthy, such rules must have some practical significance, as well as ontological identity. Our discussion in this Part shows the pervasiveness of pliability rules in the legal world, rendering pliability rules a more valuable category of analysis than grue.

Indeed, as our discussion shows, pliability rules are so ubiquitous in our legal regime that every entitlement can be viewed, in one sense or another, as falling under the protection of pliability rules, rather than property or liability rules. This, too, requires a practical approach. Property rules, liability rules, and pliability rules are not divorced from the legal context in which they arise. In some cases, the legal contingency that gives rise to a change in legal protection may be so remote that it may be safely ignored for most purposes. Pure property or liability rules are the more useful framework for examining the entitlement in such instances.

2. *Pliability and Calabresi and Melamed*

The role of pliability rules can also be illustrated in reference to Calabresi and Melamed's famous table of the four basic types of property and liability rules. Their table omitted inalienability rules. The table is meant to illustrate four possible responses to claims of nuisance. The typical case underlying each cell in the table involves a homeowner suing a nearby polluter. In cell one, the plaintiff homeowner enjoys property rule protection and is entitled to a court order enjoining the polluting activity. In cell two, the plaintiff homeowner receives liability rule protection. The polluter may continue her activities but must pay the homeowner for damages. In cell three, the defendant polluter enjoys property rule protection. The polluter may continue the activities, and the homeowner receives no relief. Cell four involves liability rule protection for the defendant. The polluter must cease her polluting activities, but the plaintiff homeowner must pay the defendant polluter for the resulting damages.

The table below illustrates these possibilities, with cases in which courts may be deemed to have employed the relevant type of protection.

TABLE 1: PROPERTY RULES AND LIABILITY RULES

1. Property Rule (Plaintiff) *Department of Health & Mental Hygiene v. Galaxy Chemical Co.*[105]; *Ensign v. Walls*[106]	2. Liability Rule (Plaintiff) *Boomer v. Atlantic Cement*[107]
3. Property Rule (Defendant) *Francisco v. Department of Institutions & Agencies*[108]; *Rose v. Socony Vacuum Corp.*[109]	4. Liability Rule (Defendant) *Spur Industries Inc. v. Dell E. Webb Development Co.*[110]

As we noted in the last Part, the Calebresi-Melamedian four-cell table has been the launching pad for many analyses of property and liability rules. In that vein, we illustrate the place of pliability rules within the traditional four-cell table. As their name implies, pliability rules are amalgamated rules that combine property and liability rule protection. Under pliability rule protection, the entitlement holder initially receives one type of rule protection — property or liability — and then upon the occurrence of a certain contingency, the nature of the protection changes to another kind of rule protection. Sometimes, pliability rules involve transfer of the entitlement itself.

The next table adds the possibility of pliability rules, illustrated by the arrows. As the table demonstrates, pliability rules involve either a simultaneous rule, in which more than one of the rules applies at the same time, or, more commonly, a changing rule, in which protection begins with one of the four types of ordinary Calabresi-Melamedian property and liability rules, and then, upon a specified event, changes to another of the four types of rules. Although there is no limit on the number of possible pliability rules, we illustrate in the chart, only the six prototypical pliability rules that we describe in this Part.

---

105. 1 ENVIR. REP. 1660 (Md. Cir. Ct. 1970) (enjoining chemical smells).

106. 34 N.W.2d 549 (Mich. 1948) (enjoining raising a dog in residential neighborhood).

107. 257 N.E.2d 870 (N.Y. 1970) (ruling that avoidance of injunction was conditioned on payment of permanent damages to plaintiffs).

108. 180 A. 843 (N.J. Ch. 1935) (holding that plaintiffs were not entitled to enjoin noise and odors of adjacent sanitarium).

109. 173 A. 627 (R.I. 1934) (finding that absent negligence, pollution of percolating waters was not enjoinable).

110. 494 P.2d 700 (Ariz. 1972) (enjoining the operator of a feedlot from continuing its operation, but ordering that a developer representing residents indemnify the tortfeasor for the cost of moving or shutting down).

TABLE 2: PROPERTY RULES, LIABILITY RULES, AND PLIABILITY
RULES

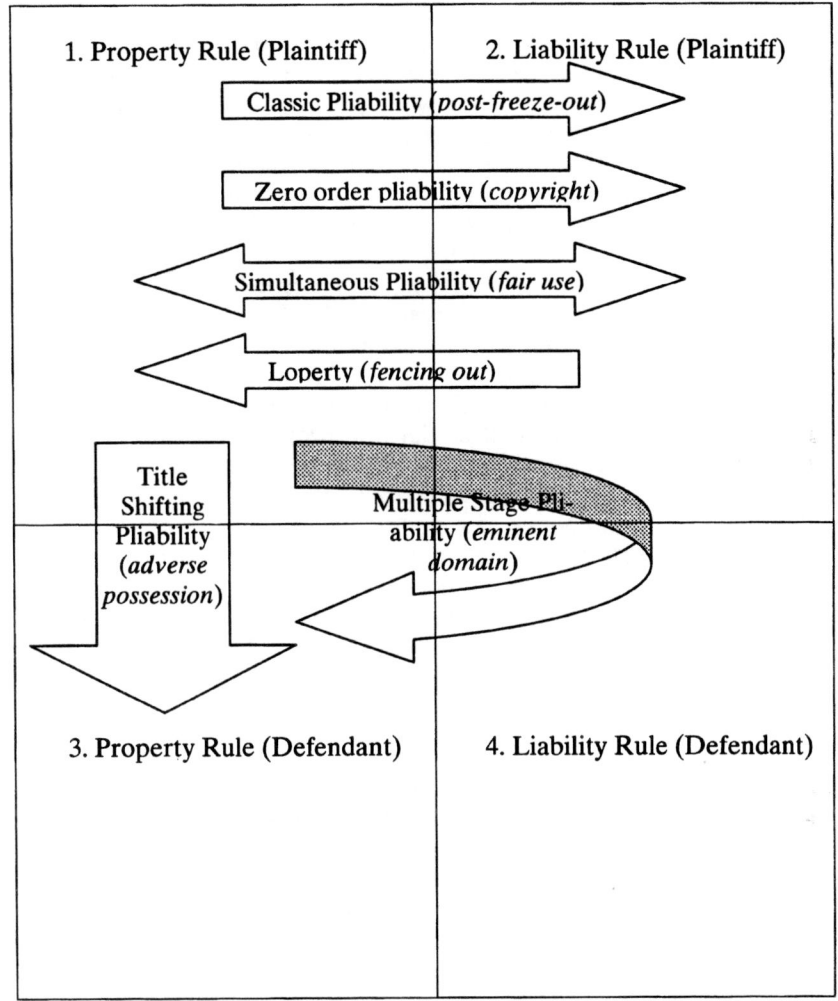

As the table demonstrates, we focus our discussion on six proto-
types of pliability rules that are common in existing law.

The first set of pliability rules involves property rules that are
transformed into liability rules — "classic pliability rules" under our
terminology. The legal protection of post-freeze-out minority shareholders provides an example of such classic pliability rule protection.

The second set comprises the particular variety of pliability rules
that we call "zero order pliability rules" — property rules that become
liability rules where the compensation for breach of the rule is zero.

An example of a zero order pliability rule is copyright protection, under which the author receives a property right for her life plus seventy years, and thereafter anybody can use the copyrighted expression free of charge.

As a third set of prototypical pliability rules, we turn to the case of "simultaneous pliability rules," in which the same entitlement holder holds one type of rule protection with respect to some potential users, but a different type of rule protection with respect to other users. For example, the fair use doctrine in copyright law reduces the usual property rule protection to zero order liability protection where the use of the copyright entitlement constitutes a "fair use."[111]

The fourth set includes "loperty rules," in which initial liability rule protection is transformed into property rule protection. The transformation of cattle-feeding rights resulting from fencing pasture in a "fencing-out" legal regime provides an example of a loperty rule.

The fifth set of pliability rules we examine consists of "title shifting pliability rules," i.e., rules that transform property rule protection in the hands of one entitlement holder into property rule protection in the hands of another entitlement holder. Adverse possession provides the classic example of this type of pliability rule.

Finally, we examine the case of "multiple stage pliability rules," in which rule protection is changed more than once. For example, we observe that eminent domain can be viewed as property rule protection followed by liability rule protection in the hands of the original owner, and then property rule protection in the hands of the subsequent entitlement holder.

B. *Classic Pliability Rules*

Classic pliability rules, as we noted, involve the transformation of an entitlement from property rule to liability rule protection. In cases involving classic pliability rules, property rules provide the baseline protection in order to advance efficient allocation of resources. By creating *in rem* rights in resources, property rules reduce the cost of defending the item against potential takers, allowing owners to invest optimally in the item's use. Where exogenous transaction costs are low, the *in rem* protection comes at low cost, since the object will still gravitate to the highest value user. Moreover, property rights themselves lower transaction costs and facilitate exchange by reducing the cost of defining ownership and usage rights in objects.

However, classic pliability rules also take into account the many instances in which the default property rule protection becomes inefficient or unfair. Classic pliability rules, by defining the triggering event

---

111. Admittedly, in framing the issue in this way, we treat users as intrinsically wedded to certain types of uses, which blurs the important distinction between uses and users.

that alters protection from property to liability rule, retains the advantages of baseline property rule protection, while creating the flexibility to adapt to changing circumstances.

We introduce the category with an examination of the most straightforward example: the rights of minority shareholders in the aftermath of mergers and acquisitions.

1. *Mergers and Acquisitions*

Ordinarily, shareholders in a corporation enjoy property rule protection over their shares. Subject to reporting and alienability restrictions established by law, shareholders may freely sell or transfer their shares, and shares may not be appropriated by nonowners without the owner's consent.[112] However, most types of corporate decisions do not require unanimous assent. This category includes key decisions such as mergers or freeze-out takeovers that force minority shareholders to surrender their shares in exchange for compensation determined by the corporation.[113] Generally, in such cases, state law entitles minority shareholders to petition for court review of the adequacy of the compensation. This right to demand review is termed an appraisal right.[114]

---

112. *See* WILLIAM L. CARY & MELVIN ARON EISENBERG, CORPORATIONS: CASES AND MATERIALS 92 (6th ed. 1992) (noting that "shares of corporate stock are freely transferable"). Cary and Eisenberg also observe that under the U.C.C., a stock certificate is a negotiable instrument. *See id.* at 92 n.4 (citing U.C.C. §§ 8-102, 8-105(1)). Therefore, "a transfer to a holder in due course cuts off most claims against the transferee." *Id.*

113. *Compare* Weinberger v. UOP, Inc., 457 A.2d 701, 713 (Del. 1983) (holding that appraisal is the only available remedy for minority shareholders in a cash-out merger, and noting that "[f]air price obviously requires consideration of all relevant factors involving the value of a company"), *with* Rabkin v. Philip A. Hunt Chem. Corp., 498 A.2d 1099, 1106, 1107-08 (Del. 1985) (holding that appraisal is not an exclusive remedy when the defendant engaged in faithless acts that were reasonably related to and have a substantial impact upon the price offered in a freeze-out merger).

114. *See* JESSE H. CHOPER ET AL., CASES AND MATERIALS ON CORPORATIONS 1167 (3d ed. 1989) (defining "dissenters' appraisal right" as the right of "[s]hareholders who dissent from a corporate merger and, in most states, shareholders who dissent from the sale of all or substantially all of their corporation's assets . . . to require the corporation to purchase their shares at a judicially determined price").

For a sample of statutes that provide for dissenters' appraisal rights, see CAL. CORP. CODE §§ 17600-17613 (West 1999) (providing for dissenters' rights with regard to certain reorganizations or mergers of limited liability corporations); FLA. STAT. ANN. § 608.4381(4)(d) (West 1999) (referring to offers required in connection with dissenters' rights); N.Y. BUS. CORP. LAW § 1005 (McKinney 1994) (providing for payments to dissenting members in the case of certain mergers or consolidations); OHIO REV. CODE ANN. § 1705.40 (Anderson 1998) (outlining members' entitlement to relief as dissenting members).

Many corporations statutes lack similar protections, notwithstanding the widespread provision of appraisal rights for minority owners in corporations. *See* Joel Seligman, *Reappraising the Appraisal Remedy*, 52 GEO. WASH. L. REV. 829, 831-32 & n.11 (1984) (reporting that all fifty states and the District of Columbia provide appraisal rights in case of a corporate merger or consolidation); *see also* Sandra K. Miller, *What Buy-Out Rights, Fiduciary Duties, and Dissolution Remedies Should Apply in the Case of the Minority Owner of a Liability Company?*, 38 HARV. J. ON LEGIS. 413, 416-17 (2001). For example, some limited liability corporations statutes do not provide for dissenters' rights in the case of certain

Consider the case of the classic tender offer accompanied by a freeze-out. The target corporation is a publicly held corporation with, let us say, 100,000 outstanding shares. An acquiring corporation desires to purchase and incorporate the business of the target corporation into its own. To this end, the acquirer issues a tender offer for the purchase of 50,001 of the target's shares. Following the success of the tender offer, the acquirer intends to use the 50,001 shares to cause the target to vote to merge itself into the acquirer. Under the terms of the merger deal, the target will sell all its assets to the acquirer for cash, and then cease to exist as an independent corporation. Since minority shareholders in the target will be forced to receive cash in exchange for their shares in the dissolving corporation, the nature of their entitlement will be transformed from property rule protection into liability rule protection. If displeased with the amount of compensation set by the majority (the acquirer's 50,001 shares), the minority shareholders may seek judicial appraisal of the value of their shares in the target. Either way, the minority shareholders lack the ability to veto the transfer of their assets and must make do with a third party determination of the amount they will receive.

Minority share ownership in the face of majoritarian corporate decisionmaking is therefore a pliability entitlement: in most cases, a share is a property interest entitled to property rule protection, but the adoption of certain corporate decisions alters the nature of the shareholder's interest in his or her shares. The provision in state law requiring majority decisions to engage in a merger, freeze-out takeover or the like, should therefore be viewed as creating a classic pliability rule.

The use of a pliability rule in this case is justifiable on grounds of both fairness and efficiency. The property rule baseline, by empowering shareholders to dispose of their shares as they please, induces investment in the stock market, and allows individuals to plan ahead. Since ordinary share trading on the market is relatively cheap, markets are liquid, and there is no inherent reason to assume that non-holding investors value shares more highly than existing shareholders, property rule protection is the optimal means for ensuring that shares are efficiently allocated.

However, in scenarios involving transfer of corporate control, property rule protection is unduly cumbersome. Obtaining unanimous consent is likely to be prohibitively costly. Additionally, strategic holdouts may bar such transactions altogether. Under a unanimous consent rule, each shareholder will find it in her interest to holdout in order to increase her expected payoff.[115] Finally, in the absence of stra-

---

mergers or acquisitions, and few corporations statutes provide an equitable dissolution or buy-out remedy in the case of illegality or fraud. *Id.* at 417.

115. *See* Zohar Goshen, *Voting (Insincerely) in Corporate Law*, 2 THEORETICAL

tegic behavior, majority decisions are the best mechanism for maximizing the wealth of the shareholders as a group. Thus, to ensure the efficient operation of the market for corporate control, corporate law replaces the property rule baseline with a liability rule triggered by majority decisions.

While a pliability rule in this context is superior to both unchanging property and liability rule protection, it still leaves open the possibility of majority abuse in the liability phase. In cases of freeze-out takeovers, for example, majority shareholders may use their power to divest minority shareholders of their assets to transfer value from the minority to the majority. Majority decisions make minorities vulnerable to unfair asset substitution, in which the majority uses a merger or takeover to substitute one set of assets underlying the share for another, less valuable set.[116] The law thus ensures the shareholders' right to adequate compensation in the liability stage of the pliability rule by means of an appraisal right.[117]

INQUIRIES L. 815, 820 (2001) (explaining the holdout problem with the example of a corporation that asks for its bondholders' consent to an interest rate decrease to ease the corporation's debt burden — a decision requiring the unanimous consent of all the bondholders: "Despite the fact that this decrease in the interest rate may be in the best interests of all the bondholders, an individual bondholder may vote strategically against the change, withholding her consent until she is paid a higher price for her support.").

116. Modern explanations of the importance of appraisal rights tend to focus on reducing the distortive effects of two-tier tender offers. *See, e.g.,* Daniel Fischel, *The Appraisal Remedy in Corporate Law,* 1983 AM. B. FOUND. RES. J. 875, 879 (1983) (arguing that appraisal rights alleviate the prisoner's dilemma in the case of a two-tier tender offer); Hideki Kanda & Saul Levmore, *The Appraisal Remedy and the Goals of Corporate Law,* 32 UCLA L. REV. 429, 463-469 (1985) (contemplating the theoretical potential of appraisal rights as a general monitoring tool against management which reduces the ex ante costs of the agency relationship). These explanations of the importance of appraisal rights also tend to focus on ensuring minority shareholders a "fair share" of value created in the corporate change. *See* Victor Brudney & Marvin A. Chirelstein, *Fair Shares in Corporate Mergers and Takeovers,* 88 HARV. L. REV. 297, 336 (1974) (arguing that in the case of a two-tier tender offer, "the function of a fairness standard should primarily be one of preventing deception"); Council of the Corporation Law Section of the Delaware State Bar Association, The Proposed Delaware Takeover Statute: A Report to the Delaware General Assembly 3 (1988) (noting that a potential bidder is able to "take over the company without the approval of the board, sell the assets, and dividend out the proceeds and have each stockholder receive his fair share of its assets"), rather than "asset substitution." For further explanation, see also Peter V. Letsou, *The Role of Appraisal in Corporate Law,* 39 B.C. L. REV. 1121 (1998); Paul Mahoney & Mark Weinstein, *The Appraisal Remedy and Merger Premiums,* 1 AM. L. & ECON. REV. 239 (1999); Barry M. Wertheimer, *The Shareholders' Appraisal Remedy and How Courts Determine Fair Value,* 47 DUKE L.J. 613 (1998).

117. Under the stock market exception, many appraisal statutes do not apply to widely held public corporations. *See, e.g.,* DEL CODE ANN. tit. 8, § 262(b)(1) (1991).

Other legal mechanisms exist to protect minority shareholders, especially in the close corporation context. For example, Delaware permits the shareholders of a close corporation to include in the certificate of incorporation a provision allowing dissolution at the request of any shareholder. *See* DEL. CODE. ANN. tit. 8, § 355 (1991). Similarly, the Model Business Corporation Act empowers courts to order the involuntary dissolution of a corporation if a shareholder establishes that (i) the directors are in a deadlock that cannot be broken by the shareholders; (ii) the directors or those in control of the corporation have acted, are acting, or will act in a manner that is "illegal, oppressive or fraudulent;" (iii) the shareholders are

2. *Essential Facilities and Antitrust Damages*

The essential facilities doctrine in antitrust law provides another example of a classic pliability rule. Originating in *United States v. Terminal Railroad Association*,[118] the doctrine renders it illegal for owners of "essential facilities" to deny others access as the result of anticompetitive motives or under conditions that reduce competition. Essential facilities are facilities that cannot practically be duplicated and are necessary for competitors' survival.[119] The case of *Terminal Railroad* is illuminating. There, financier Jay Gould established a group that acquired control over all the facilities necessary to load or unload freight or passengers, or cross the Mississippi River in the area of St. Louis. Gould's group used its monopoly power to impose premium pricing on users of the facilities owned by his group. The *Terminal Railroad* Court found in this arrangement a violation of sections 1 and 2 of the Sherman Act. However, rather than strip Gould of his property by ordering divestiture, the Court established that Gould could maintain his monopoly over the St. Louis nexus — a facility essential to trans-Mississippi traffic in the Midwest — so long as pricing (and other terms of usage) were regulated.[120]

The essential facilities doctrine has been extended to a wide array of assets, including electricity distribution networks,[121] telephone transmission and switching systems,[122] gas pipelines,[123] and the New

---

deadlocked and have been unable to elect directors for at least two consecutive annual meetings; or (iv) the corporate assets are being misapplied or wasted. *See* MODEL BUS. CORP. ACT § 14.30(2) (1969) (amended 1984); Michael P. Dooley & Michael D. Goldman, *Some Comparisons Between the Model Business Corporation Act and the Delaware General Corporation Law*, 56 BUS. LAW. 737, 747 (2001). The "oppression" ground is most often cited in petitions for dissolution, and some courts have recognized a cause of action for oppression outside of the dissolution context. *See* Robert B. Thompson, *The Shareholders Cause of Action for Oppression*, 48 BUS. LAW. 699 (1993). However, dissolution proceedings rarely result in the actual dissolution of the corporation but often result in a buyout of the petitioner's shares, or, more rarely, the petitioner's buyout of the majority's shares. *See, e.g.,* Park McGinty, *Replacing Hostile Takeovers*, 144 U. PA. L. REV. 983, 999-1002 (1996) (concluding that involuntary dissolution "either levels the terrain on which oppressed minority shareholders negotiate or (quite rarely) forces liquidation").

118. 224 U.S. 383 (1912).

119. *See, e.g.,* Hecht v. Pro-Football, Inc., 570 F.2d 982 (D.C. Cir. 1977).

120. *See generally* Abbott B. Lipsky, Jr. & J. Gregory Sidak, *Essential Facilities*, 51 STAN. L. REV. 1187 (1999).

121. *See* Otter Tail Power Co. v. United States, 410 U.S. 366 (1973); City of Anaheim v. S. Cal. Edison Co., 955 F.2d 1373 (9th Cir. 1992); City of Vernon v. S. Cal. Edison Co., 955 F.2d 1361 (9th Cir. 1992).

122. *See* MCI Communications Corp. v. Am. Tel. & Tel. Co., 708 F.2d 1081 (7th Cir. 1983); Bell Atl. Corp. v. MFS Communications Co., 901 F. Supp. 835 (D. Del. 1995).

123. *See* City of Chanute v. Williams Natural Gas Co., 955 F.2d 641 (10th Cir. 1992); Illinois *ex rel.* Burris v. Panhandle E. Pipeline Co., 935 F.2d 1469 (7th Cir. 1991); Garshman v. Universal Res. Holding, Inc., 824 F.2d 223 (3d Cir. 1987).

York Stock Exchange.[124] The aim, in all cases, has been to preserve the advantages of unified control of the essential facility, on the one hand, and to avoid the inefficiencies of monopoly pricing, on the other.[125]

The doctrine requires courts to mandate access to privately owned property once it becomes essential for competition. Thus, the essential facilities doctrine provides an example of a judicially triggered classic pliability rule. Upon a judicial finding of an essential facility, the owner's property rule protection over her essential facility changes into liability rule protection. She retains ownership of the facility but must grant access to competitors at a price determined or reviewed by a third party — the court or a regulator.

The use of a pliability rule in the instance of essential facilities enables courts to preserve the baseline advantages of property rules discussed earlier — such as encouraging optimal investment and reducing transaction costs — while introducing liability rules in those cases where circumstances make such rules more advantageous. Specifically, the liability rule stage diminishes the social deadweight loss associated with monopoly pricing by granting competitors access to necessary facilities at an approximation of competitive pricing.

In mandating a liability rule as the second stage of the pliability rule, rather than dividing the property among different firms, the essential facilities doctrine produces another benefit. Keeping the property together under one roof preserves the economies of scale produced by natural monopolies, while the liability rule avoids the cost of monopolistic pricing. In a natural monopoly, the cost of providing a service declines with output, making a single provider the optimum from a cost perspective.[126]

---

124. *See* Silver v. New York Stock Exch., 373 U.S. 341 (1963).

125. To effectuate the balance, the essential facilities doctrine imposes liability on a Sherman Act section 2 defendant when the plaintiff proves the following elements: (1) control of an essential facility by a monopolist; (2) a competitor's inability reasonably or practically to duplicate the essential facility; (3) denial of the use of the facility to the competitor; and (4) providing the competitor access to the facility is feasible. *See MCI*, 708 F.2d at 1132-33 (laying out four factors); JULIAN O. VON KALINOWSKI ET AL., ANTITRUST LAWS AND TRADE REGULATION § 25.04[3] n.114 (2d ed. 2001) (listing cases adopting or citing with approval the *MCI* formulation of the elements of an essential facilities case). However, the essential facilities doctrine has not met with universal approval. *See, e.g.*, Philip E. Areeda, *Essential Facilities: An Epithet In Need of Limiting Principles*, 58 ANTITRUST L.J. 841 (1990) (arguing that no Supreme Court case has provided a consistent rationale for the doctrine or has explored either the social costs and benefits or the administrative costs of requiring the creator of an asset to share it with a rival).

126. *See* ERNEST GELLHORN & WILLIAM E. KOVACIC, ANTITRUST LAW AND ECONOMICS IN A NUTSHELL 70 (4th ed. 1994) ("In what is known as a 'natural monopoly,' a single firm's average costs decline with output, meaning that it is always less costly for the one firm to produce any level of output rather than subdivide production among two or more firms."); Christopher Wyeth Kirkham, *Busting the Administrative Trust: An Experimentalist Approach to Universal Service Administration in Telecommunications Policy*, 98 COLUM. L. REV. 620, 621 n.4 (1998) (describing natural monopolies as "situations in which the marginal cost of production or service provision declines with increasing economies of

So far, our discussion has focused on the ex post effect of the essential facility doctrine — i.e., the outcome that results from the application of the doctrine. It is also important to note the ex ante effect of the doctrine, particularly the incentive it creates for self regulation. Because owners of facilities that may eventually be found essential know that they enjoy only pliability rule, not property rule protection, they will self-regulate in order to remain in the property rule stage of the pliability rule. They can do so either by ensuring that they do not accumulate assets in a way that stymies competition, or by voluntarily granting access to competitors.

This last point demonstrates a broader implication of pliability analysis of antitrust law. The essential facilities doctrine is not the sole antitrust remedy to employ pliability rules; indeed, pliability rules may be seen as the animating principle behind antitrust law. In a pliability

---

scale across the size of the entire market," and noting that "[i]n such a case, optimal social utility is arguably gained by concentrating production in a single enterprise"); Joseph Montiero & Gerald Robertson, *Shipping Conference Legislation in Canada, the European Economic Community and the United States: Background, Emerging Developments, Trends and a Few Major Issues*, 26 TRANSP. L.J. 141, 203 (1999) (explaining that the cost function of a natural monopolist is subadditive at output because it is more expensive for two or more firms to produce than it is for the natural monopolist to produce alone).

Natural monopolies may arise in various contexts. For telecommunications, see Daniel F. Spulber, *Deregulating Telecommunications*, 12 YALE J. ON REG. 25 (1995) (discussing natural monopoly in the context of telecommunications). *But see* Robert W. Crandall & J. Gregory Sidak, *Competition and Regulatory Policies for Interactive Broadband Networks*, 68 S. CAL. L. REV. 1203, 1214 (1995) (warning that "[w]hen formulating policies for interactive broadband networks . . . regulators should be cautious about assuming that natural monopoly will necessarily characterize such networks" because "[w]hat was once a naturally monopolistic method for delivering a particular kind of telecommunications service may be supplanted over time by a lower-cost method that does not necessarily have large sunk costs and low incremental costs"). For public utilities, see Jim Rossi, *The Common Law "Duty to Serve" and Protection of Consumers in an Age of Competitive Retail Public Utility Restructuring*, 51 VAND. L. REV. 1233, 1237 (1998) (defining a "public utility" as "a large vertically-integrated firm that provides service to all customers within its geographically-defined service area"), especially the transmission segments of public utilities, *see* Christopher G. Bond, *Shedding New Light on the Economics of Electric Restructuring: Are Retail Markets for Electricity the Answer to Rising Energy Costs?*, 33 CONN. L. REV. 1311, 1323 (2001) (noting that "[t]he transmission segments of the traditional public utilities (electricity, phone, and gas) are often cited as the best examples of natural monopolies"). For water works and cable television, see Lancaster Cmty. Hosp. v. Antelope Valley Hosp. Dist., 940 F.2d 397, 401 n.8 (9th Cir. 1991) (explaining that "electric utilities, water works, and cable television are generally highly regulated" because "these industries are paradigmatic examples of natural monopolies"). For newspaper delivery, see Roger D. Blair & John E. Lopatka, *The Albrecht Rule after Kahn: Death Becomes Her*, 74 NOTRE DAME L. REV. 123, 152 (1998) (noting that "newspaper delivery has natural monopoly characteristics in very small areas").

On the economics of natural monopoly, see generally WILLIAM J. BAUMOL ET AL., CONTESTABLE MARKETS AND THE THEORY OF INDUSTRY STRUCTURE 8 (rev. ed. 1988); SANFORD V. BERG & JOHN TSCHIRHART, NATURAL MONOPOLY REGULATION: PRINCIPLES AND PRACTICE 22 (1988); DENNIS W. CARLTON & JEFFREY M. PERLOFF, MODERN INDUSTRIAL ORGANIZATION 295-96 (2d ed. 1994); ROGER SHERMAN, THE REGULATION OF MONOPOLY 80-81 (1989); DANIEL F. SPULBER, REGULATION AND MARKETS 3 (1989); JEAN TIROLE, THE THEORY OF INDUSTRIAL ORGANIZATION 19-20 (1988); KENNETH E. TRAIN, OPTIMAL REGULATION: THE ECONOMIC THEORY OF NATURAL MONOPOLY 6-8 (1991).

analysis, antitrust law aims at defining the anticompetitive conditions that should trigger a change of legal protection from one type of property rule protection to a different type of property or liability rule. In contrast to the essential facilities doctrine, not all antitrust remedies create classic pliability rules. For example, remedies requiring the break up of the anticompetitive corporation can be seen as enforcing a title shifting pliability rule in which, upon the occurrence of a given triggering condition, property rule protection passes from the hands of one entitlement holder (the anticompetitive corporation) to one or more other entitlement holders.

3.   *Post*-Boomer *Nuisance*

Finally, we turn to the nuisance rule created by *Boomer v. Atlantic Cement Co.*[127] as yet another example of a classic pliability rule. In *Boomer*, a group of homeowners brought a lawsuit seeking to enjoin the nuisance caused by pollution from the Atlantic Cement plant. Deviating from the established rule of awarding injunctions in such cases, the New York Court of Appeals permitted the plant to continue operations, provided that Atlantic Cement pay permanent damages to the homeowners. The court reasoned that the Atlantic Cement plant was too valuable relative to the homeowners' pollution losses to follow the traditional rule. For Calabresi and Melamed, the *Boomer* decision represents an instance of liability rule protection. Effectively, the court prevented the homeowners from exercising their property rule right to exclude Atlantic Cement's pollution. Instead, the court forced them to suffer the pollution in exchange for the liability rule compensation decreed by the court.

While Calabresi and Melamed's static perspective is valid in describing the immediate effect of the *Boomer* decision, its impact from the dynamic perspective we offer is even more far reaching. In jurisdictions adopting *Boomer*'s reasoning as a rule of law, *Boomer* created a pliability rule. Under the *Boomer* pliability rule, homeowners enjoy property rule protection against all nuisances in stage one. However, once a nuisance-creating activity becomes sufficiently valuable, the *Boomer* rule downgrades the homeowners' entitlement into liability rule protection. The *Boomer* pliability rule thus aims to preserve property rules in most cases, while adopting liability rule protection where enjoining a nuisance diminishes economic efficiency. Importantly, the retention of the property rule baseline in this case would create a hold-out problem, as it would force Atlantic Cement to buy out the injunction from each of plaintiffs-homeowners. Conversely,

---

127. 257 N.E.2d 870 (N.Y. 1970).

eliminating property rule protection altogether would excessively reduce incentives for investment in the property.

C. *Zero Order Pliability Rules*

Like classic pliability rules, zero order pliability rules begin with property rule protection for the entitlement holder. However, by contrast with classic pliability rules, in the second, liability, stage of the pliability rule, the expected liability damages for use of the asset are zero. Thus, in zero order pliability rules, property rule protection is succeeded by a no-liability rule. Upon the triggering event, the initial entitlement holder loses the ability to exercise property rule protection, such as the right to exclude, over her property. Instead, all comers may use the property free of charge — that is, with zero order liability. Notwithstanding the zero order liability, no third party may gain a superior right to that of the original entitlement holder. The zero order pliability rules may therefore be seen as creating anti-exclusion, open access, or common property regimes.

As the examples we bring from copyright and patent make clear, zero order pliability rule protection is ubiquitous in the context of intellectual property. There, zero order pliability rules serve both economic efficiency and the interests of fairness. Zero order pliability preserves property rule protection necessary to encourage investment in useful inventions, while also using zero order liability to curb the deadweight loss created by monopoly power over the creation. Likewise, zero order pliability balances the claims of justice by the creator who wants exclusive control over her creation, on the one hand, and the public that claims a need to use the creation, on the other.

1. *Copyright and Patent Protection*

Nowhere is the role of property protection in inducing investment in resources more evident than in the context of copyright and patent law. Copyright law creates and protects exclusive rights in expressive works of authorship. Patent law provides protection for innovative products, processes, and designs. Both bodies of law are rooted in utilitarian philosophy, and the principal justification for their existence in the United States is widely known as the "incentive theory."[128] In-

---

128. *See, e.g.,* Kenneth Arrow, *Economic Welfare and the Allocation of Resources for Invention, in* THE RATE AND DIRECTION OF INVENTIVE ACTIVITY 609 (1962); Stanley M. Besen & Leo J. Raskind, *An Introduction to the Law and Economics of Intellectual Property,* 5 J. ECON. PERS. 3, 5 (1991); Stephen Breyer, *The Uneasy Case for Copyright: A Study of Copyrights in Books, Photocopies and Computer Programs,* 84 HARV. L. REV. 281, 291-93 (1970); Wendy J. Gordon, *Fair Use as Market Failure,* 82 COLUM. L. REV. 1600, 1602-12 (1982); Robert M. Hurt & Robert M. Schuchman, *The Economic Rationale of Copyright,* 56 AM. ECON. REV. 421, 425 (1966) (papers and proceedings); William M. Landes & Richard A. Posner, *An Economic Analysis of Copyright Law,* 18 J. LEGAL STUD. 325, 326 (1989)

deed, the utilitarian grounding of American copyright and patent law is even manifested in the Constitutional intellectual property clause, which empowers Congress to create exclusive rights in intellectual works in order "to promote the Progress of Science and useful Arts."[129]

The need for an economic incentive in the field of intellectual property stems from the "public good" characteristics of intellectual goods.[130] Unlike tangible goods, public goods share two distinctive characteristics: nonrivalry of consumption and nonexcludability of benefits.[131] A good is nonrival in consumption when a unit of that good can be consumed by one person without diminishing in the slightest the consumption opportunities available to others from that same unit.[132] A good displays nonexcludable benefits when individuals who have not paid for the production of that good cannot be prevented at a reasonable cost from availing themselves of its benefits.[133] The non-excludability property of public goods gives rise to two related problems. First, public goods are likely to be under-produced if left to the private market. Second, markets for public goods will not form.

Since inventions and expressive works are essentially information goods, they too are susceptible to the twin problems of under-production and lack of market exchange.[134] In the absence of legal pro-

---

[hereinafter Landes & Posner, *Copyright Law*]; Stewart E. Sterk, *Rhetoric and Reality in Copyright Law*, 94 MICH. L. REV. 1197, 1197 (1996); Barry W. Tyerman, *The Economic Rationale for Copyright Protection for Published Books: A Reply to Professor Breyer*, 18 UCLA L. REV. 1100, 1100-01 (1971).

129. U.S. CONST. art. 1, § 8. Edward Walterscheid points out that the intellectual property clause "is unique in being the only instance wherein the delegates prescribed a specific mode of accomplishing the particular authority granted." *See* Edward C. Walterscheid, *To Promote the Progress of Science and Useful Arts: The Background and Origin of the Intellectual Property Clause of the United States Constitution*, 2 J. INTELL. PROP. L. 1, 33 (1994).

130. *See, e.g.*, Gordon, *supra* note 128, at 1610; Landes & Posner, *Copyright Law, supra* note 128, at 326; *see also* Richard P. Adelstein & Steven I. Perez, *The Competition of Technologies in Markets for Ideas: Copyright and Fair Use in Evolutionary Perspective*, 5 INT'L REV. L. & ECON. 209, 218 (1985). For a view that intellectual works do not share the distinguishing attributes of public goods, see Tom G. Palmer, *Intellectual Property: A Non-Posnerian Law and Economics Approach*, 12 HAMLINE L. REV. 261, 273-87 (1989).

131. *See, e.g.*, ROBERT COOTER & THOMAS ULEN, LAW AND ECONOMICS 46-48 (1st ed. 1988); RICHARD CORNES & TODD SANDLER, THE THEORY OF EXTERNALITIES, PUBLIC GOODS, AND CLUB GOODS 6-7 (1986); EDWIN MANSFIELD, PRINCIPLES OF MARCROECONOMICS 400-04 (6th ed. 1989).

132. *See* CORNES & SANDLER, *supra* note 131, at 160.

133. *See id.* It should be noted that the impossibility of exclusion is hardly ever absolute. As a matter of fact, when exclusion by contract is considered, very few goods, if any, display nonexcludable benefits in the strict sense of the term. Thus, it is more accurate to describe goods as displaying nonexcludable benefits when it is prohibitively costly to bar nonpayers from enjoying the good. *See* Patrick Croskery, *Institutional Utilitarianism and Intellectual Property*, 68 CHI.-KENT L. REV. 631, 632 (1993).

134. *See, e.g.*, FRITZ MACHLUP, AN ECONOMIC REVIEW OF THE PATENT SYSTEM, Study No. 15, 85th Cong., 2d Sess. (1958); Kenneth W. Dam, *The Economic Underpinnings of Patent Law*, 23 J. LEGAL STUD. 247 (1994); John S. McGee, *Patent Exploitation: Some*

tection, competitors of the original inventors and authors would be able to copy their inventions or expressive works without incurring the initial costs of authorship and research and development. The unauthorized reproduction of successful expressive works and inventions would drive the market price down to the point where original authors and inventors would not be able to recover their initial expenditures. Thus, without intellectual property protection, the private returns to authors and inventors would fall short of the social value of their works and inventions, and too few inventions and expressive works would be created.

Worse yet, many of the inventions that would not materialize absent intellectual property protection are likely to be of great social value. Socially important inventions are often dependent not only upon large expenditures but also upon a high level of risk. Inventors often do not know, ex ante, whether their research and development will yield the anticipated result. They do not know how the invention will fare commercially. Subsequent copiers, however, face no such uncertainty. Copiers may reproduce — risk-free — only inventions with proven commercial success.[135] The same holds true of expressive works. For expressive works to make it to market, authors must generally find a publisher who believes the work is commercially viable. But publishing is a risky enterprise. Publishing involves a hit-and-miss process in which a small number of successful works subsidize the cost of publishing all other works. For publishers, commercially successful works are used as a risk spreading mechanism, enabling the publisher to bring to market various works that may not cover the publication and distribution costs. However, copiers may zero in on the successful works. By reproducing only successful works, and selling them at a lower price, copiers would deprive publishers of the ability to spread risk, and thereby force them out of business.

Patent and copyright protection solve these problems. By creating and enforcing exclusive rights in expressive works and inventions, copyright and patent law prevent unauthorized copying and thereby guarantee adequate rewards to authors and inventors. The right to exclude permits authors and inventors to engage in voluntary transactions with users and set the price of these transactions. Yet, copyright and patent are unique property regimes since they restrict the duration of the property rights they confer. Copyright protection endures for the life of the author plus seventy years;[136] patent protection lasts

---

Economic and Legal Problems, 9 J. L. & ECON. 135 (1966); Richard R. Nelson, *The Economics of Invention: A Survey of the Literature*, 32 J. BUS. 101 (1959); Dan Usher, *The Welfare Economics of Invention*, 31 ECONOMICA 279 (1964).

135. *See* Arrow, *supra* note 128, at 609, 614-15 (suggesting that the uncertainty as to the outcome of the inventive enterprise and the lack of market mechanism for risk shifting, will result in underinvestment in inventive activity).

136. 17 U.S.C. § 302(a) (1998). In the case of an anonymous work, a pseudonymous

twenty years from the date of filing an application.[137] Once the protection lapses, the formerly protected expressive works and inventions
fall into the public domain, and anyone can use, reproduce, and market them freely. Both patent and copyright are, therefore, examples of
mandatory zero order pliability rules. In both cases, the initial property rule protection changes into a zero order liability rule protection
at the end of the statutorily prescribed term.

The use of zero order pliability rules in this context serves several
important purposes. Patent and copyright law embody a fundamental
tradeoff between ex ante and ex post efficiency, or, put differently, a
tradeoff between production and access. Ex ante, patent and copyright
law seek to spur adequate production of information goods; ex post,
after the information goods have been produced, they seek to ensure
the widest possible access to these goods. As the intellectual property
clause clearly indicates, the purpose of establishing exclusive rights in
intellectual goods is not to reward authors and inventors per se, but
rather, to promote the production and dissemination of new information to the public.[138] The exclusivity conferred upon authors and inventors promotes the creation of new works and innovation, but it does so
at the cost of curtailing the dissemination of the new information
products to the public. Copyright and patent protection essentially
grant monopoly power to authors and inventors, and thus, like all monopolies, generates a social "dead-weight" loss. The same exclusivity
that induces creativity and investment also brings about supra-
competitive prices, and leads to the exclusion of certain consumers
who would have been willing to pay the competitive price.[139] Robert
Cooter and Thomas Ulen have stated the basic dilemma presented by
intellectual property is that "without a legal monopoly not enough information will be produced, but with legal monopoly too little of the
information will be used."[140]

The zero order pliability rule mitigates the tension between the
two social goals that intellectual property law seeks to promote. The
initial property rule protection — represented by the limited monopoly — underwrites the production of information goods. The subsequent zero order pliability rule — represented by the eventual fall of
expressive works and inventions into the public domain — guarantees

---

work, or a work made for hire, the copyright endures for the shorter of 95 years from the
year of its first publication, or 120 years from the year of its creation. *Id.* § 302(c).

137. 35 U.S.C. § 154(a)(2) (1999).

138. *See* CRAIG JOYCE ET AL., COPYRIGHT LAW 1-70 (5th ed. 2000).

139. *See, e.g.,* Christian Koboldt, *Intellectual Property and Optimal Copyright Protection,*
19 J. CULT. ECON. 131 (1995) (arguing that even optimal copyright protection cannot lead to
a first-best allocative efficiency solution).

140. COOTER & ULEN, *supra* note 131, at 135 (in latest edition, 3d ed. 2000, similar
proposition, but not same sentence, appears on page 128).

the public unrestricted access to information goods once the limited monopoly expires. The limited duration is supposed to guarantee that the goal of copyright and patent protection is positive because in the final analysis the goal of copyright and patent is to make more and better intellectual products available to every one.[141]

The employment of a zero order pliability rule serves another policy goal: it reduces the cost of subsequent authorship and innovation. It is important to realize that the public domain is not merely the sphere of works whose protection has expired; it is also a source of the raw materials for future authorship and invention.[142] Works whose protection has expired ensure the continuity of authorship and innovation as they perpetually replenish the supply of expression and knowledge for future authors and inventors to draw on. Furthermore, public domain works reduce the cost of creation and research for future authors and inventors, and consequently, the total cost of producing intellectual works.

The zero order pliability rule protection is also attractive on distributional grounds. Those most likely to be harmed by the monopolies wrought by copyright and especially patent protection are the least well-off. Low-income consumers can ill-afford to pay the supra-competitive prices charged for patented products and copyrighted works during the property rule protection period. The shift to a zero order liability rule opens up the market to competition and enables low-income consumers to enjoy previously over-priced goods. Consider, for example, pharmaceutical drugs. The need to recoup their initial investment in R&D prompts brand name pharmaceutical companies to charge supra-competitive prices for patented drugs. The principal victims of the monopoly pricing are the indigent [143] and the

---

141. It bears emphasis that we do *not* suggest that the current protection term is optimal. Nor do we endorse it. Our analysis has nothing to say about the issue. We merely seek to explain the use of zero order pliability rules in intellectual property law.

142. *See, e.g.*, Jessica Litman, *The Public Domain*, 39 EMORY L.J. 965, 968 (1990).

143. For analysis of the effect of monopoly pricing on poor countries see, for example, Bernard Pecoul, *Fighting for Survival*, HARV. INT'L REV., Fall 2001, at 60 (noting that international trade agreements and patenting of medicines in other parts of the world influence the global marketing and pricing policies of research-based pharmaceutical companies, which in turn impacts the availability and affordability of medicines, including AIDS medicines, in the least-developed countries); Jonathan Mann et al., *South Africa's AIDS Agreement*, CNN INT'L: INSIGHT (Apr. 19, 2001), *available at* 2001 WL 14386528 (reporting that "[t]he commercial price of the triple therapy treatment to control HIV costs up to $10,000 [per] year per patient. That dwarfs the per capita income of every African country"; also reporting that in response to a "well-organized, high-profile campaign by pressure groups, the major drug companies have slashed their prices to the poorest countries. In Zambia, about 20 percent of the population is infected with HIV. [Recently], Glaxo Smith, Bristol Myers Squibb and Merck offered the Zambian government a deal so that anti-retroviral treatment would cost two dollars a day"); Anthony Birritteri, *Intellectual Property Protection a Must for Drug Firm Success*, N.J. BUS., June 2001, at 56 (reporting the April 2001 settlement between South Africa and thirty-nine drug manufacturers, allowing the country to broaden access to medicines for the estimated 4.7 million South Africans with AIDS in exchange for

elderly,[144] who most critically need the new drugs, but lack sufficient funds to afford them. Furthermore, even those who can purchase the drugs overpay for them since the drug companies, owing to their monopoly power appropriate most, if not all, of the consumer surplus. The price of new drugs falls dramatically, however, once the patent protection expires and generic drugs enter the market. Indeed, according to some reports, two years after their introduction to the market, the price of generic substitutes is on average 35-38% of the price of the relevant brand name drug, and the market share of the generics averages 45-59%.[145] It bears emphasis, though, that without the initial inducement provided by the patent protection, neither the original drugs nor the generic substitutes would be produced. Thus, the use of pliability rule protection in this context induces scientific progress, encourages competition among various drug manufacturers in the long term, and offers significant distributive advantages relative to standard property rule protection.

2. *Genericism in Trademark Law*

The genericism doctrine in trademark law is yet another example of a zero order pliability rule. Trademark law protects symbolic information signifying the source of goods and services.[146] Unlike patent and copyright protection that seek to spur creation of inventions and

---

adherence to WTO patent laws).

144. John M.R. Bull, *Subsidized Drugs for Seniors Facing Deficit*, PITTSBURGH POST-GAZETTE, Nov. 28, 2001, at B8 (discussing the financial difficulties of Pennsylvania's program to subsidize prescription drugs for senior citizens, called Pharmaceutical Assistance Contract for the Elderly, or "PACE"); Howard Dean, *Deft Scalpel*, NAT'L J., Nov. 17, 2001, at 3617 (reviewing GEORGE D. LUNDBERG, SEVERED TRUST: WHY AMERICAN MEDICINE HASN'T BEEN FIXED (2000)) (describing the Congressional debate over prescription drug benefits for the elderly, and noting that "Democrats argue for a straight government-financed Medicare prescription drug benefit carrying a price tag of about $300 billion," while "Republicans press for a program in which the government provides vouchers so that patients can buy private insurance."); *Inside the Industry: Pfizer Announces New Pharmacy Discount Card for Seniors*, AM. HEALTH LINE, Jan. 16, 2002, *available at* Westlaw, 1/16/2002 APN-HE6 (noting the strength of "political pressure on the affordability of medicine for the elderly"); Morton Mintz, *Still Hard to Swallow*, WASH. POST, Feb. 11, 2001, at B1 (reporting that "[w]hat's new about prescription drug pricing is the attention that it's been getting in Congress, thanks partly to bus loads of elderly Americans going to Canada and Mexico to buy their medicines at sharply lower costs").

145. *See* Henry Grabowski & John Vernon, *Longer Patents for Increased Generic Competition in the U.S.: The Waxman-Hatch Act After One Decade*, 10 PHARMACOECONOMICS 110 (Supp. 2, 1996); William Haddad, *Testing Times for the U.S. Generic Industry*, SCRIP MAG., May 1992, at 26, 27; U.S. INT'L TRADE COMM'N NO. 332-302, GLOBAL COMPETITIVENESS OF U.S. ADVANCED TECHNOLOGY MFG. INDUS.: PHARMACEUTICALS 13-16 (Sept. 1991).

146. 15 U.S.C. § 1127 (1988 & Supp. IV 1992); *see also* Ralph S. Brown Jr., *Advertising and the Public Interest: Legal Protection of Trade Symbols*, 57 YALE L.J. 1165, 1185 (1948) ("The informative job of trade symbols is conventionally considered to be identification of source; and it is this capacity which courts traditionally have protected.").

expressive works, trademark protection purports to enhance competition among providers of goods and services.[147] Trademarks promote competition in two related ways. Trademarks — by themselves and in combination with other forms of advertising — convey information about the quality of products and services, reducing consumers' search costs.[148] This informational function of trademarks is especially valuable in the context of experience goods, where consumers cannot discern the attributes of products before purchasing them,[149] and must rely on prior experience in deciding among competing brands. Trademarks allow consumers to associate product and service attributes with certain firms and base their consumption decisions on this association.[150] For this reason, on the supply side, trademark protection spurs firms to maintain and improve the quality of their products and services.[151] The availability of trademark protection protects firms from free-riding by competitors, enabling them to reap the fruits of their investment in superior products and services. Furthermore, trademark protection provides firms with an incentive to establish brand recognition and loyalty, by "educating" consumers about the virtues of their products. Thus, trademarks constitute an important channel of communication between firms and consumers, with the attendant twin effects of motivating the former to improve the quality of their products and enabling the latter to differentiate among various products on the market.

---

147. *See* S. REP. NO. 79-1331, at 3 (1946); H.R. REP. NO. 79-219, at 2 (1945) ("Trademarks defeat monopoly by stimulating competition.").

148. *See, e.g.,* Nicholas Economides, *Trademarks, in* THE NEW PALGRAVE DICTIONARY OF ECONOMICS AND THE LAW 601, 602-03 (Peter Newman ed., 1998) (noting that trademarks "facilitate and enhance consumer decisions"); William P. Kratzke, *Normative Economic Analysis of Trademark Law,* 21 MEMPHIS ST. U. L. REV. 199, 214-17 (1991).

149. The term "experience goods" was coined by Philip Nelson, *Information and Consumer Behavior,* 78 J. POLITICAL ECON. 311 (1970); Philip Nelson, *Advertising as Information,* 82 J. POLITICAL ECON. 729 (1974). A search good is one whose important attributes may be ascertained before purchase or use. Besides search and experience goods, a third category, usually applied to services, is "credence." A credence quality cannot be evaluated by direct observation or use. For example, a consumer may purchase automobile repair services and never discover, before or after the purchase, whether the repair was necessary. *See* Michael Darby & Edi Karni, *Free Competition and the Optimal Amount of Fraud,* 16 J.L. & ECON. 67, 68-69 (1973).

150. *See* Mark A. Lemley, *The Modern Lanham Act and the Death of Common Sense,* 108 YALE L.J. 1687, 1690 (1999) (noting that advertising communicates the "experience" characteristics of goods directly to consumers, while "trademarks ensure that consumers associate the characteristics with the right product" when making purchasing decisions).

151. William M. Landes & Richard Posner, *Trademark Law: An Economic Perspective,* 30 J. L. & ECON. 265, 269 (1987) [hereinafter Landes & Posner, *Trademark Law*]. Landes and Posner note that trademarks have a self-enforcing quality since they denote "consistent quality, and a firm has an incentive to develop a trademark only if it is able to maintain consistent quality." *Id.* at 270.

As a general rule, any expressive term or symbol may be used as a trademark as long as it is distinctive and nondeceptive.[152] However, generic terms may not be used as trademarks.[153] The doctrine of genericism has two temporal dimensions: a prospective dimension and a retrospective dimension. Prospectively, the genericism doctrine bars the appropriation of generic terms such as "WINE" or "COMPUTER" as trademarks. Courts have applied the doctrine prospectively to deny trademark protection to terms such as, "INJURY,"[154] "386,"[155] "HONEY BROWN,"[156] "YOU HAVE MAIL," and "BUDDY LIST."[157] The genericism doctrine may also be

---

152. 15 U.S.C. § 1052(e)(1) (1988); *see also* Two Pesos, Inc. v. Taco Cabana, Inc., 505 U.S. 763, 769 (1992) ("The general rule regarding distinctiveness is clear: an identifying mark is distinctive and capable of being protected if it *either* (1) is inherently distinctive *or* (2) has acquired distinctiveness through secondary meaning."); Robert C. Denicola, *Freedom to Copy*, 108 YALE L.J. 1661, 1673 (1999) ("For word marks, the use of broad categories determinative of inherent distinctiveness avoids the administrative costs of a case-by-case balancing of the informational advantages and competitive disadvantages of protection. It also affords a degree of predictability, valued both in decisions to adopt and decisions to imitate a putative trademark.").
   Traditionally, trademark protection sprang into existence upon the use of a mark in trade. In 1988, the Lanham Act was amended to create a federal registry of trademarks, *see* Trademark Law Revision Act of 1988, Pub. L. No. 100-667, 102 Stat. 3935, and now businesses can register marks even before using them in trade upon a showing of a bona fide intent to use them in the future. *See* Lanham Act § 1(b), (codified at 15 U.S.C. § 1051(b) (1994)); J. THOMAS MCCARTHY, MCCARTHY ON TRADEMARK AND UNFAIR COMPETITION § 5 (4th ed. 2001) (noting that "[b]y far the most sweeping change [effected by the 1988 amendments] was the inclusion of an 'intent-to-use' basis for applications," which granted "United States firm[s] ... the option to apply for federal registration of a mark based on a bona fide intent to use the mark in commerce"). Descriptive marks, such as "Burger," *see In re* Nat'l Presto Indus., Inc., 197 U.S.P.Q. 188 (T.T.A.B. 1977) (holding "Burger" for cooking utensils descriptive of purpose of goods), "PM," *see* Bristol-Myers Squibb Co. v. McNeil-P.P.C., Inc., 973 F.2d 1033 (2d. Cir. 1992) (holding term "PM" descriptive of an analgesic/sleep aid designed for night-time use), and "KING SIZE," *see* King-Size, Inc. v. Frank's King Size Clothes, Inc., 547 F. Supp. 1138 (S.D. Tex. 1982) (holding the term "KING SIZE" descriptive of men's clothes), may only be registered if they have acquired a secondary meaning. *See Two Pesos*, 505 U.S. at 769 (explaining that "descriptive marks may acquire the distinctiveness which will allow them to be protected under the [Lanham] Act . . . . This acquired distinctiveness is generally called 'secondary meaning' ").

153. Originally, genericism was a court-made doctrine. *See, e.g.*, Canal Co. v. Clark, 80 U.S. (13 Wall.) 311, 323 (1871); RESTATEMENT OF TORTS § 735 (1938). Today, the doctrine is codified in the Lanham Act. *See* 15 U.S.C. § 1064(3) (1994). A generic term is one that denotes "the name of a kind of goods . . . [u]nlike a trademark, which identifies the source of a product, a generic term merely identifies the genus of which the particular product is a species." Liquid Controls Corp. v. Liquid Control Corp., 802 F.2d 934, 936 (7th Cir. 1986).

154. Dranoff-Perlstein Assocs. v. Sklar, 967 F.2d 852 (3d Cir. 1992) (stating that the "injury" portion of the mark "INJURY-1," a telephone number mnemonic, is generic and therefore unprotected as a trademark).

155. Intel Corp. v. Advanced Micro Devices, Inc., 756 F. Supp. 1292 (N.D. Cal. 1991) (ruling that Intel's mark "386" is generic and thus not protected).

156. Genesee Brewing Co. Inc. v. Stroh Brewing Co., 124 F.3d 137 (2d Cir. 1997) (concluding that the term "HONEY BROWN" is generic when applied to ale beer).

157. America Online, Inc. v. AT&T Corp., 64 F. Supp. 2d 549 (E.D. Va. 1999) (holding that service marks "YOU HAVE MAIL" and "BUDDY LIST" are generic rather than suggestive).

applied retrospectively to invalidate trademarks that were initially distinctive, but through overuse became generic. Examples of marks that initially received protection but were later nullified on genericism grounds include, among others, "aspirin,"[158] "cola,"[159] "thermos,"[160] "corn-flakes,"[161] yo-yo,"[162] "trampoline,"[163] "escalator,"[164] and "linoleum."[165] The retrospective application of the genericism doctrine effectively transforms the initial property rule protection accorded to the trademark owner into a zero order liability rule protection. Yet, the lapse of property rule protection is not automatic after the passage of time, as in the case of property and patent. Rather, the property rule stage of the zero order pliability rule is brought to a close by an event whose timing — and even existence — is uncertain: the transformation of the meaning of a term to a generic one.

The application of a zero order pliability rule in this context has several desirable efficiency effects. Although trademark protection generally promotes efficiency by fostering competition, trademarks also have a potential dark side. Excessively strong trademarks may harm competition since they constitute barriers to entry.[166] In such cases, the social cost of protecting trademarks may outweigh the social benefit. Consider, for instance, the term "cola." If the term were a protected trademark of the Coca-Cola company, competitors who produced similarly tasting beverages could not use the term "cola" to describe their products. Under this regime, competitors' marketing efforts would be stifled, and consumers would have to pay supracompetitive prices for the trademarked product.[167] The genericism

---

158. Bayer Co. v. United Drug Co., 272 F. 505 (S.D.N.Y. 1921).

159. Coca-Cola Co. v. Standard Bottling Co., 138 F.2d 788 (10th Cir. 1943); Dixi-Cola Labs., Inc. v. Coca-Cola Co., 117 F.2d 352 (4th Cir. 1941).

160. King-Seeley Thermos Co. v. Aladdin Indus., 321 F.2d 577 (2d Cir. 1963).

161. *See* PAUL GOLDSTEIN, COPYRIGHT, PATENT, TRADEMARK AND RELATED STATE DOCTRINES 243 (4th ed. 1997) (reproducing an ad by Xerox entitled, "Once a Trademark not always a trademark," that lists examples of trademarks that have become generic.).

162. *Id.*

163. *Id.*

164. *Id.*

165. *Id.*

166. In the 1930s economists believed that all forms of trademark protection were anticompetitive. The most notable champion of this view was Edward Chamberlin, who argued that the combination of trademark protection and persuasive advertising form barriers to entry. *See* EDWARD H. CHAMBERLIN, THE THEORY OF MONOPOLISTIC COMPETITION (1st ed. 1933). For an excellent review of the debate as to the effect of trademark protection on competition, see Daniel M. McClure, *The Lanham Act After Fifty Years: Trademarks and Competition: The Recent History*, LAW & CONTEMP. PROBS., Spring 1996, at 13.

167. *See* John F. Coverdale, Comment, *Trademarks and Generic Words: An Effect on Competition Test*, 51 U. CHI. L. REV. 868, 870-71 (1984) (noting that when there is only one word to describe a product, trademark protection would equate to monopoly power).

doctrine avoids this undesirable result. It empowers courts to terminate, in extreme cases, the property rule protection of marks whose value to third parties — i.e., competitors and consumers — exceeds their value to their original appropriators. Essentially, the genericism doctrine is an ex post mechanism for reallocating generic terms to a higher value user: the public, consumers, and competitors alike.[168] Hence, the genericism doctrine provides a nonmarket mechanism for improving allocative efficiency.

The ex ante effects of the genericism doctrine are even more interesting. Ex ante, the genericism doctrine gives rise to two pro-competitive effects: self-regulation and informative advertising. The key to both effects lies in the use of a conditional zero order pliability rule to protect trademarks. Trademarks do not become generic by mishap; the decisions of trademark owners determine the marks' fates. Trademark owners determine the exposure of their marks as well as which information and image to convey to consumers. Marks become generic either because there is insufficient competition in the relevant product or service market, or because trademark owners promote their brand names too aggressively. The genericism doctrine curbs the incentive of firms to engage in these types of anticompetitive behavior. To avoid the risk of losing protection, firms must ensure that the public does not associate the mark with a particular product, rather than a particular producer. The safest way to accomplish this is to ensure some degree of competition in the product, or service markets, in which dominant mark owners operate. The risk of genericism causes firms to self-regulate by introducing a winner's curse to trademarked markets. Over-aggressiveness toward existing competitors may result in the firm's mark — an asset it has labored hard to promote — becoming available to all competitors, both existing and future. Exercising restraint toward smaller competitors, on the other hand, goes a long way towards securing the longevity of the mark. Thus, the use of conditional pliability rule protection in this context encourages competition in product and service markets.

The doctrine of genericism also produces desirable information effects. In a classic article, Ralph Brown noted the symbiotic relationship between trademarks and advertising.[169] Brown argued that the scope of protection afforded to trademarks must be calibrated to the degree to which advertising promotes the public interest. Brown main-

---

168. As for the prospective dimension of genericism, Landes and Posner have suggested that by barring existing generic terms from becoming trademarks, trademark law provides an incentive to "enrich the language, by creating words or phrases that people value for their intrinsic pleasingness as well as their information value." They explicitly recognize, however, that this benefit is very "small." *See* Landes & Posner, *Trademark Law, supra* note 151, at 271.

169. *See* Brown, *supra* note 146; *see also* Symposium, *Ralph Sharp Brown, Intellectual Property and the Public Interest*, 108 YALE L.J. 1611 (1999).

tained that trademarks' chief virtue lies in their ability to promote competition through advertising. By prompting merchants to advertise, trademark protection enhances the information available to potential consumers, thus improving consumption decisions.[170] Influenced by the economists of his time, Brown distinguished between "informative advertising" and "persuasive advertising," postulating that the former was beneficial and the latter harmful.[171] Subsequent economic work called into question Brown's characterization of persuasive advertising, noting that even "persuasive" advertising may also produce various efficiency enhancing effects. Philip Nelson, for instance, pointed out that much of what Brown considered persuasive advertising serves an important signaling function, which improves the information available to consumers. Since businesses receive greater returns on advertising that produces repeat sales, the level of advertising for a product provides a useful indication of consumer satisfaction.[172] Irrespective of the ultimate desirability of persuasive advertising, Brown's basic insight about the direct effect of trademark protection on the market for commercial information remains valid.

D. *Simultaneous Pliability Rules*

Intellectual property also provides an example of a different kind of pliability rule: the simultaneous pliability rule. As usual, simultaneous pliability rules involve at least two different stages of property or liability rule protection, and the fulfillment of a predetermined condition triggers a shift from one type of protection to the other. However, unlike the other pliability rules we have discussed so far, the triggering condition does not take place at a discrete moment in time and the types of protection are not sequential chronologically. Rather, a single asset is simultaneously protected by different kinds of rules, depending on the kind of use. Vis-à-vis some uses, the entitlement holder enjoys the baseline property rule protection. However, certain kinds of uses trigger another kind of protection, such as liability rule protection.

Simultaneous pliability rules were clearly recognized by Calabresi and Melamed, albeit without being labeled as such. In fact, Calabresi

---

170. Brown, *supra* note 146, at 1186.

171. *Id.* at 1183 ("With qualifications that need not be repeated, persuasive advertising is, for the community as a whole, just a luxurious exercise in talking ourselves into spending our incomes."). Brown's view of persuasive advertising was heavily influenced by the work of the economist Edward Chamberlin, who argued that the combination of trademark protection and persuasive advertising form barriers to entry. *See* CHAMBERLIN, *supra* note 166.

172. *See* Philip J. Nelson, *The Economic Value of Advertising, in* ADVERTISING AND SOCIETY 43 (Yale Brozen ed., 1974). Other economists went even further doubting the ability of advertising to generate demand. *See, e.g.*, JULIAN L. SIMON, ISSUES IN THE ECONOMICS OF ADVERTISING 205-06 (1970).

and Melamed noted that "most entitlements to most goods are mixed," thereby admitting that protection of entitlements can hardly ever be described as falling under one of the pure rule types.[173] Our modest contribution here is to integrate Calabresi and Melamed's insight into our broader framework of pliability rules. For this reason, we limit our discussion of simultaneous pliability rules to two examples.

We emphasize that simultaneous pliability rules differ from other pliability rules we discuss in that they lack a dynamic element over time. As our examples illustrate, in simultaneous pliability rules, the type of protection depends on the type of use or the type of user, and does not change over time.

1. *Fair Use*

We illustrate simultaneous pliability rules with the example of the fair use doctrine. Ordinarily, as we noted previously, copyrighted works enjoy property rule protection for the life of the author plus seventy years, followed by a zero order liability regime.[174] However, even during the period of property rule protection, copyright law recognizes a fair use privilege.[175] An affirmative defense against copyright liability, the fair use privilege empowers courts to excuse unauthorized appropriation of a copyrighted work when doing so advances the pub-

---

173. Calabresi & Melamed, *supra* note 5, at 1093.

174. *See supra* Section II.C.1. The doctrine of experimental use is yet another example of a simultaneous pliability rule. Courts have long exempted, in principle, purely " 'experimental use[s]' of a patented invention, with no commercial purpose," from infringement liability. *See* Rebecca S. Eisenberg, *Patents and the Progress of Science: Exclusive Rights and Experimental Use*, 56 U. CHI. L. REV. 1017, 1019 (1989). This implies that patent holders do not always operate under property rule protection; as against experimental users, patent owners entitlement is protected by a zero order pliability rule. Based on the experimental use doctrine, § 271(e) of the Patent Act, which was added in 1984 as part of the Waxman-Hatch Act, now permits generic drug manufacturers to make, use, or sell "a patented invention . . . solely for uses reasonably related to the development and submission of information under a Federal law which regulates the manufacture, use, or sale of drugs." 35 U.S.C. § 271(3) (2001). The impact of the section was to dramatically expedite the introduction of generic drugs to the market upon the expiration of the patent, and thereby cabin the discretionary effects of patent grants. *Cf.* Gideon Parchomovsky & Peter Siegelman, *Towards an Integrated Theory of Intellectual Property*, 88 VA. L. REV. (forthcoming 2002) (discussing alternative measures for reducing the distortionary effects of patents).

175. 17 U.S.C. § 107 (1994). Section 107 begins with a nonexhaustive list of illustrative uses — such as comment, criticism, scholarship, research, news reporting, and teaching — that may qualify as fair, and then enumerates four factors a court should weigh in deciding whether a particular use is fair. The factors listed are: (1) the purpose of the use, including its commercial or noncommercial nature; (2) the nature of the protected work of the plaintiff; (3) the amount and importance of the parts that were reproduced; (4) the impact of the use on the potential market for the copyrighted work. *Id.*

Currently, patent law does not recognize a fair use defense. For a proposal to change this existing state of affairs by introducing a fair use defense into patent law, see Maureen A. O'Rourke, *Toward a Doctrine of Fair Use in Patent Law*, 100 COLUM. L. REV. 1177 (2000).

lic benefit without substantially impairing the economic value of the original work.[176] Thus, with respect to certain uses, the copyrighted work is placed under a zero order liability regime, rather than the ordinary property rule regime.

The "fair use" privilege serves several goals. First, it provides a safety valve that may be used to deny copyright protection when the perils of monopoly power loom large and the need for additional incentive to create is slight.[177] In this capacity, the "fair use" doctrine constitutes an effective vehicle for mitigating any anticompetitive effects copyright protection may cause. Second, the doctrine furnishes an effective means for overcoming market failures associated with high transaction costs or strategic behavior of creators.[178] In many transactional settings that involve intellectual goods, the cost of voluntary exchange is high and the benefits to both parties inconsequential. In these situations, a finding of fair use is likely to generate a net benefit to one of the parties without significantly harming the other.[179] Furthermore, the fair use privilege reduces the cost of creating subsequent works. In many cases, the party standing to benefit from a fair use finding is herself an author who borrows preexisting material to create her own work.

The incorporation of a fair use defense turns copyright law into a unique example of pliability rule protection. Essentially, the fair use privilege entitles third parties to take the intellectual property of others without paying any compensation to the property owners.[180] Due

---

176. *See* Gordon, *supra* note 128, at 1601.

177. *See, e.g.,* Sterk, *supra* note 128, at 1211. The so-called "Zapruder Film" of the assassination of John F. Kennedy is a case in point.

178. *See, e.g.,* Gordon, *supra* note 128, at 1613; Landes & Posner, *Copyright Law, supra* note 128, at 357-58; Sterk, *supra* note 128, at 1211.

179. For instance, a student who wishes to quote a phrase from a copyrighted book is likely to incur a significant cost should she choose to secure permission from the copyright owner. At the same time, quoting without permission would inflict a negligible harm on the copyright owner.

180. The incomplete privilege of private necessity available in cases of intentional tort offers an analogy to fair use. Private necessity permits a defendant to commit an intentional tort to another's rights in property to protect a higher-value interest, either in property, bodily security, or life. *See* RESTATEMENT (SECOND) OF TORTS §§ 262, 263 & cmt. d (1965). Where the higher-value interest belongs to a large class — for example, where the city must be saved from a fire — the privilege is one of public necessity and the defendant is relieved of any duty to compensate the plaintiff. *See id.* at § 262 & cmt. d. Where the higher value interest belongs to a small group or an individual, however, the privilege is one of private necessity and the defendant must compensate the plaintiff. *See id.* at § 263(2) & cmt. e. Because compensation is owing in the latter case, the privilege is said to be "incomplete."

In the well-known case of *Vincent v. Lake Erie Transportation Co.,* 124 N.W. 221 (Minn. 1910), a shipowner's ship damaged a dock when the owner attempted to moor the ship during a storm. The court invoked the incomplete privilege of private necessity to hold the shipowner liable. In pliability terms, the doctrine of private necessity transformed the dockowner's traditional property rule protection into a simultaneous pliability rule. For most uses, the dockowner retained property rule protection; but under extraordinary circumstances, the shipowner was permitted to take the dockowner's property for a sum equal to

to this unique doctrine, copyright protection is at once a zero order pliability rule — since the property right it bestows is limited in time — and a simultaneous pliability rule — since the protection copyright accords admits of nonconsensual takings.

2. *Privileged Takers*

Another instance of simultaneous pliability protection can be found in the case of privileged takers, in which property rule protection is suspended with respect to some nonconsensual users. These privileged users need only pay for their use under liability rules while property rule protection remains in force against the rest of the world.

Such a regime is illustrated by the case of *Head v. Amoskeag Manufacturing Co.*[181] There, the Supreme Court upheld a statute that permitted mill owners to dam waters, depriving riparian owners of their property, if two conditions were satisfied: first, the taking must be for a public benefit; and, second, the mill owners had to pay compensation at 150% of market value.

In pliability terms, the Supreme Court ruling established a simultaneous pliability rule regime. While the riparian owners enjoyed full property rule protection vis-à-vis all other trespassers, their right to exclude mill operators was protected by a liability rule. It is noteworthy, though, that mill owners had to show that the use effecting the taking benefited the public. The employment of a simultaneous pliability rule enabled the court to balance the right to private property against the interest of the mill owners, and the broader public in putting the land to its highest value use.

The simultaneous pliability rule described in *Head* differs from that seen in fair use in an important respect. Whereas fair use employs a zero order liability rule, the simultaneous pliability rule described in *Head* required 150% compensation for riparian owners not covered by property rule protection. The reason for this gap in compensation schemes can be discerned in the difference between the two types of uses permitted by the pliability rules. Users of copyrighted materials under the fair use provisions do not take exclusive possession of the entitlement. Although fair users utilize the copyrighted materials, the entitlement holder may continue to engage in commercial transactions regarding the copyrighted materials with other users. Fair use is not exclusive of the entitlement holder. Furthermore, fair users are only

---

the judicially-determined damages. Importantly, private necessity is distinguishable from fair use in that necessity requires compensation while a fair user need not compensate the copyright holder. Therefore, building on the typology we have developed, fair use may be termed a "zero simultaneous pliability rule" while private necessity may be called a "positive simultaneous pliability rule."

181. 113 U.S. 9 (1885).

allowed to take a small part of the entitlement. On the other hand, in the *Head* case, the use permitted by the pliability rule is exclusive. Once a mill owner dams water, the flooded or water-deprived riparian land is altered indefinitely — for as long as the dam is in operation. The riparian owner cannot continue to transact with other potential users of the land as she did prior to the damming. The condition of the land has been altered, and the pliability rule takes this into account in its compensation scheme.

E. *Loperty Rules*

Another type of pliability rule is the loperty rule. By contrast with the pliability rules we have discussed so far, loperty rules begin with liability rule protection, which, upon the occurrence of a triggering event, is transformed into property rule protection. The goal of loperty protection is generally to incentivize the entitlement holder to take some action in order to earn property rule protection. Consider the famous "fencing out" rule that governed ranging property in the American West in the nineteenth century. The fencing out regime reversed the common law rule that prevented cattle from grazing on a neighbor's land. Instead, the fencing out rule allowed cattle to roam freely on others' property until the property was fenced. Thus, landowners who wished to enjoy traditional property rule protection over their ranches bore the burden of fencing out neighbors' cattle.[182]

Analyzed in pliability terms, the fencing out regime sets a zero order liability rule as the baseline for using the land of others. Absent a fence, land was presumably part of an open access regime, and cattle grazers could use the land without paying compensation. However, any landholder could alter the baseline protection by erecting a fence. By erecting the fence, the landholder would trigger a change in protection from zero order liability to property. Under the new property regime, the landowner could exclude cattle grazers by means of injunction, and could collect damages in the event of a trespass.

By imposing the burden of exclusion on the landholder, the fencing out rule achieved two important goals. First, given the presumed mutual interest of all cattle ranchers in allowing cattle to roam freely, the fencing out rule eliminated the burden of costly negotiations among ranchers. Second, the rule created a mechanism for separating those owners for whom property rule protection was efficient from those whose land was better served by an open access regime. Specifi-

---

182. ROBERT C. ELLICKSON, ORDER WITHOUT LAW: HOW NEIGHBORS SETTLE DISPUTES 76 (1991). Fencing out is still the law in Colorado. COLO. REV. STAT. ANN. § 35-46-102(1) (Bradford 2001). *See generally* Terence J. Centner, *Reforming Outdated Fence Law Provisions: Good Fences Make Good Neighbors Only if They are Fair*, 12 J. ENVTL. L. & LITIG. 267 (1997).

cally, it induced cattle ranchers to assess and communicate to others the value of exclusive use of their land.

Additionally, a loperty rule may also be used to incentivize potential takers of the entitlement. Consider again the case of *Boomer*.[183] The Court of Appeals of New York decided to protect homeowners affected by a nuisance by means of a liability rule. Atlantic Cement was permitted to continue infringing upon homeowners' enjoyment of their property and, in exchange, pay the damage amount assessed by the court. The court was motivated in part by the concern that requiring Atlantic Cement to develop superior abatement technologies on such short notice would be inequitable. Thus, the court determined that the homeowners should permanently lose their full property rule protection. A judicially crafted loperty rule could have better balanced the equities. Under such a loperty rule, Atlantic Cement would have enjoyed the right to pollute for payment only for a limited time, say five years. Thereafter, property rule protection over the homes would be reinstated. This result achieves a better distribution of the burden of industrial uses. On the one hand, homeowners would not need to forfeit permanently their property rights. On the other hand, large industrial employers, such as Atlantic Cement, would be given several years to develop the pollution control measures necessary for their businesses to continue without unduly harming neighboring homeowners.

F. *Title Shifting Pliability Rules*

Having discussed pliability rules that involve transitions from property rules to liability rules and vice versa, we now turn to title shifting pliability rules, under which a preset condition triggers the transfer of property rule protection from one entitlement holder to another.[184] The initial holder receives no compensation. The recipient of the entitlement in the second stage, however, enjoys full property rule protection. Thus, as we discuss in our examples below, the importance of title shifting pliability rules lies in their being a nonconsensual mechanism of transferring property interests.[185]

---

183. 257 N.E.2d 870 (1970).

184. As we note in our examples in this Section, in stage 2, there may be more than one entitlement holder.

185. As we explain later in this Section, in some cases, title shifting pliability rules display several advantages over the other major nonconsensual transfer mechanism — liability rule protection. These advantages stem from the fact that the subsequent entitlement holder enjoys property rule protection under title shifting pliability rules.

1. *Adverse Possession*

Adverse possession provides a stark example of title shifting pliability protection. As Dwyer and Menell noted, adverse possession is "[p]erhaps the most startling means of acquiring property [rights]."[186] Under this doctrine, a stranger can gain title to another's land by occupying it — "but only if the occupation is indeed wrongful."[187] To succeed on an adverse possession claim, the occupier must show that her occupation is hostile to the owner's interest, actual, open and notorious, exclusive, and continuous for the statutorily mandated period of time.[188] The successful adverse possessor is not only immune against a suit for ejection; she acquires the full panoply of rights associated with ownership.[189] Effectively, therefore, adverse possession is a legal mechanism that sanctions private takings of property. Under our proposed typology, adverse possession is an example of a title shifting pliability rule. Adverse possession eliminates the legal protection accorded to the original owner from a property rule, and instead invests someone else with full property rule protection over the entitlement. As in the case of essential facilities, the reduction in

---

186. JOHN P. DWYER & PETER S. MENELL, PROPERTY LAW AND POLICY: A COMPARATIVE INSTITUTIONAL PERSPECTIVE 76 (1998). In a similar vein, Stoebuck and Whitman call adverse possession "a strange and wonderful system." WILLIAM B. STOEBUCK & DALE A. WHITMAN, THE LAW OF PROPERTY 853 (3d ed. 2000); *see also* Henry W. Ballantine, *Title by Adverse Possession*, 32 HARV. L. REV. 135, 135 (1918) ("[T]he doctrine [of adverse possession] apparently affords an anomalous instance of maturing a wrong into a right contrary to one of the most fundamental axioms of the law. 'For true it is, that neither fraud nor might/Can make a title where there wanteth right.' " (quoting Altham's case, 8 Coke Rep. 153, 77 Engl. reprint, 707)).

187. STOEBUCK & WHITMAN, *supra* note 186, at 853.

188. *See, e.g.*, DWYER & MENELL, *supra* note 186, at 77-82; *see also* Van Valkenburgh v. Lutz, 106 N.E.2d 28, 29 (N.Y. 1952) (noting that "[t]o acquire title to real property by adverse possession not founded upon a written instrument, it must be shown by clear and convincing proof that for at least fifteen years (formerly twenty years) there was an 'actual' occupation under a claim of title . . . ."); Howard v. Kunto, 477 P.2d 210, 213 (Wash. Ct. App. 1970) (restating "the oft-quoted rule that: '[T]o constitute adverse possession, there must be actual possession which is uninterrupted, open and notorious, hostile and exclusive, and under a claim of right made in good faith for the statutory period' "). *But see* O'Keefe v. Snyder, 416 A.2d 862, 870 (N.J. 1980) (noting that "[t]o establish title by adverse possession to chattels, the rule of law has been that the possession must be hostile, actual, visible, exclusive, and continuous"); Chaplin v. Sanders, 676 P.2d 431, 436 (Wash. 1984) (overruling *Howard v. Kunto* to the extent that the case suggested a good-faith requirement for adverse possession, and specifically noting that an adverse possessor's "subjective belief regarding his true interest in the land and his intent to dispossess or not dispossess another is irrelevant"). However, the *O'Keefe* court also noted that in the case of works of art, the "introduction of equitable considerations through the discovery rule," *id.* at 872, which "provides that, in an appropriate case, a cause of action will not accrue until the injured party discovers, or by exercise of reasonable diligence should have discovered, facts which form the basis of a cause of action," *id.* at 869, "provides a more satisfactory response than the doctrine of adverse possession." *Id.* at 872.

189. *See, e.g.*, STOEBUCK & WHITMAN, *supra* note 186, at 853 ("Title gained [through adverse possession] is usually in fee simple absolute.").

protection depends on the behavior of the property owner. The shift of property rule protection is not mandatory, but rather, it is triggered by the failure of the owner to assert possession over the property.[190]

In the context of adverse possession, pliability rule protection is intended to deter certain types of inaction on the part of property owners. Under the analysis of advocates of adverse possession, the use of a title shifting pliability rule in the case of adverse possession promotes both efficiency and fairness.[191] Traditionally, proponents of adverse possession have asserted that the risk of losing the property rule protection enhances efficient use of resources.[192] Adverse possession, on this theory, generates two complementary incentive effects: a negative and a positive. The negative effect targets property owners; the positive applies to potential occupiers. By penalizing negligent and dormant owners who "sleep on their rights,"[193] adverse possession induces property owners to handle their property in a socially responsible manner. By rewarding productive occupation of land, the doctrine is thought to encourage search and use of neglected property. The combination of penalty and reward effectively ensures that property is put

---

190. *See, e.g.,* Jeffery Evans Stake, *The Uneasy Case for Adverse Possession,* 89 GEO. L.J. 2419, 2443 (2001) (suggesting that "adverse possession helps deal with the problem of missing owners"); *see also* Monica Kivel Kalo & Joseph J. Kalo, *The Battle to Preserve North Carolina's Estuarine Marshes: The 1985 Legislation, Private Claims to Estuarine Marshes, Denial of Permits to Fill, and the Public Trust,* 64 N.C. L. REV. 565, 606 (1986) (noting that "landowners need not receive actual notice that their rights are in jeopardy to trigger the running of the statute of limitations . . . [where] possession . . . [is] actual, exclusive, open and notorious, and continuous and uninterrupted").

191. *See* Thomas J. Miceli & C.F. Sirmans, *An Economic Theory of Adverse Possession,* 15 INT'L REV. L. & ECON. 161, 161 (1995) (enumerating justifications for the "curious doctrine," including (1) preserving evidence, which decays over time thereby increasing the difficulty of trying cases; (2) penalizing owners for sitting on their rights or using their land inefficiently; (3) reducing transaction costs and thereby facilitating market exchange through the elimination of old claims to property; (4) supporting the reliance interest that develops among occupiers).

192. *See* Richard A. Posner, *Savigny, Holmes, and the Law and Economics of Possession,* 86 VA. L. REV. 535, 559 (2000) ("The economic rationale of adverse possession, conceived as a method of shifting ownership without benefit of negotiation or a paper transfer, can be made perspicuous by asking when property should be deemed abandoned, that is, returned to the common pool of unowned resources and so made available for appropriation through seizure by someone else. The economist's answer is that this should happen when it's likely to promote the efficient use of valuable resources."). Sprankling, however, contends that the doctrine may spur overexploitation of wild lands, and thus proposes that wild land should be exempt from the doctrine. *See* John G. Sprankling, *An Environmental Critique of Adverse Possession,* 79 CORNELL L. REV. 816, 840 (1994) (noting that "[u]nder the development model, adverse possession functions to facilitate the economic exploitation of land").

193. *See* Stake, *supra* note 190, at 2434-35 ("According to [the] 'sleeping' theory, adverse possession acts as a civil penalty for wrongdoers. The wrongdoers are those who sleep on their rights, and their penalty is to lose those rights."); *see also* Ballantine, *supra* note 186, at 135 (" 'English lawyers regard not the merit of the possessor, but the demerit of the one out of possession.' " (quoting JAMES BARR AMES, LECTURES ON LEGAL HISTORY 197 (1913))).

to socially desirable uses either by the title-holder or by the adverse possessor.[194] Adverse possession thus constitutes an informal, non-market mechanism for improving allocation of resources.

Second, the use of a title shifting pliability rule in this context has desirable information forcing effects. Carol Rose likened property to "a kind of speech, with the audience composed of all others who might be interested in claiming the object in question."[195] The group of potential claimants is not limited to adverse possessors. It also includes buyers, lessees, and creditors, who all need to know the identity of the rightful owner in order to transact. Thus, clear titles have two desirable effects: they facilitate trade and reduce conflicts. From an informational perspective, therefore, adverse possession serves the dual functions of "quieting titles" and facilitating transactions.[196] On this view, adverse possession is not intended to reward industriousness and deter slacking, but rather, to prompt property owners to communicate clearly with the rest of the world.[197] The use of a title shifting pliability rule is responsible for this result. By rewarding clear communication, and penalizing vagueness, the title shifting pliability rule preserves the informational integrity of the property system, thus leading to more transacting and less conflict. Obviously, the importance of this function varies depending on the effectiveness of the jurisdiction's recording system.

---

194. *See, e.g,* ROBERT COOTER & THOMAS ULEN, LAW AND ECONOMICS 156 (1st ed. 1988) (noting that adverse possession "tends to prevent valuable resources from being left idle for long periods of time by specifying procedures for a productive user to take title from an unproductive user"; the rule thereby "tends to move property to higher-value uses, as required for efficiency, by redistributing it to aggressive owners"). Following Holmes's suggestion that a person becomes gradually more attached to land he occupies, *see* Oliver Wendell Holmes, *The Path of the Law,* 10 HARV. L. REV. 457, 477 (1897), Richard A. Posner has argued that adverse possession is in large part about diminishing marginal utility of income. "The adverse possessor would experience the deprivation of property as a diminution in his wealth; the original owner would experience the restoration of the property as an increase in his wealth. If they have the same wealth, then probably their combined utility will be greater if the adverse possessor is allowed to keep the property." RICHARD A. POSNER, ECONOMIC ANALYSIS OF LAW 79 (4th ed. 1992). *But see* Omri Ben Shahar, *The Erosion of Rights by Past Breach,* 1 AM. L. & ECON. REV. 190, 225 (1999). Ben Shahar contends, contrary to the common wisdom, that the risk of loss of title, which he calls "erosion," is likely to prompt owners who neglect their property to "seek to evict possessors, whereas absent an erosion risk [such property owners] would potentially have allowed the efficient possessor to quietly maintain use." According to Ben Shahar the main effect of adverse possession is to "facilitate the movement of assets away from absentee owners because it makes enforcement of absentee ownership more costly." *Id.* at 225.

195. Carol M. Rose, *Possession as the Origin of Property,* 52 U. CHI. L. REV. 73, 79 (1985) [hereinafter Rose, *Origin of Property*]. For an information-based theory of property, see Thomas W. Merrill & Henry E. Smith, *Optimal Standardization in the Law of Property: The Numerus Clausus Principle,* 110 YALE L.J. 1 (2000).

196. *See* Merrill, *supra* note 102, at 1129 (noting that a "concern which has frequently been advanced in the literature on adverse possession is the interest in 'quieting titles' to property"); *id.* at 1139 (noting that the use of a mechanical entitlement determination rule in the context of adverse possession facilitates the development of a market in property rights).

197. Rose, *Origin of Property, supra* note 195, at 79-80.

Finally, the risk of losing the property rule protection deters title-holders from attempting to extort quasi-rents from adverse possessors.[198] Under standard property rule protection, and absent an effective system for conveying clear information, property owners could elicit third parties to improve their property by intentionally misrepresenting that the property has been abandoned. Such strategic behavior is a trap to innocent occupants. Believing that they will be entitled to the full value of their investment, innocent adverse possessors will expend considerable effort and resources on others' property and ultimately will lose their investment altogether when the true owner reasserts her rights.[199] The strategic misrepresentation of the true owner distorts the decision making process of the adverse possessor by creating an appearance of an economic opportunity that in reality does not exist. Adverse possession mitigates, to some extent, the ex ante incentive of property owners to engage in such strategic misrepresentation, and thus, permits "members of the public [to] rely upon their own reasonable perceptions."[200] Here, too, the importance of this function depends on the quality of the recording system and other information about the status of the property.

The use of a title shifting pliability rule to transfer the title of the property from the original owner to the adverse possessor is also justified, at times, on fairness grounds. The fairness rationale maintains that after a long period of possession, the reliance interest of the adverse possessor should outweigh the formal title of the original owner. In doing fairness to the parties, the law must consider the fact that the adverse possessor has developed an expectation to retain possession of the property, and that the original owner, intentionally or negligently, fostered this expectation. Thus, some degree of moral fault attaches to the true owner for encouraging a relationship of dependence, which she later intended to cut off.[201] As Justice Holmes famously stated, property "takes root in your being and cannot be torn away without

---

198. *See* Merrill, *supra* note 102, at 1131-1132; Miceli & Sirmans, *supra* note 191, at 161-62.

199. This problem is particularly acute in cases of boundary disputes. In such cases, a property owner permits an adjacent neighbor, who mistakenly believes she is actually building on her own land, to encroach on the property owner's land. After the encroachment occurred, the encroached upon owner can exploit her neighbor's investment to extract a much higher payment from her to settle the dispute than she otherwise would. As Merrill noted, in extreme cases, the strategically encroached upon owner "may be able to extract not only the value of the land but the full value of the addition as well." *See* Merrill, *supra* note 101, at 1131; Miceli & Sirmans, *supra* note 191, at 161-62 (noting that "when a boundary error occurs . . . allowing title to pass to the possessor after a certain period prevents the true owner from taking advantage of the possessor's initial error to extort quasi rents created by his reliance expenditures").

200. Rose, *Origin of Property, supra* note 195, at 80.

201. *See* Joseph W. Singer, *The Reliance Interest in Property*, 40 STAN. L. REV. 611, 667 (1988).

your resenting the act and trying to defend yourself, however you came by it."[202] Subsequent empirical studies have affirmed Holmes's conjecture.[203] These studies indicate that people develop an especially strong attachment to assets in their possession. This cognitive phenomenon, widely known as an "endowment effect,"[204] further tips the scale in favor of the adverse possessor. The increasing attachment of the adverse possessor to the property raises the subjective value she assigns to the property, and as time goes by her claim to the property grows stronger relative to the claim of the original owner. The title shifting pliability rule undergirding adverse possession provides the legal system with a mechanism to move the property to the adverse possessor when fairness so requires. It must be noted, however, that the requirement that the adverse possessor possess the property "hostilely" significantly undermines the adverse possessor's claim to fairness.

G. *Multiple Stage Pliability Rules*

As we noted earlier, pliability rules need not be restricted to one stage. In theory, pliability rules are unlimited in the number of property and liability rules they can aggregate into a single pliability rule. Multiple stage pliability rules serve the same functions as their two-stage cousins, and are necessary to accommodate anticipated multiple changes in circumstances or a particularly complicated balance of interests.

1. *Eminent Domain*

Arguably the most famous instance of pliability rule protection is provided by the law of eminent domain. The power of eminent domain authorizes governments to seize private property upon making a decision by a process specified in law. By exercising its power of emi-

---

202. Holmes, *supra* note 194, at 476-77.

203. *See* Robert C. Ellickson, *Bringing Culture and Human Frailty to Rational Actors: A Critique of Classical Law and Economics,* 65 CHI. KENT L. REV. 23, 39 (1986) (opining that Holmes "is more faithfully interpreted as anticipating (in a primitive way)" later developments in cognitive psychology).

204. On the endowment effect, see generally Daniel Kahneman et al., *Experimental Tests of the Endowment Effect and the Coase Theorem,* 98 J. POL. ECON. 1325 (1990); Daniel Kahneman et al., *The Endowment Effect, Loss Aversion, and Status Quo Bias,* 5 J. ECON. PERSP. 193 (1991); Richard Thaler, *Toward a Positive Theory of Consumer Choice,* 1 J. ECON. BEHAV. & ORG. 39 (1980); *see also* Owen D. Jones, *Time Shifted Rationality and the Law of Law's Leverage: Behavioral Economics Meets Behavioral Biology,* 95 NW. U. L. REV. 1141, 1154 (2001) (reporting that "people tend to value an object more highly as soon as they possess it — often twice as highly — compared to how they value the same object if they had to purchase it," or, more formally, "their indifference curves shift in a systematic manner as soon as they acquire a good, increasing the ascribed value of the endowed good relative to all other goods").

nent domain, the government may transform the property rule protection into liability rule protection, so long as it pays "just compensation," as mandated by the Constitution[205] — under current doctrine, the market value of the property taken.[206] So long as exercised for a public purpose and accompanied by "just compensation," this power is almost limitless. This makes eminent domain one of the most important pliability rules. Indeed, it can justly be said that, in light of the ubiquity of takings, all property entitlements should be viewed as protected by pliable protection, at least vis-à-vis the government.

Here, we characterize takings as resulting from a three-stage pliability rule protecting assets: property rule protection, followed by liability rule protection, and then property rule protection again.[207] In this characterization, a government decision to exercise the power of eminent domain — to "take" — effects a transition from property rule protection in the hands of the original holder to liability rule protection. Before the government's decision to take the asset, the private property holder enjoys property rule protection, even vis-à-vis the government. For example, the private property owner has the right to exclude government agents seeking to perform warrantless searches, as well as to sue the government to abate nuisances to the extent such suits are not barred by sovereign immunity. However, once the government decides to exercise its power of eminent domain, the entitlement holder enjoys only ordinary liability protection — the right to "just compensation" in exchange for the asset. After the government takes the property, however, the asset is once again protected by property rule protection, albeit this time the entitlement holder is the government.

---

205. U.S. CONST. amend. V ("[N]or shall private property be taken for public use, without just compensation.").

206. *See* Lewinsohn-Zamir, *supra* note 9, at 242 (noting that "when land is taken by the state for public use, compensation is based on the (objective) market value of the property, regardless of the unique public use intended by the government"). In the context of regulatory takings, courts have employed a "modified market value test," which measures the extent to which the regulation at issue diminished the property's market value. *See, e.g.*, A.A. Profiles, Inc. v. City of Fort Lauderdale, 253 F.3d 576, 583 n.7, 584 (11th Cir. 2001) (holding that the modified market value test was the appropriate measure of damages for a permanent regulatory taking, regardless of whether the taking had a valid public purpose). Calibrating compensation has proven contentious. *See, e.g.*, William A. Fischel, *The Offer/Ask Disparity and Just Compensation for Takings: A Constitutional Choice Perspective*, 15 INT'L REV. L. & ECON. 187, 193 (1995) (arguing that "latter-day critics who call for enhanced compensation under eminent domain would upset a solution to the offer/ask problem that had already been struck in scores of constitutional conventions"); Aaron N. Gruen, *Takings, Just Compensation, and the Efficient Use of Land, Urban, and Environmental Resources*, 33 URB. LAW. 517, 536 (2001) (suggesting that "if the government pays more than market value for a property, it may result in under-investment in beneficial public goods that the private market cannot efficiently provide").

207. Admittedly, this is not the only way of characterizing takings in a pliability analysis. *See infra* note 214 and accompanying text.

The evident enormity of the power of eminent domain has led to discomfort about its use, reflected in the constitutional requirements of "just compensation" and "public use,"[208] as well as a voluminous literature about the proper scope of the constitutional Takings Clause.[209] Yet, the power of eminent domain has also been seen as indispensable in order to allow government to fulfill its important function of providing public goods.[210] Thus, eminent domain serves a different set of goals than, for example, adverse possession. Where adverse possession aims to curb neglect of property by the original entitlement holder, eminent domain is not concerned with any "wrongdoing" of the origi-

---

208. At least as a matter of grammar, the phrasing of the Fifth Amendment's Takings Clause actually suggests that "public use" is a condition precedent to the payment of "just compensation" rather than to the exercise of the taking power. *Cf.* MORTON J. HORWITZ, THE TRANSFORMATION OF AMERICAN LAW 1780-1860, at 65 (1977) (citing arguments of nineteenth century lawyers that similar provisions in state constitutions did not limit power to take for private use). Nevertheless, the Clause has not been read to eliminate the need for just compensation where property is taken for nonpublic use. Rather, it has been seen as embodying the Anglo-American tradition of limiting the power of eminent domain to cases where the taking is for a public use. *See* BRUCE A. ACKERMAN, PRIVATE PROPERTY AND THE CONSTITUTION 190 n.5 (1977) ("[T]he modern understanding of 'public use' holds that any state purpose otherwise constitutional should qualify as sufficiently 'public' to justify a taking.") (citation omitted). In recent years, the "public use" requirement has fallen into disuse, *see, e.g.,* Richard A. Epstein, *Notice and Freedom of Contract in the Law of Servitudes*, 55 S. CAL. L. REV. 1353, 1367 n.29 (1982) (observing that "the public use limitation has little, if any, constitutional bite today, except in cases involving the condemnation of excess land"), prompting protest from some scholars. *See, e.g.,* EPSTEIN, *supra* note 101, at 161-81; Gideon Kanner, *Condemnation Blight: Just How Just Is Just Compensation?*, 48 NOTRE DAME LAWYER 765 (1973); Thomas W. Merrill, *The Economics of Public Use*, 72 CORNELL L. REV. 61 (1986).

209. *See, e.g.,* EPSTEIN, *supra* note 101; WILLIAM A. FISCHEL, REGULATORY TAKINGS (1995); Frank I. Michelman, *Property, Utility, and Fairness: Comments on the Ethical Foundations of "Just Compensation" Law*, 80 HARV. L. REV. 1165 (1967); Joseph L. Sax, *Takings and the Police Power*, 74 YALE L.J. 36 (1964). For a historical overview of takings, see William Michael Treanor, *The Original Understanding of the Takings Clause and the Political Process*, 95 COLUM. L. REV. 782 (1995). Most of the modern literature focuses on the question of what acts of government should be considered constitutional "takings" such that just compensation must be paid. Thus, the bulk of takings scholarship does not directly concern itself with the scope of the power of eminent domain; rather, it addresses the subsidiary question of when constitutional limitations apply.

210. *See* EPSTEIN, *supra* note 101, at 4-5 (arguing that the state can only validly exercise coercive power to prevent private aggression or to provide public goods); *see also* Thomas W. Merrill, *Rent Seeking and the Compensation Principle*, 80 NW. U. L. REV. 1561, 1569 (1986) (reviewing RICHARD A. EPSTEIN, TAKINGS: PRIVATE PROPERTY AND THE POWER OF EMINENT DOMAIN (1985)). Merrill's review notes Epstein's argument that "when the power of eminent domain is used to supply public goods, the surplus will tend to be divided, at least approximately, in proportion to preexisting shares of wealth. Those with large preexisting shares will obtain large benefits from public goods; those with small preexisting shares will obtain small benefits." *Id.*; *cf.* Ugo Mattei, *Efficiency as Equity: Insights from Comparative Law and Economics*, 14 INT'L REV. L. & ECON. 3, 7 (1994) ("As far as the public use requirement is concerned, the economic theory of public goods provides both a justification and a limit. The justification is that the government needs to be able to acquire the inputs that are necessary to provide public goods which the market cannot easily provide. The limit is set by the consideration that any private use of the power of eminent domain will be inefficient since it produces a result that private parties would not be able to reach by bargaining.") (internal citations omitted).

nal holder. Rather, eminent domain is used as a tool for transferring title in property to a presumed higher-value user. Eminent domain takes an asset from private hands and places it in the hands of a government that needs the asset to provide for a public good. The coercive mechanism is necessary in order to overcome strategic difficulties that impede bargaining and prevent voluntary reassignment of the asset to the government in market transactions.

The central barriers to successful negotiations overcome by eminent domain come under the heading of strategic behavior and include the closely related problems of bilateral monopoly and asymmetric information.[211]

In a situation of bilateral monopoly, there is but one potential buyer and one potential seller. Each knows that the transaction cannot take place without her cooperation, and each, therefore, attempts to extract all the profit from the transaction. The problem of bilateral monopoly can be illustrated with the example of a government decision to build a railway through an isolated valley. There is only one railway, and therefore only one potential buyer of valley land. On the other hand, the railroad must purchase all the valley parcels along the lay of the track; even one hold-out can ruin the project. Each parcel owner is thus a monopolist who may attempt to hold out for a higher price that will divert the railroad profits to her own pockets. In such a

---

211. For a comprehensive review of the literature on strategic barriers to bilateral negotiation, see Robert Cooter, *The Cost of Coase*, 11 J. LEGAL STUD. 1, 23 (1982) (pointing out that disagreements as to how to divide the contractual surplus may prevent successful Coasean bargaining); John Kennan & Robert Wilson, *Bargaining with Private Information*, 31 J. ECON. LITERATURE 45, 46 (1993) (hypothesizing that differences in private information are a primary cause of bargaining delays); Robert P. Merges, *Of Property Rules, Coase, and Intellectual Property*, 94 COLUM. L. REV. 2655, 2659 (1994) (observing that in the field of intellectual property the valuation problem heightens the possibility of strategic bargaining); Eric L. Talley, Note, *Contract Renegotiation, Mechanism Design, and the Liquidated Damages Rule*, 46 STAN. L. REV. 1195, 1198, 1219 (1994) (discussing the problem of bilateral monopoly in contract renegotiation).

On asymmetric information specifically, see Louis Kaplow & Steven Shavell, *Do Liability Rules Facilitate Bargaining? A Reply to Ayres and Talley*, 105 YALE L.J. 221, 223-29 (1995) ("When each party's own valuation is not known by the other, each party will have incentives to misrepresent its valuation in bargaining, hoping to extract more of the bargaining surplus from the other party. Parties may therefore demand too much or offer too little, with the result that efficient bargains may not be reached. In this case, one cannot say unambiguously whether property rules or liability rules will be superior."); *see also* Karen Eggleston et al., *The Design and Interpretation of Contracts: Why Complexity Matters*, 95 NW. U. L. REV. 91, 109 (2000) (defining "asymmetric information" as a situation in which "[o]ne party to a contract . . . has more information about future states of the world than does the other party"); *cf.* William Samuelson, *A Comment on the Coase Theorem*, in GAME-THEORETIC MODELS OF BARGAINING 321, 331-35 (Alvin E. Roth ed., 1985) (arguing that if an entitlement is auctioned in a particular way between the parties rather than allocated through bargaining, the problems associated with asymmetric information and bargaining can be overcome, but acknowledging that his proposed auctions may be impracticable because they would require the initial entitlement holder to share the proceeds). *See generally* RICHARD A. POSNER, ECONOMIC ANALYSIS OF LAW 56 (4th ed. 1992) ("A good economic argument for eminent domain . . . is that it is necessary to prevent monopoly.").

situation, the ex ante price is unknowable, transaction costs may become prohibitive, and the attempt to out-strategize the opponent may foil the project altogether. Eminent domain provides the solution by permitting the government to take the parcels of land in the valley and then open them for use by the railroad.

The problem of asymmetric information is particularly important in this regard. Private entities may often overcome the bilateral monopoly difficulty by using straw agents or the like to hide their plans. It is far more difficult, however, for the government to hide its plans. Parcel owners possess knowledge of the government plans, while the government can only guess at the owners' "true" selling price. This leads the parcel owners to engage in strategic behavior and rent-seeking, and burdens the opportunity to successfully negotiate a transaction.

The power of eminent domain provides a solution to these strategic barriers to efficient transactions. On the one hand, eminent domain does not disturb the property rule protection granted in ordinary circumstances. However, where there is a public need that is likely to be foiled by strategic problems, the government may exercise its power of eminent domain, triggering a change to liability rule protection, and allowing the orderly transfer of the asset. The constitutional Takings Clause prevents overutilization of this power by limiting the power of eminent domain to those cases where reasonable market transactions are unlikely. Indeed, the requirement of just compensation makes the exercise of eminent domain sufficiently costly that, in many cases, the government prefers to negotiate a transfer of the asset under ordinary property rule protection, rather than force a change to the liability stage of the pliability rule.[212]

While we classify takings as part of a three-stage pliability rule, the rule could also be classified as a title shifting pliability rule with a compensation requirement, or as a classic pliability rule as well.[213] For instance, due to the just compensation requirement, to the original asset holder, the pliability rule protection afforded vis-à-vis takings appears to consist of property rule protection followed by liability rule protection.[214] In the initial stage, the asset holder enjoys ordinary

---

212. *See* William A. Fischel, *The Political Economy of Just Compensation: Lessons from the Military Draft for the Takings Issue*, 20 HARV. J.L. & PUB. POL'Y 23, 40 (1996) (observing that "[w]hen it becomes known that compensation will be made ... the government endures" the transaction costs of making settlement (or settlement costs), including the cost of negotiating with condemnees, participating in an eminent domain trial (if negotiations fail), "the deadweight loss of additional taxes to finance the compensation and the negotiations, and the losses from moral hazard on the part of property owners who anticipate that compensation will be made") (internal citation omitted).

213. Calabresi and Melamed consider eminent domain an example of "mixed protection," or, under our terminology, a simultaneous pliability rule. Calabresi & Melamed, *supra* note 5, at 1093. For the reasons discussed in the text, we prefer a different characterization.

214. *See* Merrill, *supra* note 208, at 64 ("[I]n the eminent domain area, which so often

property rule protection. When the government makes a decision to exercise its power of eminent domain, the asset-holder's protection essentially becomes one of liability rule protection in which the asset-holder cannot prevent others from impinging upon her exclusive enjoyment of the asset, but she does have the right to reasonable compensation for such impairments of her rights in the asset. In this sense, the takings regime can be seen as a classic pliability rule, though the act that triggers the shift between the two stages of the pliability rule protection — an exercise of eminent domain — endows the new asset holder with property rule protection rather than merely liability rule protection. Alternatively, in light of the fact that the subsequent entitlement holder enjoys property rule protection like the original entitlement holder, the law of takings can be said to create a title shifting pliability rule.

We prefer the characterization of a three-stage rule in order to highlight how the pliability rule embodied in eminent domain overcomes the "reciprocal takings" difficulty engendered by liability rule protection of objects subject to possessory disputes. As we noted earlier,[215] Shavell and Kaplow favored property rules to resolve possessory disputes, lest each taking of an object protected by a liability rule engender a reciprocal taking, leading to an endless cycle of takings and retakings of the object. The pliability rule employed in eminent domain resolves this difficulty by limiting use of the liability rule protection to a single taking. Once the object is taken (in the second stage of the pliability rule), property protection is restored, albeit in the hands of a presumed higher-value user.[216]

---

parallels private law doctrine, courts have effectively declared that liability rules alone shall protect all private property rights.") (internal citation omitted).

215. *See supra* notes 56-58 and accompanying text.

216. A pliability analysis thus has an important implication for the debate between Kaplow/Shavell and Ayres/Balkin, described *supra* in note 58. Ayres and Balkin resolved the reciprocal taking difficulty by noting the possibility of an auction regime. This can be described in one of two ways in a pliability analysis. One description would see the Ayres and Balkin solution as preserving a single type of rule protection — liability rule protection — but requiring that the price paid for the taking be altered in each round in order to reflect a new value. On this view, Ayres and Balkin did not suggest a pliability rule and did not recognize that reciprocal takings could be arrested by limiting application of a liability rule.

A second description — and probably the one that would be favored by Ayres and Balkin — would view the suggested auction as a kind of protection distinct from ordinary property and liability rules. Under this description, Ayres and Balkin were suggesting a pliability rule in which the taking of an object in a possessory dispute would trigger a change in rule protection from liability to auction. Viewed in this light, Ayres and Balkin's suggestion is merely one of several ways to resolve the reciprocal takings problem by means of a pliability rule. Indeed, any rule that limited the liability rule stage of the pliability rule would foil infinite reciprocal takings.

H. *Elements of Pliability Rules*

So far, we have demonstrated the pervasiveness of pliability rules in our legal system. Before turning to the normative case for pliability rules, we summarize some salient features of pliability rules presented thus far.

Pliability rules involve at least three elements: a first stage rule (either property or liability), a triggering event causing a shift between stages, and a second stage rule. For simplicity's sake, we have focused on two-stage pliability rules, although, as we demonstrated with the case of eminent domain, there is no theoretical limitation to the number of stages in a pliability rule. Additionally, as we have noted, the stages of the pliability rule need not necessarily be chronologically sequential. Sometimes, as in the case of fair use, for example, the stages may coincide chronologically. Nevertheless, in all cases, a triggering event or fact is necessary to shift protection from one stage to another. For example, in the case of fair use, copyright is best seen as protected in the first stage by a property rule, and in the next stage by a zero order liability rule, where the trigger is a type of use that qualifies as a "fair use."

One of the important innovations of a pliability analysis therefore lies in a study of triggering mechanisms. On either side of the trigger, the protection is either by means of a liability rule or a property rule, both of which have been the subject of a rich and illuminating scholarly colloquy. However, as pliability rules have not been previously identified, there has been no previous discussion of triggering events. As we have seen, triggering mechanisms can be based in the passage of time, changed circumstances, magnitude or nature of use, or a combination of any of the three.

Time-centered triggers specify a preset period of protection in stage one at the end of which a different type of protection begins. The zero order pliability protection used in patent and copyright law employs a time-centered trigger.

Triggers based on changed circumstances are, naturally, less easily encapsulated. Thus far, among the changed circumstances that we have seen used as triggers are market power, carelessness, and the emergence of a higher value use. Excessive market power serves as a trigger both in the genericism doctrine in trademark law and in the essential facilities doctrine in the law of antitrust. Careless behavior on the part of the property owner is the triggering mechanism in the case of adverse possession. Emergence of a higher value use is the trigger in the case of eminent domain. Changed circumstances may also be combined with the time element as demonstrated by the case of adverse possession.

Triggers based in the magnitude of the use specify that the ordinary protection offered by the baseline rule are set aside with regards to certain low magnitude uses. Thus far, we have seen such a trigger employed in copyright with regard to fair use.

It is noteworthy that in some instances of pliability protection the initial entitlement holder controls the triggering mechanism, while in others she does not. Pure time-centered triggers, for example, are not subject to the control of the entitlement holder. Patent holders, for instance, lack the ability to alter the twenty year period that signals the shift from property to zero order liability protection. Other triggers, however, correlate the shift to the behavior of the initial entitlement holder. In such cases, the use of pliability rules gives the entitlement holder an incentive to self-regulate or act in accordance with socially desirable standards. For example, the doctrines of essential facilities and genericism incentivize entitlement holders not to accumulate excessive market power lest the initial property rule protection be replaced with a liability rule. The doctrine of adverse possession, on the other hand, deters careless behavior on the part of property owners by subjecting careless owners to the risk of title loss.

III. THE NORMATIVE CASE FOR PLIABILITY

Having explained and illustrated the elements of pliability rules, we now turn to the normative case for using pliability rules. First, we show that pliability rules achieve different aims than property and liability rules, and we show when pliability rules should be used. We then turn to some practical lessons to be drawn from a pliability analysis. Here, we show both how explicit recognition of the category of pliability rules suggests possible modifications of existing pliability rules and how pliability rules can be used in new areas of the law.

A. *When Pliability Rules Should Be Used*

In this Section, we take up the task of identifying those situations in which pliable rules possess a relative advantage over their static cousins.

From a normative perspective, the importance of pliability rules lies in that they significantly broaden the range of legal rules available to policy makers. We posit that pliability rules are most advantageous under the following conditions: (1) when policymakers anticipate substantially changed circumstances; (2) when competing interests must be accommodated in a single rule; and (3) when necessary to transcend the inherent limitations of property and liability rules. In all these cases, the use of a pliability rule facilitates planning by the entitlement holder, as well as bargaining between the holder and potential acquirers.

1.   *Changed Circumstances*

The utility of pliability rules is most obvious in the case of changed circumstances. Naturally, changed circumstances may necessitate a change in the initial mode of protection in order to adjust the legal rule to the changed reality. Pliability rules, due to their flexibility, are the ideal policy tool for this task. Pliability rules allow policymakers to anticipate changed circumstances and incorporate them into a legal rule by identifying the change as the trigger that shifts protection modes. Many of the examples of pliability rules that we have cited so far have been motivated primarily by changed circumstances. For example, the essential facilities doctrine, as its name suggests, aims to identify those circumstances in which a property has become "essential" to competitors, and to use that change as the trigger of a pliability rule. Neither a uniform property rule protection nor liability rule protection is capable of accommodating the challenge of changed circumstances. Uniform property rule protection preserves in perpetuity the facility owner's right to exclude. As such, uniform property rule protection is incapable of dealing with the emergence of circumstances that render such exclusion anticompetitive. Uniform liability rule protection, on the other hand, allows for nonconsensual uses, but does so at the cost of undermining the owner's incentive to develop her property. When circumstances change, therefore, either uniform rule implies some efficiency loss. Pliability rules, by contrast, preserve the efficiency advantages of both rules, despite the change in the circumstances.

Where the changed circumstances are affected by the behavior of the original entitlement holder, pliability rules have an added advantage over the pure protection modes. In such cases, pliability rules may be used to incentivize entitlement owners to avoid certain undesirable circumstances. For example, in the case of antitrust law, pliability rule protection encourages owners to avoid the anticompetitive behavior that may lead to the dilution of their property rights. Similarly, the pliability rule of genericism in trademark law incentivizes owners of strong marks to preserve competition in their field of trade, and to distinguish their products from competing ones, lest they lose their property rule protection altogether. The promotion of self-regulation also produces the added benefit of economizing on regulatory and judicial costs.

2.   *Conflicting Interests*

It is less easily seen how pliability rules are beneficial in accommodating competing interests in a single rule since pliability rules often involve sequential, rather than simultaneous, modes of protection. Yet, on more careful examination, pliability rules can prove a useful mechanism for balancing incompatible interests. For instance, pliability rules may be used to incorporate competing concerns of efficiency and justice. Consider patent protection. The time limitation on the property rule protection stage in patent law finds grounding, at least in part, in concerns of distributive justice. The legal monopoly granted by patent protection, while incentivizing inventors ex ante, also subjects the public to supra-competitive pricing of new products, such as medicines. Distributively, then, the first stage of property rule protection has the undesirable effect of denying the least well-off access to valuable, or even life saving, commodities.[217] Yet, the same legal monopoly that leads to exclusion of the poor is also responsible for the production of the invention in the first place. Additionally, many view an inventor's claim over her invention as a moral one. The use of a time-centered zero order pliability rule balances these competing interests.

3. *Inherent Limitations*

Pliability protection in patent law also provides an example of the use of pliability rules to overcome the inherent limitations in uniform property rule or liability rule protection. In addition to being subject to the tensions between concerns of efficiency, justice and fairness, patent law also must cope with the inherent tensions of efficiency within uniform property rule protection. By granting the absolute power of exclusion, property rules allow owners to invest optimally in their property. Property protection also provides the background against which voluntary exchange takes place. However, property rules may also create inefficiencies. Property rule protection of monopolies encourages underproduction, supra-competitive pricing and a deadweight loss. Patent protection illustrates both these virtues and vices. The ex ante anticipation of enjoying a property right is necessary to spur investment in research and development of new products. However, it comes at the ex post cost of supra-competitive prices. Patent law's pliability rule protection mitigates the inefficient elements of property rule protection without entirely sacrificing its beneficial as-

---

217. Distributive justice concerns are paramount in the work of philosopher John Rawls. *See* JOHN RAWLS, A THEORY OF JUSTICE 14-15 (1971) (arguing that "social and economic inequalities ... are just only if they result in compensating benefits for everyone, and in particular for the least advantaged members of society"); Steve P. Calandrillo, *Responsible Regulation: A Sensible Cost-Benefit, Risk Versus Risk Approach to Federal Health and Safety Regulation*, 81 B.U. L. REV. 957, 983 (2001) (describing the Rawlsian "veil of ignorance" by asking "If one did not know what her position in society would be — i.e., one might be among the best off, or the absolutely worst off member — what kind of a society would she choose to construct and live in?"). Calandrillo also suggests that "[t]he implicit presumption [in Rawlsianism] is that because people justifiably care about fairness and equity, and are also risk averse, they would choose a society that maximizes the position of the worst-off member," and therefore "in the regulatory arena, Rawlsianism would ask how a proposed policy affected the most disadvantaged person or group, and not whether overall social welfare increased in the aggregate." *Id.*

pects. The initial property rule protection preserves the incentive to invest in research; and the subsequent zero order liability rule stage cabins the distorting effects of monopolistic pricing.

Having identified the three primary cases in which normative considerations point toward the adoption of pliability rules, we can now suggest two sets of practical results of a pliability analysis. First, we examine the extent to which existing pliability rules can be modified to better achieve their goals. Second, we uncover situations in which pliability rules ought to be employed, but have not been.

B. *Revising Existing Pliability Rules*

In this Section, we return to some of our earlier examples of existing pliability rules to determine how their goals can be more efficiently and fairly advanced. Specifically, we discuss adverse possession, patent protection and genericism.

1. *Adverse Possession*

To review briefly, the pliability rule of adverse possession institutes property rule protection in both of the two stages of the rule, with the shift triggered by time and evidence of owner carelessness (such as exclusive, open, notorious and hostile possession by a trespasser). The pliability rule is designed to discourage underutilization of the property as well as reward adverse possessors for bringing the property back into active use.

Recognizing that adverse possession embodies a pliability rule enables one to design alternative pliability rules that might better achieve the doctrine's aims. As currently structured, the doctrine of adverse possession is stark. If the adverse possessor satisfies all the statutory elements, she may take title, free of charge, and with full property rule protection. However, if even one of the statutory elements is missing, even in part, the adverse possessor receives nothing. For example, where the statutory period is twenty years, an exclusive, open, notorious and hostile possession for nineteen years and eleven months entitles the adverse possessor to nothing.[218] At its extreme, then, the doctrine of adverse possession merely incentivizes the owner to visit the property, and possibly take corrective action, every nineteen years or so. This result may strike some of us as neither fair nor efficient.

The rigidity of current adverse possession doctrine stems from the fact that it employs a two-stage, time-limited, title shifting pliability

---

218. It is possible that the adverse possessor might have a claim for damages in unjust enrichment, or that the owner might have a claim in trespass. For the sake of the discussion, we disregard these possibilities.

rule. To introduce more flexibility into the doctrine, we note the possibility of adding several new stages to the pliability rule. This can be done is various ways. Assume that, optimally, where state law does not provide for an adequate recording system, property owners should inspect their property at least once every five years. Under this assumption, the legislature can revise the doctrine of adverse possession to give no rights to adverse possessors in the first five years of their stay, and thereafter to reduce the owner's rights vis-à-vis the adverse possessor's a certain percentage of the title. For example, the revised adverse possession rule may state that the successful adverse possessor gains twenty-five percent of the title every five years. The rule might further provide that if the adverse possession is interrupted after a certain percentage of the title was acquired by the adverse possessor, she will be entitled to purchase the remainder from the original owner. In other words, after the first five years of possession, the adverse possessor would receive a call option on the land she possessed, with the exercise price depending on how much longer the adverse possession continues. At the extreme, if the adverse possession continues successfully for twenty years, the exercise price would be zero.

Naturally, the legislature may also create a put option in the successful adverse possessor in the liability stage of the proposed pliability rule. This would mean that after five years, the adverse possessor would not only acquire twenty-five percent of the title to the land but also the right to sell this share back to the original owner. Under this regime, at the conclusion of twenty years of adverse possession, the adverse possessor would have the right to sell back the land to the original owner at market price.

States unsympathetic to adverse possession, such as New York,[219] may also employ a classic pliability rule in this context, but design it in a way that would make adverse possession less attractive. For example, New York can stipulate that the successful adverse possession gains at the end of twenty years, not the title to the land possessed, but rather a call option to buy the land at market value.[220]

Finally, it is also possible to adopt a still different classic pliability rule that introduces an auction mechanism at the liability stage. Under this variant, the adverse possessor receives no property interest whatsoever in the land possessed, but merely a right to receive a monetary award for identifying the continuous underutilization by the original owner. At the end of the statutory period, the title to the underutilized land would be auctioned off to the highest bidder, with the proceeds

---

219. *See, e.g.,* Joseph v. Whitcombe, 279 A.2d 122, 126 (2001) ("New York law has long disfavored the acquisition of title by adverse possession.") (citations omitted).

220. Alternatively, the states more sympathetic to adverse possession could give the adverse possessor a put option, thereby requiring the owner to buy the land back at market value.

divided between the original **owner** and the adverse possessor. The advantage of this system is that it transfers the land to the highest value user as determined by the auction.

2. *Patents*

As we explained, patent protection represents an example of a zero order pliability rule. Critics of the patent system have long argued that a superior way to encourage innovation would be to substitute a system of compulsory licensing for the limited property rule protection accorded to patentees. Under a system of compulsory licensing, a regulator would set the price for use of new inventions, and the patentee would have no power to deviate from that price. To compensate the patentee for the loss in revenues, the protection term could be longer than that currently provided for by law.[221] If set correctly, the compulsory license would adequately reward patentees for investing in research and development without creating a social deadweight loss. This proposed system of compulsory licenses represents a patent system that is based on liability rule protection. Thus, to date, this central debate in patent law has proceeded in terms of pure property rule versus pure liability rule arguments.

Our discussion of pliability rules introduces a third option that may be superior to the competing ones. Specifically, we propose a classic pliability rule that combines initial property rule protection and positive liability protection. Under the new rule, patentees would be accorded property rule protection for a certain period of time, and then the invention would become subject to a compulsory license for another period. For example, Congress can enact a rule under which patentees will enjoy property rule protection for ten years, and then liability rule protection for another twenty years. During the latter period, the invention would be available for a price determined by the PTO, or some arbitration tribunal.

Relative to the current patent system, the proposed pliability rule would reduce the deadweight loss associated with patent protection by cutting the exclusivity period in half; at the same time, the prolonged liability rule period would preserve the incentive to engage in innovation. Relative to a pure system of compulsory licensing, the proposed pliability rule diminishes the risk to which inventors are exposed. A fundamental problem with compulsory licenses is that it is extremely difficult to set the license rates accurately. The license rate, in order not to undermine the incentive to innovate, must reflect not only the

---

221. *See* Pankaj Tandon, *Optimal Patents with Compulsory Licensing*, 90 J. POL. ECON. 470 (1982) (contending that the optimal patent would have an indefinite life, for both process and product innovations, but even if the patent term is left at seventeen years, compulsory licensing may lead to substantial welfare improvements).

expected profits of the patentee on the current innovation, but also the expenditures incurred by the patentees in research projects that failed to yield a patentable result. Given that there is no market price for new inventions, it is very difficult to set compulsory license rates accurately. Granted, the pliability rule we propose incorporates compulsory licensing in the liability rule stage. However, it exposes patentees to a smaller risk of undercompensation by granting them ten years of property rule protection.

The proposed classic pliability rule has an additional advantage over its pure liability cousin. Assume that the liability rule equivalent of our proposed pliability rule is forty years of liability rule protection. In theory, the longer protection period can make up for the fact that patentees receive no property rule protection. In practice, however, the additional ten years may prove worthless. This is so because newer and superior inventions may render existing ones valueless. In addition, discounting of future values imposes an inherent limitation on how much patent protection may be extended. In other words, the incentive effect of the early years of protection is much stronger than that of late years.

3. *Genericism*

As we discussed, the genericism doctrine in trademark law is predicated on a zero order pliability rule. If consumers identify a dominant mark not with a particular company, but rather with the underlying product, the property rule protection of the mark holder lapses and the mark falls into the public domain. That is, once a mark is pronounced generic, competitors of the mark holder can use it free of charge.

We suggest that a classic pliability rule can improve upon existing genericism doctrine. Specifically, Congress could replace the current rule with one that grants competitors the right to use dominant marks in exchange for payment.[222] The PTO could then devise a menu of prices for the use of dominant marks, with the amount to be paid depending on the dominance of the mark: the more dominant the mark, the smaller the payment. Alternatively, once a mark becomes dominant, Congress could require the mark's owner to pay its competitors to retain the right to deny them access to the mark. Either way, the use of a classic pliability rule with a menu of prices would result in a more refined regime than that currently in place. Such a refined system would better enhance competition, and is potentially fairer to all the parties involved.

---

222. The dominance of the mark may be measured by the mark owner's market share in the relevant product or service market. Alternatively, the dominance of the mark may be a function of the strength of consumers' association of the mark with its associated product (as opposed to their association of the mark with the product's manufacturer).

C. *Introducing New Pliability Rules*

Pliability rules need not be limited to the circumstances in which they are already currently employed. In this Section, we discuss two instances of fields of law that could benefit from the introduction of pliability rules. Our first example grapples with the problem of the anti-commons — the problem of the division of property into too-small units. Our other example generalizes the anti-commons analysis and examines the possibility of exporting some of the principles of eminent domain into the private sector — in other words, the creation of a private takings power.

1. *Anti-Commons*

The familiar commons problem deals with too many owners in common of a single resource. In his "Tragedy of the Commons,"[223] Garrett Hardin posited that overexploitation of the resource would result. Hardin illustrated the phenomenon with the example of a rural pasture commonly owned by a community of shepherds. He posited that the shepherds would allow their herds to overgraze the pasture since each shepherd only bears a small fraction of the marginal cost of each use while enjoying the full marginal benefit. The result is the tragedy of the commons: property held in common will be overexploited.[224] Hardin's oft-cited conclusion was that freedom in a commons "bring[s] on universal ruin."[225] The traditional solution to commons problems is privatization, leading one owner to internalize the full marginal cost of each use.

Michael Heller noted that a converse problem — which he labeled the anti-commons problem — could result if the resource were divided into too-small pieces of property, each owned by different owners.[226] In an anti-commons, property interests in a certain asset are dispersed among multiple holders, each of whom has an effective veto over any given use of the property. Because each property owner has veto power over all competing uses, individual owners can behave strategi-

---

223. Garret Hardin, *The Tragedy of the Commons*, 162 SCIENCE 1243 (1968).

224. *But see* Carol M. Rose, *The Comedy of the Commons: Custom, Commerce, and Inherently Public Property*, 53 U. CHI. L. REV. 711, 723 (1986) [hereinafter Rose, *Comedy of the Commons*] ("[C]ustomary doctrines suggest that commerce might be thought a 'comedy of the commons' not only because it may infinitely expand our wealth, but also, at least in part, because it has been thought to enhance the sociability of the members of an otherwise atomized society.").

225. Hardin, *supra* note 223, at 1248. Having said that "[f]reedom to breed will bring ruin to all," Hardin goes on to propose that "[t]he only way we can preserve and nurture other and more precious freedoms is by relinquishing the freedom to breed." *Id.*

226. Michael A. Heller, *The Tragedy of the Anticommons: Property in the Transition from Marx to Markets*, 111 HARV. L. REV. 621 (1998).

cally with respect to their property or may fail to cooperate with other users due to high transaction costs. Heller has observed that, due to this characteristic of property rule protection, assets in an anti-commons commons regime will fall prey to underutilization.[227] The solution to an anti-commons difficulty is thus aggregation of property rights into fewer hands.

One of the most prominent examples of an anti-commons is provided by the land regime in Native American reservations. In a well-intentioned but misguided attempt to protect communal Native American lands in the late nineteenth century, Congress provided for the allocation of reservation lands among Native American households, with provisos severely limiting alienating of the parcels.[228] Over the years, as the lands became ever more divided among heirs, the parcels became increasingly fractionated, to the point where some land interests produced a lease income of as little as one cent per month, and much of the land lay fallow. In 1983, Congress passed the Indian Land Consolidation Act, which escheated small portions of highly fractionated parcels to the tribe upon death of the owner. However, in *Hodel v. Irving*,[229] the Supreme Court ruled that the escheat worked an unconstitutional uncompensated taking. As a result many Native American lands remain in an anti-commons.

A similar problem arises with respect to many other properties typically passed on to heirs as owners in common. After several cycles of intestate succession, the property is likely to have numerous owners who have little communication with one another and divergent interests. Indeed, citing Robert Brown's analysis, Heller and Hanoch Dagan recently suggested that such an anti-commons regime was responsible for the underutilization of African American-owned rural land, and, ultimately, the dissipation of African-American participation in the agricultural economy.[230]

A pliability analysis introduces additional tools to resolve anti-commons difficulties. A properly tailored pliability rule could avoid anti-commons problems by altering protection from property rules to liability rules when the value of the property interest becomes suffi-

---

227. *Id.* at 624, 626 (noting that "[w]hen there are too many owners holding rights of exclusion, the resource is prone to underuse — a *tragedy of the anticommons*" and proposing that "[p]rivatizing a commons and bundling an anticommons can solve the tragedies of misuse by better aligning individual incentives with social welfare"). Heller does note that an anti-commons regime is ideal where nonuse is the most highly valued "use" of the property.

228. *See* General Allotment Act of 1887, ch. 119, 24 Stat. 388; *see also* Act of Mar. 2, 1889, ch. 405, 25 Stat. 888 (authorizing the division of the Great Reservation of the Sioux Nation into separate reservations and the allotment of specific tracts of reservation land to individual Indians, conditioned on the consent of three-fourths of the adult male Sioux).

229. 481 U.S. 704 (1987); *see also* Youpee v. Babbitt, 519 U.S. 234 (1997).

230. *See* Hanoch Dagan & Michael A. Heller, *The Liberal Commons*, 110 YALE L.J. 549, 551 & n.3 (2001).

ciently small. For example, in the Indian Land Consolidation Act, instead of providing for an uncompensated escheat, Congress could have changed the nature of the interests in Native American Lands into a pliability rule in which owners enjoyed property rule protection only as long as the value of the interest was sufficiently large, or the number of owners in an undivided whole sufficiently small. If the value or number of owners crossed a specified threshold, however, the owner would enjoy only liability rule protection in her land vis-à-vis other tribal members or vis-à-vis the tribe. If, in the hands of the new owner, the aggregate of land interests were to become sufficiently valuable or were again concentrated in a sufficiently small number of hands, the interest could once more enjoy property rule protection.

More generally, the use of a pliability rule could help resolve the difficulties produced by successive intestate successions and the resulting multiplicity of uncoordinated heirs. In such cases, policymakers could adopt a mechanism of inter-group pliability protection, allowing, for example, heirs of intestate succession holding a too-small percentage to be subject to liability protection for their small holdings. Such liability protection, however, would only apply vis-à-vis other heirs. With regards to non-heirs, the owners would enjoy full property rule protection. To the extent that anti-commons problems were responsible for the decline of African-American farming communities, a pliability regime could have been a valuable tool in helping to preserve minority rural land ownership.

Inter-group pliability regimes would enjoy two significant advantages over the Congressional schemes of the last two decades. First, since the transition to pliability rules would still entail full compensation for takings, it would not fall afoul of the Takings Clause. Second, because different potential owners could compete for the land until it arrived in hands with sufficient other land holdings, without the necessity for potentially costly negotiation, the pliability regime would provide a more efficient market mechanism for aggregating the property holdings.[231]

2. *Eminent Domain and Private Takings*

Pliability rule protection as a solution for anti-commons underutilization can be seen as part of a broader category of pliability rule applications in the realm of private takings. A taking, in a pliability analysis, transforms property rule into liability rule protection, and

---

231. Given the immovability of the land holdings, the legislation would have to provide a mechanism by which persons could seize the land subject to the liability protection phase of the pliability rule. One possibility would be by serving notice upon a court and the person from whom the land is being seized. In cases of multiple minor holders trying to seize the same property, or cyclical takings and retakings of the same property, the court could initiate a closed auction.

then back into property rule protection in new hands — those of the government. However, a public taking is not inevitable. Condemnation could pave the way for the interest ending up in private hands in the third, property rule phase of the pliability rule. This would be a private, rather than public taking.

Notwithstanding the constitutional requirement that the government exercise its power of eminent domain for a "public use,"[232] often, the taking results in the transfer an object from one set of private hands to another. For example, in the famous case of *Poletown Neighborhood Council v. City of Detroit*,[233] the city of Detroit seized a number of private lots in order to transfer them to General Motors for building a new factory. Vis-à-vis the government, every original owner of a private lot in Poletown enjoyed the pliability rule protection shaped by the law of eminent domain. This pliability rule protection was not altered by the fact that the ultimate destination of the property was a different set of private hands. Indeed, imagine that General Motors could itself trigger the process for a taking by eminent domain by petitioning for city council approval for a private taking. In such a case, the original owner would enjoy the same pliability rule protection as in the case of a public taking, so long as the pliability rule's trigger for altering rule protection remained the same.

While private takings might produce the same incentive effects on the original owners as public takings, private takings offer two potentially significant advantages. First, by eliminating an unnecessary actor, private takings reduce surplus bureaucracy and decrease the cost of coordination. If the Poletown case had involved a private taking, General Motors could proceed on its own once it had received approval to exercise a private taking. Instead of coordinating with a government agency to undertake the project, General Motors could negotiate and interact directly with the land owners in Poletown. Importantly, as in the case of the public taking, owners dissatisfied with their compensation could seek judicial review. Thus, the lack of direct involvement of a government agency would not alter the rights available to the land owners.

Second, private takings lead the parties to a more accurate accounting of the costs of their actions, leading to fewer inefficient takings. Were Poletown a private takings case, General Motors would pay the required just compensation directly to the land owners, requiring it to internalize the full cost of the taking. By contrast, in the context of a public taking, the Poletown case permits General Motors to underestimate the cost of the takings while possibly requiring the

---

232. *But see supra* note 208.

233. 304 N.W.2d 455 (Mich. 1981).

government to overestimate the cost.[234] Indeed, the takings compensation costs for the Poletown project greatly exceeded original estimates,
leading to a depletion of public funds of in excess of $200 million.[235]

Private takings could be widely permitted, given the ubiquity of
the strategic problems justifying public takings.[236] The strategic problems afflicting government acquisitions can be seen in such private
contexts as railroad and utility land purchases. Indeed, it is for precisely this reason that private takings were a widely used tool in the
nineteenth century for railroads.[237]

An important caveat must be added here. So long as the trigger
employed by the pliability rule remains the same, the nature of the
pliability rule protection depends not at all on the actor who ends up
with the final entitlement. Thus, a pliability analysis demonstrates
that, in one sense, private takings are no less defensible than public
takings. However, when the pliability rule's trigger depends on the
discretion of a particular party, the identity of the party exercising that
discretion naturally affects the incentive effects of the pliability rule.
In our example of a private taking in the Poletown case, we vested discretion in the same actor as the real Poletown case did — the city
council. Thus, we did not have to take account of the altered incentive
effects.[238]

CONCLUSION

In this Article, we have developed the concept of pliability rules
and demonstrated its centrality to a full understanding of the entitlement theory sparked by Calebresi and Melamed's classic article. We
have also shown the pervasiveness of pliability rules in existing legal
structures, and demonstrated how pliability analysis can transform
property and intellectual property law.

Any study of a subject requires an understanding of its animating
principles. The law is no exception. In light of the widespread use of

---

234. *See* Abraham Bell & Gideon Parchomovsky, *Givings*, 111 YALE L.J. 547 (2001);
Merrill, *supra* note 208.

235. Editorial, *Protect the Taxpayers*, DETROIT NEWS, Oct. 19, 1999 at A10; Tina Lam,
Dispute Could Cause Price of Land for Stadiums to Rise, DETROIT FREE PRESS, May 17,
1999, at 1B.

236. *See, e.g.*, EPSTEIN, *supra* note 101, at 169-181 (arguing in favor of private takings
for public use); Lawrence Berger, *The Public Use Requirement in Eminent Domain*, 57 OR.
L. REV. 203, 236-37, 243 (1978) (proposing that the public use requirement in private takings
— for example, where landowners need to acquire access to their real property — should be
allowed only if fifty percent excess compensation is paid).

237. *See* Fischel, *supra* note 209, at 80-89 (1995) (discussing historical evidence of private takings by railroads in the nineteenth century).

238. A fuller analysis of the incentive effects created by discretionary triggering events
in pliability rules lies beyond the scope of this Article.

pliability rules in our legal system, it behooves the academy to update its theories to fit a complex legal reality. Given the ability of pliability rules to accommodate divergent social concerns, it is not surprising that they are already widely used, forcing the academy to play catch-up. Attention to pliability rules is thus necessary to align theory and reality. Moreover, such academic analysis of pliability rules can generate superior possibilities for decisionmakers, as we illustrated in the final Part of this Article.

Our exposition has provided a taste of the possibilities created by pliability analysis, rather than exhausted them. The prism of pliability highlights trends and features of the law that are not easily seen otherwise. Listing all the examples lies beyond the ken of this Article. But, to illustrate some possible directions for future discussions, we close by briefly touching upon a field of law that we have not yet mentioned — bankruptcy.

To be sure, the place of bankruptcy rights in Calebresi and Melamed's traditional framework is not easily determined, rendering it somewhat difficult to define precisely the various stages of the pliability rules created by bankruptcy.[239] But there is little doubt that the bankruptcy framework follows the broad outlines of pliability rules: one type of protection is altered by a trigger (the filing of the petition) and replaced by another type of protection. Bankruptcy law establishes that a certain event — the proper filing of a bankruptcy petition — alters the rights of all persons with regard to the property of the debtor. A new set of rules applies to all the debtor's and creditors' entitlements while the petition is in bankruptcy court, and after the proceeding is completed, the debtor is considered a new person, entitled to a "fresh start."

However, the importance of bankruptcy for pliability analysis lies not in its providing yet another instance of the use of pliability rules in legal practice; rather, the example of bankruptcy points to the impact of pliability rules on commercial practice, and the importance of understanding pliability rules as a category distinct from property or liability rules. Aware that a potential bankruptcy will trigger a change in protections, parties to commercial transactions shape their ex ante expectations. The possibility that a bankruptcy petition will alter the rights of owners and creditors has led to business practices such as credit ratings, risk-based interest premiums and guarantees. It has also spawned such legal fields as secured transactions, which seek to shape the rights of parties in the post-petition state of the debtor. All these

---

239. *See* Shubha Ghosh, *The Morphing of Property Rules and Liability Rules: An Intellectual Property Optimist Examines Article 9 and Bankruptcy*, 8 FORDHAM INTELL. PROP. MEDIA & ENT. L. J. 99 (1997); *see also* David Frisch, *The Implicit "Takings" Jurisprudence of Article 9 of the Uniform Commercial Code*, 64 FORDHAM L. REV. 11 (1995) (examining property rights in the context of secured transactions); *cf.* Merrill & Smith, *supra* note 94 (arguing against property analysis of *in personam* rights).

institutions are based upon the parties' awareness that the legal rights they enjoy will not necessarily extend infinitely into the future. Yet, the parties also know that if a bankruptcy petition triggers a rearrangement of their rights, they will not find themselves in unknown territory. The post-petition rules of bankruptcy are relatively clear and can be planned for.

Thus, bankruptcy provides an important guide on how the legal academy should use pliability analysis. In examining any given legal entitlement, we must reject the temptation to engage in a static analysis that freezes the entitlement at the present time. Instead, we must adopt a dynamic perspective that incorporates the change that the entitlement is due to undergo. Like the commercial actors aware of bankruptcy, we too can project change and create structures — like securities and pledges in the context of bankruptcy — that take into account the ability to change built into the rights created by law.[240]

The three decades that have elapsed since Calabresi and Melamed's landmark article have demonstrated its durability and usefulness. To retain its vitality, however, Calabresi and Melamed's model must be adapted to the dynamism of legal rules. Static property and liability rules have become basic staples of legal research. It is time for their dynamic cousins — pliability rules — to join them.

---

240. Before concluding, we note that our Article — like many based on *The Cathedral* — has focused on property and liability as the two basic building blocks identified by Calabresi and Melamed. Other combinations are, of course, possible. Consider child labor. Until a certain age, a child's labor is inalienable; after that age, a person may sell her labor at any agreed upon price, within the bounds set by labor laws. Thus, child labor laws create a type of "pliability rule" that involves a transition from inalienability to property rule protection.

Part III
Criminal Law

[12]

USING SENTENCE ENHANCEMENTS TO DISTINGUISH BETWEEN DETERRENCE AND INCAPACITATION*

DANIEL KESSLER	and	*STEVEN D. LEVITT*
Stanford University and		*University of Chicago*
National Bureau of		*and American Bar*
Economic Research		*Foundation*

ABSTRACT

Differentiating empirically between deterrence and incapacitation is difficult since both are a function of expected punishment. In this article we demonstrate that the introduction of sentence enhancements provides a direct means of measuring deterrence. Because the criminal would have been sentenced to prison even without the law change, there is no additional incapacitation effect from the sentence enhancement in the short run. Therefore, any immediate decrease in crime must be due to deterrence. We test the model using California's Proposition 8, which imposed sentence enhancements for a selected group of crimes. Proposition 8 appears to reduce eligible crimes by 4 percent in the year following its passage and 8 percent 3 years after passage. These immediate effects are consistent with deterrence. The impact of the law continues to increase 5–7 years after its passage, suggesting that incapacitation may be important as well.

I. INTRODUCTION

SINCE Gary Becker's seminal paper on the economic model of crime,[1] there have been more than 100 published studies attempting to test for deterrence.[2] While there is disagreement on the topic, many studies published

* We would like to thank John Donohue, Isaac Ehrlich, Edward Glaeser, Austan Goolsbee, John Lott, Anne Piehl, conference participants, an anonymous referee, and especially Bruce Kobayashi and the editor Sam Peltzman for comments and suggestions. Financial support of the National Science Foundation is gratefully acknowledged. David Becker and Justin Wood provided outstanding research assistance. Correspondence may be addressed either to Daniel Kessler, Graduate School of Business, Stanford University, Stanford, CA 94305 (e-mail: fkessler@GSB-pound.stanford.edu) or to Steven Levitt, Department of Economics, University of Chicago, 1126 East 59th Street, Chicago, IL 60637 (e-mail: slevitt @midway.uchicago.edu).

[1] Gary Becker, Crime and Punishment: An Economic Approach, 76 J. Pol. Econ. 169 (1968).

[2] Surveys of this literature include Samuel Cameron, The Economics of Crime Deterrence: A Survey of Theory and Evidence, 41 Kyklos 301 (1988); Issac Ehrlich, Crime, Punishment, and the Market for Offenses, 10 J. Econ. Persp. 43 (1996); and Daniel Nagin, Criminal Deter-

[*Journal of Law and Economics*, vol. XLII (April 1999)]
© 1999 by The University of Chicago. All rights reserved. 0022-2186/99/4201-0013$01.50

344   THE JOURNAL OF LAW AND ECONOMICS

in recent years have found results that are at a minimum *consistent* with the presence of an important deterrence effect using a range of different measures.[3]

One important shortcoming associated with almost all of these empirical analyses, however, is the difficulty in distinguishing between deterrence and incapacitation. As long as the primary means of punishment is imprisonment, policy changes that increase the expected punishment per crime lead to both greater deterrence and greater incapacitation. Consequently, most empirical tests of deterrence are, in practice, joint tests of deterrence and incapacitation. For example, reductions in crime associated with increased arrest rates or rising prison populations are consistent with the presence of deterrent effects, incapacitation, or both. Given the strong evidence in support of incapacitation effects,[4] caution is warranted in attributing a causal role to deterrence in such contexts.[5]

In this article, we present a novel approach to separating deterrence from incapacitation. We exploit the unique transition path associated with what are commonly termed "sentence enhancements." With sentence enhancements, additional prison time is tacked on to the basic sentence for crimes of a particular type, for example, crimes committed with a gun or

---

rence Research: A Review of the Evidence and a Research Agenda for the Outset of the Twenty-First Century (unpublished manuscript, Carnegie Mellon Univ. 1997).

[3] Isaac Ehrlich, Participation in Illegitimate Activities: A Theoretical and Empirical Investigation, 81 J. Pol. Econ. 531 (1973); Jeff Grogger, Certainty vs. Severity, 29 Econ. Inquiry 297 (1991); Steven Levitt, Using Electoral Cycles in Police Hiring to Estimate the Effect of Police on Crime, 87 Am. Econ. Rev. 270 (1997); Thomas Marvell & Carlisle Moody, Prison Population Growth and Crime Reduction, 10 J. Quant. Criminology 109 (1994); Thomas Marvell & Carlisle Moody, Police Levels, Crime Rates, and Specification Problems, 34 Criminology 609 (1996); Patricia Mayhew *et al.*, Crime in Public View (Home Office Research Study No. 49, London 1979); Helen Tauchen, Anne Witte, & Harriet Griesinger, Criminal Deterrence: Revisiting the Issue with a Birth Cohort (unpublished manuscript, Univ. North Carolina at Chapel Hill, Dep't Econ. 1993); Ann Witte, Estimating the Economic Model of Crime with Individual Data, 94 Q. J. Econ. 57 (1980).

[4] Christy Visher, The RAND Inmate Survey: A Reanalysis, in Criminal Careers and Career Criminals (A. Blumstein *et al.* eds., vol. 2 1986); John DiIulio & Anne Piehl, Does Prison Pay? The Stormy National Debate over the Cost-Effectiveness of Imprisonment, 1991 Brookings Rev. 28; William Spelman, Criminal Incapacitation (1994).

[5] There are a few studies that make an attempt to carefully differentiate between deterrence and incapacitation. Robert McCormick & Robert Tollison, Crime on the Court, 92 J. Pol. Econ. 223 (1984), analyzes the impact of increasing the number of basketball referees on the frequency with which fouls are committed. Because the punishment in this context is not incarceration, the effects are solely deterrence related. Steven Levitt, Why Do Increased Arrest Rates Appear to Reduce Crime: Deterrence, Incapacitation, or Measurement Error? 36 Econ. Inquiry 353 (1998), attempts to distinguish between deterrence and incapacitation using the impact of increased arrest rates for one crime on the frequency with which other crimes are committed.

SENTENCE ENHANCEMENTS 345

third convictions for qualifying crimes in the presence of "three strikes" laws.[6] The key insight of the analysis is that initially such laws may have a deterrent effect but will not have any impact on the amount of incapacitation. The criminal is already required to serve the basic sentence. Only after that term[7] has elapsed and the sentence enhancement takes effect will there be an added incapacitation effect. Any deterrent effect, however, will arise immediately as the criminal incorporates the increased punishment associated with the sentence enhancement into the decision calculus. Thus, by looking at changes in crime immediately following the introduction of a sentence enhancement, it is possible to isolate a pure deterrent effect that is not contaminated by incapacitation.

We begin the article by developing a theoretical model that formalizes the intuition of the preceding paragraph. We then provide an empirical test of the model using California's experiences with Proposition 8, a popular referendum passed in 1982 that increased the scope and severity of repeat-offender enhancements. In the years immediately following Proposition 8, crime rates for those offenses covered by the sentence enhancements fell sharply, both in absolute terms and relative to a set of similar offenses that were excluded from Proposition 8. In the years preceding passage of Proposition 8, the time path of eligible and noneligible crimes in California mirrors that of the United States as a whole. Immediately following Proposition 8, California's crime pattern diverges from that of the rest of the United States. These results are consistent with the presence of a deterrent effect of the sentence enhancements. Furthermore, the continued decline over the ensuing years in relative crime rates for the offenses covered by Proposition 8 are consistent with the model's prediction that the transition to a new steady state will involve a continued fall in crime as the incapacitative impact of the enhancements slowly takes effect.

Differentiating between deterrence and incapacitation is not merely an academic exercise. Rather, the distinction between those two forces is critical to determining the costs and benefits associated with sentence enhancements, particularly for three-strikes laws that entail extremely long sentences. If incapacitation is the primary force, than three-strikes laws will lead to enormous increases in the number of prisoners and eventually to a

---

[6] As discussed in the following section of the article, there has been a substantial movement toward a variety of sentence enhancements in the United States in recent years. For instance, since 1993, three-strikes laws have been adopted in 24 states and have been added to the federal sentencing guidelines. These laws are in addition to a range of repeat-offender and gun enhancements already in place in the great majority of states.

[7] Or more precisely, the proportion of that sentence that would have actually been served.

geriatric prison population that has largely aged out of crime, poses little threat to society, and requires costly health care.[8] In contrast, as demonstrated in the model, if deterrence is the operative force, then three-strikes laws will lead to an equilibrium with both lower crime and lower levels of incarceration, making them a very attractive policy. Our results provide mixed support for three-strikes laws. Although the lower bound on deterrence effects that we estimate from Proposition 8 are nontrivial (4–8 percent), we also find large lagged declines in crime that are consistent with incapacitation effects associated with a rising prison population. Thus, there is not clear evidence that increasing punishment in this instance led to a "golden" equilibrium with both lower crime and lower levels of incarceration.

The structure of the article is as follows. Section II presents the theoretical model of sentence enhancements, demonstrating formally how deterrence and incapacitation can be distinguished. The third section examines the use of sentence enhancements in the United States. Section IV provides an empirical test of the theoretical model using the response of crime rates to Proposition 8 in California and compares crime patterns in California to the rest of the United States. The final section considers the broader implications of our findings, particularly with respect to three-strikes laws.

II. THEORETICAL MODEL

In this section we develop a stylized economic model of crime incorporating sentence enhancements into the analysis. We characterize the steady-state equilibria with and without sentence enhancements, as well as the transition path when sentence enhancements are introduced into an economy.

A. The Basic Model

For simplicity, we consider a model with a continuum of infinitely-lived agents.[9] In every period, each individual chooses either to engage in a single criminal act or in the noncrime alternative (except those who are currently incarcerated, who do neither). If the agent commits a crime in period t, there is an exogenously given, predetermined likelihood of detection (p_t).

---

[8] Alfred Blumstein, Prisons, in Crime (J. Q. Wilson and J. Petersilia eds. 1995); Edith Flynn *et al.*, Three Strikes Legislation: Prevalence and Definitions in Critical Criminal Justice Issues: Task Force Reports from the American Society of Criminology to Attorney General Janet Reno (1997).

[9] The results that we derive would continue to hold in an overlapping generations framework or in a model with finite-lived agents. Limiting the focus to one cohort, however, greatly simplifies both the notation and calculations.

The punishment, conditional on being caught committing a crime, is a prison sentence of S periods that begins in period $t + 1$ and runs through period $t + S + 1$.[10] While incarcerated, the agent is unable to commit further crimes. The utility loss associated with this prison sentence is denoted $J_t(S)$. Initially, the sentence length S is assumed to be one period. Later, when sentence enhancements are introduced, the enhancement will raise the sentence length to two periods.

The private return to crime (not including the punishment if detected) is denoted r and is the only factor that varies across individuals. The return to the noncrime alternative is normalized to zero for all individuals. Agents are assumed to be risk neutral and future utilities are not discounted, although either of those factors could be incorporated into the present framework.[11] Thus, the agent's maximization problem in any period is simply

$$\underset{C_{it} \in \{0,1\}}{\text{MAX}} \ (r_i - p_t J_t(S)) C_{it}, \tag{1}$$

where i indexes individuals; C_{it} is an indicator variable equal to one if a crime is committed by agent i in period t, and zero otherwise. An agent commits crime if and only if the private return to crime r exceeds the expected punishment $(p_t J_t)$.[12] For simplicity, it is assumed that r_i is uniformly distributed over agents with a range from zero to R and a density of $1/R$. If there were no punishment, all agents would engage in criminal activities, and the total crime rate C_t would be equal to one. With a positive expected punishment, some agents will be deterred. In order to ensure an interior solution, R is chosen such that $R > p_t J_t$. Thus, some agents will commit crimes in all periods, assuming they are not already incarcerated.

Because prison sentences from one period are served in the following period(s), crime in period t depends not only on expected punishment in period t (deterrence), but also on actual levels of crime and punishment in

---

[10] Both the likelihood of punishment and the length of the prison sentence could be endogenized to allow for optimal policy determination as is standard in the literature; see, for example, Becker, *supra* note 1; Louis Kaplow & Steven Shavell, Optimal Law Enforcement with Self-Reporting of Behavior, 102 J. Pol. Econ. 583 (1994); John Lott, Should the Wealthy Be Able to Buy Justice? 95 J. Pol. Econ. 1307 (1987); A. Mitchell Polinsky & Daniel Rubinfeld, A Model of Optimal Fines for Repeat Offenders, 46 J. Pub. Econ. 291 (1991); A. Mitchell Polinsky & Steven Shavell, The Optimal Use of Fines and Imprisonment, 24 J. Pub. Econ. 89 (1984). Our interest, however, is not in deriving the optimal policy but, rather, in examining how individual criminal decisions respond to changes in observed policy, regardless of whether the policies implemented are optimal.

[11] A. Mitchell Polinsky & Steven Shavell, On the Disutility and Discounting of Imprisonment and the Theory of Deterrence (Working paper, Harvard Law School 1997).

[12] Implicit in equation (1) is the assumption that the criminal receives the utility of the criminal act even if caught and punished. This assumption is not necessary to obtain the results presented below.

the preceding period(s) (incapacitation).[13] It is relatively straightforward to demonstrate that the steady-state level of crime is as follows:[14]

$$C_t = 1 - \frac{p_t J_t}{R} - p_{t-1} C_{t-1}. \tag{2}$$

If there were neither deterrence nor incapacitation, all agents would commit crime, leading to $C_t = 1$. The second term on the right-hand side of equation (2) is deterrence; anyone with $r_i < p_t J_t$ decides against committing the crime. The final term in equation (2) is the number of crimes that do not occur as a result of incarceration (that is, the incapacitation effect). In a steady state, all agents who committed crime in the previous period will commit crime in the current period unless they are behind bars. Therefore the incapacitation effect is simply equal to the size of the prison population.

Setting crime in the current and preceding periods equal, the steady-state solution to the model solely in terms of parameters is

$$C_t = \frac{\left(1 - \dfrac{p_t J_t}{R}\right)}{1 + p_t}. \tag{3}$$

B. Adding Sentence Enhancements to the Model

We model sentence enhancements as an increase in the prison sentence from one period to two periods. We assume that the probability of detection remains constant.[15] In analyzing the effect of introducing sentence enhancements, it is critical to identify not only the new steady state but also the transition path.

Assume that sentence enhancements are introduced in period t. Also, let the disutility of a two-period prison sentence be $(1 + d)J$, where $d > 0$; there is disutility associated with the second period in prison. We allow for the marginal disutility associated with increases in the prison term to be increasing $(d > 1)$, decreasing $(d < 1)$, or constant $(d = 1)$. Crime in the first period with sentence enhancements in place is given by

---

[13] Initially we consider prison sentences that are exactly one period in length. Thus, this period's crime depends only on last period's crime and punishment levels.

[14] Out of steady state, the equation becomes more complicated because the pool of prisoners may be composed of some agents who committed a crime last period but would not engage in crime this period due to changes in the expected punishment.

[15] Although from the perspective of optimal policy design, holding p fixed would not necessarily be optimal.

$$C_t = 1 - \left[\frac{p_t J_t}{R} + \frac{dp_t J_t}{R}(1 - p_{t-1}C_{t-1}) \right] - p_{t-1}C_{t-1}. \qquad (4)$$

The only difference between equations (2) and (4) is in the deterrence term, which is in square brackets in equation (4). With sentence enhancements all agents who were previously deterred continued to be deterred. In addition, some additional agents are also deterred by the increased expected punishment. Note, however, that some agents who would be deterred if free are actually incarcerated, necessitating the $1 - p_{t-1}C_{t-1}$ term in the square brackets.

The two important observations emerging from a comparison of equations (2) and (4) are as follows. *First, crime is lower in equation (4) due to the increased deterrence associated with longer sentences resulting from the sentence enhancements. Second, in the first period following the introduction of sentence enhancements, the incapacitation effect is unaffected.* Not until the original sentence expires does the increased incapacitation associated with sentence enhancements materialize. Thus, any immediate reduction in crime associated with sentence enhancements is attributable to deterrence rather than incapacitation.

The steady-state level of crime after the introduction of sentence enhancements is

$$C_t = 1 - \frac{(1 + d)p_t J_t}{R} - (p_{t-1}C_{t-1}) - (p_{t-2}C_{t-2}). \qquad (5)$$

Comparing equations (2) and (5), the steady-state deterrence effect (the second term on the right-hand side of both equations) is greater after the sentence enhancement. This, of course, is a straightforward outcome of any economic model of crime. Comparing the first period after sentence enhancements to the steady state with such enhancements (eqq. [4] and [5]), a more subtle result emerges. *The deterrence effect associated with sentence enhancements increases over time.* The explanation for this result is that initially some of those who could be deterred are incarcerated and therefore cannot respond to the change in incentives. Over time, those agents will be released from prison and deterred thereafter.[16] Note that this channel for rising deterrence is separate from lags in behavioral changes on the part of

---

[16] In some sense, the last italicized point is a relatively minor one from a public policy perspective since these agents are not committing crime either immediately after the sentence enhancements or in the steady state. The only difference is whether the reduction in crime is assigned to deterrence or incapacitation. The reason that this distinction is important, however, is that the measured reduction in crime directly following the introduction of sentence enhancements captures only the immediate rise in deterrence, not the long-run rise.

criminals that are likely to be empirically relevant but are not explicitly modeled.

Thus, for both of these reasons, the initial change in crime represents a lower bound on the long-run increase in deterrence. This will have implications for the interpretation of the empirical results presented in later sections.

Solving for the steady-state crime rate in equation (5) solely in terms of parameters yields

$$C_t = \frac{\left(1 - \frac{(1 + d)p_t J_t}{R}\right)}{1 + 2p_t}. \tag{6}$$

Comparing equations (3) and (6), the steady-state crime rates before and after the sentence enhancements, crime is unambiguously lower with the enhancements. The change in deterrence is easily computed from equations (2) and (4) as dpJ/R. Tedious algebraic manipulation of equations (3) and (6) (not shown) demonstrates that the change in the crime rate can either be greater than or less than the change in deterrence. *Therefore, the introduction of sentence enhancements has an ambiguous impact on the incapacitation effect.* Translated into more meaningful terms, this implies that the size of the prison population may either rise or fall with sentence enhancements. There are two countervailing forces affecting the prison population. Sentences are longer, but fewer crimes are committed, so there are fewer criminals being sentenced.

III. An Overview of the Use of Sentence Enhancements in the United States

In recent years, many of the changes in sentencing policy that have been adopted have had one thing in common: they all impose mandatory, statutory increases in prison sentences on individuals who were already going to be incarcerated. Whether the new policies were called determinate sentencing laws, sentencing guidelines, gun enhancements, or repeat-offender enhancements, they all shared this common feature. By 1994, all 50 states and the federal government had adopted one or more mandatory sentencing laws.[17] In particular, repeat-offender enhancements were in use in 41 states and in the federal sentencing guidelines as of 1993.[18]

---

[17] Michael Tonry, Sentencing Matters (1996).

[18] United States Sentencing Commission, The Federal Sentencing Guidelines: A Report on the Operation of the Guidelines System and Short-Term Impacts on Disparity in Sentencing, Use of Incarceration, and Prosecutorial Discretion and Plea Bargaining (1991); Bureau of Justice Assistance, National Assessment of Structured Sentencing (1996).

In addition to those existing laws, 24 state legislatures enacted a new, more stringent breed of repeat-offender enhancements called "Three Strikes and You're Out" laws[19] between 1993 and 1995. Repeat-offender enhancements can be characterized along two dimensions: the range of current crimes and criminal histories that qualify for the enhancement (scope) and the magnitude of the enhancement imposed (severity). Three-strikes laws toughened existing repeat-offender enhancements in both dimensions, expanding the scope of the enhancements beyond the most serious felons and increasing the severity of the enhancements. In many states, three-strikes laws impose life imprisonment without parole for a third-time offender.

Furthermore, with the passage of the Violent Crime Control and Law Enforcement Act of 1994, the U.S. Congress made three-strikes sentencing a fundamental part of federal sentencing policy. First, the Act created a federal three-strikes law. The Act mandates life imprisonment for all serious violent federal felonies, if the defendant has been sentenced for two or more prior separate serious violent felonies or serious drug offenses in state or federal court.[20] Second, the Act provided incentives to states for increasing state penalties for repeat violent offenders. One way that a state can become eligible for a Truth-in-Sentencing Grant is to have in effect at the time of application laws requiring that violent felons who have been convicted of at least one prior separate serious violent felony or serious drug offence in state or federal court serve at least 85 percent of their sentence.[21]

Previous research on the impact of enhancements has reported conflicting findings on the aggregate impact of enhancements on crime. One of the few studies of the effect of a three-strikes law, undertaken by RAND, predicted that California's 1994 law would have a substantial incapacitative effect on crime.[22] Although some studies of the effect of gun enhancements report that adoption of enhancements reduces some or all gun-related crimes,[23]

---

[19] John Clark, James Austin, & D. Alan Henry, "Three Strikes and You're Out": A Review of State Legislation (NCJ 165369, U.S. Dep't of Justice, Office of Justice Statistics, 1997).

[20] 18 U.S.C. §3559(c)(1).

[21] 42 U.S.C. §13702(a)(2)(D).

[22] Peter W. Greenwood *et al.*, Three Strikes and You're Out: Estimated Benefits and Costs of California's New Mandatory Sentencing Law (RAND 1994); but see James Austin, "Three Strikes and You're Out": The Likely Consequences on the Courts, Prisons, and Crime in California and Washington State, 14 St. Louis U. Pub. L. Rev. 239 (1994), for a critique, and James Austin (presentation at the meetings of the American Criminological Society, San Diego, Cal., November 1997), for evidence that these predictions have not been realized.

[23] For example, Glen L. Pierce & William J. Bowers, The Bartley-Fox Gun Law's Short-Term Impact on Crime in Boston, 455 Annals Am. Acad. Pol. & Soc. Sci. 120 (1981); David

352 THE JOURNAL OF LAW AND ECONOMICS

other studies of gun enhancements report no effect.[24] Disagreement in the literature extends to the existence and magnitude of the impact of increasing mandatory sentences on crime generally.[25]

Previous research, however, has failed to recognize both the importance and possibility of distinguishing between deterrence and incapacitation.[26] Thus, further investigation of the effects of repeat-offender enhancements is essential to the analysis of recent changes in state and federal sentencing policy. Guided by our theoretical model, we exploit the transition path associated with the adoption of sentence enhancements. Short-run declines in crime are likely to be attributable largely or solely to deterrence since the incapacitative effect of sentence enhancements will occur only with a lag. Over time, continued declines in crime should continue as the full extent of deterrence is realized and incapacitation becomes operative. In the following section, we test the predictions of the model using California's experience with Proposition 8.[27]

IV. PROPOSITION 8 IN CALIFORNIA: THE EFFECTS OF REPEAT-OFFENDER ENHANCEMENTS[28]

Proposition 8 was passed directly by California voters through the initiative process on June 8, 1982, and went into effect the next day. By adding Sections 667(a) and 1192.7(c) to the California Penal Code, Proposition 8 substantially increased both the scope and the severity of California's existing repeat-offender enhancement.[29] Before the passage of Proposition 8,

McDowall, Colin Loftin, & Brian Wiersema, A Comparative Study of the Preventive Effects of Mandatory Sentencing Laws for Gun Crimes, 83 J. Crim. L. & Criminology 378 (1992).

[24] For example, Colin Loftin, Milton Heumann, & David McDowall, Mandatory Sentencing and Firearms Violence: Evaluating an Alternative to Gun Control, 17 L. & Soc'y Rev. 287 (1983).

[25] See, for example, Michael Tonry, Mandatory Penalties, in 16 Crime and Justice: A Review of Research (Michael Tonry ed. 1992); Tonry, supra note 17; and Bureau of Justice Assistance, supra note 18, for studies finding no effect.

[26] Indeed, the RAND study discussed above (Greenwood et al., supra note 22) assumes that the California three-strikes law will have no deterrent effect at all in its assessment of the benefits and costs of the law.

[27] As discussed in the concluding section of the article, we have also examined states' experiences with three-strikes laws. Unlike Proposition 8, however, three-strikes laws have generally not been rigorously enforced. Consequently, there is no evidence that punishments have actually increased as a result of three-strikes laws, except in California.

[28] The introduction to Section IV draws heavily on Daniel Kessler & Anne Morrison Piehl, The Role of Discretion in the Criminal Justice System, 14 J. L. Econ. & Org. 256 (1998).

[29] Before the passage of Proposition 8, California's Determinate Sentencing Law provided for several types of sentence enhancements: enhancements for causing great bodily injury, gun enhancements, and repeat-offender enhancements. At that time, § 667.5 of the California Penal Code governed repeat-offender enhancements.

SENTENCE ENHANCEMENTS   353

the existing law required a 3-year enhancement of violent felony offenders' sentences for each prior prison term served for a violent felony or a 1-year enhancement of nonviolent felony offenders' sentences for each prior prison term served for a nonviolent felony, whichever was greater. With Proposition 8, all "serious" felony offenders under Section 1192.7(c) received a 5-year enhancement for each prior *conviction* of a "serious" felony offense or a 1-year enhancement for each prior prison term served for any offense, whichever was greater.[30] In addition, Proposition 8 expanded the scope and severity of the enhancement by eliminating the statute of limitations in Section 667.5 that only considered a defendant's record for at most the past 10 years, by prohibiting judges from sentencing defendants to serve their enhancements concurrently with their base sentence and by requiring that each of the enhancements be served consecutively.[31]

Kessler and Piehl[32] show that Proposition 8 increased sentences for repeat offenders charged with serious felonies but not for repeat offenders charged with certain nonserious felonies.[33] Thus, because Proposition 8 affected punishment levels for some crimes but not for others, its passage provides an experiment with which we can evaluate the deterrent effect of repeat-offender enhancements.

The raw data for our analysis are presented in Table 1. For California, crime categories are divided into two groups: those eligible for enhancements under Proposition 8 (murder, rape, robbery, aggravated assault with a firearm, and burglary of a residence) and those that are not eligible (aggravated assault without a firearm, burglary of a nonresidence, motor vehicle

---

[30] Cal. Penal Code § 1192.7(c); "serious" felonies include all "violent" felonies covered under the previous law as well as some nonviolent felonies, in particular burglary of a residence.

[31] The only data available are aggregated by crime category. Thus we are able to make comparisons between eligible and noneligible crime categories, but not to differentiate between criminals who are or are not eligible for sentence enhancements.

[32] Kessler & Piehl, *supra* note 28.

[33] In *id.*, Kessler and Piehl also find small spillover effects of Proposition 8 affecting repeat offenders charged with "similar" nonserious felonies, where "similar" nonserious felonies are nonserious felonies that have legal elements in common with one or more serious felonies. However, spillover effects only strengthen our finding that increases in the scope and severity of repeat-offender enhancements attributable to Proposition 8 lead to decreases in crime. Because spillover effects increase sentences for "control" group crimes, they could only lead to decreases in the number of "control" group crimes, and therefore only lead to decreases in the magnitude of the estimated deterrent effect of Proposition 8 relative to rates of "control" group crimes. In contrast to Kessler and Piehl's findings, *id.*, it should be noted that earlier research found no effect of Proposition 8 on sentence lengths; see, for example, Candace McCoy & Robert Tillman, Controlling Felony Plea Bargaining in California: The Impact of the "Victims' Bill of Rights" (Cal. Dep't of Justice, Bureau of Criminal Statistics, 1986); and Robert Tillman & Candace McCoy, The Impact of California's "Prior Felony Conviction" Law (Cal. Dep't of Justice, Bureau of Criminal Statistics, 1986).

TABLE 1

CRIME RATES IN CALIFORNIA AND THE REST OF THE UNITED STATES, 1977–89

	1977	1979	1981	1983	1985	1987	1989
California:							
Eligible crimes:							
Murder	11.1	12.6	12.9	10.4	10.6	10.6	10.9
Rape	47.9	52.5	55.8	47.8	43.4	43.8	41.1
Robbery	278.3	325.3	385.9	339.1	328.1	301.5	331.8
Aggravated assault with firearm	77.6	93.0	95.6	74.8	73.7	92.0	114.4
Burglary of residence	1,418.4	1,411.1	1,521.6	1,221.7	1,141.0	1,001.8	894.1
Noneligible crimes:							
Aggravated assault with no firearm	268.8	306.6	307.6	296.4	310.9	471.1	479.1
Burglary of nonresidence	652.0	716.4	703.0	597.6	562.9	517.5	517.1
Motor vehicle theft	644.4	719.2	668.7	627.9	672.9	830.6	1,026.7
Larceny	3,388.3	3,627.0	3,791.7	3,425.9	3,387.0	3,242.7	3,344.8
United States, excluding California:							
Murder	8.6	9.4	9.5	8.0	7.6	8.0	8.4
Rape	26.9	32.4	33.2	32.0	35.8	36.6	37.7
Robbery	176.3	198.7	234.5	198.6	193.8	201.3	219.9
Aggravated assault with firearm	53.6	60.8	62.8	55.9	63.4	73.0	78.2
Burglary of residence	859.4	906.1	1,043.0	838.8	823.8	872.1	845.7
Aggravated assault with no firearm	175.9	204.0	203.7	205.5	229.5	251.1	277.4
Burglary of nonresidence	475.7	518.8	519.2	436.0	412.1	433.2	412.9
Motor vehicle theft	424.4	472.3	445.0	405.1	435.9	490.9	577.9
Larceny	2,649.9	2,911.1	3,042.7	2,798.3	2,842.3	3,060.8	3,148.6

NOTE.—Values in the table are reported crime rates per 100,000 residents. California data are taken from *Crime and Delinquency*, published annually by the California Bureau of Criminal Statistics. Data for the rest of the United States are from *Crime in the Nation*, the Uniform Crime Reports published annually by the Federal Bureau of Investigation.

theft, and larceny). Because Proposition 8 was passed by popular referendum, observed changes in crime around the time of its passage may reflect a combination of the true deterrent impact of harsher repeat-offender enhancements and of other factors correlated with but not caused by the law change, such as changes in demographics, in other state policies, and in broad social norms against crime. This makes the availability of a control group of noneligible crimes critical to the analysis. Rates for these crimes in the rest of the United States are also presented.[34] These nine crime categories exhaust the set of crimes for which comparable data are available from California and the rest of the United States. The years presented, 1977–89, provide 5 years of data before the passage of Proposition 8 and 7 years after.

Inspection of Table 1 reveals that levels of crime rates in California are higher than those in the rest of the nation, but increases and decreases in California's crime rates tend to closely parallel those of the nation. Crime rates were generally rising until 1981, falling between 1981 and 1983, and mixed thereafter. Identifying a causal impact of Proposition 8 on eligible crimes in California requires differentiating between the impact of the law change and the widespread decline in crime outside California that happens to coincide with its passage in 1982.

Table 2 presents a number of alternative estimates of the impact of Proposition 8 using a "natural experiment" framework. Eligible crimes in California are the "treatment" group. Ineligible crimes in California make up one "control" group. In addition, eligible and ineligible crime categories in the rest of the United States are also presented. The extent to which eligible and ineligible crimes outside California (neither of which should be affected by California's law change) exhibit differential time paths provides another potential control.

The first two columns of the table contain percent changes in crime rates before passage of the law; the final four columns show crime patterns after the law change. As the top row of Table 2 demonstrates, eligible crimes were rising in California before the passage of Proposition 8, then dropped sharply with the law change (a 17.5 percent decline) between 1981 and 1983, and remained roughly stable thereafter. A naive interpretation of the data might conclude that Proposition 8 had an enormous immediate effect that did not increase over time. Such a conclusion, however, is likely incor-

---

[34] Reported crime data in California include information on all of the crime categories listed. Uniform Crime Reports, which provide data on reported crime for the United States as a whole, only include overall burglary and aggravated assault for individual states. The percentage of burglaries that involve a residence for the nation as a whole, however, is reported, as is the fraction of aggravated assaults with a handgun.

TABLE 2

ESTIMATES OF THE IMPACT OF PROPOSITION 8 ON CALIFORNIA CRIME RATES

GEOGRAPHIC REGION AND CRIME CATEGORY	PRE-PROPOSITION 8		POST-PROPOSITION 8			
	1977–81	1979–81	1981–83	1981–85	1981–87	1981–89
California:						
Crimes eligible for Proposition 8	20.4	7.6	−17.5	−20.7	−19.9	−15.6
Crimes not eligible for Proposition 8	9.5	−1.0	−8.6	−7.2	9.1	17.8
California eligible − California ineligible	10.9	8.6	−8.9	−13.5	−29.0	−33.3
Rest of United States:						
Crimes that would be eligible for Proposition 8 in California	21.1	7.9	−13.0	−9.8	−4.0	.3
Crimes that would not be eligible for Proposition 8 in California	11.1	−.3	−8.0	−4.1	4.4	12.3
Rest of U.S. eligible − Rest of U.S. ineligible	10.0	8.2	−5.0	−5.7	−8.4	−12.0
(California eligible − California ineligible) − (Rest of U.S. eligible − Rest of U.S. ineligible)	.9	.4	−3.9	−7.8	−20.6	−21.3

NOTE.—Table entries are average percent changes in crime rates per 100,000 residents over the relevant crime categories in the years listed. Crimes eligible for sentence enhancements in California under Proposition 8 are murder, rape, robbery, aggravated assault with a firearm, and burglary of a residence. Ineligible crimes included in the table are aggravated assault with no firearm, burglary of a nonresidence, motor vehicle theft, and larceny. Values in the third row are the difference between rows 1 and 2. Values in the sixth row are the difference between rows 4 and 5. Values in the bottom row are the difference between rows 3 and 6. Proposition 8 took effect in June 1982.

rect given the pattern of noneligible crimes in California (row 2). These crimes also fell between 1981 and 1983. Unlike eligible crimes, ineligible crimes sharply increased in 1987 and 1989.

Row 3 of Table 2 computes the difference between patterns in eligible and ineligible crime for each time period, providing one estimate of the impact of Proposition 8 on eligible crimes. Before the passage of the law, eligible crimes were increasing at a faster rate than ineligible crimes. After passage, there is an immediate 8.9 percent reduction in eligible crimes that steadily grows over time to 33.3 percent. Under the assumption that other determinants of the two crime categories were uncorrelated with the scope and passage of Proposition 8, this approach provides an unbiased estimate of the impact of the enhancement.

Examination of the pattern of eligible and ineligible crimes in the rest of the United States, however, calls into question that assumption. The penultimate row of Table 2 presents the relative time pattern of eligible and ineligible crimes outside of California. The rest of the United States experiences changes in crime that parallel California, but with a smaller magnitude. Before 1982, eligible crimes outpace ineligible crimes, after 1982 the trend reverses.

Given that eligible and ineligible crimes exhibit systematic changes outside of California, the most convincing estimate of the true impact of Proposition 8 is the change in eligible crimes relative to ineligible crimes in California minus the corresponding change outside California (a "differences-in-differences" estimator). The bottom row of Table 2 presents that estimate. Before Proposition 8, crime patterns inside and outside of California for eligible and ineligible crimes match up closely: eligible crimes are growing less than one percentage point faster in California. After the passage of Proposition 8, an immediate decline of 3.9 percent in eligible crimes occurs. Three years after the law change, the decline has doubled to 7.9 percent. The immediacy with which crime in the eligible categories responded to the passage of Proposition 8 implies the presence of a deterrent effect. All of the immediate 3.9 percent decline in eligible crime is likely attributable to deterrence (as may be some of the later declines). It is worth noting that this finding with respect to the effectiveness of increasing the severity of punishment is unusual; most of the previous literature has found that changes in the certainty of punishment are much better predictors of changes in crime rates than are changes in severity.[35]

---

[35] For example, Grogger, *supra* note 3. Past findings of a greater impact of punishment certainty relative to punishment severity are consistent with our arguments earlier in the article that typical estimates of the economic model of crime confound deterrence and incapacitation. Increases in punishment certainty will result in an immediate increase in both deter-

Our theoretical model predicts not only an immediate fall in crime with the adoption of sentence enhancements, but also a continued decline over the longer run as incapacitation effects and further deterrence incrementally take hold. This pattern appears in the data. By 1989, a total decline of over 20 percent is observed. This result suggests that crime does not fall immediately to its steady-state level, but rather falls steadily along a transition path as the incapacitation effect is incorporated.

While the results in Table 2 are consistent with an impact of Proposition 8, it is important to consider other possible explanations for the observed patterns. One possible explanation for the patterns observed in Table 2 would be an increase in the certainty of punishment for eligible crimes relative to noneligible crimes after the passage of Proposition 8. In practice, however, just the opposite appears to have occurred. Between 1981 and 1985, the arrest rate (arrests in a crime category divided by reported crimes in that category) in California fell for two of the three eligible crime categories (homicide and robbery) for which we are able to obtain comparable arrest data.[36] In contrast, arrest rates rose between 1981 and 1985 for larceny and motor vehicle theft, the two noneligible crimes for which comparable arrest data are available.

A second possible explanation for the results involves the differential responsiveness of violent and property crimes to economic conditions. Previous research[37] finds that property crime is countercyclical, whereas violent crime is not strongly affected by the economy. Over the period analyzed, however, unemployment rates in California tracked those of the United States as a whole very closely, rising between 1981 and 1983 and then falling. Thus, while changing economic conditions might explain some of the differential trends in eligible and ineligible crime *within* California (row 3 of Table 2), the situation inside and outside of California was similar, so our preferred estimator (the bottom row of Table 2) would not be affected.

One final factor that could overstate the impact of Proposition 8 is substitution across crime categories. The more similar the crime categories, the more likely it is that criminals will substitute away from eligible crimes

---

rence and incapacitation. Increases in punishment severity, on the other hand, will only have immediate deterrence effects, with incapacitation effects occurring only with a lag.

[36] Arrest data are available only for the seven FBI Index I crime categories, not the more detailed crime categories reported in Table 1. Consequently, in the arrest data we cannot distinguish between aggravated assaults with and without a handgun, or burglaries of residences and nonresidences.

[37] David Cantor & Kenneth Land, Unemployment and Crime Rates in the Post–World War II United States: A Theoretical and Empirical Analysis, 50 Am. Soc. Rev. 317 (1985); Joel Devine, Joseph Sheley, & Dwayne Smith, Macroeconomic and Social-Control Policy Influences on Crime Rate Changes, 1948–1985, 53 Am. Soc. Rev. 407 (1988); and Levitt, *supra* note 3.

toward noneligible crimes because of the increased penalties for the former.[38] This would lead to an exaggerated increase in the ineligible crime category. In particular, aggravated assault with and without a firearm, as well as burglary of a residence and a nonresidence, are likely to be close substitutes. Empirically, the results for aggravated assault and burglary mirror the more general pattern of results. Replicating the bottom row of Table 2, but only for these four crimes (the two types of aggravated assault and the two burglary measures), in the year after Proposition 8 the eligible crimes are 4.0 percent lower, by 1985 the eligible crimes are 9.8 percent lower, and by the end of the sample period the eligible crimes are reduced by 24.8 percent. Including all crimes, the corresponding numbers are -3.9, -7.8, and -21.3. Thus, substitution from eligible to ineligible crimes does not appear to be of a magnitude great enough to substantially alter the conclusions.

V. Discussion and Conclusions

This article demonstrates theoretically that sentence enhancements provide a means of distinguishing deterrence from incapacitation. Because enhancements are tacked on to prison sentences that would have been served anyway, there is no immediate incapacitation effect associated with such enhancements. Thus any immediate decrease in crime that is observed is attributable to deterrence. In the long run, however, both the full deterrent and the incapacitation effects of sentence enhancements become operative. Consequently, crime will not fall immediately to the new steady state, but rather will decline gradually over time. The predictions of the model are borne out in an empirical application using eligible and noneligible crimes for California's Proposition 8. Crimes that were affected by the sentence enhancements in Proposition 8 fall by 4 percent relative to crimes that were not covered in the first year after the law change. The impact of the law change increases to a decline of over 20 percent in eligible crimes 7 years after it is passed. These results suggest the presence of a deterrent effect, but also a potentially important role for incapacitation.

Our results suggest that criminals respond to the severity and not just the certainty of sentences, a result that is predicted by the economic model of crime but has proven elusive empirically. This suggests that the increasing reliance on sentence enhancements in both state law and the federal sentencing guidelines may represent an effective means of reducing crime. To the extent that sentence enhancements target the most frequent and dangerous offenders, such measures may be more cost effective than further ex-

---

[38] Levitt, *supra* note 5.

360   THE JOURNAL OF LAW AND ECONOMICS

panding the prison population through the incarceration of the marginal criminal who, given the skewed distribution of crime involvement,[39] is likely to impose relatively low crime-related costs on society.

These results, if generalizable, have important implications for three-strikes laws. If deterrence is the primary reason for crime reduction with such laws, then they represent an attractive public policy option: both equilibrium crime rates and prison populations will fall. In contrast, if all of the reduction in crime were due to incapacitation, three-strikes laws would be inefficient because they lead to the long-term incarceration of individuals who are no longer criminally active. Our findings suggest that the answer likely lies somewhere in the middle. There are important behavioral responses to increased punishments on the part of criminals, but the delayed response to the law change suggests that incapacitation associated with rising prison populations may explain more than half of the drop in crime.

Unfortunately, a direct empirical test of the impact of three strikes is not possible because of the failure of states to enforce such laws in spite of having them on the books. Of the 24 states passing three-strikes laws since 1993, only California has widely applied these statutes. In California, 3,281 individuals had been sentenced under three-strikes laws as of June 1, 1997.[40] Washington, the first state to pass a three-strikes law and after California the most active state in applying the law, has sentenced only 97 prisoners under the statute. In most states, three-strikes statutes have never been enforced. Consequently, it is not surprising that passage of three-strikes laws is not associated with any discernible change in either crime rates or imprisonment rates, except perhaps in California. Between 1993 and 1996 (three-strikes laws were implemented in 1994), California has seen a 20 percent decline in violent crime per capita and a 19 percent decline in property crime per capita. In comparison, violent crime has fallen 13 percent in the rest of the nation, and property crime is down only 4 percent over the same period. California's prison population has grown at roughly the same rate as the nation as a whole since adoption (22 percent vs. 21 percent). In fact, contrary to the dire predictions of an explosion in California's prison population as a consequence of three strikes, the current prison population is at almost exactly the level projected without the passage of three-strikes law.[41] Without further investigation, however, it is difficult to know whether

---

[39] DiIulio & Piehl, *supra* note 4.

[40] Austin, "Three Strikes and You're Out": The Likely Consequences on the Courts, Prisons, and Crime in California and Washington State, *supra* note 22.

[41] In defense of Greenwood et al., *supra* note 22, one partial explanation for the lack of impact of three strikes on the prison population is the uneven application of the law by judges and prosecutors.

declining crime in California can be causally attributed to the presence of three strikes.[42]

The reasons underlying the failure to enforce three-strikes laws in most states merits greater attention, especially given that a wide variety of other enhancements are frequently enforced at both the state and federal level. The two notable differences between three-strikes laws and other enhancements are (1) the much narrower applicability of three strikes in most states and (2) the extremely harsh penalties associated with three strikes. Together, these two features lead to horizontal inequity, that is, offenders convicted of relatively similar offenses being treated in radically different manners. Combined with the fact that the third-strike penalty is often out of line with the third-strike offense (almost 40 percent of third strikes in California were for property offenses, and another 11 percent were for drug possession), prosecutors and judges appear to exercise discretion in circumventing the statutes.[43] The observed failure of most jurisdictions to enforce three-strikes laws suggests that from the perspective of fighting crime, sentence enhancements that are broader in scope and less punitive, such as Proposition 8, may ultimately prove more effective.

BIBLIOGRAPHY

Andreoni, James. "Reasonable Doubt and the Optimal Magnitude of Fines: Should the Penalty Fit the Crime?" *Rand Journal of Economics* 22, No. 3 (1991): 385–95.

Austin, James. " 'Three Strikes and You're Out': The Likely Consequences on the Courts, Prisons, and Crime in California and Washington State." *St. Louis University Public Law Review* 14 (1994): 239–57.

Austin, James. Presentation at the meetings of the American Criminological Society, San Diego, Cal., November 1997.

Becker, Gary. "Crime and Punishment: An Economic Approach." *Journal of Political Economy* 76 (1968): 169–217.

Blumstein, Alfred. "Prisons." In *Crime,* edited by J. Q. Wilson and J. Petersilia. San Francisco, Cal.: Institute for Contemporary Studies, 1995.

Bureau of Justice Assistance. *National Assessment of Structured Sentencing.* NCJ 153853. Washington, D.C.: U.S. Department of Justice, Office of Justice Programs, 1996.

California Bureau of Criminal Statistics. *Crime and Delinquency, 1979–85.* Sacramento, Cal.: California Department of Justice, 1979–85.

---

[42] Unfortunately it is not possible to conduct an analysis of the three-strikes law in California paralleling that for Proposition 8 because conviction of any felony triggers the application of the enhancement. Thus, for three strikes, there is no good counterpart to the noneligible crimes used as controls in the Proposition 8 analysis.

[43] James Andreoni, Reasonable Doubt and the Optimal Magnitude of Fines: Should the Penalty Fit the Crime? 22 Rand J. Econ. 385 (1991).

Cameron, Samuel. "The Economics of Crime Deterrence: A Survey of Theory and Evidence." *Kyklos* 41 (1988): 301–23.

Cantor, David, and Land, Kenneth. "Unemployment and Crime Rates in the Post–World War II United States: A Theoretical and Empirical Analysis." *American Sociological Review* 50 (1985): 317–32.

Clark, John; Austin, James; and Henry, D. Alan. *"Three Strikes and You're Out": A Review of State Legislation.* NCJ 165369. Washington, D.C.: U.S. Department of Justice, Office of Justice Programs, 1997.

Devine, Joel; Sheley, Joseph; and Smith, Dwayne. "Macroeconomic and Social-Control Policy Influences on Crime Rate Changes, 1948–1985." *American Sociological Review* 53 (1988): 407–20.

DiIulio, John, and Piehl, Anne. "Does Prison Pay? The Stormy National Debate over the Cost-Effectiveness of Imprisonment." *The Brookings Review* (Fall 1991), pp. 28–35.

Ehrlich, Isaac. "Participation in Illegitimate Activities: A Theoretical and Empirical Investigation." *Journal of Political Economy* 81 (1973): 531–67.

Ehrlich, Isaac. "Crime, Punishment, and the Market for Offenses." *Journal of Economic Perspectives* 10 (1996): 43–67.

Flynn, Edith E.; Flanagan, Timothy; Greenwood, Peter; and Krisberg, Barry. "Three Strikes Legislation: Prevalence and Definitions." In *Critical Criminal Justice Issues: Task Force Reports from the American Society of Criminology to Attorney General Janet Reno.* NCJ 158837. Washington, D.C.: U.S. Department of Justice, Office of Justice Programs, 1997.

Greenwood, Peter; Rydell, C. Petter; Abrahamse, Allan F.; Caulkins, Jonathan P.; Chiesa, James; Model, Karyn E.; and Klein, Stephen P. *Three Strikes and You're Out: Estimated Benefits and Costs of California's New Mandatory Sentencing Law.* Santa Monica, Cal.: RAND, 1994.

Grogger, Jeff. "Certainty vs. Severity." *Economic Inquiry* 29 (1991): 297–309.

Kaplow, Louis, and Shavell, Steven. "Optimal Law Enforcement with Self-Reporting of Behavior." *Journal of Political Economy* 102 (1994): 583–606.

Kessler, Daniel, and Piehl, Anne Morrison. "The Role of Discretion in the Criminal Justice System." *Journal of Law, Economics, and Organization* 14 (1998): 256–75.

Levitt, Steven. "Using Electoral Cycles in Police Hiring to Estimate the Effect of Police on Crime." *American Economic Review* 87 (1997): 270–90.

Levitt, Steven. "Why Do Increased Arrest Rates Appear to Reduce Crime: Deterrence, Incapacitation, or Measurement Error?" *Economic Inquiry* 36, No. 3 (1998): 353–72.

Loftin, Colin; Heumann, Milton; and McDowall, David. "Mandatory Sentencing and Firearms Violence: Evaluating an Alternative to Gun Control." *Law and Society Review* 17 (1983): 287–318.

Lott, John. "Should the Wealthy Be Able to Buy Justice?" *Journal of Political Economy* 95 (1987): 1307–16.

Marvell, Thomas, and Moody, Carlisle. "Prison Population Growth and Crime Reduction." *Journal of Quantitative Criminology* 10 (1994): 109–40.

Marvell, Thomas, and Moody, Carlisle. "Police Levels, Crime Rates, and Specification Problems." *Criminology* 34 (1996): 609–46.

Mayhew, Patricia; Clarke, Ronald; Burrows, John; Hough, J. Mike; and Winchester, Stuart. *Crime in Public View.* Home Office Research Study No. 49. London: Home Office, 1979.

McCormick, Robert, and Tollison, Robert. "Crime on the Court." *Journal of Political Economy* 92 (1984): 223–35.

McCoy, Candace, and Tillman, Robert. "Controlling Felony Plea Bargaining in California: The Impact of the 'Victims' Bill of Rights.' " Sacramento: California Department of Justice, Bureau of Criminal Statistics, 1986.

McDowall, David; Loftin, Colin; and Wiersema, Brian. "A Comparative Study of the Preventive Effects of Mandatory Sentencing Laws for Gun Crimes." *Journal of Criminal Law and Criminology* 83 (1992): 378–94.

Nagin, Daniel. "Criminal Deterrence Research: A Review of the Evidence and a Research Agenda for the Outset of the Twenty-First Century." Unpublished manuscript. Pittsburgh: Carnegie Mellon University, 1997.

Pierce, Glen L., and Bowers, William J. "The Bartley-Fox Gun Law's Short-Term Impact on Crime in Boston." *Annals of the American Academy of Political and Social Science* 455 (1981): 120–32.

Polinsky, A. Mitchell, and Rubinfeld, Daniel. "A Model of Optimal Fines for Repeat Offenders." *Journal of Public Economics* 46 (1991): 291–306.

Polinsky, A. Mitchell, and Shavell, Steven. "The Optimal Use of Fines and Imprisonment." *Journal of Public Economics* 24 (1984): 89–99.

Polinsky, A. Mitchell, and Shavell, Steven. "On the Disutility and Discounting of Imprisonment and the Theory of Deterrence." Working paper. Cambridge, Mass.: Harvard Law School, 1997.

Spelman, William. *Criminal Incapacitation.* New York: Plenum Press, 1994.

Tauchen, Helen; Witte, Anne; and Griesinger, Harriet. "Criminal Deterrence: Revisiting the Issue with a Birth Cohort." Mimeographed manuscript. Chapel Hill: University of North Carolina, Department of Economics, 1993.

Tillman, Robert, and McCoy, Candace. *The Impact of California's "Prior Felony Conviction" Law.* Sacramento: California Department of Justice, Bureau of Criminal Statistics, 1986.

Tonry, Michael. "Structuring Sentencing." In *Crime and Justice: A Review of Research.* Vol. 10, edited by Michael Tonry and Norval Morris. Chicago: University of Chicago Press, 1988.

Tonry, Michael. "Mandatory Penalties." In *Crime and Justice: A Review of Research.* Vol. 16, edited by Michael Tonry. Chicago: University of Chicago Press, 1992.

Tonry, Michael. *Sentencing Matters.* New York: Oxford University Press, 1996.

U.S. Sentencing Commission. *The Federal Sentencing Guidelines: A Report on the Operation of the Guidelines System and Short-Term Impacts on Disparity in Sentencing, Use of Incarceration, and Prosecutorial Discretion and Plea Bargaining.* Washington, D.C.: U.S. Sentencing Commission, 1991.

Visher, Christy. "The RAND Inmate Survey: A Reanalysis." In *Criminal Careers and Career Criminals.* Vol. 2, edited by A. Blumstein et al. Washington, D.C.: National Academy Press, 1986.

Witte, Ann. "Estimating the Economic Model of Crime with Individual Data." *Quarterly Journal of Economics* 94 (1980): 57–84.

[13]

THE

QUARTERLY JOURNAL OF ECONOMICS

| Vol. CXVI | May 2001 | Issue 2 |

THE IMPACT OF LEGALIZED ABORTION ON CRIME*

JOHN J. DONOHUE III AND STEVEN D. LEVITT

We offer evidence that legalized abortion has contributed significantly to recent crime reductions. Crime began to fall roughly eighteen years after abortion legalization. The five states that allowed abortion in 1970 experienced declines earlier than the rest of the nation, which legalized in 1973 with *Roe v. Wade*. States with high abortion rates in the 1970s and 1980s experienced greater crime reductions in the 1990s. In high abortion states, only arrests of those born after abortion legalization fall relative to low abortion states. Legalized abortion appears to account for as much as 50 percent of the recent drop in crime.

I. INTRODUCTION

Since 1991, the United States has experienced the sharpest drop in murder rates since the end of Prohibition in 1933. Homicide rates have fallen more than 40 percent. Violent crime and property crime have each declined more than 30 percent. Hundreds of articles discussing this change have appeared in the academic literature and popular press.[1] They have offered an array of explanations: the increasing use of incarceration, growth

* We would like to thank Ian Ayres, Gary Becker, Carl Bell, Alfred Blumstein, Jonathan Caulkins, Richard Craswell, George Fisher, Richard Freeman, James Heckman, Christine Jolls, Theodore Joyce, Louis Kaplow, Lawrence Katz, John Kennan, John Monahan, Casey Mulligan, Derek Neal, Eric Posner, Richard Posner, Sherwin Rosen, Steve Sailer, José Scheinkman, Peter Siegelman, Kenji Yoshino, and seminar participants too numerous to mention for helpful comments and discussions. Craig Estes and Rose Francis provided exceptionally valuable research assistance. Correspondence can be addressed to either John Donohue, Crown Quadrangle, Stanford Law School, Stanford, CA 94305, or Steven Levitt, Department of Economics, University of Chicago, 1126 E. 59th Street, Chicago, IL 60637. Email: jjd@stanford.edu; slevitt@midway.uchicago.edu.
1. For a sampling of the academic literature, see Blumstein and Wallman [2000] and the articles appearing in the 1998 Summer issue (Volume 88) of the *Journal of Criminal Law and Criminology,* especially Blumstein and Rosenfeld [1998], Kelling and Bratton [1998], and Donohue [1998]. See Butterfield [1997a,

The Quarterly Journal of Economics, May 2001

in the number of police, improved policing strategies such as those adopted in New York, declines in the crack cocaine trade, the strong economy, and increased expenditures on victim precautions such as security guards and alarms.

None of these factors, however, can provide an entirely satisfactory explanation for the large, widespread, and persistent drop in crime in the 1990s. Some of these trends, such as the increasing scale of imprisonment, the rise in police, and expenditures on victim precaution, have been ongoing for over two decades, and thus cannot plausibly explain the recent abrupt improvement in crime. Moreover, the widespread nature of the crime drop argues against explanations such as improved policing techniques since many cities that have not improved their police forces (e.g., Los Angeles) have nonetheless seen enormous crime declines. A similar argument holds for crack cocaine. Many areas of the country that have never had a pronounced crack trade (for instance, suburban and rural areas) have nonetheless experienced substantial decreases in crime. Finally, although a strong economy is superficially consistent with the drop in crime since 1991, previous research has established only a weak link between economic performance and violent crime [Freeman 1995] and in one case even suggested that murder rates might vary procyclically [Ruhm 2000].

While acknowledging that all of these factors may have also served to dampen crime, we consider a novel explanation for the sudden crime drop of the 1990s: the decision to legalize abortion over a quarter century ago.[2] The Supreme Court's 1973 decision in *Roe v. Wade* legalizing abortion nationwide potentially fits the criteria for explaining a large, abrupt, and continuing decrease in crime. The sheer magnitude of the number of abortions performed satisfies the first criterion that any shock underlying the recent drop in crime must be substantial. Seven years after *Roe v. Wade*, over 1.6 million abortions were being performed annually—almost one abortion for every two live births. Moreover, the legal-

---

1997b, 1999] for a selection of articles appearing in *The New York Times* and Fletcher [2000] for a recent article in *The Washington Post*.

2. We are unaware of any scholarly article that has examined this effect. We have recently learned, however, that the former police chief of Minneapolis has written that abortion is "arguably the only effective crime-prevention device adopted in this nation since the late 1960s" [Bouza 1990]. In his subsequent 1994 gubernatorial campaign, Bouza was attacked for this opinion [Short 1994]. Immediately after Bouza's view was publicized just prior to the election, Bouza fell sharply in the polls.

ization of abortion in five states in 1970, and then for the nation as a whole in 1973, were abrupt legal developments that might plausibly have a similarly abrupt influence 15–20 years later when the cohorts born in the wake of liberalized abortion would start reaching their high-crime years. Finally, any influence of a change in abortion would impact crime cumulatively as successive affected cohorts entered into their high-crime late adolescent years, providing a reason why crime has continued to fall year after year.

Legalized abortion may lead to reduced crime either through reductions in cohort sizes or through lower per capita offending rates for affected cohorts. The smaller cohort that results from abortion legalization means that when that cohort reaches the late teens and twenties, there will be fewer young males in their highest-crime years, and thus less crime. More interesting and important is the possibility that children born after abortion legalization may on average have lower subsequent rates of criminality for either of two reasons. First, women who have abortions are those most at risk to give birth to children who would engage in criminal activity. Teenagers, unmarried women, and the economically disadvantaged are all substantially more likely to seek abortions [Levine et al. 1996]. Recent studies have found children born to these mothers to be at higher risk for committing crime in adolescence [Comanor and Phillips 1999]. Gruber, Levine, and Staiger [1999], in the paper most similar to ours, document that the early life circumstances of those children on the margin of abortion are difficult along many dimensions: infant mortality, growing up in a single-parent family, and experiencing poverty. Second, women may use abortion to optimize the timing of childbearing. A given woman's ability to provide a nurturing environment to a child can fluctuate over time depending on the woman's age, education, and income, as well as the presence of a father in the child's life, whether the pregnancy is wanted, and any drug or alcohol abuse both in utero and after the birth. Consequently, legalized abortion provides a woman the opportunity to delay childbearing if the current conditions are suboptimal. Even if lifetime fertility remains constant for all women, children are born into better environments, and future criminality is likely to be reduced.

A number of anecdotal empirical facts support the existence and magnitude of the crime-reducing impact of abortion. First, we see a broad consistency with the timing of legalization of abortion and the subsequent drop in crime. For example, the peak ages for violent crime are roughly 18–24, and crime starts turning down around 1992, roughly the time at which the first cohort born following *Roe v. Wade* would hit its criminal prime. Second, as we later demonstrate, the five states that legalized abortion in 1970 saw drops in crime before the other 45 states and the District of Columbia, which did not allow abortions until the Supreme Court decision in 1973.

Third, our more formal analysis shows that higher rates of abortion in a state in the 1970s and early 1980s are strongly linked to lower crime over the period from 1985 to 1997. This finding is true after controlling for a variety of factors that influence crime, such as the level of incarceration, the number of police, and measures of the state's economic well-being (the unemployment rate, income per capita, and poverty rate). The estimated magnitude of the impact of legalized abortion on crime is large. According to our estimates, as shown on Table II, states with high rates of abortion have experienced roughly a 30 percent drop in crime relative to low-abortion regions since 1985. While one must be cautious in extrapolating our results out of sample, the estimates suggest that legalized abortion can account for about half the observed decline in crime in the United States between 1991 and 1997.

A number of factors lead us to believe that the link between abortion and crime is causal. First, there is no relationship between abortion rates in the mid-1970s and crime changes between 1972 and 1985 (prior to the point when the abortion-affected cohorts have reached the age of significant criminal involvement). Second, virtually all of the abortion-related crime decrease can be attributed to reductions in crime among the cohorts born after abortion legalization. There is little change in crime among older cohorts.

We should emphasize that our goal is to understand why crime has fallen sharply in the 1990s, and to explore the contribution to this decline that may have come from the legalization of abortion in the 1970s. In attempting to identify a link between legalized abortion and crime, we do not mean to suggest that such a link is "good" or "just," but rather, merely to show that such a relationship exists. In short, ours is a purely positive, not a normative analysis, although of course we recognize that there is an active debate about the moral and ethical implications of abortion.[3]

The structure of the paper is as follows: Section II reviews the literature and provides a brief history of abortion. Section III describes how the legalization of abortion can influence crime rates by changing the proportion of high-risk children entering the high-crime late adolescent years, and examines the likely magnitude of these effects based on past research findings. Section IV presents the basic empirical evidence that supports the proposed negative relationship between abortion and crime. Section V provides evidence that the reduction in crime comes predominantly from the lower crime rates of those born after the legalization of abortion. Section VI concludes. A Data Appendix with the sources of all variables used in the analysis is also provided.

II. BRIEF OVERVIEW OF THE HISTORY OF LEGALIZED ABORTION

Under the governing principles of English common law, abortion prior to "quickening" (when the first movements of the fetus could be felt, usually around the sixteenth to eighteenth week of the pregnancy) was lawful. This common law rule was in force throughout America until the first law in the United States restricting abortions was adopted in New York in 1828 [David et al. 1988, pp. 12–13]. Over the next 60 years, more and more states followed the lead of New York, and by 1900 abortion was illegal throughout the country.

The first modest efforts at abortion liberalization began to emerge between 1967 and 1970 when a number of states began to allow abortion under limited circumstances.[4] Legal abortion be-

---

3. For example, Paulsen [1989, pp. 49, 76–77] considers legalized abortion to be worse than slavery (since it involves death) and the Holocaust (since the 34 million post-*Roe* abortions are numerically greater than the six million Jews killed in Europe). Despite these claims, the Supreme Court has ruled that women have a fundamental constitutional right of privacy to abort an early-term fetus and that the state cannot unduly burden this right.

4. The 1962 amendments to the Model Penal Code provided for legal abortions to prevent the death or grave impairment of the physical and mental health of the woman, or if the fetus would be born with a grave physical or mental defect or in the case of rape or incest. These provisions were adopted in 1967 in Colorado, North Carolina, and California, in 1968 in Florida, Georgia, and Maryland, in 1969 in Arkansas, Kansas, New Mexico, and Oregon, and in 1970 in Delaware, South Carolina, and Virginia—a total of thirteen states. For excellent reviews of state and federal abortions laws, see Merz, Jackson, and Klerman [1995] and Alan Guttmacher Institute [1989].

384   *QUARTERLY JOURNAL OF ECONOMICS*

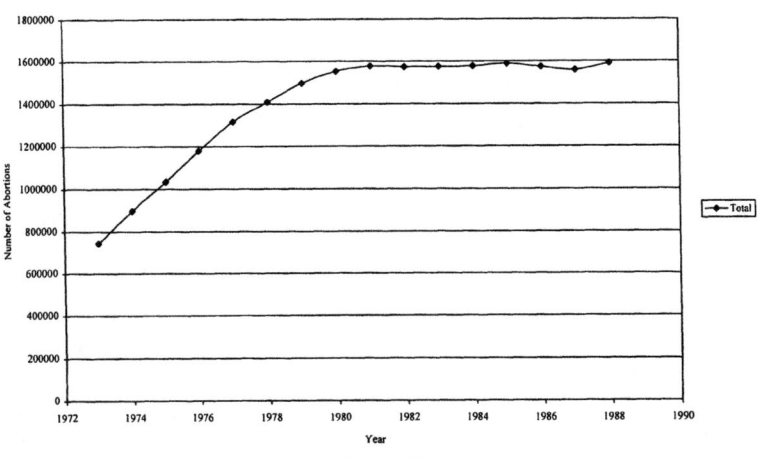

FIGURE I
Total Abortions by Year
Source: Alan Guttmacher Institute [1992].

came broadly available in five states in 1970 when New York,
Washington, Alaska, and Hawaii repealed their antiabortion
laws, and the Supreme Court of California (ruling in late 1969)
held that the state's law banning abortion was unconstitutional.
Legalized abortion was suddenly extended to the entire United
States on January 22, 1973, with the landmark ruling of the
United States Supreme Court in *Roe v. Wade.*

The Supreme Court in *Roe* explicitly considered the consequences of its decision in stating:

> The detriment that the State would impose upon the pregnant woman by
> denying this choice altogether is apparent. Specific and direct harm medi-
> cally diagnosable even in early pregnancy may be involved. Maternity, or
> additional offspring, may force upon the woman a distressful life and future.
> Psychological harm may be imminent. Mental and physical health may be
> taxed by child care. There is also the distress, for all concerned, associated
> with the unwanted child, and there is the problem of bringing a child into a
> family already unable, psychologically and otherwise, to care for it.[5]

The available data suggest that the number of abortions
increased dramatically following legalization, although there
is little direct evidence on the number of illegal abortions
performed in the 1960s. As Figure I illustrates, the total num-

5. *Roe v. Wade,* 410 U. S. 110, 153 (1973).

ber of documented abortions rose sharply in the wake of *Roe,* from under 750,000 in 1973 (when live births totaled 3.1 million) to over 1.6 million in 1980 (when live births totaled 3.6 million).[6] If illegal abortions were already being performed in equivalent numbers, one would not expect a seven-year lag in reaching a steady state. Moreover, the costs of an abortion—financial and otherwise—dropped considerably after legalization. Kaplan [1988, p. 164] notes that "an illegal abortion before *Roe v. Wade* cost $400 to $500, while today, thirteen years after the decision, the now legal procedure can be procured for as little as $80."[7] The costs of finding and traveling to an illegal abortionist and any attendant cost of engaging in illegal and therefore riskier and socially disapproved conduct were also reduced by legalization.

Perhaps the most convincing evidence that legalization increased abortion comes from Michael [1999], who finds abortion rates to be roughly an order of magnitude higher after legalization using self-reported data on pregnancy outcome histories. Thus, the first prerequisite for legalization to have an impact on crime is met—legalization increased the rate of abortion.

Consistent with this finding is a dramatic decline in the number of children put up for adoption after abortion became legal. According to Stolley [1993], almost 9 percent of premarital births were placed for adoption before 1973; that number fell to 4 percent for births occurring between 1973 and 1981. The total number of adoptions rose from 90,000 in 1957 to over 170,000 in 1970; by 1975 adoptions had fallen to 130,000.

---

6. In our analysis we use Alan Guttmacher Institute (AGI) data on abortions. Although Michael [1999] argues that the AGI may substantially overstate true abortion rates, "it is generally acknowledged [that AGI data provide] the most accurate count of induced abortions in the United States." Apparently, "reporting is less complete for nonwhites than for whites, and overall reporting . . . has declined over time" [Joyce and Kaestner 1996, p. 185].

7. The cost to the mother also depends on the availability of public funding, which was affected by the Hyde Amendment, which cut off federal funding of abortion for Medicaid recipients. The Hyde Amendment became law on September 30, 1976. The Hyde Amendment has been subject to a series of revisions and restraining orders since that time. No consensus exists as to the impact of the Hyde Amendment on the number of abortions or births, although most recent research suggests any impact is now small [Joyce and Kaestner 1996; Kane and Staiger 1996].

III. THE MECHANISM BY WHICH ABORTION LEGALIZATION
LOWERS CRIME RATES

In this section we explore in detail the theoretical link between legalization of abortion in the early 1970s and subsequent drops in crime fifteen to twenty years later. We identify a number of alternative pathways through which abortion can affect crime. We then generate "back-of-the-envelope" calculations as to the likely magnitude of the various channels based on previous research findings.

The simplest way in which legalized abortion reduces crime is through smaller cohort sizes. When those smaller cohorts reach the high-crime late adolescent years, there are simply fewer people to commit crime. Levine et al. [1996] find that legalization is associated with roughly a 5 percent drop in birth rates.[8] Assuming that the fall in births is a random sample of all births, total crime committed by this cohort would be expected to fall commensurately.

Far more interesting from our perspective is the possibility that abortion has a disproportionate effect on the births of those who are most at risk of engaging in criminal behavior.[9] To the extent that abortion is more frequent among those parents who are least willing or able to provide a nurturing home environment, as a large and growing body of evidence suggests, the impact of legalized abortion on crime might be far greater than its effect on fertility rates.[10] This is particularly true given that 6 percent of any birth cohort will commit roughly half the crime

---

8. This decline is broadly consistent with survey responses by mothers in 1973 who report that approximately 13 percent of lifetime births were unwanted [Statistical Abstract of the United States 1980, p. 65, table 99]. Note, however, that the decline in births is far less than the number of abortions, suggesting that the number of conceptions increased substantially—an example of insurance leading to moral hazard. The insurance that abortion provides against unwanted pregnancy induces more sexual conduct or diminished protections against pregnancy in a way that substantially increases the number of pregnancies. Another possible explanation for the gap between abortion rates and fertility rate changes is that illegal abortion was already suppressing the birth rate by 15–20 percent and legalization reduced it another 5–10 percent, but this would imply a higher figure for the number of illegal abortions than we think is likely, as discussed above.

9. As noted earlier, this effect can occur either because of lower lifetime fertility rates among high-risk groups, or because women delay childbearing until conditions are more favorable for successfully raising children.

10. In addition, with an estimated number of over 150,000 rapes in 1973 (often thought to be a conservative estimate), it is possible that 10,000 to 15,000 conceptions occurred that year as a result of rape, and one might expect a substantial proportion of these high-risk conceptions would end in abortion [Bureau of Justice Statistics 1985, p. 230, Table 3.2].

[Wolfgang, Figlio, and Sellin 1972; Tracy, Wolfgang, and Figlio 1990].[11]

Prior to the legalization of abortion, there was a very strong link between the number of unwanted births and low maternal education over the period from 1965 through 1970 [Commission on Population Growth and the American Future 1972, p. 98]. Levine et al. [1996] found that the drop in births associated with abortion legalization was not uniform across all groups. They estimated that the drop in births was roughly twice as great for teenage and nonwhite mothers as it was for the nonteen, white population.[12] In the years immediately following *Roe v. Wade,* data from the Centers for Disease Control [1994] indicate that almost one-third of abortions were performed on teenagers. Angrist and Evans [1996] found that while abortion reforms had relatively modest effects on the fertility of white women, "black women who were exposed to abortion reforms experienced large reductions in teen fertility and teen out-of-wedlock fertility."

A number of studies have shown that the availability of abortion improves infant outcomes by reducing the number of low birthweight babies and neonatal mortality [Grossman and Jacobowitz 1981; Corman and Grossman 1985; Joyce 1987; Grossman and Joyce 1990]. Moreover, Gruber, Levine, and Staiger [1999, p. 265] conclude that "the average living circumstances of cohorts born immediately after abortion became legalized improved substantially relative to preceding cohorts." They go on to note that "the marginal children who were not born as a result of abortion legalization would have systematically been born into less favorable circumstances if the pregnancies had not been terminated: they would have been 60 percent more likely to live in a single-parent household, 50 percent more likely to live in poverty, 45 percent more likely to be in a household collecting welfare, and 40 percent more likely to die during the first year of life."

Previous research has found that an adverse family environment is strongly linked to future criminality. Both Loeber and

---

11. The high concentration rates of crime among a relatively small number of offenders makes it more likely that legalized abortion would have larger effects on crime than on other social outcomes such as high school dropout rates or unemployment rates. A given child who has failed to complete school or secure a job counts as only one event in measuring school dropout or unemployment rates. Conversely, a single child may commit hundreds of crimes and thereby contribute far more powerfully to a higher crime rate.

12. This is not surprising since in the late 1960s the "pill" and other birth control mechanisms were far more readily available to married, educated, and affluent women [Goldin and Katz 2000].

Stouthamer-Loeber [1986] and Sampson and Laub [1993] present evidence that a variety of unfavorable parental behaviors (e.g., maternal rejection, erratic/harsh behavior on the part of parents, lack of parental supervision) are among the best predictors of juvenile delinquency. Raine, Brennan, and Medick [1994], and Raine et al. [1996] argue that birth complications combined with early maternal rejection predispose boys to violent crime at age eighteen. Rasanen et al. [1999] find that the risk of violent crime for Finnish males born in 1966 is a function of (in descending order of impact): mother's low education, teenage mother, single-parent family, mother did not want pregnancy, and mother smoked during pregnancy. It is possible that abortion could reduce the number of children born under all these circumstances: teenagers who have abortions can get more education before they give birth and may delay childbearing until they are married or want a child or both. In addition, women who inadvertently become pregnant may have engaged in behavior such as smoking, drinking, or using drugs that elevate the prospect of future criminality of their offspring.

A number of studies have looked at cases of women, living in jurisdictions in which governmental approval to have an abortion was required, who sought to have an abortion, but were denied the right to do so [David et al. 1988; Posner 1992, p. 283].[13] Dagg [1991] reports that these women overwhelmingly kept their babies, rather than giving them up for adoption, but that they often resented the unwanted children and were far less likely than other mothers to nurture, hold, and breastfeed these children. In an array of studies in Eastern Europe and Scandinavia, Dagg found that the children who were born because their mothers were denied an abortion were substantially more likely to be involved in crime and have poorer life prospects, even when controlling for the income, age, education, and health of the mother. This literature provides strong evidence that unwanted children are likely to be disproportionately involved in criminal activity, which may be the causal pathway from greater availability of abortion to lower rates of crime.

Evidence from prisoner surveys further reinforces the link between a difficult home environment as a child and later crim-

---

13. David et al. [1988] review the findings of separate studies of the effects of denied abortion for cohorts born in Goteberg, Sweden in 1939–1942, Stockholm in 1948, all of Sweden in 1960, and Prague in 1961–1963.

inality [Beck et al. 1993]. In 1991, 14 percent of prisoners reported growing up with neither parent present, and 43 percent reported having only one parent (compared with 3 percent and 24 percent, respectively, for the overall population). Thirty-eight percent of prisoners report that their parents or guardians abused alcohol or drugs; almost one-third of female inmates report being sexually abused before the age of eighteen.

A. *The Expected Magnitude of the Impact of Abortion Legalization on Crime*

Before presenting our empirical estimates in the next section, we present "back-of-the-envelope" estimates of the plausible magnitude of the impact of legalized abortion on crime. Previous researchers have studied (1) how legalized abortion affects birth rates across different groups, and (2) crime rates across groups. By combining these two sets of estimates, we can obtain a crude prediction of the impact of legalized abortion on crime.

This analysis considers four factors: race, teenage motherhood, unmarried motherhood, and unwantedness. Beginning with the first three of these factors, we use the 1990 Census to determine the proportion of children in each of the eight possible demographic categories (e.g., white children born to teenage mothers growing up in a single-parent household, or black children born to nonteenage mothers growing up in two-parent households). We then use the estimates of Levine et al. [1996] to determine what those proportions might have been in the absence of legalized abortion. Using Rasanen et al. [1999] and observed frequencies of crime by race in the United States, we generate category-specific crime rates corresponding to each of the eight cells. Combining these crime rates with the change in the number of births in each category due to abortion provides an estimate of the hypothetical reduction in crime. Finally, under the assumption that 75 percent of unwanted births are aborted (this number appears consistent with data from self-reported pregnancy histories), we estimate the contribution to lower crime from fewer unwanted births.[14] It is important to note that our calculations below isolate the *marginal* contribution of race, teenage motherhood, unmarried motherhood, and unwantedness. Thus, when

---

14. A full description of the assumptions and calculations is available from the authors on request.

computing the impact of race, we net out any racial differences in those other characteristics in order to avoid double counting.

The results of this exercise for homicide are as follows. All values reported are the hypothetical reduction in total homicides committed by members of a given cohort. Through a purely mechanical relationship, the 5.4 percent overall postlegalization decline in cohort size obtained by Levine et al. [1996] translates into a 5.4 percent reduction in homicide.

Fertility declines for black women are three times greater than for whites (12 percent compared with 4 percent). Given that homicide rates of black youths are roughly nine times higher than those of white youths, racial differences in the fertility effects of abortion are likely to translate into greater homicide reductions. Under the assumption that those black and white births eliminated by legalized abortion would have experienced the average criminal propensities of their respective races, then the predicted reduction in homicide is 8.9 percent. In other words, taking into account differential abortion rates by race raises the predicted impact of abortion legalization on homicide from 5.4 percent to 8.9 percent.[15]

Teenagers and unwed women experience reductions in fertility of 13 and 7 percent, respectively, well above that for nonteenage, married women. Rasanen et al. [1999] find, after controlling for other characteristics, that having a teenage mother roughly doubles a child's propensity to commit crime, as does growing up with a single parent.[16] Accounting for these two factors raises the estimated impact of abortion on homicide from 8.9 percent to 12.5 percent.

Adjusting for unwantedness, which more than doubles an individual's likelihood of crime based on the estimates of Rasanen et al. [1999], raises the estimates from 12.5 percent to 18.5 percent. The impact of unwantedness is large because abortion rates of unwanted pregnancies are very high, whereas wanted pregnancies are by definition not aborted.

Thus, using past estimates in the literature, we crudely estimate that crime should fall by 18.5 percent in cohorts that

15. For other crimes, the impact of race is much lower because rates of offending and victimization are much more similar across races.

16. Comanor and Phillips [1999], using the National Longitudinal Survey of Youth, find that adolescents in households with absent fathers are 2.2 times more likely to be charged with a crime as a juvenile, controlling for other observable factors. That estimate is very close to the Rasanen et al. [1999] finding for Finnish males that we use in our calculations.

have access to legalized abortion. As of 1997, roughly 60 percent of crimes were committed by individuals born after legalized abortion, implying that (thus far) the hypothetical impact of abortion on crime is only 60 percent of the impact on affected cohorts, or about an 11 percent reduction. To the extent that other factors are correlated with both criminal propensities and abortion likelihoods (e.g., poverty, maternal education, religiosity), this rough estimate is likely to understate the true impact.[17] Given that the observed declines in crime in the 1990s are 30–40 percent, abortion may be an important factor in explaining the crime drop. In the next section we present empirical estimates of the impact of abortion on crime that are roughly consistent with these hypothetical calculations.

IV. EMPIRICAL EVIDENCE OF LEGALIZED ABORTION AFFECTING CRIME RATES

We begin our empirical analysis by establishing a relationship between crime changes in the 1990s and legalized abortion in the early 1970s. We consider three different sources of variation: the national time series of crime and abortion, differential crime patterns across early legalizers and other states, and the impact of state abortion rates (properly lagged) on state crime rates. In Section V we focus on arrest rates, which allows us to decompose the effect of abortion by the age of offenders.

A. National Time Series

Figure II presents per capita crime rates for the United States for violent crime, property crime, and murder for the period 1973–1999, as measured in the Uniform Crime Reports compiled by the Federal Bureau of Investigation.[18] Between 1973

---

17. These estimates will understate the true impact of abortion on crime if there are other factors beyond the four we explicitly considered that positively covary with abortion and crime, such as religiosity, poverty, or low maternal education. Indeed, this last factor was found by Rasanen et al. [1999] to be the single most powerful factor leading to criminality by the children. Moreover, to the extent that abortion reduces crime committed by other family members as a result of the beneficial effects of a reduction in family size (since larger family size increases the likelihood of criminality), this effect would also be missed. On the other hand, a countervailing force is that a reduction in the supply of criminals will induce higher returns to entry into the criminal occupations thereby offsetting through recruitment the initial dampening effect on crime. One would suspect this effect to be limited to crimes involving active markets for illegal substances (drugs) or services (prostitution).

18. Uniform Crime Reports compile the number of crimes reported to the

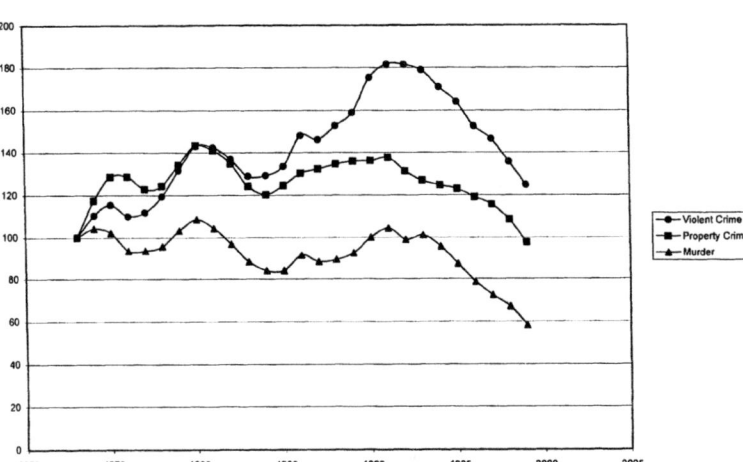

FIGURE II
Crime Rates from the Uniform Crime Reports, 1973–1999
Data are national aggregate per capita reported violent crime, property crime, and murder, indexed to equal 100 in the year 1973. All data are from the FBI's *Uniform Crime Reports,* published annually.

and 1991, violent crime nearly doubled, property crime increased almost 40 percent, and murder was roughly unchanged (despite substantial fluctuations in the intervening years). The year 1991 represents a local maximum for all three of the crime measures. Since that time, each of these crime categories has steadily fallen. Murder has fallen by 40 percent and the other two categories are down more than 30 percent.

The National Crime Victimization Survey (NCVS), which gathers information on self-reported crime victimizations, offers another perspective on national crime patterns in Figure III. According to victimization surveys, violent crime fell through the early 1980s, increased from that point until 1993, and fell sharply thereafter. Property crime fell throughout the period 1973 to 1991, and began to fall even more quickly thereafter. The crime declines in the 1990s are even greater using victimization data than the reported crime statistics. It is notable that the longer time-series patterns of UCR and victimization data do not match

police in various crime categories each year. While the potential shortcomings of these data are well recognized (e.g., O'Brien [1985]), they remain the only source of geographically disaggregated crime data available in the United States.

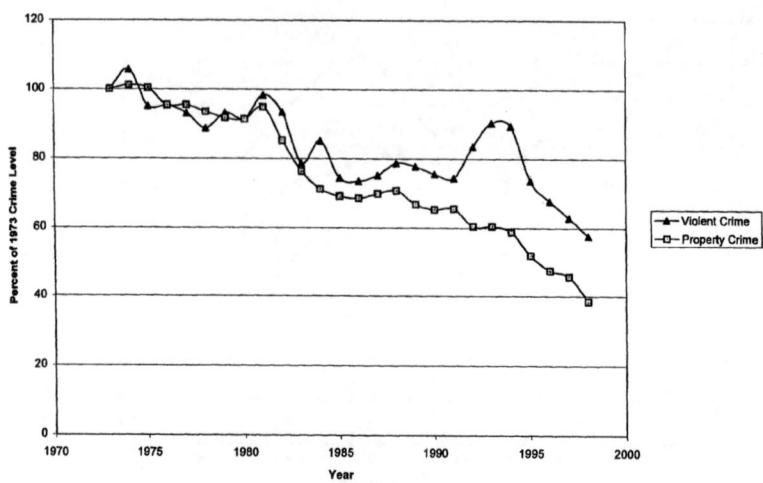

FIGURE III

National Crime Victimization Survey, 1973–1998

Data are national aggregate per capita violent crime and property crime victimizations, indexed to equal 100 in the year 1973. All data are based on the National Crime Survey, conducted annually. Data have been adjusted to correct for a one-time shift associated with the redesign of the survey in the early 1990s.

closely, yet both demonstrate a distinct break from trend in the 1990s.

The timing of the break in the national crime rate is consistent with a legalized abortion story. In 1991 the first cohort affected by *Roe v. Wade* would have been roughly seventeen years old, just beginning to enter the highest crime adolescent years.[19] In the early-legalizing states (in which slightly more than 20 percent of all Americans reside), the first cohort affected by legalized abortion would have been twenty years of age, roughly the

19. The Supreme Court handed down the decision in *Roe v. Wade* on January 22, 1973. Typically, there is a six-to-seven-month lag between the time that an abortion would be performed and the time that the birth would have occurred. Thus, the first births affected would be those born in late 1973.

If women who already had children in 1973 used abortion to prevent increases in family size, then abortion may indirectly lower criminality for the remaining children who will receive greater per child contributions of parental resources [Becker 1981; Barber, Axinn, and Thornton 1999]. Sampson and Laub [1993, p. 81] and Rasanen et al. [1999] find that family size significantly increases delinquency. Note that this family size effect suggests that criminality could be reduced for children who were born a number of years in advance of any abortion that prevents further increases in family size, and thus would allow the effect of abortion on crime to be observed prior to the time that the direct effect of abortion would be observed.

peak of the age-crime profile [Blumstein et al. 1986; Cook and Laub 1998].

The continual decrease in crime between 1991 and 1999 is also consistent with the hypothesized effects of abortion. With each passing year, the fraction of the criminal population that was born postlegalization increases. Thus, the impact of abortion will be felt only gradually. To formalize this idea, we define an index that is designed to reflect the effect of all previous abortions on crime in a particular year t. Obviously, recent abortions will not have any direct impact on crime today since infants commit little crime. As the postlegalization cohorts age, however, we can estimate the effect of abortion by seeing how much crime (proxied by the percentage of arrests committed by those of that age) is committed by the particular cohort. Thus, we define the "effective legalized abortion rate" relevant to crime in year t as the weighted average legalized abortion rate across all cohorts of arrestees, i.e.,

$$(1) \quad Effective\_Abortion_t = \sum_a Abortion^*_{t-a}(Arrests_a/Arrests_{total}),$$

where t indexes years and a indexes the age of a cohort. *Abortion* is the number of abortions per live birth, and the ratio of arrests inside the parentheses is the fraction of arrests for a given crime involving members of cohort a. In a steady state with all cohorts subjected to the same abortion rate, the effective abortion rate is equal to the actual abortion rate. For many years following the introduction of legalized abortion, the effective abortion rate will be below the actual abortion rate since many active criminal cohorts are too old to have been affected by legalized abortion. For instance, following *Roe v. Wade,* the actual abortion rate (per 1000 live births) rose to a steady state of about 400. Yet we estimate that the effective abortion rate in 1991 was only about 33 for homicide, 63 for violent crime, and 126 for property crime. Because property crime is disproportionately done by the young, the effect of abortion legalization is felt earlier.[20] The effective rates grew steadily, rising to 142, 180, and 252, respectively, by 1997. If legalized abortion reduces crime, then crime should continue to fall (all else equal) as long as the effective abortion rate

---

20. Details of this calculation are available from the authors. This effective abortion rate includes legal abortion exposure prior to 1973 in the five states that legalized in 1970.

is rising, precisely the pattern observed in actual crime data in Figures II and III.[21]

B. Comparing Crime Trends in Early-Legalizing States versus the Rest of the United States

As noted earlier in the paper, five states (Alaska, California, Hawaii, New York, and Washington) legalized or quasi-legalized abortion around 1970; in the remaining states, abortion did not become legal until 1973. The staggered timing of the introduction of legalized abortion provides a potential avenue for assessing its impact.[22] Using this source of variation to explore the consequences of abortion legalization, Levine et al. [1996] analyze the fertility effects; Angrist and Evans [1996] study the impact on female labor supply; and Gruber, Levine, and Staiger [1999] examine the effect on a variety of measures of child welfare.

For the purposes of analyzing crime, the comparison of early legalizers to all other states is less than ideal. First, criminal involvement does not jump or fall abruptly with age, but rather steadily increases through the teenage years before eventually declining. Early-legalizing states only have a three-year head start. Thus, it may be difficult to identify an impact on overall crime rates since even in the peak crime ages three cohorts account for less than 20 percent of overall arrests. Second, states that legalized abortion in 1970 continued to have higher abortion rates even after *Roe v. Wade*. For instance, in 1976, three years after *Roe v. Wade* was handed down, the early-legalizing states

---

21. It is worth noting one ostensible inconsistency between our predictions and the disaggregated time-series data. As noted by Cook and Laub [1998] and Blumstein and Rosenfeld [1998], there was a sharp spike in youth homicide rates in the late 1980s and early 1990s, especially among African-Americans. These cohorts were born after legalized abortion. Importantly, this finding is not inconsistent with the central claim that abortion legalization contributed to lower crime rates, but merely shows that this dampening effect on crime can be outweighed in the short term by factors that stimulate crime. Elevated youth homicide rates in this period appear to be clearly linked to the rise of crack and the easy availability of guns. That abortion is only one factor influencing crime in the late 1980s points out the caution required in drawing any conclusions regarding an abortion-crime link based on time-series evidence alone.

22. Evidence in Levine et al. [1996] suggests that there was a substantial amount of border crossing in order to obtain legal abortions prior to 1973. To the extent that is true, the observed differences in crime between early-legalizing states and all others will be muted. It appears, however, that the more affluent tended to travel for abortions, which probably diminishes the importance of such activity for assessments about crime. Some evidence of this is seen in the fact that abortions performed in New York on white women were cut in half in the wake of the decision in *Roe v. Wade*, but there was a far smaller drop in the number of abortions performed in New York on black women.

had a 1985 population-weighted average rate of 593 abortions per live births, compared with 308 for all other states. Given that the impact of abortion on crime happens only gradually, it is difficult to disentangle the separate impacts of early legalization and higher steady state abortion rates.[23]

Bearing in mind these important caveats, a comparison of crime trends in early-legalizing and all other states is displayed in Table I, as well as the difference between those two values. For each of three crime categories (violent, property, murder), we present percent changes in crime by six-year periods for the years 1976–1994, and for the period 1994–1997. The bottom panel of the table also presents the effective abortion rate for violent crime for the two sets of states at the end of each time period, computed using equation (1).[24]

Prior to 1982, legalized abortion should have no impact on crime since the first cohort affected by abortion is no more than twelve years old. These years are included as a check on any preexisting trends in crime rates across the two sets of states. As Table I shows, these preexisting trends are not statistically different across early-legalizing and all other states, nor is the relative pattern constant across the three crime categories. Both property and violent crime were increasing at a slower rate in early legalizing states between 1976 and 1982, whereas murder was rising faster in early-legalizing states.

As shown in the bottom panel of Table I, by 1988 the effective abortion rate for violent crime in early-legalizing states was 64.0 compared with 10.4 in the rest of the United States. To explore whether crime rates began to respond to early abortion legalization between 1982 and 1988, look at the rows labeled "Difference" in the 1982–1988 column. A negative sign for this difference suggests that crime fell faster in the states that legalized abortion earlier (consistent with the theory of this paper), while a positive sign suggests the opposite. Here we see the evidence of the impact of early legalization for the 1982–

---

23. From the broader perspective of determining whether crime rates respond to abortion, this distinction may be irrelevant. However, the inability to distinguish the two channels of impact lessens the extent to which a comparison of early legalizers to other states represents a distinct source of variation from the regression analysis using abortion rates across states after 1973.

24. The effective abortion rate for violent crime falls between the corresponding measures for property crime and homicide. The pattern of differences is similar for the other crime categories, except that the gap rises more (less) quickly for property crime (homicide).

TABLE I
CRIME TRENDS FOR STATES LEGALIZING ABORTION EARLY VERSUS
THE REST OF THE UNITED STATES

| | Percent change in crime rate over the period | | | | Cumulative, |
Crime category	1976–1982	1982–1985	1988–1994	1994–1997	1982–1997
Violent crime					
Early legalizers	16.6	11.1	1.9	−25.8	−12.8
Rest of U. S.	20.9	13.2	15.4	−11.0	17.6
Difference	−4.3	−2.1	−13.4	−14.8	−30.4
	(5.5)	(5.4)	(4.4)	(3.3)	(8.1)
Property crime					
Early legalizers	1.7	−8.3	−14.3	−21.5	−44.1
Rest of U. S.	6.0	1.5	−5.9	−4.3	−8.8
Difference	−4.3	−9.8	−8.4	−17.2	−35.3
	(2.9)	(4.0)	(4.2)	(2.4)	(5.8)
Murder					
Early legalizers	6.3	0.5	2.7	−44.0	−40.8
Rest of U. S.	1.7	−8.8	5.2	−21.1	−24.6
Difference	4.6	9.3	−2.5	−22.9	−16.2
	(7.4)	(6.8)	(8.6)	(6.8)	(10.7)
Effective abortion rate at end of period					
Early legalizers	0.0	64.0	238.6	327.0	327.0
Rest of U. S.	0.0	10.4	87.7	141.0	141.0
Difference	0.0	53.6	150.9	186.0	186.0

Early legalizing states are Alaska, California, Hawaii, New York, and Washington. These five states legalized abortion in late 1969 or 1970. In the remaining states, abortion became legal in 1973 after *Roe v. Wade*. Percent change in crime rate is calculated by subtracting the fixed 1985 population-weighted average of the natural log of the crime rate at the beginning of the period from the fixed 1985 population-weighted average of the natural log of the crime rate at the end of the period. The rows labeled "Difference" are the difference between early legalizers and the rest of the United States (standard errors are reported in parentheses). The bottom panel of the table presents the effective abortion rate for violent crime, as calculated using equation (1) in the text, based on the observed age distribution of national arrests for violent crime in 1985. Entries in the table are fixed 1985 population-weighted averages of the states. Abortion data are from the Alan Guttmacher Institute; crime data are from Uniform Crime Reports. Because of missing crime data for 1976, the 1976–1982 calculations omit the District of Columbia. Precise data sources are provided in the Data Appendix.

1988 period is mixed. Property crime fell significantly in early-legalizing states relative to the rest of the United States (−9.8 percentage points), and the difference is more than twice as large as the preexisting trend in the first column. There is no apparent impact on violent crime or murder by 1988. Nonetheless, the earlier impact on property crime is consistent with the fact that offenses committed by the very young are disproportionately concentrated in property crime. For instance, in 1995 those under age eighteen accounted for over one-third of all property crime arrests, but less than 20 percent of violent crime and murder arrests.

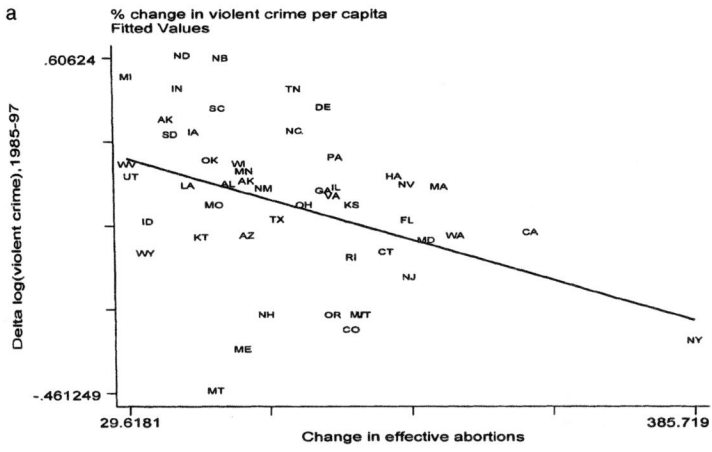

FIGURE IVa
Changes in Violent Crime and Abortion Rates, 1985–1997

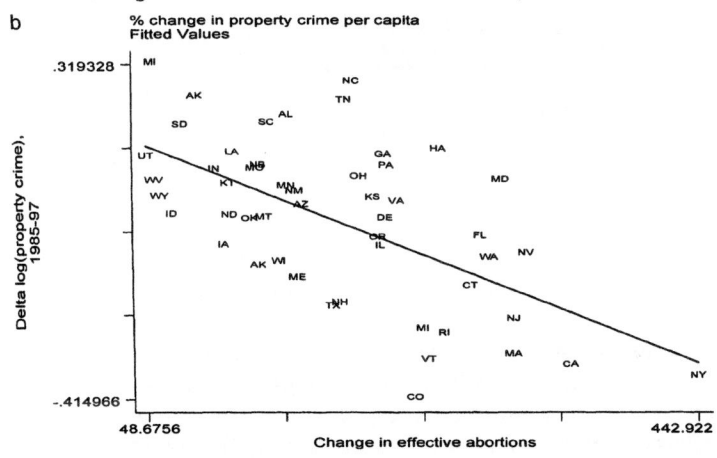

FIGURE IVb
Changes in Property Crime and Abortion Rates, 1985–1997

By 1994, the gap in the "effective abortion rate" between early-legalizing states and all others had grown to 150.9. The early-legalizing states experienced declines in crime relative to the rest of the United States in all three crime categories. The trend accelerates between 1994 and 1997, with double-digit (and highly statistically significant) differences for each of the crimes. The last column of Table I shows that the cumulative decrease in

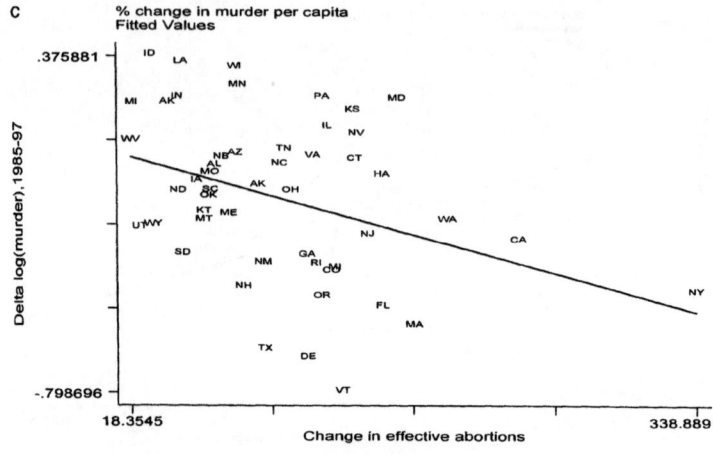

FIGURE IVc
Changes in Murder and Abortion Rates, 1985–1997

The vertical axis in Figures IVa–IVc corresponds to the log change in the named crime category between 1985 and 1997. The horizontal axis is the change in the effective abortion rate corresponding to the crime category between 1985 and 1997. The effective abortion rate is the estimated average abortion rate per 1000 live births for criminals in the state, as calculated using equation (1) in the text. Washington, DC, which is an extreme outlier with respect to abortion rates, is omitted from the figures, but is included in all other statistical analyses.

crime between 1982–1997 for early-legalizing states compared with the rest of the nation is 16.2 percent greater for murder, 30.4 percent greater for violent crime, and 35.3 percent greater for property crime. Realistically, these crime decreases are too large to be attributed to the three-year head start in the early-legalizing states. Put another way, the observed differences in the "effective abortion rate" documented in the bottom of Table I reflect not only the head start on abortion, but also higher steady state rates. Thus, the source of variation exploited in Table I is not entirely distinct from that used in the state-level panel regressions below.

C. State-Level Changes in Crime as a Function of Postlegalization Abortion Rates

The preceding discussion provides suggestive evidence of an impact of abortion on crime. In what follows, we explore this relationship more systematically by using a panel data analysis

TABLE II

CRIME CHANGES 1985–1997 AS A FUNCTION OF ABORTION RATES 1973–1976

Abortion frequency (Ranked by effective abortion rate in 1997)	Effective abortions per 1000 live births, 1997	% Change in crime rate, 1973–1985			% Change in crime rate, 1985–1997		
		Violent crime	Property crime	Murder	Violent crime	Property crime	Murder
Lowest	67.5	+31.8	+29.8	−21.1	+29.2	+9.3	+4.1
Medium	135.0	+28.8	+31.1	−19.7	+18.0	+2.2	−12.6
Highest	257.1	+32.2	+15.2	−9.7	−2.4	−23.1	−25.9

States are ranked by effective abortion rates for violent crime in 1997, with the seventeen states with lowest abortion rates classified as "lowest," the next seventeen states classified as "medium," and the highest seventeen states (including District of Columbia) classified as "highest." The effective abortion rate is the estimated average abortion rate per 1000 live births for criminals in the state, as calculated using equation (1) in the text, based on the observed age distribution of national arrests for violent crime in 1985. All values in the table are weighted averages using 1985 state populations as weights. Percent change in crime per capita is calculated by subtracting the fixed 1985 population-weighted average of the natural log of the crime rate at the beginning of the period from the fixed 1985 population-weighted average of the natural log of the crime rate at the end of the period. Because crime rates are extremely low until the midteenage years, legalized abortion is not predicted to have had a substantial impact on crime over the period 1973–1985, but would be predicted to affect crime in the period 1985–1997. Abortion data are from the Alan Guttmacher Institute; crime data are from Uniform Crime Reports. Precise data sources are provided in the Data Appendix.

to relate state abortion rates after *Roe v. Wade* to state-level changes in crime over the period from 1985 through 1997.

Before presenting regression results, Figures IVa–IVc show simple plots of log-changes in crime rates between 1985 and 1997 against the change in the state-level effective abortion rate over that same time period.[25] The three figures correspond to violent crime, property crime, and murder, respectively. In each case, there is a clear negative relationship between crime changes over the period 1985–1997 and abortion rates in the years immediately following *Roe v. Wade*. The fitted population-weighted regression lines are also included in the figures. The R^2 from these simple regressions range from .12 (murder) to .45 (property crime), as reflected in the relatively tighter fit of the regression line for the latter crime category.

The raw relationship between abortion rates in the 1970s and falling crime in the 1990s emerges even more clearly in Table II. States are ranked based on effective abortion rates in 1997 and

---

25. The figures plot the scatter diagrams for all 50 states. The District of Columbia is dropped from the graph, as it is an extreme outlier that does not accurately reflect the abortion rates of D.C. residents, as indicated in footnote 27, below. All states had effective abortion rates close to zero in 1985, so the change in the effective abortion rate between 1985 and 1997 is almost identical to the effective abortion rate in 1997.

divided into three categories: low, medium, and high. Mean effective abortion rates, and percent changes in murder, violent crime, and property crime for the periods 1973–1985 and 1985–1997 are shown in the table for the three sets of states. Crime data for the period 1973–1985 are included as a check on the validity of the results. There should be no effect of abortion on crime between 1973–1985. To the extent that high and low abortion states systematically differ in the earlier period, questions about the exogeneity of the abortion rate are raised. It is reassuring that the data reveal no clear differences in crime rates across states between 1973 and 1985 as a function of the abortion rate. In some instances crime was rising more quickly in high abortion states; in other cases the opposite is true. For the period 1985–1997, however, the results change dramatically. For each crime category, the high abortion states fell relative to the low abortion states by at least 30 percentage points. In every instance, the medium abortion states had intermediate outcomes with respect to crime.

The panel data regressions that we report are similar in spirit to Figure IV and Table II, but utilize not only the endpoints of the sample, but also information from the intervening years, as well as including a range of controls:

$$(2) \qquad \ln(CRIME_{st}) = \beta_1 ABORT_{st} + X_{st}\Theta + \gamma_s + \lambda_t + \epsilon_{st},$$

where s indexes states and t reflects time. The left-hand-side variable is the relevant logged crime rate per capita. Our measure of abortion is the effective abortion rate (defined earlier) for a given state, year, and crime category.[26] X is a vector of state-level controls that includes prisoners and police per capita, a range of variables capturing state economic conditions, lagged state welfare generosity, the presence of concealed handgun laws, and per capita beer consumption. γ_s and λ_t represent state and year fixed effects. All regressions are weighted least squares with weights based on state populations. All of the estimates we present are adjusted for serial correlation in panel data using the method of Bhargava et al. [1982].[27]

---

26. The weights used in computing the effective abortion rates are the percentage of arrests by age for a given crime category in the United States in 1985. In other words, abortion rates are state-specific, but the same weighting function is used for all states.

27. Blank, George, and London [1996] suggest that the official abortion rate in Washington, DC is artificially elevated because women from Maryland and Virginia frequently travel there to receive abortions. The CDC estimates that

Summary statistics for the sample are provided in Table III. The summary statistics on abortion correspond to the effective abortion rate, which is well below the actual abortion rate throughout the sample because much of the criminal population was born prior to legalized abortion. Actual national abortion rates in the years immediately after *Roe v. Wade* were roughly 300 abortions per 1000 live births, but with considerable variation across states. For example, over the period from 1973–1976, West Virginia had the lowest abortion rate (10 per 1000 live births), while New York (763) and Washington, D.C. (1793) had the highest rates. There is a great deal of variation in crimes per 1000 residents, both across states and within states over time. The same is true for arrest rates.

An important limitation of the data is that state abortion rates are very highly serially correlated. The correlation between state abortion rates in years t and $t + 1$ is .98. The five-year and ten-year correlations are .95 and .91, respectively. One implication of these high correlations is that it is very difficult using the data alone to distinguish the impact of 1970s abortions on current crime rates from the impact of 1990s abortions on current crime rates; if one includes both lagged and current abortion rates in the same specification, standard errors explode due to multicollinearity. Consequently, it must be recognized that our interpretation of the results relies on the assumption that there will be a fifteen-to-twenty year lag before abortion materially affects crime. This lag between the act of abortion and its impact on crime differentiates it from many other social phenomena like divorce and poverty which may have both lagged and contemporaneous effects, making it very difficult to separately identify any lagged effects.

Regression results are shown in Table IV. For each of the three crime categories, two different specifications are reported. The odd-numbered columns present results without control variables (other than the state- and year-fixed effects); the even columns add the full set of controls.

The top row of the table presents the coefficients on the abortion variable across specifications. In all six cases, the coefficient is negative, implying that higher abortion rates are asso-

---

about half of all abortions performed in the District of Columbia are on nonresidents (which is the highest percentage for any state); the comparable percentage in New Jersey is 2 percent [Dye and Presser 1999, p. 143].

TABLE III
SUMMARY STATISTICS

Variable	Mean	Standard deviation (overall)	Standard deviation (within state)
Violent crime per 1000 residents	6.73	2.81	.88
Property crime per 1000 residents	48.04	11.46	4.60
Murder per 1000 residents	0.09	0.04	0.02
"Effective" abortion rate per 1000 live births by crime:			
Violent crime	77.11	83.18	66.13
Property crime	132.26	116.46	86.89
Murder	51.00	66.57	55.39
Prisoners per 1000 residents	2.83	1.26	0.86
Police per 1000 residents	2.85	0.64	0.27
State personal income per capita ($1997)	23207	3408	1361
AFDC generosity per recipient family (t–15)	7242	2905	1364
State unemployment rate (percent unemployed)	6.15	1.55	1.21
Beer consumption per capita (gallons)	23.03	3.32	1.24
Poverty rate (percent below poverty level)	13.80	3.51	1.64
Violent crime arrests per 1000, under age 25	3.18	1.46	0.49
Property crime arrests per 1000, under age 25	12.36	3.76	1.44
Murder arrests per 1000, under age 25	0.11	0.06	0.03
Violent crime arrests per 1000, age 25 and over	2.04	1.06	0.34
Property crime arrests per 1000, age 25 and over	4.82	1.58	0.65
Murder arrests per 1000, age 25 and over	0.06	0.03	0.01

All values reported are means of annual, state-level observations for the period 1985–1997 with the following exceptions. Arrest data cover the years 1985–1996, and AFDC generosity data are for the years 1985–1998. The police and prisons data are once-lagged, and thus correspond to the years 1984–1996. The values reported in the table are population weighted averages. The effective abortion rate is a weighted average of the abortion rates for each cohort born in a state, with weights determined by the percentage of arrests by age for a given crime category in the United States in 1985 as shown in equation (1). All summary statistics are based on 663 observations, except where otherwise noted. Because of missing data, arrest statistics are based on 574 observations, compared with a theoretical maximum of 612. AFDC statistics are based on 714 observations. See Data Appendix for further details.

ciated with declining crime. These estimated effects of abortion are highly statistically significant—more so than any other variable included in the analysis. The real-world magnitude implied

TABLE IV
PANEL-DATA ESTIMATES OF THE RELATIONSHIP BETWEEN
ABORTION RATES AND CRIME

Variable	ln(Violent crime per capita)		ln(Property crime per capita)		ln(Murder per capita)	
	(1)	(2)	(3)	(4)	(5)	(6)
"Effective" abortion rate	−.137	−.129	−.095	−.091	−.108	−.121
(× 100)	(.023)	(.024)	(.018)	(.018)	(.036)	(.047)
ln(prisoners per capita)	—	−.027	—	−.159	—	−.231
(t − 1)		(.044)		(.036)		(.080)
ln(police per capita)	—	−.028	—	−.049	—	−.300
(t − 1)		(.045)		(.045)		(.109)
State unemployment rate	—	.069	—	1.310	—	.968
(percent unemployed)		(.505)		(.389)		(.794)
ln(state income per	—	.049	—	.084	—	−.098
capita)		(.213)		(.162)		(.465)
Poverty rate (percent	—	−.000	—	−.001	—	−.005
below poverty line)		(.002)		(.001)		(.004)
AFDC generosity (t −	—	.008	—	.002	—	−.000
15) (× 1000)		(.005)		(.004)		(.000)
Shall-issue concealed	—	−.004	—	.039	—	−.015
weapons law		(.012)		(.011)		(.032)
Beer consumption per	—	.004	—	.004	—	.006
capita (gallons)		(.003)		(.003)		(.008)
R^2	.938	.942	.990	.992	.914	.918

The dependent variable is the log in the per capita crime rate named at the top of each pair of columns. The first column in each pair presents results from specifications in which the only additional covariates are state- and year-fixed effects. The second column presents results using the full specification. The data set is comprised of annual state-level observations (including the District of Columbia) for the period 1985–1997. The number of observations is equal to 663 in all columns. State- and year-fixed effects are included in all specifications. The prison and police variables are once-lagged to minimize endogeneity. Estimation is performed using a two-step procedure. In the first step, weighted least squares estimates are obtained, with weights determined by state population. In the second step, a panel data generalization of the Prais-Winsten correction for serial correlation developed by Bhargava et al. [1982] is implemented. Standard errors are in parentheses. Data sources for all variables are described in the Data Appendix.

by the coefficients on abortion is substantial. An increase in the effective abortion rate of 100 per 1000 live births (the mean effective abortion rate in 1997 for violent crime is 180 with a standard deviation of 96 across states) is associated with a reduction of 12 percent in murder, 13 percent in violent crime, and 9 percent in property crime. In Table II, comparing the states in the top third with respect to abortions to the states in the bottom third, our parameter estimates imply that crime fell an additional 16–25 percent in the former states by 1997 due to greater usage of abortion. One additional abortion is associated with a reduction of 0.23 property crimes, 0.04 violent crimes, and 0.004 murders annually when a cohort is at its peak crime age. Comparing these estimates to average criminal propensities among 18–24 year olds, those on the margin for being aborted are roughly four times more criminal. These estimates are roughly consistent with, but somewhat larger than, the back-of-the-envelope predictions in Section III.

The other coefficients in the model appear plausibly estimated. The elasticities of incarceration and police with respect to crime all carry the expected sign, with prison associated with significant reductions in property crime and murder, and police associated with significant reductions in murder.[28] A higher state unemployment rate is associated with significant increases in property crime, but not violent crime, consistent with previous research [Freeman 1995]. The three other measures of state economic conditions—per capita income, the poverty rate, and AFDC generosity (lagged fifteen years to roughly correspond with the early years of life of the current teenagers) do not systematically affect crime. Shall-issue concealed carry laws appear to significantly increase the amount of property crime, but have no effect on violent crime or murder. Finally, beer consumption is weakly linked with higher crime rates, but never significantly so.

Table V investigates the sensitivity of the abortion coefficients to a range of alternative specifications. We take the specifications with the full set of controls in Table IV as a baseline. The abortion coefficients from those regressions are reported in the top row of Table V. Each row of the table represents a different specification. The sensitivity of the results to large states (since the regressions are population weighted) and states with very high or low abortion rates is examined first. Removing New York reduces the estimates for violent crime and murder, while eliminating California increases the abortion coefficient for those two crime categories. Dropping Washington, DC, which is an extreme outlier (with an abortion rate over four times the national average) increases the estimated impact of abortion.

---

28. The estimated effects of incarceration are consistent with previous correlational panel-data studies (e.g., Marvell and Moody [1994]). The prison coefficients obtained here are approximately the same magnitude as Levitt [1996] finds when correcting for the endogeneity of the prison population using prison overcrowding litigation as an instrument. Levitt [1997] finds a negative impact of police on crime using electoral cycles in large cities as an instrument for the size of the police force.

TABLE V
SENSITIVITY OF ABORTION COEFFICIENTS TO ALTERNATIVE SPECIFICATIONS

	Coefficient on the "effective" abortion rate variable when the dependent variable is		
Specification	ln (Violent crime per capita)	ln (Property crime per capita)	ln (Murder per capita)
Baseline	−.129 (.024)	−.091 (.018)	−.121 (.047)
Exclude New York	−.097 (.030)	−.097 (.021)	−.063 (.045)
Exclude California	−.145 (.025)	−.080 (.018)	−.151 (.054)
Exclude District of Columbia	−.149 (.025)	−.112 (.019)	−.159 (.053)
Exclude New York, California, and District of Columbia	−.175 (.035)	−.125 (.017)	−.273 (.052)
Adjust "effective" abortion rate for cross-state mobility	−.148 (.027)	−.099 (.020)	−.140 (.055)
Include control for flow of immigrants	−.115 (.024)	−.063 (.018)	−.103 (.047)
Include state-specific trends	−.078 (.080)	.143 (.033)	−.379 (.105)
Include region-year interactions	−.142 (.033)	−.084 (.023)	−.123 (.053)
Unweighted	−.046 (.029)	−.022 (.023)	.040 (.054)
Unweighted, exclude District of Columbia	−.149 (.029)	−.107 (.015)	−.140 (.055)
Unweighted, exclude District of Columbia, California, and New York	−.157 (.037)	−.110 (.017)	−.166 (.075)
Include control for overall fertility rate $(t - 20)$	−.127 (.025)	−.093 (.019)	−.123 (.047)
Long difference estimates using only data from 1985 and 1997	−.109 (.054)	−.077 (.034)	−.089 (.077)

Results in this table are variations on the specifications reported in columns (2), (4), and (6) of Table IV. The top row of the current table is the baseline specification that is presented in Table IV. Except where noted, all specifications are estimated using an annual, state-level panel of data for the years 1985–1997. Standard errors (in parentheses) are corrected for serial correlation using the Bhargava et al. [1982] two-step procedure for panel data. The specification that corrects for cross-state mobility does so by using an effective abortion rate that is a weighted average of the abortion rates in the state of birth for fifteen year-olds residing in a state in the PUMS 5 percent sample of the 1990 census. Controls for the flow of immigrants are derived from changes in the foreign-born population, based on the decennial censuses and 1997 estimates, linearly interpolated. Region-year interactions are for the nine census regions.

Dropping all three of those high abortion states leads to higher estimates across the board, suggesting that the crime-reducing impact of abortion may have decreasing returns.

Omitted variables may also be a concern in the regressions given the relatively limited set of covariates available. One crude way of addressing this question is to include region-year interaction terms in an attempt to absorb geographically correlated shocks. The abortion coefficients are not substantially affected by this approach.

Since we are measuring the effect of abortions in a state on crime in that state up to a quarter century later, the issue of cross-state mobility should be considered. Theoretically, the presence of such cross-state movements will tend to systematically bias the abortion coefficient toward zero since the true effective abortion rate is measured with error by our proxy that ignores mobility. In order to adjust for migration, we determined the state of birth and state of residence for all fifteen year-olds in the 1990 PUMS 5 percent sample. Using this information, we recalculated effective abortion rates as weighted average abortion rates by the actual state of birth of fifteen year-olds residing in a state. For all three crime categories the estimated impact of abortion increases with the migration correction, although the changes are not large.

We perform a range of other sensitivity checks. Controlling for the flow of immigrants to a state somewhat reduces the estimated effect of abortion on crime (particularly for property crime), but it does not change their significance. When we include state-specific time trends, the estimates change somewhat erratically, and the standard errors double for murder and property crime and triple for violent crime. Unweighted panel data regressions (as opposed to population weighted) yield sharply smaller coefficients, but this is exclusively due to Washington, DC as an outlier (owing in all likelihood to mismeasurement in the DC abortion rate). Excluding District of Columbia alone, or District of Columbia in combination with California and New York, leads to coefficients from the unweighted regressions that are greater than the baseline estimates.

Including controls for lagged changes in overall fertility rates for the same era as our abortion measures has almost no impact on our estimated coefficients. Regressions using only the 1985 and 1997 endpoints of our sample ("long-differences") yield coefficients similar to, although somewhat smaller than, the baseline coefficients for the overall panel.

V. THE IMPACT OF ABORTION ON ARRESTS BY AGE OF OFFENDER

The preceding section highlighted a strong empirical correlation between abortion rates after *Roe v. Wade* and crime changes in recent years. In this section we explore the extent to which arrest patterns substantiate a possible causal interpretation of these results. In particular, if legalized abortion is the reason for the decline in crime, then one would expect that decreases in crime should be concentrated among those cohorts born after abortion is legalized.[29]

Testing that hypothesis is complicated by the fact that the age of criminals is not directly observable. The age of arrestees, however, is reported.[30] Thus, we can analyze whether arrests by cohort are a function of the abortion rate.

The basic specifications used to explain state arrest rates by age category are identical to the crime regressions in the preceding section, except that the dependent variable is the (natural log of the) arrest rate per capita for those under age 25 rather than the overall crime rate for all ages, and 1997 is excluded from the sample because the necessary arrest data are not yet available.[31] Results from the estimation are reported in columns 1–3 of Table VI. Two specifications per crime category are presented: the top row of results just includes the effective abortion variable and year- and state-fixed effects, while the bottom row adds to these the remaining covariates that were used in Table IV above. Because the dependent variable is denominated by the population under age 25, the abortion coefficients only reflect changes in arrest rates per person. If the impact of abortion was solely through changes in cohort size, then the per capita specifications we run would yield zero coefficients on the abortion variable. In all six cases, lagged abortion rates are associated with decreases in arrests per capita by those under the age of 25, with estimates

---

29. It is possible that crime by older cohorts may be affected indirectly by abortion. For instance, if there are fewer criminals in younger cohorts, this may increase additional criminal opportunities for older individuals (particularly in activities such as drug distribution where there may be easy substitutability). On the other hand, to the extent that lower crime by the young increases the criminal justice resources available per older criminal [Sah 1991], crime among older cohorts may also fall. Moreover, as noted above, if abortion results in smaller family sizes and a concomitant increase in parental resources per child, the effect of legalization could be observed in crime reductions for older siblings. All of these effects are likely to be of second-order magnitude, however.

30. Arrest data may not accurately reflect criminal activity for a number of reasons. Greenwood [1995] argues that juvenile crime is more likely to be committed in groups so that the arrest frequency of juveniles overstates the true fraction of crime they commit. Also, if there are differences across criminals in avoiding detection, arrests will be skewed toward the less proficient criminals.

31. We use an age cutoff of 25 because it is approximately the age of the oldest cohorts affected by legalized abortion. Arrest data are available by single year of age up to age 24, but only in five-year groupings thereafter. The results presented are not sensitive to small perturbations of the age groupings.

TABLE VI

THE IMPACT OF ABORTION RATES ON ARRESTS BY AGE (ALL VALUES IN THE TABLE ARE COEFFICIENTS ON THE EFFECTIVE ABORTION RATE (× 100), OTHER COEFFICIENTS ARE NOT REPORTED)

Specification	ln (arrest per person, under age 25)			ln (arrests per person, age 25+)			ln (arrests per person, under age 25) minus ln (arrests per person, age 25+)		
	Violent crime	Property crime	Murder	Violent crime	Property crime	Murder	Violent crime	Property crime	Murder
Effective abortion rate (× 100) only, no covariates included	-.095 (.029)	-.085 (.023)	-.214 (.051)	.022 (.054)	-.019 (.037)	-.034 (.037)	-.116 (.042)	-.066 (.023)	-.180 (.034)
Effective abortion rate (× 100), including full set of covariates	-.044 (.030)	-.054 (.023)	-.180 (.062)	.033 (.046)	.008 (.031)	-.036 (.050)	-.062 (.034)	-.063 (.019)	-.137 (.046)

Regressions are identical to those in Table IV, except that the dependent variables are arrest rates broken down by age category instead of overall crime rates. The top row of the table presents results from specifications in which the only additional covariates are state- and year-fixed effects. The bottom row of the table presents results using the full specification. Covariates included in the bottom row are once-lagged police and prisoners per capita in logs, state unemployment rate, logged state income per capita, the poverty rate, lagged AFDC generosity, shall-issue concealed weapons law, and beer consumption per capita. The regressions use annual state-level data for the period 1985–1996 (1997 arrest data by age are not yet available). Because of missing data, the number of observations varies across columns between 555 and 557, compared with a theoretical maximum of 612. State- and year-fixed effects are included in all specifications. The prison and police variables are once-lagged to minimize endogeneity. Estimation is performed using a two-step procedure. In the first step, weighted least squares estimates are obtained, with weights determined by state population. In the second step, a panel data generalization of the Prais-Winsten correction for serial correlation developed by Bhargava et al. [1982] is implemented. Standard errors are in parentheses.

ranging between $-.044$ and $-.214$. The abortion coefficient is statistically significant in five out of six specifications.

If the arrest data are measured without error and there are no spillovers between the crime of the young and the old, then we would not expect legalized abortion to affect the crime of those born prior to the law change. Columns 4–6, which relate arrest rates of older cohorts to abortion rates, thus provide a natural specification test for our hypothesis. In none of the crime categories does the abortion rate variable have a statistically significant impact on arrests of older cohorts. In three instances the coefficient is positive; in the other three cases the coefficient is negative. All of the estimates are much smaller in magnitude than was the case for arrests of those under the age of 25. The last three columns of the table show "difference in differences" estimates of the impact of abortion on cohorts born after legalization relative to those born before. In all cases, the coefficients are similar to those in the first three columns of the table. This result strengthens the causal interpretation of the abortion coefficients on the arrest patterns of the young.

The implied magnitude of the abortion effects on arrests is smaller than the parallel estimates presented in the preceding section analyzing crime rates, but is of the same order of magnitude. On average, about half of those arrested are under the age of 25.[32] Thus, to generate the crime reduction in Table IV requires coefficients on young arrests that are twice as large as the coefficients on overall crime. With the exception of murder, the arrest coefficients are actually smaller than the crime coefficients. Part of this discrepancy may be attributable to the fact that the arrest regressions reflect only reductions in per capita crime by the young, not smaller youthful cohorts, but this can explain only a portion of the gap. It remains an open question as to whether this discrepancy represents a partially spurious relationship in the crime regressions, measurement error in the arrest data, or a relationship between crime and arrests that is not proportional. It is important to stress, however, that while the magnitude of the effects differs between the crime and arrest regressions, the basic story with respect to abortion is present in both cases.[33]

32. Over the sample period, those under the age of 25 accounted for an average of 49 percent of violent arrests, 62 percent of property arrests, and 48 percent of murder arrests.
33. We replicated the sensitivity tests that were presented in Table V for the baseline Table IV regressions using Table VI as the baseline estimates. These

As a further test of our hypothesis, we analyze arrest rates by state by single year of age. These data are available for the ages 15 and 24 covering the period 1985 through 1996. If abortion legalization reduces crime, then we should see the reduction begin with, say, fifteen year-olds about sixteen years after legalization, then extend to sixteen year-olds a year later, and so on. Because we observe many cohorts in a given state and year, we are able to include controls for state-year variation. Thus, unlike the preceding table, where state-year variation was our source of identification, in the analysis that follows our estimates are based on differences in abortion rates and crime rates across cohorts within a given state and year. The regression we run takes the following form:

$$(3) \quad \ln(ARRESTS_{stb}) = \beta_1 ABORT_{sb} + \gamma_s + \lambda_{tb} + \theta_{st} + \epsilon_{stb},$$

where s, t, and b index state, year, and birth cohort, respectively. The variable *ARRESTS* is the raw number of arrests for a given crime. Unlike previous tables, we do not divide arrests by population to create per capita rates because of the absence of reliable measures of state population by single year of age. As our measure of the abortion rate for a particular cohort, we use the abortion rate in the current state of residence in the calendar year most likely to have preceded the arrestees birth.[34] Cross-state migration will not be captured by this measure, but the results in earlier sections suggest that the impact of migration on the estimates is small (and that any migration correction would, if anything, strengthen our results). Because the unit of observation in the analysis is a state-birth cohort and cohorts are observed repeatedly over time, we will include controls for age, national year-cohort interactions, state-year interactions, and (in some cases) state-age interactions. We cannot, however, include state-

---

regressions again revealed the robustness of the coefficient estimates, exhibiting patterns similar to the sensitivity analysis for the full sample. These results are available from the authors on request.

34. For example, we use the abortion rate in 1980 to reflect the abortion exposure of fifteen year-olds arrested in 1996. Because the arrest data cover a calendar year, there is a possible 730-day window into which an arrestee's date of birth may fall (i.e., an arrest is made on January 1 of someone who is 16 years and 364 days old versus an arrest is made on December 31 of someone who is 16 years and 1 day old). With a six-to-seven-month lag from likely time of abortion to time of birth, this 730-day window is centered on the calendar year that we use to capture abortion exposure. More complicated attempts to measure abortion exposure yield estimates similar to the ones we present.

birth cohort interactions without absorbing all of the variation in the abortion exposure of a state-birth cohort.

Table VII presents the results of this analysis for violent crime and property crime. There are too few murder arrests per single age category per state to enable us to provide similar estimates for murder. We present estimates restricting the impact of abortion to be constant over the entire age range (odd columns) and allowing the impact of abortion to vary by age (even columns). Some of the regressions include state-age interactions, others just have state-fixed effects. All of the specifications include year-age interactions to control for national-level fluctuations in the age-crime profile.[35] In all cases, standard errors have been corrected to reflect correlation over time in a given birth cohort's observations.

The top row of Table VII presents estimates restricting the abortion coefficient to be constant across the ages 15–24. In all instances, the coefficient is strongly significantly negative, implying that higher abortion rates around the time a cohort is born are associated with lower arrest rates in their teens and twenties. When the abortion coefficient is allowed to vary by age, 38 of the 40 parameter estimates are negative; more than two-thirds of these estimates are statistically significant at the .05 level. The greatest impact of abortion appears to occur in the age range 18–22. The effects are generally weakest for the youngest ages in the sample.

The coefficients in this table are not directly comparable to those in the preceding tables. Because we are analyzing arrests by single year of age in this table, we are able to use actual abortion rates as opposed to the effective abortion rates that average over many cohorts. Comparing states in the top third and bottom third with respect to abortion frequency, the gap between those sets of states in actual abortion rates was about 350 per 1000 births. Given the estimates in the top row of Table VII, this implies that arrest rates of 15–24 year-olds in the high abortion states are estimated to have fallen between 5 and 14 percent relative to the low abortion states.

---

35. For instance, the arrival of crack appears to have temporarily raised the violent crime propensities, particularly among youths.

TABLE VII
THE RELATIONSHIP BETWEEN ABORTION RATES AND ARREST RATES, BY SINGLE YEAR OF AGE

	ln (Violent arrests)			ln (Property arrests)		
Abortion rate (× 100)	-.015 (.003)	—	-.028 (.004)	-.040 (.004)	—	-.025 (.003)
Abortion rate (× 100) interacted with						
Age = 15	—	.018 (.008)	-.008 (.010)	—	-.037 (.007)	-.005 (.008)
Age = 16	—	.008 (.007)	-.007 (.008)	—	-.043 (.006)	-.011 (.006)
Age = 17	—	-.010 (.006)	-.021 (.007)	—	-.042 (.006)	-.013 (.005)
Age = 18	—	-.035 (.004)	-.039 (.007)	—	-.053 (.005)	-.023 (.005)
Age = 19	—	-.040 (.005)	-.043 (.007)	—	-.050 (.005)	-.036 (.006)
Age = 20	—	-.043 (.006)	-.043 (.007)	—	-.038 (.006)	-.035 (.006)
Age = 21	—	-.039 (.009)	-.039 (.008)	—	-.028 (.006)	-.037 (.006)
Age = 22	—	-.028 (.013)	-.024 (.009)	—	-.020 (.008)	-.032 (.009)
Age = 23	—	-.031 (.023)	-.026 (.013)	—	-.015 (.011)	-.030 (.013)
Age = 24	—	-.027 (.040)	-.016 (.020)	—	-.024 (.019)	-.047 (.018)
R^2	.972	.972	.985	.967	.968	.984
Number of observations	5,737	5,737	5,737	5,740	5,740	5,740
State-fixed effects or State-age interactions?	State-fixed	State-fixed	State * Age interactions	State-fixed	State-fixed	State * Age interactions

Results in the table are coefficients from estimation of equation (3). The unit of observation in the regression is annual arrests by state by single year of age. The sample covers the period 1985–1996 for ages 15–24. The abortion rate for a cohort of age a in state s in year y is the number of abortions per 1000 live births in state s in year $y - a - 1$. Note that this is the actual abortion rate, rather than the "effective" abortion rate used in preceding tables. Therefore, the coefficients in this table are not directly comparable to those of earlier tables. If data were available for all states, years, and ages, the total number of observations would be 6120. Due to missing arrest data and occasional zero values for arrests, the actual number of observations is somewhat smaller. A complete set of year-birth cohort interactions are included in all specifications to capture national changes in the shape of the age-crime profile over time. State-year interactions are also included. Some specifications include state-fixed effects; in other specifications, a complete set of state-age interactions is included. Estimation is weighted least squares, with weights determined by total state population. Standard errors have been corrected to account for correlation over time within a given birth cohort in a particular state. Such a correction is necessary because the abortion rate for any given cohort is fixed over time, but multiple observations corresponding to different years of age are included in the regression. Results for murder are not included in the table because murder is infrequent, leading to many zeros when analyzed at the level of state and single year of age.

VI. Conclusion

We know that teenagers, unmarried women, and poor women are most likely to deem a pregnancy to be either mistimed or unwanted, and that a large proportion of these unintended pregnancies will be terminated through abortion.[36] According to a recent National Academy report, there appears to be "a causal and adverse effect of early childbearing on the health and social and economic well-being of children; this effect is over and above the important effects of background disadvantages" [Institute of Medicine 1995, p. 58]. Moreover, unintended pregnancies are associated with poorer prenatal care, greater smoking and drinking during pregnancy, and lower birthweights. Consequently, the life chances of children who are born only because their mothers could not have an abortion are considerably dampened relative to babies who were wanted at the time of conception. The drop in the proportion of unwanted births during the 1970s and early 1980s appears to be the result of the increasing availability and resort to abortion.

The evidence we present is consistent with legalized abortion reducing crime rates with a twenty-year lag. Our results suggest that an increase of 100 abortions per 1000 live births reduces a cohort's crime by roughly 10 percent. Extrapolating our results out of sample to a counterfactual in which abortion remained illegal and the number of illegal abortions performed remained steady at the 1960s level, we estimate that (with average national effective abortion rates in 1997 for all three crimes ranging from between 142 and 252) crime was almost 15–25 percent lower in 1997 than it would have been absent legalized abortion.

These estimates suggest that legalized abortion is a primary explanation for the large drops in murder, property crime, and violent crime that our nation has experienced over the last decade. Indeed, legalized abortion may account for as much as one-half of the overall crime reduction. Assuming that this claim is correct, existing estimates of the costs of crime (e.g., Miller, Cohen, and Rossman [1993] suggest that the social benefit to reduced crime as a result of abortion may be on the order of $30 billion dollars annually. Increased imprisonment between 1991

---

36. Roughly 75 percent of never-married women who unintentionally become pregnant will opt for abortion. Overall, almost exactly half of all unintended pregnancies—whether mistimed or unwanted—will be terminated by abortion [Institute of Medicine 1995, pp. 41–47].

and 1997 (the prison population rose about 50 percent over this period) lowered crime 10 percent based on an elasticity of $-.20$. Thus, together abortion and prison growth explain much, if not all, of the decrease in crime.[37]

Roughly half of the crimes committed in the United States are done by individuals born prior to the legalization of abortion. As these older cohorts age out of criminality and are replaced by younger offenders born after abortion became legal, we would predict that crime rates will continue to fall. When a steady state is reached roughly twenty years from now, the impact of abortion will be roughly twice as great as the impact felt so far. Our results suggest that all else equal, legalized abortion will account for persistent declines of 1 percent a year in crime over the next two decades. To the extent that the Hyde Amendment effectively restricted access to abortion, however, this prediction might be overly optimistic.

While falling crime rates are no doubt a positive development, our drawing a link between falling crime and legalized abortion should not be misinterpreted as either an endorsement of abortion or a call for intervention by the state in the fertility decisions of women. Furthermore, equivalent reductions in crime could in principle be obtained through alternatives for abortion, such as more effective birth control, or providing better environments for those children at greatest risk for future crime.

DATA APPENDIX

Crime and Police

All crime and police data used in the analysis are from Federal Bureau of Investigation *Crime in the United States* [annual], except the victimization data in Figure II, which are summarized annually in Bureau of Justice Statistics *Sourcebook of Criminal Justice Statistics* [annual].

Abortion

All abortion data are from Bureau of the Census *United States Statistical Abstract* [annual]. The primary source for the

---

37. This is not to say that other factors did not also contribute to the decline in crime. To the extent that there were other forces pushing crime higher, such as crack, then the set of factors leading to reduced crime will explain more than 100 percent of the observed decrease in crime.

abortion data is an annual survey conducted by the Alan Gutt-macher Institute.

Prisoners

Data on number of prisoners are from *Correctional Populations in the United States,* published annually by the Bureau of Justice Statistics.

Population by Age

These data are from *Estimates for the United States, Regions, Divisions, and States by 5 Year Age Groups and Sex: Annual Time Series Estimates,* U. S. Census Bureau [annual].

Poverty

Persons Below Poverty Level, by State, taken from Bureau of the Census *United States Statistical Abstract* [annual].

Unemployment

Figures used represent the percent unemployed among civilian noninstitutional population sixteen years and older, with total unemployment estimates based on the Current Population Survey, taken from Bureau of the Census, *United States Statistical Abstract* [annual].

Fertility

The number of live births per 1000 population, taken from Bureau of the Census, *United States Statistical Abstract* [annual].

Income

Per capita state personal income, converted to 1997 dollars using the Consumer Price Index, from Bureau of the Census, *United States Statistical Abstract* [annual].

AFDC Generosity

Public Assistance Payments to Families with Dependent Children, from Bureau of the Census, *United States Statistical Abstract* [annual]. The data reported in the Statistical Abstract are the average monthly payment per family receiving aid. That number is multiplied by twelve to obtain a yearly average, and then converted into 1997 dollars using the Consumer Price Index.

LEGALIZED ABORTION AND CRIME   417

Nondiscretionary Concealed Handgun Law

Indicates the year in which the state enacted a law requiring local law enforcement authorities to grant concealed weapons permits to anyone meeting certain preestablished criteria. Data come from Lott and Mustard [1997].

Beer Consumption

Consumption of Malt Beverages from the Beer Institute's *Brewer's Almanac* [1995, 1998]. In gallons consumed per capita.

Cross-State Migration

The corrections for cross-state migration are based on a comparison of the state of birth and current state of residence of fifteen year-olds in the 1990 Census Public Use Microdata 5 percent sample.

Foreign-Born Population

Prior to 1994, the decennial census was the only source of data on the number of foreign-born individuals living in the United States. Data from the three Census years and 1997 were used to interpolate intervening years. All data are from Bureau of the Census *United States Statistical Abstract* [annual].

STANFORD LAW SCHOOL
UNIVERSITY OF CHICAGO AND AMERICAN BAR FOUNDATION

REFERENCES

Alan Guttmacher Institute, *Abortion Fact Book, 1992 Edition*, Stanley Henshaw and Jennifer Van Vort, eds. (New York, NY: Alan Guttmacher Institute, 1992).
——, "An Analysis of Pre-1973 State Laws on Abortion," mimeo, March 1989.
Angrist, Joshua, and William Evans, "Schooling and Labor Market Consequences of the 1970 State Abortion Reforms," National Bureau of Economic Research, Working Paper No. 5406, January 1996.
Barber, Jennifer, William Axinn, and Arland Thornton, "Unwanted Childbearing, Health, and Mother-Child Relationships," *Journal of Health and Social Behavior*, XL (September 1999), 231–257.
Beck, Allen, et al., "Survey of State Prison Inmates, 1991," *Bureau of Justice Statistics Bulletin*, NCJ 136949, March 1993.
Becker, Gary, *A Treatise on the Family* (Chicago, IL: University of Chicago Press, 1981).
Beer Institute, *Brewers' Almanac* (New York, NY: United States Brewers Foundation, 1995 and 1998 editions).
Bhargava, A., L. Franzini, et al., "Serial Correlation and the Fixed Effects Model," *Review of Economic Studies*, XLIX (1982), 533–549.
Blank, Rebecca, C. C. George, and R. A. London, "State Abortion Rates: The Impact of Policies, Providers, Politics, Demographics, and Economic Environment," *Journal of Health Economics*, XV (1996), 513–553.

Blumstein, Alfred, Jacqueline Cohen, Jeffrey Roth, and Christy Visher, eds., *Criminal Careers and "Career Criminals"* (Washington, DC: National Academy of Sciences, 1986).

Blumstein, Alfred, and Richard Rosenfeld, "Explaining Recent Trends in U. S. Homicide Rates," *Journal of Criminal Law and Criminology,* LXXXVIII (1998), 1175–1216.

Blumstein, Alfred, and Joel Wallman, eds., *The Crime Drop in America* (New York: Cambridge University Press, 2000).

Bouza, Anthony V., *The Police Mystique: An Insider's Look at Cops, Crime, and the Criminal Justice System* (New York, NY: Plenum Press, 1990).

Bureau of the Census, "Population Estimates for the U. S., Regions, Divisions, and States by 5-year Age Groups and Sex," Population Estimates Program (annual).

——, *Statistical Abstract of the United States* (Washington, DC: U. S. Government Printing Office, annual).

Bureau of Justice Statistics, *Correctional Populations in the U. S.* (Washington, DC: U. S. Government Printing Office, annual).

——, *The Sourcebook of Criminal Justice Statistics,* Timothy Flanagan and Edmund McGarrell, eds. (Washington, DC: U. S. Government Printing Office, 1985 and annual).

Butterfield, Fox, "Number of Victims of Crime Fell Again in '96, Study Says Lowest Level Since Reports Began in 1973," *The New York Times* (November 16, 1997a), 10.

——, "Drop in Homicide Rate Linked to Crack's Decline," *The New York Times* (October 27, 1997b), A10.

——, "Crime Fell 7 Percent in '98, Continuing a 7-Year Trend," *The New York Times* (May 17, 1999), A12.

Centers for Disease Control, "Abortion Surveillance," *Morbidity and Mortality Weekly Report,* XLIII (1994), 930–939.

Comanor, William S., and Llad Phillips, "The Impact of Income and Family Structure on Delinquency," unpublished manuscript, University of California, Santa Barbara, 1999.

Commission on Population Growth and the American Future, *Population and the American Future* (Washington, DC: U. S. Government Printing Office, 1972).

Cook, Philip, and John Laub, "The Social Ecology of Youth Violence," *Youth Violence,* Michael Tonry and Mark H. Moore, eds. (Chicago: University of Chicago Press, 1998).

Corman, Hope, and Michael Grossman, "Determinants of Neonatal Mortality Rates in the U. S.: A Reduced Form Model," *Journal of Health Economics,* IV (1985), 213–236.

Dagg, P. K., "The Psychological Sequelae of Therapeutic Abortion—Denied and Completed," *American Journal of Psychiatry,* CXLVIII (1991), 578–585.

David, Henry, Zdenek Dytrych, et al., *Born Unwanted: Developmental Effects of Denied Abortion* (New York, NY: Springer, 1988).

Donohue, John J., "Understanding the Time Path of Crime," *Journal of Criminal Law and Criminology,* LXXXVIII (1998), 1423–1452.

Dye, Jane L., and Harriet B. Presser, "The State Bonus to Reward a Decrease in 'Illegitimacy:' Flawed Methods and Questionable Effects," *Family Planning Perspectives,* XXXI (1999), 142–147.

Federal Bureau of Investigation, *Uniform Crime Reports for the United States* (Washington, DC: U. S. Government Printing Office, annual).

Fletcher, Michael A., "The Crime Conundrum," *The Washington Post* (January 16, 2000), F1.

Freeman, Richard, "The Labor Market," *Crime,* James Q. Wilson and Joan Petersilia, eds. (San Francisco, CA: ICS Press, 1995).

Goldin, Claudia, and Lawrence Katz, "The Power of the Pill: Oral Contraceptives, a Women's Career and Marriage Decisions," unpublished manuscript, Harvard University, 2000.

Greenwood, Peter, "Juvenile Crime and Juvenile Justice," *Crime,* James Q. Wilson and Joan Petersilia, eds. (San Francisco, CA: ICS Press, 1995).

Grossman, Michael, and Steven Jacobowitz, "Variations in Infant Mortality Rates among Counties of the United States: The Roles of Public Policies and Programs," *Demography*, XVIII (1981), 695–713.

Grossman, Michael, and Theodore Joyce, "Unobservables, Pregnancy Resolutions, and Birth Weight Production Functions in New York City," *Journal of Political Economy*, XCVIII (1990), 983–1007.

Gruber, Jonathan, Phillip Levine, and Douglas Staiger, "Abortion Legalization and Child Living Circumstances: Who Is the 'Marginal Child?' " *Quarterly Journal of Economics*, CXIV (1999), 263–291.

Institute of Medicine, *The Best Intentions: Unintended Pregnancy and the Well-Being of Children and Families*, Sarah S. Brown and Leon Eisenberg, eds. (Washington, DC: National Academy Press, 1995).

Joyce, Theodore, "The Impact of Induced Abortion on Black and White Birth Outcomes in the United States," *Demography*, XXIV (1987), 229–244.

Joyce, Theodore, and Robert Kaestner, "The Effect of Expansions in Medicaid Income Eligibility on Abortion," *Demography*, XXXIII (1996), 181–192.

Kane, Thomas, and Douglas Staiger, "Teen Motherhood and Abortion Access," *Quarterly Journal of Economics*, CXI (1996), 467–506.

Kaplan, John, "Abortion as a Vice Crime: A 'What if' Story," *Law and Contemporary Problems*, LI (1988), 151–179.

Kelling, George L., and William J. Bratton, "Declining Crime Rates: Insiders' Views of the New York City Story," *Journal of Criminal Law and Criminology*, LXXXVIII (1998), 1217–1232.

Levine, P. B., D. Staiger, T. J. Kane, and D. J. Zimmerman, "*Roe v. Wade* and American Fertility," National Bureau of Economic Research Working Paper No. 5615, June 1996.

Levitt, Steven, "The Effect of Prison Population Size on Crime Rates: Evidence from Prison Overcrowding Litigation," *Quarterly Journal of Economics*, CXI (1996), 319–352.

——, "Using Electoral Cycles in Police Hiring to Estimate the Effect of Police on Crime," *American Economic Review*, LXXXVII (1997), 270–290.

Loeber, Rolf, and Magda Stouthamer-Loeber, "Family Factors as Correlates and Predictors of Juvenile Conduct Problems and Delinquency," *Crime and Justice*, VII, Michael Tonry and Norval Morris, eds. (Chicago, IL: University of Chicago Press, 1986).

Lott, John R., Jr., and David B. Mustard, "Crime, Deterrence, and Right-to-Carry Concealed Handguns," *Journal of Legal Studies*, XXVI (1997), 1–68.

Marvell, Thomas, and Carlisle Moody, "Prison Population Growth and Crime Reduction," *Journal of Quantitative Criminology*, X (1994), 109–140.

Matthews, Stephen, D Ribar, and M Wilhelm, "The Effects of Economic Conditions and Access to Reproductive Health Service on State Abortion Rates and Birthrates," *Family Planning Perspectives*, XXIX (1997), 52–60.

Merz, J. F., C. A. Jackson, and J. A. Klerman, "A Review of Abortion Policy: Legality, Medicaid Funding, and Parental Involvement, 1967–1994," *Women's Rights Law Reporter*, XVII (1995), 1–61.

Michael, Robert, "Abortion Decisions in the U. S.," unpublished manuscript, University of Chicago, 1999.

Miller, Ted, Mark Cohen, and Shelli Rossman, "Victim Costs of Violent Crime and Resulting Injuries," *Health Affairs*, XII (1993), 186–197.

O'Brien, Robert, *Crime and Victimization Data* (Beverly Hills, CA: Sage, 1985).

Paulsen, Michael S., "Accusing Justice: Some Variations on the Themes of Robert M. Cover's Justice Accused," *Journal of Law and Religion*, VII (1989), 33–97.

Posner, Richard, *Sex and Reason* (Cambridge, MA: Harvard University Press, 1992).

Raine, Adrian, Patricia Brennan, and Sarnoff Mednick, "Birth Complications Combined with Early Maternal Rejection at Age 1 Year Predispose to Violent Crime at Age 18 Years," *Archives of General Psychiatry*, CI (1994), 984–988.

Raine, Adrian, Patricia Brennan, Birgitte Mednick, and Sarnoff Mednick, "High Rates of Violence, Crime, Academic Problems, and Behavioral Problems in Males with Both Early Neuromotor Deficits and Unstable Family Environments," *Archives of General Psychiatry*, CIII (1996), 544–549.

Rasanen, Pijkko, et al., "Maternal Smoking during Pregnancy and Risk of Criminal Behavior among Adult Male Offspring in the Northern Finland 1966 Birth Cohort," *American Journal of Psychiatry,* CLVI (1999), 857–862.

Ruhm, Christopher, "Are Recessions Good for your Health?" *Quarterly Journal of Economics,* CXV (2000), 617–650.

Sah, Raj, "Social Osmosis and Patterns of Crime," *Journal of Political Economy,* XCIX (1991), 1272–1295.

Sampson, Robert, and John Laub, *Crime in the Making: Pathways and Turning Points through Life* (Cambridge, MA: Harvard University Press, 1993).

Short, Allen, "Hatch Calls Bouza Hypocrite on Crime," *Star Tribune,* Minneapolis, MN (August 5, 1994), 1B.

Tracy, Paul, Marvin Wolfgang, and Robert Figlio, *Delinquency Careers in Two Birth Cohorts* (Washington, DC: U. S. Department of Justice, Office of Juvenile Justice and Delinquency Prevention, National Institute for Juvenile Justice and Delinquency Prevention, 1990).

Wolfgang, Marvin, Robert F. Figlio, and Thorsten Sellin, *Delinquency in a Birth Cohort* (Chicago, IL: University of Chicago Press, 1972.)

[14]

The Economic Theory of Illegal Goods: the Case of Drugs
Gary S. Becker, Kevin M. Murphy, and Michael Grossman
NBER Working Paper No. 10976
December 2004
JEL No. D00, D11, D60, I11, I18

ABSTRACT

This paper concentrates on both the positive and normative effects of punishments that enforce laws to make production and consumption of particular goods illegal, with illegal drugs as the main example. Optimal public expenditures on apprehension and conviction of illegal suppliers obviously depend on the extent of the difference between the social and private value of consumption of illegal goods, but they also depend crucially on the elasticity of demand for these goods. In particular, when demand is inelastic, it does not pay to enforce any prohibition unless the social value is negative and not merely less than the private value. We also compare outputs and prices when a good is legal and taxed with outputs and prices when the good is illegal. We show that a monetary tax on a legal good could cause a greater reduction in output and increase in price than would optimal enforcement, even recognizing that producers may want to go underground to try to avoid a monetary tax. This means that fighting a war on drugs by legalizing drug use and taxing consumption may be more effective than continuing to prohibit the legal use of drugs.

Gary S. Becker
Department of Economics
University of Chicago
1126 East 59th Street
Chicago, IL 60637
gbecker@uchicago.edu

Kevin M. Murphy
Graduate School of Business
University of Chicago
Chicago, IL 60637
and NBER
kevin.murphy@gsb.uchicago.edu

Michael Grossman
NBER
365 Fifth Avenue
New York, NY 10016
and CUNY Graduate Center
mgrossman@gc.cuny.edu

1. Introduction

The effects of excise taxes on prices and outputs have been extensively studied. An equally large literature discusses the normative effects of these taxes measured by their effects on consumer and producer surplus. However, the emphasis has been on monetary excise taxes, while non-monetary taxes in the form of criminal and other punishments for illegal production of different goods have been discussed only a little (important exceptions are MacCoun and Reuter, 2001 and Miron, 2001).

This paper concentrates on both the positive and normative effects of punishments that enforce laws to make production and consumption of particular goods illegal. We use the supply and demand for illegal drugs as our main example, a topic of considerable interest in its own right, although our general analysis applies to the underground economy, prostitution, restrictions on sales of various goods to minors, and other illegal activities.

Drugs are a particularly timely example not only because they attract lots of attention, but also because every U.S. president since Richard Nixon has fought this war with police, the FBI, the CIA, the military, a federal agency (the DEA), and military and police forces of other nations. Despite the wide scope of these efforts–and major additional efforts in other nations–no president or drug "czar" has claimed victory, nor is a victory in sight.

Why has the War on Drugs been so difficult to win? How can international drug traffickers command the resources to corrupt some governments, and thwart the extensive efforts of the most powerful nation? Why do efforts to reduce the supply of drugs lead to violence and greater influence for street

1

gangs and drug cartels? To some extent, the answer lies in the basic theory of enforcement developed in this paper.

Section 2 sets out a simple graphical analysis that shows how the elasticity of demand for an illegal good is crucial to understanding the effects of punishment to producers on the overall cost of supplying and consuming that good. Section 3 formalizes that analysis, and adds expenditures by illegal suppliers to avoid detection and punishment.

That section also derives the optimal public expenditures on apprehension and conviction of illegal suppliers. The government is assumed to maximize a welfare function that takes account of differences between the social and private values of consumption of illegal goods. Optimal expenditures obviously depend on the extent of this difference, but they also depend crucially on the elasticity of demand for these goods. In particular, when demand is inelastic, it does not pay to enforce any prohibition unless the social value is negative and not merely less than the private value.

Section 4 compares outputs and prices when a good is legal and taxed with outputs and prices when the good is illegal. It shows that a monetary tax on a legal good could cause a greater reduction in output and increase in price than would optimal enforcement, even recognizing that producers may want to go underground to try to avoid a monetary tax. Indeed, the optimal monetary tax that maximizes social welfare tends to exceed the optimal non-monetary tax. This means, in particular, that fighting a war on drugs by legalizing drug use and taxing consumption may be more effective than continuing to prohibit the legal use of drugs.

2

Section 5 generalizes the analysis in sections 2-4 to allow producers to be heterogeneous with different cost functions. Since enforcement is costly, it is efficient to direct greater enforcement efforts toward marginal producers than toward infra-marginal producers. That implies greater enforcement against weak and small producers because marginal producers tend to be smaller and economically weaker. By contrast, if the purpose of a monetary tax partly is to raise revenue for the government, higher monetary taxes should be placed on infra-marginal producers because these taxes raise revenue without much affecting outputs and prices.

Many drugs are addictive and their consumption is greatly affected by peer pressure. Section 6 incorporates a few analytical implications of the economic theory of addiction and peer pressure. They help explain why demand elasticities for some drugs may be relatively high, and why even altruistic parents often oppose their children's desire to use drugs.

Section 7 considers when governments should to try to discourage consumption of goods through advertising, like the "just say no" campaign against drug use. Our analysis implies that advertising campaigns can be useful against illegal goods that involve enforcement expenditures to discourage production. However, they are generally not desirable against legal goods when consumption is discouraged through optimal monetary taxes.

3

Even though our analysis implies that monetary taxes on legal goods can be quite effective, drugs and many other goods are illegal. Section 8 argues that the explanation is related to the greater political clout of the middle classes.

2. A Graphical Analysis

We first analyze the effects of enforcement expenditures with a simple model of the market for illegal drugs. The demand for drugs is assumed to depend on the market price of drugs that is affected by the costs imposed on traffickers through enforcement and punishment, such as confiscation of drugs and imprisonment. The demand for drugs also depends on the costs imposed by the government on users.

Assume that drugs are supplied by a competitive drug industry with constant unit costs $c(E)$ that depend on the resources, E, that governments devote to catching smugglers and drug suppliers. In such a competitive market, the transaction price of drugs will equal unit costs, or $c(E)$, and the full price of drugs P_e, to consumers will equal $c(E) + T$, where T measures the costs imposed on users through reduced convenience and/or criminal punishments. Without a war on drugs, $T=0$ and $E=0$, so that $P_e = c(0)$. This free market equilibrium is illustrated in Figure 1 at point f.

With a war on drugs focused on interdiction and the prosecution of drug traffickers, $E>0$ but $T=0$. These efforts would raise the street price of drugs and reduce consumption from its free market level at f to the "war"

4

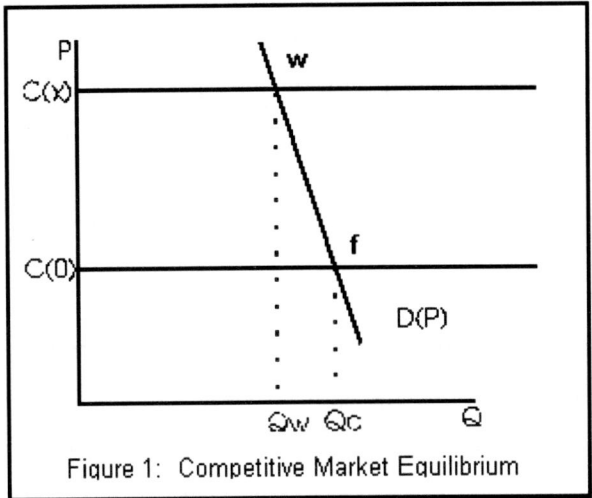

Figure 1: Competitive Market Equilibrium

equilibrium at w, as shown in Figure 1.

This figure shows that interdiction and prosecution efforts reduce consumption. In particular, if Δ measures percentage changes, the increase in costs is given by Δc, and $\Delta Q = \varepsilon \, \Delta c$, where $\varepsilon < 0$ is the price elasticity of demand for drugs. The change in expenditures on drugs from making drugs illegal is:

$$\Delta R = (1+\varepsilon) \, \Delta c.$$

When drugs are supplied in a perfectly competitive market with constant unit costs, drug suppliers earn zero profits. Therefore, resources devoted to drug production, smuggling, and distribution will equal the revenues from drug sales in both the free and illegal equilibria. Hence, the change in resources devoted to drug smuggling, including production and distribution, induced by a "war" on drugs will equal the change in consumer expenditures. Therefore, as eq. (1) shows, total resources devoted to supplying drugs will rise with a war on drugs when demand for drugs is inelastic ($\varepsilon > -1$), and total resources will fall when the demand for drugs is elastic ($\varepsilon < -1$).

When the demand for drugs is elastic, more vigorous efforts to fight the war (i.e. increases in E) will reduce the total resources spent by drug traffickers to bring drugs to market. In contrast, and paradoxically, when demand for drugs is inelastic, total resources spent by drug traffickers will increase as the war increases in severity, and consumption falls. With inelastic demand, resources are actually drawn into the drug business as enforcement reduces drug consumption.

3. The Elasticity of Demand and Optimal Enforcement

This section shows how the elasticity of demand determines optimal enforcement to reduce the consumption of specified goods -again we use the example of illegal drugs. We assume that governments maximize social welfare that depends on the social rather than consumer evaluation of the utility from consuming these goods. Producers and distributors take privately optimal actions to avoid governmental enforcement efforts. In determining optimal enforcement expenditures, the government takes into account how avoidance activities respond to changes in enforcement expenditures.

We use the following notation throughout this section:
Q = consumption of drugs

6

P = price of drugs to consumers

Demand: $Q = D(P)$

F = monetary equivalent of punishment to convicted drug traffickers

Production is assumed to be CRS. This is why we measure all cost variables per unit output.

c = competitive cost of drugs without tax or enforcement, so c=c(0) from above

A = private expenditures on avoidance of enforcement per unit output

E = level of government enforcement per unit output

$p(E,A)$ = probability that a drug trafficker is caught smuggling, with $\partial p/\partial E > 0$, and $\partial p/\partial A < 0$.

We assume that when smugglers are caught their drugs are confiscated and they are penalized F (per unit of drugs smuggled). With competition and CRS, price will be determined by minimum unit cost. For given levels of E and A, expected unit costs are given by

(2)   Expected unit cost $\equiv u = (c + A + p(E,A) F) / (1-p(E,A))$.

Working with the odds ratio of being caught rather than the probability greatly simplifies the analysis. In particular, $\theta(E,A) = p(E,A)/(1-p(E,A))$ is this odds ratio, so

(3) $u = (c + A) (1+\theta) + \theta F$.

7

Expected unit costs are linear in the odds ratio, θ, since it gives the probability of being caught per unit of drugs sold. Expected unit costs are also linear in the penalty for being caught, F.

The competitive price will be equal to the minimum level of unit cost, or

(4a) $P = \min_{A} (c + A) (1+\theta) + \theta F.$

The FOC for cost minimization (with respect to A), taking E and F as given, is

(5) $- \partial\theta/\partial A \, (c + A + F) = (1 + \theta).$

We interpret expenditures on avoidance, A, as including the entire increase in direct costs from operating an illegal enterprise. This would include costs from not being able to use the court system to enforce contracts, and costs associated with using less efficient methods of production, transportation, and distribution that have the advantage of being less easily monitored by the government. The competitive price will exceed the costs under a legal environment due to these avoidance costs, A, the loss of drugs due to confiscation, and penalties imposed on those caught.

Hence, the competitive price will equal the minimum expected unit costs, given from eq. (4a) as

(4b) $P^*(E) = (c + A^*) (1+\theta(E, A^*)) + \theta(E, A^*) F,$

where A* is the cost minimizing level of expenditures. The competitive equilibrium price, given by this equation, exceeds the competitive equilibrium legal price, c, by A (the added cost of underground production); $(c+A)\theta$, the expected value of the drugs confiscated; and θF, the expected costs of punishment.

An increase in punishment to drug offenders, F, raises the cost and lowers the profits of an individual drug producer. The second order condition for A* in eq. (5) to be a maximum implies that avoidance expenditures increase as F increases. But in competitive equilibrium, a higher F has no effect on expected profits because market price rises by the increase in expected costs due to the higher punishment. In fact, those drug producers and smugglers who manage to avoid apprehension make greater realized profits when punishment increases because the increase in market price exceeds the increase in their unit avoidance costs.

The greater profits of producers who avoid punishment, and even the absence of any effect on expected profits of all producers, does not mean that greater punishment has no desired effects. For the higher market price, given by eq. (4), induced by the increase in punishment reduces the use of drugs. The magnitude of this effect on consumption depends on the elasticity of demand: the more inelastic is demand, the smaller is this effect.

9

The role of the elasticity and the effect on consumption is seen explicitly by calculating the effect of greater enforcement expenditures on the equilibrium price. In particular, by the envelope theorem, we have[1]

(6a) $dP/dE = \partial\theta/\partial E \, (c + A^* + F) > 0$, and hence

(6b) $d\ln P/d\ln E = \varepsilon_\theta \, \theta \, (c + A^* + F)/P = \varepsilon_\theta \, [\theta(c+A^*+F)/P] = \varepsilon_\theta \, \lambda$

Here, $\lambda = \theta(c + A^* + F)/P < 1$, and ε_θ is the elasticity of the odds ratio, θ, with respect to E. Again denoting the elasticity of demand for drugs by ε_d, eq. (6b) implies that

(7) $d\ln Q/d\ln E = \varepsilon_d \, d\ln P/d\ln E = \varepsilon_d \, \varepsilon_\theta \, \lambda < 0.$

If enforcement is a pure public good, then the costs of enforcement to the government will be independent of the level of drug activity (i.e. $C(E,Q)$ $=C(E)$). On the other hand, if enforcement is a purely private good (with respect to drugs smuggled), an assumption of CRS in production implies that $C(E,Q) = QC(E)$. We adopt a mixture of these two formulations. In addition to these costs, the government has additional costs from punishing those caught. We assume that punishment costs are linear in the number caught

---

[1] Differentiate eq. 4a) with respect to E and note that in general the optimal value of A will vary as E varies:

$$\frac{dP}{dE} = (c + A^* + F)\frac{d\theta}{dE} + \left[(1+\theta) + (c + A^* + F)\frac{d\theta}{dA}\right]\frac{dA}{dE}.$$

From the first order condition for A, the sum of the terms inside the brackets on the right hand side of the equation for dP/dE is zero.

10

and punished (θQ). With a linear combination of all the enforcement cost components,

(8) $C(Q,E,\theta) = C_1 E + C_2 QE + C_3 \theta Q.$

Eq. (8) implies that enforcement costs are linear in the level of enforcement activities, although they could be convex in E without changing the basic results. Enforcement costs also depend on the level of drug activity (Q), and the fraction of drug smugglers punished (through θ).

The equilibrium level of enforcement depends on the government's objective. We assume that the government wants to reduce the consumption of goods like drugs relative to what they would be in a competitive market. We do not model the source of these preferences, but assume a "social planner" who may value drug consumption by less than the private willingness to pay of drug users, measured by the price, P. If V(Q) is the social value function, then $\partial V / \partial Q \equiv V_q \le P$, with V_q strictly $< P$ if there is a perceived externality from drug consumption, and hence drug consumption is socially valued at strictly less than the private willingness to pay. When $V_q < 0$, the negative externality from consumption exceeds the positive utility to consumers.

With these preferences, the government chooses E to maximize the value of consumption minus the sum of production and enforcement costs. Thus it chooses E to solve

11

(9) $\max_{E} W = V(Q(E)) - u(E)Q(E) - C(Q(E), E, \theta(E, A^*(E)))$.

The government incorporates into its decision the privately optimal change in avoidance costs by drug producers and smugglers to any increase in enforcement costs. With the assumption of CRS on the production side, then $u(E)Q(E) = P(E)Q(E)$, and we assume C is given by eq. (8). Thus the planner's problem simplifies to

(10) $\max_{E} W = V(Q(E)) - P(E) Q(E) - C_1 E - C_2 Q(E)E - C_3 \theta(E, A^*(E))Q(E)$

The first order condition is

(11) $V_q \, dQ/dE - MR \, dQ/dE - C_1 - C_2 (Q + (dQ/dE)E) - C_3 \left[\theta \dfrac{dQ}{dE} + Q\left(\dfrac{\partial\theta}{\partial E} + \dfrac{\partial\theta}{\partial A} \bullet \dfrac{dA}{dE} \right) \right] =$

$0 \rightarrow$

(12a) $C_1 + C_2 (Q + EdQ/dE) + C_3 (\theta \, dQ/dE + Q \, d\theta/dE) = V_q \, dQ/dE - MR \, dQ/dE$,

where $MR \equiv d(PQ)/dQ$ denotes marginal revenue.

The left hand side of eq. (12a) is the marginal cost of enforcement, including the effects on output and the odds ratio. The right hand side is the marginal benefit of the reduction in consumption, including the effect on production costs. This equation becomes more revealing if we temporarily assume that marginal enforcement costs are zero. Then the RHS of this equation equals zero, which simplifies to

12b) $V_q = MR \equiv P(1+1/\varepsilon_d)$, or $V_q/P = 1+1/\varepsilon_d$,

and V_q/P is the ratio of the social marginal willingness to pay to the private marginal willingness to pay of drug users (measured by price).

If $V_q \geq 0$, so that drug consumption has non-negative marginal social value, and if demand is inelastic, so that $MR < 0$, eq. (12b) implies that optimal enforcement would be zero, and free market consumption would be the social equilibrium. There is a loss in social utility from reduced consumption since the social value of additional consumption is positive - even if it is less than the private value–while production and distribution costs increase as output falls when demand is inelastic.

The conclusion that with positive marginal social willingness to pay–no matter how small–inelastic demand, and punishment to traffickers, the optimal social decision would be to leave the free market output unchanged does not assume the government is inefficient, or that enforcement of these taxes is costly. Indeed, the conclusion holds in the case we just discussed where governments are assumed to catch violators easily and with no cost to themselves, but costs to traffickers. Costs imposed on suppliers bring about the higher price required to reduce consumption. But since marginal revenue is negative when demand is inelastic, total costs would rise along with revenue as price rises and output is reduced, while total social value would

13

fall as output falls if V_q were positive. The optimal social decision is clearly then to do nothing, even if consumption imposes significant external costs on others.

This result differs radically from well-known optimal taxation results with monetary taxes. Then, if the monetary tax is costless to implement, and if the marginal social value of consumption is less than price–no matter how small the difference–it is always optimal to reduce output below its free market level.

Even if demand is elastic, it may not be socially optimal to reduced output if consumption of the good has positive marginal social value. For example, if the elasticity is as high as $-11/2$, eq. (12b) shows that it is still optimal to do nothing as long as the ratio of the marginal social to the marginal private value of additional consumption exceeds 1/3. It takes very low social values of consumption, or very high demand elasticities, to justify intervention, even with negligible enforcement costs.

Intervention is more likely to be justified when $V_q < 0$: when the negative external effects of consumption exceed the private willingness to pay. If demand is inelastic, marginal revenue is also negative, and eq. (12b) shows that a necessary condition to intervene in this market is that marginal social value be less than marginal revenue at the free market output level.
There are no reliable estimates of the price elasticity of demand for illegal drugs, mainly because data on prices and quantities consumed of illegal goods are scarce. However, estimates generally indicate an elasticity of less than one in absolute value, although one or two studies estimate a larger

elasticity (see Caulkins, 1995, van Ours, 1995). Moreover, few studies of drugs have utilized the theory of rational addiction, which implies that long run elasticities exceed short run elasticities for addictive goods (see section 6).[2] Since considerable resources are spent fighting the war on drugs and reducing consumption, the drug war can only be considered socially optimal with a long run demand elasticity of about −1/2 if the negative social externality of drug use is more than twice the positive value to drug users. Of course, perhaps the true elasticity is much higher, or the war may be based on interest group power rather than maximizing social welfare (see section 8).

Punishment to reduce consumption is easier to justify when demand is elastic and hence marginal revenue is positive. If enforcement costs continue to be ignored, total costs of production and distribution must then fall as output is reduced. If $V_q < 0$, social welfare would be maximized by eliminating consumption of that good because costs decline and social value rises as output falls. However, even with elastic demand and negative marginal social value, rising enforcement costs as output falls could lead to an internal equilibrium.

Figure 2 illustrates another case where it may be optimal to eliminate consumption (ignoring enforcement costs). In this case, demand is assumed

---

[2] Grossman and Chaloupka (1998) present a variety of estimates of rational addiction models of the demand for cocaine by young adults in panel data. They emphasize an estimate of the long-run price elasticity of total consumption (participation multiplied by frequency given participation) of -1.35. When, however, they include individual fixed effects to control for unmeasured area-specific effects that may be correlated with price and consumption, the elasticity becomes -0.67. One problem with the latter estimate is that biases due to random measurement error in the price of cocaine are exacerbated in the fixed-effects specification.

15

to be elastic, and at the free market equilibrium, V_q is positive and greater than MR, but it is less than the free market price. MR is assumed to rise more rapidly than V_q does as output falls, so that they intersect at Q_u. That point would equate MR and V_q, but it violates the SOC for a social maximum.

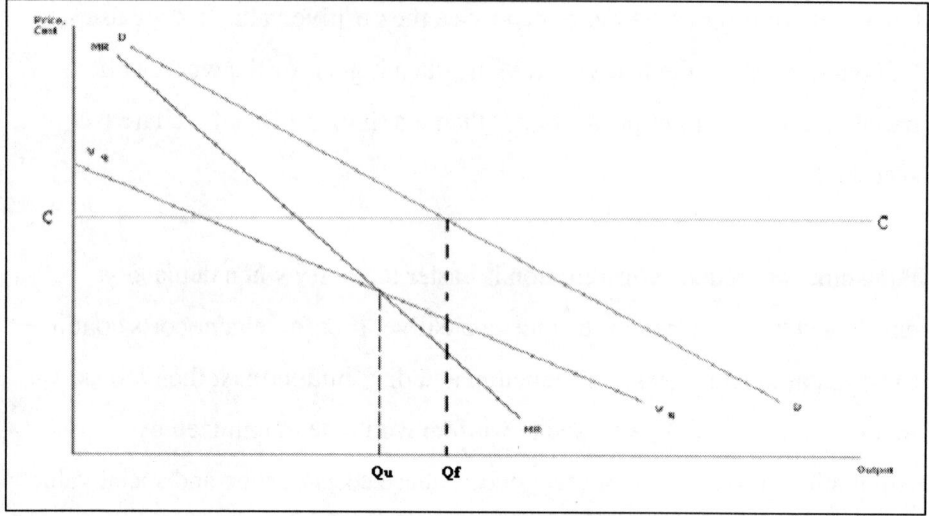

Figure 2

The optimum in this case is to go to one of the corners, and either do nothing and remain with the free market output, or fight the war hard enough to eliminate consumption. Which of these extremes is better depends on a comparison of the area between V_q and MR to the left of Q_u, with the corresponding area to the right. If the latter is bigger, output remains at the free market level, even if the social value of consumption at that point were much less than its private value. It would be optimal to remain at the free

16

market output when reducing output from the free market level lowers social value by sufficiently more than it lowers production costs.

Eq. (12a) incorporates enforcement costs into the first order conditions for a social maximum. It is interesting that marginal enforcement costs also depend on the elasticity of demand, and they too are greater when demand is more inelastic. To see this, rewrite the LHS of eq. (12a) as

$$MC_E \quad = C_1 + C_2Q + C_2EdQ/dE + C_3(\theta \; dQ/dE + Qd\theta/dE)$$

$$= C_1 + C_2Q \; (1 + dlnQ/dlnE) + C_3(\theta dQ/dE + Qd\theta/dE)$$

$$= C_1 + C_2Q \; (1 + dlnQ/dlnE) + C_3\theta \; Q/E(dlnQ/dlnE + \varepsilon_{\theta*})$$

$$(13) \qquad = C_1 + C_2Q \; (1 + \lambda \; \varepsilon_\theta \; \varepsilon_d) + C_3\theta Q/E \; \varepsilon_{\theta*} \; (1 + \lambda \; \varepsilon_d \; \varepsilon_\theta/\varepsilon_{\theta*}).$$

Here $\varepsilon_{\theta*}$ is the total elasticity of θ with respect to E, which includes the indirect effect of E on the privately optimal changes in avoidance costs, A, by producers and distributors. That is, since

$$d\theta/dE = \partial\theta/\partial E + (\partial\theta/\partial A)(dA/dE) \rightarrow \varepsilon_{\theta*} = \varepsilon_\theta + \varepsilon_A \; dlnA/dlnE.$$

Eq. (13) shows that marginal enforcement costs are greater, the smaller is ε_d in absolute value because consumption falls more rapidly as enforcement increases when demand is more elastic. Since expenditures on apprehension and punishment depend on output, a slower fall in output with more inelastic

17

demand causes enforcement expenditures to grow more rapidly. Indeed, eq.(13) implies that if demand is sufficiently elastic, marginal enforcement costs can be negative when enforcement increases since the drop in the scale of production can more than offset the increased cost per unit.

So the elasticity of demand is key on both the cost and benefit sides of enforcement. When demand is elastic, total industry costs fall as consumption is reduced, and enforcement costs increase more slowly, or they may even fall. Extensive government intervention in this market to reduce output would then be attractive if the marginal social value of consumption is low. In contrast, when demand is inelastic, total production costs rise as consumption falls, and enforcement costs rise more rapidly. With inelastic demand, a war to reduce consumption would be justified only when marginal social value is very negative. Even then, such a war will absorb a lot of resources.

4. A Comparison with Monetary Taxes

It is instructive to compare these results for enforcement effects with well-known results for monetary taxes on legal goods. The social welfare function for these monetary taxes that corresponds to the welfare function for enforcement of the prohibition against drugs in eq. 9 is, ignoring avoidance and enforcement costs,

$$(14a) \quad W_m = V(Q) - cQ - (1-\delta)\tau Q,$$

where τ is the monetary tax per unit output of drugs, and δ gives the value to society per each dollar taxed away from taxpayers. Since in competitive equilibrium $P = c + \tau$, eq. (14a) can be rewritten as

(14b) $W_m = V(Q) - cQ - (1 - \delta)(P(Q)Q - cQ)$

The first order condition for Q is

(15a) $V_q = c + (1 - \delta)(MR - c)$,

or

(15b) $\tau = P - V_q + (1 - \delta)\left(P(1 + \dfrac{1}{\varepsilon_d}) - c \right)$

If tax receipts are a pure transfer, so that $\delta=1$, eq. (15a) or (15b) gives the classical result that the optimal monetary tax equals the difference between marginal private (measured by P) and marginal social value. With a pure transfer, the elasticity of demand is irrelevant. The optimal monetary tax is positive if the marginal social value of consumption at the free market competitive position is less than the competitive price.

The elasticity of demand becomes relevant if there are net social costs or benefits from the transfer of resources to the government. If government tax receipts are socially valued at less than dollar for dollar ($\delta < 1$), and if demand is inelastic ($\varepsilon_d > -1$), the optimal tax would be positive only if the marginal

19

social value of consumption were sufficiently less than the marginal private value. The converse holds if tax revenue is highly valued so that $\delta > 1$. The optimal tax on this good might then be positive, even if demand is inelastic and social value exceeds private value.

Of course, if the monetary tax gets too high, some drug producers might try to avoid the tax by trafficking in the underground economy. An optimal monetary tax on a legal good is still always better than optimal enforcement against an illegal good. The proof assumes that the government can choose optimal punishments for producers who sell in the underground economy, and that demand for the good is not reduced by making the good illegal. Let E* denote the optimal value of enforcement that maximizes the government's welfare function given by eq. (10), and recall that this optimal value takes account of avoidance expenditures by producers. Then, from eq. (4b), the optimal price is $P^* = (c + A^*)(1 + \theta(E^*, A^*)) + \theta(E^*, A^*)F$.

Assume that enforcement against drug producers who try to avoid the monetary tax by selling in the underground economy is sufficient to raise the unit costs of these producers to the same P^*. If the monetary tax is then set at slightly less than $\tau^* = P^* - c$, firms that produce in the legal sector will be slightly more profitable than illegal underground firms. The latter would be driven out of business, or become legal producers. Even ignoring the revenue from the monetary tax, enforcement costs would then be lower with this monetary tax than with optimal enforcement since few would produce illegally. Indeed, in this case, governments only have to incur the fixed component of enforcement costs, $C_1 E^*$, since in equilibrium no one produces underground.

The government could even enforce an optimal monetary tax that raises market price above the price with optimal enforcement when drugs are illegal. This is sometimes denied with the argument that producers would go underground if monetary taxes are too high. But the logic of the analysis above on deterring underground production shows that this claim is not correct. Whatever the level of the optimal monetary tax, it could be enforced by raising punishment and apprehension sufficiently to make the net price to producers in the illegal sector below the legal price with the optimal monetary tax. Since no one would then produce in the illegal sector, actual enforcement expenditures would be limited to the fixed component, $C_1 E^*$.

To be sure, the optimal monetary tax would depend on this fixed component of enforcement expenditures. But perhaps the most important implication of this analysis relates to a comparison of optimal monetary taxes and enforcement against illegal goods. If enforcement costs are ignored, and if $\delta > 0$, a comparison of the FOC's in eqs. (12b) and (15a) clearly shows that the optimal monetary tax would exceed the optimal "tax" due to enforcement and punishment if demand were inelastic since marginal revenue is then always less than c, unit legal costs of production. The incorporation of enforcement costs only reinforces this conclusion about a higher monetary tax since enforcement costs of cutting illegal output are greater when all production is illegal rather than when some producers go underground to avoid monetary taxes.

21

If $\delta=1$ and there are no costs of enforcing the optimal monetary tax, optimal output (Q_f) satisfies $V_q = c$ (see eq. (15a)). When some enforcement costs must be incurred to insure that no one produces underground, optimal output (Q^*) satisfies

16) $(V_q - c)dQ/dE = C_1.$

Since an increase in E lowers Q, V_q must be less than c. That implies that Q^* exceeds Q_f. Note that optimal legal output is zero when V_q is negative, and there are no enforcement costs. But eq. (16) could be satisfied at a positive output level when V_q is negative as long as dQ/dE is sufficiently negative at that output.

Various wars on drugs have been only partially effective in cutting drug use, but the social cost has been large in terms of resources spent, corruption of officials, and imprisonment of many producers, distributors, and drug users. Even some individuals who are not libertarians have called for decriminalization and legalization of drugs because they believe the gain from these wars has not been worth these costs. Others prefer less radical solutions, including decriminalization only of milder drugs, such as marijuana, while preserving the war on more powerful and more addictive substances, such as cocaine.

Our analysis shows, moreover, that using a monetary tax to discourage legal drug production could reduce drug consumption by more than even an efficient war on drugs. The market price of legal drugs with a monetary excise tax could be greater than the price induced by an optimal war on

22

drugs, even when producers could ignore the monetary tax and consider producing in the underground economy. Indeed, the optimal monetary tax would exceed the optimal price due to a war on drugs if the demand for drugs is inelastic- as it appears to be- and if the demand function is unaffected by whether drugs are legal or not- the evidence on this is not clear. With these assumptions, the level of consumption that maximizes social welfare would be smaller if drugs were legalized and taxed optimally instead of the present policy of trying to enforce a ban on drugs.

5. Heterogeneous Taxes and Suppliers

The assumptions made so far of identical firms and of a constant enforcement tax per unit of output has brought out important principles that mainly continue to hold more generally. This section deals briefly with a few novel aspects of optimal enforcement when producers have different costs.

The US experience with the prohibition of alcoholic beverages shows that most companies which produced the good when it was legal exited the industry after prohibition. Legal producers of beer and other alcoholic beverages were replaced by companies who were more willing to, and more skilled at, delivering beer and liquor to underground illegal retailers, while evading or bribing the police and courts that enforced prohibition. More generally, suppliers of illegal goods would generally differ from those who would produce and sell the goods when they were illegal.
Presumably, illegal firms would have higher production costs under the contractual and other aspects of the legal and economic environment when production is legal than the firms that produced the goods when they were

23

legal. Otherwise, producers under prohibition would have been the low cost producers, and they would have dominated the legal industry.

By limiting the firms that want to enter, prohibition of a good is likely to lower the elasticity of supply. If the elasticity were less than infinite because some firms are relatively low cost producers in an illegal environment, the government should be more active in its enforcement against marginal producers and marginal outputs. Any real expenditures on more efficient infra-marginal producers and infra-marginal units is a waste and serves no efficiency purpose.

With heavier enforcement against marginal producers, the change in producer costs is less than the change in consumer expenditures as the equilibrium price is forced up by enforcement activities. Social costs would then be measured by the smaller rise in producer costs, not by the larger rise in consumer expenditures, as long as the increase in producer rents or profits are considered a transfer from consumers to producers, and not a social cost of the reduction in consumption. However, if no social value were placed on these profits–such as profits to a drug cartel–social cost would still be measured by consumer expenditures, and it would not then be possible to reduce social costs by enforcing more intensively against marginal producers than against more efficient producers.

Of course, to go after marginal producers more heavily requires information on the costs of different producers in an illegal environment. Although the direct information on such costs may be limited, indirect evidence may be considerable since marginal firms tend to be smaller, younger, less

24

profitable, and financially weaker. It would then be optimal to impose higher unit taxes on smaller, younger, and weaker suppliers. Weaker enforcement against larger producers of drugs is often taken as evidence that these producers bribed and corrupted police and other officials–which may be true. At the same time, our analysis shows that such weaker enforcement may be socially optimal. Government policy should recognize that heavy enforcement against larger and more efficient producers is a wasteful way to raise price and reduce consumption of drugs.

Note the contrast with well-known results on optimal monetary taxation of heterogeneous producers. If tax revenue is highly valued, higher monetary taxes should be extracted from infra-marginal producers than from marginal producers because more efficient producers collect profits that can be taxed away without adverse effects on their incentives. In the extreme case of completely inelastic supply, monetary taxes have no effects on incentives or output, and produce abundant tax revenue.

6. Addictions and Peer Pressure

Some drugs are highly addictive, although the degree of addiction of many of them is controversial. Most drug users start in their teens or early twenties, and peer pressure is especially strong among teenagers (see e.g., Coleman, 1961). This is why it is important to integrate both peer pressure and addiction into an analysis of the positive and normative aspects of illegal markets for drugs.

The combination of addiction to a good and peer pressure to consume that good may lower the short run elasticity of demand for drugs, but they raise

25

its long-run response to price and other shocks that are common to different consumers. These forces may raise the long run elasticity of demand for drugs to sizeable level, although not necessarily greater than one. For example, essentially all estimates of the long run demand elasticity are less than one for a highly addictive good like smoking, which is apparently also greatly affected by peer pressure.

Some models of addiction imply that individuals consume greater quantities of addictive goods than they "really" would like to. The usual claim is that multiple inconsistent selves battle for control over an individual's decision-making process, such as when they use hyperbolic discounting of future utilities. The implications for optimal excise taxes of these models are generally not unique to harmful addictive goods, and apply to the consumption of all goods that trade off present utility for future disutility. If these approaches are correct, they would provide additional reasons why the utility from the social consumption of harmful addictive goods is below private utilities.

Even if increased consumption of a good by members of a peer group lowers the utility of other members, that could stimulate greater consumption of this good by all other members through raising the good's marginal utility to these members. In this case, goods that are sensitive to peer pressure, such as drugs, would be consumed excessively from the viewpoint of members of the peer group as well. This would be a further reason why the social value of the consumption of drugs was below the private values of individuals. Of course, if greater consumption by peers raised rather than lowered utilities of other members, social utility would exceed private utilities due to the effects of peer pressure.

If parents believe their children use drugs because of the negative influence of peer pressure, this analysis provides one reason why even altruistic parents try to reduce drug use by their children. Promoting effective reductions in drug use by making drugs illegal or placing a high excise tax on drugs would then raise the utilities of their children and other members of the peer group. Also, altruistic parents may be concerned about their children consuming addictive goods that lower the children's future utilities because altruistic parents may be "forced" to help them out in the future when the children's utilities are lower.

7. Just Say No

Monetary excise tax theory leaves little room for government policies to reduce the demand function for goods that are taxed. If the purpose is to raise revenue, why try to reduce demand that reduces tax revenue? In addition, it is more efficient to cut consumption because of an externality with optimal monetary taxes that also raise revenue than with costly programs that reduce the demand function.

These advantages do not apply to illegal goods with enforcement and punishment costs. These expenditures could be reduced by successful government efforts to discourage consumption of these goods. The campaign to "just say no" to drugs is an example of an attempt to reduce consumption.

27

Illegal goods like drugs have two classes of policy instruments: enforcement and punishment strategies that reduce consumption by raising the real costs and prices of supplying the goods, and expenditures on "education," "advertising," and "persuasion" that reduce demand for these goods. If π represents these expenditures, the social value function W in eq. (10) would be modified to

$$W = V(Q(E, \pi), \pi) - P(E)Q(E, \pi) - c(\pi).$$

In this equation, $c(\pi)$ is the cost of producing π units of persuasion against consuming Q, and for simplicity we ignore enforcement costs (C). We allow W to depend directly on π as well as indirectly through π's effect on Q.

The FOC for maximizing W with respect to π is

$$(18) \quad - Q_\pi(P - V_q) + V_\pi = c_\pi,$$

where a subscript denotes a partial derivative.

The term on the RHS of this equation, $c_\pi > 0$, gives the marginal cost of producing π, and the LHS gives the marginal benefit of additional π. If persuasion is effective in reducing consumption then $Q_\pi < 0$. Reduction in consumption is desirable if the marginal social value of consumption, V_q, is less than its private value, measured by P. The sign of the term V_π is positive or negative as society likes or dislikes the "persuasion". However,

28

persuasion can have social value even if it is disliked because the LHS of eq. (18) can be positive, even if $V_\pi < 0$, if V_q is sufficiently less than P.

What is interesting about the FOC for persuasive activities to reduce demand is that these activities may be effective in raising social welfare when enforcement activities are least effective. We have shown that it is socially optimal not to spend resources to reduce consumption of an illegal good if its demand is inelastic, and if the marginal social value of its output is positive ($V_q > 0$).

Eq. (18) shows, however, that the elasticity of demand has no effect on the effectiveness of persuasive activities to reduce consumption of an illegal good. Therefore, even if demand is inelastic, and even if the marginal social value of its consumption were positive, there still could be a strong case for persuasive efforts to reduce consumption of an illegal good. This depends on whether $V_q < P$, or whether marginal social value is less than private value. If it is less, persuasion would raise social welfare if it is cheap to produce, and if persuasion efforts do not have a large negative social value. Note that $V_q < P$ is the same criterion that determines whether monetary taxes are desirable.

Persuasion may also raise the effectiveness of enforcement expenditures by raising the elasticity of demand. Becker and Murphy (1992) show that advertising tends to raise the elasticity of demand because it tries to target marginal consumers and increase their demands. It is more efficient for governments to try to reduce the demand for illegal goods of marginal consumers than of other consumers since the former are easier to affect

29

because they get little surplus from consuming these goods. This means that persuasion does not have to reduce their willingness to pay by a lot to discourage them from consuming these goods. Persuasion could be an effective instrument of government policy not only by reducing demand for illegal goods, but also by raising the effectiveness of enforcement through raising the elasticity of demand for these goods.

8. Why Are Goods Illegal Rather Than Legal And Taxed?

We demonstrated that if the social value of a good is less than its private value, it would be most effective to allow the good to be legal, and impose the right monetary tax to account for the discrepancy between private and social values. Yet throughout history goods like drugs, prostitution, and gambling have frequently been illegal. One answer to this discrepancy between actual and optimal policies depends on their different impacts on the consumption of middle class and poorer persons. Higher and middle level income families often prefer certain goods to be illegal rather than taxed, while poorer persons prefer the opposite. If the poor have much less political power, these goods would end up being illegal.

Even if the increase in money price were the same when a good was illegal and when it was legal and taxed, the consumption of richer and poorer consumers would be affected differently. Suppose a monetary tax raises the price of a good by ΔP to all consumers, and that appropriate enforcement policies prevented a black market in the good. This price increase will tend to have different income and substitution effects to members of different income groups. Even if preferences did not differ by income class, the poor would be more affected by a monetary price increase when the income

30

elasticity of demand is less than one, and when the value of the time spent consuming the good is a relatively large part of the total cost of consumption. Estimated income elasticities for cocaine, marijuana, and heroin are generally much less than one (see Grossman and Chaloupka, 1998, Liccardo Pacula, Grossman, Chaloupka, O'Malley, Johnston, and Farrelly, 2000, and Saffer and Chaloupka, 1999. However, van Ours, 1995, finds a high income elasticity for opium in the Dutch West Indies).

Up to a point the income and substitution effects work in the same way when the street price of drugs rises because it is illegal. However there is price discrimination when goods are illegal because the total price of illegal goods tends to be lower to poorer persons. Since most crimes are concentrated in poorer neighborhoods, illegal drug production and distribution also tends to be concentrated in these neighborhoods. This makes illegal goods cheaper to persons who live in these neighborhoods since access to them is easier. The total cost of drugs and other illegal goods is cheaper to poorer persons also because they are more likely to be involved in the trafficking in these goods. They are more involved because the cost of imprisonment and similar punishments from selling drugs is less to individuals with lower opportunities in the legal sector. The full cost argument is stronger if we consider enforcement against consumers. Since the non-monetary tax, i.e., punishment, is more time intensive, this corresponds to a difference in the value of the tax between classes that exacerbates the effect. There are also reputational effects that make conviction costlier for the wealthy. In fact, more than half of all persons imprisoned on drug charges are African-American (see Maguire and Pastore, 2001, and Harrison and Beck, 2003).

31

Even disclosure of use sometimes is very costly to higher income and more educated persons. During his first presidential campaign, Bill Clinton had to deny that he inhaled on the allegedly few occasions when he smoked marijuana. Marijuana use during his student days cost Judge Douglas Ginsberg a Supreme Court seat.

Our conclusion is that making goods illegal and punishing suppliers and consumers by imprisonment and other methods are more costly to higher income persons, and hence tends to reduce their consumption more than consumption of lower income persons. Even if low, middle, and higher income parents have the same desire to discourage drug use by their children, the great political influence of higher education and income groups would explain why drugs are illegal rather than subject to sizeable monetary excise taxes. It also helps explain why punishment is mainly imposed on suppliers rather than consumers of drugs since traffickers are more likely than consumers to be low-income persons.

This analysis also helps explain why prostitution and much gambling are illegal rather than legally consumed with high excise taxes. If individuals at all income levels want to discourage consumption of these goods by children and other family members or friends, the politically powerful middle and higher income persons would prefer to make them illegal rather than legal and subject to high "sin" taxes. The explanation is again that consumption of these goods by middle and richer individuals are reduced more when they are illegal than subject to the high sin taxes. The intent may not be to inflict greater harm on the poor, but making goods like drugs, gambling, and

32

prostitution illegal, and mainly punishing traffickers, has precisely that effect.

Acknowledgments

Our research has been supported by The Robert Wood Johnson Foundation (Grant I.D. # 045566 to the National Opinion Research Center), the Hoover Institution Project on Drugs, and the Stigler Center for the Study of the Economy and the State. Helpful comments were received from Steve Levitt and Ivan Werning, and at seminars at The University of Chicago and Harvard University. Steve Cicala provided excellent research assistance. This paper has not undergone the review accorded official National Bureau of Economic Research publications; in particular, it has not been submitted for approval by the Board of Directors. Any opinions expressed are ours and not those of the NBER, the Robert Wood Johnson Foundation, NORC, the Hoover Institution, or the Stigler Center.

References:

Becker, Gary S., and Murphy, Kevin M., "A Simple Theory of Advertising as a Good or Bad." Quarterly Journal of Economics, 108, No. 4 (November 1993), 941-964.

Caulkins, Jonathan, P., Estimating the Elasticities of Demand for Cocaine and Heroin with Data from 21 Cities from the Drug Use Forecasting (DUF) Program, 1987-1991 [Computer file]. ICPSR version. Santa Monica, CA: RAND (Corporation [producer], 1995. Ann Arbor, MI: Inter-university Consortium for Political and Social Research [distributor], 1996.

33

Coleman, James S., *The Adolescent Society*. Free Press. New York: 1961

Grossman, Michael and Chaloupka, Frank J., "The Demand for Cocaine by Young Adults: A Rational Addiction Approach," Journal of Health Economics, 17, No. 4, August 1998, 427-474).

Harrison, Paige M. and Beck, Allen J., *Prisoners in 2002*. The Bureau of Justice Statistics, Washington, D.C.: 2003, P. 10.

MacCoun, Robert and Reuter, Peter, Drug War Heresies: Learning from Other Vices, Times and Places (Cambridge, U.K.: Cambridge University Press, 2001).

Maguire, Kathleen and Pastore, Ann L., eds. *Sourcebook of Criminal Justice Statistics*. The Bureau of Justice Statistics, Washington, D.C.: 2001, p 515.

Jeffrey A. Miron, "Drug War Crimes", The Independent Institute, 2004.

Pacula, Rosalie Liccardo, Grossman, Michael, Chaloupka, Frank J., O'Malley, Patrick M., Johnston, Lloyd D., and Farrelly, Matthew C. "Marijuana and Youth" in Risky Behavior Among Youths: An Economic Analysis, edited by Jonathan Gruber, University of Chicago Press, 2000, pp. 271-326.

Saffer, Henry and Chaloupka, Frank J. "The Demand for Illicit Drugs," Economic Inquiry, 37, No. 3, July 1999, pp. 401-411.

van Ours, Jan C. "The Price Elasticity of Hard Drugs: The Case of Opium in the Dutch East Indies, 1923-28" Journal of Political Economy, 103, No. 2, April 1995, 261-279.